THE
CRICKETERS'
WHO'S WHO
1998

O vodafone

THE CRICKETERS' WHO'S WHO 1998

Introduction by
ANGUS FRASER

Edited by
CHRIS HAWKES

Statistics by
RICHARD LOCKWOOD

Portraits photographed or researched by
BILL SMITH

Queen Anne Press

QUEEN ANNE PRESS
a division of Lennard Associates Limited
Mackerye End, Harpenden, Herts AL5 5DR

Published in association with
The Cricketers' Who's Who Limited

First published in Great Britain 1998

© The Cricketers' Who's Who Limited

British Library Cataloguing in Publication is available

ISBN 1 85291 587 0

Typeset in Times and Univers Condensed
Editor (for Queen Anne Press): Kirsty Ennever
Quiz compiled by Chris Hawkes
Cover design by Paul Cooper

Printed and bound by
Butler and Tanner Limited, Frome and London

PICTURE ACKNOWLEDGEMENTS

Cover photographs by Allsport depict the 1997 PCA Award winners:
(main picture)
Ben Hollioake, PCA Young Player of the Year
(inset, top)
Steve James, PCA Player of the Year
(inset, middle)
Alistair Brown, PCA Special Merit Award
(inset, bottom)
Peter Willey, Goldblatt Umpires Cup

CONTENTS

The Professional Cricketers' Association are very pleased to endorse the 1998 *Cricketers' Who's Who* publication. The PCA speaks collectively for all professional cricketers while in *The Cricketers' Who's Who* they speak individually through their entries.

The PCA represents the interests of all players from uncapped county players to current internationals and plays a prominent and responsible part alongside the ECB and the county cricket clubs in promoting the game.

In the past year numerous initiatives have been introduced, in particular the formation of PCA Management Limited to develop the profile of the PCA and operate a number of commercial projects. It is our intention to expand the services to our members in many areas, particularly education, accident injury cover and benevolent support.

The PCA is also launching an initiative to introduce past professional players as associate members of the PCA.

So, we hope for a successful season both on and off the playing field.

David Graveney
General Secretary

‘Full Coverage for *English* Cricket’

O vodafone

O vodafone

It gives me great pleasure to be writing this introduction to the 1998 Cricketers' Who's Who on behalf of Vodafone. As the new sponsor of English cricket we are looking forward to forming a close and successful relationship with English cricket into the next millenium.

There are exciting times ahead for English cricket in the next 18 months. This summer we welcome both the South Africans and the Sri Lankans for both Test and One-Day Internationals. The South Africans will be keen to win the series in England after their recent disappointment in Australia. The World Champions Sri Lanka will come to England to prove thay not only are they still one of the best one-day sides in the world, but also a dominant power in Test cricket.

In September, at the end of the domestic season, the England one-day squad travel to Bangladesh for the International One-Day Tournament as a warm up to the 1999 World Cup. The senior England team will travel to Australia in October to try and reclaim the Ashes – always a battle which brings out the passion and spirit of both countries.

In 1999, England will be hosting the 7th World Cup. The recent success of England's one-day squad in Sharjah was the perfect preparation and foundation for England's bid to win this World Cup. What better way for English cricket and Vodafone to see in the new millenium by becoming the first World Champions of the 21st Century?

I wish all counties and their players a successful summer and hope that all their supporters are able to enjoy an enthralling and successful cricket season.

Chris Gent, Chief Executive, Vodafone

Without the right help David Gower might have ended up in court.

Well, that's where David Gower was heading as a law student until somebody spotted a spark of talent. In an effort to catch more people like David, NatWest are supporting the Development of Excellence programme. This identifies the brightest young hopefuls and gives them the coaching, both mental and physical, that they need to shine for their county and country. Great news for English cricket, not so good for the opposition.

NatWest
More than just a bank

INTRODUCTION

In years to come, I wonder how people will reflect on the summer of 1997. For what it is worth, I believe it will be seen as a year of missed opportunities.

England started the summer with a bang, stuffing the all-conquering Australians in both the Texaco Trophy and the first Test at Edgbaston, producing a style and quality of cricket rarely seen in recent years. To say that this was surprising following the lows of Zimbabwe five months earlier is something of an understatement, but what fun it was. Most of us, if we were totally honest, did not really believe it would last, but how nice it was for people to be talking positively about the England team. The explosion of media interest showed just how high the profile of the game can be raised when the national side is successful, so let's not ridicule some of the things the England side are doing to make themselves better; let's encourage them, because when we do win the whole game benefits.

However, the glory didn't last and Australia showed why they are the best side in the world. It wasn't that England played badly (apart from on the last day at Trent Bridge), it is just that at the moment Australia have better players than we do. There is no disgrace in losing to a side that contains players of the quality of Matthew Elliott, Steve Waugh, Ian Healy, Shane Warne and Glenn McGrath – they are players who would get into any side. Glenn McGrath, to me, was the player of the summer; he was always bowling the ball in the right areas. Isn't it amazing how easy the best players make the game look! There are lots of coaches who make cricket sound like a science, yet all the good players just do the basics right.

In the end, the Ashes were lost 3-2. This result may have given the impression that there was not much of a difference between the two sides and some people may have jumped to the conclusion that as such there isn't much wrong with the domestic game. This view, unfortunately, may have affected certain decisions that were made at the end of the summer. To my mind, a truer reflection of the difference between the two sides would have been 3-1 or 4-2. Now that may sound negative to a lot of people, but I would say it was realistic – too many times in the past one Test victory has prevented constructive changes from being implemented. This leaves us with some way to go if England are to become the best side in the world, and also makes the counties' decision to kick out the recommendations made in Lord MacLaurin's report *Raising the Standards* even harder to take. That, I believe, was a far greater missed opportunity than that which went to Graham Thorpe at Headingley last summer (sorry Thorpey!).

If you have the experience of playing cricket at every level in Australia, you realise that their structure is more conducive to producing high-quality players than ours is. I am not saying that everything they do over there is good or that we should immediately copy it, but they must be doing something right as they are not only world leaders in cricket but in other sports as well.

The majority of people within the game realise the likely benefits and the necessity of a two-divisional County Championship. It is only the self-interest of counties that is preventing the game from moving forward. This is sad, as the county game only survives on the back of international cricket and at the moment it is certainly the case that the tail is wagging the dog.

Other proposals put forward in Lord MacLaurin's report have been passed, thankfully, and county cricket boards have got a busy winter ahead of them. To me, the structural change of club cricket is one of the most important things, but it will be hard work attempting to convince both leagues and clubs that premier leagues, promotion and relegation and all-day cricket are the right way forward.

Money, or lack of it, seems to be a major problem amongst clubs at the moment. A lot of clubs are struggling financially and they as much as anybody need to feel the benefits of the extra money that appears to be coming into the game – they, after all, are responsible for producing the majority of young cricketers these days. I just wonder whether the county cricket boards will find implementing these changes easy; your voice does not carry as much weight when you ask people to do things that you yourself are not prepared to do.

This year's first-class season was as open as any, with the four domestic trophies going to four different counties. Congratulations go especially to Glamorgan for winning the Britannic Assurance County Championship – a popular win for a well-balanced side with an ambitious committee. A lot of people were scoffing at the signing of Waqar Younis, questioning whether it was wise to pay someone that much, but what an inspiration he proved to be. He wasn't the only star, though, and was brilliantly supported by the likes of Steve James, Hugh Morris (what a great note to retire on), Matthew Maynard, Robert Croft, Steve Watkin and Darren Thomas. When I made my debut for Middlesex against Glamorgan in 1984, they were considered to be an easy side, an easy 24 points – how times have changed. The only down side to this is that their supporters will be even louder now and harder to put up with than ever.

The AXA Equity & Law League was won by Warwickshire, whom many would still consider, day-in-day-out, to be the strongest side in the country. The two one-day finals at Lord's were sadly one-sided affairs, but congratulations must go, begrudgingly, to our two closest rivals, Surrey and Essex (only joking!).

One aspect of the game that will be causing great concern to the treasurers of all counties this winter will be players' wages. For years, county cricket club committees have taken great pride in keeping players' salaries as low as they possibly can, knowing that the majority of players would not move or do anything to jeopardise their chances of being awarded a benefit in years to come. This has meant that players go into contract meetings with their hands almost tied behind their backs and come out having to accept what the county has offered.

Things seem to be changing, however. With an ever-increasing onus on clubs to be successful, by members and sponsors alike, any decent player who expresses a desire to move only has to say so in the papers, and then sit back and wait for the offers to drop through the letterbox.

There is an increasing demand for high-quality cricketers and it won't be too long before counties will be asking for compensation or even a transfer fee for the loss of a player.

In some ways this is encouraging. Each of us would love to earn more than we currently do as the vast majority of cricketers have been underpaid over the years, but cricket has to be careful. The game should try and learn from rugby's mistakes. Club rugby's honeymoon period seems to be over and several clubs are in serious financial trouble. With regard to wages, the game of rugby jumped in at the deep end. The result is that some clubs are now in the sort of position we want to avoid if we possibly can. There is only so much in the pot and, although clubs should do more to increase the size of it, we have to work within the financial boundaries.

Wages are not the only area where players feel there is room for improvement. We would like to have more influence on decisions that are made about the game we play. Through the Professional Cricketers' Association (PCA) we are determined to have our voices heard; so many times decisions are made by county committees without the players ever being consulted. This has to be wrong. We accept that cricket is not all about the players, but surely we must have some say on the game we want to play. People will always do a job better if it is the one they want to do rather than the one they are told to do.

As for 1998, what has it got in store for us? Who knows. England have a tough 18 months ahead of them, but I certainly know of one player who is looking forward to it immensely. It has started well with impressive performances and an encouraging victory by the specialist one-day squad in Sharjah. It is now up to the rest of us to do the same in the Caribbean. The policy of having two specialist squads is correct as the games involve different skills, some of which come easier to some players than others. Some players can adapt their game while others are naturally suited to both. Alistair Brown is obviously going to make more of the fielding restrictions in the first 15 overs than Mike Atherton, but Mike is more likely to handle the ammunition of Messrs Ambrose and Walsh this winter.

Now I hope some of this does not read like a sad, miserable old player having a whinge. All I am trying to do is highlight some of my frustrations this year and show people that we as players do care about the game. As a game there has never been a better time to get involved. Cricket is changing for the better, but I along with others just wish that it could change a bit quicker.

Despite appearances and popular conception, I really do love the game and look forward to each summer with the same enthusiasm as my first – it's only a shame that I'm closer to the end of my career than the start. So as for advice to youngsters I would recommend a career as a professional cricketer to anybody – the lifestyle is great. You may not earn a fortune out of it and it is precarious, but it's fun. I would honestly say that if I won the lottery next week it would not change a thing. I would still ruck and moan from the Pavilion End at Lord's. There is no easy way to the top, only a lot of hard work, but yes, it is worth it.

Angus Fraser
Middlesex CCC and England

The V500 Increased strike zone with LIGHTER shoulders superbly BALANCED from finest ENGLISH WILLOW providing the ultimate strokemaker's bat.

Slazenger. V 500

Slazenger.
SHEER INSTINCT

Exclusively endorsed by the
PCA
PROFESSIONAL CRICKETERS
ASSOCIATION

THE PLAYERS

Editor's Notes

The cricketers listed in this volume include all those who played for a first-class county at least once last season, in any form of cricket, and all those registered (at the time of going to press) to play for the 18 first-class counties in 1998, even those who have yet to make a first-team appearance. All statistics are complete to the end of the last English season. Figures about 1000 runs and 50 wickets in a season refer to matches in England only. All first-class figures include figures for Test matches which are also extracted and listed separately. One-day 100s and one-day five wickets in an innings are for the English domestic competitions and all one-day Internationals, home and abroad. Career records include 'rebel' tours to South Africa.

The following abbreviations apply: * means not out; All First – all first-class matches; 1-day Int – one-day Internationals; Sunday – Sunday League; NatWest – NatWest Trophy; B&H – Benson & Hedges Cup. The figures for batting and bowling averages refer to the full first-class English list for 1997, followed in brackets by the 1996 figures. Inclusion in the batting averages depends on a minimum of six completed innings, and an average of at least 10 runs; a bowler has to have taken at least 10 wickets. The same qualification has been used for compiling the bowlers' strike rate.

Readers will notice occasional differences in the way the same kind of information is presented. This is because it has been decided to follow the way in which the cricketers themselves have provided the relevant information.

Each year in *The Cricketers' Who's Who,* in addition to those cricketers who are playing during the current season, we also include the biographical and career details of those who played in the previous season but retired at the end of it. The purpose of this is to have, on the record, the full and final cricketing achievements of every player when his career has ended.

A book of this complexity and detail has to be prepared several months in advance of the cricket season, and occasionally there are recent changes in a player's circumstances which cannot be included in time. Many examples of facts and statistics which can quickly become outdated in the period between the actual compilation of the book and its publication, months later, will spring to the reader's mind, and I ask him or her to make the necessary commonsense allowance and adjustments.

Chris Hawkes, March 1998

Name: Christopher John Adams
Role: Right-hand bat, right-arm medium
bowler, slip fielder
Born: 6 May 1970, Whitwell, Derbyshire
Height: 6ft **Weight:** 13st 7lbs
Nickname: Grizzly
County debut: 1988 (Derbyshire)
County cap: 1992 (Derbyshire)
1000 runs in season: 3
1st-Class 50s: 39
1st-Class 100s: 21
1st-Class 200s: 2
1st-Class catches: 173
One-Day 100s: 10
Place in batting averages: 116th av. 31.95
(1996 21st av. 52.78)
Strike rate: (career 90.94)
Parents: John and Eluned (Lyn)
Wife and date of marriage:
Samantha Claire, 26 September 1992
Children: Georgia Louise, 4 October 1993
Family links with cricket: Brother David played 2nd XI cricket for Derbyshire and
Gloucestershire. Father played for Yorkshire Schools and uncle played for Essex 2nd XI
Education: Tapton House School; Chesterfield Boys Grammar School; Repton School
Qualifications: 6 O-levels, NCA coaching awards
Off-season: Playing for an England XI in the Cricket Max tournament in New
Zealand
Overseas tours: Repton School to Barbados 1987; England NCA North to N Ireland 1987
Overseas teams played for: Takapuna, New Zealand 1987-88; Te Puke, New Zealand
1989-90; Primrose, Cape Town, South Africa 1991-92
Cricketers particularly admired: Ian Botham, Geoff Palmer, Adrian Kuiper
Other sports followed: Football, golf, rally driving and Formula One
Relaxations: Mountain biking, golf and squash. 'My daughter, Georgia, is very
interesting but definitely not relaxing.'
Extras: Beat Richard Hutton's 25-year-old record for most runs scored in a season at
Repton. Represented English Schools U15 and U19, MCC Schools U19 and, in 1989,
England YC. Took two catches as 12th man for England v India at Old Trafford in 1990.
Holds county records for the fastest century by a Derbyshire batsman (57 mins) and the
highest score in the Sunday League (141*). Whittingdale Young Player Award 1992.
Played for an England XI in the Cricket Max tournament in New Zealand in 1997. Was
released by Derbyshire at the end of the 1997 season and after much speculation has
joined Sussex for 1998

Opinions on cricket: 'I love it.'
Best batting: 239 Derbyshire v Hampshire, Southampton 1996
Best bowling: 4-29 Derbyshire v Lancashire, Derby 1991

1997 Season

	M	Inns	NO	Runs	HS	Avge	100s	50s	Ct	St	O	M	Runs	Wkts	Avge	Best	5wI	10wM
Test																		
All First	15	25	1	767	108	31.95	2	3	18	-	2.5	0	16	0	-	-	-	-
1-day Int																		
NatWest	3	3	2	301	129 *	301.00	2	1	-	-								
B & H	5	5	0	260	138	52.00	1	1	1	-								
Sunday	11	11	1	427	121	42.70	2	1	9	-	10	0	85	1	85.00	1-49	-	

Career Performances

	M	Inns	NO	Runs	HS	Avge	100s	50s	Ct	St	Balls	Runs	Wkts	Avge	Best	5wI	10wM
Test																	
All First	155	253	20	8431	239	36.18	21	39	173	-	1637	1088	18	60.44	4-29	-	-
1-day Int																	
NatWest	18	17	5	883	129 *	73.58	4	4	7	-	18	15	1	15.00	1-15	-	
B & H	32	29	4	866	138	34.64	2	5	10	-	24	21	0	-	-	-	
Sunday	120	113	19	3417	141 *	36.35	4	22	65	-	238	266	3	88.66	2-15	-	

AFZAAL, U.　　　Nottinghamshire

Name: Usman Afzaal
Role: Left-hand bat, slow left-arm bowler
Born: 9 June 1977, Rawalpindi, Pakistan
Height: 6ft **Weight:** 11st 7lbs
Nickname: Gulfraz
County debut: 1995
1st-Class 50s: 7
1st-Class catches: 15
Place in batting averages: 142nd av. 26.66
(1996 165th av. 29.33)
Place in bowling averages: 135th av. 49.21
Strike rate: 85.35 (career 108.70)
Parents: Mohammed and Firdous
Marital status: Single
Family links with cricket: Brother played
representative cricket for Nottinghamshire
Education: Manvers Pierrepont School
Qualifications: NCA coaching certificate

Overseas tours: England U19 to West Indies 1994-95, to Zimbabwe 1995-96
Cricketers particularly admired: Paul Johnson, Phil Tufnell, Mick Newell
Other sports followed: 'Cricket and cricket'
Relaxations: Watching movies and listening to music
Extras: Played for England U15 against South Africa and, in 1994, for England U17 against India
Best batting: 80 Nottinghamshire v Sussex, Hove 1997
Best bowling: 3-62 Nottinghamshire v Transvaal, Johannesburg 1996-97

1997 Season

	M	Inns	NO	Runs	HS	Avge	100s	50s	Ct	St	O	M	Runs	Wkts	Avge	Best	5wI	10wM
Test																		
All First	17	29	2	720	80	26.66	-	5	9	-	199.1	40	689	14	49.21	3-79	-	-
1-day Int																		
NatWest	1	0	0	0	0	-	-	-	1	-								
B & H																		
Sunday	2	2	0	29	20	14.50	-	-	-	-	2	0	21	0	-		-	-

Career Performances

	M	Inns	NO	Runs	HS	Avge	100s	50s	Ct	St	Balls	Runs	Wkts	Avge	Best	5wI	10wM
Test																	
All First	31	53	5	1159	80	24.14	-	7	15	-	2719	1537	25	61.48	3-62	-	-
1-day Int																	
NatWest	2	1	1	26	26 *	-	-	-	1	-	66	57	0	-		-	-
B & H																	
Sunday	8	4	1	31	20	10.33	-	-	3	-	216	186	8	23.25	2-25	-	

ALDRED, P. Derbyshire

Name: Paul Aldred
Role: Right-hand bat, right-arm
medium bowler
Born: 4 February 1969, Chellaston, Derby
Height: 5ft 10in **Weight:** 12st
Nickname: Aldo
County debut: 1995
1st-Class 50s: 1
1st-Class catches: 13
Place in batting averages: 195th av. 22.16
Place in bowling averages: 110th av. 37.83
Strike rate: 90.50 (career 73.57)
Parents: Harry and Lynette
Marital status: Single
Family links with cricket: None other than
father who played local cricket
Education: Chellaston Primary School;
Lady Manners, Bakenall, Derbyshire

Qualifications: 'None worth worrying about!'
Career outside cricket: Building trade – self-employed
Cricketers particularly admired: Ian Botham, Daryll Cullinan, Viv Richards
Other sports played: Golf and rugby, also played hockey for Derbyshire in 1985
Other sports followed: Rugby, golf
Relaxations: Playing sports, a beer with friends in the local pub, long distance running
with Karl Krikken
Extras: 'Had the great opportunity to play against New Zealand with the England NCA
team in 1994 which was a great day.' Represented Derbyshire U18 and U21 hockey team
at the age of 15
Opinions on cricket: 'I think a lot of injuries picked up are due to the amount of cricket
played in England. You just don't have time to recover to full fitness. I think the cricket
schedule could be lightened a little, at first-class level at least.'
Best batting: 83 Derbyshire v Hampshire, Chesterfield 1997
Best bowling: 3-28 Derbyshire v Nottinghamshire, Trent Bridge 1997

---

1. Name the two players who scored a century for their county
on the first day of the 1997 season?

1997 Season

	M	Inns	NO	Runs	HS	Avge	100s	50s	Ct	St	O	M	Runs	Wkts	Avge	Best	5wI	10wM
Test																		
All First	8	8	2	133	83	22.16	-	1	7	-	181	52	454	12	37.83	3-28	-	-
1-day Int																		
NatWest	3	2	1	4	4	4.00	-	-	1	-	23.2	2	99	4	24.75	4-30	-	
B & H																		
Sunday	10	6	1	53	17	10.60	-	-	1	-	55	1	290	7	41.42	3-40	-	

Career Performances

	M	Inns	NO	Runs	HS	Avge	100s	50s	Ct	St	Balls	Runs	Wkts	Avge	Best	5wI	10wM
Test																	
All First	20	25	4	280	83	13.33	-	1	13	-	2575	1366	35	39.02	3-28	-	-
1-day Int																	
NatWest	3	2	1	4	4	4.00	-	-	1	-	140	99	4	24.75	4-30	-	
B & H	2	1	0	7	7	7.00	-	-	-	-	54	53	2	26.50	2-35	-	
Sunday	27	11	4	87	17	12.42	-	-	5	-	862	826	23	35.91	4-41	-	

ALLEYNE, M. W. Gloucestershire

Name: Mark Wayne Alleyne
Role: Right-hand bat, right-arm medium bowler, cover fielder, occasional wicket-keeper
Born: 23 May 1968, Tottenham
Height: 5ft 11in **Weight:** 13st 7lbs
Nickname: Boo-Boo
County debut: 1986
County cap: 1990
1000 runs in a season: 5
50 wickets in a season: 1
1st-Class 50s: 54
1st-Class 100s: 14
1st-Class 200s: 1
1st-Class 5 w. in innings: 6
1st-Class catches: 170
1st-Class stumpings: 2
One-Day 100s: 3
One-Day 5 w. in innings: 3
Place in batting averages: 58th av. 40.73 (1996 137th av. 32.85)
Place in bowling averages: 38th av. 26.09 (1996 20th av. 24.37)
Strike rate: 49.11 (career 59.10)

Parents: Euclid Clevis and Hyacinth Cordeilla

Marital status: Single

Family links with cricket: Brother played for Gloucestershire 2nd XI and Middlesex YCs. Father played club cricket in Barbados and England

Education: Harrison College, Barbados; Cardinal Pole School, East London

Qualifications: 6 O-levels, NCA Senior Coaching Award, volleyball coaching certificate

Off-season: Playing for an England XI in the Cricket Max tournament in New Zealand

Overseas tours: England YC to Sri Lanka 1986-87 and Australia 1987-88

Cricketers particularly admired: Gordon Greenidge, Viv Richards

Other sports followed: Football, volleyball, athletics

Relaxations: Watching films and sport; listening to music

Extras: Youngest player to score a century for Gloucestershire. In 1990 also became the youngest to score a double hundred for the county. Graduate of Haringey Cricket College. Cricket Select Sunday League Player of the Year 1992. Highest Sunday League score for Gloucestershire. Appointed Gloucestershire captain for the 1997 season. Played for an England XI in the Cricket Max tournament in New Zealand in 1997

Best batting: 256 Gloucestershire v Northamptonshire, Northampton 1990

Best bowling: 5-32 Gloucestershire v Sussex, Bristol 1996

1997 Season

	M	Inns	NO	Runs	HS	Avge	100s	50s	Ct	St	O	M	Runs	Wkts	Avge	Best	5wI	10wM
Test																		
All First	19	30	4	1059	169	40.73	1	8	14	-	360.1	89	1148	44	26.09	6-64	3	-
1-day Int																		
NatWest	2	1	0	43	43	43.00	-	-	-	-	18	0	75	3	25.00	3-47	-	
B & H	5	4	1	74	32	24.66	-	-	4	-	35	1	206	4	51.50	2-39	-	
Sunday	15	14	3	339	58	30.81	-	1	10	-	81.1	5	430	16	26.87	3-24	-	

Career Performances

	M	Inns	NO	Runs	HS	Avge	100s	50s	Ct	St	Balls	Runs	Wkts	Avge	Best	5wI	10wM
Test																	
All First	219	359	37	10239	256	31.79	13	54	170	2	15132	8007	256	31.27	6-64	6	-
1-day Int																	
NatWest	27	22	4	416	73	23.11	-	1	9	-	953	615	22	27.95	5-30	1	
B & H	43	35	7	596	75	21.28	-	1	17	-	1681	1255	37	33.91	5-27	1	
Sunday	175	159	38	3740	134 *	30.90	3	15	65	-	5483	4686	148	31.66	5-28	1	

ALTREE, D. A.   Warwickshire

Name: Darren Anthony Altree
Role: Right-hand bat, left-arm
fast medium bowler
Born: 30 September 1974, Rugby
Height: 5ft 11in **Weight:** 12st 7lbs
Nickname: Bobby, Bobster, Dazzler
County debut: 1996
1st-Class catches: 1
Strike rate: 75.00 (career 69.00)
Parents: Tony and Margaret
Marital status: Single
Education: Ashlawn School, Rugby
Career outside cricket: Coil operator for
GEC in Rugby
Overseas tours: Warwickshire U19 to Cape
Town 1992-93
Overseas teams played for: Avendale, Cape
Town 1994-95
Cricketers particularly admired: 'Too many to list'
Young players to look out for: 'Too many to list'
Relaxations: Watching television and listening to music
Opinions on cricket: 'I have none.'
Best bowling: 3-41 Warwickshire v Pakistan, Edgbaston 1996

1997 Season

	M	Inns	NO	Runs	HS	Avge	100s	50s	Ct	St	O	M	Runs	Wkts	Avge	Best	5wl	10wM
Test																		
All First	1	0	0	0	0	-	-	-	-	-	25	3	119	2	59.50	2-108	-	-
1-day Int																		
NatWest																		
B & H																		
Sunday																		

---

2. Which three players (all still playing first-class cricket) have the
unique distinction of scoring a century on debut for two
first-class counties?

Career Performances

	M	Inns	NO	Runs	HS	Avge	100s	50s	Ct	St	Balls	Runs	Wkts	Avge	Best	5wl	10wM
Test																	
All First	4	5	2	0	0*	0.00	-	-	1	-	552	386	8	48.25	3-41	-	-
1-day Int																	
NatWest																	
B & H																	
Sunday																	

AMIN, R. M. Surrey

Name: Rupesh Amin
Role: Right-hand bat, slow left-arm bowler
Born: 20 August 1979, Clapham
County debut: 1997
1st-Class catches: 2
Strike rate: 100.87 (career 100.87)
Parents: Mahesh and Aruna
Family links with cricket: Father played club cricket
Education: Croydon College
Off-season: Playing in Australia
Overseas teams played for: Manly Warrangah, Sydney 1997-98
Best batting: 4* Surrey v Durham, The Oval 1997
Best bowling: 3-58 Surrey v Durham, The Oval 1997

1997 Season

	M	Inns	NO	Runs	HS	Avge	100s	50s	Ct	St	O	M	Runs	Wkts	Avge	Best	5wl	10wM
Test																		
All First	4	6	3	11	4*	3.66	-	-	2	-	134.3	35	348	8	43.50	3-58	-	-
1-day Int																		
NatWest																		
B & H																		
Sunday	1	0	0	0	0	-	-	-	1	-	8	0	43	2	21.50	2-43	-	

Career Performances

	M	Inns	NO	Runs	HS	Avge	100s	50s	Ct	St	Balls	Runs	Wkts	Avge	Best	5wI	10wM
Test																	
All First	4	6	3	11	4 *	3.66	-	-	2	-	807	348	8	43.50	3-58	-	-
1-day Int																	
NatWest																		
B & H																		
Sunday	1	0	0	0	0	-	-	-	1	-	48	43	2	21.50	2-43	-	

ANDREW, S. J. W. Essex

Name: Stephen Jon Walter Andrew
Role: Right-hand bat, right-arm
fast-medium bowler
Born: 27 January 1966, London
Height: 6ft 3in **Weight:** 15st
Nickname: Rip
County debut: 1984 (Hampshire),
1990 (Essex)
1st-Class 5 w. in innings: 7
1st-Class catches: 26
One-Day 5 w. in innings: 1
Place in batting averages:
(1996 303rd av. 7.62)
Place in bowling averages:
(1996 124th av. 42.73)
Strike rate: 102.00 (career 61.47)
Parents: Jon Trevor and Victoria Julia Maud
Marital status: Single
Education: Hordle House Prep School;
Milton Abbey, Portchester School for Boys
Qualifications: 3 O-levels
Career outside cricket: 'Yet to find out'
Overseas tours: England YC to West Indies 1984-85
Overseas teams played for: Pirates, Durban 1983-84; SAP, Durban 1984-86; Manly,
Sydney 1987-88; Pinetown, Durban 1988-89; Taita, Wellington 1990-91; Parnell,
Auckland, 1991-92; Primrose, Cape Town 1993-94
Cricketers particularly admired: Dennis Lillee ('god')
Other sports followed: Golf, rugby
Relaxations: Music, socialising, films and books
Opinions on cricket: 'Our Test fast bowlers have to bowl too much, our explosive
bowlers (i.e. Gough and Malcolm) should not have to bowl at all between Test matches.

Some seam bowlers need to bowl all the time, but not our fast bowlers – keep them fresh.'

Best batting: 35 Essex v Northamptonshire, Chelmsford 1990
Best bowling: 7-47 Essex v Lancashire, Old Trafford 1993

1997 Season

	M	Inns	NO	Runs	HS	Avge	100s	50s	Ct	St	O	M	Runs	Wkts	Avge	Best	5wI	10wM
Test																		
All First	3	3	0	27	24	9.00	-	-	-	-	68	17	223	4	55.75	1-16	-	-
1-day Int																		
NatWest																		
B & H																		
Sunday	2	2	1	12	7	12.00	-	-	-	-	14	0	42	3	14.00	3-20	-	

Career Performances

	M	Inns	NO	Runs	HS	Avge	100s	50s	Ct	St	Balls	Runs	Wkts	Avge	Best	5wI	10wM
Test																	
All First	132	112	42	499	35	7.12	-	-	26	-	19487	10679	317	33.68	7-47	7	-
1-day Int																	
NatWest	9	2	2	1	1 *	-	-	-	2	-	471	308	11	28.00	2-34	-	
B & H	11	3	3	5	4 *	-	-	-	1	-	654	363	20	18.15	5-24	1	
Sunday	63	22	8	140	32	10.00	-	-	3	-	2468	2030	53	38.30	4-40	-	

ARCHER, G. F.   Nottinghamshire

Name: Graeme Francis Archer
Role: Right-hand bat, right-arm 'very medium'
Born: 26 September 1970, Carlisle, Cumbria
Height: 6ft **Weight:** 13st 7lbs
Nickname: Bunka
County debut: 1992
County cap: 1995
1000 runs in season: 1
1st-Class 50s: 20
1st-Class 100s: 8
1st-Class catches: 77
Place in batting averages: 222nd av. 18.75 (1996 60th av. 43.71)
Strike rate: 79.50 (career 75.21)
Parents: Christopher William and Jean Elizabeth
Marital status: Single

Family links with cricket: Father played for Carlisle in N Lancashire League; brother Neil plays in the S Cheshire Alliance League
Education: King Edward VI High School; Stafford College
Qualifications: 3 O-levels, City & Guilds and BTEC National Diploma in Leisure Management, NCA Senior Coaching Award
Career outside cricket: 'Still not decided'
Off-season: Playing cricket for Lancaster Park, Christchurch, New Zealand
Overseas teams played for: Hutt Districts, New Zealand 1991-92; Hutt Valley representative side 1991-92, Old Collegians, Christchurch 1994-96
Cricketers particularly admired: Graeme Hick, Ian Botham, Derek Randall, Chris Cairns and Jimmy Adams

Young players to look out for: Usman Afzaal, Paul Franks and Guy Welton
Other sports followed: Football (Carlisle United and Newcastle United), rugby (Lutterworth RFC), squash and badminton
Injuries: Tendonitis in both knees, out for the last four weeks of the season
Relaxations: Music, videos and driving
Extras: Scored 200* in a 15 (8-ball) over match for Walsall U18s. Awarded the A.A.Thompson Fielding Prize by The Cricket Society in 1990. Made 2nd XI debut for Notts in 1987 aged 15. Played for Staffordshire in 1990-91. Rapid Cricketline Player of the Month April/May 1994. Awarded county cap in September 1995
Opinions on cricket: 'Must think seriously about playing more floodlit cricket to bring the crowds in. Tea should be 30 minutes … please.'
Best batting: 168 Nottinghamshire v Glamorgan, Worksop 1994
Best bowling: 3-18 Nottinghamshire v Hampshire, Southampton 1996

1997 Season

	M	Inns	NO	Runs	HS	Avge	100s	50s	Ct	St	O	M	Runs	Wkts	Avge	Best	5wI	10wM
Test																		
All First	12	22	2	375	81	18.75	-	2	15	-	53	9	188	4	47.00	1-24	-	-
1-day Int																		
NatWest	3	2	0	45	33	22.50	-	-	2	-	5	1	17	1	17.00	1-17	-	
B & H	3	3	1	125	111 *	62.50	1	-	1	-	12.5	1	73	1	73.00	1-34	-	
Sunday	11	10	3	319	104 *	45.57	1	1	4	-	9	0	70	2	35.00	1-28	-	

Career Performances

	M	Inns	NO	Runs	HS	Avge	100s	50s	Ct	St	Balls	Runs	Wkts	Avge	Best	5wl	10wM
Test																	
All First	72	128	13	4072	168	35.40	8	20	77	-	1053	648	14	46.28	3-18	-	-
1-day Int																	
NatWest	6	4	0	99	39	24.75	-	-	3	-	30	17	1	17.00	1-17	-	
B & H	8	7	1	259	111 *	43.16	1	1	1	-	113	117	1	117.00	1-34	-	
Sunday	50	44	7	798	104 *	21.56	1	2	16	-	222	216	8	27.00	2-16	-	

ASTLE, N. J.   Nottinghamshire

Name: Nathan John Astle
Role: Right-hand bat, right-arm medium bowler
County debut: 1997
Test debut: 1995-96
Tests: 11
One-Day Internationals: 46
1st-Class 50s: 10
1st-Class 100s: 8
1st-Class 5 w. in innings: 2
1st-Class catches: 33
One-Day 100s: 4
Place in batting averages: 62nd av. 40.25
Place in bowling averages: 29th av. 23.86
Strike rate: 57.00 (career 86.19)
Overseas tours: New Zealand to India and Pakistan (World Cup) 1995-96, to West Indies 1995-96, to Pakistan 1996-97, to Zimbabwe 1997-98, to Australia 1997-98
Overseas teams played for: Canterbury 1991-98
Best batting: 191 Canterbury v Wellington, Christchurch 1994-95
Best bowling: 6-22 Canterbury v Otago, Christchurch 1996-97

3. Who won the ICC Trophy in 1997?

O vodafone

1997 Season

	M	Inns	NO	Runs	HS	Avge	100s	50s	Ct	St	O	M	Runs	Wkts	Avge	Best	5wI	10wM
Test																		
All First	10	16	0	644	100	40.25	2	3	11	-	209	44	525	22	23.86	5-46	1	-
1-day Int																		
NatWest	3	2	0	83	56	41.50	-	1	-	-	27	7	61	4	15.25	3-20	-	
B & H																		
Sunday	6	6	0	192	75	32.00	-	2	3	-	39	3	203	9	22.55	3-22	-	

Career Performances

	M	Inns	NO	Runs	HS	Avge	100s	50s	Ct	St	Balls	Runs	Wkts	Avge	Best	5wI	10wM
Test	11	21	1	633	125	31.65	3	2	8	-	654	264	8	33.00	2-26	-	-
All First	48	77	7	2635	191	37.64	8	10	33	-	5258	1869	61	30.63	6-22	2	-
1-day Int	46	46	1	1460	120	32.44	4	8	13	-	1523	1130	37	30.54	4-43	-	
NatWest	3	2	0	83	56	41.50	-	1	-	-	162	61	4	15.25	3-20	-	
B & H																	
Sunday	6	6	0	192	75	32.00	-	2	3	-	234	203	9	22.55	3-22	-	

ATHERTON, M. A.   Lancashire

Name: Michael Andrew Atherton
Role: Right-hand bat, leg-break bowler
Born: 23 March 1968, Manchester
Height: 6ft **Weight:** 12st 7lbs
Nickname: Athers, Dread
County debut: 1987
County cap: 1989
Test debut: 1989
Tests: 73
One-Day Internationals: 53
1000 runs in a season: 7
1st-Class 50s: 84
1st-Class 100s: 44
1st-Class 5 w. in innings: 3
1st-Class catches: 196
One-Day 100s: 11
Place in batting averages: 109th av. 32.80
(1996 82nd av. 38.52)
Strike rate: (career 83.15)
Parents: Alan and Wendy
Marital status: Single
Family links with cricket: Father and brother both play league cricket

Education: Briscoe Lane Primary; Manchester GS; Downing College, Cambridge

Qualifications: 10 O-levels, 3 A-levels; BA (Hons) (Cantab)

Off-season: Captain of the England touring party to West Indies

Overseas tours: England YC to Sri Lanka 1986-87, to Australia 1987-88; England A to Zimbabwe 1989-90; England to Australia and New Zealand 1990-91, to India and Sri Lanka 1992-93, to West Indies 1993-94, to Australia 1994-95, to South Africa 1995-96, to India and Pakistan (World Cup) 1995-96, to Zimbabwe and New Zealand 1996-97, to West Indies 1997-98

Cricketers particularly admired: Graham Gooch

Other sports followed: Golf, squash, football

Relaxations: 'Decent novels (Heller, Kundera, etc.), good movies, food and wine, travelling, most sports, music'

Extras: In 1987 was first player to score 1000 runs in his debut season since Paul Parker in 1976. Youngest Lancastrian to score a Test century (151 v NZ at Trent Bridge in 1990); second Lancastrian to score a Test century at Old Trafford (138 v India in 1990). First captained England U19 aged 16. Selected for England tour to New Zealand and also England A tour to Bermuda and West Indies in 1991-92 but ruled out of both through injury. Appointed England captain in 1993. Cornhill England Player of the Year 1994. Voted England's Player of the Series against the West Indies in 1995. Hit 185 not out in the second Test against South Africa in Johannesburg in 1995-96 series. The innings lasted 645 minutes and was the fourth longest by an Englishman in Test matches. Passed Peter May's long-standing record of most Tests as England captain against Australia during the Ashes campaign in 1997

Best batting: 199 Lancashire v Durham, Gateshead Fell 1992

Best bowling: 6-78 Lancashire v Nottinghamshire, Trent Bridge 1990

1997 Season

	M	Inns	NO	Runs	HS	Avge	100s	50s	Ct	St	O	M	Runs	Wkts	Avge	Best	5wI	10wM
Test	6	12	1	257	77	23.36	-	2	2	-								
All First	16	28	2	853	149	32.80	2	5	8	-	1	0	7	0	-	-	-	-
1-day Int	3	3	1	118	113 *	59.00	1	-	1	-								
NatWest	2	2	0	10	8	5.00	-	-	1	-								
B & H	4	4	0	61	24	15.25	-	-	3	-								
Sunday	10	10	1	260	90 *	28.88	-	1	2	-								

Career Performances

	M	Inns	NO	Runs	HS	Avge	100s	50s	Ct	St	Balls	Runs	Wkts	Avge	Best	5wI	10wM
Test	73	134	5	5243	185 *	40.64	11	33	49	-	408	302	2	151.00	1-20	-	-
All First	249	431	39	16725	199	42.66	44	84	196	-	8981	4733	108	43.82	6-78	3	-
1-day Int	53	53	3	1727	127	34.54	2	11	15	-							
NatWest	22	22	2	790	115	39.50	2	4	8	-	188	154	6	25.66	2-15	-	
B & H	54	53	4	1807	121 *	36.87	3	11	29	-	252	228	7	32.57	4-42	-	
Sunday	83	81	6	2630	111	35.06	4	13	28	-	216	248	7	35.42	3-33	-	

ATHEY, C. W. J. Sussex

Name: Charles William Jeffrey Athey
Role: Right-hand bat, occasional right-arm
medium bowler, occasional wicket-keeper
Born: 27 September 1957, Middlesbrough
Height: 5ft 10in **Weight:** 12st 7lbs
Nickname: Bumper, Wingnut, Ath
County debut: 1976 (Yorkshire),
1984 (Gloucestershire), 1993 (Sussex)
County cap: 1980 (Yorkshire), 1985
(Gloucestershire), 1993 (Sussex)
Benefit: 1990
Test debut: 1980
Tests: 23
One-Day Internationals: 31
1000 runs in a season: 13
1st-Class 50s: 126
1st-Class 100s: 55
1st-Class catches: 429
1st-Class stumpings: 2
One-Day 100s: 11

One-Day 5 w. in innings: 1
Place in batting averages: 87th av. 35.89 (1996 135th av. 33.06)
Strike rate: (career 100.20)
Parents: Peter and Maree
Wife and date of marriage: Janet Linda, 9 October 1982
Family links with cricket: 'Father played league cricket in North Yorkshire and South
Durham League for 29 years, 25 of them with Middlesbrough, and has been President
of Middlesbrough CC since 1975. Brother-in-law Colin Cook played for Middlesex,
other brother-in-law (Martin) plays in Thames Valley League. Father-in-law deeply
involved in Middlesex Youth cricket'
Education: Linthorpe Junior; Stainsby Secondary School; Acklam Hall High School
Qualifications: 4 O-levels, some CSEs, NCA coaching certificate
Overseas tours: England YC to West Indies 1975-76; England to West Indies 1980-81,
to Australia 1986-87, to Pakistan, Australia and New Zealand 1987-88; England B to Sri
Lanka 1985-86; unofficial English XI to South Africa 1989-90; MCC to Bahrain 1994-
95; BSI World Cup, India 1994-95
Cricketers particularly admired: 'Too many to mention, but those with enthusiasm for
the game'
Young players to look out for: 'Several young players at Sussex'
Other sports followed: Most sports, especially football (Middlesbrough FC)
Relaxations: Gardening, sport and military history

33

Extras: Played for Teeside County Schools U16 at age 12. Played for Yorkshire Colts 1974. Played football for Middlesbrough Schools U16 and Junior XI. Offered but declined apprenticeship terms with Middlesbrough FC. Captain of Gloucestershire in 1989. Suspension for playing in South Africa in 1990 was remitted in 1992. 'Scored four hundreds in four innings for Gloucestershire CCC.' Passed 25,000 first-class runs with his 138 not out against Somerset at Taunton in 1997 and retired at the end of the season
Opinions on cricket: 'Must play county cricket on better wickets.'
Best batting: 184 England B v Sri Lanka XI, Galle 1985-86
Best bowling: 3-3 Gloucestershire v Hampshire, Bristol 1985

1997 Season

	M	Inns	NO	Runs	HS	Avge	100s	50s	Ct	St	O	M	Runs	Wkts	Avge	Best	5wI	10wM
Test																		
All First	12	21	2	682	138 *	35.89	1	5	9	-	7	0	21	0	-	-	-	-
1-day Int																		
NatWest	4	4	1	95	30	31.66	-	-	1	-								
B & H	5	4	0	121	66	30.25	-	1	-	-								
Sunday	9	9	1	252	109 *	31.50	1	1	-	-								

Career Performances

	M	Inns	NO	Runs	HS	Avge	100s	50s	Ct	St	Balls	Runs	Wkts	Avge	Best	5wI	10wM
Test	23	41	1	919	123	22.97	1	4	13	-							
All First	467	784	71	25453	184	35.69	55	126	429	2	4810	2673	48	55.68	3-3	-	-
1-day Int	31	30	3	848	142 *	31.40	2	4	16	-	6	10	0	-	-	-	
NatWest	53	52	9	1860	115	43.25	2	14	22	-	199	168	1	168.00	1-18	-	
B & H	84	79	11	2551	118	37.51	1	20	34	1	478	364	16	22.75	4-48	-	
Sunday	269	258	23	7504	121 *	31.93	7	47	97	-	913	857	30	28.56	5-35	1	

AUSTIN, I. D.   Lancashire

Name: Ian David Austin
Role: Left-hand bat, right-arm medium bowler
Born: 30 May 1966, Haslingden, Lancs
Height: 5ft 10in **Weight:** 14st 7lbs
Nickname: Oscar, Bully
County debut: 1986
County cap: 1990
1st-Class 50s: 18
1st-Class 100s: 2
1st-Class 5 w. in innings: 5
1st-Class 10 w. in match: 1

1st-Class catches: 26
One-Day 5 w. in innings: 1
Place in batting averages: 66th av. 39.28
(1996 35th av. 48.55)
Place in bowling averages: 48th av. 27.06
(1996 53rd av. 29.31)
Strike rate: 59.82 (career 65.78)
Parents: Jack and Ursula
Wife and date of marriage:
Alexandra, 27 February 1993
Children: Victoria, 28 January 1995
Family links with cricket: Father opened
batting for Haslingden CC
Education: Haslingden High School
Qualifications: 4 O-levels, NCA coaching
certificate
Off-season: 'Nothing certain as yet'
Overseas tours: NAYC to Bermuda 1985;

Lancashire to Jamaica 1986-87, 1987-88, to Zimbabwe 1988-89, to Tasmania and
Western Australia 1989-90, 1990-91
Overseas teams played for: Maroochydore, Queensland 1987-88, 1991-92;
Randwick, Sydney 1990-91
Cricketers particularly admired: Ian Botham, Hartley Alleyne
Young players to look out for: Andrew Flintoff
Other sports followed: Football (Burnley), golf
Relaxations: Golf, and listening to music
Extras: Holds amateur Lancashire League record for highest individual score (147*).
Broke Lancashire CCC record for most wickets in the Sunday League in 1991. Scored
quickest first-class century in 1991 off authentic bowling (64 balls). Man of the Match
in the 1996 Benson and Hedges final and the NatWest semi-final. Lancashire Player of
the Year for 1997. Played for an England XI in the Cricket Max tournament in New
Zealand in 1997
Opinions on cricket: 'Fitness is now the most important part of the game. It seems that
it is even more important than having the ability to play the game and takes over the time
that should be spent developing skills.'
Best batting: 115* Lancashire v Derbyshire, Blackpool 1992
Best bowling: 5-23 Lancashire v Middlesex, Old Trafford 1994

---

4. Which three non-Test-playing nations have
qualified for the 1999 World Cup in England?

 vodafone

1997 Season

	M	Inns	NO	Runs	HS	Avge	100s	50s	Ct	St	O	M	Runs	Wkts	Avge	Best	5wI	10wM
Test																		
All First	17	25	4	825	95	39.28	-	8	6	-	448.4	131	1218	45	27.06	4-44	-	-
1 day Int																		
NatWest	2	2	0	99	97	49.50	-	1	-	-	23	5	67	3	22.33	2-45	-	
B & H	5	5	0	138	35	27.60	-	-	3	-	49	7	172	9	19.11	3-33	-	
Sunday	16	13	4	119	27 *	13.22	-	-	2	-	105.5	7	432	19	22.73	3-25	-	

Career Performances

	M	Inns	NO	Runs	HS	Avge	100s	50s	Ct	St	Balls	Runs	Wkts	Avge	Best	5wI	10wM
Test																	
All First	105	146	31	3349	115 *	29.12	2	18	26	-	14143	6501	215	30.23	5-23	5	1
1-day Int																	
NatWest	23	17	8	321	97	35.66	-	2	1	-	1503	920	27	34.07	3-32	-	
B & H	50	32	9	549	80	23.86	-	2	12	-	2925	1867	63	29.63	4-8	-	
Sunday	155	97	38	1069	48	18.11	-	-	31	-	6408	4879	167	29.21	5-56	1	

AVERIS, J. M. M.   Gloucestershire

Name: James Max Michael Averis
Role: Right-hand bat, right-arm
medium-fast bowler
Born: 28 May 1974, Hong Kong
Height: 5ft 10in **Weight:** 12st 8lb
Nickname: Beaveris, Braveheart, Avo, Fish,
Ladder, Step
County debut: 1994 (one-day), 1997 (first-class)
1st-Class 5 w. in innings: 1
1st-Class catches: 2
Place in batting averages: 162nd av. 25.09
Place in bowling averages: 146th av. 69.00
Strike rate: 102.12 (career 102.12)
Parents: Michael and Carol
Marital status: Single
Family links with cricket: 'Father "The Cat"
was local club legend. Member of the
infamous Frenchay Falcons'
Education: Bristol Cathedral School, Portsmouth University, St Cross College,
Oxford University
Qualifications: 10 GCSEs, 3 A-levels, BSc (Hons) Geography, DipSoc (Oxon)

Off-season: Working and playing rugby for Bristol RFC
Overseas tours: Bristol Schools to Australia 1990-91; Gloucestershire to Zimbabwe 1996; Oxford University RFC to Japan and Australia 1996
Cricketers particularly admired: 'Apart from "The Cat", Andy Roberts, Pete Morgan and Ian Botham'
Young players to look out for: James Fulton, Mark Wagh and Alex Screni
Other sports followed: Rugby (Bristol RFC) and football (Liverpool FC)
Injuries: Broken toe and bruised heel, out for total of three weeks
Relaxations: Watching *The Simpsons* and shooting
Extras: Double Oxford Blue in 1996-97 and played for Bristol RFC 1st XV in 1995. Was captain of South West U21 rugby in 1995
Opinions on cricket: 'Cricket is not professional enough in terms of training and fitness, but with less games this would be remedied. Also, why can't we play in shorts?'
Best batting: 42 Oxford University v Sussex, The Parks 1997
Best bowling: 5-98 Oxford University v Hampshire, The Parks 1997

1997 Season

	M	Inns	NO	Runs	HS	Avge	100s	50s	Ct	St	O	M	Runs	Wkts	Avge	Best	5wI	10wM
Test																		
All First	10	15	4	276	42	25.09	-	-	2	-	272.2	40	1104	16	69.00	5-98	1	-
1-day Int																		
NatWest																		
B & H																		
Sunday	2	0	0	0	0	-	-	-	-	-	9	0	53	2	26.50	2-43	-	

Career Performances

	M	Inns	NO	Runs	HS	Avge	100s	50s	Ct	St	Balls	Runs	Wkts	Avge	Best	5wI	10wM
Test																	
All First	10	15	4	276	42	25.09	-	-	2	-	1634	1104	16	69.00	5-98	1	-
1-day Int																	
NatWest																	
B & H																	
Sunday	5	2	2	3	2 *	-	-	-	1	-	174	175	6	29.16	2-35	-	

AYMES, A. N.   Hampshire

Name: Adrian Nigel Aymes
Role: Right-hand bat, wicket-keeper
Born: 4 June 1964, Southampton
Height: 6ft **Weight:** 12st 7lbs
Nickname: Aymser, Adi
County debut: 1987
County cap: 1991
1st-Class 50s: 23
1st-Class 100s: 3
1st-Class catches: 321
1st-Class stumpings: 31
Place in batting averages: 185th av. 23.26
(1996 73rd av. 40.05)
Strike rate: (career 96.00)
Parents: Michael and Barbara
Wife and date of marriage: Marie, 12
November 1992

Children: Lucie, 9 November 1994
Family links with cricket: 'Father once walked into a Holt and Haskell Sports Shop'
Education: Shirley Middle; Bellemoor Secondary; Hill College
Qualifications: 4 O-levels, 1 A-level, NCA coaching award
Career outside cricket: Selling cricket equipment and coaching
Overseas tours: Hampshire CCC to Isle of Wight 1992, to Portugal 1993, to Guernsey 1994
Cricketers particularly admired: Malcolm Marshall, Cardigan Connor, Jimmy Cook and 'wicket-keepers past and present'
Young players to look out for: Ashley Cowan, Andrew Flintoff
Other sports followed: Boxing and non-sport martial arts
Relaxations: Watching videos, exercising
Extras: Half century on debut v Surrey; equalled club record of 6 catches in an innings and 10 in a match. Hampshire Exiles Young Player of the Year 1990
Opinions on cricket: 'Great game.'
Best batting: 113 Hampshire v Essex, Southampton 1996
Best bowling: 1-75 Hampshire v Sussex, Southampton 1992

---

5. Who holds the record for the highest score in a one-day International?

O vodafone

1997 Season

	M	Inns	NO	Runs	HS	Avge	100s	50s	Ct	St	O	M	Runs	Wkts	Avge	Best	5wI	10wM
Test																		
All First	18	23	4	442	96 *	23.26	-	1	35	7	9	0	76	0	-		-	-	-
1-day Int																		
NatWest	2	1	1	11	11 *	-	-	-	4	-								
B & H	5	4	1	57	22 *	19.00	-	-	6	2								
Sunday	17	11	4	107	30	15.28	-	-	14	6								

Career Performances

	M	Inns	NO	Runs	HS	Avge	100s	50s	Ct	St	Balls	Runs	Wkts	Avge	Best	5wI	10wM
Test																	
All First	145	212	56	4771	113	30.58	3	23	321	31	96	151	1	151.00	1-75	-	-
1-day Int																	
NatWest	15	5	1	75	34	18.75	-	-	22	2							
B & H	31	17	5	226	38	18.83	-	-	31	9							
Sunday	109	76	33	1127	54	26.20	-	1	103	27							

BAILEY, R. J. Northamptonshire

Name: Robert John Bailey
Role: Right-hand bat, off-spin bowler
Born: 28 October 1963, Biddulph, Stoke-on-Trent
Height: 6ft 3in **Weight:** 14st 7lbs
Nickname: Biff, Nose Bag
County debut: 1982
County cap: 1985
Benefit: 1993
Test debut: 1988
Tests: 4
One-Day Internationals: 4
1000 runs in a season: 13
1st-Class 50s: 99
1st-Class 100s: 42
1st-Class 200s: 4
1st-Class 5 w. in innings: 2
1st-Class catches: 240
One-Day 100s: 9
Place in batting averages: 46th av. 43.12 (1996 103rd av. 36.10)
Place in bowling averages: 107th av. 36.70
Strike rate: 67.50 (career 80.61)

Parents: Marie, father deceased
Wife and date of marriage: Rachel, 11 April 1987
Children: Harry John, 7 March 1991; Alexandra Joy, 13 November 1993
Family links with cricket: 'Brother professional for Haslington/North Staffs in the South Cheshire League'
Education: Biddulph High School
Qualifications: 6 CSEs, 1 O-level, NCA advanced cricket coach
Overseas tours: England to Sharjah 1984-85 and 1986-87, to West Indies 1989-90; Northants to Durban 1991-92, to Cape Town 1992-93, to Zimbabwe 1994-95; Singapore Sixes October 1994
Overseas teams played for: Rhodes University, South Africa 1982-83; Uitenhage, Melbourne 1983-84, 1984-85; Fitzroy, Melbourne, 1985-86; Gosnells, Perth 1987-88
Young players to look out for: David Roberts
Other sports followed: Football (Stoke City)
Relaxations: Walking and drinking at the local village pub
Extras: Played for Young England v Young Australia 1983. Selected for cancelled tour of India 1988-89. Youngest Northamptonshire player to score 10,000 runs. Won three consecutive Man of the Match Awards in the Nat West Trophy in 1995. Took over the Northamptonshire captaincy in 1996 season but relinquished the captaincy at the end of the 1997 season
Best batting: 224* Northamptonshire v Glamorgan, Swansea 1986
Best bowling: 5-54 Northamptonshire v Nottinghamshire, Northampton 1993

1997 Season

	M	Inns	NO	Runs	HS	Avge	100s	50s	Ct	St	O	M	Runs	Wkts	Avge	Best	5wI	10wM
Test																		
All First	17	30	5	1078	117 *	43.12	3	5	18	-	112.3	19	367	10	36.70	4-10	-	-
1-day Int																		
NatWest	2	2	0	33	23	16.50	-	-	2	-	12	0	67	3	22.33	3-55	-	
B & H	6	6	2	282	73 *	70.50	-	3	3	-	5	0	17	1	17.00	1-1	-	
Sunday	13	12	2	381	75	38.10	-	5	2	-	21	0	121	3	40.33	1-18	-	

Career Performances

	M	Inns	NO	Runs	HS	Avge	100s	50s	Ct	St	Balls	Runs	Wkts	Avge	Best	5wI	10wM
Test	4	8	0	119	43	14.87	-	-	-	-							
All First	317	537	80	19099	224 *	41.79	42	99	240	-	8465	4561	105	43.43	5-54	2	-
1-day Int	4	4	2	137	43 *	68.50	-	-	1	-	36	25	0	-	-	-	-
NatWest	46	46	12	1562	145	45.94	1	10	17	-	654	407	16	25.43	3-47	-	
B & H	64	61	10	2538	134	49.76	4	19	18	-	390	260	3	86.66	1-1	-	
Sunday	210	198	31	6016	125 *	36.02	4	41	54	-	1294	1229	38	32.34	3-23	-	

BAILEY, T. M. B.   Northamptonshire

Name: Tobin Michael Barnaby Bailey
Role: Right-hand bat, wicket-keeper
Born: 28 August 1976, Kettering
Height: 5ft 10in **Weight:** 12st 6lbs
Nickname: Bill, Mad Dog, Scruff
County debut: 1996
1st-Class catches: 4
Parents: Terry and Penny
Marital status: Single
Family links with cricket: 'Step-dad
watches a lot'
Education: Bedford School;
Loughborough University
Qualifications: 3 A-levels
Overseas tours: Bedford to South Africa 1994
Cricketers particularly admired: Jack
Russell, Mike Atherton, Alan Knott
Young players to look out for:
Michael Davies
Other sports followed: 'Played county hockey and tennis at youth level for
Bedfordshire.' Rugby (Bedford RFC) and football (Leicester City FC)
Relaxations: 'Sleeping in the winter, drinking and spending time with friends'
Extras: Bedfordshire Young Player of the Year in 1995. Northants County League
Young Player of the Year in 1995. Holmwoods Schools Cricketer of the Year. Played for
England Schools U19 and was a reserve for the England U19 tour to Zimbabwe. Won
the BUSA cricket cup with Loughborough in 1996
Opinions on cricket: 'BBC and ITV should put more games on television. Lunch and
tea should be five minutes longer.'
Best batting: 31* Northamptonshire v Lancashire, Northampton 1996

1997 Season

	M	Inns	NO	Runs	HS	Avge	100s	50s	Ct	St	O	M	Runs	Wkts	Avge	Best	5wl	10wM
Test																		
All First																		
1-day Int																		
NatWest																		
B & H	5	4	0	74	52	18.50	-	1	3	3								
Sunday	3	0	0	0	0	-	-	-	4	1								

Career Performances

	M	Inns	NO	Runs	HS	Avge	100s	50s	Ct	St	Balls	Runs	Wkts	Avge	Best	5wl	10wM
Test																	
All First	2	2	1	33	31 *	33.00	-	-	4	-							
1-day Int																	
NatWest																	
B & H	5	4	0	74	52	18.50	-	1	3	3							
Sunday	3	0	0	0	0	-	-	-	4	1							

BALL, M. C. J.   Gloucestershire

Name: Martyn Charles John Ball
Role: Right-hand bat, off-spin bowler,
slip fielder
Born: 26 April 1970, Bristol
Height: 5ft 9in **Weight:** 12st 4lbs
Nickname: Benny, Barfo
County debut: 1988
1st-Class 50s: 4
1st-Class 5 w. in innings: 8
1st-Class 10 w. in match: 1
1st-Class catches: 122
Place in batting averages: 169th av. 24.25
(1996 273rd av. 13.88)
Place in bowling averages: 129th av. 43.82
(1996 141st av. 49.15)
Strike rate: 99.17 (career 74.48)
Parents: Kenneth Charles and Pamela Wendy
Wife and date of marriage: Mona, 28
September 1991
Children: Kristina, 9 May 1990; Alexandra, 2 August 1993
Education: King Edmund Secondary School, Yate; Bath College of Further Education
Qualifications: 6 O-levels, 2 AO-levels
Overseas tours: Gloucestershire to Namibia 1991, to Kenya 1992, to Sri Lanka 1993
Overseas teams played for: North Melbourne, Australia 1988-89; Old Hararians,
Zimbabwe 1990-91
Cricketers most admired: Ian Botham, John Emburey, Vic Marks
Other sports followed: All sports except show-jumping
Relaxations: Music, watching sport and celebrating a victory for AFC Horton.
Extras: Played for Young England against New Zealand in 1989. Produced best bowling
figures in a match for the Britannic County Championship 1993 season – 14-169 against
Somerset

Opinions on cricket: 'Things seem to be moving in the right direction, but I believe that if a club allows a player to run out of contract then he should be a free agent like in any other profession and not be restricted by regulations like those of contested registration.'
Best batting: 71 Gloucestershire v Nottinghamshire, Bristol 1993
Best bowling: 8-46 Gloucestershire v Somerset, Taunton 1993

1997 Season

	M	Inns	NO	Runs	HS	Avge	100s	50s	Ct	St	O	M	Runs	Wkts	Avge	Best	5wI	10wM
Test																		
All First	18	27	3	587	50	24.45	-	1	24	-	479.2	129	1271	29	43.82	5-66	1	-
1-day Int																		
NatWest	2	1	1	9	9 *	-	-	-	1	-	24	1	99	1	99.00	1-51	-	
B & H	5	2	0	37	28	18.50	-	-	2	-	43	4	197	6	32.83	4-23	-	
Sunday	15	10	2	54	12	6.75	-	-	3	-	86	0	402	12	33.50	4-26	-	

Career Performances

	M	Inns	NO	Runs	HS	Avge	100s	50s	Ct	St	Balls	Runs	Wkts	Avge	Best	5wI	10wM
Test																	
All First	103	158	28	2231	71	17.16	-	4	122	-	15304	7337	195	37.62	8-46	8	1
1-day Int																	
NatWest	10	5	2	72	31	24.00	-	-	6	-	558	347	10	34.70	3-42	-	
B & H	22	13	1	138	28	11.50	-	-	10	-	1140	738	20	36.90	4-23	-	
Sunday	83	57	18	383	28 *	9.82	-	-	23	-	2786	2389	58	41.18	4-26	-	

6. Who leads the way with the most centuries in one-day Internationals?

43

BARNETT, K. J.   Derbyshire

Name: Kim John Barnett
Role: Right-hand bat, leg-break bowler
Born: 17 July 1960, Stoke-on-Trent
Height: 6ft **Weight:** 13st 3lbs
Nickname: Barn
County debut: 1979
County cap: 1982
Benefit: 1993 (£37,056)
Test debut: 1988
Tests: 4
One-Day Internationals: 1
1000 runs in a season: 14
1st-Class 50s: 131
1st-Class 100s: 52
1st-Class 200s: 4
1st-Class 5 w. in innings: 3
1st-Class catches: 242
One-Day 100s: 12
One-Day 5 w. in innings: 1
Place in batting averages: 19th av. 50.23 (1996 48th av. 45.50)
Place in bowling averages: (1996 122nd av. 42.25)
Strike rate: (career 74.56)
Parents: Derek and Doreen
Wife: Janet
Children: Michael Nicholas, 24 April 1990; Christina, 11 June 1996
Education: Leek High School, Staffs
Qualifications: 7 O-levels
Career outside cricket: Bank clerk
Overseas tours: English Schools to India 1977-78; England YC to Australia 1978-79; England B to Sri Lanka 1985-86 (vice-captain); unofficial English XI to South Africa 1989-90
Overseas teams played for: Boland 1980-81, 1982-83
Cricketers particularly admired: Eddie Barlow, Gordon Greenidge
Young players to look out for: Vikram Solanki, Andrew Harris and Kevin Dean
Other sports followed: Football, golf, horse racing
Relaxations: Golf and horse racing
Extras: Played for Northamptonshire 2nd XI when aged 15, Staffordshire and Warwickshire 2nd XI. Became youngest captain of a first-class county when appointed in 1983. One of *Wisden*'s Five Cricketers of the Year 1989. Banned from Test cricket after joining tour to South Africa, suspension remitted in 1992. Relinquished captaincy at the end of the 1995 season. Leading century maker and run scorer in all competitions

in the history of Derbyshire cricket

Opinions on cricket: 'We will not produce enough bowlers for the Test arena until we produce pitches that encourage the fast bowlers and leg spinners etc., not just for the batsmen.'

Best batting: 239* Derbyshire v Leicestershire, Leicester 1988

Best bowling: 6-28 Derbyshire v Glamorgan, Chesterfield 1991

1997 Season

	M	Inns	NO	Runs	HS	Avge	100s	50s	Ct	St	O	M	Runs	Wkts	Avge	Best	5wI	10wM
Test																		
All First	15	24	3	1055	210 *	50.23	3	5	3	-								
1-day Int																		
NatWest	3	2	0	129	111	64.50	1	-	1	-	10	0	48	0	-		-	-
B & H	5	5	1	325	112 *	81.25	1	2	-	-	10	1	52	3	17.33	3-52	-
Sunday	8	7	0	297	99	42.42	-	1	1	-	2	0	20	2	10.00	2-20	-

Career Performances

	M	Inns	NO	Runs	HS	Avge	100s	50s	Ct	St	Balls	Runs	Wkts	Avge	Best	5wI	10wM
Test	4	7	0	207	80	29.57	-	2	1	-	36	32	0	-	-	-	-
All First	414	670	62	24327	239 *	40.01	52	131	242	-	13422	6717	180	37.31	6-28	3	-
1-day Int	1	1	0	84	84	84.00	-	1	-	-							
NatWest	39	37	3	1253	113 *	36.85	2	8	15	-	544	369	21	17.57	6-24	2	
B & H	81	72	5	2595	115	38.73	4	18	30	-	438	294	10	29.40	3-52	-	
Sunday	263	251	39	7389	131 *	34.85	6	40	89	-	1189	1100	38	28.94	3-26	-	

7. Which former county player detailed a high life of drugs and sex in a *Sunday Mirror* article in May 1997?

BATES, J. J.   Sussex

Name: Justin Jonathan Bates
Role: Right-hand bat, off-spin bowler
Born: 9 April 1976, Farnborough, Hants
Height: 6ft **Weight:** 11st 7lbs
County debut: 1996 (one-day),
1997 (first-class)
1st-Class 5 w. in innings: 1
1st-Class catches: 6
Place in batting averages: 243rd av. 16.14
Place in bowling averages: 52nd av. 27.63
Strike rate: 71.78 (career 71.78)
Parents: Barry and Sandra
Marital status: Single
Family links with cricket: Father played
club cricket and brother played for Sussex
Young Cricketers

Education: St Mark's Primary School;
Warden Park Secondary School;
Hurstpierpoint College
Qualifications: 8 GCSEs, 3 A-levels, NCA coaching award
Career outside cricket: Freelance graphic designer
Overseas tours: Sussex YC to India 1990-91, to Barbados 1992-93, to Sri Lanka 1994-95
Cricketers particularly admired: Sachin Tendulkar, Eddie Hemmings, Shane Warne
Other sports followed: Golf and rugby
Relaxations: Reading, computing and music
Opinions on cricket: 'Second XI championship cricket should be played over four days and not three.'
Best batting: 47 Sussex v Gloucestershire, Hove 1997
Best bowling: 5-89 Sussex v Nottinghamshire, Hove 1997

1997 Season

	M	Inns	NO	Runs	HS	Avge	100s	50s	Ct	St	O	M	Runs	Wkts	Avge	Best	5wl	10wM
Test																		
All First	7	9	2	113	47	16.14	-	-	6	-	227.2	71	525	19	27.63	5-89	1	-
1-day Int																		
NatWest																		
B & H																		
Sunday	3	3	1	8	5 *	4.00	-	-	1	-	10	0	53	1	53.00	1-24	-	

Career Performances

	M	Inns	NO	Runs	HS	Avge	100s	50s	Ct	St	Balls	Runs	Wkts	Avge	Best	5wl	10wM
Test																	
All First	7	9	2	113	47	16.14	-	-	6	-	1364	525	19	27.63	5-89	1	-
1-day Int																	
NatWest																	
B & H																	
Sunday	4	4	1	16	8	5.33	-	-	2	-	78	99	1	99.00	1-24	-	

BATES, R. T.   Nottinghamshire

Name: Richard Terry Bates
Role: Right-hand bat, off-spin bowler, slip fielder
Born: 17 June 1972, Stamford, Lincs
Height: 6ft 1in **Weight:** 13st 7lbs
Nickname: Blast, Batesy, Roland, La-La
County debut: 1993
1st-Class 5 w. innings: 1
1st-Class catches: 18
Place in batting averages: 286th av. 9.85 ·
(1996 259th av. 16.35)
Place in bowling averages: 138th av. 52.36
(1996 131st av. 46.14)
Strike rate: 123.09 (career 93.50)
Parents: Terry and Sue
Marital status: Suzanne, 16 March 1996
Family links with cricket: Father works for the ECB
Education: Bourne Grammar School; Stamford College for Further Education
Qualifications: 8 GCSEs, BTEC in Business and Finance, NCA Advanced Coach
Career outside cricket: Employed by Notts CCC to coach during the winter
Off-season: Coaching and keeping fit
Overseas tours: Lincolnshire Colts (U19) to Australia 1989-90; Notts CCC to Johannesburg April 1997
Overseas teams played for: Redwood, New Zealand 1991-92
Cricketers particularly admired: Ian Botham, Derek Randall, Viv Richards
Young players to look out for: Matt Dowman
Other sports followed: Football (Liverpool FC) and squash
Injuries: Severe bruising to index finger, out for five weeks
Relaxations: 'Good food, films, having a beer with mates, travelling to Anfield to watch Liverpool and walking my dogs'

Best batting: 34 Nottinghamshire v Worcestershire, Worcester 1996
Best bowling: 5-88 Nottinghamshire v Durham, Chester-le-Street 1995

1997 Season

	M	Inns	NO	Runs	HS	Avge	100s	50s	Ct	St	O	M	Runs	Wkts	Avge	Best	5wI	10wM
Test																		
All First	8	12	5	69	21	9.85	-	-	6	-	225.4	51	576	11	52.36	3-89	-	-
1-day Int																		
NatWest	1	1	0	11	11	11.00	-	-	2	-	9	0	38	0	-		-	-
B & H	3	2	1	8	4 *	8.00	-	-	-	-	29.5	2	155	2	77.50	2-40	-	
Sunday	13	9	1	32	9	4.00	-	-	4	-	65.5	1	349	9	38.77	3-33	-	

Career Performances

	M	Inns	NO	Runs	HS	Avge	100s	50s	Ct	St	Balls	Runs	Wkts	Avge	Best	5wI	10wM
Test																	
All First	30	43	10	433	34	13.12	-	-	18	-	4675	2339	50	46.78	5-88	1	-
1-day Int																	
NatWest	2	2	0	12	11	6.00	-	-	2	-	120	94	0	-		-	-
B & H	7	5	1	53	27	13.25	-	-	4	-	401	283	9	31.44	3-21	-	
Sunday	38	19	4	108	16	7.20	-	-	15	-	1276	1134	36	31.50	3-30	-	

BATTY, J. N. Surrey

Name: Jonathan Neil Batty
Role: Right-hand bat, wicket-keeper
Born: 18 April 1974, Chesterfield
Height: 5ft 10in **Weight:** 11st 7lbs
Nickname: Batts, Lizard, Nora, Mutant
County debut: 1997
1st-Class 50s: 2
1st-Class catches: 18
1st-Class stumpings: 3
Place in batting averages: 158th av. 30.20
Parents: Roger and Gill
Marital status: Single
Family links with cricket: Father played for
Nottinghamshire Schools and played a good
standard of club cricket
Education: Repton School; Durham
University (St Chad's); Keble College,
Oxford

Qualifications: 10 GCSEs, 4 A-levels, BSc (Hons) in Natural Sciences, Diploma in Social Studies
Overseas tours: Repton School to Holland 1990; MCC to Bangladesh 1996
Cricketers particularly admired: David Gower, Bruce French, Alec Stewart
Young players to look out for: David Roberts, Stephen Peters, Alex Tudor
Other sports followed: Football (Nottingham Forest), rugby union (Leicester Tigers) and squash
Relaxations: Going to the cinema, listening to music and reading
Extras: Oxford Blue in 1996. Has also played Minor Counties cricket for Oxfordshire
Opinions on cricket: '2nd XI games should be played on 1st XI wickets.'
Best batting: 56 Oxford University v Northamptonshire, The Parks 1996

1997 Season

	M	Inns	NO	Runs	HS	Avge	100s	50s	Ct	St	O	M	Runs	Wkts	Avge	Best	5wl	10wM
Test																		
All First	3	3	1	54	23 *	27.00	-	-	7	1	4	0	9	0	-	-	-	-
1-day Int																		
NatWest																			
B & H																			
Sunday	4	3	1	15	8	7.50	-	-	1	-								

Career Performances

	M	Inns	NO	Runs	HS	Avge	100s	50s	Ct	St	Balls	Runs	Wkts	Avge	Best	5wl	10wM
Test																	
All First	15	19	5	396	56	28.28	-	2	18	3	24	9	0	-	-	-	-
1-day Int																	
NatWest	1	1	0	1	1	1.00	-	-	-	-							
B & H	10	8	3	83	26 *	16.60	-	-	9	-							
Sunday	4	3	1	15	8	7.50	-	-	1	-							

8. Name the five players, all of whom played first-class cricket in 1997, who have passed 25,000 first-class runs?

O vodafone

BELL, M. A. V.   Warwickshire

Name: Michael Anthony Vincent Bell
Role: Right-hand bat, left-arm
fast-medium bowler
Born: 19 December 1967, Birmingham
Height: 6ft 2in **Weight:** 13st 2lbs
Nickname: Belly, Nelly, Breezer
County debut: 1992
1st-Class 5 w. in innings: 3
1st-Class catches: 8
One-Day 5 w. in innings: 2
Strike rate: 159.00 (career 61.46)
Parents: Vincent and Adelheid
Marital status: Single
Family links with cricket: Father played
cricket mainly for Mitchells & Butler in the
Birmingham League. An uncle played a few
games for Jamaica

Education: Bishop Milner Comprehensive;
Dudley Technical College
Qualifications: 5 O-levels, City and Guilds in Recreation and Leisure Parts 1 & 2
Career outside cricket: Casino croupier, worked with the PE staff at Earls High
School and also worked in the corporate hospitality department at EMP plc for two
years
Overseas tours: BWIA to Barbados and Trinidad & Tobago 1989; John Morris's
Madcap CC to Australia 1992
Overseas teams played for: Swanbourne, Perth 1986-87; Norwood, Melbourne 1989-
90; Phoenix, Perth 1992-93; Sunshine Heights 1993-94
Cricketers particularly admired: Dennis Lillee, Viv Richards, Michael Holding,
Imran Khan, Wasim Akram, Shane Warne
Other sports followed: Any sport played by the best in that particular field
Relaxations: 'Golf (although I'm no Calvin Peete), good movies and going to a hot
country before winter sets in.'
Opinions on cricket: 'When are the batsmen going to be prevented from taking the
initiative over the bowlers and get limited to, for instance, one extra-cover drive – on the
up – per over ... and when will a cow jump over the moon!'
Best batting: 22* Warwickshire v Gloucestershire, Edgbaston 1993
Best bowling: 7-48 Warwickshire v Gloucestershire, Edgbaston 1993

1997 Season

	M	Inns	NO	Runs	HS	Avge	100s	50s	Ct	St	O	M	Runs	Wkts	Avge	Best	5wl	10wM
Test																		
All First	3	2	0	30	30	15.00	-	-	1	-	79.3	14	232	3	77.33	1-12	-	-
1-day Int																		
NatWest																		
B & H																		
Sunday																		

Career Performances

	M	Inns	NO	Runs	HS	Avge	100s	50s	Ct	St	Balls	Runs	Wkts	Avge	Best	5wl	10wM
Test																	
All First	20	23	10	109	30	8.38	-	-	8	-	3012	1565	49	31.93	7-48	3	-
1-day Int																	
NatWest	1	0	0	0	0	-	-	-	-	-	53	41	2	20.50	2-41	-	
B & H	2	0	0	0	0	-	-	-	1	-	66	34	2	17.00	2-34	-	
Sunday	13	5	2	27	8 *	9.00	-	-	1	-	570	411	22	18.68	5-19	2	

BENJAMIN, J. E.   Surrey

Name: Joseph Emmanuel Benjamin
Role: Right-hand bat, right-arm
fast-medium bowler
Born: 2 February 1961, Christchurch,
St Kitts, West Indies
Height: 6ft 2in **Weight:** 12st 7lbs
Nickname: Boggy, Moon Man
County debut: 1988 (Warwickshire), 1992
(Surrey)
County cap: 1993 (Surrey)
Test debut: 1994
Tests: 1
One-Day Internationals: 2
50 wickets in a season: 3
1st-Class 5 w. in innings: 16
1st-Class 10 w. in match: 1
1st-Class catches: 23
Place in batting averages: 238th av. 16.88
(1996 247th av. 17.62)
Place in bowling averages: 144th av. 58.38 (1996 67th av. 31.20)
Strike rate: 97.38 (career 58.84)
Parents: Henry and Judith

Marital status: Single
Education: Cayon High School, St Kitts; Mount Pleasant, Highgate, Birmingham
Qualifications: 4 O-levels
Career outside cricket: Landscape gardener, store manager
Overseas teams played for: Prahran, Melbourne 1992-93
Overseas tours: England to Australia 1994-95
Cricketers particularly admired: Imran Khan, Viv Richards, Malcolm Marshall
Other sports followed: Rugby, squash, football
Relaxations: Music, going to the cinema, reading
Extras: Released by Warwickshire at the end of the 1991 season and signed up by Surrey for 1992. Surrey Player of the Year in 1993
Opinions on cricket: 'The four-day game has been very beneficial to county cricket. It helps batters and bowlers to achieve individual milestones and gives players more time to recover after the game.'
Best batting: 49 Surrey v Essex, The Oval 1995
Best bowling: 6-19 Surrey v Nottinghamshire, The Oval 1993

1997 Season

	M	Inns	NO	Runs	HS	Avge	100s	50s	Ct	St	O	M	Runs	Wkts	Avge	Best	5wI	10wM
Test																		
All First	11	15	6	152	35	16.88	-	-	-	-	211	39	759	13	58.38	3-52	-	-
1-day Int																		
NatWest																		
B & H	6	2	2	5	5 *	-	-	-	2	-	58	4	228	10	22.80	4-19	-	
Sunday	12	3	1	18	13 *	9.00	-	-	1	-	69	1	321	7	45.85	2-40	-	

Career Performances

	M	Inns	NO	Runs	HS	Avge	100s	50s	Ct	St	Balls	Runs	Wkts	Avge	Best	5wI	10wM
Test	1	1	0	0	0	0.00	-	-	-	-	168	80	4	20.00	4-42	-	-
All First	116	134	40	1095	49	11.64	-	-	23	-	21421	10884	364	29.90	6-19	16	1
1-day Int	2	1	0	0	0	0.00	-	-	-	-	72	47	1	47.00	1-22	-	
NatWest	18	8	3	64	25	12.80	-	-	3	-	1086	652	21	31.04	4-20	-	
B & H	24	6	4	32	20	16.00	-	-	8	-	1458	939	31	30.29	4-19	-	
Sunday	91	36	15	190	24	9.04	-	-	16	-	3873	2895	89	32.52	4-44	-	

BETTS, M. M.   Durham

Name: Melvyn Morris Betts
Role: Right-hand bat, right-arm
medium-fast bowler
Born: 26 March 1975, Durham
Height: 5ft 11in **Weight:** 12st 2lbs
Nickname: Betsy, Alpha
County debut: 1993
1st-Class 50s: 1
1st-Class 5 w. in innings: 3
1st-Class 10 w. in a match: 1
1st-Class catches: 7
Place in batting averages: 276th av. 11.50
(1996 253rd av. 17.11)
Place in bowling averages: 17th av. 22.14
(1996 112th av. 39.84)
Strike rate: 40.28 (career 49.71)
Parents: Melvyn and Shirley
Marital status: Engaged
Family links with cricket: Father and uncle played for local club, Sacriston
Education: Fyndoune Comprehensive
Qualifications: 9 GCSEs, plus qualifications in engineering and sports and
recreational studies
Overseas tours: England U19 to Sri Lanka 1993-94
Other sports followed: Football (Newcastle United FC)
Relaxations: Football
Extras: Played for England U19 in home series against India in 1994
Opinions on cricket: 'I think that it is getting harder for bowlers due to the reduction in
the seam on the cricket ball and now the one-bouncer-per-over rule.'
Best batting: 57* Durham v Sussex, Hove 1996
Best bowling: 9-64 Durham v Northamptonshire, Northampton 1997

1997 Season

	M	Inns	NO	Runs	HS	Avge	100s	50s	Ct	St	O	M	Runs	Wkts	Avge	Best	5wI	10wM
Test																		
All First	13	19	1	207	35	11.50	-	-	1	-	329	77	1085	49	22.14	9-64	3	1
1-day Int																		
NatWest	1	1	0	3	3	3.00	-	-	-	-	9	0	73	1	73.00	1-73	-	
B & H	2	2	1	6	5*	6.00	-	-	-	-	14	3	65	1	65.00	1-44	-	
Sunday	6	5	2	35	21	11.66	-	-	1	-	40	2	193	5	38.60	3-22	-	

Career Performances

	M	Inns	NO	Runs	HS	Avge	100s	50s	Ct	St	Balls	Runs	Wkts	Avge	Best	5wl	10wM
Test																	
All First	37	57	10	574	57 *	12.21	-	1	7	-	5518	3710	111	33.42	9-64	5	1
1-day Int																	
NatWest	4	4	1	24	11	8.00	-	-	-	-	258	240	7	34.28	3-33	-	
B & H	4	2	1	6	5 *	6.00	-	-	1	-	138	101	3	33.66	2-36	-	
Sunday	23	16	11	96	21	19.20	-	-	3	-	949	811	22	36.86	3-22	-	

BEVAN, M. G. Sussex

Name: Michael Gwyl Bevan
Role: Left-hand bat, slow left-arm bowler, county vice-captain
Born: 8 May 1970, Canberra, Australia
County debut: 1995
Test debut: 1994-95
Tests: 17
One-Day Internationals: 59
1000 runs in a season: 2
1st-Class 50s: 51
1st-Class 100s: 31
1st-Class 200s: 1
1st-Class catches: 77
Place in batting averages: 89th av. 35.61 (1996 7th av. 64.47)
Place in bowling averages: 140th av. 55.09
Strike rate: 83.27 (career 74.54)
Marital status: Single
Education: Australian Cricket Academy

Off-season: Playing for New South Wales and Australia
Overseas teams played for: South Australia 1989-90, New South Wales 1990-95
Overseas tours: Australia to Sharjah 1994, to Pakistan 1994-95, to India and Pakistan (World Cup) 1995-96, to South Africa 1996-97, to England 1997
Extras: In 1990-91 he became the first player to score a century in five successive Sheffield Shield matches. Made 82 on his Test debut against Pakistan in Karachi, 1994-95. Played for Rawtenstall in the Lancashire League in 1993 and 1994. Appointed Yorkshire's vice-captain for the 1996 season. Has been appointed as overseas player for Sussex for the 1998 season
Best batting: 203* New South Wales v Western Australia, Sydney 1993-94
Best bowling: 6-82 Australia v West Indies, Adelaide 1996-97

1997 Season

	M	Inns	NO	Runs	HS	Avge	100s	50s	Ct	St	O	M	Runs	Wkts	Avge	Best	5wI	10wM
Test	3	5	0	43	24	8.60	-	-	1	-	34.4	6	121	2	60.50	1-14	-	-
All First	11	16	3	463	104 *	35.61	1	3	6	-	152.4	23	606	11	55.09	3-73	-	-
1-day Int	3	3	1	146	108 *	73.00	1	-	-	-	12	0	70	1	70.00	1-43	-	
NatWest																		
B & H																		
Sunday																		

Career Performances

	M	Inns	NO	Runs	HS	Avge	100s	50s	Ct	St	Balls	Runs	Wkts	Avge	Best	5wI	10wM
Test	17	29	3	773	91	29.73	-	6	8	-	1129	629	27	23.29	6-82	1	1
All First	134	226	38	9750	203 *	51.86	31	51	77	-	5069	3003	68	44.16	6-82	1	1
1-day Int	59	53	19	1912	108 *	56.23	2	11	20	-	1005	810	18	45.00	3-36	-	
NatWest	8	8	2	388	91 *	64.66	-	4	-	-	114	89	3	29.66	2-47	-	
B & H	10	9	4	544	95 *	108.80	-	7	1	-	31	25	1	25.00	1-25	-	
Sunday	29	27	5	1108	103 *	50.36	2	7	9	-	445	399	23	17.34	5-29	1	

BICKNELL, D. J.   Surrey

Name: Darren John Bicknell
Role: Left-hand opening bat, slow left-arm
Born: 24 June 1967, Guildford
Height: 6ft 4in **Weight:** 14st
Nickname: Denzil
County debut: 1987
County cap: 1990
1000 runs in a season: 6
1st-Class 50s: 59
1st-Class 100s: 30
1st-Class 200s: 2
1st-Class catches: 75
One-Day 100s: 7
Place in batting averages: 67th av. 39.60
(1996 117th av. 34.60)
Place in bowling averages:
(1996 16th av. 23.00)
Strike rate: 72.00 (career 53.26)
Parents: Vic and Valerie
Wife and date of marriage: Rebecca, 26 September 1992
Children: Lauren Elizabeth, 21 October 1993
Family links with cricket: Brother Martin plays a bit, dad is a qualified umpire and

youngest brother plays club cricket

Education: Robert Haining County Secondary; Guildford County College of Technology

Qualifications: 8 O-levels, 2 A-levels, senior coaching award

Career outside cricket: Marketing and sales for Scottish Courage Ltd

Overseas tours: Surrey to Sharjah 1988, 1989, to Dubai 1990, to Perth 1995; England A to Zimbabwe and Kenya 1989-90, to Pakistan 1990-91, to Bermuda and West Indies 1991-92

Overseas teams played for: Coburg, Melbourne 1986-87

Cricketers particularly admired: Mark Taylor, Graham Gooch, Mark Butcher

Young players to look out for: Mark Butcher, Adam Hollioake

Other sports followed: Football ('follow West Ham United'), golf (12 handicap)

Relaxations: Golf, DIY, 'looking after my family'

Extras: Shared county record third-wicket stand of 413 with David Ward v Kent at Canterbury in 1990 – both made career bests. Surrey batsman of the year four times. Hit the fastest hundred of the year in 1990

Opinions on cricket: 'Too much cricket played. Must have two divisions, the best players must play against each other as often as possible.'

Best batting: 235* Surrey v Nottinghamshire, Trent Bridge 1994

Best bowling: 3-7 Surrey v Sussex, Hove 1996

1997 Season

	M	Inns	NO	Runs	HS	Avge	100s	50s	Ct	St	O	M	Runs	Wkts	Avge	Best	5wI	10wM
Test																		
All First	9	15	0	594	162	39.60	2	1	1	-	12	1	38	1	38.00	1-12	-	-
1-day Int																		
NatWest																		
B & H																		
Sunday	4	4	1	79	49 *	26.33	-	-	3	-								

Career Performances

	M	Inns	NO	Runs	HS	Avge	100s	50s	Ct	St	Balls	Runs	Wkts	Avge	Best	5wI	10wM
Test																	
All First	200	352	34	12696	235 *	39.92	30	59	75	-	1232	789	23	34.30	3-7	-	-
1-day Int																	
NatWest	20	20	4	778	135 *	48.62	1	5	1	-							
B & H	33	32	3	1241	119	42.79	2	9	11	-							
Sunday	96	93	13	2915	125	36.43	4	17	24	-	36	39	2	19.50	1-11	-	

BICKNELL, M. P.   Surrey

Name: Martin Paul Bicknell
Role: Right-hand bat, right-arm
fast-medium bowler
Born: 14 January 1969, Guildford
Height: 6ft 4in **Weight:** 14st 7lbs
Nickname: Bickers
County debut: 1986
County cap: 1989
Benefit: 1997
Test debut: 1993
Tests: 2
One-Day Internationals: 7
50 wickets in a season: 6
1st-Class 50s: 10
1st-Class 5 w. in innings: 27
1st-Class 10 w. in match: 2
1st-Class catches: 63
Place in batting averages: 207th av. 20.33
(192nd av. 25.61)

Place in bowling averages: 45th av. 26.68 (1996 22nd av. 24.74)
Strike rate: 52.54 (career 54.58)
Parents: Vic and Valerie
Wife and date of marriage: Loraine, 29 September 1995
Children: Eleanor, 31 March 1995; Charlotte, 22 July 1996
Family links with cricket: 'Brother plays, but with no luck'
Education: Robert Haining County Secondary
Qualifications: 2 O-levels, NCA coach
Career outside cricket: Amateur golfer
Overseas tours: England YC to Sri Lanka 1986-87, to Australia 1987-88; England A
to Zimbabwe and Kenya 1989-90, to Bermuda and West Indies 1991-92, to South
Africa 1993-94; England to Australia 1990-91
Cricketers particularly admired: Ian Botham, Dennis Lillee, Richard Hadlee, Jason
Ratcliffe
Young players to look out for: Ben Hollioake
Other sports followed: 'Leeds United and golf'
Relaxations: Playing golf and spending time with the family
Extras: Youngest player to play for Surrey since David Smith. His figures of 9 for 45
were the best for the county for 30 years. One of four players on stand-by as reserves for
England's World Cup squad 1991-92. Supporters' Player of the Year 1993. Was awarded
a benefit year for 1997
Opinions on cricket: 'There is still too much cricket. Two divisions are a must.'

Best batting: 88 Surrey v Hampshire, Southampton 1992
Best bowling: 9-45 Surrey v Cambridge University, Fenner's 1988

1997 Season

	M	Inns	NO	Runs	HS	Avge	100s	50s	Ct	St	O	M	Runs	Wkts	Avge	Best	5wl	10wM
Test																		
All First	15	20	5	305	74	20.33	-	2	8	-	385.2	94	1174	44	26.68	5-34	1	-
1-day Int																		
NatWest	2	1	0	24	24	24.00	-	-	-	-	22	5	53	3	17.66	2-28	-	
B & H	8	4	3	26	13	26.00	-	-	-	-	75	9	316	15	21.06	4-41	-	
Sunday	14	7	5	107	57 *	53.50	-	1	4	-	84	1	389	18	21.61	4-28	-	

Career Performances

	M	Inns	NO	Runs	HS	Avge	100s	50s	Ct	St	Balls	Runs	Wkts	Avge	Best	5wl	10wM
Test	2	4	0	26	14	6.50	-	-	-	-	522	263	4	65.75	3-99	-	-
All First	181	215	58	2979	88	18.97	-	10	63	-	34387	16405	630	26.03	9-45	27	2
1-day Int	7	6	2	96	31 *	24.00	-	-	2	-	413	347	13	26.69	3-55	-	
NatWest	28	14	6	126	66 *	15.75	-	1	13	-	1779	984	38	25.89	4-35	-	
B & H	44	23	6	208	43	12.23	-	-	8	-	2568	1692	69	24.52	4-41	-	
Sunday	137	60	30	485	57 *	16.16	-	1	33	-	5821	4200	165	25.45	5-12	1	

BLACKWELL, I. D. Derbyshire

Name: Ian David Blackwell
Role: Left-hand bat, slow left-arm bowler
Born: 10 June 1978, Chesterfield
Height: 6ft 1in **Weight:** 13st 7lbs
Nickname: Blackie
County debut: 1997
Strike rate: 156.00 (career 156.00)
Parents: John and Marilyn
Marital status: Single
Family links with cricket: Father plays
for Derbyshire Over 50s and at local level
Education: Old Hall Primary School;
Manor Community College; Brookfield
Community School
Qualifications: 8 GCSEs, 1 A-level, NCA
coaching course
Cricketers particularly admired: Dominic
Cork and Brian Lara
Young players to look out for: David Sales and Kevin Dean

58

Other sports followed: Football ('played for Sheffield Wednesday Young Owls') and golf
Relaxations: Golf and 'visiting Brampton Manor Health and Fitness Club'
Extras: Played for Derbyshire from the age of eight through to the 2nd XI
Opinions on cricket: 'Approve of the influx of Australians into our game, bringing their superior ideas and knowledge to the county game.'
Best batting: 42 Derbyshire v Lancashire, Derby 1997
Best bowling: 1-27 Derbyshire v Lancashire, Derby 1997

1997 Season

	M	Inns	NO	Runs	HS	Avge	100s	50s	Ct	St	O	M	Runs	Wkts	Avge	Best	5wI	10wM
Test																		
All First	4	5	0	51	42	10.20	-	-	-	-	52	10	227	2	113.50	1-27	-	-
1-day Int																		
NatWest																		
B & H	1	0	0	0	0	-	-	-	-	-	5	0	38	0	-		-	-
Sunday	4	4	0	54	29	13.50	-	-	-	-								

Career Performances

	M	Inns	NO	Runs	HS	Avge	100s	50s	Ct	St	Balls	Runs	Wkts	Avge	Best	5wI	10wM
Test																	
All First	4	5	0	51	42	10.20	-	-	-	-	312	227	2	113.50	1-27	-	-
1-day Int																	
NatWest																	
B & H	1	0	0	0	0	-	-	-	-	-	30	38	0	-		-	-
Sunday	4	4	0	54	29	13.50	-	-	-	-							

9. Which England player became the third generation
of his family to play Test cricket during 1997,
and who were his predecessors?

BLAIN, J. A. R.   Northamptonshire

Name: John Angus Rae Blain
Role: Right-hand bat, right-arm
medium-fast bowler
Born: 4 January 1979, Edinburgh
Height: 6ft 1in   **Weight:** 12st 10lbs
Nickname: Blainey, Haggis
County debut: 1997
1st-Class catches: 2
Strike rate: 90.00 (career 156.00)
Parents: John and Elma
Marital status: Single
Education: Eastfield Primary School;
Penicuik High School; Jewel and Esk Valley
College
Qualifications: 8 GCSEs, 2 O-levels, NC
Leisure and Recreation, NCA coaching
certificate
Off-season: Scotland U19 tour to South

Africa for Youth World Cup
Overseas tours: Scotland U19 to Holland for International Youth Tournament 1994-
95, to Bermuda 1997; Scotland to Denmark for European Championships 1996, to
Malaysia 1997
Cricketers particularly admired: Allan Donald, Dougie Brown, Jim Love, Mark
Waugh
Young players to look out for: David Roberts, David Sales, Michael Davies
Other sports followed: Football (schoolboy forms with Hibernian and Falkirk making
youth and reserve team appearances)
Relaxations: Playing football or golf and listening to music
Extras: Youngest ever player to play for Scotland national side at 17 years old. Played
for Scotland in the Benson & Hedges and NatWest competitions. Made his first-class
debut for Scotland against Ireland in 1996. Took 5 for 24 on Sunday League debut
against Derbyshire
Opinions on cricket: 'Have a blend of youth and experience in a side, but give
youngsters the chance because the top level is the only real place to learn. More
day/night matches is a must – it's the way ahead.'
Best bowling: 1-18 Northamptonshire v Worcestershire, Northampton 1997

1997 Season

	M	Inns	NO	Runs	HS	Avge	100s	50s	Ct	St	O	M	Runs	Wkts	Avge	Best	5wI	10wM
Test																		
All First	1	1	0	0	0	0.00	-	-	1	-	30	8	105	2	52.50	1-18	-	-
1-day Int																		
NatWest																		
B & H	1	0	0	0	0	-	-	-	-	-	6	0	82	2	41.00	2-82	-	
Sunday	3	0	0	0	0	-	-	-	1	-	24	0	110	7	15.71	5-24	1	

Career Performances

	M	Inns	NO	Runs	HS	Avge	100s	50s	Ct	St	Balls	Runs	Wkts	Avge	Best	5wI	10wM
Test																	
All First	2	1	0	0	0	0.00	-	-	2	-	312	208	2	104.00	1-18	-	-
1-day Int																	
NatWest	1	0	0	0	0	-	-	-	1	-	66	56	2	28.00	2-56	-	
B & H	3	2	1	14	10 *	14.00	-	-	-	-	90	140	3	46.66	2-82	-	
Sunday	3	0	0	0	0	-	-	-	1	-	144	110	7	15.71	5-24	1	

BLAKEY, R. J. Yorkshire

Name: Richard John Blakey
Role: Right-hand bat, wicket-keeper
Born: 15 January 1967, Huddersfield
Height: 5ft 10in **Weight:** 11st 4lbs
Nickname: Dick
County debut: 1985
County cap: 1987
Test debut: 1992-93
Tests: 2
One-Day Internationals: 3
1000 runs in a season: 4
1st-Class 50s: 67
1st-Class 100s: 10
1st-Class 200s: 2
1st-Class catches: 517
1st-Class stumpings: 46
One-Day 100s: 3
Place in batting averages: 75th av. 37.77
(1996 115th av. 34.95)
Strike rate: (career 63.00)
Parents: Brian and Pauline
Wife and date of marriage: Michelle, 28 September 1991

Children: Harrison Brad, 22 September 1993
Family links with cricket: Father played local cricket
Education: Woodhouse Primary; Rastrick Grammar School
Qualifications: 4 O-levels, Senior NCA Coach
Career outside cricket: Started own leisure company
Overseas tours: England YC to West Indies 1984-85; Yorkshire to Barbados 1986-87, to Cape Town 1990-91; England A to Zimbabwe and Kenya 1989-90, to Pakistan 1990-91; England to India and Sri Lanka 1992-93
Overseas teams played for: Waverley, Sydney 1985-87; Mt Waverley, Sydney 1987-88; Bionics, Zimbabwe 1989-90
Cricketers particularly admired: Martyn Moxon, Dermot Reeve, Ian Botham, Alan Knott
Other sports followed: All
Relaxations: All sports, particularly golf and squash, eating out, drawing, photography
Extras: Established himself in Huddersfield League. Made record 2nd XI score – 273* v Northamptonshire 1986. Yorkshire's Young Player of the Year 1989. Made Test debut in second Test against India at Madras, February 1993. He was awarded a citation by the International Committee for Fair Play in 1995. He was the only cricketer among the 25 winners worldwide
Opinions on cricket: 'Four-day game is much more enjoyable and the best team wins. National anthem should be played before the start of every international, like football.'
Best batting: 221 England A v Zimbabwe, Bulawayo 1989-90
Best bowling: 1-68 Yorkshire v Nottinghamshire, Sheffield 1986

1997 Season

	M	Inns	NO	Runs	HS	Avge	100s	50s	Ct	St	O	M	Runs	Wkts	Avge	Best	5wl	10wM
Test																		
All First	18	24	6	680	92	37.77	-	6	49	4								
1-day Int																		
NatWest	3	3	2	23	20*	23.00	-	-	2	-								
B & H	6	6	3	60	23*	20.00	-	-	6	1								
Sunday	16	15	3	231	56	19.25	-	1	18	4								

Career Performances

	M	Inns	NO	Runs	HS	Avge	100s	50s	Ct	St	Balls	Runs	Wkts	Avge	Best	5wl	10wM
Test	2	4	0	7	6	1.75	-	-	2	-							
All First	258	413	65	11364	221	32.65	10	67	517	46	63	68	1	68.00	1-68	-	-
1-day Int	3	2	0	25	25	12.50	-	-	2	1							
NatWest	27	21	6	388	75	25.86	-	2	30	2							
B & H	46	40	8	914	80*	28.56	-	6	40	3							
Sunday	150	134	26	4055	130*	37.54	3	24	121	22							

BLANCHETT, I. N. Middlesex

Name: Ian Neale Blanchett
Role: Right-hand bat, right-arm
fast-medium bowler
Born: 2 October 1975, Melbourne, Australia
Height: 6ft 4in **Weight:** 14st 3lbs
Nickname: Blanchy, Noisy, 'and other
descriptive names created by uni housemates
based around being very clumsy'
County debut: 1997 (one-day)
Parents: Edward Arthur Blanchett and Susan
Anne Billows
Marital status: Single
Family links with cricket: 'Uncle Steve
played for Surrey YC when he was younger –
a long time ago!'
Education: Feltwell Primary, Norfolk;
Methwold High School, Norfolk; Downham
Market High School; Luton University
Qualifications: 8 GCSEs, 2 A-levels, 'in process of completing a Health
Science/Leisure degree'
Career outside cricket: 'I'd like to hold the position of personal manager, accountant
and agent for Louise Nurding for £200,000-a-year, although I think I'd better just
concentrate on my cricket right now!'
Off-season: Improving my BSc degree up to honours level
Cricketers particularly admired: I.T. Botham, G.A. Gooch, 'Gussy and Tim
Bloomfield for his nice but amazing transformation'
Young players to look out for: Owais Shah, Aaron Laraman, James Hewitt, Tim
Walton, Kevin Innes
Other sports followed: Football (Norwich City), snooker, swimming
Injuries: 'In a rather rough challenge with a sightscreen at Harrow, came off worst
funnily enough, in a certain place often recognised with spermatogenesis'
Relaxations: 'Enjoy trips to my grandparents in Malaga immensely, where a choice of
diving, sailing, swimming and tannich is available. Also enjoy bashing up a nice spag
bol for myself and Rob Watson, listening to good music. Relaxation often occurs away
from my hectic university household'
Extras: Voted Player of the Year four times successively by his club in Norfolk.
Awarded a special achievement prize in the 1994 NAYC Cambridge Festival. 'Last year
playing goalkeeper for Luton University 1st XI let in a goal from the half-way line –
actually the kick-off after going 1-0 up. I was just trying to congratulate my stern
defenders and he chipped me – not happy!'
Opinions on cricket: 'It gets better every day. More day/night cricket is a must.'

1997 Season

	M	Inns	NO	Runs	HS	Avge	100s	50s	Ct	St	O	M	Runs	Wkts	Avge	Best	5wI	10wM
Test																		
All First																		
1-day Int																		
NatWest																		
B & H	1	0	0	0	0	-	-	-	-	-	6	0	44	1	44.00	1-44	-	
Sunday	5	2	1	2	1 *	2.00	-	-	2	-	27	0	184	1	184.00	1-51	-	

Career Performances

	M	Inns	NO	Runs	HS	Avge	100s	50s	Ct	St	Balls	Runs	Wkts	Avge	Best	5wI	10wM
Test																	
All First																	
1-day Int																	
NatWest																	
B & H	1	0	0	0	0	-	-	-	-	-	36	44	1	44.00	1-44	-	
Sunday	5	2	1	2	1 *	2.00	-	-	2	-	162	184	1	184.00	1-51	-	

BLOOMFIELD, T. F.   Middlesex

Name: Timothy Francis Bloomfield
Role: Right-hand bat, right-arm
fast-medium bowler
Height: 6ft 3in **Weight:** 14st
Nickname: Nice, BT, Frank
County debut: 1997
1st-Class 5 w. in innings: 1
1st-Class catches: 2
Place in bowling averages: 8th av. 19.84
Strike rate: 39.23 (career 39.23)
Parents: Richard (deceased) and Pauline
Education: Halliford Secondary School
Qualifications: GCSEs
Off-season: Working, training, keeping fit
Overseas tours: Berkshire U25 to Barbados
Cricketers particularly admired: Ian
Botham, Viv Richards, Angus Fraser
Other sports followed: Football (Liverpool)
Relaxations: 'Playing other sports and
spending time with Emma'
Extras: Has also played for Sussex 2nd XI and Berkshire
Opinions on cricket: 'We play too much cricket. The powers-that-be need to be more
forward thinking.'

Best batting: 4 Middlesex v Australia, Lord's 1997
Best bowling: 5-77 Middlesex v Essex, Chelmsford 1997

1997 Season

	M	Inns	NO	Runs	HS	Avge	100s	50s	Ct	St	O	M	Runs	Wkts	Avge	Best	5wI	10wM
Test																		
All First	4	3	2	4	4	4.00	-	-	2	-	85	17	258	13	19.84	5-77	1	-
1-day Int																		
NatWest	1	0	0	0	0	-	-	-	-	-	8	2	25	1	25.00	1-25	-	
B & H																		
Sunday	6	1	0	1	1	1.00	-	-	1	-	39	1	198	6	33.00	2-8	-	

Career Performances

	M	Inns	NO	Runs	HS	Avge	100s	50s	Ct	St	Balls	Runs	Wkts	Avge	Best	5wI	10wM
Test																	
All First	4	3	2	4	4	4.00	-	-	2	-	510	258	13	19.84	5-77	1	-
1-day Int																	
NatWest	1	0	0	0	0	-	-	-	-	-	48	25	1	25.00	1-25	-	
B & H																	
Sunday	6	1	0	1	1	1.00	-	-	1	-	234	198	6	33.00	2-8	-	

BOILING, J. Durham

Name: James Boiling
Role: Right-hand bat, right-arm off-spin
bowler, 'wicket-keeper in benefit matches'
Born: 8 April 1968, New Delhi
Height: 6ft 4in **Weight:** 15st 2lbs
Nickname: Roget, Fatman, Nancy, Randy
Timmy Tiger, Keltie, The Beermonster,
Alehead, Rowdy, Brainbox, Frecklehead,
Carrott Top, Gingernut, The Gambler
County debut: 1988 (Surrey), 1995
(Durham)
1st-Class 50s: 2
1st-Class 5 w. in innings: 4
1st-Class 10 w. in match: 1
1st-Class catches: 70
One-Day 5 w. in innings: 1
Place in batting averages: 257th av. 15.18
(1996 285th av. 11.28)

Place in bowling averages: 130th av. 44.04
Strike rate: 96.00 (career 105.75)
Parents: Graham and Geraldine
Wife and date of marriage: Rachael, 7 October 1995
Family links with cricket: 'Met wife, Rachael, whilst she had a summer holiday job at the Foster's Oval. Mother-in-law, Brenda, lives a stone's throw away from Parkhead Cricket Club in Sheffield. Sister-in-law, Gail, has a business selling clothes that could be worn whilst watching cricket. Father likes to wear my old cricket sweaters whilst gardening. Brother Ed sometimes speaks to Neville Scott (a cricket "journalist") in the course of his daily duties at work. Dog likes cricket'
Education: Poplar Primary School, Merton; Joseph Hood Middle School, Merton; Rutlish School, Merton; Durham University (College of St Hild and Bede)
Qualifications: 'Some O- and A-levels, a history degree, senior NCA coaching award, St John Ambulance emergency first-aid certificate, dog handling and obedience'
Career outside cricket: Sports
Off-season: 'We're going to spend a weekend with Alan and Claire in November: Brenda (mother-in-law) is coming to ours for Christmas; we'll probably see my folks over the New Year; if we're lucky we might get down to see Stuart, Carolyn and the boys before the start of the season'
Overseas tours: Surrey Schools to Australia 1985-86; England YC to Australia (Youth World Cup) 1987-88; England A to Australia 1992-93
Overseas teams played for: Bionics, Harare 1991-92; St Augustine, Cape Town 1992-93; Watsonians, California 1996-97
Cricketers particularly admired: Derrick Brett. ' The great Old Rutlishians CC team of the 1980s who taught me so much – players like Andy Ray, Lance and Perry Keene, Micky Way, Dave Doerr, Dave Bradford, Mel Taylor'
Young players to look out for: Mel Betts
Other sports followed: 'None. Just cricket'
Injuries: 'Wounded pride, bruised ego, knocked confidence, broken heart every time I was hit for six'
Relaxations: 'We have just acquired a whippet puppy, so most of my spare time revolves around walking her, feeding her, playing with her, cleaning up after her and training her to fetch the ball after I have been hit out of the ground'
Extras: 'Voted Durham's "top fielder" in 1997. Could have played Test cricket for India but chose to go on England A tour to Australia instead. Left Surrey at the end of the 1994 season. Has been hit for more sixes than any other Durham bowler in the Sunday League. Described by David Boon as "a genuine eccentric"'
Opinions on cricket: 'I would like to see a week in July or August set aside specifically for players' weddings. Every married cricketer I know has had his big weekend during the last weekend in September or the first weekend in October, which is very unfair on the bride and her family who would undoubtedly prefer a "summer" wedding. Having a week set aside in July or August would also enable us to practise and rehearse properly for what is, after all, the most important day of our lives. You could also have the reception at the county ground and invite the sponsors, members and committee and

have a really good knees-up.'
Best batting: 69 Durham v West Indies, Chester-le-Street 1995
Best bowling: 6-84 Surrey v Gloucestershire, Bristol 1992

1997 Season

	M	Inns	NO	Runs	HS	Avge	100s	50s	Ct	St	O	M	Runs	Wkts	Avge	Best	5wI	10wM
Test																		
All First	17	26	4	334	62	15.18	-	1	13	-	336	98	925	21	44.04	3-21	-	-
1-day Int																		
NatWest	1	1	1	6	6 *	-	-	-	-	-	12	0	54	0	-		-	-
B & H	4	1	0	11	11	11.00	-	-	3	-	37	3	152	4	38.00	2-26	-	
Sunday	16	10	5	54	19 *	10.80	-	-	8	-	101.3	1	530	11	48.18	3-33	-	

Career Performances

	M	Inns	NO	Runs	HS	Avge	100s	50s	Ct	St	Balls	Runs	Wkts	Avge	Best	5wI	10wM
Test																	
All First	88	125	38	1160	69	13.33	-	2	70	-	14806	6633	140	47.37	6-84	4	1
1-day Int																	
NatWest	16	7	3	112	46 *	28.00	-	-	8	-	1024	558	13	42.92	4-22	-	
B & H	38	22	13	99	15	11.00	-	-	16	-	2020	1391	33	42.15	3-9	-	
Sunday	99	47	22	305	27	12.20	-	-	39	-	4029	3188	96	33.20	5-24	1	

BOON, D. C.   Durham

Name: David Clarence Boon
Role: Right-hand bat, right-arm medium bowler, county captain
Born: 29 December 1960, Launceston, Tasmania
County debut: 1997
Test debut: 1984-85
Tests: 107
One-Day Internationals: 181
1000 runs in a season: 1
1st-Class 50s: 95
1st-Class 100s: 63
1st-Class 200s: 3
1st-Class catches: 251
One-Day 100s: 6
Place in batting averages: 51st av. 42.37
Strike rate: 37.00 (career 79.25)

Off-season: Playing for Tasmania
Overseas teams played for:
Tasmania, 1978-98
Overseas tours: Young Australia to Zimbabwe 1982-83; Australia to England 1985, 1989 and 1993, to New Zealand 1985-86, 1989-90, 1992-93, to India 1986-87, to Pakistan 1988-89, 1994-95, to West Indies 1990-91, 1994-95, to Sri Lanka 1992-93, to South Africa 1993-94, to India and Pakistan (World Cup) 1986-87
Extras: David Boon first toured England in 1985, and his early struggles to establish his position in the Test side were overcome when he was paired with Geoff Marsh. They went on to become Australia's most successful opening pair since Bill Lawry and Bobby Simpson. Dropped from the Test series for poor form against England in 1986-87, he came back to win the International Cricketer of the Year the following season. In 1988-89 he was the leading run-scorer in the series against West Indies, and followed that with a successful tour of England in 1989. He made his highest Test score against New Zealand at Perth in 1989-90, but had the rest of the season ruined by a knee injury. He recovered to score over 500 runs in successive series against England and India, now batting at No. 3. He returned to opener against the West Indies in 1991-92, scoring 490 runs at an average of over 60. Also one of the world's finest close to the wicket fieldsmen. Retired from Test cricket in 1995-96. Agreed to play for Gloucestershire in the 1995 season, but withdrew through injury and his overseas berth was taken by Javagal Srinath. Signed a two-year deal with Durham as captain for the 1997 and 1998 seasons
Best batting: 227 Tasmania v Victoria, Melbourne 1983-84
Best bowling: 2-18 Durham v Kent, Darlington 1997

1997 Season

	M	Inns	NO	Runs	HS	Avge	100s	50s	Ct	St	O	M	Runs	Wkts	Avge	Best	5wI	10wM
Test																		
All First	18	30	3	1144	117	42.37	3	8	19	-	12.2	3	39	2	19.50	2-18	-	-
1-day Int																		
NatWest	1	1	0	57	57	57.00	-	1	1	-								
B & H	4	3	1	171	103	85.50	1	1	1	-								
Sunday	16	16	3	448	76	34.46	-	2	3	-	7	0	46	0	-		-	-

Career Performances

	M	Inns	NO	Runs	HS	Avge	100s	50s	Ct	St	Balls	Runs	Wkts	Avge	Best	5wI	10wM
Test	107	190	20	7422	200	43.65	21	32	99	-	36	14	0	-	-	-	-
All First	296	496	44	20583	227	45.53	63	95	251	-	951	569	12	47.41	2-18	-	-
1-day Int	181	177	16	5964	122	37.04	5	37	45	-	12	11	0	-	-	-	-
NatWest	1	1	0	57	57	57.00	-	1	1	-							
B & H	4	3	1	171	103	85.50	1	1	1	-							
Sunday	16	16	3	448	76	34.46	-	2	3	-	42	46	0	-		-	-

BOSWELL, S. A. J.   Northamptonshire

Name: Scott Antony John Boswell
Role: Right-hand bat, right-arm
fast-medium bowler
Born: 11 September 1974, York
Height: 6ft 5in   **Weight:** 14st
Nickname: Joey, Bossy, Retro
County debut: 1995 (one-day),
1996 (first-class)
1st-Class 5 w. in innings: 1
1st-Class catches: 2
Place in batting averages: 268th av. 13.55
Place in bowling averages: 137th av. 51.26
Strike rate: 74.33 (career 70.71)
Parents: Tony and Judy
Marital status: Single
Education: Pocklington School;
Wolverhampton University
Qualifications: 9 GCSEs, 3 A-levels
Overseas teams played for: Hutt Valley,
New Zealand 1994-95

Cricketers particularly admired: Dennis Lillee, Richard Hadlee and Kevin Curran
Young players to look out for: David Sales
Other sports followed: Football (York City), rugby union, golf
Relaxations: Watching most sports, playing golf, socialising and spending time with friends and family
Opinions on cricket: 'Overseas players should be allowed in the county championship because they are essential for younger players, like myself, to learn from and to play with and against. Also for the crowds to be able to watch top international players perform. I think most second team cricket should be played at first-class grounds which have been prepared to the quality of first-class cricket.'
Best batting: 35 Northamptonshire v Leicestershire, Northampton 1997
Best bowling: 5-94 Northamptonshire v Worcestershire, Northampton 1997

1997 Season

	M	Inns	NO	Runs	HS	Avge	100s	50s	Ct	St	O	M	Runs	Wkts	Avge	Best	5wI	10wM
Test																		
All First	9	12	3	122	35	13.55	-	-	2	-	185.5	26	769	15	51.26	5-94	1	-
1-day Int																		
NatWest																		
B & H	4	1	0	3	3	3.00	-	-	-	-	34.3	3	177	3	59.00	3-39	-	
Sunday																		

Career Performances

	M	Inns	NO	Runs	HS	Avge	100s	50s	Ct	St	Balls	Runs	Wkts	Avge	Best	5wI	10wM
Test																	
All First	12	16	5	127	35	11.54	-	-	4	-	1557	1012	22	46.00	5-94	1	-
1-day Int																	
NatWest																	
B & H	10	6	1	24	14	4.80	-	-	1	-	536	485	6	80.83	3-39	-	
Sunday	4	1	0	2	2	2.00	-	-	-	-	138	104	3	34.66	1-20	-	

BOULTON, N. R.   Somerset

Name: Nicholas Ross Boulton
Role: Left-hand bat, right-arm slow-medium bowler
Born: 22 March 1979, Johannesburg, South Africa
Height: 6ft 1in **Weight:** 12st 6lbs
Nickname: Boults
County debut: No first-team appearance
Parents: Michael and Pauline
Marital status: Single
Education: Ridge School, Johannesburg, South Africa; King's School, Taunton
Qualifications: 8 GCSEs and 'hopefully 3 A-levels'
Career outside cricket: Hopefully university student
Off-season: 'Hope to play cricket in South Africa'
Overseas tours: King's School 1st XI to Australia 1995, to South Africa 1997
Overseas teams played for: Wanderers CC, Johannesburg, South Africa 1996-98
Young players to look out for: Marcus Trescothick
Other sports followed: Hockey, rugby, golf, flyfishing, Liverpool FC
Relaxations: 'Flyfishing, reading, spending time with my girlfriend, going back to South Africa'
Extras: Awarded Holmwoods Schoolboy Cricketer of the Year. Played ESCA U19 and Transvaal U14

BOVILL, J. N. B. Hampshire

Name: James Noel Bruce Bovill
Role: Right-hand bat, right-arm fast-medium bowler
Born: 2 June 1971, High Wycombe
Height: 6ft **Weight:** 13st
Nickname: Jimma, Ned
County debut: 1993
1st-Class 5 w. in innings: 4
1st-Class 10 w. in match: 1
1st-Class catches: 7
Place in batting averages: 290th av. 9.28 (1996 302nd av. 7.70)
Place in bowling averages: 118th av. 39.21 (1996 96th av. 35.26)
Strike rate: 60.95 (career 54.97)
Parents: Mike and Anne
Marital status: Single
Family links with cricket: Father played for Dorset 1957-60
Education: Sandroyd Preparatory School; Charterhouse; Durham University
Qualifications: 8 O-levels, 3 A-levels, BA (Hons) in Combined Social Sciences
Career outside cricket: 'Pursuing'
Overseas tours: Hampshire Maniacs to Guernsey and Jersey 1989; Bucks to Zimbabwe 1991-92; Durham University to South Africa 1992-93; MCC to Far East and India 1995-96
Overseas teams played for: Western Province CC, South Africa 1989-90, Tigers Parow, South Africa 1994-95; Durban HS Old Boys 1996
Cricketers particularly admired: Cardigan Connor, Paul Terry, Reg Peacock, Aubrey Martyn
Young players to look out for: Derek Kenway, Kevan James
Other sports followed: Soccer (Brian Humber's XI 1994-96)
Injuries: Stress fracture of back, out for August and September
Relaxations: 'Claire and Balearic sound'
Extras: First first-class match was David Gower's last. Made *Sunday Sport* headlines following Ralgex gag by Shaun Udal during a match – 'My balls are boiling'
Opinions on cricket: 'Self-interest among players is inevitable due to poor salaries and uncertain futures. However, self-interest among many of the counties is stalling our national game and hindering necessary changes to its structure.'
Best batting: 31 Hampshire v Worcestershire, Southampton 1995
Best bowling: 6-29 Hampshire v Durham, Stockton 1995

1997 Season

	M	Inns	NO	Runs	HS	Avge	100s	50s	Ct	St	O	M	Runs	Wkts	Avge	Best	5wI	10wM
Test																		
All First	9	9	2	65	27	9.28	-	-	5	-	233.4	37	902	23	39.21	4-62	-	-
1-day Int																		
NatWest																		
B & H																		
Sunday	4	1	0	2	2	2.00	-	-	1	-	25	0	180	5	36.00	4-44	-	

Career Performances

	M	Inns	NO	Runs	HS	Avge	100s	50s	Ct	St	Balls	Runs	Wkts	Avge	Best	5wI	10wM
Test																	
All First	38	49	16	324	31	9.81	-	-	7	-	5717	3384	104	32.53	6-29	4	1
1-day Int																	
NatWest																	
B & H	7	1	1	14	14 *	-	-	-	1	-	373	249	5	49.80	2-21	-	
Sunday	16	6	2	16	7 *	4.00	-	-	2	-	587	558	15	37.20	4-44	-	

BOWEN, M. N.　　　　　Nottinghamshire

Name: Mark Nicholas Bowen
Role: Right-hand bat, right-arm
medium bowler
Born: 6 December 1967, Redcar
Height: 6ft 1in **Weight:** 13st
Nickname: Jim
County debut: 1991-92 (Northamptonshire),
1996 (Nottinghamshire)
1st-Class 5 w. in innings: 3
1st-Class 10 w. in match: 1
1st-Class catches: 11
Place in batting averages: 280th av. 11.15
(1996 293rd av. 10.81)
Place in bowling averages: 94th av. 34.00
(1996 106th av. 38.81)
Strike rate: 68.39 (career 64.46)
Parents: Keith
Wife and date of marriage: Lesley, 11
October 1997

Family links with cricket: 'Father always keen player and watcher'
Education: St Mary's, Redcar; Sacred Heart, Redcar; Teesside Polytechnic
Qualifications: 8 O-levels, 3 A-levels, BSc (Hons) in Chemical Engineering

Career outside cricket: Chemical engineer
Off-season: Working at BNFL Sellafield
Overseas tours: Northamptonshire to Durban 1992, to Cape Town 1993; Christians in Sport to Zimbabwe 1994-95; Nottinghamshire CCC to Johannesburg 1997
Cricketers particularly admired: Richard Hadlee, Dennis Lillee, Viv Richards, Graham Gooch, Malcolm Marshall
Young players to look out for: Paul Franks, Andy Oram
Other sports followed: Football (Middlesbrough FC), golf, hockey (played for Durham County)
Injuries: Shoulder problem and broken hand, missed one game for each injury
Relaxations: 'Keeping fit, watching television and a good pint of ale'
Extras: Made debut for Northants first team in Natal on 1991-92 tour to South Africa before playing in the 2nd XI. Released by Northamptonshire at the end of the 1995 season and joined Nottinghamshire for the start of the 1996 season
Opinions on cricket: 'Perhaps a return to three-day cricket on uncovered pitches may be the answer if counties are not prepared to have two divisions with promotion and relegation.'
Best batting: 32 Nottinghamshire v Northamptonshire, Northampton 1997
Best bowling: 7-75 Nottinghamshire v Derbyshire, Trent Bridge 1997

1997 Season

	M	Inns	NO	Runs	HS	Avge	100s	50s	Ct	St	O	M	Runs	Wkts	Avge	Best	5wI	10wM
Test																		
All First	15	19	6	145	32	11.15	-	-	5	-	467.2	107	1394	41	34.00	7-75	3	1
1-day Int																		
NatWest	2	1	1	8	8 *	-	-	-	-	-	15	0	55	3	18.33	3-38	-	
B & H																		
Sunday	11	6	3	44	14	14.66	-	-	2	-	66.2	0	429	17	25.23	4-29	-	

Career Performances

	M	Inns	NO	Runs	HS	Avge	100s	50s	Ct	St	Balls	Runs	Wkts	Avge	Best	5wI	10wM
Test																	
All First	42	52	13	462	32	11.84	-	-	11	-	7156	3970	111	35.76	7-75	5	1
1-day Int																	
NatWest	3	2	2	8	8 *	-	-	-	1	-	126	97	3	32.33	3-38	-	
B & H	1	1	0	0	0	0.00	-	-	-	-	60	39	1	39.00	1-39	-	
Sunday	45	20	10	182	27 *	18.20	-	-	9	-	1730	1548	47	32.93	4-29	-	

BOWLER, P. D. Somerset

Name: Peter Duncan Bowler
Role: Right-hand opening bat, occasional
off-spin bowler, wicket-keeper,
county captain
Born: 30 July 1963, Plymouth
Height: 6ft 2in **Weight:** 13st
Nickname: Tom
County debut: 1986 (Leicestershire), 1988
(Derbyshire), 1995 (Somerset)
County cap: 1989 (Derbyshire), 1995
(Somerset)
1000 runs in a season: 8
1st-Class 50s: 70
1st-Class 100s: 28
1st-Class 200s: 3
1st-Class catches: 120
1st-Class stumpings: 1
One-Day 100s: 5
Place in batting averages: 144th av. 26.64

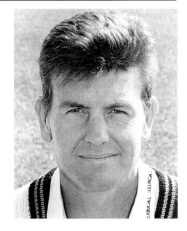

(1996 70th av. 40.93)
Strike rate: 88.66 (career 109.70)
Parents: Peter and Etta
Wife and date of marriage: Joanne, 10 October 1992
Children: Peter Robert, 21 September 1993; Rebekah, 25 August 1995
Education: Scots College, Sydney, Australia; Daramalan College, Canberra, Australia
Qualifications: Australian Year 12 certificate
Cricketers particularly admired: Gus Valence, Rob Jeffery, Bill Carracher, Phil
Russell
Young players to look out for: Marcus Trescothick
Other sports followed: Rugby union
Relaxations: Family and reading
Extras: First Leicestershire player to score a first-class century on debut (100* v
Hampshire 1986). Moved to Derbyshire at end of 1987 season and scored a hundred on
his debut v Cambridge University in 1988. First batsman to 2000 runs in 1992, finishing
equal leading run-scorer (2044) with Mike Roseberry of Middlesex. Derbyshire Player
of the Year 1992. Signed a five-year contract with Somerset starting in 1995. Took over
the Somerset captaincy mid-season after Andy Hayhurst was released
Best batting: 241* Derbyshire v Hampshire, Portsmouth 1992
Best bowling: 3-41 Derbyshire v Leicestershire, Leicester 1991

1997 Season

	M	Inns	NO	Runs	HS	Avge	100s	50s	Ct	St	O	M	Runs	Wkts	Avge	Best	5wI	10wM
Test																		
All First	16	26	1	666	123	26.64	1	5	20	-	44.2	20	145	3	48.33	2-48	-	-
1-day Int																		
NatWest	2	2	0	101	87	50.50	-	1	2	-								
B & H	5	5	0	159	79	31.80	-	1	2	-	6	1	24	1	24.00	1-24	-	
Sunday	14	13	2	353	61	32.09	-	2	5	-	7	0	56	1	56.00	1-33	-	

Career Performances

	M	Inns	NO	Runs	HS	Avge	100s	50s	Ct	St	Balls	Runs	Wkts	Avge	Best	5wI	10wM
Test																	
All First	212	368	33	13438	241 *	40.11	29	75	140	1	2962	1901	27	70.40	3-41	-	-
1-day Int																	
NatWest	18	18	0	510	111	28.33	1	3	8	-	36	26	0	-		-	-
B & H	46	45	1	1364	109	31.00	2	11	21	1	309	182	5	36.40	1-15	-	
Sunday	158	153	17	4700	138 *	34.55	2	38	61	1	284	293	8	36.62	3-31	-	

BRIMSON, M. T.　　　　Leicestershire

Name: Matthew Thomas Brimson
Role: Right-hand bat, slow left-arm bowler
Born: 1 December 1970, Plumstead, London
Height: 6ft **Weight:** 11st 7lbs
Nickname: Brimmo, Doogie
County debut: 1993
1st-Class 5 w. in innings: 2
1st-Class catches: 6
Place in batting averages:
(1996 298th av. 8.50)
Place in bowling averages: 124th av. 41.00
(1996 70th av. 31.60)
Strike rate: 93.18 (career 73.10)
Parents: David and Jennifer
Wife and date of marriage: Lyn, 29
December 1993
Children: Poppy Lilian, 14 July 1996
Family links with cricket: Brother played a
little in Kent League and South Thames League
Education: St Joseph's Preparatory School, Blackheath; Chislehurst and Sidcup
Grammar School, Sidcup; Van Mildert College, Durham University
Qualifications: 8 O-levels, 3 A-levels, BA (Hons) degree in Geography

Off-season: At home doing some part-time work
Overseas tours: Kent Schools U17 to Singapore and New Zealand 1987-88;
Leicestershire to South Africa 1994 and 1995, to Potchefstroom, Western Province,
South Africa 1996 and 1997
Cricketers particularly admired: Derek Underwood, Phil Tufnell and Luke Hatter
Other sports followed: Football (Charlton Athletic), tennis and golf
Relaxations: 'Family life is all the relaxation I need'
Extras: Was on the Kent staff in 1991, Rapidline 2nd XI Player of the Month, July 1995
Opinions on cricket: 'The 60-over game is too long and goes against all that the one-day game stands for. 2nd XI cricket is essential for bringing on young players.'
Best batting: 30* Leicestershire v Durham, Leicester 1997
Best bowling: 5-12 Leicestershire v Sussex, Leicester 1996

1997 Season

	M	Inns	NO	Runs	HS	Avge	100s	50s	Ct	St	O	M	Runs	Wkts	Avge	Best	5wI	10wM
Test																		
All First	7	7	2	59	30 *	11.80	-	-	3	-	170.5	48	451	11	41.00	3-49	-	-
1-day Int																		
NatWest	1	0	0	0	0	-	-	-	-	-	12	4	16	2	8.00	2-16	-	
B & H	5	1	0	0	0	0.00	-	-	1	-	47.5	2	186	6	31.00	2-36	-	
Sunday	6	1	1	12	12 *	-	-	-	2	-	39	3	201	7	28.71	3-37	-	

Career Performances

	M	Inns	NO	Runs	HS	Avge	100s	50s	Ct	St	Balls	Runs	Wkts	Avge	Best	5wI	10wM
Test																	
All First	34	36	15	217	30	* 10.33	-	-	6	-	4898	2384	67	35.58	5-12	2	-
1-day Int																	
NatWest	2	1	0	9	9	9.00	-	-	-	-	136	50	5	10.00	3-34	-	
B & H	6	1	0	0	0	0.00	-	-	1	-	347	242	7	34.57	2-36	-	
Sunday	12	2	2	16	12 *	-	-	-	2	-	492	383	13	29.46	3-23	-	

BROWN, A. D. Surrey

Name: Alistair Duncan Brown
Role: Right-hand bat, occasional
leg-break bowler, occasional wicket-keeper
Born: 11 February 1970, Beckenham
Height: 5ft 10in **Weight:** 12st 6lbs
Nickname: Lordy
County debut: 1992
One-Day Internationals: 3
1000 runs in a season: 3

1st-Class 50s: 23
1st-Class 100s: 14
1st-Class catches: 92
One-Day 100s: 9
One-Day 200s: 1
Place in batting averages: 50th av. 42.40
(1996 202nd av. 24.13)
Parents: Robert and Ann
Marital status: Single
Family links with cricket: Father played for
Surrey Young Amateurs
Education: Cumnor House School;
Caterham School
Qualifications: 5 O-levels, NCA
Senior Coach
Career outside cricket: 'Actor, thespian and
all round good egg'
Off-season: Going to Sharjah with England
for the one-day competition

Overseas tours: England Six-a-side to Singapore 1993, 1994, 1995, to Hong Kong 1997; England to Sharjah 1997
Overseas teams played for: North Perth, Australia 1989-90
Cricketers particularly admired: Ian Botham, Viv Richards
Other sports followed: Football (West Ham United), rugby (Harlequins and London Broncos) and golf
Relaxations: 'Watching Jason Ratcliffe bat and listening to Martin Bicknell telling me that Leeds are a good football team'
Extras: Scored three of the eight fastest centuries of the 1992 season (71, 78 & 79 balls). Awarded Man of the Match for 118 against India in the third One-Day International, 'followed by Most Disastrous Season Award at the end of term prize-giving.' Played for England in the 1997 Hong Kong Sixes competition in which England finished runners-up to Pakistan. Recorded the highest-ever score in the Sunday League with 203 off 119 balls against Hampshire at Guildford and received an individual award at the PCA Dinner at the end of the season for that achievement
Opinions on cricket: 'Four-day cricket is essential. Over-rate fines should be put back into the game in the form of prize money for the Championship and should be distributed evenly between first and ninth. The three one-day trophies should remain the same.'
Best batting: 187 Surrey v Gloucestershire, The Oval 1995

---

10. Which former England international returned to county cricket
in 1997 after an absence of three years?

 vodafone

1997 Season

	M	Inns	NO	Runs	HS	Avge	100s	50s	Ct	St	O	M	Runs	Wkts	Avge	Best	5wI	10wM
Test																		
All First	14	21	1	848	170 *	42.40	3	2	11	-	16	4	37	0	-	-	-	-
1-day Int																		
NatWest	2	2	0	63	44	31.50	-	-	1	-								
B & H	8	8	0	256	71	32.00	-	2	4	-								
Sunday	14	14	1	558	203	42.92	2	2	1	-								

Career Performances

	M	Inns	NO	Runs	HS	Avge	100s	50s	Ct	St	Balls	Runs	Wkts	Avge	Best	5wI	10wM
Test																	
All First	93	150	14	5628	187	41.38	14	23	92	-	324	176	0	-	-	-	-
1-day Int	3	3	0	155	118	51.66	1	-	1	-							
NatWest	15	12	1	377	72	34.27	-	2	3	-							
B & H	30	30	6	987	117 *	41.12	1	5	9	-							
Sunday	107	103	4	3419	203	34.53	8	15	26	-							

BROWN, D. R.   Warwickshire

Name: Douglas Robert Brown
Role: Right-hand bat, right-arm
fast-medium bowler
Born: 29 October 1969, Stirling
Height: 6ft 2in **Weight:** 13st 7lbs
Nickname: Hoots
County debut: 1992
County cap: 1995
50 wickets in a season: 1
1st-Class 50s: 12
1st-Class 5 w. in innings: 8
1st-Class 10 w. in match: 3
1st-Class catches: 34
One-Day 5 w. in innings: 1
Place in batting averages: 175th av. 24.00
(1996 218th av. 22.36)
Place in bowling averages: 6th av. 19.25
(1996 94th av. 35.25)
Strike rate: 38.82 (career 45.72)
Parents: Alastair and Janette
Wife and date of marriage: Brenda,
2 October 1993

Family links with cricket: Both grandfathers played club cricket. 'Siamese twin, Ash, plays a bit!'
Education: Alloa Academy; West London Institute of Higher Education (Borough Road College)
Qualifications: 9 O-Grades, 5 Higher Grades; BEd (Hons) Physical Education
Career outside cricket: PE teacher
Off-season: Playing in Sharjah with England and touring Kenya and Sri Lanka with England A
Overseas tours: Scotland XI to Pakistan 1988-89; England Six-a-side to Hong Kong 1997; England to Sharjah 1997-98, to West Indies 1997-98; England A to Kenya and Sri Lanka 1997-98
Overseas teams played for: Primrose, Cape Town 1992-93; Uredenburg Salohana, Cape Town 1994; Eastern Suburbs, Wellington 1995-96; Wellington, New Zealand 1995-96
Cricketers particularly admired: 'Everyone that plays for their team and gives it 100 per cent'
Young players to look out for: Darren Altree, Anurag Singh
Other sports followed: Football (Alloa Athletic) and golf
Relaxations: Playing golf, learning to play the guitar
Extras: Played football at Hampden Park for Scotland U18. Played first-class and B & H cricket for Scotland in 1989, and played again for Scotland against Ireland in 1992. Played for England in the 1997 Hong Kong Sixes competition in which England finished runners-up to Pakistan. Played for the victorious England side in Sharjah in 1997 and was called up to the England A tour of Kenya and Sri Lanka after the promotion of Chris Silverwood to England's tour of the West Indies following the withdrawal of Darren Gough through injury
Opinions on cricket: 'Great game!'
Best batting: 85 Warwickshire v Essex, Ilford 1995
Best bowling: 8-89 First-Class Counties v Pakistan A, Chelmsford 1997

1997 Season

	M	Inns	NO	Runs	HS	Avge	100s	50s	Ct	St	O	M	Runs	Wkts	Avge	Best	5wI	10wM
Test																		
All First	17	24	3	504	79	24.00	-	4	9	-	521.3	135	1560	81	19.25	8-89	4	1
1-day Int																		
NatWest	5	4	0	46	37	11.50	-	-	-	-	47	6	163	3	54.33	2-34	-	
B & H	6	6	0	194	62	32.33	-	2	1	-	49.3	4	216	8	27.00	5-31	1	
Sunday	17	17	1	374	68	23.37	-	2	4	-	96	4	432	17	25.41	4-42	-	

Career Performances

	M	Inns	NO	Runs	HS	Avge	100s	50s	Ct	St	Balls	Runs	Wkts	Avge	Best	5wI	10wM
Test																	
All First	64	97	11	2143	85	24.91	-	12	34	-	9191	4804	201	23.90	8-89	8	3
1-day Int																	
NatWest	11	10	1	216	67	24.00	-	2	1	-	510	339	6	56.50	2-34	-	
B & H	18	13	1	336	62	28.00	-	2	5	-	903	609	20	30.45	5-31	1	
Sunday	59	52	7	929	78*	20.64	-	4	12	-	1797	1378	48	28.70	4-42	-	

BROWN, J. F.   Northamptonshire

Name: Jason Fred Brown
Role: Right-hand bat, off-spin bowler
Born: 10 October 1974, Stoke-on-Trent
Height: 6ft 1in   **Weight:** 12st
Nickname: Macey, Brown Fish
County debut: 1996
1st-Class catches: 3
Place in bowling averages: 84th av. 32.55
Strike rate: 61.10 (career 61.70)
Parents: Peter and Cynthia
Marital status: Engaged to Samantha
Education: St Margaret Ward RC School
Qualifications: 9 O-levels
Overseas tours: Kidsgrove League U18 to
Australia 1991
Cricketers particularly admired:
John Emburey
Other sports followed: Football, golf, snooker
Relaxations: Watching videos and listening
to music. Playing and watching all sports, socialising

Extras: Represented Staffordshire at all junior levels and Staffordshire's Minor Counties.
'Once took 10 for 16 in a Kidsgrove League game against Haslington Under 18 playing
for Sandyford Under 18.' Played for Staffordshire in the 1995 NatWest competition
Best batting: 16* Northamptonshire v Durham, Northampton 1997
Best bowling: 4-50 Northamtonshire v Cambridge University, Fenner's 1997

---

11. Which player took a hat-trick for Oxford University in their game against
Warwickshire – the first hat-trick for the side for 30 years?

1997 Season

	M	Inns	NO	Runs	HS	Avge	100s	50s	Ct	St	O	M	Runs	Wkts	Avge	Best	5wI	10wM
Test																		
All First	6	8	4	25	16 *	6.25	-	-	2	-	203.4	39	651	20	32.55	4-50	-	-
1-day Int																		
NatWest																		
B & H																		
Sunday	1	0	0	0	0	-	-	-	-	-	7	0	26	4	6.50	4-26	-	

Career Performances

	M	Inns	NO	Runs	HS	Avge	100s	50s	Ct	St	Balls	Runs	Wkts	Avge	Best	5wI	10wM
Test																	
All First	7	9	5	25	16 *	6.25	-	-	3	-	1354	715	20	35.75	4-50	-	-
1-day Int																	
NatWest	1	0	0	0	0	-	-	-	-	-	72	72	1	72.00	1-72	-	
B & H																	
Sunday	1	0	0	0	0	-	-	-	-	-	42	26	4	6.50	4-26	-	

BROWN, K. R.   Middlesex

Name: Keith Robert Brown
Role: Right-hand bat, wicket-keeper
Born: 18 March 1963, Edmonton
Height: 5ft 11in **Weight:** 13st 7lbs
Nickname: Browny, Scarface, Stally
County debut: 1984
County cap: 1990
1000 runs in a season: 2
1st-Class 50s: 54
1st-Class 100s: 13
1st-Class 200s: 1
1st-Class catches: 425
1st-Class stumpings: 28
One-Day 100s: 2
Place in batting averages: 123rd av. 30.05
(1996 112th av. 35.26)
Strike rate: (career 53.50)
Parents: Kenneth William and Margaret Sonia
Wife and date of marriage: Marie, 3
November 1984
Children: Zachary, 24 February 1987; Rosanna, 18 December 1989;
Alex, 29 December 1992

Family links with cricket: Brother Gary was on Middlesex staff for three years and then played for Durham. Father is a qualified umpire
Education: Chace Comprehensive School, Enfield
Qualifications: French O-level; NCA Senior Coaching Award; qualified plasterer
Career outside cricket: Plasterer, PE instructor, coach
Off-season: Coaching and working on benefit
Overseas tours: NCA Youth tour to Denmark; Middlesex pre-season tours to La Manga 1985, 1986 and Portugal 1991, 1992, 1993
Overseas teams played for: Sydney University, Australia 1988-89; Motueka Cricket Association, Nelson, New Zealand 1991-92
Cricketers particularly admired: Clive Radley and Derek Randall
Other sports followed: Most sports apart from motor racing
Injuries: Fractured fingers, missed two Sunday League games
Relaxations: 'Long country walks with family and pet greyhound, finishing with a couple of pints in local.'
Extras: Had promising boxing career but gave it up in order to concentrate on cricket. Picked to play rugby for Essex. 1996 Middlesex Player of the Year
Opinions on cricket: 'Over rate fines should be scrapped. Day/night cricket needs to be more widely introduced to generate a different type of spectator – i.e. people can come after work and bring their children etc.'
Best batting: 200* Middlesex v Nottinghamshire, Lord's 1990
Best bowling: 2-7 Middlesex v Gloucestershire, Bristol 1987

1997 Season

	M	Inns	NO	Runs	HS	Avge	100s	50s	Ct	St	O	M	Runs	Wkts	Avge	Best	5wl	10wM
Test																		
All First	19	29	9	601	144 *	30.05	1	2	47	3								
1-day Int																		
NatWest	3	3	0	88	50	29.33	-	1	8	-								
B & H	4	4	1	91	42 *	30.33	-	-	5	2								
Sunday	13	12	4	159	44 *	19.87	-	-	11	2								

Career Performances

	M	Inns	NO	Runs	HS	Avge	100s	50s	Ct	St	Balls	Runs	Wkts	Avge	Best	5wl	10wM
Test																	
All First	230	348	69	9911	200 *	35.52	13	54	425	28	321	276	6	46.00	2-7	-	-
1-day Int																	
NatWest	24	21	3	536	103 *	29.77	1	1	23	6	6	8	0	-		-	-
B & H	39	36	7	726	75	25.03	-	2	28	9	6	0	0	-		-	-
Sunday	162	137	41	2805	102	29.21	1	10	101	28	28	29	0	-		-	-

BROWN, S. J. E. Durham

Name: Simon John Emmerson Brown
Role: Right-hand bat, left-arm medium pace bowler, gully fielder
Born: 29 June 1969, Cleadon Village, Sunderland
Height: 6ft 3in **Weight:** 13st
Nickname: Chubby
County debut: 1987 (Northamptonshire), 1992 (Durham)
Test debut: 1996
Tests: 1
50 wickets in a season: 5
1st-Class 50s: 2
1st-Class 5 w. in innings: 25
1st-Class 10 w. in match: 2
1st-Class catches: 36
Place in batting averages: 301st av. 6.36 (1996 266th av. 15.53)
Place in bowling averages: 53rd av. 27.68 (1996 39th av. 26.96)
Strike rate: 52.88 (career 54.51)

Parents: Ernest and Doreen
Wife and date of marriage: Sarah, 3 October 1992
Education: Boldon Comprehensive, Tyne & Wear; South Tyneside College
Qualifications: 6 O-levels, qualified electrician
Career outside cricket: Electrician
Overseas tours: England YC to Sri Lanka 1986-87, to Australia for Youth World Cup 1987-88; MCC to Bahrain 1994-95
Overseas teams played for: Marist, Christchurch, New Zealand
Cricketers particularly admired: John Lever, Dennis Lillee
Other sports followed: Basketball and golf
Relaxations: Playing basketball and golf
Extras: Offered basketball scholarship in America. Durham Supporters' Player of the Year 1992. Durham Player of the Year 1994. Made his Test debut for England against Pakistan at Lord's in 1996
Best batting: 69 Durham v Leicestershire, Durham University 1994
Best bowling: 7-70 Durham v Australians, Durham University 1993

1997 Season

	M	Inns	NO	Runs	HS	Avge	100s	50s	Ct	St	O	M	Runs	Wkts	Avge	Best	5wI	10wM
Test																		
All First	17	24	5	121	30	6.36	-	-	2	-	590.3	126	1855	67	27.68	5-58	4	1
1-day Int																		
NatWest	1	0	0	0	0	-	-	-	-	-	10	0	42	2	21.00	2-42	-	
B & H	4	1	1	8	8 *	-	-	-	3	-	38.2	3	130	10	13.00	6-30	1	
Sunday	12	8	1	25	8	3.57	-	-	4	-	82.3	3	420	13	32.30	2-34	-	

Career Performances

	M	Inns	NO	Runs	HS	Avge	100s	50s	Ct	St	Balls	Runs	Wkts	Avge	Best	5wI	10wM
Test	1	2	1	11	10 *	11.00	-	-	1	-	198	138	2	69.00	1-60	-	-
All First	124	172	50	1490	69	12.21	-	2	36	-	22243	12692	408	31.10	7-70	25	2
1-day Int																	
NatWest	10	6	3	12	7 *	4.00	-	-	1	-	640	450	18	25.00	5-22	1	
B & H	19	8	4	38	12	9.50	-	-	4	-	1031	626	27	23.18	6-30	1	
Sunday	72	34	12	152	18	6.90	-	-	15	-	3099	2586	79	32.73	4-20	-	

BULBECK, M. P.   Somerset

Name: Matthew Paul Bulbeck
Role: Left-hand bat, left-arm medium-fast bowler
Born: 8 November 1979, Taunton
Height: 6ft 3in **Weight:** 12st 7lbs
Nickname: Bully, Pigeon
County debut: No first-team appearance
Parents: Paul and Carolyn
Marital status: Single
Family links with cricket: Father plays for local club
Education: Bishops Hall Primary School; Taunton School; Richard Huish College
Qualifications: 8 GCSEs
Off-season: Training with Somerset CCC Academy and studying for A-levels at Richard Huish College
Overseas tours: West of England U15 to West Indies; Somerset U16 to South Africa
Young players to look out for: Matthew Gitsham (Somerset U16)
Other sports followed: Football (Manchester United), rugby union (Bath RFC), golf (16 handicap)

Relaxations: Playing golf and listening to music
Extras: Went to Madras Pace Foundation and was coached by Dennis Lillee and Jeff Thompson in September 1997
Opinions on cricket: 'The County Championship should be split into two divisions.'

BURNS, M. Somerset

Name: Michael Burns
Role: Right-hand bat, right-arm medium bowler, wicket-keeper
Born: 6 February 1969, Barrow-in-Furness
Height: 6ft **Weight:** 13st
Nickname: George, Red Hot
County debut: 1991 (Warwickshire), 1997 (Somerset)
1st-Class 50s: 8
1st-Class catches: 49
1st-Class stumpings: 6
One-Day 100s: 1
Place in batting averages: 156th av. 25.50 (1996 200th av. 24.64)
Strike rate: 74.40 (career 86.40)
Parents: Robert and Linda, stepfather Stan
Wife and date of marriage: Carolyn, 9 October 1994
Children: 'Wife Caroline expecting January 1997'
Family links with cricket: 'Grandfather was a great back-garden bowler'
Education: Walney Comprehensive; Barrow College of Further Education
Qualifications: 'Few CSEs, couple of GCEs', qualified fitter at VSEL in Barrow, coaching award
Career outside cricket: 'Signing autographs for DHSS'
Overseas teams played for: Gill College, South Africa 1991-92; Motueka, Nelson, New Zealand 1992-93; Alex CC, Harare
Cricketers particularly admired: Dermot Reeve, Allan Donald, Pop Welch and 'Frosty'
Young players to look out for: Tony Frost, Darren Altree
Other sports followed: Rugby league ('had trials for Barrow RLFC and Carlisle RLFC') and golf
Relaxations: 'Eating Indians, socialising with friends. One or two pints with Pop Welch'
Extras: Played for Cumberland 1989-90. Had a trial with Glamorgan, went to La Manga with Lancashire junior side 1984. Player of the Tournament at Benson and Hedges

Thailand International Cricket Sixes in 1989. Left Warwickshire and joined Somerset for the 1997 season

Opinions on cricket: 'More should be done to help players in the winter and to help players find work after cricket.'

Best batting: 82 Somerset v Northamptonshire, Northampton 1997

Best bowling: 2-18 Somerset v Kent, Taunton 1997

1997 Season

	M	Inns	NO	Runs	HS	Avge	100s	50s	Ct	St	O	M	Runs	Wkts	Avge	Best	5wI	10wM
Test																		
All First	14	21	1	510	82	25.50	-	4	8	1	62	13	266	5	53.20	2-18	-	-
1-day Int																		
NatWest	2	2	0	9	6	4.50	-	-	-	-	6	0	27	0	-		-	-
B & H	5	5	0	256	91	51.20	-	3	-	-	21.4	0	95	5	19.00	3-18	-	
Sunday	15	14	1	362	115 *	27.84	1	2	5	-	58.1	0	324	13	24.92	4-39	-	

Career Performances

	M	Inns	NO	Runs	HS	Avge	100s	50s	Ct	St	Balls	Runs	Wkts	Avge	Best	5wI	10wM
Test																	
All First	34	55	3	1150	82	22.11	-	8	49	6	432	287	5	57.40	2-18	-	-
1-day Int																	
NatWest	4	4	1	46	37 *	15.33	-	-	-	-	36	27	0	-		-	-
B & H	13	11	0	311	91	28.27	-	3	6	2	130	95	5	19.00	3-18	-	
Sunday	46	40	5	699	115 *	19.97	1	2	33	8	349	324	13	24.92	4-39	-	

BUTCHER, G. P.   Glamorgan

Name: Gary Paul Butcher

Role: Right-hand opening bat, right-arm medium bowler

Born: 11 March 1975, Clapham, South London

Height: 5ft 9in **Weight:** 11st

Nickname: Marcellus

County debut: 1994

1st-Class 50s: 6

1st-Class 100s: 1

1st-Class 5 w. in innings: 1

1st-Class catches: 11

Place in batting averages: 108th av. 32.88 (1996 123rd av. 33.95)

Place in bowling averages: 116th av. 38.83 (1996 100th av. 39.33)

Strike rate: 57.08 (career 65.20)

Parents: Alan and Elaine

Marital status: Engaged to Annie Griffiths

Children: Edwin Griffiths, 6 June 1997
Family links with cricket: Father Alan played for Surrey, Glamorgan and England and is now with Essex; brother Mark plays for Surrey and England and uncle Ian played for Gloucestershire and Leicestershire
Education: Cumnor House; Trinity School; Riddlesdown Comprehensive; Heath Clark College and 'away trips with Steve Barwick'
Qualifications: 4 GCSEs, BTEC 1st Diploma in Leisure Studies
Career outside cricket: Chef
Off-season: 'Chef/carver in restaurant on the spit roast'
Overseas tours: England U18 to Denmark 1993; England U19 to Sri Lanka 1993-94; Glamorgan to Portugal 1994, to Zimbabwe 1995, to Pretoria 1996

Cricketers particularly admired: David Gower, Viv Richards, Brian Lara, Curtly Ambrose, Ian Botham, Sachin Tendulkar
Young players to look out for: Alun Evans – 'who has a face like a clock'
Other sports followed: 'Once went to Stuttgart in the Spit Roast Championships'
Relaxations: 'Mincing, on the pull, drinking, nightclubbing, smoking and general fitness'
Extras: Won Glamorgan's Most Improved Player Award 1996, recorded batting and bowling personal bests during the 1996 season. Appeared on *Gower's Cricket Monthly* with brother Mark
Opinions on cricket: 'Too much cricket.'
Best batting: 101* Glamorgan v Oxford University, The Parks 1997
Best bowling: 7-77 Glamorgan v Gloucestershire, Bristol 1996

1997 Season

	M	Inns	NO	Runs	HS	Avge	100s	50s	Ct	St	O	M	Runs	Wkts	Avge	Best	5wI	10wM
Test																		
All First	11	11	2	296	101*	32.88	1	1	1	-	114.1	21	466	12	38.83	3-87	-	-
1-day Int																		
NatWest	3	2	1	29	18*	29.00	-	-	-	-	14	0	72	3	24.00	2-33	-	
B & H	4	3	1	27	17	13.50	-	-	-	-	14.1	0	76	1	76.00	1-20	-	
Sunday	13	10	2	192	47	24.00	-	-	1	-	40.4	0	305	6	50.83	2-28	-	

Career Performances

	M	Inns	NO	Runs	HS	Avge	100s	50s	Ct	St	Balls	Runs	Wkts	Avge	Best	5wl	10wM
Test																	
All First	31	44	8	1046	101 *	29.05	1	6	11	-	2282	1559	35	44.54	7-77	1	-
1-day Int																	
NatWest	4	3	1	77	48	38.50	-	-	-	-	120	122	4	30.50	2-33	-	
B & H	9	6	2	39	17	9.75	-	-	-	-	169	136	3	45.33	2-21	-	
Sunday	25	17	4	251	47	19.30	-	-	2	-	456	513	14	36.64	4-32	-	

BUTCHER, M. A. Surrey

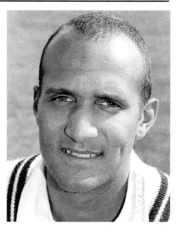

Name: Mark Alan Butcher
Role: Left-hand bat, right-arm medium bowler
Born: 23 August 1972, Croydon
Height: 5ft 11in **Weight:** 12st 7lbs
Nickname: Butch, Baz
County debut: 1991
Test debut: 1997
Tests: 5
1000 runs in a season: 3
1st-Class 50s: 37
1st-Class 100s: 7
1st-Class catches: 91
Place in batting averages: 114th av. 32.36
(1996 24th av. 51.74)
Strike rate: 35.14 (career 63.29)
Parents: Alan and Elaine
Wife: Judy
Family links with cricket: Father Alan
played for Glamorgan, Surrey and England
and is now with Essex; brother Gary plays for Glamorgan; uncle Ian played for
Gloucestershire and Leicestershire
Education: Cumnor House School; Trinity School; Archbishop Tenison's, Croydon
Qualifications: 5 O-levels, senior coaching award
Career outside cricket: Singer, guitar player, female impersonator
Off-season: Touring West Indies with England
Overseas tours: England YC to New Zealand 1990-91; Surrey to Dubai 1990 and
1993, to Perth 1995; England A to Australia 1996-97; England to West Indies 1997-98
Overseas teams played for: South Melbourne, Australia 1993-94; North Perth 1994-95
Cricketers particularly admired: Carl Rackemann, Mark and Steve Waugh,
Ian Botham, David Gower, Michael Holding, Jason Ratcliffe for his driving skills
('behind the wheel')

Other sports followed: Football, tennis, rhythmic gymnastics

Relaxations: 'Books, collecting CDs and records, playing guitar and singing in my band with my brother Gary, Peter James and Jo Fullman'

Extras: Played his first game for Surrey against his father's Glamorgan in the Refuge Assurance League at The Oval, the first-ever match of any sort between first-class counties in which a father and son have been in opposition

Opinions on cricket: 'Since introducing four-day cricket, the aim of those involved in producing the directives for pitches and the pitches themselves seems to be to have the game finish as soon as possible. The standard of first-class pitches is extremely poor and if they are not improved, neither will the standard of the players. Surely a hard-fought draw over four days is more beneficial to producing Test cricketers than a game which is over in two days. Secondly, why in England are first-class games played over 110 overs? Nowhere else in the world do cricketers play so many games let alone over so many overs. Fewer overs would produce a better quality of cricket throughout the day.'

Best batting: 167 Surrey v Durham, The Oval 1995

Best bowling: 4-31 Surrey v Worcestershire, The Oval 1994

1997 Season

	M	Inns	NO	Runs	HS	Avge	100s	50s	Ct	St	O	M	Runs	Wkts	Avge	Best	5wI	10wM
Test	5	10	0	254	87	25.40	-	2	8	-	2	0	14	0	-	-	-	-
All First	19	34	1	1068	153	32.36	1	7	28	-	41	8	97	7	13.85	3-24	-	-
1-day Int																		
NatWest	2	2	0	35	35	17.50	-	-	3	-								
B & H	6	5	1	124	48	31.00	-	-	2	-								
Sunday	10	10	1	227	81	25.22	-	1	6	-	8	0	35	1	35.00	1-24	-	

Career Performances

	M	Inns	NO	Runs	HS	Avge	100s	50s	Ct	St	Balls	Runs	Wkts	Avge	Best	5wI	10wM
Test	5	10	0	254	87	25.40	-	2	8	-	12	14	0	-	-	-	-
All First	78	139	11	5029	167	39.28	7	37	91	-	4311	2494	68	36.67	4-31	-	-
1-day Int																	
NatWest	10	10	2	370	91	46.25	-	3	6	-	216	127	3	42.33	2-57	-	
B & H	15	11	3	187	48	23.37	-	-	4	-	343	291	6	48.50	3-37	-	
Sunday	52	40	11	681	81	23.48	-	2	17	-	1381	1305	28	46.60	3-23	-	

12. Who was England's Man of the Series in the 1997 Texaco Trophy against Australia?

 vodafone

BYAS, D.   Yorkshire

Name: David Byas
Role: Left-hand bat, right-arm medium bowler, county captain
Born: 26 August 1963, Middledale, Kilham
Height: 6ft 4in **Weight:** 14st 7lbs
Nickname: Bingo, Gadgett
County debut: 1986
County cap: 1991
1000 runs in a season: 5
1st-Class 50s: 64
1st-Class 100s: 20
1st-Class 200s: 1
1st-Class catches: 247
One-Day 100s: 4
Place in batting averages: 31st av. 45.48
(1996 152nd av. 31.10)
Strike rate: (career 91.00)
Parents: Richard and Anne
Wife and date of marriage:
Rachael Elizabeth, 27 October 1990
Children: Olivia Rachael, 16 December 1991; Georgia Elizabeth, 30 December 1993; Benjamin
Family links with cricket: Father played local league cricket
Education: Kilham Primary School; Lisvane School, Scarborough; Scarborough College
Qualifications: 1 O-level (Engineering)
Career outside cricket: Partner in family farming business
Off-season: 'Farming and with my wife and family'
Overseas teams played for: Papatoetoe, Auckland 1988
Cricketers particularly admired: David Gower, Viv Richards, Ian Botham
Young players to look out for: Anthony McGrath, Paul Hutchison
Other sports followed: Hockey, motor racing, rugby union
Relaxations: 'Looking after my two active daughters and son. Dining out with my wife. Gardening.'
Extras: Became youngest captain (aged 21) of Scarborough CC in 1985. Broke John Hampshire's Sunday League record with 702 runs in 1994, which had stood since 1976. Runner-up in the Sunday League averages 1994. Played hockey for England Under 21. Has just completed end of first season as captain of Yorkshire
Best batting: 213 Yorkshire v Worcestershire, Scarborough 1995
Best bowling: 3-55 Yorkshire v Derbyshire, Chesterfield 1990

1997 Season

	M	Inns	NO	Runs	HS	Avge	100s	50s	Ct	St	O	M	Runs	Wkts	Avge	Best	5wI	10wM
Test																		
All First	20	33	4	1319	128	45.48	3	9	24	-								
1-day Int																		
NatWest	3	3	0	17	10	5.66	-	-	3	-								
B & H	6	6	0	142	72	23.66	-	1	1	-								
Sunday	16	16	0	409	83	25.56	-	2	7	-								

Career Performances

	M	Inns	NO	Runs	HS	Avge	100s	50s	Ct	St	Balls	Runs	Wkts	Avge	Best	5wI	10wM
Test																	
All First	200	337	32	11232	213	36.82	20	64	247	-	1092	719	12	59.91	3-55	-	-
1-day Int																	
NatWest	23	21	2	625	73 *	32.89	-	6	12	-	18	23	1	23.00	1-23	-	
B & H	36	33	2	933	116 *	30.09	1	4	9	-	283	155	5	31.00	2-38	-	
Sunday	156	151	22	3936	111 *	30.51	3	20	43	-	529	463	19	24.36	3-19	-	

CADDICK, A. R.   Somerset

Name: Andrew Richard Caddick
Role: Right-hand bat, right-arm
fast-medium bowler
Born: 21 November 1968, Christchurch,
New Zealand
Height: 6ft 5in **Weight:** 14st 13lbs
Nickname: Des, Shack
County debut: 1991
County cap: 1992
Test debut: 1993
Tests: 16
One-Day Internationals: 9
50 wickets in a season: 5
1st-Class 50s: 5
1st-Class 5 w. in innings: 26
1st-Class 10 w. in match: 8
1st-Class catches: 37
One-Day 5 w. in innings: 3
Place in batting averages: 229th av. 17.83
(1996 275th av. 13.26)
Place in bowling averages: 44th av. 26.61 (1996 43rd av. 27.79)
Strike rate: 52.04 (51.39)

Parents: Christopher and Audrey
Wife and date of marriage: Sarah, 27 January 1995
Education: Papanui High School, Christchurch, New Zealand
Qualifications: Qualified plasterer and tiler
Career outside cricket: Plasterer and tiler
Off-season: Touring West Indies with England
Overseas tours: New Zealand YC to Australia (Youth World Cup) 1987-88, to England 1988; England A to Australia 1992-93; England to West Indies 1993-94, to Zimbabwe and New Zealand 1996-97, to West Indies 1997-98
Cricketers particularly admired: Dennis Lillee, Richard Hadlee, Robin Smith, Jimmy Cook
Young players to look out for: Nasser Hussain, Nick Knight, Marcus Trescothick
Other sports followed: 'Mostly all'
Relaxations: Golf
Extras: Rapid Cricketline Player of the Year 1991. Whyte and Mackay Bowler of the Year 1997
Opinions on cricket: 'For a bowler it's a very hard game. We play far too much cricket at the top level, producing stale, soft cricketers.'
Best batting: 92 Somerset v Worcestershire, Worcester 1995
Best bowling: 9-32 Somerset v Lancashire, Taunton 1993

1997 Season

	M	Inns	NO	Runs	HS	Avge	100s	50s	Ct	St	O	M	Runs	Wkts	Avge	Best	5wI	10wM
Test	5	8	2	59	26 *	9.83	-	-	1	-	179.5	27	634	24	26.41	5-42	2	-
All First	18	22	4	321	56 *	17.83	-	1	5	-	702.4	139	2156	81	26.61	6-65	6	-
1-day Int																		
NatWest	2	1	0	5	5	5.00	-	-	-	-	18.5	3	57	2	28.50	1-27	-	
B & H	5	3	2	47	38	47.00	-	-	1	-	46.3	3	214	9	23.77	3-43	-	
Sunday	10	3	0	13	8	4.33	-	-	4	-	74	3	374	21	17.80	4-19	-	

Career Performances

	M	Inns	NO	Runs	HS	Avge	100s	50s	Ct	St	Balls	Runs	Wkts	Avge	Best	5wI	10wM
Test	16	26	4	272	29 *	12.36	-	-	6	-	3890	2006	61	32.88	6-65	4	-
All First	103	132	23	1797	92	16.48	-	5	37	-	21329	11187	415	26.95	9-32	26	8
1-day Int	9	5	4	35	20 *	35.00	-	-	2	-	522	498	15	33.20	3-35	-	
NatWest	14	8	2	26	8	4.33	-	-	2	-	848	458	29	15.79	6-30	2	
B & H	17	12	8	114	38	28.50	-	-	3	-	999	669	25	26.76	5-51	1	
Sunday	58	20	6	192	39	13.71	-	-	12	-	2475	1952	80	24.40	4-18	-	

CAMPBELL, C. L.   Durham

Name: Colin Lockey Campbell
Role: Right-hand bat, right-arm
fast-medium bowler
Born: 11 August 1977, Newcastle-upon-Tyne
Height: 6ft 6in **Weight:** 15st 10lbs
Nickname: Scunner, Big Col, Big'un,
Funkster, Funky Col
County debut: 1996
Strike rate: 72.00 (career 82.00)
Parents: Paul and Jacqueline
Marital status: Single
Education: West Lane, Winlayton Primary
School; Blaydon Comprehensive; Blaydon
Comprehensive Sixth Form
Qualifications: 9 GCSEs, 2 A-levels, NCA
Coaching Award

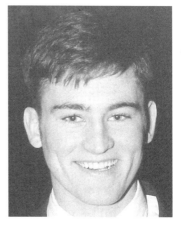

Off-season: 'Keeping fit, working on
strengthening the back, playing football.
Trying to get a job to bring some sort of
money in. Working with Durham Cricket Academy'
Overseas tours: Durham to South Africa 1995; England U19 to Zimbabwe 1995-96;
Durham U19 to Sri Lanka 1996-97
Cricketers particularly admired: Graeme Hick, Allan Donald, Ian Somerville
Young players to look out for: 'All the lads on the Durham Academy'
Other sports followed: Golf ('playing with the rest of the lads – bandits') and football
('watching Newcastle United and wishing the Maccums get beat each week')
Injuries: Stiff back, missed the first month and the last three weeks of the season
Relaxations: 'Playing golf, listening to dance music. Socialising with Somers, Biffa
and The Duck. Having a good laugh and dance with Phil Carlin to *Freed from Desire*'
Extras: Top of the bowling averages for Blaydon 1st XI for three years and Blaydon
U18 for two years. Once took 6 for 5 and 8 for 3 in successive games for his club. Had
match figures of 9 for 86 on his debut for Durham 2nd XI
Opinions on cricket: 'I think the introduction of day/night cricket was a good move.
Eight- or nine-month contracts need to be considered, as lads train and practise from
January and February as well as having to do a job.'
Best batting: 7 Durham v Gloucestershire, Chester-le-Street 1996
Best bowling: 1-29 Durham v Gloucestershire, Chester-le-Street 1996

1997 Season

	M	Inns	NO	Runs	HS	Avge	100s	50s	Ct	St	O	M	Runs	Wkts	Avge	Best	5wI	10wM
Test																		
All First	1	0	0	0	0	-	-	-	-	-	12	0	92	1	92.00	1-92	-	-
1-day Int																		
NatWest																		
B & H																		
Sunday																		

Career Performances

	M	Inns	NO	Runs	HS	Avge	100s	50s	Ct	St	Balls	Runs	Wkts	Avge	Best	5wI	10wM
Test																	
All First	2	1	0	7	7	7.00	-	-	-	-	164	136	2	68.00	1-29	-	-
1-day Int																	
NatWest																	
B & H																	
Sunday	2	1	0	0	0	0.00	-	-	-	-	96	89	3	29.66	2-45	-	

CAPEL, D. J.　　　　　　　Northamptonshire

Name: David John Capel
Role: Right-hand bat, right-arm medium bowler, all-rounder, slip fielder
Born: 6 February 1963, Northampton
Height: 5ft 11in **Weight:** 12st 8lbs
Nickname: Capes, Fiery, Fireball
County debut: 1981
County cap: 1986
Benefit: 1994
Test debut: 1987
Tests: 15
One-Day Internationals: 23
1000 runs in a season: 3
50 wickets in a season: 4
1st-Class 50s: 72
1st-Class 100s: 16
1st-Class 5 w. in innings: 14
1st-Class catches: 156
One-Day 100s: 4
Place in batting averages: 209th av. 20.00 (1996 168th av. 29.07)
Place in bowling averages: (1996 84th av. 33.74)
Strike rate: 117.00 (career 60.53)
Parents: John and Angela

Wife and date of marriage: Deborah Jane, 21 September 1985
Children: Jennifer Anne, 21 October 1987; Jordan David, 18 May 1993
Family links with cricket: Father and brother Andrew both captained
their local league sides. Brother plays for Old Northamptonians
Education: Roade Primary School; Roade Comprehensive School
Qualifications: 3 O-levels, 4 CSEs, NCA advanced coaching certificate
Off-season: Coaching and doing some commercial work for Northamptonshire CCC
Overseas tours: England to Sharjah 1986-87, to Pakistan 1987-88, to New Zealand
and Australia 1987-88, to India (Nehru Cup) 1989-90, to West Indies 1989-90;
England A to Australia 1992-93; MCC to Bangladesh 1996
Overseas teams played for: Eastern Province, South Africa 1985-87; Petersham-
Marrickville, Sydney 1991-92
Young players to look out for: Graham Swann
Other sports followed: Golf and rugby (Northampton RFC)
Injuries: Broken hand and dislocated shoulder, missed a total of 12 weeks
Relaxations: Fishing, listening to music and 'spending time watching family grow up'
Extras: Only second Northampton-born man to play for England. Two centuries in a
match against Sussex 1989. All-Rounder of the Year 'Wetherall Award' 1989. Broke
Northants records for fourth wicket in Sunday League with K.M. Curran and for fifth
wicket in NatWest Trophy with A.J. Lamb. Record Northants CCC benefit of £192,000
Opinions on cricket: 'Too much unnecessary tinkering with the game. Should play
NatWest as a 50-over competition in line with World Cup regulations and play it earlier
in the season. Have zonal games, much as with the Benson & Hedges format, but with
the B & H disappearing from view. Leave the championship as it is.'
Best batting: 175 Northamptonshire v Leicestershire, Northampton 1995
Best bowling: 7-44 Northamptonshire v Warwickshire, Edgbaston 1995

1997 Season

	M	Inns	NO	Runs	HS	Avge	100s	50s	Ct	St	O	M	Runs	Wkts	Avge	Best	5wI	10wM
Test																		
All First	4	7	0	140	57	20.00	-	1	1	-	39	4	180	2	90.00	1-22	-	-
1-day Int																		
NatWest																		
B & H	5	5	0	182	68	36.40	-	2	3	-	35	3	154	10	15.40	5-51	1	
Sunday	7	6	0	79	54	13.16	-	1	2	-	32	0	195	5	39.00	2-42	-	

Career Performances

	M	Inns	NO	Runs	HS	Avge	100s	50s	Ct	St	Balls	Runs	Wkts	Avge	Best	5wI	10wM
Test	15	25	1	374	98	15.58	-	2	6	-	2000	1064	21	50.66	3-88	-	-
All First	311	477	66	12202	175	29.68	16	72	156	-	32992	17507	545	32.12	7-44	14	-
1-day Int	23	19	2	327	50 *	19.23	-	1	6	-	1038	805	17	47.35	3-38	-	
NatWest	39	34	8	916	101	35.23	1	4	10	-	1702	1120	33	33.93	3-21	-	
B & H	61	55	5	1181	97	23.62	-	5	14	-	2632	1699	64	26.54	5-51	1	
Sunday	185	167	33	3981	121	29.70	3	16	46	-	5485	4453	133	33.48	4-30	-	

CARPENTER, J.   Sussex

Name: James Carpenter
Role: Left-hand bat, slow left-arm bowler
Born: 20 October 1975, Birkenhead
Height: 6ft 2in **Weight:** 12st 7lbs
Nickname: Carps, Harry, Scouse
County debut: 1997
1st-Class 50s: 1
1st-Class catches: 2
Place in batting averages: 157th av. 25.50
Strike rate: 129.00 (career 129.00)
Parents: John and Joanne
Marital status: Single
Family links with cricket: Father played
Minor Counties cricket for Cheshire
Education: Gayton Primary School;
Birkenhead School
Qualifications: 9 GCSEs and 4 A-levels
Off-season: Playing grade cricket in Sydney,
Australia
Overseas teams played for: Randwick CC, Sydney, Australia 1996-98
Young players to look out for: Brett Lee (Mosman CC, New South Wales), Jamie
Keggin (Bootle CC)
Other sports followed: Played county schools rugby for Cheshire and schoolboy
football with Liverpool FC. Had schoolboy forms with Everton and trials with Bolton
Wanderers. Played football for Runcorn FC in Vauxhall Conference
Relaxations: Golf and 'lying on Coogee beach, Sydney, in the off-season'
Extras: Captained MCC Young Professionals at Lord's. *Daily Telegraph* Bowling
Award. Awarded the Wetherall Trophy by the Cricket Society for the year's outstanding
schoolboy cricketer
Opinions on cricket: 'More floodlit cricket. More competition for mid-table sides in the
Championship when it is clear that they cannot win the Championship.'
Best batting: 63 Sussex v Hampshire, Southampton 1997
Best bowling: 1-50 Sussex v Nottinghamshire, Hove 1997

13. Who was Australia's Man of the Series in the
1997 Texaco Trophy against England?

O vodafone

1997 Season

	M	Inns	NO	Runs	HS	Avge	100s	50s	Ct	St	O	M	Runs	Wkts	Avge	Best	5wl	10wM
Test																		
All First	3	6	0	153	63	25.50	-	1	2	-	21.3	5	81	1	81.00	1-50	-	-
1-day Int																		
NatWest																		
B & H																		
Sunday	2	2	1	35	18	35.00	-	-	-	-	1	0	15	0	-		-	-

Career Performances

	M	Inns	NO	Runs	HS	Avge	100s	50s	Ct	St	Balls	Runs	Wkts	Avge	Best	5wl	10wM
Test																	
All First	3	6	0	153	63	25.50	-	1	2	-	129	81	1	81.00	1-50	-	-
1-day Int																	
NatWest																	
B & H																	
Sunday	2	2	1	35	18	35.00	-	-	-	-	6	15	0	-		-	-

CASSAR, M. E.   Derbyshire

Name: Matthew Edward Cassar
Role: Right-hand bat, right-arm
fast-medium bowler
Born: 16 October 1972, Sydney, Australia
Height: 6ft **Weight:** 13st
Nickname: Charchie, Oz
County debut: 1994
1st-Class 50s: 3
1st-Class catches: 4
Place in batting averages: 113th av. 32.42
Strike rate: 39.12 (career 40.12)
Parents: Edward and Joan
Wife and date of marriage: Jane, 5 October
1996
Family links with cricket: Wife, Jane, is the
England Ladies wicket-keeper
Education: Punchbowl Primary School,
Sydney; Sir Joseph Banks High School,
Sydney
Qualifications: School certificate and NCA coaching certificate
Overseas teams played for: Petersham/Marrickville, Sydney 1988-95
Cricketers particularly admired: Jane

Other sports followed: Football (Derby County), golf, racquet ball

Relaxations: Playing social sports, listening to music, watching television, sleeping 'and spending as much time as possible with Jane'

Extras: Played for New South Wales Colts

Opinions on cricket: 'Overseas players are a vital part of the English game. Playing with and against the greatest players in the world can only be to our advantage.'

Best batting: 78 Derbyshire v Somerset, Derby 1997

Best bowling: 4-54 Derbyshire v Oxford University, The Parks 1995

1997 Season

	M	Inns	NO	Runs	HS	Avge	100s	50s	Ct	St	O	M	Runs	Wkts	Avge	Best	5wI	10wM
Test																		
All First	7	8	1	227	78	32.42	-	2	2	-	52.1	6	224	8	28.00	3-31	-	-
1-day Int																		
NatWest																		
B & H																		
Sunday	4	3	0	36	33	12.00	-	-	2	-	11	1	85	2	42.50	1-15	-	

Career Performances

	M	Inns	NO	Runs	HS	Avge	100s	50s	Ct	St	Balls	Runs	Wkts	Avge	Best	5wI	10wM
Test																	
All First	10	12	1	361	78	32.81	-	3	4	-	642	409	16	25.56	4-54	-	-
1-day Int																	
NatWest																	
B & H																	
Sunday	4	3	0	36	33	12.00	-	-	2	-	66	85	2	42.50	1-15	-	

CATTERALL, D. N.   Worcestershire

Name: Duncan Neil Catterall
Role: Right-hand bat, right-arm
medium-fast bowler
Born: 19 September 1978, Preston
Height: 6ft **Weight:** 10st 7lbs
Nickname: Cats, Felix
County debut: No first-team appearance
Parents: David and Christine
Marital status: Single
Family links with cricket: Father and
brother play for Leyland DAF in the Northern
League
Education: Horncliffe School, Blackburn;
Queen Elizabeth's Grammar School,
Blackburn; Loughborough University
Qualifications: 11 GCSEs and 4 A-levels
Off-season: Studying
Overseas tours: Queen Elizabeth Grammar
School to Australia, December 1996
Cricketers particularly admired: Ian Botham, Steve Waugh
Other sports followed: Football (Blackburn Rovers) and badminton
Relaxations: Pop music
Opinions on cricket: 'More must be done to attract spectators'

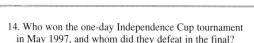

14. Who won the one-day Independence Cup tournament
in May 1997, and whom did they defeat in the final?

CAWDRON, M. J.   Gloucestershire

Name: Michael John Cawdron
Role: Left-hand bat, right-arm
medium-fast bowler
Born: 7 October 1974, Luton
Height: 6ft 3in **Weight:** 12st 7lbs
Nickname: Muscles
County debut: 1995 (one-day)
Parents: William and Mandy
Marital status: Single
Family links with cricket: Father and
brother played local village cricket
Education: Cheltenham College
Qualifications: 10 GCSEs, 3 A-Levels,
NCA coaching award
Career outside cricket: 'Vocationally
challenged'
Overseas tours: West of England U14 to
Holland; Cheltenham College to Zimbabwe
1992; Gloucestershire YC to Sri Lanka 1993-
94; Gloucestershire Gypsies to Zimbabwe 1994-95
Cricketers particularly admired: David Gower, Richard Hadlee, Reg Williams 'for
his disco antics'
Young players to look out for: Rob Cunliffe
Other sports followed: Rugby, hockey, racquets, clay-pigeon shooting, golf
Relaxations: Cinema, videos, eating and going out with friends
Extras: Winner of the *Daily Telegraph* Regional Bowling Award 1993. Captain of MCC
Schools and ESCA U19, 1993. 'Made 50 off 32 balls on Sunday League debut against
Essex at my old school' (Cheltenham College)
Opinions on cricket: 'Twelve-month contracts would be of great benefit to those
players who do not wish to winter abroad, as work opportunities are not secure, as other
employers are not eager to take on people on such a temporary basis.'

---

15. Who was voted Man of the Series in the Independence
Cup in May 1997, as a result of his tournament
total of 306 runs?

 vodafone

1997 (did not make any first-class or one-day appearances)

Career Performances

	M	Inns	NO	Runs	HS	Avge	100s	50s	Ct	St	Balls	Runs	Wkts	Avge	Best	5wI	10wM
Test																	
All First																	
1-day Int																	
NatWest																	
B & H	1	0	0	0	0	-	-	-	-	-	36	48	2	24.00	2-48	-	
Sunday	8	6	1	134	50	26.80	-	1	2	-	288	225	3	75.00	1-23	-	

CHAPMAN, C. A. Yorkshire

Name: Colin Anthony Chapman
Role: Right-hand bat, wicket-keeper
Born: 8 June 1971, Bradford
Height: 5ft 8in **Weight:** 11st 7lbs
Nickname: Chappy
County debut: 1990
1st-Class 50s: 1
1st-Class catches: 8
1st-Class stumpings: 3
Parents: Mick and Joyce
Wife and date of marriage:
Amanda, 11 November 1996
Education: Nabwood Middle; Beckfoot
Grammar; Bradford & Ilkley Community
College
Qualifications: 5 O-levels, BTEC Diploma
in Graphic Design, senior coaching certificate
Overseas teams played for: Waitamata,
Auckland 1989-91
Overseas tours: Yorkshire CCC to South Africa 1993 and 1995
Cricketers particularly admired: Phil Carrick, Alan Knott, Mark Nicklin
Young players to look out for: Alex Wharf, Alex Morris
Other sports followed: Football (Liverpool FC)
Relaxations: 'A few beers or a meal out, DIY, playing and watching sport'
Opinions on cricket: 'Too much travelling'
Best batting: 80 Yorkshire v Lancashire, Headingley 1997

1997 Season

	M	Inns	NO	Runs	HS	Avge	100s	50s	Ct	St	O	M	Runs	Wkts	Avge	Best	5wl	10wM
Test																		
All First	2	4	0	139	80	34.75	-	1	3	1								
1-day Int																		
NatWest																		
B & H																		
Sunday																		

Career Performances

	M	Inns	NO	Runs	HS	Avge	100s	50s	Ct	St	Balls	Runs	Wkts	Avge	Best	5wl	10wM
Test																	
All First	6	11	1	211	80	21.10	-	1	8	3							
1-day Int																	
NatWest	1	0	0	0	0	-	-	-	1	-							
B & H																	
Sunday	7	6	3	89	36 *	29.66	-	-	2	-							

CHAPMAN, R. J. Worcestershire

Name: Robert James Chapman
Role: Right-hand bat, right-arm
fast-medium bowler
Born: 28 July 1972, Nottingham
Height: 6ft 1in **Weight:** 13st
Nickname: Bobby Chap, Bobby C
County debut: 1992 (Nottinghamshire),
1997 (Worcestershire)
1st-Class catches: 6
Place in bowling averages: 104th av. 36.00
Strike rate: 47.76 (career 64.47)
Parents: Sammy and Hazel
Marital status: Single
Family links with cricket: Father Sammy
plays club cricket for Clifton CC and was a
pro footballer with Nottingham Forest, Notts
County and Shrewsbury Town
Education: South Wilford C of E School;
Farnborough School, Clifton, Nottingham;
South Nottinghamshire College
Qualifications: 7 O-levels, 2 A-levels, NCA Coaching Award
Overseas tours: Worcestershire CCC to Zimbabwe 1997

Overseas teams played for: South Barwon, Geelong, Australia 1995-96
Cricketers particularly admired: Graeme Hick, Stuart Law, Matthew Dowman
Young players to look out for: Vikram Solanki, Ismail Dawood
Other sports followed: Football (Nottingham Forest), indoor cricket, fishing, 'darts with my Dad'
Injuries: Calf and Achilles problems, out for three weeks
Relaxations: Cinema, reading, fishing and listening to music (U2, Radiohead, Oasis, Paul Weller, Smashing Pumpkins, The Verve)
Extras: Left Nottinghamshire at the end of the 1996 season and joined Worcestershire for 1997
Best batting: 25 Nottinghamshire v Lancashire, Trent Bridge 1994
Best bowling: 4-109 Nottinghamshire v South Africa A, Trent Bridge 1996

1997 Season

	M	Inns	NO	Runs	HS	Avge	100s	50s	Ct	St	O	M	Runs	Wkts	Avge	Best	5wI	10wM
Test																		
All First	6	3	0	3	3	1.00	-	-	2	-	103.3	18	468	13	36.00	3-26	-	-
1-day Int																		
NatWest	1	0	0	0	0	-	-	-	-	-								
B & H	1	1	0	0	0	0.00	-	-	-	-	6	0	27	0	-		-	-
Sunday	9	2	0	0	0	0.00	-	-	-	-	49	2	214	7	30.57	3-27	-	

Career Performances

	M	Inns	NO	Runs	HS	Avge	100s	50s	Ct	St	Balls	Runs	Wkts	Avge	Best	5wI	10wM
Test																	
All First	21	20	4	124	25	7.75	-	-	6	-	2450	1759	38	46.28	4-109	-	-
1-day Int																	
NatWest	2	0	0	0	0	-	-	-	-	-	72	40	0	-		-	-
B & H	1	1	0	0	0	0.00	-	-	-	-	36	27	0	-		-	-
Sunday	20	5	2	6	4 *	2.00	-	-	-	-	663	582	14	41.57	3-27	-	

16. Who was Ian Healy's 100th Ashes Test victim
during the third Test at Old Trafford in 1997?

CHAPPLE, G.   Lancashire

Name: Glen Chapple
Role: Right-hand bat, right-arm
medium bowler
Born: 23 January 1974, Skipton, Yorkshire
Height: 6ft 2in **Weight:** 12st 7lbs
Nickname: Chappy, Boris, Boomor, Cheeky
County debut: 1992
50 wickets in a season: 2
1st-Class 50s: 3
1st-Class 100s: 1
1st-Class 5 w. in innings: 6
1st-Class catches: 24
One-Day 5 w. in innings: 1
Place in batting averages: 180th av. 23.70
(1996 238th av. 19.35)
Place in bowling averages: 90th av. 33.33
(1996 82nd av. 33.38)
Strike rate: 61.29 (career 57.27)
Parents: Eileen and Michael
Marital status: Single
Family links with cricket: Father played in Lancashire League for Nelson and was a professional for Darwen and Earby
Education: West Craven High School; Nelson and Colne College
Qualifications: 8 GCSEs, 2 A-levels (geography and economics)
Overseas tours: England U18 to Canada 1991; England U19 to New Zealand 1990-91, to Pakistan 1991-92, to India 1992-93; England A to India 1994-95, to Australia 1996-97
Cricketers particularly admired: Dennis Lillee, Robin Smith
Other sports followed: Football (Liverpool), golf
Relaxations: 'Watching films, cinema, music, socialising'
Extras: Hit fastest century (21 minutes) against Glamorgan at Old Trafford 1993. Man of the Match in the 1996 NatWest final against Essex after taking 6 for 18
Best batting: 109* Lancashire v Glamorgan, Old Trafford 1993
Best bowling: 6-48 Lancashire v Durham, Stockton 1994

---

17. Who broke Danny Morrison's undistinguished record as the
player to have scored the most Test-match ducks?

O vodafone

1997 Season

	M	Inns	NO	Runs	HS	Avge	100s	50s	Ct	St	O	M	Runs	Wkts	Avge	Best	5wl	10wM
Test																		
All First	11	14	4	237	66	23.70	-	2	2	-	275.5	45	900	27	33.33	4-80	-	-
1-day Int																		
NatWest	2	1	1	2	2 *	-	-	-	-	-	10.1	0	46	1	46.00	1-28	-	
B & H	1	0	0	0	0	-	-	-	-	-	5	1	23	0	-	-	-	
Sunday	11	4	3	26	13 *	26.00	-	-	3	-	67	2	382	10	38.20	3-22	-	

Career Performances

	M	Inns	NO	Runs	HS	Avge	100s	50s	Ct	St	Balls	Runs	Wkts	Avge	Best	5wl	10wM
Test																	
All First	74	102	38	1386	109 *	21.65	1	3	24	-	12256	6470	214	30.23	6-48	8	-
1-day Int																	
NatWest	9	5	1	6	4	1.50	-	-	2	-	480	355	12	29.58	6-18	1	
B & H	14	4	3	20	8	20.00	-	-	2	-	750	584	13	44.92	3-31	-	
Sunday	53	19	10	146	43	16.22	-	-	9	-	1968	1582	50	31.64	3-22	-	

CHILTON, M. J.   Lancashire

Name: Mark James Chilton
Role: Right-hand bat, right-arm medium bowler
Born: 2 October 1976, Sheffield
Height: 6ft 3in **Weight:** 12st 10lbs
Nickname: Chill, Prof, Chilly
County debut: 1997
Parents: Jim and Sue
Marital status: Single
Family links with cricket: 'Father played local cricket'
Education: Brooklands Primary School; Manchester Grammar School; Durham University
Qualifications: 10 GCSEs, 3 A-levels, NCA coaching award
Career outside cricket: Student
Off-season: 'Studying, but no plans after I finish'

Overseas tours: Manchester Grammar School to Barbados 1993-94, to South Africa 1995-96; Durham University to Zimbabwe 1997-98
Cricketers particularly admired: Alec Stewart

Young players to look out for: Stuart Adamson, Jon Humphreys
Other sports followed: Football (Manchester United), tennis and golf
Relaxations: Darts, videos, music, socialising
Extras: Represented England U14, U15, U17. Played for North of England v New Zealand U19 in 1996. Awarded England U15 Batsman of the Year in 1992. Played for British Universities in 1997 Benson & Hedges Cup winning the Gold Award against Sussex. Played for Lancashire in the first day/night game held in Britain
Opinions on cricket: 'Still too much cricket played. Need a structure so that the season remains competitive throughout. An improvement in weather conditions would be nice!'
Best batting: 9 Lancashire v Glamorgan, Liverpool 1997

1997 Season

	M	Inns	NO	Runs	HS	Avge	100s	50s	Ct	St	O	M	Runs	Wkts	Avge	Best	5wl	10wM
Test																		
All First	1	1	0	9	9	9.00	-	-	-	-	4	0	23	0	-		-	-
1-day Int																		
NatWest																		
B & H	5	5	0	104	43	20.80	-	-	-	-	28.3	0	159	8	19.87	5-26	1	
Sunday	3	3	0	31	22	10.33	-	-	-	-	16	0	80	3	26.66	2-27	-	

Career Performances

	M	Inns	NO	Runs	HS	Avge	100s	50s	Ct	St	Balls	Runs	Wkts	Avge	Best	5wl	10wM
Test																	
All First	1	1	0	9	9	9.00	-	-	-	-	24	23	0	-		-	-
1-day Int																	
NatWest																	
B & H	5	5	0	104	43	20.80	-	-	-	-	171	159	8	19.87	5-26	1	
Sunday	3	3	0	31	22	10.33	-	-	-	-	96	80	3	26.66	2-27	-	

CHURCH, M. J.   Gloucestershire

Name: Matthew John Church
Role: Right-hand bat, right-arm medium bowler
Born: 26 July 1972, Guildford
Height: 6ft 2in **Weight:** 13st
Nickname: Money, Churchy, Loose Unit, Maddy, Larse
County debut: 1994 (Worcestershire), 1997 (Gloucestershire)
1st-Class 50s: 1
1st-Class 100s: 1
1st-Class catches: 8
Place in batting averages: 195th av. 25.45 (1995 244th av. 15.75)

Strike rate: 26.11 (career 26.77)
Parents: Anthony and Annette
Marital status: Single
Education: St George's College, Weybridge;
Guildford Technical College; Stuart Cricket
Academy
Qualifications: 4 GCSEs, 1 A-level ('Thanks
Mr Dav and Les')
Overseas tours: Surrey Young Cricketers to
Australia 1989-90; St George's College to
Zimbabwe 1990-91
Overseas teams played for: Harmony,
Orange Free State 1991-92; North Shore,
Geelong 1992-93; Adelaide University 1994-
95
Cricketers particularly admired: Ian
Glover, Graham Thorpe, Robin Smith, Tim
Edwards and Karl Thomas
Other sports followed: All sports

Extras: Former MCC Young Cricketer, signed by Worcestershire at the beginning of the
1994 season. Sold scorecards at the 1993 Benson & Hedges Cup final and was 12th Man
for Worcestershire at the NatWest final the following year. Fielded for England as substitute
in 1995 Lord's Test against South Africa. Played for Surrey from U12 to U19. Released by
Worcestershire at the end of the 1996 season and joined Gloucestershire in 1997
Best batting: 152 Worcestershire v Oxford University, The Parks 1996
Best bowling: 4-50 Worcestershire v Oxford University, The Parks 1996

1997 Season

	M	Inns	NO	Runs	HS	Avge	100s	50s	Ct	St	O	M	Runs	Wkts	Avge	Best	5wI	10wM
Test																		
All First	2	4	0	73	53	18.25	-	1	-	-								
1-day Int																		
NatWest																		
B & H																		
Sunday	1	1	0	25	25	25.00	-	-	-	-								

Career Performances

	M	Inns	NO	Runs	HS	Avge	100s	50s	Ct	St	Balls	Runs	Wkts	Avge	Best	5wI	10wM
Test																	
All First	16	29	1	544	152	19.42	1	1	8	-	241	163	9	18.11	4-50	-	-
1-day Int																	
NatWest	1	1	0	35	35	35.00	-	-	-	-	30	34	0	-		-	-
B & H	1	0	0	0	0	-	-	-	-	-							
Sunday	15	11	0	98	25	8.90	-	-	7	-	6	12	0	-		-	-

CLARKE, V. P.   Derbyshire

Name: Vincent Paul Clarke
Role: Right-hand bat, leg-break bowler
Born: 11 November 1971, Liverpool
Height: 6ft 3in **Weight:** 15st 10lbs
County debut: 1994 (Somerset), 1995
(Leicestershire), 1997 (Derbyshire)
1st-Class 50s: 5
1st-Class catches: 11
Place in batting averages: 90th av. 35.29
Place in bowling averages: 145th av. 64.23
Strike rate: 103.30 (career 99.40)
Parents: Vinnie and Sandra
Marital status: Single
Family links with cricket: Father played
representative schoolboy cricket
Education: Craigie Primary School; Sacred
Heart College, Sorrento; Perth College,
Western Australia
Qualifications: Diploma in Social Training
Overseas teams played for: Wanneroo District, Perth 1990-94
Cricketers particularly admired: Shane Warne, Ian Botham
Other sports followed: Windsurfing, Aussie Rules football, most sports
Relaxations: Playing the guitar, golf, watching sport
Extras: Brought up in Australia but has English birth qualification. Was in Western Australian Development Squads from U14 to U19. Represented Western Australia at indoor cricket in 1991. Played for Bridgwater and Somerset 2nd XI in 1993. Joined Leicestershire at the start of the 1995 season but was released at the end of the 1996 season. Joined Derbyshire for the 1997 season
Best batting: 99 Derbyshire v Warwickshire, Edgbaston 1997
Best bowling: 3-47 Derbyshire v Cambridge University, Fenner's 1997

1997 Season

	M	Inns	NO	Runs	HS	Avge	100s	50s	Ct	St	O	M	Runs	Wkts	Avge	Best	5wI	10wM
Test																		
All First	19	30	6	847	99	35.29	-	5	9	-	223.5	48	835	13	64.23	3-47		-
1-day Int																		
NatWest	3	2	1	35	24 *	35.00	-	-	2	-	27	2	92	2	46.00	1-38	-	
B & H	5	5	1	81	52	20.25	-	1	2	-	28	0	142	7	20.28	4-49	-	
Sunday	13	13	3	244	77 *	24.40	-	2	4	-	52	2	292	9	32.44	2-28	-	

Career Performances

	M	Inns	NO	Runs	HS	Avge	100s	50s	Ct	St	Balls	Runs	Wkts	Avge	Best	5wI	10wM
Test																	
All First	26	43	7	991	99	27.52	-	5	11	-	1988	1276	20	63.80	3-47	-	-
1-day Int																	
NatWest	3	2	1	35	24 *	35.00	-	-	2	-	162	92	2	46.00	1-38	-	
B & H	6	6	1	103	52	20.60	-	1	2	-	168	142	7	20.28	4-49	-	
Sunday	23	23	3	304	77 *	15.20	-	2	6	-	452	428	12	35.66	2-28	-	

COLLINGWOOD, P. D. Durham

Name: Paul Davis Collingwood
Role: Right-hand bat, right-arm medium bowler
Born: 26 May 1976, Shotley Bridge, Tyneside
Height: 5ft 11in **Weight:** 11st 4lbs
Nickname: Colly, Shep
County debut: 1995 (one-day), 1996 (first-class)
1st-Class 50s: 3
1st-Class 100s: 1
1st-Class catches: 17
Place in batting averages: 148th av. 26.63 (1996 212th av. 23.20)
Strike rate: 48.00 (career 68.88)
Parents: David and Janet
Marital status: Single
Family links with cricket: Father and brother play in the Tyneside Senior League for Shotley Bridge CC
Education: Benfieldside Junior School; Blackfyne Comprehensive School; Derwentside College
Qualifications: 9 GCSEs and 2 A-levels
Cricketers particularly admired: Dermot Reeve, Graham Thorpe and Ian Botham
Other sports followed: Football (Sunderland AFC) and table tennis
Relaxations: 'I enjoy watching most sports programmes and listening to music. Also going to Sunderland matches home and away'
Opinions on cricket: 'I believe there is far too much cricket played during the season. Surely if there was less first-class cricket played the standard would improve overall.'
Best batting: 107 Durham v Oxford University, The Parks 1997
Best bowling: 3-46 Durham v Lancashire, Old Trafford 1997

1997 Season

	M	Inns	NO	Runs	HS	Avge	100s	50s	Ct	St	O	M	Runs	Wkts	Avge	Best	5wI	10wM
Test																		
All First	8	13	1	316	107	26.33	1	1	11	-	48	4	203	6	33.83	3-46	-	-
1-day Int																		
NatWest	1	1	0	15	15	15.00	-	-	-	-								
B & H	4	4	0	123	49	30.75	-	-	1	-	14	0	64	2	32.00	1-12	-	
Sunday	8	7	0	63	19	9.00	-	-	3	-	20.4	0	104	3	34.66	1-2	-	

Career Performances

	M	Inns	NO	Runs	HS	Avge	100s	50s	Ct	St	Balls	Runs	Wkts	Avge	Best	5wI	10wM
Test																	
All First	19	33	1	780	107	24.37	1	3	17	-	620	384	9	42.66	3-46	-	-
1-day Int																	
NatWest	3	3	0	69	28	23.00	-	-	-	-	12	20	0	-		-	-
B & H	9	8	1	165	49	23.57	-	-	2	-	265	224	7	32.00	3-28	-	
Sunday	24	23	3	368	61 *	18.40	-	2	11	-	262	210	4	52.50	1-2	-	

CONNOR, C. A.   Hampshire

Name: Cardigan Adolphus Connor
Role: Right-hand bat, right-arm
fast-medium bowler
Born: 24 March 1961, West End, Anguilla
Height: 5ft 10in **Weight:** 12st 8lbs
Nickname: Cardy, CC
County debut: 1984
County cap: 1988
50 wickets in a season: 5
1st-Class 50s: 2
1st-Class 5 w. in innings: 18
1st-Class 10 w. in match: 4
1st-Class catches: 61
Place in batting averages:
(1996 265th av. 15.55)
Place in bowling averages: 88th av. 33.07
(1996 11th av. 21.85)
Strike rate: 56.69 (career 60.60)
Parents: Ethleen
Wife and date of marriage: Jacqui, 18 March 1995
Education: The Valley Secondary School, Anguilla; Windsor and Langley College
Qualifications: Engineer, trainer

Career outside cricket: Keep-fit instructor and masseur
Overseas teams played for: Merewether DCC, Newcastle, Australia 1983-93; Valley Secondary School, Anguilla 1992-98
Cricketers particularly admired: Malcolm Marshall, Viv Richards
Young players to look out for: Andrew Flintoff, Ben Hollioake
Other sports followed: Football (Arsenal)
Injuries: Knee, out for four months
Relaxations: Keeping fit
Extras: Played for Buckinghamshire in Minor Counties before joining Hampshire. First Anguillan-born player to appear in the County Championship
Best batting: 59 Hampshire v Surrey, The Oval 1993
Best bowling: 9-38 Hampshire v Gloucestershire, Southampton 1996

1997 Season

	M	Inns	NO	Runs	HS	Avge	100s	50s	Ct	St	O	M	Runs	Wkts	Avge	Best	5wl	10wM
Test																		
All First	5	4	2	34	12 *	17.00	-	-	-	-	122.5	18	430	13	33.07	7-46	1	-
1-day Int																		
NatWest	2	0	0	0	0	-	-	-	-	-	19.4	4	66	3	22.00	2-55	-	
B & H	1	1	0	2	2	2.00	-	-	-	-	10	0	61	1	61.00	1-61	-	
Sunday	8	3	2	1	1 *	1.00	-	-	-	-	55.5	2	300	6	50.00	2-35	-	

Career Performances

	M	Inns	NO	Runs	HS	Avge	100s	50s	Ct	St	Balls	Runs	Wkts	Avge	Best	5wl	10wM
Test																	
All First	217	205	53	1814	59	11.93	-	2	61	-	37091	19338	612	31.59	9-38	18	4
1-day Int																	
NatWest	34	7	4	37	13	12.33	-	-	10	-	2196	1299	69	18.82	4-11	-	
B & H	55	15	7	39	11	4.87	-	-	10	-	3091	2063	80	25.78	4-19	-	
Sunday	187	55	18	239	25	6.45	-	-	33	-	8243	6196	228	27.17	5-25	1	

18. To whom was Dennis Lillee referring when he said, 'The only fellow I've met who fell in love with himself at a young age and has remained faithful ever since?'

vodafone

COOK, S. J.   Middlesex

Name: Simon James Cook
Role: Right-hand bat, right-arm
medium-fast bowler
Born: 15 January 1977, Oxford
Height: 6ft 4in **Weight:** 12st
Nickname: Cookie
County debut: 1997 (one-day)
Parents: Phil and Sue
Marital status: Single
Education: Botley Primary School; Matthew
Arnold School
Qualifications: GCSEs, NVQ Business
Administration II
Career outside cricket: Sales and marketing
within the computer industry
Off-season: Working and training
Cricketers particularly admired:
Angus Fraser, Allan Donald, Mark Waugh
Young players to look out for: Owais Shah,
Neil Martin, David Nash
Other sports followed: Football (Liverpool), 'any other ball sport'
Injuries: Shin splints, missed a total of three weeks during the season
Relaxations: Sleeping, playing any sport, watching television and videos
Opinions on cricket: 'Cut down the number of games that we play and have more short,
sharp quality training sessions.'

1997 Season

	M	Inns	NO	Runs	HS	Avge	100s	50s	Ct	St	O	M	Runs	Wkts	Avge	Best	5wI	10wM
Test																		
All First																		
1-day Int																		
NatWest																		
B & H	1	1	0	6	6	6.00	-	-	-	-	9	0	71	0	-		-	-
Sunday																		

Career Performances

	M	Inns	NO	Runs	HS	Avge	100s	50s	Ct	St	Balls	Runs	Wkts	Avge	Best	5wI	10wM
Test																	
All First																	
1-day Int																	
NatWest																	
B & H	1	1	0	6	6	6.00	-	-	-	-	54	71	0	-		-	-
Sunday																	

CORK, D. G. Derbyshire

Name: Dominic Gerald Cork
Role: Right-hand bat, right-arm,
fast-medium bowler, county captain
Born: 7 August 1971, Newcastle-under-
Lyme, Staffordshire
Height: 6ft 3in **Weight:** 13st
Nickname: Corky
County debut: 1990
County cap: 1993
Test debut: 1995
Tests: 19
One-Day Internationals: 25
50 wickets in a season: 3
1st-Class 50s: 24
1st-Class 100s: 2
1st-Class 5 w. in innings: 12
1st-Class 10 w. in match: 2
1st-Class catches: 87
Place in batting averages: 176th av. 24.00
(1996 124th av. 33.86)
Place in bowling averages: 126th 41.54 (1996 79th av. 33.17)
Strike rate: 72.00 (career 53.55)
Parents: Gerald and Mary
Children: Gregory Theodore Gerald, 29 September 1994
Family links with cricket: 'Father and two brothers play for Betley CC in the North
Staffs and South Cheshire League'
Education: St Joseph's College, Stoke-on-Trent; Newcastle College of Further
Education
Qualifications: History O-level, leisure and recreation, qualified coach
Career outside cricket: 'None at the moment but I would love to work in the media
or in television'

Overseas tours: England YCs to Australia 1989-90; England A to Bermuda and West Indies 1991-92, to Australia 1992-93, to South Africa 1993-94, to India 1994-95; England to South Africa 1995-96, to India and Pakistan (World Cup) 1995-96, to New Zealand 1996-97

Overseas teams played for: East Shirley, Christchurch, New Zealand 1990-91

Cricketers particularly admired: Ian Botham, Kim Barnett, 'and particularly Shane Warne'

Young players to look out for: Vikram Solanki, Andrew Harris and Phil DeFreitas ('off-spin')

Other sports followed: Horse racing, football (Stoke 'Premier League soon'), rugby union (England and Bath RFC)

Relaxations: Gardening ('I love weeding'), listening to music, 'watching Lou Macari rally the mighty men'

Extras: First played cricket for Betley CC in the North Staffs & South Cheshire League. In 1990 he took a wicket in his first over in first-class cricket v New Zealand at Derby and scored a century as nightwatchman for England U19 v Pakistan at Taunton. Played Minor Counties cricket for Staffordshire in 1989 and 1990. Selected for England A in 1991 – his first full season of first-class cricket. The Cricket Association Young Player of 1991. Took eight wickets for 53 runs on 20th birthday. Achieved first-class hat-trick against Kent, 1994. Took seven wickets for 43 runs on Test debut against West Indies at Lord's. Achieved hat-trick against the West Indies at Old Trafford in the fourth Test – the first by an Englishman in Test cricket for thirty years. Won two Man of the Match awards in three Test matches. Voted Player of the Year by the Professional Cricketers' Association for 1995. Finished at the top of the Whyte and Mackay ratings for bowling in 1995. Withdrew from the Zimbabwe leg of England's 1996-97 winter tour through personal reasons, but joined up with the team in New Zealand. Appointed Derbyshire captain for the 1998 season

Opinions on cricket: 'Counties should be amalgamated together, giving us nine counties. Squads would get stronger and there would be no need for overseas players. England players and fringe players should be contracted to the TCCB and batsmen should stop hitting bowlers for boundaries.'

Best batting: 104 Derbyshire v Gloucestershire, Cheltenham 1993

Best bowling: 9-43 Derbyshire v Northamptonshire, Derby 1995

1997 Season

	M	Inns	NO	Runs	HS	Avge	100s	50s	Ct	St	O	M	Runs	Wkts	Avge	Best	5wI	10wM
Test																		
All First	6	9	1	192	55 *	24.00	-	2	4	-	132	28	457	11	41.54	4-48	-	-
1-day Int																		
NatWest	1	1	0	16	16	16.00	-	-	-	-	11.2	0	67	1	67.00	1-67	-	
B & H																		
Sunday	3	3	0	67	33	22.33	-	-	-	-	17	1	80	6	13.33	6-21	1	

Career Performances

	M	Inns	NO	Runs	HS	Avge	100s	50s	Ct	St	Balls	Runs	Wkts	Avge	Best	5wI	10wM
Test	19	27	4	482	59	20.95	-	2	10	-	4345	2249	74	30.39	7-43	3	-
All First	137	201	30	4216	104	24.65	2	24	87	-	22973	11468	429	26.73	9-43	12	2
1-day Int	25	15	2	132	31 *	10.15	-	-	6	-	1440	1071	35	30.60	3-27	-	
NatWest	12	10	0	290	62	29.00	-	3	3	-	757	481	26	18.50	5-18	2	
B & H	18	14	5	281	92 *	31.22	-	2	8	-	1076	712	20	35.60	5-49	1	
Sunday	69	55	6	867	66	17.69	-	2	26	-	2874	2293	79	29.02	6-21	1	

COSKER, D. A.   Glamorgan

Name: Dean Andrew Cosker
Role: Right-hand bat, slow left-arm bowler
Born: 7 January 1978, Weymouth, Dorset
Height: 5ft 11in   **Weight:** 12st 7lbs
County debut: 1996
1st-Class catches: 7
Place in bowling averages: 112th av. 37.93
(1996 107th av. 38.87)
Strike rate: 77.65 (career 70.80)
Parents: Des and Carol
Marital status: 'Associated with Claire Evans'
Family links with cricket: Brother Gareth is keen, grandfather is an avid supporter of Glamorgan CCC
Education: Preston Primary School, Yeovil; Ravenswood Prep School, Devon; Millfield School
Qualifications: 10 GCSEs, 3 A-levels, Class 3 soccer referee
Career outside cricket: 'Lurking with intent, touring and sleeping'
Off-season: England A tour to Kenya and Sri Lanka
Overseas tours: West of England U15 to West Indies 1993-94; Millfield School to Sri Lanka 1994-95; England U17 to Holland 1995; England U19 to Pakistan 1996-97; England A to Kenya and Sri Lanka 1997-98
Overseas teams played for: Gordon, Sydney 1996-97
Cricketers particularly admired: 'My good old friend, Quintin,' and Waqar Younis
Young players to look out for: David 'half man half goat' Nash, John Derrick
Other sports followed: Soccer (Tottenham Hotspur FC)
Injuries: Strained neck playing soccer in a warm-up at Leicester. Spent three days in a neck brace

115

Relaxations: 'Eating out, especially at Ramon's Cafe, Cardiff. Spending time with my very attractive girlfriend Claire and shopping'

Extras: *Daily Telegraph* Regional Bowling Award, England U15 and U17. Played for U19 TCCB Development of Excellence XI against South Africa U19 in 1995. Played for England U19 against Zimbabwe in 1997

Opinions on cricket: 'The size of playing staffs should be cut. When international or any other form of cricket is shown on national television commentators should comment on the game and not criticise the players' techniques or attitudes. They should let the audience enjoy the cricket.'

Best batting: 24 Glamorgan v Lancashire, Cardiff 1996
Best bowling: 4-60 Glamorgan v Lancashire, Cardiff 1996

1997 Season

	M	Inns	NO	Runs	HS	Avge	100s	50s	Ct	St	O	M	Runs	Wkts	Avge	Best	5wl	10wM
Test																		
All First	16	9	5	16	7	4.00	-	-	4	-	375.2	92	1100	29	37.93	4-64	-	-
1-day Int																		
NatWest	1	1	1	3	3 *	-	-	-	-	-	12	3	26	3	8.66	3-26	-	
B & H	1	1	0	0	0	0.00	-	-	-	-	6	0	38	1	38.00	1-38	-	
Sunday	7	2	0	5	5	2.50	-	-	2	-	52	3	250	6	41.66	2-40	-	

Career Performances

	M	Inns	NO	Runs	HS	Avge	100s	50s	Ct	St	Balls	Runs	Wkts	Avge	Best	5wl	10wM
Test																	
All First	21	15	6	61	24	6.77	-	-	7	-	3186	1722	45	38.26	4-60	-	-
1-day Int																	
NatWest	1	1	1	3	3 *	-	-	-	-	-	72	26	3	8.66	3-26	-	
B & H	1	1	0	0	0	0.00	-	-	-	-	36	38	1	38.00	1-38	-	
Sunday	8	3	0	9	5	3.00	-	-	2	-	360	288	8	36.00	2-38	-	

COTTEY, P. A.   Glamorgan

Name: Phillip Anthony Cottey
Role: Right-hand bat
Born: 2 June 1966, Swansea
Height: 5ft 5in **Weight:** 10st 7lbs
Nickname: Cotts, Baba Oily
County debut: 1986
County cap: 1992
1000 runs in season: 6
1st-Class 50s: 54
1st-Class 100s: 19

1st-Class 200s: 1
1st-Class catches: 121
Place in batting averages: 134th av. 27.94
(1996 25th av. 51.43)
Strike rate: (career 84.61)
Parents: Bernard John and Ruth
Wife and date of marriage: Gail, 5 October 1992
Children: Lowri Rhiannon, 16 October 1993; Seren Nia, 6 August 1997
Family links with cricket: Father played club cricket for Swansea CC
Education: Bishopston Comprehensive School, Swansea
Qualifications: 9 O-levels, advanced coach
Career outside cricket: Cricket Development Officer for Dyfed
Overseas tours: Glamorgan to La Manga, Barbados, Trinidad, Zimbabwe and Cape Town 1987-96
Overseas teams played for: Penrith, Sydney 1986-88; Benoni, Johannesburg 1990-93; Eastern Transvaal 1991-92
Cricketers particularly admired: Ian Botham, Wasim Akram, Stuart Law
Young players to look out for: Wayne Law, Dean Cosker, Darren Thomas
Other sports followed: Golf, soccer (Swansea City), rugby union (Dunvant RFC) and marathon running
Injuries: Torn ligament in hand, out for ten days
Relaxations: Videos, golf, marathon running and 'lager tasting'
Extras: Left school at 16 to play for Swansea City FC for three years as a professional. Three Welsh Youth caps (one as captain). Glamorgan Player of the Year in 1994. Ran the New York Marathon in 1995, the Athens Marathon in 1996 and is planning to run the Las Vegas Marathon in February 1998
Opinions on cricket: 'England sides should be selected on present form and good previous records. Not potential players who have no performances to back up their selection.'
Best batting: 203 Glamorgan v Leicestershire, Swansea 1996
Best bowling: 4-49 Glamorgan v Leicestershire, Swansea 1996

1997 Season

	M	Inns	NO	Runs	HS	Avge	100s	50s	Ct	St	O	M	Runs	Wkts	Avge	Best	5wI	10wM
Test																		
All First	17	21	4	475	83	27.94	-	2	15	-	3.3	1	19	0	-	-	-	-
1-day Int																		
NatWest	4	4	1	92	56	30.66	-	1	2	-	8	0	37	1	37.00	1-9	-	
B & H	4	4	1	45	21 *	15.00	-	-	-	-								
Sunday	13	12	2	327	61	32.70	-	2	3	-	22	0	127	2	63.50	1-29	-	

Career Performances

	M	Inns	NO	Runs	HS	Avge	100s	50s	Ct	St	Balls	Runs	Wkts	Avge	Best	5wI	10wM
Test																	
All First	184	297	46	9607	203	38.27	19	54	121	-	1100	767	13	59.00	4-49	-	-
1-day Int																	
NatWest	23	22	6	439	61 *	27.43	-	3	8	-	150	96	3	32.00	1-9	-	
B & H	29	27	5	462	68	21.00	-	1	8	-	66	50	1	50.00	1-49	-	
Sunday	117	97	19	1957	92 *	25.08	-	10	39	-	455	456	13	35.07	4-56	-	

COUSINS, D. M. Essex

Name: Darren Mark Cousins
Role: Right-hand bat, right-arm fast-medium
bowler, outfielder
Born: 24 September 1971, Cambridge
Height: 6ft 1in **Weight:** 13st 7lbs
Nickname: Mad Dog, Cuz, Cuzzi, Skuz
County debut: 1993
1st-Class 5 w. in innings: 1
1st-Class catches: 5
Strike rate: 88.00 (career 72.69)
Parents: Dennis Charles and Deanna
Maureen (deceased)
Marital status: Single
Family links with cricket: Father opened the
bowling and was capped for Cambridgeshire
Education: Milton Primary School;
Impington Village College
Qualifications: 7 GCSEs
Career outside cricket: Coaching and
teaching PE in local secondary school
Overseas teams played for: Gold Coast Dolphins, Queensland 1994-95; Maritzburg
Old Boys, Pietermaritzburg, South Africa 1995–96
Cricketers particularly admired: Neil Foster, Geoff Arnold, Alan Butcher, Keith
Fletcher and 'anyone else who has given me help, advice and guidance during my
career'
Young players to look out for: Robert Rollins, Ashley Cowan, Stephen Peters,
Darren Robinson
Other sports followed: Football (Liverpool, Cambridge United), 'I used to be a
county swimmer and a county footballer but had to give up all other sports due to
glass back syndrome'
Relaxations: 'Socialising. Listening to all types of music from Indie to soul to swing'

Extras: Represented Cambridgeshire at football and swimming and every level at cricket. Played for a Bull Development Squad against Australia in 1991, taking four wickets in each innings. Played 2nd XI cricket for Northants and Worcs. Holds the record for both number of wickets in any single Colts festival (21) and number of wickets taken in the Hilda Overy Festival overall (74). Awarded 2nd XI cap and Essex Young Player of the Year, 1994. Essex Cricket Society 2nd XI Player of the Year, 1994. Leading Essex wicket-taker in Sunday League and top of the bowling averages in 1994. Underwent third back operation in 22 months and missed his third season of cricket
Best batting: 18* Essex v Durham, Chelmsford 1995
Best bowling: 6-35 Essex v Cambridge University, Fenner's 1994

1997 Season

	M	Inns	NO	Runs	HS	Avge	100s	50s	Ct	St	O	M	Runs	Wkts	Avge	Best	5wI	10wM
Test																		
All First																		
1-day Int																		
NatWest	1	0	0	0	0	-	-	-	-	-	3	0	28	0	-		-	-
B & H																		
Sunday	1	1	0	1	1	1.00	-	-	-	-	8	0	42	1	42.00	1-42	-	

Career Performances

	M	Inns	NO	Runs	HS	Avge	100s	50s	Ct	St	Balls	Runs	Wkts	Avge	Best	5wI	10wM
Test																	
All First	14	23	5	145	18 *	8.05	-	-	5	-	1890	1086	26	41.76	6-35	1	-
1-day Int																	
NatWest	4	2	1	1	1 *	1.00	-	-	-	-	150	145	1	145.00	1-33	-	
B & H	6	2	1	22	12 *	22.00	-	-	1	-	239	171	2	85.50	1-33	-	
Sunday	29	11	4	18	6	2.57	-	-	2	-	1203	930	38	24.47	3-18	-	

20. Which player became only the fourth Englishman to score a double century on debut for his county?

O vodafone

COWAN, A. P.   Essex

Name: Ashley Preston Cowan
Role: Right-hand bat, right-hand
fast-medium bowler
Born: 7 May 1975, Hitchin, Hertfordshire
Height: 6ft 5in **Weight:** 14st
Nickname: Victor, Dic Dic
County debut: 1995
50 w. in a season: 1
1st-Class 50s: 1
1st-Class 5 w. in innings: 4
1st-Class catches: 14
Place in batting averages: 194th av. 22.35
(1996 274th av. 13.42)
Place in bowling averages: 34th av. 25.65
(1996 104th av. 36.60)

Strike rate: 48.46 (career 55.05)
Parents: Jeff and Pam
Marital status: Single
Family links with cricket: 'Father tried to
play in local village team'
Education: Kingshott Prep; Framlingham College
Qualifications: 5 GCSEs, 1 A-level; Business Vocation Degree
Career outside cricket: Family business
Off-season: Touring West Indies with England
Overseas tours: England to West Indies 1997-98
Overseas teams played for: Zingan CC, Pietermaritzburg, South Africa 1995-97
Cricketers particularly admired: Ian Botham, Graham Dilley, Curtly Ambrose
Young players to look out for: Steve Andrew, Robert Rollins
Other sports followed: Rugby, hockey, golf, football (Newcastle United)
Relaxations: Socialising, playing golf, 'having fun'
Extras: Played rugby and hockey for East of England U18. The youngest person to play
for Cambridgeshire. First-class hat-trick at Colchester in 1996. Was the joint leading
scorer in the 1996 NatWest final
Opinions on cricket: 'Looking for a younger and more dedicated cricket crowd who
will inspire the players through their enthusiasm.'
Best batting: 77 Essex v Middlesex, Chelmsford 1997
Best bowling: 5-45 Essex v Sussex, Hove 1997

1997 Season

	M	Inns	NO	Runs	HS	Avge	100s	50s	Ct	St	O	M	Runs	Wkts	Avge	Best	5wI	10wM
Test																		
All First	16	26	6	447	77	22.35	-	1	7	-	420	106	1334	52	25.65	5-45	3	-
1-day Int																		
NatWest	5	3	2	22	17 *	22.00	-	-	2	-	56	7	220	8	27.50	3-29	-	
B & H	4	2	1	10	8	10.00	-	-	1	-	37	3	196	5	39.20	2-35	-	
Sunday	16	12	4	113	22	14.12	-	-	5	-	109.2	4	560	23	24.34	4-31	-	

Career Performances

	M	Inns	NO	Runs	HS	Avge	100s	50s	Ct	St	Balls	Runs	Wkts	Avge	Best	5wI	10wM
Test																	
All First	33	50	13	682	77	18.43	-	1	14	-	5120	2911	93	31.30	5-45	4	-
1-day Int																	
NatWest	7	4	2	33	17 *	16.50	-	-	4	-	456	297	9	33.00	3-29	-	
B & H	6	2	1	10	8	10.00	-	-	1	-	336	262	6	43.66	2-35	-	
Sunday	26	19	7	161	22 *	13.41	-	-	8	-	964	797	27	29.51	4-31	-	

COWDREY, G. R.   Kent

Name: Graham Robert Cowdrey
Role: Right-hand bat, right-arm medium
bowler, cover fielder
Born: 27 June 1964, Farnborough, Kent
Height: 5ft 11in **Weight:** 13st 9lbs
Nickname: Van, Cow
County debut: 1984
County cap: 1988
1000 runs in season: 3
1st-Class 50s: 46
1st-Class 100s: 17
1st-Class catches: 97
One-Day 100s: 3
Place in batting averages: 127th av. 29.46
(1996 151st av. 31.11)
Strike rate: (career 100.50)
Parents: Michael Colin and Penelope Susan
Wife and date of marriage: Maxine, 20
February 1993
Family links with cricket: Father (M.C.) and brother (C.S.) played for, and captained,
Kent and England
Education: Wellesley House, Broadstairs; Tonbridge School; Durham University

Qualifications: Potter
Off-season: Working with Caribbean holiday firm, Caribtours, taking trips to the West Indies
Overseas tours: Christians in Sport to India 1985-86, 1989-90; MCC to West Indies 1991-92
Overseas teams played for: Avendale, Cape Town 1983-84; Mossman, Sydney 1985-86; Randwick, Sydney 1986-87
Cricketers particularly admired: Aravinda De Silva, Steve Marsh, Mark Waugh
Young players to look out for: Ed Smith, Colin Johns
Other sports followed: Horse racing, golf ('I am Frank Nobilo's greatest fan') and rugby league
Injuries: Hamstring, out for eight weeks
Relaxations: Music, theatre and carp fishing
Extras: Played for England YC. Made 1000 runs for Kent 2nd XI first season on staff, and broke 2nd XI record with 1300 runs in 26 innings in 1985. Plays in contact lenses. Holds Kent record partnership for any wicket with Aravinda De Silva, 382 runs against Derbyshire 1995
Opinions on cricket: 'I am a traditionalist and so am delighted to see the same format kept for the Championship. Let's get back to three-day cricket and uncovered wickets.'
Best batting: 147 Kent v Gloucestershire, Bristol 1992
Best bowling: 1-5 Kent v Warwickshire, Edgbaston 1988

1997 Season

	M	Inns	NO	Runs	HS	Avge	100s	50s	Ct	St	O	M	Runs	Wkts	Avge	Best	5wI	10wM
Test																		
All First	9	15	0	442	101	29.46	1	1	7	-	5	0	31	0	-		-	-	-
1-day Int																		
NatWest																		
B & H	7	7	1	200	77	33.33	-	1	1	-								
Sunday	13	11	2	354	82	39.33	-	3	2	-	8	0	35	2	17.50	2-35	-	

Career Performances

	M	Inns	NO	Runs	HS	Avge	100s	50s	Ct	St	Balls	Runs	Wkts	Avge	Best	5wI	10wM
Test																	
All First	179	284	29	8858	147	34.73	17	46	97	-	1206	872	12	72.66	1-5	-	-
1-day Int																	
NatWest	23	20	4	416	65	26.00	-	1	3	-	303	157	8	19.62	2-4	-	
B & H	55	50	4	1064	77	23.13	-	6	19	-	202	139	2	69.50	1-8	-	
Sunday	165	146	23	3529	105 *	28.69	3	17	56	-	690	544	24	22.66	4-15	-	

COX, D. M. Durham

Name: David Matthew Cox
Role: Left-hand bat, slow left-arm bowler
Born: 2 March 1972, Southall, Middlesex
Height: 5ft 10in **Weight:** 13st
Nickname: Coxy, Cocker
County debut: 1994
1st-Class 50s: 4
1st-Class 5 w. in innings: 2
1st-Class 10 w. in match: 1
1st-Class catches: 4
Place in batting averages:
(1996 36th av. 48.22)
Place in bowling averages:
(1996 88th av. 33.96)
Strike rate: 59.57 (career 77.35)
Parents: Charles and Georgina
Wife and date of marriage: Hazel Jennifer,
1 October 1994
Family links with cricket: Father played for
Old Actonians

Education: Lady Margaret Primary School; Greenford High School
Qualifications: 5 GCSEs, cricket coaching certificate, part-qualified plasterer
Career outside cricket: Warehouse supervisor
Off-season: Working and getting fit for next season
Cricketers particularly admired: Phil Bainbridge, Wayne Larkins and Dean Jones
Other sports followed: Snooker, darts, football (QPR), golf and horse racing
Relaxations: 'Watching football, spending time with my wife and watching horse racing'
Extras: First Durham player to get more than 50 2nd XI Championship wickets in a
season (1995). Player of the Month for Durham CCC in August 1996
Best batting: 95* Durham v Somerset, Weston-super-Mare 1996
Best bowling: 5-97 Durham v Warwickshire, Edgbaston 1996

1997 Season

	M	Inns	NO	Runs	HS	Avge	100s	50s	Ct	St	O	M	Runs	Wkts	Avge	Best	5wI	10wM
Test																		
All First	4	3	0	46	24	15.33	-	-	1	-	69.3	18	202	7	28.85	3-72	-	-
1-day Int																		
NatWest																			
B & H																			
Sunday																			

Career Performances

	M	Inns	NO	Runs	HS	Avge	100s	50s	Ct	St	Balls	Runs	Wkts	Avge	Best	5wl	10wM
Test																	
All First	17	25	5	535	95 *	26.75	-	4	4	-	3481	1852	45	41.15	5-97	2	1
1-day Int																	
NatWest																		
B & H																		
Sunday	6	2	0	7	7	3.50	-	-	1	-	264	195	3	65.00	2-34	-	

CRAWLEY, J. P.   Lancashire

Name: John Paul Crawley
Role: Right-hand bat, occasional wicket-keeper, county vice-captain
Born: 21 September 1971, Malden, Essex
Height: 6ft 2in **Weight:** 13st 2lbs
Nickname: Creeps, Jonty, JC
County debut: 1990
Test debut: 1994
Tests: 22
One-Day Internationals: 10
1000 runs in a season: 6
1st-Class 50s: 69
1st-Class 100s: 22
1st-Class 200s: 3
1st-Class catches: 124
One-Day 100s: 2
Place in batting averages: 21st av. 49.60 (1996 29th av. 50.09)
Strike rate: (career 78.00)
Parents: Frank and Jean
Marital status: Single
Family links with cricket: Father played in Manchester Association; brother Mark played for Lancashire before moving to Nottinghamshire; other brother Peter plays for Warrington CC and has played for Scottish Universities and Cambridge University; uncle was excellent fast bowler; godfather umpires in Manchester Association
Education: Manchester Grammar School; Trinity College, Cambridge
Qualifications: 10 O-levels, 2 AO-Levels, 3 A-levels, 2 S-levels, BA in History
Off-season: Touring West Indies with England
Overseas tours: England YC to Australia 1989-90, to New Zealand 1990-91; England A to South Africa 1993-94; England to Australia 1994-95, to South Africa 1995-96, to Zimbabwe and New Zealand 1996-97, to West Indies 1997-98

Overseas teams played for: Midland Guildford, Perth 1990
Cricketers particularly admired: Michael Atherton, Neil Fairbrother, Graham Gooch, Alec Stewart, David Gower, Allan Donald, Ian Salisbury
Other sports followed: Football (Manchester United), golf
Relaxations: 'Playing or trying to play the guitar'
Extras: Captained England YC (U19) to New Zealand 1990-91 and played for England YC in three home series v New Zealand 1989, Pakistan 1990 and Australia (as captain) 1991. Made his maiden first-class century for Cambridge University on the same day that brother Mark made his for Notts. First to score 1000 runs in U19 Tests. Scored 286 for England A against Eastern Province at Port Elizabeth in 1994, the highest score by an Englishman on an England or England A tour for almost 30 years. Finished top of the first-class batting averages on England's tour to South Africa in 1995-96 with 336 runs at 67.20, but had to fly home after suffering a hamstring injury whilst fielding in the third Test at Durban. Scored his maiden Test match hundred (106) in the third Test against Pakistan at The Oval in 1996, followed by 112 in England's next Test against Zimbabwe in Bulawayo in 1996-97. Appointed Lancashire vice-captain for the 1998 season
Best batting: 286 England A v Eastern Province, Port Elizabeth 1993-94
Best bowling: 1-90 Lancashire v Sussex, Hove 1992

1997 Season

	M	Inns	NO	Runs	HS	Avge	100s	50s	Ct	St	O	M	Runs	Wkts	Avge	Best	5wI	10wM
Test	5	9	1	243	83	30.37	-	2	3	-								
All First	16	25	2	1141	133	49.60	3	7	11	-								
1-day Int	1	1	0	52	52	52.00	-	1	-	-								
NatWest	2	2	1	124	113 *	124.00	1	-	-	-	1	0	4	0	-	-	-	
B & H	5	5	0	39	37	7.80	-	-	3	-								
Sunday	11	11	1	267	83	26.70	-	2	3	-								

Career Performances

	M	Inns	NO	Runs	HS	Avge	100s	50s	Ct	St	Balls	Runs	Wkts	Avge	Best	5wI	10wM
Test	22	35	4	1028	112	33.16	2	7	21	-							
All First	154	252	26	11111	286	49.16	22	69	124	-	78	108	1	108.00	1-90	-	-
1-day Int	10	9	0	180	73	20.00	-	2	1	-							
NatWest	11	11	1	362	113 *	36.20	1	2	2	-	6	4	0	-	-	-	
B & H	30	29	1	957	114	34.17	1	4	10	-							
Sunday	58	56	2	1368	91	25.33	-	10	17	-							

CROFT, R. D. B.   Glamorgan

Name: Robert Damien Bale Croft
Role: Right-hand bat, off-spinner
Born: 25 May 1970, Swansea
Height: 5ft 11in **Weight:** 11st 5lbs
Nickname: Crofty
County debut: 1989
County cap: 1992
Test debut: 1996
Tests: 10
One-Day Internationals: 14
50 wickets in a season: 5
1st-Class 50s: 24
1st-Class 100s: 2
1st-Class 5 w. in innings: 20
1st-Class 10 w. in match: 2
1st-Class catches: 93
Place in batting averages: 151st av. 26.08
(1996 184th av. 26.95)
Place in bowling averages:
51st av. 27.38 (1996 76th av. 32.71)
Strike rate: 64.46 (career 79.00)
Parents: Malcolm and Susan
Family links with cricket: Father and grandfather played local cricket
Education: St John Lloyd Catholic School; Neath Trinity College; West Glamorgan Institute of Higher Education
Qualifications: 6 O-levels; OND Business Studies; HND Business Studies; NCA senior coaching certificate
Career outside cricket: Personnel management ('not as yet!')
Off-season: Touring West Indies with England
Overseas tours: England A to Bermuda and West Indies 1991-92, to South Africa 1993-94; England to Zimbabwe and New Zealand 1996-97, to West Indies 1997-98
Cricketers particularly admired: Alan Jones, Tom Cartwright, Don Shepherd, John Steele, John Emburey
Other sports followed: Rugby, soccer
Relaxations: Shooting, fishing, driving, music, golf
Extras: Captained England South to victory in International Youth Tournament 1989 and was voted Player of the Tournament. Glamorgan Young Player of the Year 1992. Made his Test debut in the third Test against Pakistan at The Oval in 1996
Opinions on cricket: 'Enjoyment is of the utmost importance.'
Best batting: 143 Glamorgan v Somerset, Taunton 1995
Best bowling: 8-66 Glamorgan v Warwickshire, Swansea 1992

1997 Season

	M	Inns	NO	Runs	HS	Avge	100s	50s	Ct	St	O	M	Runs	Wkts	Avge	Best	5wI	10wM
Test	5	8	0	75	24	9.37	-	-	1	-	161.5	41	439	8	54.87	3-125	-	-
All First	18	26	1	652	86	26.08	-	4	14	-	666.1	159	1698	62	27.38	5-33	1	-
1-day Int	3	0	0	0	0	-	-	-	-	-	30	3	106	2	53.00	1-39	-	
NatWest	4	4	0	133	64	33.25	-	2	-	-	48	6	136	4	34.00	2-45	-	
B & H	4	4	0	89	43	22.25	-	-	1	-	40	0	172	4	43.00	2-38	-	
Sunday	10	9	0	230	50	25.55	-	1	3	-	76	1	339	8	42.37	2-31	-	

Career Performances

	M	Inns	NO	Runs	HS	Avge	100s	50s	Ct	St	Balls	Runs	Wkts	Avge	Best	5wI	10wM
Test	10	14	1	138	31	10.61	-	-	6	-	2350	904	28	32.28	5-95	1	-
All First	185	269	49	5621	143	25.55	2	24	93	-	39266	18172	497	36.56	8-66	20	2
1-day Int	14	9	3	89	30 *	14.83	-	-	4	-	780	516	15	34.40	2-26	-	
NatWest	22	18	5	339	64	26.07	-	3	4	-	1336	730	20	36.50	3-30	-	
B & H	23	19	7	327	50 *	27.25	-	1	7	-	1337	841	29	29.00	4-30	-	
Sunday	100	75	22	1155	68	21.79	-	3	25	-	4012	3020	90	33.55	6-20	1	

CROWE, C. D. Leicestershire

Name: Carl Daniel Crowe
Role: Right-hand bat, off-spin bowler
Born: 25 November 1975, Leicester
Height: 6ft **Weight:** 12st 7lbs
Nickname: Scuba
County debut: 1995
1st-Class catches: 1
Parents: Edward Patrick and Jeannette
Marital status: Single
Family links with cricket: Brother Craig progressing through Leicestershire's youth ranks
Education: Lutterworth High School; Lutterworth Grammar School
Qualifications: 11 GCSEs, 2 A-levels, NCA Senior Coach
Off-season: Playing in Australia
Overseas tours: Leicestershire U19 to South Africa 1993-94; Leicestershire to Holland 1996
Cricketers particularly admired: Greg Blewett, Graeme Hick, Mark and Steve Waugh

Young players to look out for: Jimmy Ormond, David Roberts
Other sports followed: Try all sports, 'had a hole in one'. 'Support Leicester at everything and follow Spurs'
Relaxations: Cinema, ten-pin bowling and basic yoga
Extras: Played for Leicestershire U12-U19 and Midlands Schools U14-U19. One of the Cricketers of the Festival at Cambridge U19 Festival 1994
Opinions on cricket: 'The experiment of four-day cricket in 2nd XI cricket seemed to be the best way forward if that level of cricket is going to survive.'
Best batting: 9 Leicestershire v Warwickshire, Leicester 1995

1997 (no first-class or one-day appearances)

Career Performances

	M	Inns	NO	Runs	HS	Avge	100s	50s	Ct	St	Balls	Runs	Wkts	Avge	Best	5wI	10wM
Test																	
All First	1	2	0	10	9	5.00	-	-	1	-	18	4	0	-		-	-	-
1-day Int																	
NatWest																	
B & H																	
Sunday	1	0	0	0	0	-	-	-	-	-							

CUNLIFFE, R. J. Gloucestershire

Name: Robert John Cunliffe
Role: Right-hand bat, cover fielder, occasional wicket-keeper
Born: 8 November 1973, Oxford
Height: 5ft 10in **Weight:** 13st
Nickname: 'Too rude to mention'
County debut: 1993 (one-day), 1994 (first-class)
1st-Class 100s: 2
1st-Class 50s: 5
1st-Class catches: 15
One-Day 100s: 3
Place in batting averages: 206th av. 21.00 (1996 214th av. 22.90)
Parents: Barry and Janet
Marital status: Engaged to Claire
Family links with cricket: 'Dad played in his younger days for his wife's village team and was groundsman for nine years at

Banbury Twenty CC'
Education: Banbury School and Banbury Technical College
Qualifications: 'Not too many'
Overseas tours: England U19 to India 1992-93
Overseas teams played for: Richmond City CC, Melbourne 1996-97
Cricketers particularly admired: Robin Smith
Young players to look out for: Michael Vaughan
Other sports followed: Football, squash ('not the best'), 'can't watch any sport'
Relaxations: 'Being with Claire'
Extras: Played in England U19 home series against West Indies in 1993
Best batting: 190* Gloucestershire v Oxford University, The Parks 1995

1997 Season

	M	Inns	NO	Runs	HS	Avge	100s	50s	Ct	St	O	M	Runs	Wkts	Avge	Best	5wI	10wM
Test																		
All First	9	14	1	273	61	21.00	-	1	4	-								
1-day Int																		
NatWest	2	1	0	33	33	33.00	-	-	-	-								
B & H	5	5	1	181	113	45.25	1	-	2	-								
Sunday	9	9	1	225	56	28.12	-	2	-	-								

Career Performances

	M	Inns	NO	Runs	HS	Avge	100s	50s	Ct	St	Balls	Runs	Wkts	Avge	Best	5wI	10wM
Test																	
All First	29	46	5	1291	190 *	31.48	2	5	15	-							
1-day Int																	
NatWest	5	4	0	110	40	27.50	-	-	1	-							
B & H	10	10	3	534	137 *	76.28	3	1	3	-							
Sunday	14	14	1	328	56	25.23	-	3	2	-							

21. When Ian Healy completed a tally of 100 victims in Ashes Tests, he became only the third player to do so. Who were the other two?

O vodafone

CURRAN, K. M.   Northamptonshire

Name: Kevin Malcolm Curran
Role: Right-hand bat, right-arm
fast-medium bowler, county captain
Born: 7 September 1959, Rusape, Rhodesia
Height: 6ft 2in **Weight:** 14st
Nickname: KC
County debut: 1985 (Glos),
1991 (Northamptonshire)
County cap: 1985 (Glos),
1992 (Northamptonshire)
One-Day Internationals: 11
1000 runs in a season: 7
50 wickets in a season: 5
1st-Class 50s: 76
1st-Class 100s: 25
1st-Class 5 w. in innings: 15
1st-Class 10 w. in match: 4
1st-Class catches: 179
One-Day 100s: 1
One-Day 5 w. in innings: 1

Place in batting averages: 29th av. 46.90 (1996 14th av. 59.14)
Place in bowling averages: 68th av. 29.79 (1996 152nd av. 58.27)
Strike rate: 53.83 (career 52.53)
Parents: Kevin and Sylvia
Wife and date of marriage: Sarah, 5 June 1993
Children: Thomas Kevin, 12 March 1995; Benjamin Jack, 7 June 1996
Family links with cricket: Father played for Rhodesia 1947-54. Cousin Patrick
Curran played for Rhodesia 1975
Education: Marandellas High School, Zimbabwe
Qualifications: 6 O-levels, 2 M-levels
Career outside cricket: Tobacco buyer/farmer
Overseas tours: Zimbabwe to Sri Lanka 1982 and 1984, to England 1982 and for
World Cup 1983, to Pakistan and India for World Cup 1987
Overseas teams played for: Zimbabwe and Natal 1988-92, Boland 1994-95
Other sports followed: Rugby union
Relaxations: 'Game fishing, especially along the North Natal coast, the Mozambique
coast, and Magaruque Island'
Extras: First player to take a Sunday League hat-trick, and score 50 in the same match,
Gloucestershire v Warwickshire, Edgbaston 1989. Released by Gloucestershire at end of
1990 after he had completed the season's double of 1000 runs and 50 wickets. Chose to
join Northamptonshire for the 1991 season after he had been approached by several counties.

Best batting: 159 Northamptonshire v Glamorgan, Abergavenny 1997
Best bowling: 7-47 Northamptonshire v Yorkshire, Harrogate 1993

1997 Season

	M	Inns	NO	Runs	HS	Avge	100s	50s	Ct	St	O	M	Runs	Wkts	Avge	Best	5wl	10wM
Test																		
All First	15	26	4	1032	159	46.90	2	6	8	-	215.2	57	715	24	29.79	4-32	-	-
1-day Int																		
NatWest	2	2	0	30	21	15.00	-	-	-	-	16	4	54	2	27.00	2-31	-	
B & H	6	6	1	96	49 *	19.20	-	-	2	-	31	0	137	0	-		-	-
Sunday	12	12	2	440	78 *	44.00	-	3	3	-	49	0	292	9	32.44	4-36	-	

Career Performances

	M	Inns	NO	Runs	HS	Avge	100s	50s	Ct	St	Balls	Runs	Wkts	Avge	Best	5wl	10wM
Test																	
All First	297	467	78	14722	159	37.84	25	76	179	-	30787	16234	586	27.70	7-47	15	4
1-day Int	11	11	0	287	73	26.09	-	2	1	-	506	398	9	44.22	3-65	-	
NatWest	41	35	7	809	78 *	28.89	-	3	11	-	2123	1204	41	29.36	4-34	-	
B & H	53	48	8	1002	57	25.05	-	6	10	-	2448	1701	52	32.71	4-38	-	
Sunday	185	175	37	4569	119 *	33.10	1	26	38	-	5691	4693	169	27.76	5-15	1	

CURTIS, T. S. Worcestershire

Name: Timothy Stephen Curtis
Role: Right-hand bat, leg-spin bowler
Born: 15 January 1960, Chislehurst, Kent
Height: 5ft 11in **Weight:** 11st 10lbs
Nickname: TC, Duracell, Professor
County debut: 1979
County cap: 1984
Benefit: 1994 (£129,501)
Test debut: 1988
Tests: 5
1000 runs in a season: 11
1st-Class 50s: 103
1st-Class 100s: 43
1st-Class 200s: 2
1st-Class catches: 191
One-Day 100s: 6
Place in batting averages: 79th av. 37.10
(1996 138th av. 32.82)
Strike rate: 72.00 (career 80.92)

Parents: Bruce and Betty

Wife and date of marriage: Philippa, 21 September 1985

Children: Jennifer May, 9 February 1991; Andrew Stephen Neild, 17 February 1993

Family links with cricket: Father played good club cricket in Bristol and Stafford

Education: Royal Grammar School, Worcester; Durham University; Cambridge University

Qualifications: 12 O-levels, 4 A-levels, BA (Hons) in English, PCGE in English and Games

Off-season: In retirement, teaching

Overseas tours: NCA U19 tour of Canada 1979; 'Worcestershire to most parts of the cricketing world'

Cricketers particularly admired: 'So many, but watching Hicky from 22 yards has been awesome'

Young players to look out for: Vikram Solanki, Reuben Spiring, Phil Weston

Other sports followed: Golf, tennis, squash

Injuries: Age

Relaxations: All sports, novels, family life, food and wine

Extras: Captained Durham University to UAU Championship in 1981. Appointed county captain in 1992. Worcestershire Supporters' Player of the Year 1992. A century against Durham in 1993 meant that he had scored a century against every other first-class county. Raised £129,501 from his benefit in 1994. Relinquished the captaincy during the 1995 season. Retired as Chairman of the PCA as from September 1996 and from first-class cricket at the end of the 1997 season to teach full time at RGS Worcester

Opinions on cricket: 'Four-day cricket needs time to bring the best out of our cricketers. Better pitches (bounce) are crucial at all levels of the game.'

Best batting: 248 Worcestershire v Somerset, Taunton 1991

Best bowling: 2-17 Worcestershire v Oxford University, The Parks 1991

1997 Season

	M	Inns	NO	Runs	HS	Avge	100s	50s	Ct	St	O	M	Runs	Wkts	Avge	Best	5wI	10wM
Test																		
All First	13	21	1	742	160	37.10	4	1	9	-	12	1	65	1	65.00	1-55	-	-
1-day Int																		
NatWest	2	2	0	69	41	34.50	-	-	-	-								
B & H																			
Sunday	5	5	0	195	93	39.00	-	1	3	-								

Career Performances

	M	Inns	NO	Runs	HS	Avge	100s	50s	Ct	St	Balls	Runs	Wkts	Avge	Best	5wI	10wM
Test	5	9	0	140	41	15.55	-	-	3	-	18	7	0	-	-	-	-
All First	339	579	67	20832	248	40.68	43	103	191	-	1133	813	14	58.07	2-17	-	-
1-day Int																	
NatWest	42	41	5	1761	136 *	48.91	4	10	11	-	36	31	2	15.50	1-6	-	
B & H	62	62	5	1936	97	33.96	-	18	14	-	2	4	0	-	-	-	
Sunday	192	186	28	6423	124	40.65	2	54	59	-							

DAKIN, J. M. — Leicestershire

Name: Jonathan Michael Dakin
Role: Left-hand bat, right-arm
medium-fast bowler
Born: 28 February 1973, Hitchin, Herts
Height: 6ft 5in **Weight:** 15st 8lb
Nickname: Babe
County debut: 1993
1st-Class 100s: 3
1st-Class 50s: 2
1st-Class catches: 9
One-Day 100s: 1
Strike rate: 81.60 (career 78.35)
Parents: Fred John and Gloria May
Marital status: Single
Family links with cricket: Brother plays for
Wanderers CC in
South Africa
Education: King Edward VII School,
Johannesburg, South Africa
Qualifications: Matriculation
Off-season: Playing for Villagers CC in Pretoria, South Africa
Overseas tours: Rutland Tourists to Jersey 1992; Leicestershire CCC to South Africa
1996 and 1997
Overseas teams played for: Wanderers, South Africa, 1986-92; Alberts, South Africa
1993; Kaponga CC, New Zealand 1995-96
Cricketers particularly admired: Phil Simmons, Vince 'Legend' Wells
Young players to look out for: Darren 'Roasting' Maddy, Gary Outram
Other sports followed: Football (Leicester City and Qwa Qwa Stars FC), rugby union
(Leicester Tigers)
Injuries: Broken toe, but missed no cricket
Relaxations: Cinema, television, golf, having *a* drink in a pub
Extras: Won three Bain Hogg trophies in four years. Scored 193 against Middlesex in
the Bain Hogg in 1996. Won the Gold Award against Durham in the 1996 Benson and
Hedges
Opinions on cricket: 'Tea should be 30 minutes.'
Best batting: 190 Leicestershire v Northamptonshire, Northampton 1997
Best bowling: 4-45 Leicestershire v Cambridge University, Fenner's 1993

1997 Season

	M	Inns	NO	Runs	HS	Avge	100s	50s	Ct	St	O	M	Runs	Wkts	Avge	Best	5wl	10wM
Test																		
All First	4	5	1	311	190	77.75	2	-	2	-	68	17	204	5	40.80	2-12	-	-
1-day Int																		
NatWest	1	1	0	6	6	6.00	-	-	-	-								
B & H	5	5	2	115	45 *	38.33	-	-	5	-	31	0	176	7	25.14	2-16	-	
Sunday	14	13	2	224	41 *	20.36	-	-	3	-	56	1	330	13	25.38	3-38	-	

Career Performances

	M	Inns	NO	Runs	HS	Avge	100s	50s	Ct	St	Balls	Runs	Wkts	Avge	Best	5wl	10wM
Test																	
All First	16	24	3	706	190	33.61	3	2	9	-	1332	733	17	43.11	4-45	-	-
1-day Int																	
NatWest	4	4	0	63	26	15.75	-	-	-	-	144	100	1	100.00	1-63	-	
B & H	8	8	3	251	108 *	50.20	1	-	5	-	198	203	7	29.00	2-16	-	
Sunday	51	46	6	570	45	14.25	-	-	12	-	1206	1190	39	30.51	3-23	-	

DALE, A.   Glamorgan

Name: Adrian Dale
Role: Right-hand bat, right-arm medium bowler
Born: 24 October 1968, Johannesburg, South Africa
Height: 5ft 11in **Weight:** 11st 8lbs
Nickname: Arthur
County debut: 1989
County cap: 1992
1000 runs in a season: 2
1st-Class 50s: 34
1st-Class 100s: 14
1st-Class 200s: 1
1st-Class 5 w. in innings: 1
1st-Class catches: 59
One-Day 100s: 2
One-Day 5 w. in innings: 2
Place in batting averages: 76th av. 3739
(1996 170th av. 28.75)
Place in bowling averages: (1996 109th av. 39.16)
Strike rate: (career 74.97)
Parents: John and Maureen

Marital status: Single
Family links with cricket: Father played for Chepstow CC and the odd game for Glamorgan 2nd XI
Education: Pembroke Primary; Chepstow Comprehensive; Swansea University
Qualifications: 9 O-levels, 3 A-levels, BA (Hons) in Economics
Off-season: Working for Darlowa Estate Agents
Overseas tours: Welsh Schools U16 to Australia 1986-87; Combined Universities to Barbados 1988-89; Glamorgan to Trinidad 1989-90, to Zimbabwe 1990-91, to Trinidad 1991-92, to Cape Town 1992-93; England A to South Africa 1993-94
Overseas teams played for: Bionics, Zimbabwe 1990-91; Cornwall, New Zealand 1991-93, 1995-97
Cricketers particularly admired: Ian Botham, Michael Holding, Mike Gatting
Other sports followed: Football (Arsenal), athletics, US basketball, rugby league (Auckland Warriors and Wales), rugby union (Wales), ice hockey (Cardiff Devils)
Injuries: 'The odd back problem'
Relaxations: Eating out, following other sports, travelling
Extras: Played in successful Combined Universities sides of 1989 and 1990. Only batsman to score two half-centuries against the West Indies tourists in the same match in 1991. Took a wicket with his first delivery at Lord's. Recorded Glamorgan's best one-day bowling figures, 6-22 against Durham 1993. Recorded Glamorgan's highest ever partnership, 425, with Viv Richards against Middlesex, 1993
Opinions on cricket: 'The four-day game is working to produce better cricket. Although I enjoy one-day cricket, we play too much.'
Best batting: 214* Glamorgan v Middlesex, Cardiff 1993
Best bowling: 6-18 Glamorgan v Warwickshire, Cardiff 1993

1997 Season

	M	Inns	NO	Runs	HS	Avge	100s	50s	Ct	St	O	M	Runs	Wkts	Avge	Best	5wI	10wM
Test																		
All First	19	27	4	860	142 *	37.39	2	5	6	-	71.1	14	261	0	-	-	-	-
1-day Int																		
NatWest	4	3	0	122	71	40.66	-	1	-	-	17	0	100	1	100.00	1-61		
B & H	4	4	0	199	100	49.75	1	-	2	-	33.2	2	155	8	19.37	3-30	-	
Sunday	13	13	1	400	65	33.33	-	3	2	-	66.5	6	350	13	26.92	2-18	-	

Career Performances

	M	Inns	NO	Runs	HS	Avge	100s	50s	Ct	St	Balls	Runs	Wkts	Avge	Best	5wI	10wM
Test																	
All First	146	240	23	7129	214 *	32.85	14	34	59	-	9897	5358	132	40.59	6-18	1	-
1-day Int																	
NatWest	24	21	2	565	110	29.73	1	2	6	-	1036	730	21	34.76	3-54	-	
B & H	29	28	4	709	100	29.54	1	1	10	-	1220	867	36	24.08	5-41	1	
Sunday	114	99	13	2408	67 *	28.00	-	14	27	-	3555	3212	99	32.44	6-22	1	

DALEY, J. A.   Durham

Name: James Arthur Daley
Role: Right-hand bat
Born: 24 September 1973, Sunderland
Height: 5ft 11in **Weight:** 12st
Nickname: Bebs, Jonty
County debut: 1992
1st-Class 50s: 13
1st-Class 100s: 1
1st-Class catches: 26
Place in batting averages: 188th av. 26.50
(1995 53rd av. 43.50)
Parents: William and Christine
Marital status: Single
Family links with cricket: Brother played
representative cricket for Durham
Education: Hetton Comprehensive
Qualifications: 5 GCSEs
Career outside cricket: Travel agent
Overseas tours: Durham to Zimbabwe,

1991-92; England U19 to India 1992-93; England XI to Holland 1993
Cricketers particularly admired: David Graveney, Wayne Larkins, Jimmy Adams
Other sports followed: Most sports
Relaxations: Socialising, listening to all types of music
Extras: Scored three centuries in 1991 for MCC Young Cricketers at Lord's. Northern
Electric Foundation for Sport award winner 1992
Best batting: 159* Durham v Hampshire, Portsmouth 1994

1997 Season

	M	Inns	NO	Runs	HS	Avge	100s	50s	Ct	St	O	M	Runs	Wkts	Avge	Best	5wI	10wM
Test																		
All First	2	2	0	46	39	23.00	-	-	2	-								
1-day Int																		
NatWest																		
B & H																		
Sunday																		

> 22. Curtly Ambrose joined the list of élite players who have
> taken 300 Test wickets, but who was his 300th Test victim
> in June 1997 in the first Test against Sri Lanka?

O vodafone

	M	Inns	NO	Runs	HS	Avge	100s	50s	Ct	St	Balls	Runs	Wkts	Avge	Best	5wl	10wM
Test																	
All First	46	79	8	2224	159 *	31.32	1	13	26	-	12	9	0	-	-	-	-
1-day Int																	
NatWest																	
B & H	6	5	0	72	33	14.40	-	-	-	-	12	19	0	-	-	-	
Sunday	20	18	6	461	98 *	38.41	-	3	5	-	1	4	0	-	-	-	

DAVIES, A. P. Glamorgan

Name: Andrew Philip Davies
Role: Left-hand bat, right-arm
medium-fast bowler
Born: 7 November 1976, Neath
Height: 6ft **Weight:** 12st
County debut: 1995
Strike rate: 156.00 (career 174.00)
Parents: Philip and Anne
Marital status: Single
Family links with cricket: Dad played for
Ywysygerwn and B.P. Llandarcy. Mum used
to do the teas
Education: Dwr-y-felin Comprehensive
School; Christ College, Brecon
Qualifications: 6 GCSEs, 1 A-level
Overseas tours: Wales to Barbados;
Glamorgan to South Africa 1995-96
Overseas teams played for: Marist CC,
Whangarei, New Zealand 1995-96
Cricketers particularly admired: Graeme Hick
Young players to look out for: Alun 'face like a clock' Evans – 'hits the ball hard,
mainly due to the amount of Big Macs and quarter-pounders he eats'
Other sports followed: Football (had trials at Birmingham City), 'used to be a season
ticket holder at Neath RFC, in the days of the great winger Adrian Shaw – he's sadly
missed at the Gnoll'
Relaxations: 'Over the last two seasons, my interests have been sadly ruined by the
loss of Adrian Shaw on the Neath wing. An influential player whose ability was sorely
neglected on the international front'
Extras: Trials at Birmingham City FC. Rugby trials for Wales U17. Welsh U19 Player
of the Year 1995
Opinions on cricket: 'Not enough time is actually spent on coaching youngsters,

especially in the 2nd XI, because of the amount of cricket played. If a young player has a problem, it is hard to get time to sort the problem out.'
Best batting: 11* Glamorgan v Pakistan, Pontypridd 1996
Best bowling: 1-25 Glamorgan v Oxford University, The Parks 1996

1997 Season (no first-class or one-day appearances)

Career Performances

	M	Inns	NO	Runs	HS	Avge	100s	50s	Ct	St	Balls	Runs	Wkts	Avge	Best	5wI	10wM
Test																	
All First	3	2	1	19	11 *	19.00	-	-	-	-	174	135	1	135.00	1-25	-	-
1-day Int																	
NatWest																		
B & H																		
Sunday																		

DAVIES, M. K. Northamptonshire

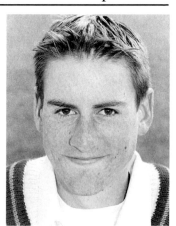

Name: Michael Kenton Davies
Role: Right-hand bat, slow left-arm bowler
Born: 17 July 1976, Ashby-de-la-Zouch
Height: 6ft **Weight:** 12st
Nickname: Dickie, Spaceman
County debut: 1997
1st-Class 5 w. in innings: 1
1st-Class catches: 2
Place in bowling averages: 65th av. 29.30
Strike rate: 61.13 (career 61.13)
Parents: Lyndon and Ann
Marital status: Single
Family links with cricket: None
Education: Fairfield Primary School; Loughborough Grammar School; Loughborough University
Qualifications: 8 GCSEs and 4 A-levels
Career outside cricket: Student
Off-season: Studying at university
Cricketers particularly admired: Phil Edmonds, David Gower
Young players to look out for: Tobin Bailey, Scott Boswell
Other sports followed: Golf (handicap 8), football (Derby County) and 'Wales at anything especially rugby'
Relaxations: 'Playing a relaxing 18 holes, listening to music and walking my dogs'

Extras: Leicestershire U19 Player of the Year. Was a member of BUSA's cricket squad in the 1997 Benson & Hedges Cup. 'Was once coached by the editor of this book, Chris Hawkes'

Opinions on cricket: 'The game needs to be more commercialised and marketed better if we are to compete against other sports.'

Best batting: 17 Northamptonshire v Glamorgan, Abergavenny 1997

Best bowling: 5-46 Northamptonshire v Derbyshire, Derby 1997

1997 Season

	M	Inns	NO	Runs	HS	Avge	100s	50s	Ct	St	O	M	Runs	Wkts	Avge	Best	5wI	10wM
Test																		
All First	6	9	4	49	17	9.80	-	-	2	-	234.2	71	674	23	29.30	5-46	1	-
1-day Int																		
NatWest																			
B & H	1	1	1	1	1 *	-	-	-	-	-	8.2	1	69	1	69.00	1-69	-	
Sunday																			

Career Performances

	M	Inns	NO	Runs	HS	Avge	100s	50s	Ct	St	Balls	Runs	Wkts	Avge	Best	5wI	10wM
Test																	
All First	6	9	4	49	17	9.80	-	-	2	-	1406	674	23	29.30	5-46	1	-
1-day Int																	
NatWest																		
B & H	1	1	1	1	1 *	-	-	-	-	-	50	69	1	69.00	1-69	-	
Sunday																		

23. Name the two Nottinghamshire players to take
hat-tricks during the 1997 season.

DAVIS, R. P.   Gloucestershire

Name: Richard Peter Davis
Role: Right-hand bat, slow left-arm bowler
Born: 18 March 1966, Westbrook, Margate
Height: 6ft 4in **Weight:** 14st 4lbs
Nickname: Dicky
County debut: 1986 (Kent), 1994
(Warwickshire), 1996 (Gloucestershire)
County Cap: 1990 (Kent), 1994
(Warwickshire)
50 wickets in a season: 2
1st-Class 50s: 4
1st-Class 5 w. in innings: 16
1st-Class 10 w. in match: 2
1st-Class catches: 155
One-Day 5 w. in innings: 1
Place in batting averages: 278th av. 11.25
(1996 268th av. 15.40)
Place in bowling averages: 102nd av. 35.70
(1996 130th av. 45.78)

Strike rate: 85.05 (career 74.87)
Parents: Brian and Sylvia
Wife and date of marriage: Samantha Jane, 3 March 1990
Family links with cricket: Father played club cricket and is an NCA coach; father-in-law, Colin Tomlin, helped with England's fitness training for tours from 1990-93; brother-in-law, Raj Sharma, played for Derbyshire
Education: King Ethelbert's School, Birchington; Thanet Technical College
Qualifications: CSEs, NCA Coaching Certificate
Overseas tours: Kent Schools to Canada 1983; Kent to Zimbabwe 1992-93; Warwickshire to Zimbabwe 1993-94, to Cape Town 1994-95
Young players to look out for: Vikram Solanki
Other sports followed: Football (Derby County), rugby, squash, golf, badminton
Relaxations: Eating out with my wife, Sam, television and reading
Extras: Moved to Warwickshire at the end of the 1993 season after nine years with Kent. Released by Warwickshire at the end of the 1995 season and joined Gloucestershire for the 1996 season. Retired from first-class cricket at the end of the 1997 season to take up a coaching position
Best batting: 67 Kent v Hampshire, Southampton 1989
Best bowling: 7-64 Kent v Durham, Gateshead Fell 1992

1997 Season

	M	Inns	NO	Runs	HS	Avge	100s	50s	Ct	St	O	M	Runs	Wkts	Avge	Best	5wI	10wM
Test																		
All First	9	12	0	135	39	11.25	-	-	9	-	241	76	607	17	35.70	4-35	-	-
1-day Int																		
NatWest	1	1	1	1	1 *	-	-	-	-	-	12	0	44	0	-		-	-
B & H	4	1	1	8	8 *	-	-	-	3	-	40	3	190	3	63.33	2-48	-	
Sunday	6	4	2	24	12 *	12.00	-	-	3	-	19	0	139	5	27.80	2-29	-	

Career Performances

	M	Inns	NO	Runs	HS	Avge	100s	50s	Ct	St	Balls	Runs	Wkts	Avge	Best	5wI	10wM
Test																	
All First	169	208	46	2452	67	15.13	-	4	155	-	30998	14543	414	35.12	7-64	16	2
1-day Int																	
NatWest	14	7	2	47	22	9.40	-	-	10	-	801	436	15	29.06	3-19	-	
B & H	27	11	5	65	18 *	10.83	-	-	12	-	1466	1018	20	50.90	2-26	-	
Sunday	95	47	19	255	40 *	9.10	-	-	31	-	3506	2768	100	27.68	5-52	1	

DAWOOD, I.   Glamorgan

Name: Ismail Dawood
Role: Right-hand bat, wicket-keeper
Born: 23 July 1976, Dewsbury
Nickname: Hectic
County debut: 1994 (Northamptonshire), 1996 (Worcestershire)
1st-Class catches: 4
1st-Class stumpings: 2
Parents: Saleem and Rashida
Marital status: Single
Family links with cricket: Grandfather and father played local league cricket
Education: Batley Grammar School
Qualifications: 8 GCSEs, NCA Coaching Award
Overseas tours: England U19 to Sri Lanka 1993-94, to West Indies 1994-95
Overseas teams played for: Grafton, Auckland 1992-93
Cricketers particularly admired: Mohammed Azharuddin, Allan Border, Ian Healy 'and many others'
Other sports followed: Local soccer team

Relaxations: 'Spending time with family and friends'
Extras: Left Northamptonshire at the end of 1995 season and joined Worcestershire in 1996. Has joined Glamorgan for the 1998 season
Opinions on cricket: 'The game should be played in good spirit and enjoyed at all levels from junior to Test cricket.'
Best batting: 10* Worcestershire v Pakistan A, Worcester 1997

1997 Season

	M	Inns	NO	Runs	HS	Avge	100s	50s	Ct	St	O	M	Runs	Wkts	Avge	Best	5wI	10wM
Test																		
All First	1	2	1	10	10 *	10.00	-	-	1	2								
1-day Int																		
NatWest																		
B & H																		
Sunday	1	1	0	1	1	1.00	-	-	-	-								

Career Performances

	M	Inns	NO	Runs	HS	Avge	100s	50s	Ct	St	Balls	Runs	Wkts	Avge	Best	5wI	10wM
Test																	
All First	3	4	2	13	10 *	6.50	-	-	4	2							
1-day Int																	
NatWest																	
B & H																	
Sunday	2	2	0	3	2	1.50	-	-	-	-							

DAWSON, R. I.   Gloucestershire

Name: Robert Ian Dawson
Role: Right-hand bat, right-arm medium bowler
Born: 29 March 1970, Exmouth, Devon
Height: 5ft 11in **Weight:** 12st 7lbs
Nickname: Daws, Giggsy
County debut: 1991 (one-day), 1992 (first-class)
1000 runs in a season: 1
1st-Class 50s: 12
1st-Class 100s: 3
1st-Class catches: 27
Place in batting averages: 183rd av. 23.50 (1996 283rd av. 11.75)
Strike rate: (career 102.66)
Parents: Barry and Shirley

Marital status: Single
Family links with cricket: Father and brother both played club cricket
Education: Millfield School; Newcastle Polytechnic
Qualifications: 8 O-levels, 3 A-levels
Off-season: Playing for Val Tech in Johannesburg, South Africa
Overseas teams played for: Amanzimtoti, South Africa, 1993-94; Strathfield CC, Sydney 1996-97; Val Tech CC, Johannesburg 1997-98
Overseas tours: Gloucestershire CCC to Zimbabwe 1996 and 1997; Gloucestershire Gypsies to Cape Town 1996
Cricketers particularly admired: Ian Botham, David Gower, Viv Richards
Young players to look out for: Jon Lewis (Gloucestershire CCC)

Other sports followed: Football ('big fan of Manchester United, although definitely not Leeds'), most other sports, 'but not motor racing'
Relaxations: 'Watching or playing sport. Watching Leeds lose. Bird watching'
Extras: Played in NatWest for Devon (from 1988), before joining Gloucestershire
Opinions on cricket: 'Three conferences – rubbish. Banning 2nd XI cricket – stupid. Club cricket is not good enough. The jump from there to first-class cricket is too big and young players would be way out of their depth.'
Best batting: 127* Gloucestershire v Cambridge University, Bristol 1994
Best bowling: 2-38 Gloucestershire v Derbyshire, Chesterfield 1994

1997 Season

	M	Inns	NO	Runs	HS	Avge	100s	50s	Ct	St	O	M	Runs	Wkts	Avge	Best	5wI	10wM
Test																		
All First	8	14	0	329	100	23.50	1	1	3	-	3	0	22	0	-		-	-	-
1-day Int																		
NatWest																		
B & H	4	3	0	38	24	12.66	-	-	-	-								
Sunday	7	5	1	116	45	29.00	-	-	1	-								

24. Who won the International U19 tournament in Bermuda in July 1997?

143

Career Performances

	M	Inns	NO	Runs	HS	Avge	100s	50s	Ct	St	Balls	Runs	Wkts	Avge	Best	5wI	10wM
Test																	
All First	55	98	7	2375	127 *	26.09	3	12	27	-	308	132	3	44.00	2-38	-	-
1-day Int																	
NatWest	5	4	0	73	60	18.25	-	1	-	-	24	37	1	37.00	1-37	-
B & H	14	13	0	258	38	19.84	-	-	1	-	18	12	0	-	-	-
Sunday	68	60	6	1138	85	21.07	-	4	12	-	86	95	1	95.00	1-19	-

DEAN, K. J.   Derbyshire

Name: Kevin James Dean
Role: Left-hand bat, left-arm
medium-fast bowler
Born: 16 October 1975, Derby
Height: 6ft 5in **Weight:** 13st 7lbs
Nickname: Deane, Baby Giraffe
County debut: 1996
1st-Class catches: 1
Place in batting averages: 277th av. 11.28
(1996 315th av. 4.71)
Place in bowling averages: 64th av. 28.96
(1996 57th av. 29.43)
Strike rate: 50.28 (career 51.65)
Parents: Kenneth and Dorothy
Marital status: Engaged to Clare
Family links with cricket: None
Education: Waterhouses First School; Leek
High School; Leek College
Qualifications: 8 GCSEs, 3 A-levels, 1 AS-
level

Career outside cricket: Deputy manager for Ladbrokes
Overseas teams played for: Sturt CC, Adelaide 1996-97
Cricketers particularly admired: Dominic Cork, Wasim Akram, Courtney Walsh
Young players to look out for: Andrew Harris, Vikram Solanki
Other sports followed: Football (Derby County), golf, tennis, horse racing
Relaxations: Horse racing, golf, going to cinema
Extras: A member of the Staffordshire U16 Texaco winning team
Opinions on cricket: 'Come and enjoy Derbyshire's famous lunches and teas.'
Best batting: 21* Derbyshire v Australia, Derby 1997
Best bowling: 4-39 Derbyshire v Cambridge University, Fenner's 1997

1997 Season

	M	Inns	NO	Runs	HS	Avge	100s	50s	Ct	St	O	M	Runs	Wkts	Avge	Best	5wI	10wM
Test																		
All First	10	12	5	79	21 *	11.28	-	-	2	-	234.4	47	811	28	28.96	4-39	-	-
1-day Int																		
NatWest	1	0	0	0	0	-	-	-	-	-	9	2	24	1	24.00	1-24	-	
B & H	5	1	0	6	6	6.00	-	-	-	-	30	2	149	3	49.66	1-16	-	
Sunday	10	3	2	2	1 *	2.00	-	-	3	-	69.3	4	329	10	32.90	3-24	-	

Career Performances

	M	Inns	NO	Runs	HS	Avge	100s	50s	Ct	St	Balls	Runs	Wkts	Avge	Best	5wI	10wM
Test																	
All First	18	20	6	112	21	* 8.00-		3	-	2273	1282		44	29.13	4-39	-	-
1-day Int																	
NatWest	4	1	1	0	0 *	-	-	-	1	-	222	189	6	31.50	3-52	-	
B & H	5	1	0	6	6	6.00	-	-	-	-	180	149	3	49.66	1-16	-	
Sunday	22	4	3	10	8 *	10.00	-	-	7	-	879	688	23	29.91	5-32	1	

DEFREITAS, P. A. J.   Derbyshire

Name: Phillip Anthony Jason DeFreitas
Role: Right-hand bat, right-arm fast bowler
Born: 18 February 1966, Scotts Head, Dominica
Height: 6ft **Weight:** 13st 7lbs
Nickname: Daffy, Lunchy
County debut: 1985 (Leics), 1989 (Lancs), 1994 (Derbys)
County cap: 1986 (Leics), 1989 (Lancs), 1994 (Derbys)
Test debut: 1986-87
Tests: 44
One-Day Internationals: 103
50 wickets in a season: 10
1st-Class 50s: 38
1st-Class 100s: 6
1st-Class 5 w. in innings: 47
1st-Class 10 w. in match: 5
1st-Class catches: 96
One-Day 5 w. in innings: 6
Place in batting averages: 205th av. 21.04 (1996 246th av. 17.90)
Place in bowling averages: 47th av. 27.01 (1996 32nd av. 26.35)

Strike rate: 51.41 (career 57.15)
Parents: Sybil and Martin
Wife and date of marriage: Nicola, 10 December 1990
Children: Alexandra Elizabeth Jane, 5 August 1991
Family links with cricket: Father played in Windward Islands. All six brothers play
Education: Willesden High School
Qualifications: 2 O-levels
Overseas tours: England YC to West Indies 1984-85; England to Australia 1986-87, to Pakistan, Australia and New Zealand 1987-88, to India and West Indies 1989-90, to Australia 1990-91, to New Zealand 1991-92, to India and Sri Lanka 1992-93, to Australia 1994-95, to South Africa 1995-96, to India and Pakistan (World Cup) 1995-96
Overseas teams played for: Port Adelaide, South Australia 1985; Mossman, Sydney 1988; Boland, South Africa 1993-94, 1995-96
Cricketers particularly admired: Ian Botham, Graham Gooch, Geoff Boycott, Mike Gatting
Other sports followed: Football (Manchester City) and rugby league (Warrington)
Relaxations: 'Golf, gardening, visiting stately homes, spending spare time with wife and daughter Alexandra'
Extras: Left Leicestershire and joined Lancashire at end of 1988 season. Originally agreed to join unofficial English tour of South Africa 1989-90, but withdrew under pressure. Man of the Match in 1990 NatWest Trophy final. One of *Wisden*'s Five Cricketers of the Year 1992. Man of the Tournament in the Hong Kong Sixes 1993. Left Lancashire at the end of the 1993 season. Player of the Series against New Zealand 1994. He was called up to the England one-day squad in South Africa 1996-97 after spending the winter with Boland and went on to play in the World Cup. Captained Derbyshire after the departure of Dean Jones during the 1997 season. Played for an England XI in the Cricket Max tournament in New Zealand in 1997
Best batting: 113 Leicestershire v Nottinghamshire, Worksop 1988
Best bowling: 7-21 Lancashire v Middlesex, Lord's 1989

1997 Season

	M	Inns	NO	Runs	HS	Avge	100s	50s	Ct	St	O	M	Runs	Wkts	Avge	Best	5wI	10wM
Test																		
All First	19	24	1	484	96	21.04	-	2	5	-	574.1	132	1810	67	27.01	7-64	5	2
1-day Int	2	0	0	0	0	-	-	-	-	-	17	1	82	0	-	-	-	
NatWest	3	2	0	50	26	25.00	-	-	1	-	31	5	102	2	51.00	1-20	-	
B & H	5	3	1	44	32 *	22.00	-	-	1	-	49	7	171	5	34.20	2-43	-	
Sunday	12	10	1	140	45	15.55	-	-	4	-	63.5	6	309	10	30.90	3-19	-	

25. Which current player holds the record for bowling the most overs in a County Championship innings?

Career Performances

	M	Inns	NO	Runs	HS	Avge	100s	50s	Ct	St	Balls	Runs	Wkts	Avge	Best	5wI	10wM
Test	44	68	5	934	88	14.82	-	4	14	-	9838	4700	140	33.57	7-70	4	-
All First	273	385	35	7624	113	21.78	6	38	96	-	52356	25616	916	27.96	7-21	47	5
1-day Int	103	66	23	690	67	16.04	-	1	26	-	5712	3775	115	32.82	4-35	-	
NatWest	32	22	4	323	69	17.94	-	1	6	-	2015	976	48	20.33	5-13	4	
B & H	55	36	7	593	75 *	20.44	-	2	14	-	3145	1767	81	21.81	5-16	1	
Sunday	154	113	22	1692	72 *	18.59	-	3	29	-	6099	4578	172	26.61	5-26	1	

DIBDEN, R.R. Hampshire

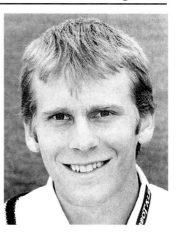

Name: Richard Rockley Dibden
Role: Right-hand bat, right-arm
off-spin bowler
Born: 29 January 1975, Southampton
Height: 6ft **Weight:** 11st 7lbs
Nickname: Dibbers, Rocky, The Vicar
County debut: 1995
Strike rate: 108.00 (career 104.37)
Parents: Keith and Nancy
Marital status: Single
Family links with cricket: 'Dad played
competitive club cricket'
Education: Mountbatten School, Romsey;
Loughborough University
Qualifications: 10 GCSEs, 4 A-levels, 2:1 in
Recreational Management, NCA coaching
award
Career outside cricket: Student
Off-season: Tours to South Africa and New
Zealand
Overseas tours: Hampshire 2nd XI to Denmark 1996
Overseas teams played for: Techs, South Africa 1994
Cricketers particularly admired: David Gower, Malcolm Marshall, Robin Smith
Young players to look out for: Michael Davies (Northants), Ben Tragett (Kent)
Other sports followed: Football (Southampton FC – 'European Champions in the year
2005')
Relaxations: 'Pint of Guinness with the lads' and golf
Extras: *Daily Telegraph* Under-15 Bowling Award winner
Opinions on cricket: 'Tea should be extended to thirty minutes. Great idea to have
Academy-type tour during the winter for future England players. Day/night cricket will
be a much-needed boost for the image of the game.'

Best batting: 1 British Universities v India, Fenner's 1996
Best bowling: 2-36 Hampshire v Yorkshire, Scarborough 1995

1997 (no first-class or first-team appearance)

Career Performances

	M	Inns	NO	Runs	HS	Avge	100s	50s	Ct	St	Balls	Runs	Wkts	Avge	Best	5wI	10wM
Test																	
All First	5	8	2	1	1	0.16	-	-	-	-	835	592	8	74.00	2-36	-	-
1-day Int																	
NatWest																		
B & H																		
Sunday																		

DIMOND, M. Somerset

Name: Matthew Dimond
Role: Right-hand bat, right-arm fast bowler
Born: 24 September 1975, Taunton
Height: 6ft 1in **Weight:** 12st
Nickname: Dougie Howser MD, Dominic
County debut: 1994
1st-Class catches: 4
Strike rate: (career 80.50)
Parents: Roger and Gill
Marital status: Single
Family links with cricket: Father and
brother play for local club
Education: Castle School, Taunton; Richard
Huish Sixth Form College, Taunton
Qualifications: 8 GCSEs, 3 A-levels
Overseas tours: West of England U15 to
Trinidad and Tobago, 1991-92; Somerset
Youth to Holland, 1992; England U19 to
West Indies 1994-95

Cricketers particularly admired: Allan Donald, Andy Caddick, Graham Gooch
Young players to look out for: Chris Silverwood, Andrew Harris, Owais Shah
Other sports followed: Football (Yeovil Town and Southampton), golf, American
football (Kansas City)
Relaxations: 'Spending time with my girlfriend, Rachel, enjoying nights out with my
college friends, IB, JB and AW'
Extras: Released by Somerset at the end of the 1997 season

Opinions on cricket: 'I feel that all 2nd XI games should be played on county grounds and treated in the same way as a first-class game – by reducing the overs from 110 to 100/104 in a day.'

Best batting: 26 Somerset v Derbyshire, Derby 1995
Best bowling: 4-73 Somerset v Yorkshire, Bradford 1994

1997 Season

	M	Inns	NO	Runs	HS	Avge	100s	50s	Ct	St	O	M	Runs	Wkts	Avge	Best	5wI	10wM
Test																		
All First	1	1	0	4	4	4.00	-	-	-	-	11	3	30	0	-		-	-
1-day Int																		
NatWest																		
B & H																		
Sunday																		

Career Performances

	M	Inns	NO	Runs	HS	Avge	100s	50s	Ct	St	Balls	Runs	Wkts	Avge	Best	5wI	10wM
Test																	
All First	5	5	1	71	26	17.75	-	-	4	-	483	316	6	52.66	4-73	-	-
1-day Int																	
NatWest																	
B & H	1	0	0	0	0	-	-	-	-	-	18	26	0	-		-	-
Sunday	3	0	0	0	0	-	-	-	-	-	60	76	0	-		-	-

26. Which wicket-keeper broke the record for the most dismissals in the Sunday League during the 1997 season and whose record did he take?

O vodafone

DOBSON, A. M.   Northamptonshire

Name: Andrew Michael Dobson
Role: Left-hand bat, right-hand
medium-fast bowler
Born: 6 April 1980, Scunthorpe
Height: 6ft **Weight:** 12st 11lbs
County debut: No first-team appearance
Nickname: Dobbo
Parents: David and Susan
Marital status: Single
Family links with cricket: 'My father played
second-class cricket for a while and brother
plays to a high level'
Education: Bottesford School; Frederick
Gough Comprehensive; Oundle School
Qualifications: 10 GCSEs, NCA coaching
award
Off-season: Studying for A-levels at Oundle
School
Cricketers particularly admired: Ian
Botham, Richard Hadlee, Nasser Hussain
Young players to look out for: Martyn Dobson (brother)
Other sports followed: Football (Tottenham Hotspur and Scunthorpe United) and
rugby (Northampton Saints)
Relaxations: Playing other sports, listening to music, spending time with friends
Extras: Played for England at U14, U15 and U17 level. Was the best bowler in North
region at U15 level in 1995. Was a member of both the Northamptonshire U17 and U19
national winners in 1997
Opinions on cricket: 'The game is possibly a little too sedate. It does not have enough
competition, publicity or marketing.'

DONALD, A. A.   Warwickshire

Name: Allan Anthony Donald
Role: Right-hand bat, right-arm fast bowler
Born: 20 October 1966, Bloemfontein,
South Africa
Height: 6ft 3in **Weight:** 14st
County debut: 1987
County cap: 1989

Test debut: 1991-92
Tests: 33
One-Day Internationals: 87
50 wickets in a season: 5
1st-Class 5 w. in innings: 51
1st-Class 10 w. in match: 8
1st-Class catches: 92
One-Day 5 w. in innings: 10
Place in batting averages: 210th av. 20.00
(1996 229th av. 16.07)
Place in bowling averages: 2nd av. 15.63
(1996 1st av. 16.07)
Strike rate: 38.78 (career 47.361)
Parents: Stuart and Francine
Wife and date of marriage: Tina, 21
September 1991
Family links with cricket: Father and uncle
played club cricket
Education: Grey College High School;
Technical High School, Bloemfontein
Qualifications: Matriculation
Off-season: Playing for South Africa
Overseas tours: South Africa to India 1991-92, to Australia and New Zealand (World Cup) 1991-92, to West Indies 1991-92, to Sri Lanka 1992-93, to Australia 1992-93, to England 1994, to New Zealand 1994-95, to Zimbabwe 1995-96, to India and Pakistan (World Cup) 1995-96, to India 1996-97, to Pakistan 1997-98, to Australia 1997-98
Overseas teams played for: Orange Free State, South Africa 1985-98
Cricketers particularly admired: Richard Hadlee, Malcolm Marshall, Gladstone Small, Andy Lloyd, Eddie Barlow
Other sports followed: Rugby, golf, tennis
Relaxations: 'Listening to music, having a barbecue, playing golf and having a few beers with my friends'
Extras: Played for South African XI v Australian XI in 1986-87 and v English XI in 1989-90. Retained by Warwickshire for 1991 season ahead of Tom Moody. Toured with South Africa on first-ever visit to India and to West Indies in 1991-92. One of *Wisden*'s Five Cricketers of the Year 1992. Accepted the appointment of fitness coach for Warwickshire for the 1996 season. Took his 100th Test wicket against England in Johannesburg 1995-96. Voted Man of the Series against England finishing with 19 wickets at an average of 26.15. Returned as overseas player for Warwickshire in 1997 after spending a year as fitness coach. Took his 500th wicket for Warwickshire during the 1997 season. Was awarded his country's highest sporting honour when he was presented with a Gold Medal by Nelson Mandela at an awards ceremony in Pretoria on 15 August 1997
Best batting: 46* Orange Free State v Western Province, Cape Town 1990-91
Best bowling: 8-37 Orange Free State v Transvaal, Johannesburg 1986-87

1997 Season

	M	Inns	NO	Runs	HS	Avge	100s	50s	Ct	St	O	M	Runs	Wkts	Avge	Best	5wI	10wM
Test																		
All First	11	13	6	140	29	20.00	-	-	5	-	387.5	123	938	60	15.63	6-55	3	1
1-day Int																		
NatWest	5	3	2	4	3 *	4.00	-	-	1	-	52.1	6	223	15	14.86	5-37	1	
B & H	6	4	3	28	17 *	28.00	-	-	1	-	48	11	159	8	19.87	5-25	1	
Sunday	14	2	2	5	5 *	-	-	-	4	-	85.5	4	336	30	11.20	5-10	1	

Career Performances

	M	Inns	NO	Runs	HS	Avge	100s	50s	Ct	St	Balls	Runs	Wkts	Avge	Best	5wI	10wM
Test	33	44	18	334	33	12.84	-	-	7	-	7609	3621	155	23.36	8-71	8	2
All First	241	279	107	2126	46 *	12.36	-	-	92	-	44762	21160	945	22.39	8-37	51	8
1-day Int	87	21	10	40	7 *	3.63	-	-	12	-	4710	3211	147	21.84	6-23	2	
NatWest	29	10	6	32	14 *	8.00	-	-	4	-	1829	1023	73	14.01	5-12	5	
B & H	26	15	8	87	23 *	12.42	-	-	4	-	1489	996	38	26.21	5-25	1	
Sunday	71	24	12	139	18 *	11.58	-	-	16	-	3109	2074	102	20.33	6-15	2	

DOWMAN, M. P. Nottinghamshire

Name: Matthew Peter Dowman
Role: Left-hand bat, right-arm medium bowler
Born: 10 May 1974, Grantham, Lincs
Height: 5ft 11in **Weight:** 12st
Nickname: Doomer, Rid Rod
County debut: 1993 (one-day), 1994 (first-class)
1000 runs in a season: 1
1st-Class 50s: 7
1st-Class 100s: 6
1st-Class catches: 22
Place in batting averages: 100th av. 34.09 (1996 203rd av. 24.07)
Strike rate: 81.00 (career 100.50)
Parents: Clive and Jackie
Marital status: Single
Family links with cricket: Dad played for Grantham Town. Three brothers also play for Grantham, two of them representing Lincolnshire Schools and Lincolnshire U19
Education: Earl of Dysart Primary; St Hugh's Comprehensive; Grantham College
Qualifications: Senior coach

Career outside cricket: Undecided
Off-season: Playing for East Shirley in Christchurch
Overseas tours: England U19 to India 1992-93; Lincolnshire U16 to Zimbabwe 1988-89; Nottinghamshire to Cape Town 1992-93, to Johannesburg 1996-97; also to Guernsey for Tim Robinson's benefit 1992
Overseas teams played for: South Burwon, Geelong, Melbourne 1995-96
Cricketers particularly admired: Robin Smith, Mike Gatting, Malcolm Marshall, Jimmy Adams
Young players to look out for: Owais Shah, James Ormond, Andy Oram
Other sports followed: Golf, 'follow Notts Forest and County and Lincoln City'
Injuries: Stress fracture of left leg, but missed no cricket
Relaxations: Watching films, playing golf, listening to music
Extras: Played for England U19 in home series against West Indies in 1993, scoring 267 in second 'Test'. Played in winning Midlands team at ESCA Festival 1989. Most runs in a season for Lincolnshire Schools and holds record for most runs in Lincolnshire Schools career. Winner of the 1997 Uncapped Whyte and Mackay Batting Award
Opinions on cricket: 'None of any value.'
Best batting: 149 Nottinghamshire v Leicestershire, Leicester 1997
Best bowling: 3-10 Nottinghamshire v Pakistan A, Trent Bridge 1997

1997 Season

	M	Inns	NO	Runs	HS	Avge	100s	50s	Ct	St	O	M	Runs	Wkts	Avge	Best	5wI	10wM
Test																		
All First	19	33	1	1091	149	34.09	3	5	11	-	81	15	260	6	43.33	3-10	-	-
1-day Int																		
NatWest	1	1	0	14	14	14.00	-	-	-	-								
B & H	3	3	0	151	92	50.33	-	1	-	-	21	0	115	3	38.33	2-46	-	
Sunday	13	13	0	222	71	17.07	-	1	3	-	44.5	0	254	4	63.50	2-31	-	

Career Performances

	M	Inns	NO	Runs	HS	Avge	100s	50s	Ct	St	Balls	Runs	Wkts	Avge	Best	5wI	10wM
Test																	
All First	40	70	3	2087	149	31.14	6	7	22	-	804	457	8	57.12	3-10	-	-
1-day Int																	
NatWest	1	1	0	14	14	14.00	-	-	-	-							
B & H	10	7	2	190	92	38.00	-	1	3	-	242	201	8	25.12	3-21	-	
Sunday	37	37	2	638	74 *	18.22	-	3	8	-	533	524	11	47.63	2-31	-	

DRAKES, V. C. Sussex

Name: Vasbert Conniel Drakes
Role: Right-hand bat, right-arm fast bowler
Born: 5 August 1969, St Michael's, Barbados
Height: 6ft 2in **Weight:** 12st
County debut: 1996
One-Day Internationals: 5
1st-Class 50s: 6
1st-Class 100s: 4
1st-Class catches: 17
1st-Class 5 w. in innings: 6
1st-Class 10 w. in match: 1
One-Day 5 w. in innings: 1
Place in batting averages: 271st av. 13.00
(1996 183rd av. 27.41)
Place in bowling averages: 92nd av. 33.64
(1996 83rd av. 30.16)
Strike rate: 58.06 (career 52.84)
Parents: Leon and Caroline
Marital status: Engaged

Family links with cricket: 'Sir Francis Drake is the famous bowler in the family – the only bowler to receive a knighthood. Introduced cricket to Barbados on an away day'
Education: St Lucy Secondary and College School, Barbados
Qualifications: NCA Coach
Career outside cricket: Electrician
Overseas tours: Barbados U19 to UK 1987; Barbados U21 to UK 1990; Barbados to South Africa 1992; West Indies to England 1995
Overseas teams played for: Barbados 1991-95; Border, South Africa 1996-97
Cricketers particularly admired: Desmond Haynes, Malcolm Marshall 'and all successful fast bowlers throughout the world'
Young players to look out for: Ben Hurley (Barbados) and Danny Law
Other sports followed: Tennis, golf, basketball, football (Arsenal) and volleyball
Relaxations: Listening to music, 'spending time with Mrs Washing-up'
Extras: Was called up to the West Indies squad as a replacement for Winston Benjamin on the 1995 tour to England. Played for West Indies in one-day international series against Australia in 1994-95. Once took 9 for 2 for Lamhey CC
Opinions on cricket: 'Too many wickets are prepared for batsmen. Make the four-day game more interesting and more competitive and have less cricket so that the players would be more enthusiastic all season.'
Best batting: 180* Barbados v Leeward Islands, Anguilla 1994-95
Best bowling: 8-59 Border v Natal, Durban 1996-97

1997 Season

	M	Inns	NO	Runs	HS	Avge	100s	50s	Ct	St	O	M	Runs	Wkts	Avge	Best	5wI	10wM
Test																		
All First	10	18	1	221	48	13.00	-	-	7	-	300	60	1043	31	33.64	4-55	-	-
1-day Int																		
NatWest	4	1	0	15	15	15.00	-	-	-	-	43	13	148	9	16.44	4-62	-	
B & H	4	3	0	75	58	25.00	-	1	-	-	31	2	146	4	36.50	3-46	-	
Sunday	9	8	2	48	12 *	8.00	-	-	-	-	57	5	282	7	40.28	2-21	-	

Career Performances

	M	Inns	NO	Runs	HS	Avge	100s	50s	Ct	St	Balls	Runs	Wkts	Avge	Best	5wI	10wM
Test																	
All First	63	100	15	2048	180 *	24.09	4	6	17	-	10463	6027	198	30.43	8-59	6	1
1-day Int	5	2	0	25	16	12.50	-	-	1	-	239	204	3	68.00	1-36	-	
NatWest	7	4	1	104	35	34.66	-	-	-	-	441	250	15	16.66	4-62	-	
B & H	8	6	1	130	58	26.00	-	1	-	-	396	289	11	26.27	5-19	1	
Sunday	23	20	4	213	37	13.31	-	-	2	-	962	862	24	35.91	4-50	-	

DRIVER, R. K.   Worcestershire

Name: Ryan Keith Driver
Role: Left-hand bat, right-arm medium bowler
Born: 30 April 1979, Truro
Height: 6ft 4in **Weight:** 13st 7lbs
Nickname: Bambi, TJ, Screw
County debut: No first-team appearance
Parents: Les and Jan
Marital status: Single
Family links with cricket: Grandfather, uncle and father all played club cricket. Father was captain of Truro CC for six years. Mother a keen supporter
Education: Trewirge Junior School, Redruth; Redruth School; Durham University
Qualifications: 9 GCSEs, 3 A-levels, NCA coaching award
Off-season: At university studying for a sports degree
Overseas tours: ESCA West U14 to West Indies 1993-94; Cornwall U17 to South Africa 1996 and 1997
Cricketers particularly admired: Brian Lara, Graeme Hick, Allan Donald

Young players to look out for: Patrick Ellis, Adam Barber, Carl Gazzard
Other sports followed: Football (Derby County) and basketball
Relaxations: 'Music, videos, socialising and running up my parents' phone bill on the Internet'
Extras: CSCA Batting Award 1993-96. Played for ESCA U19 and MCC Schools in 1997. Has played for Cornwall CCC since 1995. The opening bat for Truro CC (Cornwall Champions in 1996 and 1997). 'I owe a lot to Malcolm Broad, Peter Bolland and the CSCA'
Opinions on cricket: 'The emphasis should be on quality rather than quantity at all levels. There should be closer links between first-class and minor counties. 2nd XI matches should be played at county grounds wherever possible.'

DUTCH, K. P. Middlesex

Name: Keith Peter Dutch
Role: Right-hand bat, off-spin bowler
Born: 21 March 1973, Harrow, Middlesex
Height: 5ft 9in Weight: 11st 6lbs
Nickname: Dutchy, Double, Zoro
County debut: 1993
1st-Class 50s: 1
1st-Class catches: 8
Place in batting averages: 216th av. 19.71
Strike rate: 58.77 (career 65.08)
Parents: Alan and Ann
Marital status: Single
Family links with cricket: Father is a qualified coach
Education: Nower Hill High School, Pinner; Weald College, Harrow
Qualifications: 5 GCSEs and 1 AS-level
Overseas teams played for: Worcester United, South Africa 1992-93; Geelong City, Australia, 1994

Cricketers particularly admired: Mark Ramprakash, John Emburey
Young players to look out for: Owais Shah, David Nash, Stephen Peters
Other sports followed: Football (Arsenal FC)
Relaxations: Music, pubs, clubbing
Extras: On MCC groundstaff for one year before becoming a contracted player. Rapid Cricketline 2nd XI Player of the Year 1993, Middlesex 2nd XI Player of the Year 1995. In 1996 scored over 1,000 2nd XI Championship runs and took 65 wickets. During this time he achieved highest-ever batting total and bowling figures by a Middlesex player in the history of the 2nd XI Championship with 261 against Somerset and 15 for 157

against Leicestershire – each was the fourth highest in the championship record books.
Named 2nd XI Player of the Year in 1996
Best batting: 79 Middlesex v Gloucestershire, Bristol 1997
Best bowling: 3-25 Middlesex v Somerset, Uxbridge 1996

1997 Season

	M	Inns	NO	Runs	HS	Avge	100s	50s	Ct	St	O	M	Runs	Wkts	Avge	Best	5wI	10wM
Test																		
All First	7	9	2	138	79	19.71	-	1	2	-	88.1	15	289	9	32.11	3-79	-	-
1-day Int																		
NatWest	2	2	1	9	6 *	9.00	-	-	1	-	22	1	78	1	78.00	1-24	-	
B & H	4	4	0	30	20	7.50	-	-	-	-	16	0	85	6	14.16	4-42	-	
Sunday	14	10	3	114	58	16.28	-	1	1	-	75.5	0	375	10	37.50	2-19	-	

Career Performances

	M	Inns	NO	Runs	HS	Avge	100s	50s	Ct	St	Balls	Runs	Wkts	Avge	Best	5wI	10wM
Test																	
All First	12	13	2	177	79	16.09	-	1	8	-	781	416	12	34.66	3-25	-	-
1-day Int																	
NatWest	2	2	1	9	6 *	9.00	-	-	1	-	132	78	1	78.00	1-24	-	
B & H	5	5	0	43	20	8.60	-	-	-	-	126	118	6	19.66	4-42	-	
Sunday	26	20	5	181	58	12.06	-	1	6	-	684	581	17	34.17	3-10	-	

27. Who became the fastest player to score 4,000 runs in the Sunday League?

O vodafone

EALHAM, M. A. Kent

Name: Mark Alan Ealham
Role: Right-hand bat, right-arm
medium bowler
Born: 27 August 1969, Willesborough, Kent
Height: 5ft 10in **Weight:** 13st 9lbs
Nickname: Ealy, Skater
County debut: 1989
County cap: 1992
Test debut: 1996
Tests: 6
One-Day Internationals: 5
1000 runs in a season: 1
1st-Class 50s: 32
1st-Class 100s: 4
1st-Class 5 w. in innings: 8
1st-Class 10 w. in match: 1
1st-Class catches: 44
One-Day 5 w. in innings: 1
One-Day 100s: 1
Place in batting averages: 15th av. 52.75 (1996 141st av. 32.52)
Place in bowling averages: 77th av. 30.95 (1996 9th av. 21.17)
Strike rate: 61.15 (career 60.31)
Parents: Alan and Sue
Wife and date of marriage: Kirsty, 24 February 1996
Family links with cricket: Father played county cricket for Kent
Education: Stour Valley Secondary School
Qualifications: 9 CSEs
Off-season: England to Sharjah and then England A tour to Kenya and Sri Lanka
Overseas tours: England A to Australia 1996-97, to Kenya and Sri Lanka 1997-98;
England to Sharjah 1997-98; England VI to Hong Kong 1997
Overseas teams played for: South Perth, Australia 1992-93; University, Perth,
Australia 1993-94
Cricketers particularly admired: Ian Botham, Viv Richards, Robin Smith, Paul
Blackmore and Albert 'for his F and G'
Other sports followed: Football (Manchester United) and most other sports
Injuries: Rib muscle strain, missed four weeks
Relaxations: Playing golf and snooker, watching films
Extras: Scored fastest Sunday League century off 44 balls. Made his Test debut against
India in the third Test at Trent Bridge in 1996. Represented England in the 1997 Hong
Kong Sixes tournament in which England finished as runners-up to Pakistan
Best batting: 139 Kent v Leicestershire, Canterbury 1997
Best bowling: 8-36 Kent v Warwickshire, Edgbaston 1996

1997 Season

	M	Inns	NO	Runs	HS	Avge	100s	50s	Ct	St	O	M	Runs	Wkts	Avge	Best	5wI	10wM
Test	4	6	3	105	53 *	35.00	-	1	3	-	58.4	11	191	8	23.87	3-60	-	-
All First	18	30	10	1055	139	52.75	3	6	12	-	407.4	80	1238	40	30.95	4-47	-	-
1-day Int	3	0	0	0	0	-	-	-	1	-	27	5	108	4	27.00	2-21	-	
NatWest	1	1	0	46	46	46.00	-	-	-	-	12	0	45	1	45.00	1-45	-	
B & H	8	8	3	185	52	37.00	-	1	5	-	62	2	284	10	28.40	2-31	-	
Sunday	12	10	1	201	61	22.33	-	2	3	-	62.2	3	280	12	23.33	5-41	1	

Career Performances

	M	Inns	NO	Runs	HS	Avge	100s	50s	Ct	St	Balls	Runs	Wkts	Avge	Best	5wI	10wM
Test	6	9	3	186	53 *	31.00	-	2	4	-	832	383	15	25.53	4-21	-	-
All First	106	171	28	4689	139	32.79	4	32	44	-	14234	7037	236	29.81	8-36	8	1
1-day Int	5	1	0	40	40	40.00	-	-	1	-	198	131	4	32.75	2-21	-	
NatWest	14	14	4	298	58 *	29.80	-	2	4	-	767	387	16	24.18	4-10	-	
B & H	34	31	8	618	75	26.86	-	4	14	-	1775	1195	49	24.38	4-29	-	
Sunday	105	85	23	1535	112	24.75	1	7	24	-	4023	3087	98	31.50	6-53	2	

ECCLESTONE, S. C.   Somerset

Name: Simon Charles Ecclestone
Role: Left-hand bat, right-arm
fast-medium bowler, county vice-captain
Born: 16 July 1971, Great Dunmow, Essex
Height: 6ft 3in **Weight:** 14st 7lbs
Nickname: Major
County debut: 1994
1st-Class 50s: 11
1st-Class 100s: 3
1st-Class catches: 18
One-Day 100s: 3
Place in batting averages: 33rd av. 45.28
(1996 177th av. 27.83)
Strike rate: (career 73.54)
Parents: Jonathan and Pippa
Marital status: Single
Family links with cricket: Brother Giles
played for Essex and Cambridgeshire
Education: Bryanston School; Durham
University; Keble College, Oxford

Qualifications: 9 O-levels, 3 A-levels, BA (Hons) Social Sciences, Dip Soc (Oxon)
Overseas tours: Bryanston to West Indies 1989; Durham University to South Africa

1992-93
Cricketers particularly admired: David Gower
Other sports followed: Rugby and all other sports
Relaxations: 'Continuous cycle of cooking it, eating it, drinking it and getting rid of the evidence'
Extras: Played for Essex from U11 to U19/2nd XI and for ESCA U19 v New Zealand 1989; captained Durham University, played for Cambridgeshire, Blue for Oxford University 1994, 'brother of first *Daily Telegraph* Fantasy League winner'
Best batting: 133 Somerset v Oxford University, Taunton 1997
Best bowling: 4-66 Oxford University v Surrey, The Oval 1994

1997 Season

	M	Inns	NO	Runs	HS	Avge	100s	50s	Ct	St	O	M	Runs	Wkts	Avge	Best	5wI	10wM
Test																		
All First	13	23	2	951	133	45.28	3	4	12	-	1	1	0	0	-		-	-
1-day Int																		
NatWest	2	2	0	188	101	94.00	1	1	-	-								
B & H	5	5	0	130	92	26.00	-	1	1	-								
Sunday	12	11	1	236	96 *	23.60	-	1	1	-								

Career Performances

	M	Inns	NO	Runs	HS	Avge	100s	50s	Ct	St	Balls	Runs	Wkts	Avge	Best	5wI	10wM
Test																	
All First	41	67	9	2091	133	36.05	3	11	18	-	2427	1208	33	36.60	4-66	-	-
1-day Int																	
NatWest	7	7	0	295	101	42.14	1	2	-	-	66	53	0	-		-	-
B & H	14	13	2	465	112 *	42.27	1	3	4	-	210	155	3	51.66	2-44	-	
Sunday	42	41	4	997	130	26.94	1	3	7	-	590	593	18	32.94	4-31	-	

EDMOND, M. D.   Warwickshire

Name: Michael Dennis Edmond
Role: Right-hand bat, right-arm medium-fast bowler
Born: 30 July 1969, Barrow-in-Furness
Weight: 14st 7lbs
Nickname: Eddo, Aus
County debut: 1996
1st-Class catches: 1
Strike rate: 87.00 (career 89.80)
Parents: Tom and Carol
Marital status: Single
Children: Ryen

Family links with cricket: 'My brother plays'
Education: Briar Road Public School, Campbelltown, NSW; Airds High School, Campbelltown, NSW
Qualifications: Level O coach in Australia
Career outside cricket: Barman
Overseas teams played for: Campbelltown, Sydney 1988-93; Fairfield, Sydney 1994
Cricketers particularly admired: Ian Botham, Viv Richards, Len Pascoe
Young players to look out for: 'All with an ambition to play for England'
Other sports followed: Indoor cricket (played for Australia 1993-96), football (Manchester United), rugby league (Manly-Warringam)
Relaxations: Spending time with friends, going out and listening to music

Best batting: 21 Warwickshire v Kent, Tunbridge Wells 1997
Best bowling: 2-26 Warwickshire v Oxford University, The Parks 1997

1997 Season

	M	Inns	NO	Runs	HS	Avge	100s	50s	Ct	St	O	M	Runs	Wkts	Avge	Best	5wI	10wM
Test																		
All First	3	3	1	35	21	17.50	-	-	1	-	58	14	175	4	43.75	2-26	-	-
1-day Int																		
NatWest																		
B & H																		
Sunday	5	3	1	34	19	17.00	-	-	1	-	30.5	0	146	9	16.22	2-4	-	

Career Performances

	M	Inns	NO	Runs	HS	Avge	100s	50s	Ct	St	Balls	Runs	Wkts	Avge	Best	5wI	10wM
Test																	
All First	4	4	2	43	21	21.50	-	-	1	-	449	254	5	50.80	2-26	-	-
1-day Int																	
NatWest	1	1	0	0	0	0.00	-	-	-	-	48	24	1	24.00	1-24	-	
B & H																	
Sunday	8	5	2	43	19	14.33	-	-	2	-	311	233	12	19.41	2-4	-	

EDWARDS, A. D.　　　　　　　　Sussex

Name: Alexander David Edwards
Role: Right-hand bat, right-arm
fast-medium bowler
Born: 2 August 1975, Cuckfield, Sussex
Height: 6ft **Weight:** 12st 9lbs
Nickname: Al, Steads, Elvis
County debut: 1994 (one-day),
1995 (first-class)
1st-Class 5 w. in innings: 1
1st-Class catches: 2
Place in batting averages: 293rd av. 8.25
Place in bowling averages: 20th av. 22.88
Strike rate: 36.47 (career 49.00)
Parents: Richard John and Angela Janet
Marital status: Single
Family links with cricket: 'Parents drove
me everywhere to play or practise cricket and
have been absolutely wonderful'

Education: Felbridge Primary; Imberhorne
Comprehensive; Loughborough University
Qualifications: 10 GCSEs, 4 A-levels
Career outside cricket: Studying at Loughborough
Overseas tours: Sussex U18 to India 1990-91; England U18 to South Africa 1992-93,
to Denmark 1993
Cricketers particularly admired: Dennis Lillee, Michael Holding, Viv Richards,
Stan Berry and Pat Cale 'for their tremendous support, belief and encouragement'
Other sports followed: Football (Liverpool FC)
Relaxations: Snooker, swimming, training, listening to a variety of music, watching
sports on television
Extras: Lord's Taverners U15 Young Cricketer of the Year 1991 and a *Cricketer*
magazine Young Cricketer of the Month in the same year. Played for England U19
against India U19 in 1994
Opinions on cricket: 'Second XI cricket should mirror the first-class game, e.g. same
grounds, practice facilities and duration of matches in the championship (four days).
This would help young players to make the transition from 2nd XI to first-class cricket.
Young players should be given ample opportunity to prove themselves in first-class
cricket. They shouldn't be afraid of initial failure.'
Best batting: 22 Sussex v Young Australia, Hove 1995
Best bowling: 5-34 Sussex v Pakistan A, Hove 1997

1997 Season

	M	Inns	NO	Runs	HS	Avge	100s	50s	Ct	St	O	M	Runs	Wkts	Avge	Best	5wI	10wM
Test																		
All First	6	10	2	66	20	8.25	-	-	5	-	103.2	19	389	17	22.88	5-34	1	-
1-day Int																		
NatWest																		
B & H	2	2	1	9	9	9.00	-	-	-	-	20	1	109	0	-		-	-
Sunday	4	4	1	11	9 *	3.66	-	-	1	-	17.5	1	82	3	27.33	2-44	-	

Career Performances

	M	Inns	NO	Runs	HS	Avge	100s	50s	Ct	St	Balls	Runs	Wkts	Avge	Best	5wI	10wM
Test																	
All First	9	13	2	104	22	9.45	-	-	7	-	980	699	20	34.95	5-34	1	-
1-day Int																	
NatWest																	
B & H	7	6	2	30	9	7.50	-	-	5	-	444	341	5	68.20	2-51	-	
Sunday	5	4	1	11	9 *	3.66	-	-	1	-	137	106	3	35.33	2-44	-	

ELLIS, S. W. K.   Worcestershire

Name: Scott William Kenneth Ellis
Role: Right-hand bat, right-arm
fast-medium bowler
Born: 3 October 1975, Newcastle-under-Lyme
Height: 6ft 4in **Weight:** 14st 7lbs
Nickname: Llama, Fleece Head
County debut: 1996
1st-Class catches: 7
1st-Class 5 w. in innings: 1
Place in batting averages: 295th av. 10.50
Place in bowling averages: 139th av. 49.00
Strike rate: 72.85 (career 64.73)
Parents: Tony and Valerie Anne
Marital status: Single
Education: Shrewsbury School;
Warwick University
Qualifications: 9 GCSEs, 3 A-levels, 2:1 in
Ancient History and Philosophy
Off-season: Playing in South Africa
Overseas tours: England U19 to West Indies 1994-95
Cricketers particularly admired: Courtney Walsh, Alec Stewart
Other sports followed: Football

Injuries: Pulled hamstring, out for one month
Relaxations: Listening to music, reading
Extras: Played for England U18 against India U19 in 1994. Made first-class debut for Combined Universities against West Indies in 1995
Opinions on cricket: 'We missed a great opportunity to improve the game when we rejected the two-tier system.'
Best batting: 15 Worcestershire v Middlesex, Lord's 1996
Best bowling: 5-59 Combined Universities v West Indies, The Parks 1995

1997 Season (did not make any first-class or one-day appearances)

Career Performances

	M	Inns	NO	Runs	HS	Avge	100s	50s	Ct	St	Balls	Runs	Wkts	Avge	Best	5wl	10wM
Test																	
All First	10	11	4	63	15	9.00	-	-	7	-	1230	832	19	43.78	5-59	1	-
1-day Int																	
NatWest	1	1	1	0	0 *	-	-	-	-	-	42	34	2	17.00	2-34	-	
B & H	1	1	0	4	4	4.00	-	-	-	-	54	50	1	50.00	1-50	-	
Sunday	6	1	0	1	1	1.00	-	-	2	-	156	141	4	35.25	2-35	-	

EMBUREY, J. E. Northamptonshire

Name: John Ernest Emburey
Role: Right-hand bat, off-spin bowler
Born: 20 August 1952, Peckham
Height: 6ft 2in **Weight:** 14st
Nickname: Embers, Ern
County debut: 1973 (Middlesex),
1996 (Northamptonshire)
County cap: 1977
Benefit: 1986
Testimonial: 1995
Test debut: 1978
Tests: 64
One-Day Internationals: 61
50 wickets in a season: 17
1st-Class 50s: 55
1st-Class 100s: 7
1st-Class 5 w. in innings: 72
1st-Class 10 w. in match: 12
1st-Class catches: 459

One-Day 5 w. in innings: 3
Place in batting averages: (1996 220th av. 22.22)
Place in bowling averages: (1996 105th av. 38.59)
Strike rate: 165.75 (career 70.21)
Parents: John (deceased) and Rose
Wife and date of marriage: Susie, 20 September 1980
Children: Clare, 1 March 1983; Chloë, 31 October 1985
Education: Peckham Manor Secondary School
Qualifications: O-levels, advanced cricket coaching certificate
Overseas tours: England to Australia 1978-79, to Australia and India 1979-80, to West Indies 1980-81, to India and Sri Lanka 1981-82, to West Indies 1985-86, to Australia 1986-87, to Pakistan, Australia and New Zealand 1987-88, to India 1992-93; unofficial English XI to South Africa 1981-82 and 1989-90
Overseas teams played for: Prahran, Melbourne 1977-78; St Kilda, Melbourne 1984-85; Western Province 1982-84
Cricketers particularly admired: Ken Barrington, Alan Knott
Other sports followed: Golf
Relaxations: Reading, golf
Extras: Played for Surrey YC 1969-70. Phil Edmonds of Middlesex and England was the best man at his wedding. Middlesex vice-captain 1983-93. One of *Wisden*'s Five Cricketers of the Year 1983. Captain of England v West Indies for two Tests in 1988. Banned from Test cricket for three years for touring South Africa in 1981-82, and for five more for touring in 1989-90, suspension remitted in 1992. Published autobiography *Emburey* in 1988. In the match against Somerset at Lord's in 1992 he became only the 9th player to take 1,000 wickets for Middlesex. Middlesex Player of the Year 1993. Manager of the England A tour to Pakistan 1995-96. Left Middlesex at the end of the 1995 season to join Northamptonshire as the club's chief coach
Opinions on cricket: 'Young players seem very uptight. They should relax and enjoy the game. The less pressure you put yourself under, the easier it will become. Good players don't become bad players, bad players can become good players. They just have to work a little harder.'
Best batting: 133 Middlesex v Essex, Chelmsford 1983
Best bowling: 8-40 Middlesex v Hampshire, Lord's 1993

1997 Season

	M	Inns	NO	Runs	HS	Avge	100s	50s	Ct	St	O	M	Runs	Wkts	Avge	Best	5wI	10wM
Test																		
All First	3	3	0	39	39	13.00	-	-	1	-	110.3	39	259	4	64.75	2-36	-	-
1-day Int																		
NatWest	2	2	0	2	1	1.00	-	-	-	-	24	3	83	1	83.00	1-61	-	
B & H	6	3	1	33	19 *	16.50	-	-	3	-	55	5	187	6	31.16	3-34	-	
Sunday	11	7	2	25	8	5.00	-	-	3	-	72.3	2	350	13	26.92	4-28	-	

Career Performances

	M	Inns	NO	Runs	HS	Avge	100s	50s	Ct	St	Balls	Runs	Wkts	Avge	Best	5wI	10wM
Test	64	96	20	1713	75	22.53	-	10	34	-	15391	5646	147	38.40	7-78	6	-
All First	513	644	130	12021	133	23.38	7	55	459	-	112904	41958	1608	26.09	8-40	72	12
1-day Int	61	45	10	501	34	14.31	-	-	19	-	3425	2346	76	30.86	4-37	-	
NatWest	61	39	11	521	46	18.60	-	-	21	-	4082	1907	71	26.85	3-11	-	
B & H	93	62	19	679	50	15.79	-	1	45	-	5002	2666	98	27.20	5-37	1	
Sunday	277	179	62	1901	50	16.24	-	1	85	-	11780	8635	368	23.46	5-23	2	

EVANS, A. W. Glamorgan

Name: Alun Wyn Evans
Role: Right-hand bat, right-arm medium bowler
Height: 5ft 8in **Weight:** 11st 10lbs
Born: 20 August 1975, Glanammen, Dyfed
County debut: 1996
1st-Class 50s: 1
1st-Class catches: 6
Place in batting averages:
(1996 90th av. 37.60)
Parents: Gareth and Lynfa
Marital status: Single
Family links with cricket: Father formerly with Ammanford CC. Brother played Welsh Schools at all ages and now plays for Ammanford
Education: Fishguard County High School; Neath Tertiary College
Qualifications: 11 GCSEs, BTEC National Diploma in Sports Science
Overseas tours: Welsh Schools U17 to Australia 1992-93
Overseas teams played for: Marist, Whangarei 1995-96
Cricketers particularly admired: Brian Lara, Wasim Akram
Young players to look out for: Ricky Fay
Other sports followed: Rugby, football (Tottenham Hotspur FC)
Relaxations: Music, reading magazines
Extras: Welsh Schools Player of the Year 1994, MCC Young Cricketer 1995. Balconiers 2nd XI Player of the Year. ASW Young Player of the Year
Opinions on cricket: 'In the 2nd XI Championship, I think the extra hour rule that has been brought in is out of order.'
Best batting: 71* Glamorgan v Oxford University, The Parks 1996

1997 Season

	M	Inns	NO	Runs	HS	Avge	100s	50s	Ct	St	O	M	Runs	Wkts	Avge	Best	5wI	10wM
Test																		
All First	2	3	0	61	31	20.33	-	-	1	-								
1-day Int																		
NatWest																		
B & H																		
Sunday	7	6	1	70	25	14.00	-	-	1	-								

Career Performances

	M	Inns	NO	Runs	HS	Avge	100s	50s	Ct	St	Balls	Runs	Wkts	Avge	Best	5wI	10wM
Test																	
All First	9	16	3	437	71 *	33.61	-	2	6	-							
1-day Int																	
NatWest																	
B & H																	
Sunday	13	12	3	169	50 *	18.77	-	1	3	-							

EVANS, K. P.   Nottinghamshire

Name: Kevin Paul Evans
Role: Right-hand bat, right-arm medium bowler
Born: 10 September 1963, Calverton, Nottingham
Height: 6ft 2in **Weight:** 13st
Nickname: Ghost, Texas
County debut: 1984
County cap: 1990
1st-Class 50s: 21
1st-Class 100s: 3
1st-Class 5 w. in innings: 8
1st-Class catches: 108
One-Day 5 w. in innings: 2
Place in batting averages: 274th av. 12.23 (1996 145th av. 32.13)
Place in bowling averages: 59th av. 28.37 (1996 114th av. 40.56)
Strike rate: 61.04 (career 69.02)
Parents: Eric and Eileen
Wife and date of marriage: Sandra, 19 March 1988
Children: Ryan Matthew, 24 January 1997

Family links with cricket: Brother Russell played for Nottinghamshire and still plays for Minor Counties and Lincolnshire. Father played local cricket
Education: William Lee Primary; Colonel Frank Seely Comprehensive, Calverton
Qualifications: 10 O-levels, 3 A-levels, qualified coach
Off-season: 'Unemployed'
Overseas teams played for: Wanuiomata, New Zealand 1989-91
Cricketers particularly admired: Richard Hadlee, Clive Rice
Young players to look out for: Guy Welton
Other sports followed: Football (Leeds United), tennis, squash
Injuries: 'Hit by a non-pitching ball from an international bowler in a very painful area.' Out for two weeks
Relaxations: Listening to music, reading, DIY, gardening
Extras: With brother, Russell, first brothers to bat together for Nottinghamshire in first-class cricket for 50 years. Kept wicket for the first time in the Championship match against Essex at Colchester in 1992. Second Notts cricketer to bowl Sunday League hat-trick v Glamorgan at Trent Bridge, Mark Saxelby was the other
Opinions on cricket: 'The two-tier system will eventually take over from the present system, but the logistics of this must be looked at in far more detail. Four-day cricket on covered wickets should remain the norm.'
Best batting: 104 Nottinghamshire v Surrey, Trent Bridge 1992
104 Nottinghamshire v Sussex, Trent Bridge 1994
Best bowling: 6-40 Nottinghamshire v Lancashire, Old Trafford 1997

1997 Season

	M	Inns	NO	Runs	HS	Avge	100s	50s	Ct	St	O	M	Runs	Wkts	Avge	Best	5wI	10wM
Test																		
All First	15	18	1	208	47	12.23	-	-	6	-	457.5	103	1277	45	28.37	6-40	2	-
1-day Int																		
NatWest	3	1	0	11	11	11.00	-	-	-	-	30.4	9	78	5	15.60	2-22	-	
B & H	3	2	0	20	13	10.00	-	-	2	-	27	2	127	4	31.75	3-61	-	
Sunday	12	10	2	74	20	9.25	-	-	3	-	86	2	436	12	36.33	4-26	-	

Career Performances

	M	Inns	NO	Runs	HS	Avge	100s	50s	Ct	St	Balls	Runs	Wkts	Avge	Best	5wI	10wM
Test																	
All First	151	207	44	4069	104	24.96	3	21	108	-	23053	11292	334	33.80	6-40	8	-
1-day Int																	
NatWest	22	15	2	126	21	9.69	-	-	6	-	1346	724	31	23.35	6-10	1	
B & H	33	21	5	243	47	15.18	-	-	10	-	1838	1261	45	28.02	4-19	-	
Sunday	133	81	31	776	30	15.52	-	-	26	-	5456	4613	141	32.71	5-29	1	

FAIRBROTHER, N. H. Lancashire

Name: Neil Harvey Fairbrother
Role: Left-hand bat, left-arm medium bowler
Born: 9 September 1963, Warrington, Cheshire
Height: 5ft 8in **Weight:** 11st 4lbs
Nickname: Harvey
County debut: 1982
County cap: 1985
Benefit: 1995
Test debut: 1987
Tests: 10
One-Day Internationals: 56
1000 runs in a season: 10
1st-Class 50s: 93
1st-Class 100s: 37
1st-Class 200s: 3
1st-Class 300s: 1
1st-Class catches: 220
One-Day 100s: 6

Place in batting averages: 61st av. 40.31 (1996 20th av. 53.40)
Strike rate: (career 134.60)
Parents: Les and Barbara
Wife and date of marriage: Audrey, 23 September 1988
Children: Rachael Elizabeth, 4 April 1991; Sam, 3 April 1994
Family links with cricket: Father and two uncles played local league cricket
Education: St Margaret's Church of England School, Oxford; Lymm Grammar School
Qualifications: 5 O-levels
Overseas tours: England to Sharjah 1986-87, to India and Pakistan (World Cup)1987, Australia and New Zealand 1987-88; England A to Pakistan 1990-91; England to New Zealand 1991-92, to India 1992-93, to Australia 1994-95, to South Africa 1995-96, to India and Pakistan (World Cup) 1995-96
Cricketers particularly admired: Clive Lloyd, Allan Border, David Gower
Other sports followed: Football, rugby union, rugby league
Relaxations: Music and playing sport
Extras: 'I was named after the Australian cricketer Neil Harvey, who was my mum's favourite cricketer.' Played for England YC v Australia 1983. His innings of 366 in 1990 was the third highest score ever made in the County Championship, the second highest first-class score by a Lancashire batsman and the best at The Oval. Appointed Lancashire captain for 1992 but resigned in 1993. Called up to join England tour party as a replacement in Australia 1994-95 but was immediately injured in a collision with Steven Rhodes while fielding and forced to return home. Played in the one-day series between England and South Africa and represented England in the World Cup in 1996-97
Opinions on cricket: 'There is too much cricket. The game has to be made more

entertaining.'
Best batting: 366 Lancashire v Surrey, The Oval 1990
Best bowling: 2-91 Lancashire v Nottinghamshire, Old Trafford 1987

1997 Season

	M	Inns	NO	Runs	HS	Avge	100s	50s	Ct	St	O	M	Runs	Wkts	Avge	Best	5wI	10wM
Test																		
All First	16	24	2	887	132	40.31	2	4	19	-								
1-day Int																		
NatWest																		
B & H	5	5	2	246	75 *	82.00	-	3	1	-								
Sunday	15	15	5	546	88	54.60	-	6	3	-								

Career Performances

	M	Inns	NO	Runs	HS	Avge	100s	50s	Ct	St	Balls	Runs	Wkts	Avge	Best	5wI	10wM
Test	10	15	1	219	83	15.64	-	1	4	-	12	9	0	-	-	-	-
All First	303	483	68	17182	366	41.40	37	93	220	-	673	440	5	88.00	2-91	-	-
1-day Int	56	54	13	1539	113	37.53	1	11	24	-	6	9	0	-	-	-	-
NatWest	34	33	5	1254	93 *	44.78	-	9	18	-	48	44	1	44.00	1-28	-	
B & H	69	66	21	2471	116 *	54.91	1	20	33	-	54	67	1	67.00	1-17	-	
Sunday	200	186	45	5552	116 *	39.37	4	36	60	-	48	48	1	48.00	1-33	-	

FAY, R. A.   Middlesex

Name: Richard Anthony Fay
Role: Right-hand bat, right-arm
medium-fast bowler
Born: 14 May 1974, Kilburn, London
Height: 6ft 4in **Weight:** 15st
Nickname: Red, Two Dofs
County debut: 1995
1st-Class catches: 5
Place in batting averages:
(1996 306th av. 7.40)
Place in bowling averages:
(1996 101st av. 36.16)
Strike rate: 69.67 (career 70.25)
Parents: James Peter and Margaret Christine
Marital status: Single
Family links with cricket: Father played for
Combined Services. Great uncle was
Maurice Tate

Education: Kilburn Park; Brondesbury and Kilburn, Queen's Park Community School; City of Westminster College

Qualifications: 4 GCSEs, BTEC in Business Studies, BTEC in Design and Realisation Finance

Career outside cricket: 'Haven't thought'

Off-season: Training, working, 'spending time with my girlfriend Julie'

Cricketers particularly admired: Mark Garaway, Darren Wyrill, Angus Fraser, Scott Moffatt, Ian Kidd, Mark Lowrey, Kenyon Jones-Ginn

Young players to look out for: Owais Shah, Jamie Hewitt, David Nash, Alun Evans

Other sports followed: Football (Chelsea), table tennis, pool, darts, baseball

Injuries: Lower back problem, out for 10 weeks

Relaxations: 'Having a few pints in my local and watching videos with my girlfriend Julie'

Extras: Best league performance of nine wickets for 45 runs against Wembley CC. MCC YC 1992-95

Opinions on cricket: 'There are too many people ready to stab you in the back. If anyone has anything to say, say it to the individual's face. When you have time off, it may be wise to have time to yourself, rather than train or come in to practise. 2nd XI cricket should be played over four days to prepare the younger members of the side for first-class cricket.'

Best batting: 26 Middlesex v Glamorgan, Lord's 1996

Best bowling: 4-53 Middlesex v Glamorgan, Lord's 1996

1997 Season

	M	Inns	NO	Runs	HS	Avge	100s	50s	Ct	St	O	M	Runs	Wkts	Avge	Best	5wl	10wM
Test																		
All First																		
1-day Int																		
NatWest																		
B & H	1	1	1	3	3 *	-	-	-	-	-	10	0	63	1	63.00	1-63	-	
Sunday	2	0	0	0	0	-	-	-	-	-	16	1	50	3	16.66	2-23	-	

Career Performances

	M	Inns	NO	Runs	HS	Avge	100s	50s	Ct	St	Balls	Runs	Wkts	Avge	Best	5wl	10wM
Test																	
All First	16	25	3	164	26	7.45	-	-	5	-	2178	1146	31	36.96	4-53	-	-
1-day Int																	
NatWest	2	1	0	0	0	0.00	-	-	2	-	102	63	3	21.00	2-43	-	
B & H	5	3	1	4	3 *	2.00	-	-	1	-	264	186	4	46.50	1-13	-	
Sunday	22	8	5	36	12 *	12.00	-	-	2	-	906	656	22	29.81	4-33	-	

FISHER, I. D.   Yorkshire

Name: Ian Douglas Fisher
Role: Left-hand bat, slow left-arm bowler
Born: 31 March 1976, Bradford
Height: 5ft 11in **Weight:** 13st 6lbs
Nickname: Fish, Fishcake
County debut: 1996
1st-Class 5 w. in innings: 1
Strike rate: 234.00 (career 52.20)
Parents: Geoff and Linda
Marital status: Single
Family links with cricket: Father played
club cricket
Education: Parkside Middle School;
Beckfoot Grammar School
Qualifications: 8 GCSEs, NCA coaching
award, Sports Leaders Award
Off-season: Playing club cricket in New
Zealand

Overseas tours: Yorkshire to Zimbabwe 1996
Overseas teams played for: Somerset West, South Africa 1994-95
Cricketers particularly admired: Darren Lehman, Phil Tufnell
Young players to look out for: Matthew Wood
Other sports followed: Football (Leeds United), golf
Injuries: Broken thumb, missed the first two games
Relaxations: Television, films, socialising, music, watching football
Extras: Played England U17 and Yorkshire Schools U15, U16 and Yorkshire U19
Opinions on cricket: '2nd XI cricket should be four days on first-class grounds.
Should have gone for the two-league system.'
Best batting: 37 Yorkshire v Derbyshire, Derby 1997
Best bowling: 5-35 Yorkshire v Lancashire, Old Trafford 1996

1997 Season

	M	Inns	NO	Runs	HS	Avge	100s	50s	Ct	St	O	M	Runs	Wkts	Avge	Best	5wI	10wM
Test																		
All First	2	4	0	75	37	18.75	-	-	-	-	39	7	103	1	103.00	1-26	-	-
1-day Int																		
NatWest																		
B & H																		
Sunday	2	0	0	0	0	-	-	-	-	-	16	0	47	4	11.75	2-23	-	

	M	Inns	NO	Runs	HS	Avge	100s	50s	Ct	St	Balls	Runs	Wkts	Avge	Best	5wI	10wM
Test																	
All First	5	5	1	75	37	18.75	-	-	-	-	624	285	12	23.75	5-35	1	-
1-day Int																	
NatWest																	
B & H																	
Sunday	2	0	0	0	0	-	-	-	-	-	96	47	4	11.75	2-23	-	

FLANAGAN, I. N. Essex

Name: Ian Nicholas Flanagan
Role: Left-hand bat, off-spin bowler
Born: 5 June 1980, Colchester
Height: 6ft **Weight:** 12st
Nickname: Bud, Flanners, Schlong, Crudsky
County debut: 1997
Parents: Roy and Anita
Marital status: Single
Family links with cricket: 'Old man played
cricket for Colchester and Carlisle. Mum
does teas at Colchester, and has been known
to "lick it in the bush" for Colchester Ladies
cricket team'
Education: Millfield County Primary School;
The Colne Community School; The Sixth
Form College, Colchester; 'away trips with
Stephen Andrew'
Qualifications: 10 GCSEs

Off-season: Touring South Africa with England U19 for the Test series and the
International Youth World Cup
Overseas tours: England U19 to Pakistan 1996-97, to South Africa 1997-98
Cricketers particularly admired: Stephen Andrew, Nasser Hussain, Carl Hooper,
Stuart Law
Young players to look out for: Paul Franks, David Sales, Graham Napier
Other sports followed: Rugby, football (Tottenham Hotspur and Colchester United)
Relaxations: Watching films, music, going out, cinema, sleeping
Extras: Also played for England U17, U18 and U19
Opinions on cricket: 'Tea should be 30 minutes. 2nd XI games should be played on 1st
XI grounds. Two divisions should have been introduced, but a lot of people running
county cricket are too afraid of radical change.'
Best batting: 40 Essex v Lancashire, Old Trafford 1997

	M	Inns	NO	Runs	HS	Avge	100s	50s	Ct	St	O	M	Runs	Wkts	Avge	Best	5wI	10wM
Test																		
All First	2	3	1	72	40	36.00	-	-	-	-								
1-day Int																		
NatWest																		
B & H																		
Sunday																		

Career Performances

	M	Inns	NO	Runs	HS	Avge	100s	50s	Ct	St	Balls	Runs	Wkts	Avge	Best	5wI	10wM
Test																	
All First	2	3	1	72	40	36.00	-	-	-	-							
1-day Int																	
NatWest																	
B & H																	
Sunday																	

FLEMING, M. V.   Kent

Name: Matthew Valentine Fleming
Role: Right-hand bat, right-arm
medium bowler
Born: 12 December 1964, Macclesfield
Height: 5ft 11ins **Weight:** 12st 6lbs
Nickname: Jazzer, Swan Vesta
County debut: 1988
County cap: 1990
1st-Class 50s: 36
1st-Class 100s: 9
1st-Class catches: 60
1st-Class 5 w. in innings: 2
One-Day 100s: 1
Place in batting averages: 128th av. 29.95
(1996 156th av. 30.53)
Place in bowling averages: 76th av. 30.94
(1996 37th av. 26.88)
Strike rate: 64.59 (career 81.90)
Parents: Valentine and Elizabeth
Wife and date of marriage: Caroline, 23 September 1989
Children: Hannah, 9 October 1992; Victoria, 16 June 1994
Family links with cricket: Great-grandfather C.F. Leslie played for England in 1880s;

father played for Eton 2nd XI; mother opened the bowling for Heathfield School
Education: St Aubyns School, Rottingdean; Eton College
Qualifications: 8 O-levels, 3 A-levels, commissioned Royal Green Jackets in 1985
Career outside cricket: 'Unemployable'
Off-season: Playing in the one-day competition for England in Sharjah
Overseas tours: England to Sharjah 1997-98, to West Indies 1997-98 (one-day series); England VI to Hong Kong 1997
Overseas teams played for: Avendale, Cape Town 1983-84
Cricketers particularly admired: 'All who play to win yet with a smile'
Young players to look out for: Matthew Walker, Ben Phillips
Other sports followed: Football (Arsenal), golf
Relaxations: Fishing, shooting, stalking, building bonfires
Extras: Ex-army officer in the Royal Green Jackets. First two scoring shots in Championship cricket were sixes. Vice-chairman of the Professional Cricketers' Association. Out twice before lunch batting at number three for Kent against West Indies in 1995. Played for England in the 1997 Hong Kong Sixes tournament in which England finished runners-up to Pakistan and was named Player of the Tournament. Called up to the England squad for the one-day competition in Sharjah after the withdrawal of Darren Gough
Opinions on cricket: 'The NatWest competition should go. Benson and Hedges format for world one-day cricket should become the premier one-day competition.'
Best batting: 138 Kent v Essex, Canterbury 1997
Best bowling: 5-51 Kent v Nottinghamshire, Trent Bridge 1997

1997 Season

	M	Inns	NO	Runs	HS	Avge	100s	50s	Ct	St	O	M	Runs	Wkts	Avge	Best	5wI	10wM
Test																		
All First	18	31	4	790	138	29.25	1	4	5	-	398.2	97	1145	37	30.94	5-51	2	-
1-day Int																		
NatWest	1	1	0	41	41	41.00	-	-	-	-	12	3	22	1	22.00	1-22	-	
B & H	8	8	0	167	63	20.87	-	1	3	-	61.4	5	257	17	15.11	5-27	2	
Sunday	17	14	2	192	40	16.00	-	-	2	-	107.5	5	530	26	20.38	3-14	-	

Career Performances

	M	Inns	NO	Runs	HS	Avge	100s	50s	Ct	St	Balls	Runs	Wkts	Avge	Best	5wI	10wM
Test																	
All First	149	244	27	6689	138	30.82	9	36	60	-	14169	6726	173	38.87	5-51	2	-
1-day Int																	
NatWest	18	18	1	326	53	19.17	-	1	10	-	693	428	18	23.77	3-28	-	
B & H	42	39	2	922	72	24.91	-	5	12	-	2046	1449	58	24.98	5-27	2	
Sunday	140	129	15	2706	112	23.73	1	12	36	-	5181	4567	174	26.24	4-13	-	

FLINTOFF, A. Lancashire

Name: Andrew Flintoff
Role: Right-hand bat, right-arm
medium bowler
Born: 6 December 1977, Preston
Height: 6ft 4in **Weight:** 13st 10lb
County debut: 1995
1st-Class 50s: 1
1st-Class 100s: 1
1st-Class catches: 7
Place in batting averages: 121st av. 30.37
Strike rate: 60.00 (career 126.00)
Parents: Colin and Susan
Family links with cricket: Brother Chris and
father both play local league cricket
Education: Greenlands County Primary;
Ribbleton Hall High School
Qualifications: 9 GCSEs
Off-season: Touring with England A
Overseas tours: England Schools U15 to South Africa 1993; England U19 to West
Indies 1994-95, to Zimbabwe 1995-96, to Pakistan 1996-97; England A to Kenya and
Sri Lanka 1997-98
Cricketers particularly admired: Jason Gallian, John Crawley, Stephen Titchard,
Warren Hegg
Other sports followed: Football (Preston North End and Liverpool FC)
Relaxations: Listening to music and sleeping
Extras: Won a *Daily Telegraph* regional award for batting. Represented England U14
to U19 and played for U17 against India in 1994. Captained the England U19 tour to
Pakistan in 1996-97 and again in the series against Zimbabwe in 1997
Opinions on cricket: 'Cricket should be promoted more in state schools.'
Best batting: 117 Lancashire v Hampshire, Southampton 1997
Best bowling: 1-11 Lancashire v Yorkshire, Headingley 1997

1997 Season

	M	Inns	NO	Runs	HS	Avge	100s	50s	Ct	St	O	M	Runs	Wkts	Avge	Best	5wI	10wM
Test																		
All First	5	8	0	243	117	30.37	1	1	4	-	10	6	11	1	11.00	1-11	-	-
1-day Int																		
NatWest	1	1	0	2	2	2.00	-	-	-	-	5.5	0	21	0	-		-	-
B & H	1	1	0	0	0	0.00	-	-	-	-	4	0	17	0	-		-	-
Sunday	4	4	0	83	31	20.75	-	-	2	-								

Career Performances

	M	Inns	NO	Runs	HS	Avge	100s	50s	Ct	St	Balls	Runs	Wkts	Avge	Best	5wI	10wM
Test																	
All First	7	11	0	252	117	22.90	1	1	7	-	126	50	1	50.00	1-11	-	-
1-day Int																	
NatWest	1	1	0	2	2	2.00	-	-	-	-	35	21	0	-		-	-
B & H	2	1	0	0	0	0.00	-	-	-	-	60	27	1	27.00	1-10	-	
Sunday	7	7	0	119	31	17.00	-	-	2	-							

FOLLETT, D.   Northamptonshire

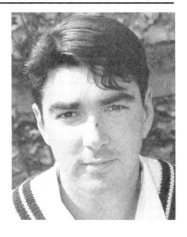

Name: David Follett
Role: Right-hand bowler, right-arm
medium-fast bowler
Born: 14 October 1968, Hanley,
Stoke-on-Trent
Height: 6ft 2in **Weight:** 12st 10lbs
Nickname: Foll
County debut: 1995 (Middlesex), 1997
(Northamptonshire)
1st-Class 5 w. in innings: 3
1st-Class 10 w. in match: 1
1st-Class catches: 3
Place in bowling averages:
(1996 29th av. 25.60)
Strike rate: 73.50 (career 46.57)
Parents: Gordon and Sandra
Marital status: Single
Family links with cricket: 'Dad played for
Burslem CC in Stoke-on-Trent'
Education: Clarence Street Middle School, Stoke-on-Trent; Moorland Road High
School, Burslem, Stoke-on-Trent; Stoke-on-Trent Technical College
Qualifications: 2 O-levels
Career outside cricket: Engineer
Off-season: Coaching
Overseas teams played for: Australian Capital Territory 1994; Queenbeyan, New
South Wales, Australia, 1994-95
Cricketers particularly admired: Imran Khan, Derek Randall
Young players to look out for: Tony Naylor, Gareth Ainsworthy
Other sports followed: Football (Port Vale)
Injuries: Torn muscle in side, out for five weeks
Relaxations: Current affairs and 'vegging out in front of the television'

Extras: Played for Staffordshire in the Minor Counties before joining Middlesex. Was first team Player of the Month for April and May in 1996. Took 8 for 22 in the Championship game against Durham. Has moved to Northamptonshire for the 1996 season

Best batting: 17 Middlesex v Yorkshire, Lord's 1996
Best bowling: 8-22 Middlesex v Durham, Chester-le-Street 1996

1997 Season

	M	Inns	NO	Runs	HS	Avge	100s	50s	Ct	St	O	M	Runs	Wkts	Avge	Best	5wI	10wM
Test																		
All First	1	2	0	3	3	1.50	-	-	-	-	24.3	1	123	2	61.50	2-123	-	-
1-day Int																		
NatWest																		
B & H	2	1	0	4	4	4.00	-	-	-	-	15	1	69	6	11.50	4-39	-	
Sunday	4	2	1	2	1*	2.00	-	-	2	-	26	0	138	5	27.60	2-28	-	

Career Performances

	M	Inns	NO	Runs	HS	Avge	100s	50s	Ct	St	Balls	Runs	Wkts	Avge	Best	5wI	10wM
Test																	
All First	8	10	6	30	17	7.50	-	-	3	-	1211	807	26	31.03	8-22	3	1
1-day Int																	
NatWest																	
B & H	9	3	0	8	4	2.66	-	-	-	-	408	302	12	25.16	4-39	-	
Sunday	7	2	1	2	1*	2.00	-	-	4	-	294	260	10	26.00	2-27	-	

28. When Alisdair Brown scored 203 in Surrey's Sunday League game against Hampshire at Guildford, the first double century in the competition, how many balls did it take him?

O vodafone

FORD, J. A.

Kent

Name: James Anthony Ford
Role: Right-hand bat, slow left-arm bowler
Born: 30 March 1976, Penbury, Kent
Height: 5ft 9in **Weight:** 12st 4lbs
Nickname: Fordy, Didge
County debut: 1996
1st-Class catches: 1
Parents: Anthony and Linda
Marital status: Single
Family links with cricket: Father is a keen
follower
Education: Sevenoaks Prep School;
Tonbridge School; University of Durham
Qualifications: 11 GCSEs, 3 A-levels
Overseas tours: Tonbridge School to
Australia 1992-93
Cricketers particularly admired: Viv
Richards, Malcolm Marshall, Steve Waugh
Young players to look out for: Anurag Singh, Tim Hodgson
Other sports followed: Football (Tottenham Hotspur), hockey (plays for Durham
University and England Students), 'all sports'
Relaxations: Socialising and playing sport
Extras: Played for British Universities in the B&H Cup in 1997. Played for HMC
Schools
Opinions on cricket: 'We play too much cricket. As batsmen know they will have three
innings per week they are perhaps not as hungry as their Australian counterparts who
play far less.'

1997 Season

	M	Inns	NO	Runs	HS	Avge	100s	50s	Ct	St	O	M	Runs	Wkts	Avge	Best	5wl	10wM
Test																		
All First																		
1-day Int																		
NatWest																		
B & H	4	4	0	63	38	15.75	-	-	2	-	5	0	27	0	-		-	-
Sunday																		

Career Performances

	M	Inns	NO	Runs	HS	Avge	100s	50s	Ct	St	Balls	Runs	Wkts	Avge	Best	5wl	10wM
Test																	
All First	1	0	0	0	0	-	-	-	1	-	67	54	0	-	-	-	-
1-day Int																	
NatWest																	
B & H	4	4	0	63	38	15.75	-	-	2	-	30	27	0	-	-	-	-
Sunday																	

FORDHAM, A.   Northamptonshire

Name: Alan Fordham
Role: Right-hand bat, occasional right-arm medium bowler
Born: 9 November 1964, Bedford
Height: 6ft 1in **Weight:** 13st
Nickname: Forders
County debut: 1986
County cap: 1990
1000 runs in a season: 5
1st-Class 50s: 54
1st-Class 100s: 25
1st-Class 200s: 1
1st-Class catches: 117
One-Day 100s: 6
Place in batting averages: 34th av. 44.86 (1996 130th av. 33.46)
Strike rate: (career 107.75)
Parents: Clifford and Ruth

Wife and date of marriage: Claire Louise, 29 September 1996
Family links with cricket: Brother John played school and college cricket
Education: Bedford Modern School; Durham University
Qualifications: 9 O-levels, 3 A-levels, BSc (Hons) Chemistry, NCA senior coaching award
Off-season: Taking up full employment at the ECB
Overseas tours: Bedford Modern to Barbados 1983; Gentlemen of Leicestershire to Jersey and Guernsey 1987; International Ambassadors XI/Christians in Sport to India 1989-90, to Zimbabwe 1994-95; MCC to Leeward Islands 1991-92, to Bangladesh 1995-96; Northamptonshire to Natal 1991-92; Singapore Sixes 1995
Overseas teams played for: Richmond, Melbourne 1983-84; Camberwell, Melbourne 1987-88; Curtin University, Perth, Western Australia 1988; Nirman Schools XI, Dhaka, Bangladesh 1989-90; Montrose, Cape Town, South Africa 1992-93 and 1996-97

180

Cricketers particularly admired: Allan Lamb, Bob Willis, Mike Brearley
Young players to look out for: Alun Evans, Michael Davies
Other sports followed: Rugby union (Bedford RFC) and football (Aston Villa)
Injuries: Broken thumb, missed two weeks
Relaxations: Television, music, travel
Extras: Has appeared for Bedfordshire in Minor Counties Championship. Played for Combined Universities in B&H Cup 1987. Shared county third-wicket record stand of 393 with Allan Lamb v Yorkshire at Headingley in 1990. First white man to have played league cricket in Bangladesh. Treasurer of the Professional Cricketers' Association. Retired from first-class cricket at the end of the 1997 season to take up full-time employment at the ECB
Opinions on cricket: 'Pitch quality remains a huge concern. The health of county cricket depends on the surfaces we play on to a great extent, so if pitches are sub-standard then English and ultimately England cricket will under-achieve. I'm sure no one wants that.'
Best batting: 206* Northamptonshire v Yorkshire, Headingley 1990
Best bowling: 1-0 Northamptonshire v West Indies, Northampton 1995

1997 Season

	M	Inns	NO	Runs	HS	Avge	100s	50s	Ct	St	O	M	Runs	Wkts	Avge	Best	5wI	10wM
Test																		
All First	9	17	2	673	85 *	44.86	-	6	10	-	4.3	1	8	0	-	-	-	-
1-day Int																		
NatWest																		
B & H																		
Sunday	5	5	0	114	43	22.80	-	-	2	-								

Career Performances

	M	Inns	NO	Runs	HS	Avge	100s	50s	Ct	St	Balls	Runs	Wkts	Avge	Best	5wI	10wM
Test																	
All First	167	297	24	10939	206 *	40.06	25	54	117	-	431	297	4	74.25	1-0	-	-
1-day Int																	
NatWest	24	24	1	1158	132 *	50.34	3	6	4	-	21	6	1	6.00	1-3	-	
B & H	27	26	1	732	108	29.28	2	4	6	-							
Sunday	112	105	1	2731	111	26.25	1	17	31	-	6	10	0	-	-	-	

29. Who was voted Man of the Match in the 1997 Benson & Hedges Cup final?

FOSTER, M. J.   Durham

Name: Michael James Foster
Role: Right-hand bat, right arm
medium-fast bowler
Born: 17 September 1972, Leeds
Height: 6ft 2in **Weight:** 15st
Nickname: Foz, Bear
County debut: 1993 (Yorkshire), 1995
(Northamptonshire, one-day), 1996 (Durham)
1st-Class 50s: 4
1st-Class 100s: 1
1st-Class catches: 8
One-Day 100s: 1
Place in batting averages: 177th av. 23.95
(1996 286th av. 11.16)
Place in bowling averages: 96th av. 34.23
Strike rate: 55.13 (career 57.81)
Parents: Paul and Margaret
Wife and date of marriage:
Lynne, 7 March 1998
Family links with cricket: 'Sister played for Yorkshire. Grandfather played in the
Forces and for Great Preston. Father played for Great Preston'
Education: 'Las Vegas College'
Qualifications: 7 GCSEs, 2 A-levels
Career outside cricket: 'Digging holes and lifting heavy things'
Off-season: 'Getting fit and working hard'
Overseas tours: England U19 to Pakistan 1992; Yorkshire to West Indies
Overseas teams played for: Fremantle, Perth, Western Australia; Queenstown, New
Zealand; Ringswood, Melbourne, Australia
Cricketers particularly admired: Jeff Thomson, Ian Botham, Steve Waugh, Richie
Richardson
Young players to look out for: David Boon
Other sports followed: Rugby league (Castleford Tigers), football (Huddersfield
Town), squash, 'various drinking games'
Injuries: 'Pain in the arse for most of the season, but played through it'
Relaxations: Socialising, sleeping, eating and keeping fit
Extras: 'Captained all the junior sides I played in up to and including Yorkshire
Academy.' Off the mark with a six in first first-class game
Opinions on cricket: 'One-day cricket is a pain in the arse.'
Best batting: 129 Durham v Glamorgan, Cardiff 1997
Best bowling: 4-21 Durham v Middlesex, Lord's 1996

1997 Season

	M	Inns	NO	Runs	HS	Avge	100s	50s	Ct	St	O	M	Runs	Wkts	Avge	Best	5wl	10wM
Test																		
All First	14	24	0	575	129	23.95	1	3	2	-	275.4	55	1027	30	34.23	4-58	-	-
1-day Int																		
NatWest	1	1	1	56	56 *	-	-	-	1	-	8	1	37	2	18.50	2-37	-	
B & H	2	2	1	74	73 *	74.00	-	1	-	-	16	1	91	1	91.00	1-27	-	
Sunday	10	8	0	66	18	8.25	-	-	1	-	50	0	315	8	39.37	3-52	-	

Career Performances

	M	Inns	NO	Runs	HS	Avge	100s	50s	Ct	St	Balls	Runs	Wkts	Avge	Best	5wl	10wM
Test																	
All First	22	37	1	807	129	22.41	1	4	8	-	2544	1488	44	33.81	4-21	-	-
1-day Int																	
NatWest	1	1	1	56	56 *	-	-	-	1	-	48	37	2	18.50	2-37	-	
B & H	7	7	3	179	73 *	44.75	-	2	-	-	332	274	5	54.80	2-52	-	
Sunday	38	29	2	375	118	13.88	1	-	8	-	990	955	20	47.75	3-52	-	

FRANCIS, S. R. G.   Hampshire

Name: Simon Richard George Francis
Role: Right-hand bat, right-arm
medium-fast bowler
Born: 15 August 1978, Bromley
Height: 6ft 1in **Weight:** 14st
Nickname: Frankie
County debut: 1997
Parents: Daniel and Linda
Marital status: Single
Family links with cricket: 'Brother was the
leading run-scorer in the 1996 U15 World
Cup for England U15. Father and grandfather
played club cricket'
Education: Yardley Court, Tonbridge; King
Edward VI, Southampton; Durham University
Qualifications: 10 GCSEs, 3 A-levels, NCA
coaching award

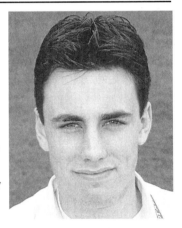

Off-season: At university and winter cricket
tour to Zimbabwe with university 1st XI
Overseas tours: England U17 to Holland for International Youth Tournament 1995
Cricketers particularly admired: Matthew Hayden, Malcolm Marshall
Young players to look out for: Thomas Hansen, Andrew Flintoff

Other sports followed: Hockey (played for England U17 and for Durham University 1st XI), golf
Injuries: Lower back, out from April until the end of June
Relaxations: Going out, socialising, playing golf and sleeping
Extras: *Daily Telegraph* West Region Bowling Award U15
Best batting: 4 Hampshire v Worcestershire, Southampton 1997

1997 Season

	M	Inns	NO	Runs	HS	Avge	100s	50s	Ct	St	O	M	Runs	Wkts	Avge	Best	5wI	10wM
Test																		
All First	1	2	0	8	4	4.00	-	-	-	-	19	1	97	0	-		-	-
1-day Int																		
NatWest																		
B & H																		
Sunday	1	0	0	0	0	-	-	-	-	-	8	0	31	2	15.50	2-31	-	

Career Performances

	M	Inns	NO	Runs	HS	Avge	100s	50s	Ct	St	Balls	Runs	Wkts	Avge	Best	5wI	10wM
Test																	
All First	1	2	0	8	4	4.00	-	-	-	-	114	97	0	-		-	-
1-day Int																	
NatWest																	
B & H																	
Sunday	1	0	0	0	0	-	-	-	-	-	48	31	2	15.50	2-31	-	

FRANKS, P. J. Nottinghamshire

Name: Paul John Franks
Role: Left-hand bat, right-arm fast-medium bowler
Born: 3 February 1979, Sutton-in-Ashfield
Height: 6ft 1in **Weight:** 13st
Nickname: Beardo, Pike, Franksie
County debut: 1996
1st-Class 50s: 1
1st-Class catches: 7
Place in batting averages: 200th av. 21.53
Place in bowling averages: 114th av. 38.60
Strike rate: 74.53 (career 75.21)
Parents: John and Patricia
Marital status: Single
Family links with cricket: 'Dad played league cricket for thirty years'
Education: Walter D'Ayncourt Primary School; Southwell Minster; West Notts

College
Qualifications: 7 GCSEs, NCA coaching
award
Career outside cricket: 'None yet'
Off-season: England U19 tour to South
Africa
Overseas tours: England U19 to Pakistan
1996-97, to South Africa 1997-98
Cricketers particularly admired: Allan
Donald, Brian Lara, Darren Gough, Matt
Dowman
Young players to look out for: Matthew
Whiley, Stephen Randall and 'Trig'
Other sports followed: Golf and football
(Mansfield Town)
Injuries: Shins and back, missed a total of
three weeks
Relaxations: Going out, cinema
Extras: Youngest ever Notts player to take a hat-trick (aged 18 years 163 days) against
Warwickshire in 1997
Opinions on cricket: 'We still need a wider range of sponsors to allow the game to
continue to develop as it needs to.'
Best batting: 50 Nottinghamshire v Derbyshire, Trent Bridge 1997
Best bowling: 4-47 Nottinghamshire v Surrey, The Oval 1997

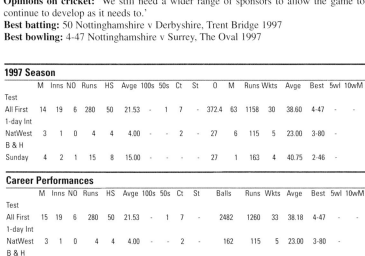

1997 Season

	M	Inns	NO	Runs	HS	Avge	100s	50s	Ct	St	O	M	Runs	Wkts	Avge	Best	5wI	10wM
Test																		
All First	14	19	6	280	50	21.53	-	1	7	-	372.4	63	1158	30	38.60	4-47	-	-
1-day Int																		
NatWest	3	1	0	4	4	4.00	-	-	2	-	27	6	115	5	23.00	3-80	-	
B & H																		
Sunday	4	2	1	15	8	15.00	-	-	-	-	27	1	163	4	40.75	2-46	-	

Career Performances

	M	Inns	NO	Runs	HS	Avge	100s	50s	Ct	St	Balls	Runs	Wkts	Avge	Best	5wI	10wM
Test																	
All First	15	19	6	280	50	21.53	-	1	7	-	2482	1260	33	38.18	4-47	-	-
1-day Int																	
NatWest	3	1	0	4	4	4.00	-	-	2	-	162	115	5	23.00	3-80	-	
B & H																	
Sunday	4	2	1	15	8	15.00	-	-	-	-	162	163	4	40.75	2-46	-	

FRASER, A. R. C.   Middlesex

Name: Angus Robert Charles Fraser
Role: Right-hand bat, right-arm medium-fast bowler, outfielder 'specialist'
Born: 8 August 1965, Billinge, Lancashire
Height: 6ft 6in **Weight:** 15st 10lbs (at the start of the season)
Nickname: Gus, Soup, Wiggy, Recall
County debut: 1984
County cap: 1988
Test debut: 1989
Tests: 32
One-Day Internationals: 33
50 wickets in a season: 6
1st-Class 50s: 1
1st-Class 5 w. in innings: 26
1st-Class 10 w. in match: 3
1st-Class catches: 42
One-Day 5 w. in innings: 1
Place in batting averages: 260th av. 14.35 (1996 292nd av. 10.81)
Place in bowling averages: 78th av. 31.06 (1996 81st av. 33.38)
Strike rate: 73.00 (career 63.82)
Parents: Don and Irene
Wife: Denise
Children: Alexander Charles Mitchell; Bethan Louise
Family links with cricket: Brother Alastair played for Middlesex and Essex. Parents are keen followers
Education: Weald First School; Gayton High School, Harrow; Orange Senior High School, Edgware
Qualifications: 7 O-levels, qualified cricket coach
Career outside cricket: 'Worked for Whittingdale Holding Ltd. 1991-93 when injured. Enjoy writing and television work that I do'
Off-season: 'On tour with England and attending my benefit functions'
Overseas tours: Thames Valley Gentlemen to Barbados 1985; Middlesex to La Manga 1985 and 1986, to Portugal 1991-93; England to India (Nehru Cup) 1989-90, to West Indies 1989-90, to Australia 1990-91, to West Indies 1993-94, to Australia 1994-95, to South Africa 1995-96, to West Indies 1997-98
Overseas teams played for: Plimmerton, Wellington 1985-86 and 1987-88; Western Suburbs, Sydney 1988-89 and 1994-95
Cricketers particularly admired: Richard Hadlee, Allan Border, Graham Gooch and Curtly Ambrose
Young players to look out for: David Nash 'if you can see him in the long grass' and

Jason Pooley 'in one-day cricket'

Other sports followed: 'Follow Liverpool FC keenly. Enjoy watching rugby internationals at my local rugby club, Harrow'

Injuries: 'Twisted ankle playing basketball, but manfully played through it'

Relaxations: 'Watching Liverpool FC, Harrow RFC and internationals. Watch most sport to the annoyance of my wife, Denise. Didn't have much time to relax last summer as the batsmen didn't bat for long enough. A good glass of red with the Middlesex physio, S. Shepherd'

Extras: Middlesex Player of the Year 1988 and 1989. Took a hat-trick in the Benson and Hedges Cup in 1989. Selected for England tour to New Zealand 1991-92 but ruled out by injury. Originally left out of England tour party to Australia 1994-95 but called up when Martin McCague was injured. Took his 100th Test wicket (Brian Lara) against West Indies in 1995. Finished 2nd in the Whyte and Mackay bowling ratings for 1995. *Wisden* Cricketer of the Year 1996. Awarded benefit by Middlesex in 1997. 'Possibly the unluckiest bowler in the world'

Opinions on cricket: 'Well done Glamorgan. No change is a step backwards. Disappointed counties are so short sighted, one day they will realise they have a responsibility to look after themselves financially and not look to the ECB to bail them out each year. Congratulations G.A. Gooch on an outstanding career. I ruck and moan but there is nothing I would rather do than play cricket – even if it does test you at times.'

Best batting: 92 Middlesex v Surrey, The Oval 1990

Best bowling: 8-75 England v West Indies, Bridgetown, 1994

1997 Season

	M	Inns	NO	Runs	HS	Avge	100s	50s	Ct	St	O	M	Runs	Wkts	Avge	Best	5wI	10wM
Test																		
All First	19	23	6	244	35	14.35	-	-	4	-	571.5	155	1460	47	31.06	6-77	2	-
1-day Int																		
NatWest	3	1	1	9	9 *	-	-	-	1	-	35	8	103	3	34.33	2-22	-	
B & H	4	4	2	35	30 *	17.50	-	-	-	-	37	7	114	4	28.50	1-23	-	
Sunday	14	7	2	65	33	13.00	-	-	2	-	108	9	430	20	21.50	3-10	-	

Career Performances

	M	Inns	NO	Runs	HS	Avge	100s	50s	Ct	St	Balls	Runs	Wkts	Avge	Best	5wI	10wM
Test	32	46	10	265	29	7.36	-	-	7	-	7967	3509	119	29.48	8-75	8	-
All First	220	258	63	2175	92	11.15	-	1	42	-	42126	18208	660	27.58	8-75	26	3
1-day Int	33	14	6	80	38 *	10.00	-	-	1	-	1876	1132	38	29.78	4-22	-	
NatWest	28	10	8	65	19	32.50	-	-	4	-	1833	927	41	22.60	4-34	-	
B & H	39	22	11	100	30 *	9.09	-	-	7	-	2295	1313	49	26.79	4-49	-	
Sunday	145	56	24	366	33	11.43	-	-	21	-	6392	4277	151	28.32	5-32	1	

FROST, T.   Warwickshire

Name: Tony Frost
Role: Right-hand bat, wicket-keeper
Born: 17 November 1975, Stoke-on-Trent
Height: 5ft 10in **Weight:** 10st 6lbs
County debut: 1997
1st-Class 50s: 1
1st-Class catches: 26
1st-Class stumpings: 2
Place in batting averages: 232nd av. 17.55
Parents: Ivan and Christine
Marital status: Single
Family links with cricket: Father played for
Staffordshire
Education: James Brinkley High School;
Stoke-on-Trent College
Qualifications: 5 GCSEs
Overseas tours: Kidsgrove U18 to Australia
1990-91

Cricketers particularly admired: Ashley Giles 'could be described as a legend',
'Pop' Welch and George Burns 'in the JT bracket'
Other sports followed: Football, golf
Relaxations: Listening to music, watching films, reading aircraft magazines
Extras: Has represented Staffordshire at all levels from U11 to U19. Won Texaco U16
competition with Staffordshire in 1992. Played for Development of Excellence XI U17
v South Africa and U18 v West Indies and U19 v India
Opinions on cricket: 'A lot of people are too critical. If they spent more time building
up the players' confidence instead of putting the player down then they may get better
results. '
Best batting: 56 Warwickshire v Somerset, Edgbaston 1997

1997 Season

	M	Inns	NO	Runs	HS	Avge	100s	50s	Ct	St	O	M	Runs	Wkts	Avge	Best	5wl	10wM
Test																		
All First	9	11	2	158	56	17.55	-	1	26	2								
1-day Int																		
NatWest	1	1	0	0	0	0.00	-	-	2	1								
B & H	2	2	1	11	10*	11.00	-	-	1	-								
Sunday	7	2	1	2	2*	2.00	-	-	7	-								

Career Performances

	M	Inns	NO	Runs	HS	Avge	100s	50s	Ct	St	Balls	Runs	Wkts	Avge	Best	5wI	10wM
Test																	
All First	9	11	2	158	56	17.55	-	1	26	2							
1-day Int																	
NatWest	1	1	0	0	0	0.00	-	-	2	1							
B & H	2	2	1	11	10 *	11.00	-	-	1	-							
Sunday	7	2	1	2	2 *	2.00	-	-	7	-							

FULTON, D. P.   Kent

Name: David Paul Fulton
Role: Right-hand bat, 'The most versatile bowler on the circuit. Also the worst'
Born: 15 November 1971, Lewisham
Height: 6ft 2in **Weight:** 12st
Nickname: Raver, Tav
County debut: 1992
1st-Class 50s: 16
1st-Class 100s: 4
1st-Class catches: 90
Place in batting averages: 80th av. 36.65 (1996 150th av. 31.55)
Strike rate: (career 67.00)
Parents: John and Ann
Marital status: Single
Family links with cricket: 'Dad plays for village side. Anyone who has watched him will realise my tendency to aim consistently through mid-wicket is hereditary'
Education: Otford County Primary; The Judd School, Tonbridge; University of Kent
Qualifications: 10 GCSEs, 3 A-levels, BA (Hons) Politics and International Relations, senior cricket coach, rugby coach, gym instructor
Career outside cricket: Personal trainer. 'Eventually a diplomat'
Overseas tours: Kent Schools U17 to Singapore and New Zealand
Overseas teams played for: Avendale, Cape Town 1993-94; Victoria, Cape Town 1994-95, University of WA, Perth 1995-96
Cricketers particularly admired: Gordon Greenidge, Graham Gooch, Viv Richards, Robin Smith, Curtly Ambrose, Courtney Walsh, Ian Bishop, Steve Waugh
Young players to look out for: Ben Phillips, 'The Musketeers at Kent'
Other sports followed: Rugby (Harlequins) and football (Nottingham Forest), tennis, table tennis ('top 10 in UK as a junior'), chess (England junior), golf, boxing

Relaxations: 'Pursuing money-making schemes.' Clubs, pubs, golf and working out

Extras: 'Helped Dean Headley's hat-trick against Derbyshire by catching Kim Barnett and Chris Adams. Was the last person to catch the great Viv Richards in a first-class match. Opened the batting and the bowling against South Africa in their first county game. Once scored 2000 runs without being dismissed against my little sister in the back garden'

Opinions on cricket: 'As one of the game's deepest thinkers I could be here all day – suffice it to say that it is a game which should be enjoyed more because in the whole scheme of things it seems rather daft to me.'

Best batting: 134* Kent v Oxford University, Canterbury 1996

Best bowling: 1-37 Kent v Oxford University, Canterbury 1996

1997 Season

	M	Inns	NO	Runs	HS	Avge	100s	50s	Ct	St	O	M	Runs	Wkts	Avge	Best	5wI	10wM
Test																		
All First	16	29	3	953	110	36.65	1		4	23	-							
1-day Int																		
NatWest	1	1	0	9	9	9.00	-	-	-	-								
B & H	1	1	0	17	17	17.00	-	-	2	-								
Sunday	3	3	0	19	9	6.33	-	-	-	-								

Career Performances

	M	Inns	NO	Runs	HS	Avge	100s	50s	Ct	St	Balls	Runs	Wkts	Avge	Best	5wI	10wM
Test																	
All First	59	106	8	3105	134 *	31.68	4	16	90	-	67	65	1	65.00	1-37	-	-
1-day Int																	
NatWest	4	4	0	50	19	12.50	-	-	-	-	6	9	0	-		-	-
B & H	2	2	0	42	25	21.00	-	-	3	-							
Sunday	12	12	0	96	29	8.00	-	-	4	-							

GALLIAN, J. E. R.   Nottinghamshire

Name: Jason Edward Riche Gallian
Role: Right-hand bat, right-arm medium bowler
Born: 25 June 1971, Manly, NSW, Australia
Height: 6ft **Weight:** 13st
Nickname: Gally
County debut: 1990 (Lancashire)
Test debut: 1995
Tests: 3
1000 runs in a season: 2

1st-Class 50s: 28
1st-Class 100s: 12
1st-Class 300s: 1
1st-Class 5 w. in innings: 1
1st-Class catches: 62
One-Day 100s: 5
One-Day 5 w. in innings: 1
Place in batting averages: 124th av. 29.76
(1996 54th av. 44.46)
Place in bowling averages:
(1996 100th av. 36.00)
Strike rate: 62.50 (career 68.98)
Parents: Ray and Marilyn
Marital status: Single
Family links with cricket: Father played for
Stockport
Education: The Pittwater House Schools,
Australia; Oxford University
Qualifications: Higher School Certificate, Diploma in Social Studies
(Keble College, Oxford)
Overseas tours: Australia U20 to West Indies 1989-90; England A to India 1994-95, to
Pakistan 1995-96, to Australia 1996-97; England to South Africa 1995-96
Overseas teams played for: NSW and Australia U19 1988-89; NSW Colts and NSW
2nd XI 1990-91; Australia U20 and U21 1991-92; Manly 1993-94
Cricketers particularly admired: Desmond Haynes, Mike Gatting
Other sports followed: Rugby league and union, football
Relaxations: Listening to music, playing golf
Extras: Played for Oxford University in 1992 and for Combined Universities in the
B&H Cup. Captained Oxford University 1993. Was called up to the England squad in
South Africa in 1995-96 as a replacement for the injured John Crawley and played in the
fourth Test at Port Elizabeth. He was dogged by finger injuries throughout the England
A tour to Australia in 1996-97. Left Lancashire during the off-season and has joined
Nottinghamshire for 1998
Best batting: 312 Lancashire v Derbyshire, Old Trafford 1996
Best bowling: 6-115 Lancashire v Surrey, Southport 1996

1997 Season

	M	Inns	NO	Runs	HS	Avge	100s	50s	Ct	St	O	M	Runs	Wkts	Avge	Best	5wl	10wM
Test																		
All First	11	19	2	506	106	29.76	1	3	12	-	83.2	12	375	8	46.87	3-51	-	-
1-day Int																		
NatWest	1	1	0	1	1	1.00	-	-	-	-	7	0	37	0	-		-	-
B & H	5	5	0	151	59	30.20	-	2	1	-	12	1	60	1	60.00	1-13	-	
Sunday	10	10	3	424	104	60.57	2	2	5	-	28	1	144	4	36.00	1-23	-	

Career Performances

	M	Inns	NO	Runs	HS	Avge	100s	50s	Ct	St	Balls	Runs	Wkts	Avge	Best	5wl	10wM
Test	3	6	0	74	28	12.33	-	-	1	-	84	62	0	-	-	-	-
All First	91	159	13	5728	312	39.23	12	28	62	-	5657	3332	82	40.63	6-115	1	-
1-day Int																	
NatWest	8	8	1	212	101 *	30.28	1	-	3	-	120	88	1	88.00	1-11	-	
B & H	25	24	1	763	134	33.17	2	5	4	-	479	383	13	29.46	5-15	1	
Sunday	46	45	7	1402	104	36.89	2	9	18	-	694	653	26	25.11	2-10	-	

GANNON, B. W. Gloucestershire

Name: Benjamin Ward Gannon
Role: Right-hand bat, right-arm
medium bowler
Born: 5 September 1975, Oxford
Height: 6ft 3in **Weight:** 13st
Nickname: Moon Cat, Ganja
Parents: Martin and Jane
Marital status: Single
Education: Dragon School, Oxford;
Abingdon School; Cheltenham and
Gloucester School of Higher Education
Qualifications: 10 GCSEs, 3 A-levels, BSc
(Hons) Physical Geography and Sports
Science
Career outside cricket: 'Self-unemployed,
open to offers'
Off-season: 'Relaxing, keeping fit and
walking the dog'
Overseas teams played for: Waverley, Sydney 1993-94
Cricketers particularly admired: Courtney Walsh, Curtly Ambrose, Shane Warne,
Glen McGrath, Paul Reiffel, Allan Donald
Young players to look out for: Darren Thomas, Vikram Solanki, Darren Altree
Other sports followed: Rugby, boxing and tennis
Injuries: Bad back, out for four weeks
Relaxations: Listening to music, keeping fit and eating
Extras: 'Striving to score a 50 at any level'
Opinions on cricket: 'Would like to see a wider use of sports science in the game in
terms of preparation and closer monitoring of young fast bowlers to avoid injuries
which occur far too frequently.'

GARAWAY, M.   Hampshire

Name: Mark Garaway
Role: Right-hand bat, wicket-keeper
Born: 20 July 1973, Swindon, Wilts
Height: 5ft 7in **Weight:** 12st
Nickname: Wolf, Garas, Scenariohead
County debut: 1996
1st-Class catches: 9
1st-Class stumpings: 1
Parents: Sam and Val
Marital status: Single ('hugely')
Family links with cricket: 'Sam still whacks
it for Ventnor CC. Grandfather was a steady
player. Sister is still popular with many Isle
of Wight cricketers'
Education: Carhampton Primary, Somerset;
Ventnor Middle and Sandown High School,
Isle of Wight, 'Ventnor CC, the Astoria
(Hermanus, SA)'
Qualifications: 10 O-levels, 3 A-levels, NCA cricket coach
Off-season: 'Training, holidaying in the Canary Islands with Reg, Dog, Armani et al'
Overseas tours: Isle of Wight U14 and U17 to Jersey and Guernsey 1988-91; Ventnor
to Winchester 1994; Hampshire to Val de Lobo 1994
Overseas teams played for: Worcester, Boland, South Africa 1991-93; Hermanus,
South Africa 1993, 1995-97; 'Ventnor, Isle of Wight 1982-94'
Cricketers particularly admired: Ian Botham, Robin Smith, Mark Brumer, Simon
Rodney, Jeff Hose, Kevan James
Young players to look out for: Dimitri Mascarenhas, Simon Francis
Other sports followed: Football (Swindon Town), squash
Injuries: Back, out for four weeks
Relaxations: Music, art
Extras: Represented England at U15, U17 and U19 level. Played for Isle of Wight at
U16, U17, U21 and senior level in the same season. Spent two years (1991 and 1992) as
MCC Young Professional. Hampshire Schools Wicketkeepers Award 1988. Andrew
Swallow Memorial Cup 1987. Wight Waters Sports Award 1989-91. 2nd XI Player of
the Month June 1997
Opinions on cricket: 'Apparently first-class cricket is a good game.'
Best batting: 44 Hampshire v Cambridge University, Fenner's 1996

	M	Inns	NO	Runs	HS	Avge	100s	50s	Ct	St	O	M	Runs	Wkts	Avge	Best	5wI	10wM
Test																		
All First	1	1	0	5	5	5.00	-	-	5	-								
1-day Int																		
NatWest																		
B & H																		
Sunday																		

Career Performances

	M	Inns	NO	Runs	HS	Avge	100s	50s	Ct	St	Balls	Runs	Wkts	Avge	Best	5wI	10wM
Test																	
All First	2	2	0	49	44	24.50	-	-	9	1							
1-day Int																	
NatWest																	
B & H																	
Sunday																	

GATTING, M. W.   Middlesex

Name: Michael William Gatting
Role: Right-hand bat, right-arm medium bowler, slip fielder
Born: 6 June 1957, Kingsbury, Middlesex
Height: 5ft 10in **Weight:** 15st 7lbs
Nickname: Gatt, Jabba
County debut: 1975
County cap: 1977
Benefit: 1988 (£205,000)
Test debut: 1977-78
Tests: 79
One-Day Internationals: 92
1000 runs in a season: 17
1st-Class 50s: 174
1st-Class 100s: 92
1st-Class 200s: 9
1st-Class 5 w. in innings: 2
1st-Class catches: 474
One-Day 100s: 12
Place in batting averages: 71st av. 39.00 (1996 104th av. 36.04)
Strike rate: 42.00 (career 63.89)
Parents: Bill and Vera

Wife and date of marriage: Elaine, 9 September 1980
Children: Andrew, 21 January 1983; James, 11 July 1986
Family links with cricket: Father used to play club cricket. Brother Steve played for Middlesex 2nd XI
Education: Wykeham Primary School; John Kelly Boys' High School
Qualifications: 4 O-levels
Off-season: Travelling with the England A side as coach
Overseas tours: England to New Zealand and Pakistan 1977-78, to West Indies 1980-81, to India and Sri Lanka 1981-82, to New Zealand and Pakistan 1983-84, to India 1984-85, to West Indies 1985-86, to Australia 1986-87, to India and Pakistan (World Cup), Australia and New Zealand 1987-88; unofficial English XI to South Africa 1989-90; England to India and Sri Lanka 1992-93, to Australia 1994-95
Cricketers particularly admired: Gary Sobers, Len Hutton
Young players to look out for: David Nash, Owais Shah
Other sports followed: Football, golf, tennis, swimming, indoor cricket, rugby
Injuries: Knee surgery for torn ligament and a virus, missed a total of five weeks
Relaxations: Golf, swimming, reading, music
Extras: Awarded OBE in Queen's Birthday Honours 1987 for services to cricket. Captain of Middlesex since 1983. Captain of England from 1986 to 1988. Published autobiography *Leading From the Front* in 1988. Won a bronze medal for ballroom dancing at the Neasden Ritz. Played football for Edgware Town as a teenager. Started as a goalkeeper, but also played centre-half for Middlesex Schools. Was recommended to West Ham, had a trial with QPR and offered an apprenticeship by Watford. His brother Steve has had a successful football career with Arsenal and Brighton. Mike started his cricket career as wicket-keeper for his school team. He toured West Indies with England Young Cricketers in 1976 and 'to my immense pleasure (and to most other people's total disbelief) I was given the job of opening the bowling in the "Test" matches.' One of *Wisden*'s Five Cricketers of the Year 1983. His finest achievement was as captain of England on victorious tour of Australia, 1986-87, when they won the Ashes, the Perth Challenge Cup and World Series Cup. Was relieved of England captaincy after the First Test against West Indies in 1988. Captain of unofficial English team in South Africa in 1989-90 and was banned from Test cricket for five years; suspension remitted in 1992. Captained Middlesex to Championship title in 1990 and 1993. Retired from Test cricket after the final Test of the 1994-95 series against Australia. Relinquished Middlesex captaincy during the 1997 season. Is now a Test selector and is the England A coach
Opinions on cricket: 'Four-day cricket has been an eye-opener.'
Best batting: 258 Middlesex v Somerset, Bath 1984
Best bowling: 5-34 Middlesex v Glamorgan, Swansea 1982

---

30. Who was the first player to complete 1000 runs in 1997?

O vodafone

1997 Season

	M	Inns	NO	Runs	HS	Avge	100s	50s	Ct	St	O	M	Runs	Wkts	Avge	Best	5wI	10wM
Test																		
All First	19	29	2	1053	160 *	39.00	2	4	23	-	7	1	46	1	46.00	1-46	-	-
1-day Int																		
NatWest	3	3	0	30	20	10.00	-	-	1	-								
B & H	4	4	0	62	23	15.50	-	-	2	-								
Sunday	11	10	1	164	82 *	18.22	-	1	5	-								

Career Performances

	M	Inns	NO	Runs	HS	Avge	100s	50s	Ct	St	Balls	Runs	Wkts	Avge	Best	5wI	10wM
Test	79	138	14	4409	207	35.55	10	21	59	-	752	317	4	79.25	1-14	-	-
All First	534	832	120	35410	258	49.73	92	174	474	-	10031	4694	157	29.89	5-34	2	-
1-day Int	92	88	17	2095	115 *	29.50	1	9	22	-	392	336	10	33.60	3-32	-	
NatWest	64	62	13	2113	132 *	43.12	2	15	25	-	1004	643	19	33.84	2-14	-	
B & H	96	90	18	2921	143 *	40.56	3	18	30	-	1382	940	41	22.92	4-49	-	
Sunday	268	241	30	6671	124 *	31.61	6	40	89	-	3196	2730	90	30.33	4-30	-	

GIDDINS, E. S. H. Warwickshire

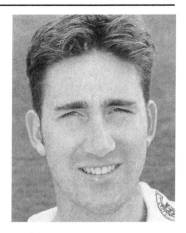

Name: Edward Simon Hunter Giddins
Role: Right-hand bat, right-arm medium-fast bowler
Born: 20 July 1971, Eastbourne
Height: 6ft 4in **Weight:** 13st 7lbs
Nickname: Geezer
County debut: 1991 (Sussex)
County cap: 1994
50 wickets in a season: 2
1st-Class 5 w. in innings: 13
1st-Class 10 w. in match: 1
1st-Class catches: 12
Place in batting averages:
(1996 313th av. 5.50)
Place in bowling averages:
(1996 24th av. 25.08)
Strike rate: 45.95 (career 53.46)
Parents: Simon and Pauline
Marital status: Single
Family links with cricket: None
Education: St Bede's Prep School; Eastbourne College
Qualifications: 'Various O- and A-levels, national coaching certificate, recorder

(grade 2), shorthand and typing 100/60'
Career outside cricket: None
Overseas tours: England A to Pakistan 1995-96
Overseas teams played for: Mossman, Sydney 1994-95
Cricketers particularly admired: Derek Randall
Young players to look out for: Alan Wells
Other sports followed: Brighton & Hove Albion FC, 'fingers crossed'
Relaxations: Gym, fitness and mountain biking
Best batting: 34 Sussex v Essex, Hove 1995
Best bowling: 6-47 Sussex v Yorkshire, Eastbourne 1996

1997 Season (did not make any first-class or one-day appearances)

Career Performances

	M	Inns	NO	Runs	HS	Avge	100s	50s	Ct	St	Balls	Runs	Wkts	Avge	Best	5wI	10wM
Test																	
All First	80	96	39	321	34	5.63	-	-	12	-	13259	7427	248	29.94	6-47	13	1
1-day Int																	
NatWest	10	4	2	25	13	12.50	-	-	-	-	665	393	11	35.72	3-24	-	
B & H	12	3	2	0	0 *	0.00	-	-	3	-	704	468	11	42.54	3-28	-	
Sunday	62	28	11	25	9 *	1.47	-	-	8	-	2604	2255	70	32.21	4-23	-	

GIE, N. A. Nottinghamshire

Name: Noel Addison Gie
Role: Right-hand bat, right-arm
medium bowler
Born: 12 April 1977, Pretoria, South Africa
Height: 6ft **Weight:** 12st 8lbs
County debut: 1995
1st-Class 50s: 1
1st-Class catches: 3
Place in batting averages: 262nd av. 14.16
Parents: Clive and Lindy
Marital status: Single
Family links with cricket: Father played
first-class cricket in South Africa for Western
Province, Northern Transvaal and Natal
Education: Fornwood School, Nottingham;
Trent College, Nottingham; Nottingham Trent
University
Qualificatons: Studying for degree in

Business Studies from October 1996, NCA coaching award
Overseas tours: Trent College to Australia 1993-94; England U19 to Zimbabwe 1995-96
Overseas teams played for: Berea Rovers, Durban, South Africa 1995
Cricketers particularly admired: Robin Smith
Other sports followed: Squash, tennis, rugby league
Relaxations: Reading and cycling
Extras: Scored 3,153 runs for the Ist XI during his time at Trent College
Opinions on cricket: 'Counties need to be more competitive i.e. fewer in "top league" and fewer players on full-time staff.'
Best batting: 50 Nottinghamshire v Oxford University, The Parks 1997

1997 Season

	M	Inns	NO	Runs	HS	Avge	100s	50s	Ct	St	O	M	Runs	Wkts	Avge	Best	5wl	10wM
Test																		
All First	3	6	0	85	50	14.16	-	1	4	-								
1-day Int																		
NatWest																		
B & H	3	3	0	61	47	20.33	-	-	-	-								
Sunday	8	6	1	149	75 *	29.80	-	1	3	-								

Career Performances

	M	Inns	NO	Runs	HS	Avge	100s	50s	Ct	St	Balls	Runs	Wkts	Avge	Best	5wl	10wM
Test																	
All First	7	12	0	183	50	15.25	-	1	4	-							
1-day Int																	
NatWest																	
B & H	3	3	0	61	47	20.33	-	-	-	-							
Sunday	8	6	1	149	75 *	29.80	-	1	3	-							

GILES, A. F.   Warwickshire

Name: Ashley Fraser Giles
Role: Right-hand bat, slow left-arm bowler
Born: 19 March 1973, Chertsey, Surrey
Height: 6ft 4in **Weight:** 15st 7lbs
Nickname: Splash, Skinny, Melink, Medog, Savo Melinkovic
County debut: 1993
One-Day Internationals: 1
50 wickets in a season: 1
1st-Class 50s: 9
1st-Class 100s: 1

1st-Class 5 w. in innings: 4
1st-Class catches: 15
One-Day 5 w. in innings: 2
Place in batting averages: 72nd av. 39.00
(1996 132nd av. 33.33)
Place in bowling averages: 83rd av. 32.23
(1996 26th av. 25.23)
Strike rate: 79.92 (career 67.10)
Parents: Michael and Paula
Marital status: 'Girlfriend Ally'
Family links with cricket: 'Brother Andrew
and brother-in-law Nigel play club cricket.
Dad used to slog it. Sister Tracy gets it
through'
Education: Kingfield Primary School, Old
Woking; George Abbot County Secondary,
Guildford

Qualifications: 9 GCSEs, 2 A-levels, NCA
coaching award
Off-season: England to Sharjah and then the A tour to Kenya and Sri Lanka
Overseas tours: Surrey U19 to Barbados 1990-91; Warwickshire to Cape Town 1993
and 1996; England A to Australia 1996-97, to Kenya and Sri Lanka 1997-98; England
to Sharjah 1997-98, to West Indies 1997-98 (one-day series)
Overseas teams played for: Vredenburg/Saldanha, South Africa 1992-95; Avendale
CC, Cape Town 1995-96
Cricketers particularly admired: Dermot Reeve, Ian Botham, Phil Tufnell, Allan
Donald and Dougie Brown
Young players to look out for: Darren Altree
Other sports followed: Football (QPR), golf, basketball
Relaxations: Listening to music, playing golf, socialising, 'getting premiered up with
Dougie and spending valuable time with Ally'
Extras: Surrey Young Cricketer of the Year 1991, NBC Denis Compton Award for
Warwickshire in 1996. Whyte and Mackay Bowler of the Month for August.
Warwickshire Player of the Year in 1996. Warwickshire Most Improved Player 1996
Opinions on cricket: 'Great game. Should be played harder and marketed better.'
Best batting: 106* Warwickshire v Lancashire, Edgbaston 1996
Best bowling: 6-45 Warwickshire v Durham, Edgbaston 1996

31. Who is the leading run-scorer in the history of one-day Internationals?

1997 Season

	M	Inns	NO	Runs	HS	Avge	100s	50s	Ct	St	O	M	Runs	Wkts	Avge	Best	5wl	10wM
Test																		
All First	16	20	4	624	97	39.00	-	5	4	-	506.1	155	1225	38	32.23	4-54	-	-
1-day Int	1	0	0	0	0	-	-	-	-	-	9	0	48	0	-		-	
NatWest	5	3	0	103	69	34.33	-	1	-	-	49.3	9	195	10	19.50	5-21	1	
B & H	6	5	2	93	29	31.00	-	-	4	-	51.2	4	211	7	30.14	2-26	-	
Sunday	15	9	3	159	57	26.50	-	1	2	-	76.1	2	398	18	22.11	4-25	-	

Career Performances

	M	Inns	NO	Runs	HS	Avge	100s	50s	Ct	St	Balls	Runs	Wkts	Avge	Best	5wl	10wM
Test																	
All First	44	60	14	1427	106 *	31.02	1	9	15	-	8522	3521	127	27.72	6-45	4	-
1-day Int	1	0	0	0	0	-	-	-	-	-	54	48	0	-		-	
NatWest	8	5	1	127	69	31.75	-	1	-	-	429	278	14	19.85	5-21	1	
B & H	10	7	2	110	29	22.00	-	-	6	-	422	316	8	39.50	2-26	-	
Sunday	34	17	5	269	57	22.41	-	1	11	-	931	751	40	18.77	5-36	1	

GOOCH, G. A.   Essex

Name: Graham Alan Gooch
Role: Right-hand bat, right-arm
medium bowler
Born: 23 July 1953, Leytonstone
Height: 6ft **Weight:** 13st
Nickname: Zap, Goochie
County debut: 1973
County cap: 1975
Benefit: 1985 (£153,906)
Testimonial: 1995
Test debut: 1975
Tests: 118
One-Day Internationals: 125
1000 runs in a season: 20
1st-Class 50s: 217
1st-Class 100s: 128
1st-Class 200s: 12
1st-Class 300s: 1
1st-Class 5 w. in innings: 3
1st-Class catches: 555
One-Day 100s: 41
One-Day 5 w. in innings: 1

Place in batting averages: 186th av. 23.06 (1996 3rd av. 67.03)
Strike rate: (career 76.36)
Parents: Alfred and Rose
Wife and date of marriage: Brenda, 23 October 1976
Children: Hannah; Megan and Sally (twins)
Family links with cricket: Father played local cricket for East Ham Corinthians. Second cousin, Graham Saville, played for Essex CCC and was England U19 team manager
Education: Cannhall School and Norlington Junior High School, Leytonstone; Redbridge Technical College
Qualifications: 6 CSEs; four-year apprenticeship in tool-making
Overseas tours: England YC to West Indies 1971-72; England to Australia 1978-79, to Australia and India 1979-80, to West Indies 1980-81, to India and Sri Lanka 1981-82, to World Cup and Pakistan 1987-88, to India and West Indies 1989-90, to Australia 1990-91, to New Zealand 1991-92, to Australia (World Cup) 1991-92, to India 1992-93, to Australia 1994-95; unofficial English XI to South Africa 1981-82
Overseas teams played for: Western Province, South Africa 1982-84
Cricketers particularly admired: Bob Taylor, a model sportsman; Mike Procter for his enthusiasm; Barry Richards for his ability
Other sports followed: Squash, soccer, golf. Has trained with West Ham United FC
Relaxations: 'Relaxing at home'
Extras: One of *Wisden*'s Five Cricketers of the Year 1979. Captained English rebel team in South Africa in 1982 and was banned from Test cricket for three years. Hit a hole in one at Tollygunge Golf Club during England's tour in India, 1981-82. Appointed Essex captain 1986, but resigned captaincy at end of 1987, being reappointed in 1989 following retirement of Keith Fletcher. Captain of England for last two Tests of 1988 season against West Indies and Sri Lanka in 1988 and chosen to captain England on the cancelled tour of India in 1988-89. Reappointed captain for the tour to India and West Indies in 1989-90, and led England to their first Test victory over West Indies for 16 years. His 333 in the Lord's Test v India was the third highest score ever by an England batsman in a Test match, and by hitting 123 in the second innings he created a record Test aggregate of 456 runs and became the first man to hit a triple century and a century in the same first-class match. His aggregate for the season (2746 runs at 101.70) was the best since 1961 and he was only the fourth batsman to finish an English season with an average better than 100. When he first joined Essex, he was a wicket-keeper and batted at No 11 in his first match. He went on a Young England tour to the West Indies as second wicket-keeper to Andy Stovold of Gloucestershire. Autobiography *Out of the Wilderness* published in 1988; *Test of Fire,* an account of the West Indies tour, published in 1990; *Captaincy* published in 1992. Scored his 100th century in 1993. Resigned as England captain after Australia had retained the Ashes in 1993. Became the 15th player to pass 40,000 runs in first-class cricket. Resigned as Essex captain at end of 1994 season. Retired from Test cricket after final Test of 1994-95 series against Australia. *Graham Gooch: My Autobiography* written with Frank Keating was published in 1995. Retired from first-class cricket during the 1997 season and is currently part of the England selection panel

Best batting: 333 England v India, Lord's 1990
Best bowling: 7-14 Essex v Worcestershire, Ilford 1982

1997 Season

	M	Inns	NO	Runs	HS	Avge	100s	50s	Ct	St	O	M	Runs	Wkts	Avge	Best	5wI	10wM
Test																		
All First	10	17	1	369	56	23.06	-	2	12	-	2	1	3	0	-		-	-	-
1-day Int																		
NatWest																		
B & H	4	4	1	70	40	23.33	-	-	-	-								
Sunday	1	1	0	28	28	28.00	-	-	-	-								

Career Performances

	M	Inns	NO	Runs	HS	Avge	100s	50s	Ct	St	Balls	Runs	Wkts	Avge	Best	5wI	10wM
Test	118	215	6	8900	333	42.58	20	46	103	-	2655	1069	23	46.47	3-39	-	-
All First	580	988	75	44841	333	49.11	128	217	555	-	18785	8457	246	34.37	7-14	3	-
1-day Int	125	122	6	4290	142	36.98	8	23	45	-	2066	1516	36	42.11	3-19	-	
NatWest	57	56	4	2547	144	48.98	6	17	27	-	1655	855	33	25.90	5-8	1	
B & H	115	114	15	5176	198 *	52.28	15	30	68	-	3770	2195	69	31.81	3-24	-	
Sunday	274	268	23	8573	176	34.99	12	58	100	-	2576	4244	143	29.67	4-33	-	

GOODCHILD, D. J.   Middlesex

Name: David John Goodchild
Role: Right-hand bat, right-arm
medium bowler
Born: 17 September 1976, Harrow
Height: 6ft 2in **Weight:** 15st
County debut: 1996
Nickname: Golden, G, Goody
Parents: John and Brenda
Marital status: Single
Family links with cricket: 'Father played
club cricket. Mum does the teas'
Education: Vaughan First and Middle
School; Whitmore High School; Weald
College; North London University
Qualifications: 9 GCSEs, 3 A-levels and
NCA coaching award
Off-season: 'Training hard, practising and
improving my game. Studying at university'
Cricketers particularly admired: Graham

Gooch, Mike Gatting, Mark Ramprakash

Young players to look out for: Stefan and Rod James, Owais Shah

Other sports followed: Football (Arsenal), golf, fishing, American football (Miami Dolphins)

Injuries: Shin splints, out for five weeks

Relaxations: 'Having a few drinks with my friends. Going to the cinema with my girlfriend Sarah and watching television'

Extras: Holds the top score for Middlesex U11 side (153) and the top total aggregate for that age group (563). Awarded 2nd XI county cap at the end of the 1996 season. First-ever game for Middlesex was for the 1st XI against Gloucestershire at Lord's in 1996

Opinions on cricket: 'I think the lunch and tea intervals are too short. We play a lot of cricket and I feel that because of this not enough time is free to be devoted to basic cricket skills i.e. techniques and fielding practices.'

Best batting: 4 Middlesex v Gloucestershire, Lord's 1996

1997 Season (did not make any first-class or one-day appearances)

Career Performances

	M	Inns	NO	Runs	HS	Avge	100s	50s	Ct	St	Balls	Runs	Wkts	Avge	Best	5wI	10wM
Test																	
All First	1	2	0	4	4	2.00	-	-	-	-	29	26	0	-	-	3	-
1-day Int																	
NatWest																	
B & H																	
Sunday																	

---

32. Who won the Lord's Taverners Cricketer Colts Trophy in 1997 and whom did they beat in the final?

 vodafone

GOUGH, D.   Yorkshire

Name: Darren Gough
Role: Right-hand bat, right-arm fast bowler
Born: 18 September 1970, Barnsley
Height: 5ft 11in **Weight:** 13st 3lbs
Nickname: Dazzler, Rhino
County debut: 1989
County cap: 1993
Test debut: 1994
Tests: 21
One-Day Internationals: 38
50 wickets in a season: 3
1st-Class 50s: 9
1st-Class 100s: 1
1st-Class 5 w. in innings: 19
1st-Class 10 w. in innings: 3
1st-Class catches: 34
One-Day 5 w. in innings: 4
Place in batting averages: 269th av. 13.06
(1996 215th av. 22.77)
Place in bowling averages: 46th av. 26.72 (1996 14th av. 22.91)
Strike rate: 46.69 (career 51.88)
Parents: Trevor and Christine
Wife and date of marriage: Anna Marie, 16 October 1993
Children: Liam James, 24 November 1994; 'second due Christmas 1997'
Education: St Helens Junior; Priory Comprehensive; Airedale and Wharfdale College (part-time)
Qualifications: 2 O-levels, 5 CSEs, BTEC Leisure, NCA coaching award
Off-season: 'Going to Lapland with son Liam and getting to know addition to family'
Overseas tours: England YC to Australia 1989-90; Yorkshire to Barbados 1989-90, to South Africa 1991-92 and 1992-93; England A to South Africa 1993-94; England to Australia 1994-95, to South Africa 1995-96, to India and Pakistan (World Cup) 1995-96, to Zimbabwe and New Zealand 1996-97
Overseas teams played for: East Shirley, Christchurch, New Zealand 1991-92
Cricketers particularly admired: Ian Botham, Steve Waugh, Shane Warne, Michael Atherton ('mental strength')
Young players to look out for: Paul Hutchinson, Andrew Flintoff, Gareth Batty, Ryan Sidebottom, Liam James Gough (aged 2¾)
Other sports followed: Football (Tottenham Hotspur and Barnsley) and golf
Injuries: Knee, out for five weeks and hamstring on comeback
Relaxations: 'Spending time at home, especially at Christmas with family'
Extras: England Cornhill Player of the Year 1994. Yorkshire Sports Personality of the

Year 1994. Voted Man of the Match in England's third Test match against Australia at Sydney in 1994-95. Took a hat-trick against Kent in 1995. Named Player of the Year by Cornhill Insurance for 1995 season. Whyte and Mackay Bowler of the Year in 1996. Had to withdraw from the England tour to West Indies due to a persistent hamstring injury which required surgery

Opinions on cricket: 'Read my book – *My Guide to your Success.*'
Best batting: 121 Yorkshire v Warwickshire, Headingley 1996
Best bowling: 7-28 Yorkshire v Lancashire, Headingley 1995

1997 Season

	M	Inns	NO	Runs	HS	Avge	100s	50s	Ct	St	O	M	Runs	Wkts	Avge	Best	5wI	10wM
Test	4	6	0	17	10	2.83	-	-	-	-	142	27	511	16	31.93	5-149	1	-
All First	12	16	1	196	58	13.06	-	1	-	-	334.4	70	1149	43	26.72	5-56	3	-
1-day Int	3	0	0	0	0	-	-	-	-	-	30	5	119	7	17.00	5-44	1	
NatWest	3	2	0	50	46	25.00	-	-	-	-	30.5	5	85	13	6.53	7-27	1	
B & H	6	4	3	40	22 *	40.00	-	-	4	-	53	1	223	7	31.85	3-38	-	
Sunday	9	7	3	69	23 *	17.25	-	-	2	-	63	1	325	14	23.21	3-21	-	

Career Performances

	M	Inns	NO	Runs	HS	Avge	100s	50s	Ct	St	Balls	Runs	Wkts	Avge	Best	5wI	10wM
Test	21	30	4	363	65	13.96	-	2	8	-	4522	2401	85	28.24	6-49	3	-
All First	136	182	31	2475	121	16.39	1	9	34	-	24023	12625	463	27.26	7-28	19	3
1-day Int	38	24	7	203	45	11.94	-	-	4	-	2120	1438	58	24.79	5-44	2	
NatWest	21	11	0	183	46	16.63	-	-	3	-	1338	735	41	17.92	7-27	1	
B & H	24	14	5	130	48 *	14.44	-	-	7	-	1260	786	26	30.23	3-38	-	
Sunday	88	57	14	571	72 *	13.27	-	1	18	-	3770	2833	105	26.98	5-13	1	

33. Who won the one-day International Asia Cup in July 1997 and whom did they beat in the final?

O vodafone

GRAHAM, J. A.   Durham

Name: John Alexander Graham
Role: Right-hand bat
Born: 4 March 1978, Newcastle-upon-Tyne
County debut: No first-team appearance
Parents: Bill and Jennifer
Marital status: Single
Education: Woodlands First School,
Wideopen Middle; Seaton Burn Community
High School; University of Leeds
Qualifications: 9 GCSEs, 3 A-levels
Career outside cricket: Student
Off-season: Studying geography at university
Overseas tours: England U19 to Pakistan
1996-97
Cricketers particularly admired: David
Gower, Graham Thorpe
Young players to look out for: David Nash,
Andrew Flintoff

Other sports followed: Football (Newcastle United)
Injuries: Stress injury to right forefinger, out for five weeks
Relaxations: Music, cinema, watching Newcastle United FC

GRAYSON, A. P.   Essex

Name: Adrian Paul Grayson
Role: Right-hand bat, slow left-arm
bowler, slip fielder
Born: 31 March 1971, Ripon
Height: 6ft 2in **Weight:** 12st 2lbs
Nickname: PG, Laz, Ravi
County debut: 1990 (Yorkshire),
1996 (Essex)
County cap: 1996 (Essex)
1000 runs in a season: 2
1st-Class 50s: 21
1st-Class 100s: 4
1st-Class catches: 75
Place in batting averages: 57th av. 40.88 (1996 116th av. 34.77)
Place in bowling averages: 105th av. 36.03 (1996 121st av. 42.16)

Strike rate: 84.60 (career 97.61)
Parents: Adrian and Carol
Wife and date of marriage: Alison, 30 September 1994
Family links with cricket: 'Dad played good league cricket and is also an NCA staff coach; brother also plays when free from football commitments'
Education: Bedale Comprehensive School
Qualifications: 8 CSEs, BTEC in Leisure, NCA Senior Coaching Award
Overseas tours: England YC to Australia 1989-90; Yorkshire to Barbados 1989-90, to Cape Town 1991-92, to Cape Town 1992-93, to Leeward Islands 1993-94, to Cape Town 1994-95
Overseas teams played for: Petone, Wellington 1991-92 and 1995-96
Cricketers particularly admired: Graham Gooch, Martyn Moxon, Darren Gough 'and all the Essex playing staff'
Young players to look out for: Stephen Peters, Jason Laney
Other sports followed: Football 'turned down apprentice terms with Middlesbrough at 16. Support Leeds United and Leicester City. Brother Simon plays for Leicester'
Relaxations: Playing golf, spending time with my wife
Extras: Played for England YC v New Zealand 1989 and Pakistan 1990. Brother plays football for Leicester City. Scored 1000 runs for first time in 1994. Yorkshire Player of the Year 1994. Released by Yorkshire at end of 1995 but joined Essex for 1996 season. Awarded county cap 1996
Opinions on cricket: 'More cricket should be played in schools. Tea break should be longer. Short run-ups in the Sunday League.'
Best batting: 140 Essex v Middlesex, Lord's 1996
Best bowling: 4-53 Essex v Northamptonshire, Northampton 1997

1997 Season

	M	Inns	NO	Runs	HS	Avge	100s	50s	Ct	St	O	M	Runs	Wkts	Avge	Best	5wI	10wM
Test																		
All First	19	28	3	1022	105	40.88	1	6	20	-	394.5	112	1009	28	36.03	4-53	-	-
1-day Int																		
NatWest	5	4	1	179	82 *	59.66	-	2	4	-	42	1	207	7	29.57	3-40	-	
B & H	4	3	1	70	49 *	35.00	-	-	2	-	38	0	166	7	23.71	3-39	-	
Sunday	16	15	1	333	69 *	23.78	-	1	4	-	100	1	572	19	30.10	4-63	-	

Career Performances

	M	Inns	NO	Runs	HS	Avge	100s	50s	Ct	St	Balls	Runs	Wkts	Avge	Best	5wI	10wM
Test																	
All First	88	138	16	3919	140	32.12	4	21	75	-	5759	2614	59	44.30	4-53	-	-
1-day Int																	
NatWest	17	14	1	301	82 *	23.15	-	2	7	-	809	629	20	31.45	3-24	-	
B & H	18	14	4	222	49 *	22.20	-	-	6	-	630	440	15	29.33	3-30	-	
Sunday	82	65	10	878	69 *	15.96	-	2	25	-	2420	2224	69	32.23	4-25	-	

GREEN, R. J. Lancashire

Name: Richard James Green
Role: Right-hand bat, right-arm medium-fast bowler
Born: 13 March 1976, Grappenhall, Warrington
Height: 6ft **Weight:** 12st 12lbs
Nickname: Slimey, Greendog, Spotty, Captain Darling
County debut: 1995
1st-Class 50s: 1
1st-Class 5 w. in innings: 1
1st-Class catches: 3
Place in batting averages: (1996 277th av. 13.00)
Place in bowling averages: (1996 41st av. 27.22)
Strike rate: 122.80 (career 62.03)
Parents: Jim and Christina
Marital status: Single
Family links with cricket: 'Father Manchester Association League legend'
Education: Bridgewater County High School, Warrington; Hartford College
Qualifications: 5 GCSEs, BTEC National Business and Finance
Career outside cricket: 'One day will own a wine bar'
Off-season: 'Resting until Christmas and then training'
Overseas tours: Lancashire to Jamaica 1996, to Cape Town, South Africa 1997
Overseas teams played for: Waratah-Mayfield CC, Newcastle, NSW 1994-95; Paramn CC, Melbourne, Australia 1996-97
Cricketers particularly admired: Warren Hegg
Young players to look out for: David Sales
Other sports followed: Football (Manchester United)
Injuries: Ankle spur, out for nearly three months and broken thumb, out for two

weeks at the end of the season
Relaxations: Music, fast Rover cars, the occasional night out
Extras: Cheshire County League's youngest century-maker. Played for England U17 and England U19. Denis Compton Award winner in 1996
Opinions on cricket: 'Staffs of 16 players and pay them more money. Should be a two-division league system and more day/night cricket.'
Best batting: 51 Lancashire v Essex, Old Trafford 1997
Best bowling: 6-41 Lancashire v Yorkshire, Old Trafford 1996

1997 Season

	M	Inns	NO	Runs	HS	Avge	100s	50s	Ct	St	O	M	Runs	Wkts	Avge	Best	5wI	10wM
Test																		
All First	4	5	2	93	51	31.00	-	1	1	-	102.2	25	320	5	64.00	3-66	-	-
1-day Int																		
NatWest																			
B & H	5	3	1	13	7	6.50	-	-	1	-	41.3	1	231	6	38.50	2-33	-	
Sunday	5	0	0	0	0	-	-	-	1	-	26	0	150	6	25.00	3-18	-	

Career Performances

	M	Inns	NO	Runs	HS	Avge	100s	50s	Ct	St	Balls	Runs	Wkts	Avge	Best	5wI	10wM
Test																	
All First	12	16	5	185	51	16.81	-	1	3	-	1861	1006	30	33.53	6-41	1	-
1-day Int																	
NatWest																		
B & H	5	3	1	13	7	6.50	-	-	1	-	249	231	6	38.50	2-33	-	
Sunday	12	1	1	0	0 *	-	-	-	1	-	462	405	17	23.82	3-18	-	

---

34. Name the two Sri Lankan players who set a new Test second-wicket partnership record of 576 runs against India in Colombo in August 1997.

GREENFIELD, K.   Sussex

Name: Keith Greenfield
Role: Right-hand bat, right-arm
off-spin bowler, emergency wicket-keeper
Born: 6 December 1968, Brighton
Height: 6ft **Weight:** 12st 12lbs
Nickname: Grubby, G-Man, Grav
County debut: 1987
1st-Class 50s: 13
1st-Class 100s: 9
1st-Class catches: 65
One-Day 100s: 2
Place in batting averages: 230th av. 17.71
(1996 67th av. 41.63)
Strike rate: (career 162.80)
Parents: Leslie Ernest and Sheila
Wife and date of marriage: Caroline
Susannah, 22 February 1992
Family links with cricket: Father keen
spectator, father-in-law played club cricket for 20 years and now umpires and spectates
Education: Coldean First and Middle Schools; Falmer High School
Qualifications: 3 O-levels, BTEC National Diploma in Leisure and Management,
junior, senior and advanced coaching certificates
Career outside cricket: Cricket coach
Overseas tours: Sussex U16 to Guernsey 1985; Select XI to Malaga 1993; Sussex to
Malaga 1993-94; David Smith Testimonial XI to Malaga 1994; MCC Tour to SE Asia
and Far East 1994-95, to Bangladesh 1996
Overseas teams played for: Cornwall, Auckland 1988-90
Cricketers particularly admired: Derek Randall, Ian Botham, Chris Tugwell,
Malcolm Eldridge (St Peters), Ray Bierber (Brighton & Hove) and Chris Pickett
Young players to look out for: Giles Haywood, Matthew Prior, James Chadburn,
Jonathan Armitage 'all from Sussex Youth teams'
Other sports followed: Liverpool FC and 'a big watcher of golf'
Relaxations: 'Eating out with friends. DIY, music and concerts. Spending time with
Caroline and lads at St Peters and Brighton and Hove CC'
Extras: First person taken on Youth Training Scheme to become a professional cricketer
at Sussex. Only uncapped player to have captained Sussex at Hove (v Cambridge U),
scored century in this game. Captained 2nd XI to Championship title in 1990. Sussex
Team Man of the Year 1990, 1993. Joined Bill Athey on a trip to Belarus to take aid to
the cancer hospital near Chernobyl
Opinions on cricket: 'As players we seem to be forever rushing around between overs
just so that we can manage the current over-rate and not end up with large fines. The
over-rate should be reduced to a realistic amount. Teams no longer seem to socialise

after matches anywhere near as much as in years gone by, thus taking away an important part of county cricket – making friends from other counties.'

Best batting: 154* Sussex v India, Hove 1996
Best bowling: 2-40 Sussex v Essex, Hove 1993

1997 Season

	M	Inns	NO	Runs	HS	Avge	100s	50s	Ct	St	O	M	Runs	Wkts	Avge	Best	5wI	10wM
Test																		
All First	11	21	0	372	108	17.71	1	-	12	-	10	2	45	0	-	-	-	-
1-day Int																		
NatWest	4	4	1	223	129	74.33	1	1	2	-	20	0	121	0	-	-	-	
B & H	5	5	0	123	44	24.60	-	-	1	-	5	0	27	1	27.00	1-17	-	
Sunday	15	15	2	426	69 *	32.76	-	4	3	-	7	0	38	0	-	-	-	

Career Performances

	M	Inns	NO	Runs	HS	Avge	100s	50s	Ct	St	Balls	Runs	Wkts	Avge	Best	5wI	10wM
Test																	
All First	78	135	15	3550	154 *	29.58	9	13	65	-	814	524	5	104.80	2-40	-	-
1-day Int																	
NatWest	15	14	3	431	129	39.18	1	2	7	-	402	303	3	101.00	2-35	-	
B & H	23	22	2	518	62	25.90	-	3	8	-	432	354	2	177.00	1-17	-	
Sunday	111	109	10	2634	102	26.60	1	16	34	-	964	954	21	45.42	3-34	-	

GRIFFITHS, S. P. Derbyshire

Name: Stephen Paul Griffiths
Role: Right-hand bat, wicket-keeper
Born: 31 May 1973, Hereford
Height: 5ft 11in **Weight:** 12st
Nickname: 'Too many to name'
County debut: 1995
1st-Class catches: 17
Parents: Paul and Lesley
Marital status: Single
Family links with cricket: 'Father has played a good standard of club cricket for years'
Education: Bathford Primary School; Beechen Cliff School, Bath; Brunel College of Art and Technology
Qualifications: 7 GCSEs, basic coaching award
Career outside cricket: Studying antique

furniture restoration and conservation

Overseas tours: Bath Schools to Zimbabwe and Kenya 1989

Overseas teams played for: CBC Old Boys, Bloemfontein, South Africa 1992-93

Cricketers particularly admired: Jack Russell, Bob Taylor, Alan Knott, Doug C. Storey, Gregg Brown

Young players to look out for: Andrew Harris, Kevin Dean

Other sports followed: Rugby (Bath RFC) and golf

Relaxations: 'Music (listening to and collecting blues, jazz, reggae, Irish, Motown), roaming through flea markets, reading, going to pubs in Bath with friends, spending time with girlfriend Ceri, eating foreign food and doing up old furniture'

Extras: Took six catches on first-class debut against Worcestershire in 1995 (five of them in the first innings). Played for Somerset 2nd XI before joining Derbyshire. Member of Bath CC and Buccaneers CC

Opinions on cricket: 'It is far too easy for young cricketers to slip through the net. The standard of coaching in many schools is very poor and luck plays a big part in being spotted.'

Best batting: 20 Derbyshire v Surrey, Derby 1995

1997 Season

	M	Inns	NO	Runs	HS	Avge	100s	50s	Ct	St	O	M	Runs	Wkts	Avge	Best	5wI	10wM
Test																		
All First	1	1	0	1	1	1.00	-	-	3	-								
1-day Int																		
NatWest																		
B & H																			
Sunday	1	0	0	0	0	-	-	-	1	-								

Career Performances

	M	Inns	NO	Runs	HS	Avge	100s	50s	Ct	St	Balls	Runs	Wkts	Avge	Best	5wI	10wM
Test																	
All First	6	10	0	76	20	7.60	-	-	17	-							
1-day Int																	
NatWest																	
B & H																	
Sunday	1	0	0	0	0	-	-	-	1	-							

---

35. Which former Test player celebrated a £200,000 win on the Barbados lottery with the words: 'I do not think it will change my life'?

O vodafone

GROVE, J. O.

Name: Jamie Oliver Grove
Role: Right-hand bat, right-arm
fast-medium bowler
Born: 3 July 1979, Bury St Edmunds
Height: 6ft 3in **Weight:** 12st 1lb
Nickname: Grover, Groover
County debut: No first-team appearance
Parents: Chris John and Patricia Susan
Marital status: Single
Family links with cricket: Father played in
the local leagues for many years
Education: Whepstead Primary School; St
James Middle School, Bury St Edmunds;
County Upper School, Bury St Edmunds
Qualifications: 8 GCSEs, City and Guilds in
Basic Engineering
Career outside cricket: Mechanical engineer
Off-season: Touring South Africa with
England U19
Overseas tours: England U19 to South Africa 1997-98
Cricketers particularly admired: Dennis Lillee
Young players to look out for: Stephen Peters, Paul Franks
Other sports followed: Hockey and football (West Ham United)
Injuries: Knee problems, out for one week at start of the season
Relaxations: Listening to music and going out with friends
Extras: Played for England at U15, U17 and U19 level. Was part of the successful
England U19 World Cup-winning squad in South Africa in 1997-98
Opinions on cricket: 'The pitches favour the batsman too much.'

---

36. Which player holds the record for the most sixes in
a one-day International innings?

HABIB, A.   Leicestershire

Name: Aftab Habib
Role: Right-hand bat, right-arm slow-
medium bowler
Born: 7 February 1972, Reading, Berks
Height: 5ft 11in **Weight:** 12st
Nickname: Afie, Tabby, Scabby, Habbiby,
Alvin, Inzaman
County debut: 1992 (Middlesex), 1995
(Leicestershire)
1st-Class 50s: 3
1st-Class 100s: 3
1st-Class 200s: 1
1st-Class catches: 14
Place in batting averages: 66th av. 39.70
(1996 105th av. 36.00)
Parents: Hussain and Tahira
Marital status: Single

Family links with cricket: Cousin of Zahid
Sadiq (ex-Surrey and Derbyshire)
Education: Alfred Sutton Primary School; Millfield Junior School; Taunton School
Qualifications: 7 GCSEs, NCA coaching certificate
Career outside cricket: Salesman for Sewards
Off-season: Playing club and district cricket in New Zealand and coaching
Overseas tours: England YC to Australia 1989-90, to New Zealand 1990-91;
Berkshire CCC to South Africa 1996
Overseas teams played for: Globe Wakatu, Nelson, New Zealand, 1992-93 and 1996-
97; Riccarton CC, Christchurch, New Zealand 1997-98
Cricketers particularly admired: Vince Wells, Mark Waugh, Steve Waugh, Saeed
Anwar, Paul Nixon, Darren Maddy, Graham Lloyd, Sachin Tendulkar, Phil Simmons
Young players to look out for: Darren Maddy, James Ormond, Chris Schofield
Other sports followed: 'Follow Reading FC and enjoy watching Liverpool'
Injuries: Knee, out for seven weeks
Relaxations: Music, cinema, reading, books, playing golf
Extras: 2nd XI Seaxe Player of the Year 1992. Released by Middlesex at end of 1994 season.
Leicestershire 2nd XI Player of the Year in 1995. Championship medal with Leicestershire
in 1996. Gold Award-winner in the Benson & Hedges Cup with 111 against Durham in 1997.
Holds Leicestershire's fifth-wicket partnership record with James Whitaker of 320 set against
Worcestershire at Leicester in 1996
Best batting: 215 Leicestershire v Worcestershire, Leicester 1996

1997 Season

	M	Inns	NO	Runs	HS	Avge	100s	50s	Ct	St	O	M	Runs	Wkts	Avge	Best	5wI	10wM
Test																		
All First	9	14	4	397	175 *	39.70	1	1	4	-	4	0	37	0	-	-	-	-
1-day Int																		
NatWest																		
B & H	6	6	1	249	111	49.80	1	1	3	-								
Sunday	6	6	3	114	45 *	38.00	-	-	2	-								

Career Performances

	M	Inns	NO	Runs	HS	Avge	100s	50s	Ct	St	Balls	Runs	Wkts	Avge	Best	5wI	10wM
Test																	
All First	29	45	9	1438	215	39.94	3	3	14	-	24	37	0	-	-	-	-
1-day Int																	
NatWest	2	2	0	38	35	19.00	-	-	-	-							
B & H	6	6	1	249	111	49.80	1	1	3	-							
Sunday	18	16	6	338	99 *	33.80	-	2	5	-	1	4	0	-	-	-	-

HAMILTON, G. M. Yorkshire

Name: Gavin Mark Hamilton
Role: Right-hand bat, right-arm fast bowler
Born: 16 September 1974, Broxburn
Height: 6ft 1in **Weight:** 13st
Nickname: Hammy, Scotty, Jock, 'anything Scottish'
County debut: 1994
1st-Class 50s: 1
1st-Class catches: 10
1st-Class 5 w. in innings: 2
Place in batting averages: 235th av. 17.14
Place in bowling averages: 91st av. 33.59
Strike rate: 53.55 (career 60.49)
Parents: Gavin and Wendy
Marital status: Single
Family links with cricket: Father long-serving player for West Lothian CC. Brother another long-term player for Aberdeenshire CC and opening bat for Scotland
Education: Hurstmere School, Sidcup
Qualifications: 10 GCSEs and 'numerous coaching awards'
Overseas teams played for: Municipals, Orange Free State, South Africa; Wellington,

Cape Town, South Africa; Stellenbosch University, Boland, South Africa
Cricketers particularly admired: Craig White, Alan Mullally
Young players to look out for: Danny Law
Other sports followed: Golf, football (Arsenal YTS)
Relaxations: Listening to most kinds of music, 'playing golf on a hot day'
Opinions on cricket: 'Nowhere near enough days off. Cricketers should be allowed or forced to come off when it is too cold, it shouldn't have to rain.'
Best batting: 61 Yorkshire v Essex, Headingley 1996
Best bowling: 5-65 Scotland v Ireland, Eglinton 1993

1997 Season

	M	Inns	NO	Runs	HS	Avge	100s	50s	Ct	St	O	M	Runs	Wkts	Avge	Best	5wI	10wM
Test																		
All First	11	16	2	240	49	17.14	-	-	3	-	241	53	907	27	33.59	5-89	1	-
1-day Int																		
NatWest																		
B & H																			
Sunday	6	3	3	28	18 *	-	-	-	-	-	31	0	222	5	44.40	3-30	-

Career Performances

	M	Inns	NO	Runs	HS	Avge	100s	50s	Ct	St	Balls	Runs	Wkts	Avge	Best	5wI	10wM
Test																	
All First	25	32	7	476	61	19.04	-	1	10	-	3569	2033	59	34.45	5-65	2	-
1-day Int																	
NatWest	2	1	0	2	2	2.00	-	-	1	-	120	86	4	21.50	2-42	-
B & H	2	1	1	8	8 *	-	-	-	-	-	78	42	0	-	-	-
Sunday	22	12	5	74	18 *	10.57	-	-	2	-	775	772	25	30.88	4-27	-

HANCOCK, T. H. C.   Gloucestershire

Name: Timothy Harold Coulter Hancock
Role: Right-hand bat, occasional right-arm medium bowler, short-leg or cover fielder
Born: 20 April 1972, Reading
Height: 5ft 11in **Weight:** 12st 12lbs
Nickname: Herbie
County debut: 1991
1st-Class 50s: 24
1st-Class 100s: 4
1st-Class catches: 58
Place in batting averages: 120th av. 30.50 (1996 161st av. 29.54)
Strike rate: 119.80 (career 82.50)
Parents: John and Jennifer

Marital status: Single
Family links with cricket: 'Dad still plays'
Education: St Edward's, Oxford;
Henley College
Qualifications: 8 GCSEs
Overseas tours: Gloucestershire to Kenya
1991, to Sri Lanka 1993
Overseas teams played for: CBC Old Boys,
Bloemfontein 1991-92; Wynnum Manley,
Brisbane 1992-93
Cricketers particularly admired: Ian
Botham, Viv Richards
Other sports followed: Rugby union, golf,
hockey
Relaxations: Playing golf, watching
television, 'having a pint or two with friends'
Extras: Played hockey for Oxfordshire U19
Best batting: 123 Gloucestershire v Essex,
Chelmsford 1994

Best bowling: 3-10 Gloucestershire v Glamorgan, Abergavenny 1993

1997 Season

	M	Inns	NO	Runs	HS	Avge	100s	50s	Ct	St	O	M	Runs	Wkts	Avge	Best	5wl	10wM
Test																		
All First	19	31	3	854	100 *	30.50	1	5	10	-	99.5	22	386	5	77.20	1-24	-	-
1-day Int																		
NatWest	2	1	0	4	4	4.00	-	-	-	-	12	0	58	6	9.66	6-58	1	
B & H	5	4	1	69	24 *	23.00	-	-	-	-	23.1	2	99	2	49.50	2-34	-	
Sunday	15	13	0	332	57	25.53	-	2	8	-	20.4	0	94	2	47.00	1-22	-	

Career Performances

	M	Inns	NO	Runs	HS	Avge	100s	50s	Ct	St	Balls	Runs	Wkts	Avge	Best	5wl	10wM
Test																	
All First	94	165	13	4015	123	26.41	4	24	58	-	1485	945	18	52.50	3-10	-	-
1-day Int																	
NatWest	6	5	0	88	45	17.60	-	-	3	-	113	97	8	12.12	6-58	1	
B & H	21	18	3	357	71 *	23.80	-	1	2	-	217	150	6	25.00	3-13	-	
Sunday	68	62	1	984	57	16.13	-	2	28	-	327	307	9	34.11	2-6	-	

HANSEN, T. M.   Hampshire

Name: Thomas Munkholt Hansen
Role: Right-hand bat, left-arm
fast-medium bowler
Born: 25 March 1976, Glostrup, Denmark
Height: 6ft **Weight:** 14st
County debut: 1997
Parents: Lars and Brigitte
Marital status: Single
Family links with cricket: 'My father played
in the 1st XI at Svanholm Cricket Club for 20
years and made four appearances for
Denmark. He runs the only shop in Denmark
that sells cricket equipment'
Education: Norregaard; Falkonergaarden
Career outside cricket: Student
Off-season: 'Playing club cricket in Australia
or touring with Denmark'
Cricketers particularly admired:
Ian Botham, Steve Waugh
Other sports followed: Football (Brondby IF and Manchester United), handball
(Denmark) and tennis
Relaxations: 'All kinds of sports and a good day on the beach'
Extras: Has played for Denmark at U17 and U19 level (as captain) and the national side
in the European Championships where they finished third behind Ireland and Holland.
Also played for Denmark in the ICC Trophy in Malaysia winning the Man of the Match
Award against Canada and Holland
Best batting: 19 Hampshire v Worcestershire, Southampton 1997

1997 Season

	M	Inns	NO	Runs	HS	Avge	100s	50s	Ct	St	O	M	Runs	Wkts	Avge	Best	5wI	10wM
Test																		
All First	1	2	1	31	19	31.00	-	-	-	-	26	10	75	0	-		-	--
1-day Int																		
NatWest																		
B & H																		
Sunday																		

	M	Inns	NO	Runs	HS	Avge	100s	50s	Ct	St	Balls	Runs	Wkts	Avge	Best	5wI	10wM
Test																	
All First	1	2	1	31	19	31.00	-	-	-	-	156	75	0	-		-	-	-
1-day Int																	
NatWest																	
B & H																	
Sunday																	

HARDEN, R. J.   Somerset

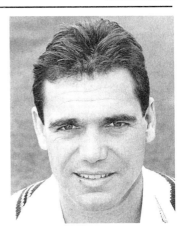

Name: Richard John Harden
Role: Right-hand bat, left-arm medium bowler
Born: 16 August 1965, Bridgwater
Height: 5ft 11in **Weight:** 13st 7lbs
Nickname: Sumo, Curtis
County debut: 1985
County cap: 1989
1000 runs in a season: 6
1st-Class 50s: 65
1st-Class 100s: 28
1st-Class catches: 172
One-Day 100s: 4
Place in batting averages: 42nd av. 43.88 (1996 109th av. 39.74)
Strike rate: (career 72.70)
Parents: Chris and Anne
Wife and date of marriage: Nicki Rae, 25 September 1992
Family links with cricket: Grandfather played club cricket for Bridgwater
Education: King's College, Taunton
Qualifications: 8 O-levels, 2 A-levels, coaching award
Career outside cricket: Print broker for Pennine Dataforms
Overseas teams played for: Central Districts, New Zealand
Cricketers particularly admired: Viv Richards, Jimmy Cook
Other sports followed: Squash, golf, rugby
Relaxations: 'Love my domestic duties (dusting, Hoovering, etc.) rather than golf. Good food and the odd drink.'
Best batting: 187 Somerset v Nottinghamshire, Taunton 1992
Best bowling: 2-7 Central Districts v Canterbury, Blenheim 1987-88

1997 Season

	M	Inns	NO	Runs	HS	Avge	100s	50s	Ct	St	O	M	Runs	Wkts	Avge	Best	5wI	10wM
Test																		
All First	7	11	2	395	136 *	43.88	2	1	3	-								
1-day Int																		
NatWest																		
B & H	5	5	0	235	68	47.00	-	3	3	-								
Sunday	8	8	2	244	85	40.66	-	3	7	-								

Career Performances

	M	Inns	NO	Runs	HS	Avge	100s	50s	Ct	St	Balls	Runs	Wkts	Avge	Best	5wI	10wM
Test																	
All First	229	374	58	12596	187	39.86	28	65	172	-	1454	1011	20	50.55	2-7	-	-
1-day Int																	
NatWest	21	19	2	733	108 *	43.11	3	2	12	-	18	23	0	-		-	-
B & H	52	50	4	1036	76	22.52	-	6	14	-							
Sunday	160	154	28	4130	100 *	32.77	1	26	51	-	1	0	0	-		-	-

HARRIS, A. J.   Derbyshire

Name: Andrew James Harris
Role: Right-hand bat, right-arm fast bowler
Born: 26 June 1973, Ashton-under-Lyne
Height: 6ft **Weight:** 11st 7lbs
Nickname: AJ
County debut: 1994
County cap: 1996
1st-Class 5 w. in innings: 2
1st-Class 10 w. in match: 1
1st-Class catches: 12
Place in batting averages: 291st av. 8.55
(1996 301st av. 7.84)
Place in bowling averages: 132nd av. 48.50
(1996 31st av. 26.03)
Strike rate: 82.54 (career 55.71)
Parents: Norman and Joyce
Marital status: Single
Education: Tintwistle Primary School;
Hadfield Comprehensive School;
Glossopdale Community College
Qualifications: 6 GCSEs, 1 A-level
Overseas tours: England A to Australia 1996-97

Overseas teams played for: Ginninderra, West Belconnen, Australia 1992-93
Cricketers particularly admired: Kim Barnett, 'Brian Lara – he's top drawer – and Merv Hughes for his effort and determination'
Young players to look out for: Vikram Solanki
Other sports followed: 'Soccer, as my brother plays for Altrincham, but I support the True Blues, Manchester City, and every sport I will view with great determination'
Relaxations: 'Playing any sport, golf in particular. As relaxing goes, watching television, playing on my Sega, and how could I forget having quite a few beers, although I have never been to the Pink Coconut'
Extras: Awarded county cap in 1996
Best batting: 36 Derbyshire v Worcestershire, Worcester 1997
Best bowling: 6-40 Derbyshire v Middlesex, Derby 1996

1997 Season

	M	Inns	NO	Runs	HS	Avge	100s	50s	Ct	St	O	M	Runs	Wkts	Avge	Best	5wI	10wM
Test																		
All First	18	24	4	171	36	8.55	-	-	9	-	481.3	98	1694	35	48.40	3-66	-	-
1-day Int																		
NatWest	2	1	1	5	5 *	-	-	-	-	-	18	2	79	3	26.33	2-12	-	
B & H	5	2	1	6	4 *	6.00	-	-	-	-	47.5	1	234	8	29.25	3-41	-	
Sunday	13	7	4	27	10 *	9.00	-	-	2	-	88.2	2	479	21	22.80	4-22	-	

Career Performances

	M	Inns	NO	Runs	HS	Avge	100s	50s	Ct	St	Balls	Runs	Wkts	Avge	Best	5wI	10wM
Test																	
All First	37	51	11	335	36	8.37	-	-	12	-	5961	3647	107	34.08	6-40	2	1
1-day Int																	
NatWest	4	2	2	16	11 *	-	-	-	1	-	234	156	6	26.00	3-58	-	
B & H	7	3	1	11	5	5.50	-	-	1	-	395	322	10	32.20	3-41	-	
Sunday	35	12	6	31	10 *	5.16	-	-	9	-	1398	1207	51	23.66	4-22	-	

38. Who was voted Man of the Match in the 1997 NatWest final?

HART, J. P.   Nottinghamshire

Name: Jamie Paul Hart
Role: Right-hand bat, right-arm
medium bowler
Born: 31 December 1975, Blackpool
Height: 6ft 2in **Weight:** 13st 8lbs
Nickname: Harty
County debut: 1995 (one-day),
1996 (first-class)
Parents: Paul and Vicky
Marital status: Single
Education: Grosvenor School, Nottingham;
Millfield School
Qualifications: 8 GCSEs and 1 A-level
Career outside cricket: Sales
Overseas tours: Millfield School to Sri
Lanka 1993
Cricketers particularly admired: Ian
Botham, Dermot Reeve

Other sports followed: Football (Leeds United)
Relaxations: Listening to music and reading
Extras: Father played professional football and is now at Leeds United on the coaching staff
Opinions on cricket: 'The different standards of second-class pitches compared with first-class pitches and grounds often make the step-up harder i.e. more often than not one can get more out of a 2nd XI pitch than a first-class one (as a bowler).'
Best batting: 18* Nottinghamshire v Yorkshire, Scarborough 1996

1997 Season (did not make any first-class or one-day appearances)

Career Performances

	M	Inns	NO	Runs	HS	Avge	100s	50s	Ct	St	Balls	Runs	Wkts	Avge	Best	5wI	10wM
Test																	
All First	1	2	2	18	18 *	-	-	-	-	-	108	51	0	-		-	-	-
1-day Int																	
NatWest																	
B & H																	
Sunday	2	0	0	0	0	-	-	-	-	-	72	87	1	87.00	1-48	-	

HARTLEY, P. J. — Hampshire

Name: Peter John Hartley
Role: Right-hand bat, right-arm medium-fast bowler
Born: 18 April 1960, Keighley
Height: 6ft **Weight:** 13st 7lbs
Nickname: Jack
County debut: 1982 (Warwickshire), 1985 (Yorkshire)
County cap: 1987 (Yorkshire)
Benefit: 1996 (Yorkshire)
50 wickets in a season: 6
1st-Class 50s: 13
1st-Class 100s: 2
1st-Class 5 w. in innings: 21
1st-Class 10 w. in match: 2
1st-Class catches: 62
One-Day 5 w. in innings: 4
Place in batting averages: 275th av. 12.10 (1996 217th av. 22.66)
Place in bowling averages: 21st av. 23.13 (1996 58th av. 29.66)
Strike rate: 44.34 (career 54.04)
Parents: Thomas and Molly
Wife and date of marriage: Sharon Louise, 12 March 1988
Children: Megan Grace, 25 April 1992; Courtney, 25 June 1995
Family links with cricket: Father played local league cricket
Education: Hartington/Greenhead Grammar School; Bradford College
Qualifications: City & Guilds in textile design and management, NCA coaching award
Career outside cricket: Textiles
Overseas tours: Yorkshire pre-season tours to Barbados 1986-87, to South Africa 1991-92, 1992-93
Overseas teams played for: Melville, New Zealand 1983-84; Adelaide, Australia 1985-86; Harmony and Orange Free State, South Africa 1988-89
Cricketers particularly admired: Malcolm Marshall, Richard Hadlee
Young players to look out for: Peter Hartley, Nick Faldo, Ernie Els
Other sports followed: Rugby league (Keighley Cougars), football (Chelsea FC)
Relaxations: Golf, walking
Extras: Released by Yorkshire at the end of the 1997 season and has joined Hampshire for the 1998 season
Opinions on cricket: 'Underpaid, overworked.'
Best batting: 127* Yorkshire v Lancashire, Old Trafford 1988
Best bowling: 9-41 Yorkshire v Derbyshire, Chesterfield 1995

1997 Season

	M	Inns	NO	Runs	HS	Avge	100s	50s	Ct	St	O	M	Runs	Wkts	Avge	Best	5wI	10wM
Test																		
All First	9	10	0	121	39	12.10	-	-	3	-	170	39	532	23	23.13	5-34	1	-
1-day Int																		
NatWest	3	2	0	86	83	43.00	-	1	1	-	22	1	81	3	27.00	2-49	-	
B & H	6	6	1	65	22	13.00	-	-	1	-	49.4	2	239	8	29.87	3-31	-	
Sunday	14	12	2	200	48 *	20.00	-	-	7	-	85.4	4	490	12	40.83	3-42	-	

Career Performances

	M	Inns	NO	Runs	HS	Avge	100s	50s	Ct	St	Balls	Runs	Wkts	Avge	Best	5wI	10wM
Test																	
All First	198	241	52	3875	127 *	20.50	2	13	62	-	31401	17653	581	30.38	9-41	21	2
1-day Int																	
NatWest	28	17	8	250	83	27.77	-	2	2	-	1715	1108	45	24.62	5-46	1	
B & H	43	26	10	195	29 *	12.18	-	-	12	-	2343	1539	61	25.22	5-43	1	
Sunday	146	102	31	1164	52	16.39	-	2	25	-	6201	4798	174	27.57	5-36	2	

HARVEY, M. E.   Lancashire

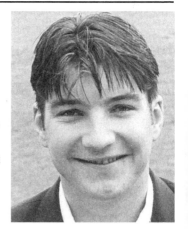

Name: Mark Edward Harvey
Role: Right-hand bat, off-spin bowler
Born: 26 June 1974, Burnley, Lancs
Height: 5ft 9in **Weight:** 13st
Nickname: Harv, Vadge, Baz
County debut: 1994
1st-Class catches: 2
Parents: David and Wendy
Marital status: Single
Family links with cricket: Brother Jonathan spent four years as MCC young player and was professional for Greenmount CC in the Bolton League, 'father, David, is still playing local club cricket, 50 n.o.'
Education: Worsthorne County Primary; Habergham High School, Burnley; Loughborough University
Qualifications: 8 GCSEs, 3 A-levels, BSc Honours in PE Sports Management and Recreational Management
Career outside cricket: 'None yet!'
Overseas tours: England U19 to India 1992-93

Overseas teams played for: Queanbeyan CC, Canberra, Australia 1996-97
Cricketers particularly admired: 'David Gower (someone who makes it all look so easy), Dean Jones (exciting both batting and fielding), Mudassar Nazar (an admired professional for many years at Burnley), Les "The Whirlwind" Seal'
Young players to look out for: Andrew Flintoff
Other sports followed: Football (Manchester United, Burnley and Oxford United)
Relaxations: 'I'd love to say that watching Burnley FC was a relaxation, but unfortunately it's very frustrating, drinking at the Crooked Billet, Workthorne with father and brother'
Extras: Captained England U17, represented England at U17, U18 and U19 levels, represented Lancashire from U13 to U19. In an attempt to produce a result in a rain-affected 2nd XI match v Yorkshire at Todmorden, he bowled an over costing 108 runs from 18 no-balls, all of which went for four without hitting the bat. 'This allowed both teams to contrive a game in five rather than 50 minutes. A claim to fame which earns me never-ending stick at the local pub!' Played for Combined Universities in 1995
Opinions on cricket: 'The increasing introduction of top class, ex-Test playing coaches, and the like, whether foreign or British, can only be a good thing, allowing young players such as myself to benefit from their vast knowledge and experience. Different methods and approaches can only serve to widen our horizons of the game.'
Best batting: 25 Lancashire v Gloucestershire, Bristol 1997

1997 Season

	M	Inns	NO	Runs	HS	Avge	100s	50s	Ct	St	O	M	Runs	Wkts	Avge	Best	5wI	10wM
Test																		
All First	2	4	0	49	25	12.25	-	-	1	-								
1-day Int																		
NatWest	1	1	0	86	86	86.00	-	1	1	-								
B & H																			
Sunday	2	1	0	8	8	8.00	-	-	-	-								

Career Performances

	M	Inns	NO	Runs	HS	Avge	100s	50s	Ct	St	Balls	Runs	Wkts	Avge	Best	5wI	10wM
Test																	
All First	5	8	0	116	25	14.50	-	-	2	-							
1-day Int																	
NatWest	1	1	0	86	86	86.00	-	1	1	-							
B & H	4	4	0	9	5	2.25	-	-	3	-							
Sunday	2	1	0	8	8	8.00	-	-	-	-							

HAYDEN, M. L.   Hampshire

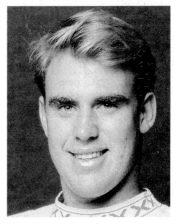

Name: Matthew Lawrence Hayden
Role: Left-hand bat, right-arm medium bowler
Born: 29 October 1971, Kingaroy, Australia
County debut: 1997
Test debut: 1993-94
Tests: 7
One-Day Internationals: 13
1000 runs in a season: 1
1st-Class 50s: 39
1st-Class 100s: 28
1st-Class 200s: 3
1st-Class catches: 92
One-Day 100s: 3
Place in batting averages: 14th av. 53.55
Strike rate: 66.00 (career 92.75)
Overseas tours: Australia to England 1993, to South Africa 1993-94, 1996-97
Overseas teams played for: Queensland 1991-1997
Extras: Scored 149 on his first-class debut for Queensland against South Australia and went on to become the youngest Australian to score 1000 runs in his first season. Played in his first Test match in South Africa in 1994 after a sequence of impressive run-scoring in the Sheffield Shield forced his inclusion in the tour squad, but has failed to hold down a regular place in the Test side. Was given another chance after opener Matthew Elliott was injured and played in the Test series against West Indies in 1996-97 and solid performances warranted his inclusion in the squad to tour South Africa. Has played league cricket for Greenmount in the Bolton League, breaking the club record with an aggregate of 1483 runs
Best batting: 235* Hampshire v Warwickshire, Southampton 1997
Best bowling: 2-17 Hampshire v Sussex, Southampton 1997

1997 Season

	M	Inns	NO	Runs	HS	Avge	100s	50s	Ct	St	O	M	Runs	Wkts	Avge	Best	5wI	10wM
Test																		
All First	17	30	3	1446	235 *	53.55	4	7	13	-	33	0	166	3	55.33	2-17	-	-
1-day Int																		
NatWest	2	2	0	110	90	55.00	-	1	1	-								
B & H	5	5	1	216	120 *	54.00	1	-	3	-	9	0	45	2	22.50	2-45	-	
Sunday	16	15	0	654	118	43.60	2	3	7	-	13.3	0	78	2	39.00	2-38	-	

	M	Inns	NO	Runs	HS	Avge	100s	50s	Ct	St	Balls	Runs	Wkts	Avge	Best	5wI	10wM
Test	7	12	0	261	125	21.75	1	-	8	-							
All First	108	194	23	9280	235 *	54.26	28	39	92	-	371	282	4	70.50	2-17	-	-
1-day Int	13	12	1	286	67	26.00	-	2	4	-							
NatWest	2	2	0	110	90	55.00	-	1	1	-							
B & H	5	5	1	216	120 *	54.00	1	-	3	-	54	45	2	22.50	2-45	-	
Sunday	16	15	0	654	118	43.60	2	3	7	-	81	78	2	39.00	2-38	-	

HAYHURST, A. N. Derbyshire

Name: Andrew Neil Hayhurst
Role: Right-hand bat, right-arm
medium bowler
Born: 23 November 1962, Davyhulme,
Manchester
Height: 6ft **Weight:** 13st 10lbs
Nickname: Bull
County debut: 1985 (Lancashire), 1990
(Somerset), 1997 (Derbyshire)
County cap: 1990 (Somerset)
1000 runs in a season: 3
1st-Class 50s: 40
1st-Class 100s: 14
1st-Class catches: 56
One-Day 5 w. in innings: 1
Place in batting averages: (1996 240th av.
18.66)
Strike rate: 54.00 (career 81.45)
Parents: William and Margaret
Wife and date of marriage: April, 17 February 1990
Children: Myles William David, 30 March 1992
Family links with cricket: Father played club cricket for Worsley. 'We played in the
same side.' Grew up in house lived in by Tyldesley brothers (Lancashire and England)
Education: St Mark's Primary School; Worsley Wardley High; Eccles Sixth Form
College; Leeds Polytechnic (Carnegie College of PE)
Qualifications: 8 O-levels, 4 A-levels, BA (Hons) Human Movement, advanced
cricket coach, qualified financial consultant
Overseas tours: Lancashire to Jamaica 1986-87 and 1987-88, to Zimbabwe 1988-89;
Somerset to Bahamas 1989-90
Overseas teams played for: South Launceston, Tasmania 1987-89
Cricketers particularly admired: Dermot Reeve, Jimmy Cook, Clive Lloyd, Jack

Bond, Andy Caddick

Young players to look out for: Vikram Solanki, Andy Harris

Other sports followed: Football (Manchester United) and rugby league (Salford)

Relaxations: Animals and statistics

Extras: Made 110* on his first-class debut for Somerset and was appointed captain for the 1994 season. His first scoring shot in first-class cricket was a six off the bowling of Kapil Dev whilst opening the batting. Was released by Somerset at the end of the 1996 season and joined Derbyshire for the 1997 season. Has been appointed Director of Cricket at Derbyshire

Opinions on cricket: 'The huge gap between 2nd XI and 1st XI needs to be closed. The players are there, it's just the attitude. Four-day cricket has worked.'

Best batting: 172* Somerset v Gloucestershire, Bath 1991

Best bowling: 4-27 Lancashire v Middlesex, Old Trafford 1987

1997 Season

	M	Inns	NO	Runs	HS	Avge	100s	50s	Ct	St	O	M	Runs	Wkts	Avge	Best	5wI	10wM
Test																		
All First	2	2	0	6	6	3.00	-	-	3	-	9	2	30	1	30.00	1-12	-	-
1-day Int																		
NatWest																		
B & H																		
Sunday	2	2	0	20	12	10.00	-	-	-	-	7	0	37	2	18.50	2-37	-	

Career Performances

	M	Inns	NO	Runs	HS	Avge	100s	50s	Ct	St	Balls	Runs	Wkts	Avge	Best	5wI	10wM
Test																	
All First	166	265	34	7825	172*	33.87	14	40	56	-	8960	4991	110	45.37	4-27	-	-
1-day Int																	
NatWest	22	20	4	588	91*	36.75	-	3	4	-	809	543	24	22.62	5-60	1	
B & H	34	30	5	736	95	29.44	-	6	3	-	1114	770	32	24.06	4-50	-	
Sunday	121	103	24	2253	84	28.51	-	12	16	-	2958	2607	74	35.22	4-37	-	

HAYNES, G. R.   Worcestershire

Name: Gavin Richard Haynes

Role: Right-hand bat, right-arm
medium bowler

Born: 29 September 1969, Stourbridge

Height: 5ft 10in **Weight:** 12st

Nickname: Splash

County debut: 1991

County cap: 1994

1000 runs in a season: 1
1st-Class 50s: 19
1st-Class 100s: 3
1st-Class catches: 37
One-Day 100s: 1
Place in batting averages: 85th av. 36.09
Place in bowling averages: 57th av. 28.22
Strike rate: 55.58 (career 76.23)
Parents: Nicholas and Dorothy
Wife and date of marriage: Joanne, 25
October 1997
Family links with cricket: Father played
club cricket and manages Worcester U14
side. Cousin Peter Haynes played very good
club cricket
Education: Gigmill Junior School; High Park
Comprehensive; King Edward VI College,
Stourbridge
Qualifications: 5 O-levels, 1 A-level, NCA advanced coaching award
Overseas tours: Worcestershire to Zimbabwe, to South Africa. to Guernsey 1997
Overseas teams played for: Sunrise Sports Club, Zimbabwe 1989-90
Cricketers particularly admired: Ian Botham, Graham Dilley, Graham Gooch,
Malcolm Marshall, Viv Richards, Graeme Hick
Young players to look out for: 'The good ones'
Other sports followed: Football (Aston Villa), golf
Injuries: Sore facet joint, out for two weeks
Relaxations: Playing golf, watching television
Extras: Represented England Schools U15. Worcestershire Uncapped Player of the Year
1993
Opinions on cricket: 'We must have two leagues, but whilst the power in English
cricket stays as it is nothing will change.'
Best batting: 158 Worcestershire v Kent, Worcester 1993
Best bowling: 4-33 Worcestershire v Kent, Worcester 1995

1997 Season

	M	Inns	NO	Runs	HS	Avge	100s	50s	Ct	St	O	M	Runs	Wkts	Avge	Best	5wI	10wM
Test																		
All First	17	25	3	794	70	36.09	-	6	5	-	287.1	68	875	31	28.22	3-46	-	-
1-day Int																		
NatWest	1	1	0	32	32	32.00	-	-	1	-	9	2	18	1	18.00	1-18	-	
B & H	5	5	0	112	39	22.40	-	-	-	-	46	9	160	3	53.33	1-15	-	
Sunday	13	12	3	355	64 *	39.44	-	1	1	-	72	3	326	15	21.73	4-13	-	

	M	Inns	NO	Runs	HS	Avge	100s	50s	Ct	St	Balls	Runs	Wkts	Avge	Best	5wI	10wM
Test																	
All First	80	122	9	3464	158	30.65	3	19	37	-	5108	2558	67	38.17	4-33	-	-
1-day Int																	
NatWest	9	7	1	309	116 *	51.50	1	1	3	-	318	204	5	40.80	1-9	-	
B & H	17	15	3	303	65	25.25	-	1	4	-	719	423	15	28.20	3-17	-	
Sunday	63	52	6	1141	83	24.80	-	3	17	-	1810	1246	45	27.68	4-13	-	

HAYNES, J. J.   Lancashire

Name: Jamie Jonathan Haynes
Role: Right-hand bat, wicket-keeper
Born: 5 July 1974, Bristol
Height: 5ft 10in **Weight:** 12st 2lbs
Nickname: Thrush, Amos, Quito, Stinky
County debut: 1996
1st-Class catches: 12
1st-Class stumpings: 1
Parents: Steve Haynes and Moiya Ford
Marital status: Single
Family links with cricket: Father and uncle
both played for Gloucestershire CCC
Education: Garran Primary; St Edmunds
College; University of Canberra, Australia
Qualifications: Year 12 Certificate.
'Currently studying for a BA in sports media'
Career outside cricket: Bar work
Off-season: 'Holiday in Australia to catch up
with family and friends'
Overseas teams played for: Tuggeranong Valley CC, Australia 1995-96; South
Canberra CC, Australia 1996-97
Cricketers particularly admired: Graham Lloyd, Warren Hegg, Jack Russell, Alan
Knott, Alec Stewart, Steve Titchard
Young players to look out for: Chris Schofield, Steve Titchard
Other sports followed: Football (Manchester United, Burnley) and Australian rules
Injuries: Chipped eye socket, out for two weeks
Relaxations: Golf, music, movies, socialising in old-fashioned pubs
Opinions on cricket: 'Not enough consideration is given to wicketkeepers in relation
to man of the match awards.'
Best batting: 21 Lancashire v Yorkshire, Headingley 1997

1997 Season

	M	Inns	NO	Runs	HS	Avge	100s	50s	Ct	St	O	M	Runs	Wkts	Avge	Best	5wI	10wM
Test																		
All First	2	3	0	41	21	13.66	-	-	12	-								
1-day Int																		
NatWest																		
B & H																		
Sunday																		

Career Performances

	M	Inns	NO	Runs	HS	Avge	100s	50s	Ct	St	Balls	Runs	Wkts	Avge	Best	5wI	10wM
Test																	
All First	3	5	0	67	21	13.40	-	-	12	1							
1-day Int																	
NatWest																	
B & H																	
Sunday	1	0	0	0	0	-	-	-	1	-							

HAYWOOD, G. R. Sussex

Name: Giles Ronald Haywood
Role: Left-hand bat, right-arm medium bowler
Born: 8 September 1979, Chichester
Height: 6ft 1in **Weight:** 12st
County debut: 1996 (one-day)
Parents: Ronald and Shirley
Family links with cricket: Father and brother currently play club cricket
Education: The Prebendal, Chichester; Lancing College
Qualifications: 11 GCSEs
Career outside cricket: Student
Overseas tours: Sussex U19 to Sri Lanka 1995
Cricketers particularly admired: David Gower, Sachin Tendulkar
Young players to look out for: Danny Law, Russell Staves
Other sports followed: Football (Bognor Regis Town FC), hockey and squash
Relaxations: Listening to music, relaxing at home and going out for a drink with friends

Extras: Played for ESCA U15, England U16. Made Sunday League debut at the age of 17

Opinions on cricket: 'Higher player salaries would mean more competition in county sides and ultimately a higher standard of cricket.'

1997 Season (did not make any first-class or one-day appearances)

Career Performances

	M	Inns	NO	Runs	HS	Avge	100s	50s	Ct	St	Balls	Runs	Wkts	Avge	Best	5wI	10wM
Test																	
All First																	
1-day Int																	
NatWest																	
B & H																	
Sunday	1	1	0	4	4	4.00	-	-	-	-							

HEADLEY, D. W. Kent

Name: Dean Warren Headley
Role: Right-hand bat, right-arm medium-fast bowler
Born: 27 January 1970, Stourbridge
Height: 6ft 5in **Weight:** 13st 10lbs
Nickname: Frog
County debut: 1991 (Middlesex), 1993 (Kent)
County cap: 1993 (Kent)
Test debut: 1997
Tests: 3
One-Day Internationals: 3
50 wickets in a season: 1
1st-Class 50s: 4
1st-Class 5 w. in innings: 18
1st-Class 10 w. in match: 2
1st-Class catches: 38
One-Day 5 w. in innings: 2

Place in batting averages: 266th av. 13.83 (1996 237th av. 19.46)
Place in bowling averages: 75th av. 30.84 (1996 40th av. 27.19)
Strike rate: 55.47 (career 56.94)
Parents: Ronald George Alphonso and Gail
Marital status: Single

Family links with cricket: Grandfather (George) and father (Ron) both played for West Indies
Education: Gigmill Junior School; Oldswinford Hospital School; Royal Grammar School, Worcester
Qualifications: 7 O-levels
Career outside cricket: 'None yet'
Off-season: England to Sharjah and West Indies
Overseas tours: RGS Worcester to Zimbabwe 1988; Christians in Sport to India 1989-90; England A to Pakistan 1995-96, to Australia 1996-97; England to Sharjah 1997-98, to West Indies 1997-98
Overseas teams played for: Melbourne, Jamaica 1991-92; Primrose CC, South Africa 1993-95
Cricketers particularly admired: Malcolm Marshall, 'my dad', Ian Botham, Gavin O'Hanlon, Adam Patrick, Min Patel
Young players to look out for: Matthew Walker, Owais Shah, Andrew Harris
Other sports followed: 'Have a go at anything'
Relaxations: Socialising, watching films, playing golf and eating out
Extras: Took five wickets on debut including a wicket with his first ball in Championship cricket. Played for Worcestershire 2nd XI 1988-89. Left Middlesex at the end of 1992 season and signed for Kent. Called up as a replacement for the England A tour to Pakistan. Took a record-breaking three hat-tricks during the summer of 1996. The third generation of his family to play Test cricket, both his father and grandfather played Test cricket for West Indies
Opinions on cricket: 'I am a bowler, I have none.'
Best batting: 91 Middlesex v Leicestershire, Leicester 1992
Best bowling: 8-98 Kent v Derbyshire, Derby 1996

1997 Season

	M	Inns	NO	Runs	HS	Avge	100s	50s	Ct	St	O	M	Runs	Wkts	Avge	Best	5wI	10wM
Test	3	6	2	39	22	9.75	-	-	1	-	131.2	20	444	16	27.75	4-72	-	-
All First	12	17	5	166	40	13.83	-	-	3	-	425.2	75	1419	46	30.84	5-92	1	-
1-day Int	1	0	0	0	0	-	-	-	-	-	8	0	36	1	36.00	1-36	-	
NatWest	1	1	0	1	1	1.00	-	-	-	-	12	1	31	3	10.33	3-31	-	
B & H	8	1	1	3	3 *	-	-	-	1	-	69	7	294	8	36.75	3-36	-	
Sunday	8	5	3	12	7 *	6.00	-	-	1	-	59	6	220	12	18.33	4-27	-	

Career Performances

	M	Inns	NO	Runs	HS	Avge	100s	50s	Ct	St	Balls	Runs	Wkts	Avge	Best	5wl	10wM
Test	3	6	2	39	22	9.75	-	-	1	-	788	444	16	27.75	4-72	-	-
All First	98	127	33	1655	91	17.60	-	4	38	-	18110	9419	318	29.61	8-98	18	2
1-day Int	3	1	1	3	3 *	-	-	-	-	-	150	120	1	120.00	1-36	-	
NatWest	12	7	5	51	24 *	25.50	-	-	-	-	733	454	21	21.61	5-20	1	
B & H	23	8	3	60	26	12.00	-	-	5	-	1301	859	25	34.36	4-19	-	
Sunday	74	25	14	129	29 *	11.72	-	-	15	-	3131	2477	92	26.92	6-42	1	

HEGG, W. K.   Lancashire

Name: Warren Kevin Hegg
Role: Right-hand bat, wicket-keeper
Born: 23 February 1968, Radcliffe, Lancashire
Height: 5ft 9in **Weight:** 12st 10lbs
Nickname: Chucky
County debut: 1986
1st-Class 50s: 31
1st-Class 100s: 4
1st-Class catches: 536
1st-Class stumpings: 63
Place in batting averages: 159th av. 25.33 (1996 91st av. 37.52)
Parents: Kevin and Glenda
Wife and date of marriage: Joanne, 29 October 1994
Family links with cricket: Father and brother Martin play in local leagues

Education: Unsworth High School; Stand College, Whitefield
Qualifications: 5 O-levels, 7 CSEs, qualified coach
Overseas tours: NCA North U19 to Bermuda 1985; England YC to Sri Lanka 1986-87, to Australia (Youth World Cup) 1987-88; England A to Pakistan and Sri Lanka 1990-91, to Australia 1996-97
Overseas teams played for: Sheffield, Tasmania 1988-90, 1992-93
Cricketers particularly admired: Ian Botham, Alan Knott, Bob Taylor, Gehan Mendis
Young players to look out for: Paddy McKeown, Richard Green, Peter Martin, Ian Austin
Other sports followed: Football (Manchester United), rugby league (Wigan), golf, fishing, Aussie rules football
Relaxations: Listening to music, walking on my own, sleep, and 'beating Oscar and Digger at golf'
Extras: First player to make county debut from Lytham CC. Youngest player for 30 years to score a century for Lancashire, 130 v Northamptonshire in his fourth first-class game. Eleven victims in match v Derbyshire, equalling world record. Wombwell Cricket Lovers' Society joint Wicket-keeper of the Year 1993
Best batting: 134 Lancashire v Leicestershire, Old Trafford 1996

---

39. Who won the 1997 Village Championship?

O vodafone

	M	Inns	NO	Runs	HS	Avge	100s	50s	Ct	St	O	M	Runs	Wkts	Avge	Best	5wI	10wM
Test																		
All First	17	23	5	456	77 *	25.33	-	5	37	2								
1-day Int																		
NatWest	2	1	0	37	37	37.00	-	-	2	-								
B & H	5	5	2	83	54 *	27.66	-	1	5	-								
Sunday	15	11	3	141	31 *	17.62	-	-	18	8								

Career Performances

	M	Inns	NO	Runs	HS	Avge	100s	50s	Ct	St	Balls	Runs	Wkts	Avge	Best	5wI	10wM
Test																	
All First	223	325	63	6745	134	25.74	4	31	536	63	6	7	0	-	-	-	-
1-day Int																	
NatWest	27	16	1	288	37	19.20	-	-	35	2							
B & H	54	24	10	371	81	26.50	-	2	75	5							
Sunday	159	92	42	1120	52	22.40	-	1	160	24							

HEMP, D. L.   Warwickshire

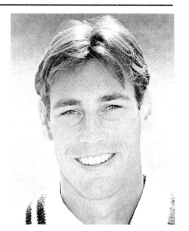

Name: David Lloyd Hemp
Role: Left-hand bat, right-arm medium bowler
Born: 15 November 1970, Bermuda
Height: 6ft **Weight:** 12st 7lbs
Nickname: Hempy, Soc, Mad Dog
County debut: 1991
1000 runs in a season: 2
1st-Class 50s: 27
1st-Class 100s: 9
1st-Class catches: 57
One-Day 100s: 3
Place in batting averages: 56th av. 41.00 (1996 96th av. 36.81)
Strike rate: (career 51.60)
Parents: Clive and Elisabeth
Wife and date of marriage: Angie, 16 March 1996
Family links with cricket: Father plays for Ffynone, brother Tim plays for Swansea and Wales Minor Counties, sister Charlotte played for Parklands Junior School
Education: Olchfa Comprehensive School; Millfield School; West Glamorgan

Institute of Further Education
Qualifications: 5 O-levels, 2 A-levels, NCA coaching award
Career outside cricket: Working in accountancy firm
Overseas tours: Welsh Schools U19 to Australia 1986-87; Welsh Cricket Association U18 to Barbados 1987; Glamorgan to Trinidad 1990; South Wales Cricket Association to New Zealand and Australia 1991-92; England A to India 1994-95
Overseas teams played for: Hirsh Crusaders, Durban, South Africa 1992-94, 1995-96
Cricketers particularly admired: Viv Richards, David Gower, Keith Arthurton, Mark Waugh
Other sports followed: Football (Swansea City)
Relaxations: Watching football and television, going to movies
Extras: Scored 258* for Wales v MCC 1991. In 1990 scored 104* and 101* for Welsh Schools U19 v Scottish Schools U19 and 120 and 102* v Irish Schools U19. Left Glamorgan at the end of the 1996 season and has joined Warwickshire on a three-year contract
Opinions on cricket: 'All 2nd XI games should be played on county grounds rather than club grounds as the quality of wickets is usually poorer at clubs, also they do not have such good facilities for covering wickets. If third umpires are going to be used in semi-finals and finals then they should be used in all the previous rounds. There is too much cricket being played.'
Best batting: 157 Glamorgan v Gloucestershire, Abergavenny 1995
Best bowling: 3-23 Glamorgan v South Africa A, Cardiff 1996

1997 Season

	M	Inns	NO	Runs	HS	Avge	100s	50s	Ct	St	O	M	Runs	Wkts	Avge	Best	5wI	10wM
Test																		
All First	18	31	4	1107	138	41.00	3	5	9	-	23	4	120	0	-	-	-	-
1-day Int																		
NatWest	5	5	1	273	112	68.25	2	-	2	-								
B & H	6	6	0	59	23	9.83	-	-	-	-								
Sunday	17	17	4	370	70 *	28.46	-	2	7	-								

Career Performances

	M	Inns	NO	Runs	HS	Avge	100s	50s	Ct	St	Balls	Runs	Wkts	Avge	Best	5wI	10wM
Test																	
All First	94	164	16	4984	157	33.67	9	27	57	-	516	450	10	45.00	3-23	-	-
1-day Int																	
NatWest	11	10	1	435	112	48.33	2	1	3	-							
B & H	13	12	0	294	121	24.50	I	1	1								
Sunday	64	53	6	947	74	20.14	-	5	32	-	38	43	1	43.00	1-14	-	

HERZBERG, S.   Somerset

Name: Steven Herzberg
Role: Right-hand bat, off-spin bowler
Born: 25 May 1967, Carshalton, Surrey
Height: 6ft 4in **Weight:** 13st
Nickname: Hertzy
County debut: 1991 (Worcs), 1995 (Kent),
1997 (Somerset)
1st-Class 50s: 2
1st-Class 5 w. in innings: 1
1st-Class catches: 6
Place in bowling averages: 55th av. 28.10
Strike rate: 61.20 (career 75.91)
Parents: Louis and Brenda
Marital status: Single
Family links with cricket: 'Father keen
follower and a useful all-rounder in his day.

Mother invented the flipper'
Education: Claremont Primary School,
Perth, WA; Hollywood Senior High School,
Perth, WA; Curtin University, Perth, WA
Qualifications: Bachelor of Business (Marketing), Level 2 coach
Career outside cricket: Teaching physical education full time in Sydney
Overseas teams played for: Western Australia 1991-92; Tasmania 1993-94
Cricketers particularly admired: Steve Waugh, Mark Atkinson (Tasmania), Alistair
Storie
Young players to look out for: Mike Hussey (Western Australia), Graham Rose, Jo
Betsworth
Other sports followed: Golf, tennis
Injuries: Shoulder tear, three weeks without bowling. 'Emotional distress at never
getting a regular first team spot'
Relaxations: Music, reading, talking, being with friends and family
Extras: Has now played for five first-class teams. 'Took a wicket with my first ball
for Somerset'
Opinions on cricket: 'County cricket is an animal in itself. Players focus on
individual security rather than the team's goal. Australia has won the past five Ashes
series because players who represent them have passion and tremendous pride.
England can beat Australia if they focus on four-day cricket at county level and play
far less one-day cricket which distorts and disturbs cricketers' techniques.'
Best batting: 57* Western Australia v New South Wales, Sydney 1992-93
Best bowling: 5-33 Kent v Leicestershire, Canterbury 1995

1997 Season

	M	Inns	NO	Runs	HS	Avge	100s	50s	Ct	St	O	M	Runs	Wkts	Avge	Best	5wI	10wM
Test																		
All First	7	8	3	207	56	41.40	-	1	2	-	102	25	281	10	28.10	3-100	-	-
1-day Int																		
NatWest																		
B & H	1	0	0	0	0	-	-	-	-	-	3	0	20	0	-		-	-
Sunday	2	0	0	0	0	-	-	-	1	-	5	0	37	1	37.00	1-37	-	

Career Performances

	M	Inns	NO	Runs	HS	Avge	100s	50s	Ct	St	Balls	Runs	Wkts	Avge	Best	5wI	10wM
Test																	
All First	21	26	8	394	57 *	21.88	-	2	6	-	3568	1813	47	38.57	5-33	1	-
1-day Int																	
NatWest																	
B & H	1	0	0	0	0	-	-	-	-	-	18	20	0	-		-	-
Sunday	3	0	0	0	0	-	-	-	1	-	60	65	1	65.00	1-37	-	

HEWITT, J. P.   Middlesex

Name: James Peter Hewitt
Role: Left-hand bat, right-arm medium-fast bowler
Born: 26 February 1976, London
Height: 6ft 3in **Weight:** 12st 8lbs
Nickname: Hewiey
County debut: 1995 (one-day), 1996 (first-class)
50 wickets in a season: 1
1st-Class 50s: 2
1st-Class 5 w. in innings: 2
1st-Class catches: 11
Place in batting averages: 244th av. 15.52 (1996 172nd av. 28.36)
Place in bowling averages: 23rd av. 23.15 (1996 48th av. 28.27)
Strike rate: 43.70 (career 44.03)
Parents: Mr T.D. Hewitt and Mrs G.J. Underhay
Marital status: Single
Family links with cricket: Father played club cricket and had trials with Surrey. Grandfather played club cricket and had trials with Surrey

Education: Buckingham School, Hampton; Teddington School, Middlesex; Richmond College; Kingston College; City of Westminster College
Qualifications: GCSEs; City and Guilds Part I, II and III in Recreation and Leisure; GNVQ Leisure and Tourism; coaching awards in cricket intermediate and advanced; squash, basketball, hockey, gymnastics, badminton, football, volleyball and referee qualifications; Community Sports Leadership Award
Career outside cricket: Retail, cricket and coaching
Cricketers particularly admired: Richard Hadlee, David Gower, Curtly Ambrose, Dominic Cork, Richard Johnson, Philip Hudson
Other sports followed: Athletics ('represented South of England at cross-country'), football ('played for Chelsea Youth'), badminton, volleyball, rugby (Harlequins)
Relaxations: Watching and playing a number of sports and sports quiz programmes
Extras: 'I was invited back to my old school, Teddington, to present the sports awards to the pupils – I consider this to be an honour'
Opinions on cricket: 'I am pleased to see the injection of youth into the game at Test level as well as county. I think the young blood together with the more experienced players can only be good for the game.'
Best batting: 75 Middlesex v Essex, Chelmsford 1997
Best bowling: 6-14 Middlesex v Glamorgan, Cardiff 1997

1997 Season

	M	Inns	NO	Runs	HS	Avge	100s	50s	Ct	St	O	M	Runs	Wkts	Avge	Best	5wl	10wM
Test																		
All First	18	21	4	264	75	15.52	-	1	6	-	439	97	1393	60	23.21	6-14	2	-
1-day Int																		
NatWest	3	2	2	18	14 *	-	-	-	1	-	25	1	117	2	58.50	1-37	-	
B & H	4	4	0	22	14	5.50	-	-	1	-	35	1	178	4	44.50	2-49	-	
Sunday	14	6	2	69	32 *	17.25	-	-	2	-	103	1	435	17	25.58	2-24	-	

Career Performances

	M	Inns	NO	Runs	HS	Avge	100s	50s	Ct	St	Balls	Runs	Wkts	Avge	Best	5wl	10wM
Test																	
All First	28	36	8	576	75	20.57	-	2	11	-	3711	2074	84	24.69	6-14	2	-
1-day Int																	
NatWest	3	2	2	18	14 *	-	-	-	1	-	150	117	2	58.50	1-37	-	
B & H	4	4	0	22	14	5.50	-	-	1	-	210	178	4	44.50	2-49	-	
Sunday	27	13	4	118	32 *	13.11	-	-	8	-	999	737	29	25.41	3-26	-	

HEWSON, D. R.   Gloucestershire

Name: Dominic Robert Hewson
Role: Right-hand bat, right-arm
medium bowler
Born: 3 October 1974, Cheltenham
Height: 5ft 10in **Weight:** 13st
Nickname: Chopper, Popa, Con
County debut: 1996
1st-Class 50s: 3
1st-Class catches: 5
Place in batting averages: (1996 207th av.
23.72)
Parents: Robert and Julie
Marital status: Single
Children: Peter (aged 7); Debbie (aged 3)
Family links with cricket: Dad played for
Upper Fathergill CC near Chopperton
Education: Cheltenham College; University
of West of England
Qualifications: 10 GCSEs, 3 A-levels
Cricketers particularly admired: Jon Lewis, Jack Russell, Courtney Walsh, Mark
Snape
Young players to look out for: Jon Lewis, Dom Hewson, Matt Windows, Rob
Cunliffe, Andrew Symonds
Other sports followed: Rugby, ice hockey, Aussie rules, football
Relaxations: Seeing friends
Extras: Made debut for Gloucestershire 2nd XI in July 1993
Opinions on cricket: 'We play too much cricket and Australians should be banned.
Baseball-style fighting should be allowed.'
Best batting: 87 Gloucestershire v Hampshire, Southampton 1996

1997 Season

	M	Inns	NO	Runs	HS	Avge	100s	50s	Ct	St	O	M	Runs	Wkts	Avge	Best	5wI	10wM
Test																		
All First	3	4	0	56	42	14.00	-	-	3	-								
1-day Int																		
NatWest																		
B & H																		
Sunday	1	0	0	0	0	-	-	-	-	-	-							

	M	Inns	NO	Runs	HS	Avge	100s	50s	Ct	St	Balls	Runs	Wkts	Avge	Best	5wI	10wM
Test																	
All First	9	16	1	317	87	21.13	-	3	5	-							
1-day Int																	
NatWest																	
B & H																	
Sunday	2	1	0	3	3	3.00	-	-	-	-							

HIBBERT, A. J. E. Essex

Name: Andrew James Edward Hibbert
Role: Right-hand bat, right-arm
medium bowler
Born: 17 December 1974, Harold Wood,
Essex
Height: 6ft **Weight:** 13st 10lbs
Nickname: Buns, Hibby
County debut: 1995
1st-Class 50s: 1
1st-Class catches: 3
Parents: Tony and Thelma (both deceased)
Marital status: Single
Family links with cricket: 'Dad played club
cricket and Mum followed avidly'
Education: St Edward's C of E
Comprehensive, Romford
Qualifications: 8 GCSEs, NCA senior
coaching award
Off-season: Playing and coaching for
University of Newcastle, New South Wales, Australia
Overseas tours: England U18 to Denmark (International Youth Tournament) 1993
Overseas teams played for: University of Newcastle, New South Wales, Australia
1995-96, 1997-98
Cricketers particularly admired: Graham Thorpe, Graham Gooch, Stuart Law
Young players to look out for: Richard Clinton
Other sports followed: Golf, football (Tottenham Hotspur), snooker
Relaxations: Music 'would love to be a DJ'
Extras: Played for Essex from U14 upwards. *Daily Telegraph* (South) Batting Award
1990. Hartwell 2nd XI Player of the Year 1996. Awarded 2nd XI cap in 1996. Scored
607 runs at an average of 101.4 in Bain Hogg Trophy. Essex Cricket Society 2nd XI
Player of the Year in 1996

Opinions on cricket: 'Too many overs in a day. The England Test team is going in the right direction. All hotel rooms should be like the Mount Somerset in Taunton.'
Best batting: 85 Essex v Cambridge University, Fenner's 1996

1997 Season

	M	Inns	NO	Runs	HS	Avge	100s	50s	Ct	St	O	M	Runs	Wkts	Avge	Best	5wl	10wM
Test																		
All First	1	1	0	17	17	17.00	-	-	3	-	1	0	1	0	-	-	-	-
1-day Int																		
NatWest																		
B & H																		
Sunday																		

Career Performances

	M	Inns	NO	Runs	HS	Avge	100s	50s	Ct	St	Balls	Runs	Wkts	Avge	Best	5wl	10wM
Test																	
All First	4	7	1	151	85	25.16	-	1	3	-	6	1	0	-	-	-	-
1-day Int																	
NatWest																	
B & H																	
Sunday	6	6	2	45	25	11.25	-	-	1	-							

HICK, G. A. Worcestershire

Name: Graeme Ashley Hick
Role: Right-hand bat, off-spin bowler
Born: 23 May 1966, Salisbury, Rhodesia
Height: 6ft 3in **Weight:** 14st 7lbs
Nickname: Hicky, Ash
County debut: 1984
County cap: 1986
Test debut: 1991
Tests: 46
One-Day Internationals: 62
1000 runs in a season: 13
1st-Class 50s: 107
1st-Class 100s: 96
1st-Class 200s: 10
1st-Class 300s: 1
1st-Class 400s: 1
1st-Class 5 w. in innings: 5
1st-Class 10 w. in match: 1

1st-Class catches: 416
One-Day 100s: 21
Place in batting averages: 1st av. 69.27 (1996 53rd av. 44.46)
Strike rate: 128.66 (career 89.02)
Parents: John and Eve
Wife and date of marriage: Jackie, 5 October 1991
Children: Lauren Amy, 12 September 1992
Family links with cricket: Father has served on Zimbabwe Cricket Union Board of Control since 1984 and played representative cricket in Zimbabwe
Education: Banket Primary; Prince Edward Boys' High School, Zimbabwe
Qualifications: 4 O-levels, NCA coaching award
Off-season: England to Sharjah for the one-day competition, playing for Auckland and then going to the West Indies for the one-day series
Overseas tours: Zimbabwe to England (World Cup) 1983, to Sri Lanka 1983-84, to England 1985; England to New Zealand and Australia (World Cup) 1991-92, to India and Sri Lanka 1992-93, to West Indies 1993-94, to Australia 1994-95, to South Africa 1995-96, to India and Pakistan (World Cup) 1995-96, to Sharjah 1997-98, to West Indies 1997-98 (one-day series)
Overseas teams played for: Old Hararians, Zimbabwe 1982-90; Northern Districts, New Zealand 1987-89; Queensland, Australia 1990-91; Auckland 1997-98
Cricketers particularly admired: Duncan Fletcher (Zimbabwe captain) for approach and understanding of the game, David Houghton, Basil D'Oliveira
Other sports followed: Follows Liverpool FC, golf, tennis, squash, hockey
Relaxations: 'Leaning against Steve Rhodes at first-slip'
Extras: Made first century aged six for school team; youngest player participating in 1983 Prudential World Cup (aged 17); youngest player to represent Zimbabwe. Scored 1234 runs in Birmingham League and played for Worcestershire 2nd XI in 1984 – hitting six successive centuries. In 1986, at age 20, he became the youngest player to score 2000 runs in an English season. One of *Wisden*'s Five Cricketers of the Year 1986. In 1988 he made 405* v Somerset at Taunton, the highest individual score in England since 1895, and scored 1000 first-class runs by end of May, hitting a record 410 runs in April. In 1990 became youngest batsman ever to make 50 first-class centuries and scored 645 runs without being dismissed – a record for English cricket. Also in 1990 became the fastest to 10,000 runs in county cricket (179 innings). Qualified as an English player in 1991. Scored first Test century v India in Bombay 1992-93 and was England's leading batsman, bowler and fielder. Published *Hick 'n' Dilley Circus* and *A Champion's Diary*. Also played hockey for Zimbabwe. Finished third in the Whyte and Mackay batting ratings in 1995 and top of the first-class batting averages in 1997
Opinions on cricket: 'What a great game.'
Best batting: 405* Worcestershire v Somerset, Taunton 1988
Best bowling: 5-18 Worcestershire v Leicestershire, Worcester 1995

1997 Season

	M	Inns	NO	Runs	HS	Avge	100s	50s	Ct	St	O	M	Runs	Wkts	Avge	Best	5wI	10wM
Test																		
All First	18	28	6	1524	303 *	69.27	6	4	20	-	193	46	629	9	69.88	4-70	-	
1-day Int																		
NatWest	2	2	0	153	146	76.50	1	-	1	-	16.2	0	54	2	27.00	2-14	-	
B & H	5	5	0	89	40	17.80	-	-	-	-	27	0	139	3	46.33	1-26	-	
Sunday	16	16	2	549	119 *	39.21	1	1	7	-	48.4	0	251	9	27.88	2-12	-	

Career Performances

	M	Inns	NO	Runs	HS	Avge	100s	50s	Ct	St	Balls	Runs	Wkts	Avge	Best	5wI	10wM
Test	46	80	6	2672	178	36.10	4	15	62	-	2973	1247	22	56.68	4-126	-	-
All First	346	565	59	28473	405 *	56.27	96	107	416	-	18695	9218	210	43.89	5-18	5	1
1-day Int	62	61	7	2105	105 *	38.98	2	16	32	-	840	696	18	38.66	3-41	-	
NatWest	35	35	6	1532	172 *	52.82	4	8	19	-	1193	716	22	32.54	4-54	-	
B & H	58	57	11	2589	127 *	56.28	7	16	34	-	732	562	12	46.83	3-36	-	
Sunday	168	162	30	6128	130	46.42	8	46	44	-	2403	2050	74	27.70	4-21	-	

HINDSON, J. E.   Nottinghamshire

Name: James Edward Hindson
Role: Right-hand bat, slow left-arm bowler
Born: 13 September 1973, Huddersfield, Yorkshire
Height: 6ft 1in **Weight:** 12st 4lbs
Nickname: Nugget, Gerrard, Cyril
County debut: 1992
50 wickets in a season: 1
1st-Class 50s: 1
1st-Class 5 w. in innings: 7
1st-Class 10 w. in match: 2
1st-Class catches: 14
Place in bowling averages: 39th av. 26.09
Strike rate: 52.72 (career 62.65)
Parents: Robert and Gloria
Marital status: Single
Family links with cricket: Both brothers play
Education: St Peter's Primary School, East Bridgford; Toot Hill Comprehensive School, Bingham
Qualifications: 10 GCSEs, 3 A-levels, senior cricket coach
Off-season: Coaching at Trent Bridge

Overseas tours: England U19 to India 1992-93
Overseas teams played for: Lancaster Park, Christchurch, New Zealand 1995-96
Cricketers particularly admired: Andy Afford, Courtney Walsh
Young players to look out for: Guy Welton
Other sports followed: Ice hockey (Nottingham Panthers), football (Notts County)
Injuries: Dislocated spinning finger, bruised hand, out for a total of five weeks
Relaxations: 'I enjoy dot balls'
Extras: Took five wickets on first-class debut (eight in the match) v Cambridge University. Converted from right-arm to left-arm bowler at age six, still throws right-handed and bowled left-arm medium until 15 years old. Received 2nd team cap at end of 1993 season
Opinions on cricket: 'Free admission for four-day cricket.'
Best batting: 53* Nottinghamshire v Oxford University, The Parks 1995
Best bowling: 5-42 Nottinghamshire v Cambridge University, Trent Bridge 1992

1997 Season

	M	Inns	NO	Runs	HS	Avge	100s	50s	Ct	St	O	M	Runs	Wkts	Avge	Best	5wI	10wM
Test																		
All First	3	4	2	54	42 *	27.00	-	-	2	-	96.4	24	287	11	26.09	4-28	-	-
1-day Int																		
NatWest	1	0	0	0	0	-	-	-	-	-	5	0	37	0	-		-	-
B & H																		
Sunday	1	1	1	3	3 *	-	-	-	-	-								

Career Performances

	M	Inns	NO	Runs	HS	Avge	100s	50s	Ct	St	Balls	Runs	Wkts	Avge	Best	5wI	10wM
Test																	
All First	28	36	7	384	53 *	13.24	-	1	14	-	5827	3045	93	32.74	5-42	7	2
1-day Int																	
NatWest	3	1	1	16	16 *	-	-	-	-	-	150	120	2	60.00	2-57	-	
B & H	1	1	1	41	41 *	-	-	-	-	-	60	69	1	69.00	1-69	-	
Sunday	21	8	4	61	21	15.25	-	-	5	-	768	639	16	39.93	4-19	-	

HOCKLEY, J. B.   Kent

Name: James Bernard Hockley
Role: Right-hand bat, off-spin bowler
Born: 16 April 1979, Beckenham
Height: 6ft 2in **Weight:** 13st
Nickname: Hockers, Ice
County debut: No first-team appearance
Parents: Bernard and Joan
Marital status: Single
Family links with cricket: None
Education: Churchfields Primary School,
Beckenham; Kelsey Park School, Beckenham
Qualifications: 7 GCSEs, NCA coaching
award
Career outside cricket: Working for Legal
Aid Board
Off-season: 'Hope to play cricket abroad'
Cricketers particularly admired: Ian
Botham, Carl Hooper, Neil Mobey, Peter
Gouch, David Pask
Other sports followed: Football (Arsenal), tennis, golf, snooker, rugby and squash
Relaxations: Playing golf and snooker. Listening to music
Extras: AKCL Player of the Year Award in 1995. Equalled Trevor Ward's Kent U15
batting record with a total of 1,000 runs in the season. Kent Schools Player of the Year
in 1996
Opinions on cricket: 'The 2nd XI Championship should be played over four days, to
give the younger players the experience of playing the longer game.'

HODGSON, T. P.   Essex

Name: Timothy Philip Hodgson
Role: Left-hand bat
Born: 27 March 1975, Guildford
Height: 5ft 10in **Weight:** 12st
Nickname: TP, Wiggy, Hodge
County debut: 1996 (one-day), 1997 (first-class)
Place in batting averages: 239th av. 16.83
Parents: Simon and Victoria
Marital status: Single
Family links with cricket: 'Dad bowls leg-spin off 24 yards. Brother Jamie played for

Cambridge University, Mark for Surrey 2nds and Charlie for England Schools U19'

Education: Milbourne Lodge, Esher; Wellington College, Berkshire; Durham University

Qualifications: GCSEs, A-levels, 2:2 in Sociology

Off-season: Playing in Sydney

Overseas tours: Wellington College to South Africa; Durham University to Vienna for European Indoor Cricket Championships

Cricketers particularly admired: Graham Gooch, Stuart Law

Young players to look out for: Graham Napier

Other sports followed: Football (Southampton FC and Woking FC) and golf

Relaxations: Watching or playing most sports, spending time at home

Extras: Highest first wicket partnership in second team (366). Played Surrey U12 to U19 and several second team games. Member of Wellington Cricketer Cup winning side in 1995. Member of Durham University's UAU winning side in 1995 and 1997. Scored the highest ever score on 'The Turf'(Wellington school ground) with 205 not out. Played for British Universities XI in 1997

Opinions on cricket: 'Durham University should be granted first-class status and never again be subjected to the traumas of playing Hull University away (and should never have a northerner as their captain!).'

Best batting: 44 Essex v Nottinghamshire, Worksop 1997

1997 Season

	M	Inns	NO	Runs	HS	Avge	100s	50s	Ct	St	O	M	Runs	Wkts	Avge	Best	5wl	10wM
Test																		
All First	3	6	0	101	44	16.83	-	-	-	-								
1-day Int																		
NatWest	1	1	0	2	2	2.00	-	-	-	-								
B & H	5	5	0	237	113	47.40	1	1	2	-								
Sunday	1	1	0	12	12	12.00	-	-	-	-								

40. Who, to date, has the best batting record as England captain?

Career Performances

	M	Inns	NO	Runs	HS	Avge	100s	50s	Ct	St	Balls	Runs	Wkts	Avge	Best	5wl	10wM
Test																	
All First	3	6	0	101	44	16.83	-	-	-	-							
1-day Int																	
NatWest	1	1	0	2	2	2.00	-	-	-	-							
B & H	5	5	0	237	113	47.40	1	1	2	-							
Sunday	5	4	0	39	21	9.75	-	-	-	-							

HOGGARD, M. J. Yorkshire

Name: Matthew James Hoggard
Role: Right-hand bat, right-arm fast bowler
Born: 31 December 1976, Leeds
Height: 6ft 2in **Weight:** 13st 7lbs
Nickname: Ming
County debut: 1996
Strike rate: 81.00 (career 84.00)
Parents: John and Margaret
Marital status: Single
Education: Pudsey Grangefield; Pudsey
Grangefield Sixth Form
Qualifications: GCSEs and A-levels
Off-season: 'Sleeping'
Overseas tours: England U19 to Zimbabwe
1995-96
Overseas teams played for: Johannesburg
Pirates 1995-97
Cricketers particularly admired: Richard
Thorpe, Chris Simpson

Other sports followed: Rugby league (Leeds), football, athletics, rugby
Injuries: Groin strain, missed eight weeks
Relaxations: 'Sleeping'
Extras: Joined England U19 tour to Zimbabwe as a replacement in 1995-96
Opinions on cricket: 'More day/night games and one-day games and less four-day cricket.'
Best batting: 10 Yorkshire v South Africa A, Headingley 1996
Best bowling: 1-41 Yorkshire v South Africa A, Headingley 1996

1997 Season

	M	Inns	NO	Runs	HS	Avge	100s	50s	Ct	St	O	M	Runs	Wkts	Avge	Best	5wI	10wM
Test																		
All First	1	2	1	2	1*	2.00	-	-	-	-	27	4	155	2	77.50	1-45	-	-
1-day Int																		
NatWest																		
B & H																		
Sunday																		

Career Performances

	M	Inns	NO	Runs	HS	Avge	100s	50s	Ct	St	Balls	Runs	Wkts	Avge	Best	5wI	10wM
Test																		
All First	2	3	1	12	10	6.00	-	-	-	-	252	196	3	65.33	1-41	-	-
1-day Int																		
NatWest																		
B & H																		
Sunday																		

HOLLIOAKE, A. J. Surrey

Name: Adam John Hollioake
Role: Right-hand bat, right-arm
fast-medium bowler, county captain
Born: 5 September 1971, Melbourne,
Australia
Height: 5ft 11in **Weight:** 13st 4lbs
Nickname: Smokey, Smokin' Joe, Wolf,
Rock, Rambo, Holly, Strong Dance,
Millionaire, Oaky, The Oak, Hokey Cokey,
Abo, Bong, Stumpy, Raj Maru, Gatt, Judgy
County debut: 1992 (one-day),
1993 (first-class)
County cap: 1995
Test debut: 1997
Tests: 2
One-Day Internationals: 5
1000 runs in a season: 2
1st-Class 50s: 28
1st-Class 100s: 11
1st-Class catches: 63
Place in batting average: 78th av. 37.12 (1996 5th av. 66.17)
Place in bowling averages: 73rd av. 30.53 (1996 156th av. 66.08)

Strike rate: 53.06 (career 73.37)
Parents: John and Daria
Marital status: Single
Family links with cricket: 'Brother Ben tries to play but is far too skinny to really progress any further'
Education: St Joseph's College, Sydney; St Patrick's College, Ballarat, Australia; St George's School, Weybridge; Surrey Tutorial College, Guildford
Qualifications: 'Some GCSEs and A-levels'
Off-season: Captaining England in one-day tournament in Sharjah and then going on to tour West Indies
Overseas tours: School trip to Zimbabwe; Surrey YC to Australia; England YC to New Zealand 1990-91; England A to Australia 1996-97; England to Sharjah 1997-98, to West Indies 1997-98
Overseas teams played for: Fremantle, Western Australia 1990-91; North Shore, Sydney 1992-93; Geelong, Victoria; North Perth, Western Australia 1995-97
Cricketers particularly admired: Steve Waugh, 'anyone who gives 100 per cent'
Young players to look out for: Alex Tudor
Other sports followed: Rugby, boxing, Aussie rules football, American football, 'chess and mind games'
Relaxations: 'Spending time with a gorgeous little Indon'
Extras: Played rugby for London Counties, Middlesex and South of England as well as having a trial for England U18. Scored a century on first-class debut against Derbyshire. Surrey Young Player of the Year 1993. Fastest ever one-day 50 – in 15 balls v Yorkshire. Surrey Supporters' Player of the Year 1996 and Surrey Players' Player of the Year 1996. Captained the England A side on their 1996-97 tour to Australia. His 39 wickets in the Sunday league in 1996 was a record for the competition. Man of the Match in the first One-Day International against Australia at Headingley in 1997. Along with brother Ben became the first brothers to make their England Test debut together this century at the fifth Test against Australia at Trent Bridge. Captained England in the 1997 Hong Kong Sixes tournament in which England finished runners-up to Pakistan
Opinions on cricket: 'Boundaries are too small and outfields are too short – it is too easy to score runs. How come everyone in England knows we are playing too much quantity and not enough quality cricket, but no one has the balls to do anything about it?'
Best batting: 182 Surrey v Middlesex, Lord's 1997
Best bowling: 4-22 Surrey v Yorkshire, The Oval 1995
4-22 Surrey v Yorkshire, The Oval 1997

---

41. Who was England's Player of the Series against Australia in 1997?

O vodafone

1997 Season

	M	Inns	NO	Runs	HS	Avge	100s	50s	Ct	St	O	M	Runs	Wkts	Avge	Best	5wI	10wM
Test	2	4	0	51	45	12.75	-	-	4	-	19	2	55	2	27.50	2-31	-	-
All First	16	25	1	891	182	37.12	1	6	15	-	132.4	23	458	15	30.53	4-22	-	-
1-day Int	3	3	3	123	66*	-	-	2	1	-	15.2	0	82	4	20.50	2-22	-	
NatWest	2	2	0	41	34	20.50	-	-	-	-	13	0	66	0	-	-	-	
B & H	8	6	0	217	80	36.16	-	2	1	-	40.2	1	209	11	19.00	3-40	-	
Sunday	12	12	0	288	63	24.00	-	2	3	-	58	2	375	16	23.43	5-38	1	

Career Performances

	M	Inns	NO	Runs	HS	Avge	100s	50s	Ct	St	Balls	Runs	Wkts	Avge	Best	5wI	10wM
Test	2	4	0	51	45	12.75	-	-	4	-	114	55	2	27.50	2-31	-	-
All First	76	123	12	4691	182	42.26	11	28	63	-	6017	3324	82	40.53	4-22	-	-
1-day Int	5	5	3	151	66*	75.50	-	2	1	-	185	150	12	12.50	4-23	-	
NatWest	12	10	2	302	60	37.75	-	2	6	-	500	388	14	27.71	4-53	-	
B & H	21	15	1	318	80	22.71	-	2	5	-	692	602	21	28.66	4-34	-	
Sunday	70	61	10	1506	93	29.52	-	8	13	-	2519	2445	105	23.28	5-38	3	

HOLLIOAKE, B. C. Surrey

Name: Ben Caine Hollioake
Role: Right-hand bat, right-arm
medium-fast bowler
Born: 11 November 1977, Melbourne,
Australia
Height: 6ft 2in **Weight:** 12st 7lbs
Nickname: Bedroom Bully, Big Dog,
Pelican, Snoop, Oaky
County debut: 1996
Test debut: 1997
Tests: 1
One-Day Internationals: 1
1st-Class 50s: 3
1st-Class catches: 16
One-Day 5 w. in innings: 1
Place in batting averages: 145th av. 26.61
Place in bowling averages: 95th av. 34.00
(1996 25th av. 25.20)
Strike rate: 55.91 (career 50.78)
Parents: John and Daria
Marital status: Single
Family links with cricket: 'Dad played for Victoria, brother for Surrey and England'

Education: Edgarley Hall; Millfield School; Wesley College, Perth, Western Australia; 'Joey Benjamin's house'

Qualifications: 'A couple of GCSEs and NCA coaching award'

Career outside cricket: 'Beach lizard'

Off-season: England to Sharjah and then England A to Kenya and Sri Lanka

Overseas tours: Millfield to Zimbabwe 1992; West of England to West Indies 1992; England U19 to Pakistan 1996-97; England A to Kenya and Sri Lanka 1997-98; England to Sharjah 1997-98, to West Indies 1997-98 (one-day series)

Overseas teams played for: Mellville, Perth 1992-95; North Perth 1996-97

Cricketers particularly admired: Waugh brothers, Waqar Younis, Graham Dilley, 'brother and the old man' and Neil 'Lionheart' Sargeant

Young players to look out for: Owais 'Youngster' Shah, Alex Tudor, David Sales

Other sports followed: Rugby 7s, league and union, Aussie rules

Injuries: 'Useless ankle, out for three weeks'

Relaxations: Playing the guitar, surfing, 'making sexy chit-chat with women'

Extras: Played England U14 and U15. Played Western Australia U17 and U19. The youngest player to take five wickets in a Sunday League game (5 for 10). His first two appearances at Lord's both resulted in him winning Man of the Match awards – his 63 off 48 balls in the third One-Day International against Australia in 1997 and his 98 off 113 balls for Surrey against Kent in the Benson & Hedges Cup final in 1997. Became the youngest player (aged 19) to make his Test debut for England since Brian Close in 1949 and he and brother Adam became the first brothers to make their Test debuts together for England this century. Played for England during the 1997 Hong Kong Sixes tournament in which they finished runners-up to Pakistan. Was voted the Young Cricketer of the Year by both the Cricket Writers' Club and the PCA in 1997

Opinions on cricket: 'Youngsters are still not backed enough in the "big" games.'

Best batting: 76 Surrey v Middlesex, Lord's 1997

Best bowling: 4-54 Surrey v Kent, Canterbury 1997

1997 Season

	M	Inns	NO	Runs	HS	Avge	100s	50s	Ct	St	O	M	Runs	Wkts	Avge	Best	5wI	10wM
Test	1	2	0	30	28	15.00	-	-	1	-	15	2	83	2	41.50	1-26	-	-
All First	14	22	1	559	76	26.61	-	3	13	-	214.2	42	782	23	34.00	4-54	-	-
1-day Int	1	1	0	63	63	63.00	-	1	-	-	7	0	36	0	-	-	-	
NatWest	2	1	0	0	0	0.00	-	-	1	-	16	2	70	1	70.00	1-39	-	
B & H	8	8	0	259	98	32.37	-	2	-	-	51.2	1	271	6	45.16	2-15	-	
Sunday	11	10	1	213	61	23.66	-	1	1	-	77	0	444	13	34.15	3-47	-	

42. Who was England's leading wicket-taker during the 1997 Ashes campaign?

 vodafone

Career Performances

	M	Inns	NO	Runs	HS	Avge	100s	50s	Ct	St	Balls	Runs	Wkts	Avge	Best	5wI	10wM
Test	1	2	0	30	28	15.00	-	-	1	-	90	83	2	41.50	1-26	-	-
All First	17	26	1	622	76	24.88	-	3	16	-	1676	1034	33	31.33	4-54	-	-
1-day Int	1	1	0	63	63	63.00	-	1	-	-	42	36	0	-	-	-	
NatWest	3	1	0	0	0	0.00	-	-	3	-	120	95	1	95.00	1-39	-	
B & H	9	8	0	259	98	32.37	-	2	-	-	350	296	7	42.28	2-15	-	
Sunday	22	18	3	283	61	18.86	-	1	6	-	814	712	26	27.38	5-10	1	

HOLLOWAY, P. C. L.   Somerset

Name: Piran Christopher Laity Holloway
Role: Left-hand bat, off-spin bowler, wicket-keeper
Born: 1 October 1970, Helston, Cornwall
Height: 5ft 8in **Weight:** 11st 5lbs
Nickname: Oggy, Leg, Piras
County debut: 1988 (Warwickshire), 1994 (Somerset)
1st-Class 50s: 17
1st-Class 100s: 5
1st-Class catches: 54
1st-Class stumpings: 1
One-Day 100s: 1
Place in batting averages: 122nd av. 30.16 (1996 108th av. 35.66)
Parents: Chris and Mary
Marital status: 'Engaged to the lovely Nikki'
Family links with cricket: 'Mum and Dad are keen'

Education: Nansloe CP School, Helston; Millfield School; Taunton School; Loughborough University
Qualifications: 7 O-levels, 2 A-levels, BSc Hons in Sports Science
Off-season: Playing for Claremont Nedlands in Perth
Overseas tours: Millfield School to Barbados 1986; England YC to Australia 1989-90; Warwickshire CCC to Cape Town 1992 and 1993; Somerset CCC to Holland 1994
Overseas teams played for: North Perth, 1993-94; Nedlands, Perth 1994-96; Claremont Nedlands 1996-97
Cricketers particularly admired: Neil 'Noddy' Holder
Young players to look out for: Matthew Elliot
Other sports followed: Squash, football, rugby, tennis, surfing
Injuries: Back break, missed no cricket

Relaxations: Surfing or watching videos

Extras: Joined Somerset for the 1995 season. Won the Jack Hobbs Trophy in 1990, played Young England for three years, was fourth in the county averages in 1991. 1995 Somerset Young Player of the Year. Scored the most runs in A-grade cricket in Perth last season in which Claremont Nedlands won the Bank West Cup

Opinions on cricket: 'Present format is unacceptable. It is no longer enough just to moan about it. We as players must take responsibility for the future of our game. It is simply not enough to make suggestions and rely on businessmen to decide whether it's a good idea – after all, if you were a turkey you wouldn't vote for Christmas. As far as I am concerned there should be two groups in the Championship with play-offs for the top two or three teams in each group. Sunday League should be the same as the above. The free days this allows would mean that you could play more Benson & Hedges and NatWest games at weekends, changing the NatWest competition to 50 overs. There may be less cricket as a result, but hopefully it will have more meaning and create more interest. It's too mundane at the moment.'

Best batting: 168 Somerset v Middlesex, Uxbridge 1996

1997 Season

	M	Inns	NO	Runs	HS	Avge	100s	50s	Ct	St	O	M	Runs	Wkts	Avge	Best	5wI	10wM
Test																		
All First	19	34	4	905	106	30.16	1	5	12	-								
1-day Int																		
NatWest	2	2	0	128	90	64.00	-	1	1	-								
B & H																		
Sunday	11	10	2	267	117	33.37	1	-	3	-								

Career Performances

	M	Inns	NO	Runs	HS	Avge	100s	50s	Ct	St	Balls	Runs	Wkts	Avge	Best	5wI	10wM
Test																	
All First	59	99	18	2921	168	36.06	5	17	54	1	40	46	0	-	-	-	-
1-day Int																	
NatWest	6	5	1	196	90	49.00	-	2	4	1							
B & H	6	6	1	67	27	13.40	-	-	7	-							
Sunday	54	45	11	769	117	22.61	1	2	28	7							

HOOPER, C. L.   Kent

Name: Carl Llewellyn Hooper
Role: Right-hand bat, off-spin bowler
Born: 15 December 1966, Guyana
Height: 6ft **Weight:** 13st
County debut: 1992
County cap: 1992
Test debut: 1987-88
Tests: 64
One-Day Internationals: 155
1000 runs in a season: 6
1st-Class 50s: 73
1st-Class 100s: 37
1st-Class 200s: 1
1st-Class 5 w. in innings: 12
1st-Class catches: 260
One-Day 100s: 8
One-Day 5 w. in innings: 1
Place in batting averages: (1996 41st av. 44.88)
Place in bowling averages: (1996 60th av. 30.34)
Strike rate: 74.19 (career 80.06)
Off-season: Playing for West Indies
Overseas tours: West Indies to India and Pakistan 1987-88, to Australia 1988-89, to Pakistan 1990-91, to England 1991, to Pakistan and Australia (World Cup) 1991-92, to Australia and South Africa 1992-93, to Sharjah, India (Hero Cup) and Sri Lanka 1993-94, to India 1994-95, to England 1995, to Australia 1996-97, to Pakistan 1997-98
Overseas teams played for: Guyana 1984-96
Extras: AXA Equity & Law Award 1993. Withdrew from the West Indies squad for tours to Australia and the World Cup in 1995-96 through illness. Unable to play the 1997 county season due to commitments with the West Indies. His overseas slot was taken by Zimbabwe's Paul Strang, but he returns for the 1998 season
Best batting: 236* Kent v Glamorgan, Canterbury 1993
Best bowling: 5-26 West Indies v Sri Lanka, St Vincent 1996-97

---

43. When Adam and Ben Hollioake made their Test debuts in the Trent Bridge Test of 1997, they became the first brothers to make their England debuts simultaneously for a century – which cricketing brothers preceded them in 1880?

vodafone

1997 Season (did not make any first-class or one-day appearances)

Career Performances

	M	Inns	NO	Runs	HS	Avge	100s	50s	Ct	St	Balls	Runs	Wkts	Avge	Best	5wl	10wM
Test	64	108	10	3303	178 *	33.70	7	15	72	-	7648	3307	63	52.49	5-26	3	-
All First	229	363	35	14689	236 *	44.78	37	73	260	-	29991	13178	367	35.90	5-26	12	-
1-day Int	155	139	33	3600	113 *	33.96	3	20	76	-	6263	4536	134	33.85	4-34	-	
NatWest	11	11	1	423	136 *	42.30	1	1	7	-	651	383	5	76.60	2-12	-	
B & H	12	12	0	454	98	37.83	-	4	4	-	654	385	12	32.08	3-28	-	
Sunday	65	62	7	2482	145	45.12	4	19	34	-	2785	1898	57	33.29	5-41	1	

HOUSE, W. J.   Kent

Name: William John House
Role: Left-hand bat, right-arm
medium bowler
Born: 16 March 1976, Sheffield
Height: 5ft 11in   **Weight:** 13st 4lbs
Nickname: Housey, Wendy, Curry
County debut: 1997
1st-Class 50s: 4
1st-Class 100s: 2
1st-Class catches: 13
Place in batting averages: 158th av. 25.46
(1996 22nd av. 52.60)
Strike rate: (career 473.50)
Parents: Bill and Anna
Marital status: Single
Education: British School in the
Netherlands, The Hague; Sevenoaks School;
University of Cambridge (Gonville and Caius
College)
Qualifications: 11 GCSEs, International Baccalaureate, NCA coaching award
Off-season: Studying and playing overseas
Overseas teams played for: Royal Hague CC 1985-89; University CC, Adelaide
1994-95
Cricketers particularly admired: Ian Botham, David Gower
Young players to look out for: Anurag Singh, Robert Key
Other sports followed: Rugby (Cambridge University U21 XV), football (Cambridge
University and support Sheffield Wednesday), golf
Relaxations: Golf and history
Extras: Cricket Societies leading all-rounder in schools cricket in 1993. Kent CCC's

Most Improved Player 1996. Cambridge University's Player of the Year 1996
Opinions on cricket: 'Sooner or later a shift to two divisions will ensure meaningful competitive cricket right through to September.'
Best batting: 136 Cambridge University v Derbyshire, Fenner's 1996
Best bowling: 1-44 Cambridge University v Essex, Fenner's 1996

1997 Season

	M	Inns	NO	Runs	HS	Avge	100s	50s	Ct	St	O	M	Runs	Wkts	Avge	Best	5wI	10wM
Test																		
All First	10	14	1	331	94	25.46	-	2	11	-	68.5	9	284	0	-		-	-
1-day Int																		
NatWest																		
B & H	5	5	0	155	93	31.00	-	1	-	-	3	0	14	0	-		-	-
Sunday	1	1	0	0	0	0.00	-	-	-	-								

Career Performances

	M	Inns	NO	Runs	HS	Avge	100s	50s	Ct	St	Balls	Runs	Wkts	Avge	Best	5wI	10wM
Test																	
All First	18	29	6	857	136	37.26	2	4	13	-	947	696	2	348.00	1-44	-	-
1-day Int																	
NatWest																	
B & H	6	6	0	177	93	29.50	-	1	1	-	18	14	0	-		-	-
Sunday	5	5	1	46	19 *	11.50	-	-	1	-							

HUGHES, J. G.   Northamptonshire

Name: John Gareth Hughes
Role: Right-hand bat, right-arm medium-fast bowler
Born: 3 May 1971, Wellingborough
Height: 6ft 2in **Weight:** 13st 7lbs
Nickname: Yozzer
1st-Class 5 w. in innings: 1
1st-Class catches: 5
Strike rate: 69.00 (career 77.85)
Parents: John and Jennifer
Wife and date of marriage: Helen, 28 September 1996
Family links with cricket: 'My grandad, Dad and brother all play or have played for Little Harrowden, whilst two of my uncles umpire for the same club'
Education: Little Harrowden Primary School; Westfield Boys/Sir Christopher Hatton School, Wellingborough; Sheffield Hallam University
Qualifications: 7 O-levels, 2 A-levels, BEd (Hons) in Physical Education
Career outside cricket: Physical education teacher
Overseas tours: Northamptonshire CA U15 to Holland 1986; Northamptonshire to Durban 1991-92, to Cape Town 1992-93, to Zimbabwe 1994-95, to Johannesburg 1996
Overseas teams played for: Mana and Wellington B 1994-95
Cricketers particularly admired: Nick Cook, Alan Walker, David Capel, Greg Thomas, Bob Carter, Curtly Ambrose
Other sports followed: 'Football especially, but I enjoy most sports'
Relaxations: Going out for a pint and a meal
Extras: Represented both English Schools and England YC at various age groups. Also represented Northamptonshire at football and basketball at schoolboy level. Grandfather played international football for Wales
Best batting: 17 Northamptonshire v Hampshire, Southampton 1994
Best bowling: 5-69 Northamptonshire v Hampshire, Southampton 1994

44. Who was Australia's leading run-scorer during the 1997 Ashes campaign?

1997 Season

	M	Inns	NO	Runs	HS	Avge	100s	50s	Ct	St	O	M	Runs	Wkts	Avge	Best	5wI	10wM
Test																		
All First	2	1	1	5	5*	-	-	-	-	-	46	11	141	4	35.25	2-15	-	-
1-day Int																		
NatWest																		
B & H																		
Sunday																		

Career Performances

	M	Inns	NO	Runs	HS	Avge	100s	50s	Ct	St	Balls	Runs	Wkts	Avge	Best	5wI	10wM
Test																	
All First	20	26	2	128	17	5.33	-	-	5	-	2725	1622	37	43.83	5-69	1	-
1-day Int																	
NatWest																	
B & H	4	3	0	11	9	3.66	-	-	1	-	116	106	2	53.00	2-47	-	
Sunday	6	5	2	31	21	10.33	-	-	1	-	174	127	3	42.33	2-39	-	

HUMPHRIES, S. Sussex

Name: Shaun Humphries
Role: Right-hand bat, right-arm net bowler, wicket-keeper
Born: 11 January 1973, Horsham, West Sussex
Height: 5ft 11in **Weight:** 10st 8lbs
Nickname: Stan, Gooner
County debut: 1993
1st-Class catches: 9
Parents: Peter John and Marilyn Christine
Marital status: Single
Education: The Weald School, Billingshurst; Kingston College of Further Education
Qualifications: 5 GCSEs, BTEC National Diploma in Leisure Studies
Overseas tours: Sussex U13 to Barbados 1987; Sussex U18 to India 1990-91
Overseas teams played for: Sutherland, Sydney 1994-95
Cricketers particularly admired: Peter Moores, Alec Stewart, John Berry, Geoff Kirkham, Ian Healy
Young players to look out for: Giles Haywood

Other sports followed: 'Away trips with the Gunners', cycling, LA Raiders
Relaxations: Music, raves, Kate, 'being in awe of Spurs' trophy cabinet'
Opinions on cricket: '2nd XI cricketers are continually playing in sub-standard conditions, wet wickets, bad light. It must be on a par with first-class cricket.'
Best batting: 41* Sussex v Oxford University, The Parks 1997

1997 Season

	M	Inns	NO	Runs	HS	Avge	100s	50s	Ct	St	O	M	Runs	Wkts	Avge	Best	5wI	10wM
Test																		
All First	2	3	1	52	41 *	26.00	-	-	6	-								
1-day Int																		
NatWest																		
B & H																		
Sunday																		

Career Performances

	M	Inns	NO	Runs	HS	Avge	100s	50s	Ct	St	Balls	Runs	Wkts	Avge	Best	5wI	10wM
Test																	
All First	4	3	1	52	41 *	26.00	-	-	9	-							
1-day Int																	
NatWest																	
B & H																	
Sunday																	

HUSSAIN, N.   Essex

Name: Nasser Hussain
Role: Right-hand bat, declaration bowler, county vice-captain
Born: 28 March 1968, Madras, India
Height: 6ft **Weight:** 12st
Nickname: Nashwani
County debut: 1987
Test debut: 1989-90
Tests: 23
One-Day Internationals: 12
1000 runs in a season: 5
1st-Class 50s: 61
1st-Class 100s: 35
1st-Class 200s: 1
1st-Class catches: 261
One-Day 100s: 3
Place in batting averages: 73rd av. 38.60 (1996 46th av. 46.20)

Strike rate: (career 138.00)
Parents: Joe and Shireen
Wife and date of marriage: Karen, 24 September 1993
Family links with cricket: Father played for Madras in Ranji Trophy 1966-67. Brother Mel played for Hampshire, brother Abbas played for Essex 2nd XI
Education: Forest School, Snaresbrook; Durham University
Qualifications: 10 O-levels, 3 A-levels; BSc (Hons) in Natural Sciences; NCA cricket coaching award
Off-season: Touring West Indies with England
Overseas tours: England YC to Sri Lanka 1986-87, to Australia (Youth World Cup) 1987-88; England to India (Nehru Cup) 1989-90, to West Indies 1989-90 and 1993-94, to

Zimbabwe and New Zealand 1996-97, to West Indies 1997-98; England A to Pakistan and Sri Lanka 1990-91, to Bermuda and West Indies 1991-92, to Pakistan 1995-96
Overseas teams played for: Madras 1986-87; Petersham, Sydney 1992-93; Adelaide University 1990; Stellenbosch University, South Africa 1994-95; Primrose, Cape Town; Petersham, Sydney
Cricketers particularly admired: Graham Gooch, Mark Waugh
Young players to look out for: Robert Rollins, Anthony McGrath
Other sports followed: Golf (10 handicap), football (Leeds)
Injuries: Broken finger during Trent Bridge Test, out for three weeks
Relaxations: Listening to music. Listening to Mark Ilott. Watching television
Extras: Played for England Schools U15 for two years (one as captain). Youngest player to play for Essex Schools U11 at the age of eight and U15 at the age of 12. At 15, was considered the best young leg-break bowler in the country. Cricket Writers' Club Young Cricketer of the Year, 1989. Holds record for third, fourth and fifth wicket partnerships for Essex (with Mark Waugh, Salim Malik and Mike Garnham). Essex Player of the Year 1993. Appointed Essex's vice-captain for 1996. Captained the England A tour to Pakistan in 1995-96. Finished 2nd in the Whyte and Mackay batting ratings in 1995. Appointed England's vice-captain in 1996-97
Opinions on cricket: 'Too much soft cricket. Quality not quantity. Better one-day wickets, especially in September at Lord's.'
Best batting: 207 England v Australia, Edgbaston 1997
Best bowling: 1-38 Essex v Worcestershire, Kidderminster 1992

1997 Season

	M	Inns	NO	Runs	HS	Avge	100s	50s	Ct	St	O	M	Runs	Wkts	Avge	Best	5wI	10wM
Test	6	11	0	431	207	39.18	2	-	8	-								
All First	16	28	0	1081	207	38.60	4	3	17	-								
1-day Int																		
NatWest	5	5	2	221	89 *	73.66	-	2	2	-								
B & H	3	2	1	84	52	84.00	-	1	3	-								
Sunday	12	12	2	206	45 *	20.60	-	-	3	-								

Career Performances

	M	Inns	NO	Runs	HS	Avge	100s	50s	Ct	St	Balls	Runs	Wkts	Avge	Best	5wI	10wM
Test	23	40	3	1391	207	37.59	5	3	23	-							
All First	210	331	34	13107	207	44.13	35	61	261	-	276	307	2	153.50	1-38	-	-
1-day Int	12	12	4	155	49 *	19.37	-	-	5	-							
NatWest	23	22	3	857	108	45.10	2	4	14	-							
B & H	40	36	8	1238	118	44.21	1	11	18	-							
Sunday	122	111	17	2838	83	30.19	-	17	48	-							

HUTCHISON, P. M. Yorkshire

Name: Paul Michael Hutchison
Role: Left-hand bat, left-arm fast bowler
Born: 9 June 1977, Leeds
Height: 6ft 3in **Weight:** 12st
Nickname: Hutch, Hooch
County debut: 1996
1st-Class 5 w. in innings: 3
1st-Class 10 w. in match: 1
1st-Class catches: 2
Place in bowling averages: 10th av. 20.02
Strike rate: 37.81 (career 36.97)
Parents: David Hutchison and Rita Laycock
Marital status: 'Long-term girlfriend Emma'
Family links with cricket: 'Brother Richard played for Pudsey St Lawrence in the Bradford League'
Education: Pudsey Greenside; Pudsey Crawshaw; Yorkshire Cricket School
Qualifications: 7 GCSEs, sports leadership coaching award, qualified cricket coach
Career outside cricket: 'No thanks'
Off-season: 'England A tour to Kenya and Sri Lanka. Holiday with friends. Get fit and

strong'

Overseas tours: England U19 to Zimbabwe 1995-96; Yorkshire CCC to Zimbabwe and Botswana 1996; England A to Kenya and Sri Lanka 1997-98

Cricketers particularly admired: Ian Botham, Mark Ramprakash, Darren Lehmann, Mark Ilott

Young players to look out for: Ryan Sidebottom, David Sales and Alex Wharf

Other sports followed: Football (Leeds United), rugby league (Leeds Rhinos) and golf

Relaxations: Sleeping, socialising with friends and going to the cinema

Extras: Represented England at U17, U18 and U19 levels. Played for Pudsey St Lawrence in the Bradford League. Had a place at the Yorkshire Academy. Took 7 for 50 on county debut against Hampshire at Portsmouth, only bettered by Wilfred Rhodes 99 years previously. Took 7 for 38 on first first-class appearance in 1997 against Pakistan A. Voted Wombwell Cricket Lovers' Young Player of the Year for 1997

Opinions on cricket: 'There is too much cricket played in the season, which destroys quality and increases injury. Contracts should be nine or 12 months instead of the present six. Better marketing of the game is required if we are to make it more attractive to youngsters.'

Best batting: 15* Yorkshire v Derbyshire, Derby 1997

Best bowling: 7-38 Yorkshire v Pakistan A, Headingley 1997

1997 Season

	M	Inns	NO	Runs	HS	Avge	100s	50s	Ct	St	O	M	Runs	Wkts	Avge	Best	5wI	10wM
Test																		
All First	7	8	7	29	15 *	29.00	-	-	1	-	233.1	56	741	37	20.02	7-38	3	1
1-day Int																		
NatWest																		
B & H																			
Sunday																			

Career Performances

	M	Inns	NO	Runs	HS	Avge	100s	50s	Ct	St	Balls	Runs	Wkts	Avge	Best	5wI	10wM
Test																	
All First	10	10	7	29	15 *	9.66	-	-	2	-	1812	1028	49	20.97	7-38	3	1
1-day Int																	
NatWest																	
B & H																	
Sunday																	

HUTTON, B. L. — Middlesex

Name: Benjamin Leonard Hutton
Role: Left-hand bat, right-arm
medium-fast bowler
Born: 29 January 1977, Johannesburg,
South Africa
Height: 6ft 2in **Weight:** 12st
Nickname: Gibbs, Bouff, Hutts,
Jazzer, Funky
County debut: No first-team appearances
Parents: Richard and Charmaine
Marital status: 'Very single'
Family links with cricket: 'Grandfather and
father played a bit!' Uncle captains
Falconhurst CC
Education: Holmewood House Primary
School; Radley College; Durham University
Qualifications: Grade one recorder, 10
GCSEs, 3 A-levels, NCA coaching award
Career outside cricket: Student

Off-season: 'Concentrate on getting a degree and touring Zimbabwe'
Overseas tours: Durham University to Zimbabwe 1997-98; Middlesex to Portugal 1997
Overseas teams played for: Wanderers CC, Johannesburg 1995-96; Pirates CC, Johannesburg 1995-96
Cricketers particularly admired: Leonard Hutton, Richard Hutton, Brian Lara, Matthew Elliott, Michael Atherton, Mark Ramprakash, Graeme Fowler
Young players to look out for: Owais Shah, David Nash, Oliver Hutton, Matthew Wilson, Robert Guide, Mark Chilton, John Bond, Paul Hutchison
Other sports followed: Football (Ipswich Town), hockey, golf
Injuries: Shin splints, but missed no cricket
Relaxations: 'Reading around my subject in the library! Mon–Wed in Rixy's, Thurs–Fri in Klute!'
Extras: BUSA Halifax medal 1997
Opinions on cricket: 'Middlesex should play 2nd XI games at Lord's. More emphasis should be placed on the need for specific cricket fitness (using testing and training programmes). The counties should have backed Lord MacLaurin's proposals for "raising the standards".'

HUTTON, S.   Durham

Name: Stewart Hutton
Role: Left-hand bat, cover fielder
Born: 30 November 1969, Stockton-on-Tees
Height: 6ft **Weight:** 12st
Nickname: Len
County debut: 1992
1st-Class 50s: 12
1st-Class 100s: 3
1st-Class catches: 33
Place in batting averages: 201st av. 21.50
(1996 126th av. 33.83)
Parents: Leonard and Mavis
Marital status: Single
Education: De Brus Comprehensive;
Cleveland Technical College
Qualifications: 6 O-levels (equivalent), A-
level Economics
Overseas tours: Durham to Zimbabwe
1991-92
Cricketers particularly admired: Mike Gatting
Other sports followed: Golf, football
Relaxations: Playing golf
Extras: Scored century for Durham on pre-season tour to Zimbabwe in 1991-92.
Appeared as 12th man for England in the 4th Test against West Indies at Old Trafford in
1995
Best batting: 172* Durham v Oxford University, The Parks 1996

1997 Season

	M	Inns	NO	Runs	HS	Avge	100s	50s	Ct	St	O	M	Runs	Wkts	Avge	Best	5wI	10wM
Test																		
All First	7	13	1	258	95	21.50	-	1	1	-								
1-day Int																		
NatWest																		
B & H																		
Sunday	7	7	0	188	57	26.85	-	1	3	-								

---

45. Who was Australia's leading wicket-taker during the 1997 Ashes campaign?

Career Performances

	M	Inns	NO	Runs	HS	Avge	100s	50s	Ct	St	Balls	Runs	Wkts	Avge	Best	5wl	10wM
Test																	
All First	65	118	6	3241	172 *	28.93	3	13	34	-	25	18	0	-	-	-	-
1-day Int																	
NatWest	8	8	1	287	125	41.00	1	1	3	-							
B & H	2	2	0	44	36	22.00	-	-	-	-							
Sunday	56	53	5	1219	81	25.39	-	4	16	-							

HYAM, B. J.   Essex

Name: Barry James Hyam
Role: Right-hand bat, wicket-keeper
Born: 9 September 1975, Romford, Essex
Height: 5ft 11in **Weight:** 11st 7lbs
Nickname: Bazza
County debut: 1993
1st-Class catches: 20
1st-Class stumpings: 1
Place in batting averages: 285th av. 9.87
Parents: Peter and Gloria
Marital status: Single
Family links with cricket: Brother Matthew plays for Harold Wood, brother Richard plays for Gidea Park, 'Matt also has NCA coaching award. Mum and Dad are keen fans'
Education: Marshalls Park; Havering Sixth Form College; Westminster College
Qualifications: 9 GCSEs, 1 A-level, NCA coaching award
Cricketers particularly admired: Graham Gooch, Jack Russell
Young players to look out for: Stephen Peters, Jonathan Powell
Other sports followed: Football (West Ham), hockey and golf
Relaxations: Playing any sport and socialising with friends
Extras: Made first-class debut on his 18th birthday
Opinions on cricket: 'Second XI should play more four-day cricket to prepare them for first-class cricket. They should also play less friendlies on bad wickets.'
Best batting: 49 Essex v Pakistan, Chelmsford 1996

1997 Season

	M	Inns	NO	Runs	HS	Avge	100s	50s	Ct	St	O	M	Runs	Wkts	Avge	Best	5wI	10wM
Test																		
All First	7	10	2	79	26	9.87	-	-	15	-								
1-day Int																		
NatWest																		
B & H																		
Sunday	4	2	1	4	3	4.00	-	-	6	-								

Career Performances

	M	Inns	NO	Runs	HS	Avge	100s	50s	Ct	St	Balls	Runs	Wkts	Avge	Best	5wI	10wM
Test																	
All First	10	16	2	153	49	10.92	-	-	20	1							
1-day Int																	
NatWest																	
B & H																	
Sunday	5	3	1	4	3	2.00	-	-	6	-							

IGGLESDEN, A. P.　　　　　Kent

Name: Alan Paul Igglesden
Role: Right-hand bat, right-arm
fast-medium bowler
Born: 8 October 1964, Farnborough, Kent
Height: 6ft 6in **Weight:** 15st 8lbs
Nickname: Iggy, Norm, Silver Spice
County debut: 1986
Test debut: 1989
Tests: 3
One-Day Internationals: 4
50 wickets in a season: 4
1st-Class 5 w. in innings: 23
1st-Class 10 w. in match: 4
1st-Class catches: 38
One-Day 5 w. in innings: 2
Place in bowling averages: 70th av. 29.88
Strike rate: 50.66 (career 52.21)
Parents: Alan Trevor and Gillian Catherine
Family links with cricket: 'Brother Kevin
due to failing eyesight has been reduced to the ranks of the complete hacker that bowls
dibbley dobbleys'
Education: St Mary's Primary School, Westerham; Churchill School, Westerham; 'the

Kent dressing-room'
Qualifications: Advanced coaching certificate
Off-season: 'Coaching and working on my testimonial'
Overseas tours: England A to Kenya and Zimbabwe 1990; England to West Indies 1994; Fred Rumsey's XI to Barbados 1993
Overseas teams played for: Avendale CC, Cape Town 1984-89, Green Point CC, Cape Town 1990-91, Western Province 1986-90; Boland Cricket Union 1991-92
Cricketers particularly admired: Dennis Lillee, Terry Alderman, Carl Hooper, Aravinda De Silva, Paul Strang
Young players to look out for: Robert Key
Other sports followed: Football (Crystal Palace FC), rugby union and golf
Injuries: Slipped disc, out for six weeks
Relaxations: 'Walking and cycling with Sara and Jessica'
Extras: 'Lots of runners-up medals but working on it.' Testimonial in 1998
Opinions on cricket: 'Might have a few more next year.'
Best batting: 41 Kent v Surrey, Canterbury 1988
Best bowling: 7-28 Boland v Griqualand West, Kimberley 1992-93

1997 Season

	M	Inns	NO	Runs	HS	Avge	100s	50s	Ct	St	O	M	Runs	Wkts	Avge	Best	5wl	10wM
Test																		
All First	6	8	3	6	3	1.20	-	-	1	-	152	23	538	18	29.88	4-67	-	-
1-day Int																		
NatWest																		
B & H																		
Sunday	6	0	0	0	0	-	-	-	-	-	43	1	195	9	21.66	3-29	-	

Career Performances

	M	Inns	NO	Runs	HS	Avge	100s	50s	Ct	St	Balls	Runs	Wkts	Avge	Best	5wl	10wM
Test	3	5	3	6	3 *	3.00	-	-	1	-	555	329	6	54.83	2-91	-	-
All First	151	166	62	868	41	8.34	-	-	38	-	26159	13286	501	26.51	7-28	23	4
1-day Int	4	3	1	20	18	10.00	-	-	1	-	168	122	2	61.00	2-12	-	
NatWest	14	4	3	23	12 *	23.00	-	-	3	-	728	375	18	20.83	4-29	-	
B & H	25	10	7	43	26 *	14.33	-	-	5	-	1457	892	35	25.48	3-24	-	
Sunday	87	27	17	93	13 *	9.30	-	-	19	-	3954	2632	113	23.29	5-13	2	

ILLINGWORTH, R. K. Worcestershire

Name: Richard Keith Illingworth
Role: Right-hand bat, slow left-arm bowler
Born: 23 August 1963, Bradford
Height: 6ft **Weight:** 13st
Nickname: Lucy, Harry
County debut: 1982
County cap: 1986
Test debut: 1991
Tests: 9
One-Day Internationals: 25
50 wickets in a season: 5
1st-Class 50s: 16
1st-Class 100s: 4
1st-Class 5 w. in innings: 27
1st-Class 10 w. in match: 6
1st-Class catches: 146
One-Day 5 w. in innings: 2
Place in batting averages:

(1996 143rd av. 32.30)
Place in bowling averages: 30th av. 24.55 (1996 85th av. 33.74)
Strike rate: 68.72 (career 76.73)
Parents: Keith and Margaret
Wife and date of marriage: Anne, 20 September 1985
Children: Miles, 28 August 1987; Thomas, 20 April 1989
Family links with cricket: Father played Bradford League cricket
Education: Wrose Brow Middle; Salts Grammar School ('same school as the late Jim Laker')
Qualifications: 6 O-levels, advanced coaching award
Off-season: 'Working on benefit to the end of the year, then recover'
Overseas tours: England A to Zimbabwe and Kenya 1989-90, to Pakistan and Sri Lanka 1990-91; England to New Zealand and Australia (World Cup) 1991-92, to South Africa 1995-96, to India and Pakistan (World Cup) 1995-96
Overseas teams played for: Natal 1988-89
Cricketers particularly admired: Ian Botham, Wasim Akram, Derek Underwood
Young players to look out for: Reuben Spring, Alamgir Sheriyar
Other sports followed: 'Watching Miles and Thomas play rugby, football and cricket.' Most sports – football (Leeds United), rugby league (Bradford Bulls) and rugby union (Worcester RFC)
Injuries: Dislocated shoulder, out for approximately 14 weeks
Relaxations: Gardening, DIY, Monday night football
Extras: Took 11 for 108 on South African first-class debut for Natal B v Boland 1988.

Scored 120 not out as nightwatchman for Worcestershire v Warwickshire 1988 and 106 for England A v Zimbabwe 1989-90. In 1991, v West Indies, became 11th person in history to take a wicket with first ball in Test cricket. Took a hat-trick in Sunday League v Sussex in 1993, the first Worcestershire player to do this in one-day cricket. Won 1993 Dick Lygon award for contribution to Worcestershire CCC. Has made three centuries as a nightwatchman

Opinions on cricket: 'I've been very fortunate to play this game for 15 years and enjoyed most of it. I hope everyone gets the same enjoyment as myself.'

Best batting: 120* Worcestershire v Warwickshire, Worcester 1987

Best bowling: 7-50 Worcestershire v Oxford University, The Parks 1985

1997 Season

	M	Inns	NO	Runs	HS	Avge	100s	50s	Ct	St	O	M	Runs	Wkts	Avge	Best	5wI	10wM
Test																		
All First	5	4	2	157	112	78.50	1	-	3	-	206.1	79	442	18	24.55	7-79	1	1
1-day Int																		
NatWest																		
B & H																		
Sunday	4	1	1	2	2*	-	-	-	-	-	27	0	119	3	39.66	2-29	-	

Career Performances

	M	Inns	NO	Runs	HS	Avge	100s	50s	Ct	St	Balls	Runs	Wkts	Avge	Best	5wI	10wM
Test	9	14	7	128	28	18.28	-	-	5	-	1485	615	19	32.36	4-96	-	-
All First	330	368	108	5818	120*	22.37	4	16	146	-	59927	23794	780	30.50	7-50	27	6
1-day Int	25	11	5	68	14	11.33	-	-	8	-	1501	1059	30	35.30	3-33	-	
NatWest	33	16	6	139	29*	13.90	-	-	10	-	1969	1014	28	36.21	4-20	-	
B & H	54	26	15	214	36*	19.45	-	-	12	-	2794	1619	51	31.74	4-27	-	
Sunday	181	80	42	542	31	14.26	-	-	41	-	6964	5013	211	23.75	5-24	2	

ILOTT, M. C. Essex

Name: Mark Christopher Ilott
Role: Left-hand bat, left-arm
fast-medium bowler
Born: 27 August 1970, Watford
Height: 6ft 1in **Weight:** 13st 4lbs
Nickname: Ramble, Choock
County debut: 1988
County cap: 1993
Test debut: 1993
Tests: 5
50 wickets in a season: 4
1st-Class 50s: 4
1st-Class 5 w. in innings: 22
1st-Class 10 w. in match: 3
1st-Class catches: 32
One-Day 5 w. in innings: 1
Place in batting averages: 220th av. 19.33
(1996 264th av. 15.59)
Place in bowling averages: 16th av. 22.00
(1996 80th av. 33.32)
Strike rate: 46.32 (career 55.27)
Parents: John and Glenys
Wife and date of marriage: Sandra Jane, 16 October 1994
Children: James, 6 October 1996
Family links with cricket: 'Dad played for years and now umpires in the Minor
Counties. Brother has played for Hertfordshire but his face didn't fit in. Mum has made
many a good tea'
Education: Francis Combe School; 'Essex changing-room'
Qualifications: 6 O-levels, 2 A-levels, 2 AO-levels, coaching qualification, diploma in
Fitness and Nutrition
Career outside cricket: Hole-in-One Worldwide Insurance Air Packaging Europe,
GNI Money Brokers and Centremark Graphic Design
Off-season: 'Coaching and working for various companies in a selling/marketing role'
Overseas tours: England A to Sri Lanka 1990-91, to Australia 1992-93, to South
Africa 1993-94, to India 1994-95; England to South Africa 1995-96
Overseas teams played for: East Torrens District, Adelaide 1989-91
Cricketers particularly admired: Graham Gooch, Stuart Law, Ronnie Irani, John
Lever, Geoff Arnold
Other sports followed: Golf, football (Liverpool), badminton, snooker
Injuries: Heel injury, out for five weeks
Relaxations: 'Playing with my … guitar, my son and my wife (but not in that order)'

Extras: Youngest player ever to play for Hertfordshire. Missed almost all 1991 season with stress fracture of the back
Opinions on cricket: 'No one listens to me anyway – not even my son.'
Best batting: 60 England A v Warwickshire, Edgbaston 1995
Best bowling: 9-19 Essex v Northamptonshire, Luton 1995

1997 Season

	M	Inns	NO	Runs	HS	Avge	100s	50s	Ct	St	O	M	Runs	Wkts	Avge	Best	5wI	10wM
Test																		
All First	13	20	5	290	47	19.33	-	-	1	-	332	91	946	43	22.00	7-59	1	-
1-day Int																		
NatWest	3	1	1	1	1 *	-	-	-	-	-	36	6	113	2	56.50	1-29	-	
B & H	4	2	0	4	4	2.00	-	-	-	-	39	4	182	9	20.22	3-28	-	
Sunday	12	8	3	65	15 *	13.00	-	-	-	-	84	1	432	9	48.00	2-10	-	

Career Performances

	M	Inns	NO	Runs	HS	Avge	100s	50s	Ct	St	Balls	Runs	Wkts	Avge	Best	5wI	10wM
Test	5	6	2	28	15	7.00	-	-	-	-	1042	542	12	45.16	3-48	-	-
All First	137	168	39	1883	60	14.59	-	4	32	-	25869	13008	468	27.79	9-19	22	3
1-day Int																	
NatWest	18	10	5	111	54 *	22.20	-	1	5	-	1153	728	18	40.44	2-23	-	
B & H	26	9	1	69	21	8.62	-	-	3	-	1409	813	41	19.82	5-21	1	
Sunday	86	56	18	404	56 *	10.63	-	1	14	-	3680	2757	99	27.84	4-15	-	

INNES, K. J.   Northamptonshire

Name: Kevin John Innes
Role: Right-hand bat, right-arm
medium bowler
Born: 24 September 1975, Wellingborough
Height: 5ft 10in **Weight:** 10st 5lbs
Nickname: Ernie, Ken, Milkman, KJ
County debut: 1994
1st-Class 50s: 1
1st-Class catches: 3
Strike rate: (career 66.75)
Parents: Peter and Jane
Marital status: Engaged to Caroline Pinnock
Education: Boothville Middle School;
Weston Favell Upper School, Northampton
Qualifications: 6 GCSEs, 4 O-levels, NCA
coaching award
Off-season: Staying at home, coaching in
Northamptonshire, training for the coming
season

Overseas tours: England U18 to South Africa 1992-93, to Denmark 1993; England U19 to Sri Lanka 1993-94
Cricketers particularly admired: Mark Waugh, Carl Hooper, Greg Blewett, Curtly Ambrose
Young players to look out for: Owais Shah, Vikram Solanki, Melvyn Betts
Other sports followed: 'Snooker, golf, tennis and many more'
Relaxations: 'Spending time with my friends, watching and playing most sports, music, sleeping and reading magazines'
Extras: Played for England U19 in home series against India in 1994. Won the MCC Lord's Taverners Award U13 and U15
Opinions on cricket: 'It is a shame that employment is not found at the end of the season for a lot more cricketers.'
Best batting: 63 Northamptonshire v Lancashire, Northampton 1996
Best bowling: 4-61 Northamptonshire v Lancashire, Northampton 1996

---

46. Who captained the England Women's cricket team in the 1997 World Cup?

1997 Season

	M	Inns	NO	Runs	HS	Avge	100s	50s	Ct	St	O	M	Runs	Wkts	Avge	Best	5wI	10wM
Test																		
All First	1	1	1	8	8 *	-	-	-	-	-	20	6	49	0	-		-	-
1-day Int																		
NatWest	1	1	0	25	25	25.00	-	-	-	-								
B & H																		
Sunday	4	2	2	26	19 *	-	-	-	-	1	-	4	0	36	0	-		-	-

Career Performances

	M	Inns	NO	Runs	HS	Avge	100s	50s	Ct	St	Balls	Runs	Wkts	Avge	Best	5wI	10wM
Test																	
All First	6	8	1	116	63	16.57	-	1	3	-	534	275	8	34.37	4-61	-	-
1-day Int																	
NatWest	1	1	0	25	25	25.00	-	-	-	-							
B & H	1	0	0	0	0	-	-	-	-	-	36	25	1	25.00	1-25	-	
Sunday	11	4	2	34	19 *	17.00	-	-	4	-	256	309	3	103.00	1-35	-	

IRANI, R. C.   Essex

Name: Ronald Charles Irani
Role: Right-hand bat, right-arm
medium bowler
Born: 26 October 1971, Leigh, Lancashire
Height: 6ft 4in **Weight:** 13st 10lbs
Nickname: Reggie, Ledge
County debut: 1990 (Lancashire),
1994 (Essex)
County cap: 1994 (Essex)
Test debut: 1996
Tests: 2
One-Day Internationals: 10
1000 runs in a season: 2
1st-Class 50s: 29
1st-Class 100s: 7
1st-Class catches: 37
1st-Class 5 w. in innings: 3
One-Day 100s: 2
Place in batting averages: 97th av. 34.47
(1996 83rd av. 38.48)
Place in bowling averages: 115th av. 38.61 (1996 45th av. 29.40)
Strike rate: 87.27 (career 63.54)

Parents: Jimmy and Anne
Marital status: Single
Family links with cricket: 'Father played local league cricket in Bolton for 30 years; mother did teas for many years!'
Education: Church Road Primary School; Smithills Comprehensive School
Qualifications: 9 GCSEs
Overseas tours: England YC to Australia 1989-90; England A to Pakistan 1995-96; England to Zimbabwe and New Zealand 1996-97
Overseas teams played for: Technicol Natal, Durban, South Africa 1992-93; Eden-Roskill, Auckland 1993-94
Cricketers particularly admired: Mark Waugh, Javed Miandad, Wasim Akram, John Crawley, Graham Gooch
Other sports followed: 'Most sports especially football'
Relaxations: Sleeping and watching football
Extras: Played for England U19 in home series v Australia 1991, scoring a century and three 50s in six innings and being named Bull Man of the Series. Made his Test debut in the first Test against India at Edgbaston in 1996
Opinions on cricket: 'Too much cricket played by English county cricket professionals'
Best batting: 123* Essex v Hampshire, Chelmsford 1997
Best bowling: 5-27 Essex v Nottinghamshire, Chelmsford 1996

1997 Season

	M	Inns	NO	Runs	HS	Avge	100s	50s	Ct	St	O	M	Runs	Wkts	Avge	Best	5wI	10wM
Test																		
All First	16	24	1	793	123 *	34.47	3	3	5	-	261.5	73	695	18	38.61	3-51	-	-
1-day Int																		
NatWest	5	4	1	168	79 *	56.00	-	2	-	-	52.2	6	207	5	41.40	2-61	-	
B & H	4	3	1	165	82 *	82.50	-	1	-	-	32	2	169	6	28.16	3-42	-	
Sunday	15	15	3	321	52	26.75	-	1	3	-	88.2	3	421	20	21.05	3-23	-	

Career Performances

	M	Inns	NO	Runs	HS	Avge	100n	50s	Ct	Ct	Balls	Runs	Wkts	Avge	Best	5wI	10wM
Test	2	3	0	76	41	25.33	-	-	-	-	126	74	2	37.00	1-22	-	-
All First	86	139	16	4334	123 *	35.23	7	29	37	-	8578	4547	135	33.68	5-19	3	-
1-day Int	10	10	2	78	45 *	9.75	-	-	2	-	330	246	4	61.50	1-23	-	
NatWest	14	13	2	461	124	41.90	1	4	2	-	854	574	14	41.00	4-55	-	
B & H	16	11	2	391	82 *	43.44	-	2	2	-	768	582	24	24.25	4-30	-	
Sunday	68	63	6	1306	101 *	22.91	1	6	14	-	2099	1702	68	25.02	3-22	-	

JAMES, K. D.   Hampshire

Name: Kevan David James
Role: Left-hand bat, left-arm medium bowler
Born: 18 March 1961, Lambeth, South London
Height: 6ft ½in **Weight:** 13st 8lbs
Nickname: Jambo, Jaimo, Jockey
County debut: 1980 (Middlesex), 1985 (Hampshire)
County cap: 1989
1000 runs in a season: 2
1st-Class 50s: 39
1st-Class 100s: 10
1st-Class 5 w. in innings: 11
1st-Class 10 w. in match: 1
1st-Class catches: 70
One-Day 5 w. in innings: 2
Place in batting averages: 138th av. 27.61
(1996 129th av. 33.54)
Place in bowling averages: 5th av. 18.66
(1996 55th av. 29.40)

Strike rate: 35.81 (career 62.50)
Parents: David (deceased) and Helen
Wife and date of marriage: Debbie, October 1987
Children: Natalie Ann, 8 October 1992; Naomi Claire, 25 October 1995
Family links with cricket: Late father played club cricket in North London; brother Martin plays for Hertfordshire
Education: Edmonton County High School
Qualifications: 5 O-levels, qualified coach, City and Guilds in Electric Theories
Career outside cricket: 'Still working on it'
Off-season: 'Have had a couple of offers of full-time employment and shall be taking one of them up along with freelance work with Radio Solent'
Overseas tours: England YC to Australia 1978-79, to West Indies 1979-80; England to Hong Kong Sixes 1996
Overseas teams played for: Wellington, New Zealand 1982-83, 1983-84
Cricketers particularly admired: Chris Smith
Young players to look out for: Simon Francis
Other sports followed: 'Football but never achieved anything – about the same as cricket'
Injuries: Torn tendon in shoulder, out for three months
Relaxations: 'Enjoy my work with local radio. Find it a welcome relaxation during the summer when I am writing my scripts'

Extras: Left Middlesex at end of 1984 season and joined Hampshire. Achieved a world record in 1996 when he became the first player in a first-class match to score a century and take four wickets in four balls in Hampshire's game against India at Southampton

Opinions on cricket: 'I worry about the players who want to play less cricket. The season is short enough as it is. To want to play less cricket is an easy option to get away with less work. Some of those same players should also work out that less cricket means fewer jobs.'

Best batting: 162 Hampshire v Glamorgan, Cardiff 1989
Best bowling: 8-49 Hampshire v Somerset, Basingstoke 1997

1997 Season

	M	Inns	NO	Runs	HS	Avge	100s	50s	Ct	St	O	M	Runs	Wkts	Avge	Best	5wI	10wM
Test																		
All First	10	15	2	359	85	27.61	-	5	5	-	161.1	37	504	27	18.66	8-49	2	1
1-day Int																		
NatWest																		
B & H	3	2	1	23	13 *	23.00	-	-	1	-	20	1	112	1	112.00	1-48	-	
Sunday	8	3	0	57	50	19.00	-	1	-	-	40	3	221	8	27.62	3-16	-	

Career Performances

	M	Inns	NO	Runs	HS	Avge	100s	50s	Ct	St	Balls	Runs	Wkts	Avge	Best	5wI	10wM
Test																	
All First	205	307	48	7928	162	30.61	10	39	70	-	22316	11323	357	31.71	8-49	11	1
1-day Int																	
NatWest	23	14	3	159	42	14.45	-	-	4	-	1426	896	34	26.35	4-42	-	
B & H	42	29	6	430	56	18.69	-	1	10	-	2017	1364	32	42.62	3-31	-	
Sunday	159	107	31	1590	66	20.92	-	5	43	-	6331	4671	157	29.75	6-35	2	

JAMES, S. P.   Glamorgan

Name: Stephen Peter James
Role: Right-hand opening bat
Born: 7 September 1967, Lydney
Height: 6ft **Weight:** 13st
Nickname: Sid, Jamo
County debut: 1985
County cap: 1992
1000 runs in a season: 5
1st-Class 50s: 38
1st-Class 100s: 31
1st-Class 200s: 2
1st-Class catches: 133
One-Day 100s: 6
Place in batting averages: 2nd av. 68.26
(1996 40th av. 47.72)
Parents: Peter and Margaret
Wife and date of marriage: Jane Louise,
26 September 1997
Family links with cricket: Father played for
Gloucestershire 2nd XI. Distant relative of Dominic Ostler
Education: Monmouth School; University College, Swansea; Cambridge University
Qualifications: BA (Hons) Wales – Classics; BA (Hons) Cantab – Land Economy
Career outside cricket: Journalism
Off-season: England A tour to Kenya and Sri Lanka as vice-captain
Overseas tours: Welsh Schools to Barbados 1984; Monmouth Schools to Sri Lanka
1985; Combined Universities to Barbados 1989; Glamorgan to Trinidad 1989-90, to
Zimbabwe 1990-91, Cape Town 1993-94, to Pretoria 1996; England A to Kenya and
Sri Lanka 1997-98
Overseas teams played for: Bionics, Zimbabwe 1990-92; Universals Sports Club,
Zimbabwe 1992-96
Cricketers particularly admired: Michael Atherton, Graham Burgess
Young players to look out for: Mike Powell, Dean Cosker
Other sports followed: Rugby union ('played for Lydney, Gloucestershire and
Cambridge University and was on bench for Varsity Match')
Relaxations: Reading, *Telegraph* crosswords, videos, weight-training
Extras: Scored maiden century in only second first-class game. Broke Matthew
Maynard's club record for number of one-day runs in a season in 1995. Also broke Hugh
Morris's club record for number of Sunday League runs in a season. First player to reach
1000 runs in 1997 and was voted the Cricketer of the Year by both the Wombwell
Cricket Lovers' Society and the PCA. Appointed vice-captain for the England A tour to
Kenya and Sri Lanka

Best batting: 235 Glamorgan v Nottinghamshire, Worksop 1996

1997 Season

	M	Inns	NO	Runs	HS	Avge	100s	50s	Ct	St	O	M	Runs	Wkts	Avge	Best	5wl	10wM
Test																		
All First	18	30	4	1775	162	68.26	7	8	14	-								
1-day Int																		
NatWest	4	3	0	178	109	59.33	1	1	3	-								
B & H	4	4	1	30	15	10.00	-	-	2	-								
Sunday	11	10	4	230	75 *	38.33	-	1	5	-								

Career Performances

	M	Inns	NO	Runs	HS	Avge	100s	50s	Ct	St	Balls	Runs	Wkts	Avge	Best	5wl	10wM
Test																	
All First	168	296	25	10485	235	38.69	31	38	133	-	2	3	0	-	-	-	-
1-day Int																	
NatWest	19	18	1	708	123	41.64	2	4	5	-							
B & H	29	29	2	984	135	36.44	2	8	10	-							
Sunday	89	86	11	2763	107	36.84	2	20	22	-							

JARVIS, P. W. Sussex

Name: Paul William Jarvis
Role: Right-hand bat, right-arm
fast-medium bowler
Born: 29 June 1965, Redcar, North Yorkshire
Height: 5ft 11in **Weight:** 12st 5lbs
Nickname: Jarv, Gnasher
County debut: 1981 (Yorkshire),
1994 (Sussex)
County cap: 1986 (Yorkshire)
Test debut: 1987-88
Tests: 9
One-Day Internationals: 16
50 wickets in a season: 4
1st-Class 50s: 6
1st-Class 5 w. in innings: 22
1st-Class 10 w. in match: 3
1st-Class catches: 59
One-Day 5 w. in innings: 5
Place in batting averages: 184th av. 23.37
(1996 210th av. 23.42)

Place in bowling averages: 106th av. 36.36 (1996 64th av. 31.15)
Strike rate: 63.76 (career 53.85)
Parents: Malcolm and Marjorie
Wife and date of marriage: Wendy Jayne, 3 December 1988
Children: Alexander Michael, 13 June 1989; Isabella Grace, 21 March 1993
Family links with cricket: Father still plays league cricket for Sudbrooke CC in Gwent. Brother plays in Yorkshire (Selby Londesborough)
Education: Bydales Comprehensive School, Marske, Cleveland
Qualifications: 4 O-levels, advanced coaching awards
Career outside cricket: Agent for Adidas eye protection
Overseas tours: Yorkshire to St Lucia and Barbados 1987, to South Africa 1991; England to India/Pakistan (World Cup) and Pakistan 1986-87, to Australia and New Zealand 1987-88, to India and Sri Lanka 1992-93; unofficial English XI to South Africa 1989-90
Overseas teams played for: Mossman Middle Harbour, Sydney 1984-85; Avendale, Cape Town 1985-86; Manly Warringah, Sydney 1987; Onslow, Wellington 1994-95
Cricketers particularly admired: Ian Botham, Malcolm Marshall
Young players to look out for: James Kirtley, Danny Law
Other sports followed: Football
Relaxations: DIY, cooking, golf, fishing, music, eating out, going to the pub
Extras: Youngest player ever to play for Yorkshire in County Championship (16 years, 2 months, 13 days) and youngest player to take hat-trick in Sunday League (1982) and Championship (1985). Played for England YC v West Indies 1982 and Australia 1983. Banned from Test cricket for joining 1989-90 tour of South Africa, suspension remitted in 1992
Opinions on cricket: 'You could write a book on them, but still too much one-day cricket.'
Best batting: 80 Yorkshire v Northamptonshire, Scarborough 1992
Best bowling: 7-55 Yorkshire v Surrey, Headingley 1986

1997 Season

	M	Inns	NO	Runs	HS	Avge	100s	50s	Ct	St	O	M	Runs	Wkts	Avge	Best	5wI	10wM
Test																		
All First	11	18	2	374	64	23.37	-	4	5	-	318.5	46	1091	30	36.36	5-44	2	-
1-day Int																		
NatWest	2	1	0	16	16	16.00	-	-	-	-	19	0	129	0	-		-	-
B & H	5	5	3	144	63	72.00	-	1	-	-	48	6	221	10	22.10	4-60	-	
Sunday	11	11	0	51	14	4.63	-	-	1	-	73.2	2	355	12	29.58	3-32	-	

47. Who won the 1997 Cricketer Cup and whom did they beat in the final?

Career Performances

	M	Inns	NO	Runs	HS	Avge	100s	50s	Ct	St	Balls	Runs	Wkts	Avge	Best	5wI	10wM
Test	9	15	2	132	29 *	10.15	-	-	2	-	1912	965	21	45.95	4-107	-	-
All First	201	252	66	3189	80	17.14	-	10	59	-	33444	17786	621	28.64	7-55	22	3
1-day Int	16	8	2	31	16 *	5.16	-	-	1	-	879	672	24	28.00	5-35	1	
NatWest	21	13	3	139	34 *	13.90	-	-	4	-	1327	890	22	40.45	4-41	-	
B & H	45	25	9	336	63	21.00	-	1	4	-	2582	1553	74	20.98	4-34	-	
Sunday	138	83	28	592	43	10.76	-	-	30	-	5804	4326	197	21.95	6-27	4	

JOHNSON, N. C. Leicestershire

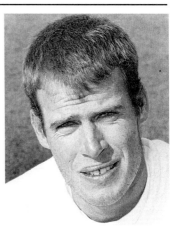

Name: Neil Clarkson Johnson
Role: Left-hand bat, right-arm
fast-medium bowler
Born: 24 January 1970, Salisbury, Rhodesia
County debut: 1997
1st-Class debut: 1989-90
1st-Class 50s: 18
1st-Class 100s: 4
1st-Class 5 w. in innings: 2
Place in batting averages: 6th av. 63.00
Strike rate: 87.00 (career 60.07)
Overseas teams played for: Natal
Extras: Has also played for South Africa A.
Called up as a late replacement for Phil
Simmons as the Leicestershire overseas
player for 1997
Best batting: 150 Leicestershire v
Hampshire, Leicester 1997
Best bowling: 5-79 Natal v Boland,
Stellenbosch 1993-94

1997 Season

	M	Inns	NO	Runs	HS	Avge	100s	50s	Ct	St	O	M	Runs	Wkts	Avge	Best	5wI	10wM
Test																		
All First	12	18	5	819	150	63.00	2	5	13	-	116	18	420	8	52.50	3-61	-	-
1-day Int																		
NatWest	2	2	0	19	15	9.50	-	-	1	-	3	0	19	0	-	-	-	
B & H	5	5	1	73	58	18.25	-	1	1	-	36	0	205	6	34.16	2-38	-	
Sunday	11	11	1	300	80 *	30.00	-	2	6	-	47.2	0	325	14	23.21	3-37	-	

Career Performances

	M	Inns	NO	Runs	HS	Avge	100s	50s	Ct	St	Balls	Runs	Wkts	Avge	Best	5wI	10wM
Test																	
All First	64	97	14	2777	150	33.45	4	18	72	-	6608	3308	110	30.07	5-79	2	-
1-day Int																	
NatWest	2	2	0	19	15	9.50	-	-	1	-	18	19	0	-	-	-	-
B & H	5	5	1	73	58	18.25	-	1	1	-	216	205	6	34.16	2-38	-	
Sunday	11	11	1	300	80 *	30.00	-	2	6	-	284	325	14	23.21	3-37	-	

JOHNSON, P.   Nottinghamshire

Name: Paul Johnson
Role: Right-hand bat, right-arm medium 'occasional' bowler, county captain
Born: 24 April 1965, Newark
Height: 'Below average' **Weight:** 'Above average'
Nickname: Johno, Midget, Gus
County debut: 1982
County cap: 1986
Benefit: 1995
1000 runs in a season: 7
1st-Class 50s: 98
1st-Class 100s: 34
1st-Class catches: 188
1st-Class stumpings: 1
One-Day 100s: 13
Place in batting averages: 49th av. 42.81 (1996 149th av. 31.61)
Strike rate: (career 105.66)
Parents: Donald Edward and Joyce
Wife's name and date of marriage: Jackie, 24 December 1993
Children: Ruth, 28 September 1994; Eve, 9 September 1996
Family links with cricket: Father played local cricket and is a qualified coach
Education: Grove Comprehensive School, Newark
Qualifications: 9 CSEs, NCA advanced coach
Overseas tours: England A to Bermuda and West Indies 1991-92
Overseas teams played for: RAU Johannesburg, 1985-86; Hutt District, Wellington, New Zealand 1988-89
Cricketers particularly admired: Clive Rice and Mike Gatting
Young players to look out for: Usman Afzaal, Noel Gie
Other sports followed: Watches ice-hockey (Nottingham Panthers), football

(Nottingham Forest and Notts County)
Relaxations: 'Listening to music, crosswords and reading autobiographies'
Extras: Played for English Schools in 1980-81 and England YC 1982 and 1983. Youngest player ever to join the Nottinghamshire staff. Made 235 for Nottinghamshire 2nd XI, July 1982, aged 17. Won Man of the Match award in his first NatWest game (101* v Staffordshire) in 1985, but missed the final owing to appendicitis. Sunday morning soccer referee in Nottingham. Took over the Nottinghamshire captaincy from Tim Robinson at the start of the 1996 season
Opinions on cricket: 'Who would take any notice?'
Best batting: 187 Nottinghamshire v Lancashire, Old Trafford 1993
Best bowling: 1-9 Nottinghamshire v Oxford University, Trent Bridge 1984

1997 Season

	M	Inns	NO	Runs	HS	Avge	100s	50s	Ct	St	O	M	Runs	Wkts	Avge	Best	5wI	10wM
Test																		
All First	16	27	5	942	96 *	42.81	-	8	12	-	14	5	34	0	-	-	-	-
1-day Int																		
NatWest	2	2	0	110	106	55.00	1	-	3	-								
B & H	3	3	0	60	34	20.00	-	-	-	-								
Sunday	12	12	1	467	117	42.45	2	2	7	-	0.1	0	1	0	-	-	-	

Career Performances

	M	Inns	NO	Runs	HS	Avge	100s	50s	Ct	St	Balls	Runs	Wkts	Avge	Best	5wI	10wM
Test																	
All First	301	501	49	16755	187	37.06	34	98	188	1	634	595	6	99.16	1-9	-	-
1-day Int																	
NatWest	31	31	2	879	146	30.31	3	1	10	-	12	16	0	-	-	-	
B & H	53	50	11	1364	104 *	34.97	2	9	15	-							
Sunday	202	191	24	5554	167 *	33.25	8	31	70	-	1	1	0	-	-	-	

JOHNSON, R. L.   Middlesex

Name: Richard Leonard Johnson
Role: Right-hand bat, right-arm fast-medium bowler, outfielder
Born: 29 December 1974, Chertsey, Surrey
Height: 6ft 2in **Weight:** 13st 6lbs
Nickname: Jono, Lenny
County debut: 1992
50 wickets in a season: 1
1st-Class 50s: 1
1st-Class 5 w. in innings: 4
1st-Class 10 w. in match: 2
1st-Class catches: 23
Place in batting averages: 263rd av. 13.91 (1996 278th av. 12.78)
Place in bowling averages: 61st av. 28.58 (1996 93rd av. 35.12)
Strike rate: 51.52 (career 52.97)
Parents: Roger and Mary Ann
Marital status: Single
Family links with cricket: Father and grandfather played club cricket
Education: Sunbury Manor School; Spelthorne College
Qualifications: 9 GCSEs, A-Level in Physical Education, NCA senior coaching award
Overseas tours: England U18 to South Africa 1992-93; England U19 to South Africa 1993-94; England A to India 1994-95
Cricketers particularly admired: Ian Botham, Richard Hadlee and Angus Fraser 'for his quality bowling and his dedication to moaning'
Young players to look out for: David Nash, Owais Shah
Other sports followed: Basketball, soccer, snooker and most other sports
Relaxations: Sport and music
Extras: Plays for Sunbury CC, has represented Middlesex at all levels since U11. Took 10 for 45 v Derbyshire in July 1994, first person to take 10 wickets in an innings since Ian Thomson (Sussex) in 1964, also most economical figures since Hedley Verity's 10 for 10. Had to pull out of England's 1995-96 tour to South Africa due to a persistent back injury
Best batting: 50* Middlesex v Cambridge University, Fenner's 1994
Best bowling: 10-45 Middlesex v Derbyshire, Derby 1994

---

48. Name the former county captain who led his side to the 1997 Cricketer Cup.

1997 Season

	M	Inns	NO	Runs	HS	Avge	100s	50s	Ct	St	O	M	Runs	Wkts	Avge	Best	5wI	10wM
Test																		
All First	18	24	1	320	39	13.91	-	-	6	-	427.2	79	1425	50	28.50	4-26	-	-
1-day Int																		
NatWest	3	2	0	8	8	4.00	-	-	-	-	26	1	130	8	16.25	5-50	1	
B & H	3	3	0	39	19	13.00	-	-	-	-	29	0	154	3	51.33	2-50	-	
Sunday	10	7	2	72	29	14.40	-	-	-	-	63	1	366	12	30.50	3-35	-	

Career Performances

	M	Inns	NO	Runs	HS	Avge	100s	50s	Ct	St	Balls	Runs	Wkts	Avge	Best	5wI	10wM
Test																	
All First	56	77	8	1005	50 *	14.56	-	1	23	-	8358	4413	158	27.93	10-45	4	2
1-day Int																	
NatWest	11	9	2	106	33	15.14	-	-	-	-	600	416	17	24.47	5-50	1	
B & H	9	8	0	58	19	7.25	-	-	1	-	456	380	5	76.00	2-50	-	
Sunday	51	31	12	256	29	13.47	-	-	6	-	2088	1872	50	37.44	4-66	-	

JONES, D. M.   Derbyshire

Name: Dean Mervyn Jones
Role: Right-hand bat, off-spin bowler
Born: 24 March 1963, Melbourne, Australia
Height: 6ft 1in   **Weight:** 13st 5lbs
Nickname: Deano
County debut: 1992 (Durham),
1996 (Derbys)
Test debut: 1983-84
Tests: 52
One-Day Internationals: 164
1st-Class 50s: 83
1st-Class 100s: 52
1st-Class 200s: 4
1st-Class 300s: 1
1st-Class 5 w. in innings: 1
1st-Class catches: 171
One-Day 100s: 15
Place in batting averages: 53rd av. 41.63
(1996 23rd av. 51.79)
Strike rate: (career 100.14)
Parents: Barney and Gaynor
Wife and date of marriage: Jane, 24 April 1986

Children: Phoebe, 26 June 1991; Isabella, 14 April 1996
Family links with cricket: Father was a captain/coach of Carlton, Victoria for 18 years and played district cricket for Victoria
Education: Mt Waverley High School, Victoria
Qualifications: High School Certificate
Career outside cricket: Work for Foxtel cable television and radio
Overseas tours: Young Australians to Zimbabwe 1983 and 1985; Australia to West Indies 1984 and 1991, to England 1985 and 1989, to India 1986 and 1987 (World Cup), to Sharjah 1986 and 1990, to Pakistan 1988, to New Zealand 1989, to USA 1990
Overseas teams played for: Victoria, Australia
Cricketers particularly admired: David Boon, Steve and Mark Waugh, Allan Border, Shane Warne, Ian Healy, Waqar Younis, Wasim Akram
Young players to look out for: Andrew Harris, Chris Adams, Karl Krikken
Other sports followed: Golf, fishing and Aussie rules (Carlton FC)
Relaxations: Watching golf, family, reading and 'walking my Rottweiler, Stanley'
Extras: Played for Durham in their first season as a first-class county in 1992. Appointed captain of Derbyshire for the 1996 season. He is the highest run-scorer in the history of the Sheffield Shield competition. Resigned from both captaincy and coaching duties on 12 June 1997
Opinions on cricket: 'Greatest game in the world'
Best batting: 324* Victoria v South Australia, Melbourne 1994-95
Best bowling: 5-112 Derbyshire v Hampshire, Southampton 1996

1997 Season

	M	Inns	NO	Runs	HS	Avge	100s	50s	Ct	St	O	M	Runs	Wkts	Avge	Best	5wI	10wM
Test																		
All First	7	12	1	458	99 *	41.63	-	5	8	-	6	2	20	0	-		-	-
1-day Int																		
NatWest																		
B & H	5	5	0	105	35	21.00	-	-	5	-								
Sunday	5	5	0	189	58	37.80	-	1	1	-	4	0	45	0	-		-	-

Career Performances

	M	Inns	NO	Runs	HS	Avge	100s	50s	Ct	St	Balls	Runs	Wkts	Avge	Best	5wI	10wM
Test	52	89	11	3631	216	46.55	11	14	34	-	198	64	1	64.00	1-5	-	-
All First	234	394	41	18292	324 *	51.81	52	83	182	-	2704	1533	27	56.77	5-112	1	-
1-day Int	164	161	25	6068	145	44.61	7	46	54	-	106	81	3	27.00	2-34	-	
NatWest	4	3	1	171	100 *	85.50	1	-	5	-	14	16	2	8.00	2-0	-	
B & H	14	14	0	432	142	30.85	1	2	11	-	54	52	2	26.00	2-34	-	
Sunday	31	30	5	1594	118	63.76	6	7	13	-	224	246	5	49.20	2-15	-	

JONES, P. S.   Somerset

Name: Philip Steffan Jones
Role: Right-hand bat, right-arm fast bowler
Born: 9 February 1974, Llangennech,
Llanelli
Height: 6ft 2in **Weight:** 14st 8lbs
Nickname: Cracker
County debut: 1997
1st-Class 5 w. in innings: 1
1st-Class catches: 4
Place in batting averages: 261st av. 14.20
Place in bowling averages: 81st av. 32.13
Strike rate: 54.21 (career 54.21)
Parents: Lyndon and Anne
Marital status: Single
Family links with cricket: Father played for
Wales U19 and Glamorgan 2nd XI
Education: Llangennech Primary School;
Ysgay Strade, Llanelli; Loughborough
University; Cambridge University

Qualifications: BSc sports science, PGCE
Career outside cricket: Professional rugby player for Bristol RFC
Off-season: Playing rugby
Overseas tours: Wales Minor Counties to Barbados 1995
Cricketers particularly admired: Dermot Reeve, Courtney Walsh
Young players to look out for: Ed Smith
Other sports followed: Rugby (Wales Schoolboy and Youth caps and was in the
Cambridge Varsity squad)
Relaxations: Swimming, cycling
Extras: Took nine wickets in the Varsity match at Lord's in 1997
Opinions on cricket: 'Exciting and invigorating.'
Best batting: 36 Cambridge University v Essex, Fenner's 1997
Best bowling: 6-67 Cambridge University v Oxford University, Lord's 1997

1997 Season

	M	Inns	NO	Runs	HS	Avge	100s	50s	Ct	St	O	M	Runs	Wkts	Avge	Best	5wI	10wM
Test																		
All First	10	13	3	142	36	14.20	-	-	4	-	207.5	37	739	23	32.13	6-67	1	-
1-day Int																		
NatWest																		
B & H	5	3	2	26	12	26.00	-	-	2	-	43	7	188	5	37.60	2-51	-	
Sunday	1	0	0	0	0	-	-	-	1	-	2	0	19	0	-	-	-	

	M	Inns	NO	Runs	HS	Avge	100s	50s	Ct	St	Balls	Runs	Wkts	Avge	Best	5wl	10wM
Test																	
All First	10	13	3	142	36	14.20	-	-	4	-	1247	739	23	32.13	6-67	1	-
1-day Int																	
NatWest	1	1	1	26	26 *	-	-	-	-	-	18	30	0	-		-	-
B & H	5	3	2	26	12	26.00	-	-	2	-	258	188	5	37.60	2-51	-	
Sunday	1	0	0	0	0	-	-	-	1	-	12	19	0	-		-	-

JONES, S. P.   Glamorgan

Name: Simon P. Jones
Role: Left-hand bat, right-arm fast bowler
Born: 25 December 1978
Height: 6ft 3in **Weight:** 13st 7lbs
Nickname: Jonsey
County debut: No first-team appearance
Parents: Jeff and Irene
Marital status: Single
Family links with cricket: Father former
Glamorgan and England left-arm fast bowler
Education: Half Way CP School; Coedcar
Comprehensive; Millfield School
Career outside cricket: Student
Cricketers particularly admired: Allan
Donald
Other sports followed: Football (Manchester
United)

KALLIS, J. H.   Middlesex

Name: Jacques Henry Kallis
Role: Right-hand bat, right-arm medium bowler
Born: 16 October 1975, Pinelands, South Africa
County debut: 1997
1st-Class debut: 1993-94
Test debut: 1995-96
Tests: 5
One-Day Internationals: 25

1st-Class 50s: 19
1st-Class 100s: 8
1st-Class 5 w. in innings: 1
One-Day 100s: 1
Place in batting averages: 28th av. 47.00
Place in bowling averages: 12th av. 20.46
Strike rate: 43.96 (career 59.51)
Overseas tours: Western Province to
Queensland 1995-96; South Africa U24 to Sri
Lanka 1995-96; South Africa A to England
1996; South Africa to India and Pakistan
(World Cup) 1995-96, to Sharjah 1995-96, to
Pakistan 1997-98, to Australia 1997-98
Extras: Signed as overseas player for
Middlesex after Greg Blewett, the county's
original choice, was selected for the 1997
Ashes series. He was struck down with
appendicitis during South Africa's 1997-98
tour of Pakistan. Hit both his maiden Test and one-day International centuries during
South Africa's winter tour of Australia

Best batting: 186* Western Province v Queensland, Brisbane 1995-96
Best bowling: 5-54 Middlesex v Kent, Lord's 1997

1997 Season

	M	Inns	NO	Runs	HS	Avge	100s	50s	Ct	St	O	M	Runs	Wkts	Avge	Best	5wI	10wM
Test																		
All First	16	25	3	1034	172 *	47.00	4	4	15	-	234.3	61	655	32	20.46	5-54	1	-
1-day Int																		
NatWest	3	3	0	116	100	38.66	1	-	1	-	23	1	107	5	21.40	4-47	-	
B & H	2	2	0	82	72	41.00	-	1	-	-	15	1	79	2	39.50	2-49	-	
Sunday	11	10	0	140	24	14.00	-	-	4	-	34.2	1	124	5	24.80	2-19	-	

Career Performances

	M	Inns	NO	Runs	HS	Avge	100s	50s	Ct	St	Balls	Runs	Wkts	Avge	Best	5wI	10wM
Test	5	7	0	57	39	8.14	-	-	1	-	376	136	5	27.20	3-29	-	-
All First	54	80	8	3271	186 *	45.43	8	19	36	-	4523	2079	76	27.35	5-54	2	-
1-day Int	25	24	6	700	82	38.88	-	6	5	-	570	459	8	57.37	3-21	-	
NatWest	3	3	0	116	100	38.66	1	-	1	-	138	107	5	21.40	4-47	-	
B & H	2	2	0	82	72	41.00	-	1	-	-	90	79	2	39.50	2-49	-	
Sunday	11	10	0	140	24	14.00	-	-	4	-	206	124	5	24.80	2-19	-	

KEECH, M. Hampshire

Name: Matthew Keech
Role: Right-hand bat, right-arm 'military medium' bowler
Born: 21 October 1970, Hampstead
Height: 6ft **Weight:** 13st 4lbs
County debut: 1991 (Middlesex), 1994 (Hampshire)
1st-Class 50s: 11
1st-Class 100s: 3
1st-Class catches: 36
Place in batting averages: 45th av. 43.16 (1996 58th av. 44.05)
Strike rate: 72.00 (career 94.50)
Parents: Ron and Brenda
Marital status: Single
Family links with cricket: 'Mother and father like to watch a good game'
Education: Northumberland Park School, Tottenham; 'Middlesex and Hampshire dressing-rooms'

Qualifications: 5 O-levels, NCA coaching certificate
Career outside cricket: Coaching
Overseas tours: England YC to Australia 1989-90
Overseas teams played for: Mossman, Sydney 1988-89; Lancaster Park, Christchurch NZ 1990-91
Cricketers particularly admired: Mike Gatting, Robin Smith and Tony Middleton
Young players to look out for: Jason Laney, Owais Shah
Other sports followed: Football, golf, squash
Relaxations: Caffreys, 'avoiding jobs to be done around the house'
Opinions on cricket: 'Format for four days is now right with wickets improving. Surely the third umpire should be present in every round of both the Benson & Hedges and NatWest competitions.'
Best batting: 127 Hampshire v Oxford University, The Parks 1997
Best bowling: 2-28 Middlesex v Gloucestershire, Bristol 1993

---

49. Who won the 1997 Hong Kong Sixes tournament and whom did they defeat in the final?

O vodafone

1997 Season

	M	Inns	NO	Runs	HS	Avge	100s	50s	Ct	St	O	M	Runs	Wkts	Avge	Best	5wI	10wM
Test																		
All First	10	16	4	518	127	43.16	2	1	10	-	12	1	51	1	51.00	1-12	-	-
1-day Int																		
NatWest	2	2	0	59	34	29.50	-	-	1	-	1	0	6	0	-		-	-
B & H	3	3	0	63	32	21.00	-	-	1	-								
Sunday	11	11	3	295	53 *	36.87	-	2	1	-	6	0	40	2	20.00	2-29	-	

Career Performances

	M	Inns	NO	Runs	HS	Avge	100s	50s	Ct	St	Balls	Runs	Wkts	Avge	Best	5wI	10wM
Test																	
All First	49	84	11	2136	127	29.26	3	11	36	-	756	383	8	47.87	2-28	-	-
1-day Int																	
NatWest	4	3	0	62	34	20.66	-	-	3	-	66	47	0	-		-	-
B & H	9	8	0	191	47	23.87	-	-	7	-	66	47	1	47.00	1-37	-	
Sunday	66	61	9	1217	98	23.40	-	4	11	-	492	393	9	43.66	2-22	-	

KEEDY, G.   Lancashire

Name: Gary Keedy
Role: Left-hand bat, slow left-arm 'with a few revs on it'
Born: 27 November 1974, Wakefield
Height: 6ft **Weight:** 11st 7lbs
Nickname: Bod, Seedy, Linus, Binbag
County debut: 1994 (Yorkshire), 1995 (Lancashire)
1st-Class 5 w. in innings: 1
1st-Class 10 w. in match: 1
1st-Class catches: 10
Place in batting averages: (1996 280th av. 12.16)
Place in bowling averages: 93rd av. 33.96 (1996 146th av. 52.82)
Strike rate: 65.03 (career 87.69)
Parents: Roy and Pat
Marital status: Single
Family links with cricket: Twin brother plays for Castleford in the Yorkshire League
Education: Garforth Comprehensive
Qualifications: 4 GCSEs, junior coaching award

Career outside cricket: 'Self unemployed'
Overseas tours: England U18 to South Africa 1992-93, to Denmark 1994; England U19 to Sri Lanka 1993-94
Overseas teams played for: Frankston, Melbourne 1995-96
Cricketers particularly admired: Shane Warne, Graham Gooch
Other sports followed: Rugby league (Leeds), football (Leeds United)
Extras: Player of the Series for England U19 v West Indies U19 in 1993. Graduate of the Yorkshire Cricket Academy. Played for England U19 in the home series against India in 1994. Signed a three-year contract to play for Lancashire from 1995
Opinions on cricket: 'I reckon that two divisions wouldn't go amiss! Keep the Benson & Hedges and the NatWest but sack the Sunday League.'
Best batting: 26 Lancashire v Essex, Chelmsford 1996
Best bowling: 6-79 Lancashire v Surrey, The Oval 1997

1997 Season

	M	Inns	NO	Runs	HS	Avge	100s	50s	Ct	St	O	M	Runs	Wkts	Avge	Best	5wI	10wM
Test																		
All First	8	8	7	11	6 *	11.00	-	-	1	-	292.4	60	917	27	33.96	6-79	1	1
1-day Int																		
NatWest																		
B & H																		
Sunday	1	0	0	0	0	-	-	-	-	-	5.1	0	47	0	-	-	-	

Career Performances

	M	Inns	NO	Runs	HS	Avge	100s	50s	Ct	St	Balls	Runs	Wkts	Avge	Best	5wI	10wM
Test																	
All First	38	40	27	158	26	12.15	-	-	10	-	7805	3703	89	41.60	6-79	1	1
1-day Int																	
NatWest																	
B & H																	
Sunday	5	0	0	0	0	-	-	-	-	-	175	175	1	175.00	1-40	-	

KENDALL, W. S.   Hampshire

Name: William Salwey Kendall
Role: Right-hand bat, right-arm medium bowler, occasional wicket-keeper
Born: 18 December 1973, Wimbledon
Height: 5ft 10in **Weight:** 12st 7lbs
Nickname: Villy, Lemon
County debut: 1996
1000 runs in a season: 1
1st-Class 50s: 10

1st-Class 100s: 4
1st-Class catches: 32
Place in batting averages: 172nd av. 24.29 (1996 18th av. 55.00)
Strike rate: (career 63.00)
Parents: Tom and Sue
Marital status: Single
Family links with cricket: Father played club cricket with East Horsley, Hampshire Hogs and MCC. Older brother James played for Durham University
Education: Bradfield College, Berkshire; Keble College, Oxford University
Qualifications: 10 GCSEs, 3 A-levels, 1 AS-level, BA (Hons) Modern History
Career outside cricket: None as yet
Off-season: Playing for Frankston Peninsular CC in Melbourne, Australia and coaching at schools in the area
Overseas tours: Bradfield College to Barbados, 1991; Troubadours to Argentina 1997; Hampshire CCC to Anguilla 1997
Cricketers particularly admired: Robin Smith, Graham Thorpe, Mark Ramprakash
Young players to look out for: Simon Francis, Lee Savident, Derek Kenway
Other sports followed: Hockey for Oxford University, football (offered terms by Reading) and golf
Relaxations: Playing or watching sport, socialising with friends, relaxing at home
Extras: Surrey Young Cricketer of the Year 1992. Awarded Gray-Nicolls Trophy for Schoolboy Cricketer of the Year in memory of Len Newbury 1992. Made first-class debut for Oxford University in 1994. Played football for Independent Schools 1992. Offered one-year contract with Reading FC. Hampshire Exiles Player of the Year for 1996
Best batting: 145* Oxford University v Cambridge University, Lord's 1996
Best bowling: 3-37 Oxford University v Derbyshire, The Parks 1995

1997 Season

	M	Inns	NO	Runs	HS	Avge	100s	50s	Ct	St	O	M	Runs	Wkts	Avge	Best	5wI	10wM
Test																		
All First	12	19	2	413	76	24.29	-	1	6	-	5	0	46	0	-	-	-	-
1-day Int																		
NatWest	2	2	1	16	16	16.00	-	-	-	-								
B & H	4	4	0	67	26	16.75	-	-	-	-								
Sunday	16	13	0	235	55	18.07	-	1	15	-	2	0	22	0	-	-	-	

Career Performances

	M	Inns	NO	Runs	HS	Avge	100s	50s	Ct	St	Balls	Runs	Wkts	Avge	Best	5wI	10wM
Test																	
All First	44	68	11	2168	145 *	38.03	4	10	32	-	630	383	10	38.30	3-37	-	-
1-day Int																	
NatWest	2	2	1	16	16	16.00	-	-	-	-							
B & H	7	7	0	121	26	17.28	-	-	-	-							
Sunday	24	21	1	365	55	18.25	-	1	18	-	12	22	0	-		-	-

KENNIS, G. J. Surrey

Name: Gregor John Kennis
Role: Right-hand bat, right-arm
off-spin bowler
Born: 9 March 1974, Yokohama, Japan
Height: 6ft 2in **Weight:** 12st
Nickname: Nesty
County debut: 1994
1st-Class catches: 6
Parents: Michael and Sally
Marital status: Single
Family links with cricket: 'Dad played for
his company side and is now a qualified
coach'
Education: Tiffin Boys' School; Stewart
Cricket Academy
Qualifications: 9 GCSEs, 1 A-level, NCA
senior coach
Career outside cricket: 'Interior designing'
Overseas tours: Surrey U19 to Barbados
1991
Overseas teams played for: Claremont Nedlands, Perth 1995-96; Marist Newman
Old Boys CC, Perth 1996-97
Cricketers particularly admired: David Boon, James Bond, Alec Stewart, Neil
Stewart, Neil 'what a brave man' Sargeant
Other sports followed: Horse racing and football (West Ham)
Relaxations: Horse racing, drinking with friends
Extras: 1995 Surrey 2nd XI Batsman of the Year. Scored 258 against Leicestershire in
1995, a record for Surrey 2nd XI
Opinions on cricket: 'We should be grateful. We are getting paid for something we
enjoy doing, although getting paid more would be good.'
Best batting: 29 Surrey v Kent, Canterbury 1995

1997 Season

	M	Inns	NO	Runs	HS	Avge	100s	50s	Ct	St	O	M	Runs	Wkts	Avge	Best	5wI	10wM
Test																		
All First	3	5	0	49	24	9.80	-	-	3	-	1	0	4	0	-	-	-	-
1-day Int																		
NatWest																		
B & H																		
Sunday																		

Career Performances

	M	Inns	NO	Runs	HS	Avge	100s	50s	Ct	St	Balls	Runs	Wkts	Avge	Best	5wI	10wM
Test																		
All First	6	11	1	140	29	14.00	-	-	6	-	24	4	0	-	-	-	-
1-day Int																		
NatWest																		
B & H																		
Sunday	1	1	0	5	5	5.00	-	-	-	-								

KENWAY, D. A. Hampshire

Name: Derek Anthony Kenway
Role: Right-hand bat, right-arm medium bowler, occasional wicket-keeper
Born: 12 June 1978, Fareham
Height: 5ft 11in **Weight:** 13st
Nickname: Kenners, Prince, Squeeler, Bananaman
County debut: 1997
1st-Class catches: 1
Strike rate: 27.00 (career 27.00)
Parents: Keith and Geraldine
Family links with cricket: Brother plays Southern League cricket for Hambledon
Education: Botley Primary School; St George's, Southampton
Qualifications: 6 GCSEs, NCA coaching award, qualified snowboard instructor
Off-season: Playing for Beaumaris CC in Melbourne
Overseas tours: West of England U15 to West Indies 1993
Overseas teams played for: Beaumaris CC, Melbourne 1997-98
Cricketers particularly admired: Robin Smith, Derek Lane, Billy Taylor

Young players to look out for: David Sales, Alex Tudor
Other sports followed: Football (Southampton FC), kickboxing and boxing
Injuries: Shin splints, out for one month
Relaxations: 'The occasional social beer with my mates and spending time with my girlfriend'
Extras: *Daily Telegraph* Batting Award (West) 1994. Southern League Player of the Year in 1996. Made 1st XI debut in 1997 against Warwickshire
Opinions on cricket: 'Longer breaks during lunch and tea and between innings.'
Best batting: 20* Hampshire v Warwickshire, Southampton 1997
Best batting: 1-5 Hampshire v Warwickshire, Southampton 1997

1997 Season

	M	Inns	NO	Runs	HS	Avge	100s	50s	Ct	St	O	M	Runs	Wkts	Avge	Best	5wI	10wM
Test																		
All First	1	2	1	22	20*	22.00	-	-	1	-	9	2	58	2	29.00	1-5	-	-
1-day Int																		
NatWest																		
B & H																		
Sunday																		

Career Performances

	M	Inns	NO	Runs	HS	Avge	100s	50s	Ct	St	Balls	Runs	Wkts	Avge	Best	5wI	10wM
Test																	
All First	1	2	1	22	20*	22.00	-	-	1	-	54	58	2	29.00	1-5	-	-
1-day Int																	
NatWest																	
B & H																	
Sunday																	

KERR, J. I. D.   Somerset

Name: Jason Ian Douglas Kerr
Role: Right-hand bat, right-arm
fast-medium bowler
Born: 7 April 1974, Bolton, Lancashire
Height: 6ft 3in **Weight:** 12st 6lbs
Nickname: Junior B
County debut: 1993
1st-Class 50s: 3
1st-Class 5 w. in innings: 1
1st-Class catches: 10
Place in batting averages: (1996 164th av. 29.33)

Place in bowling averages: 109th av. 37.40 (1996 147th av. 53.27)
Strike rate: 61.80 (career 60.40)
Parents: Len and Janet
Marital status: Single
Family links with cricket: 'Brother Andy is becoming a young legend'
Education: Withins High School; Bolton Met College
Qualifications: 5 GCSEs, BTEC National Diploma in Business Studies, cricket coach
Off-season: Training in Perth, Western Australia
Overseas tours: England U19 to India 1992-93; Lancashire U19 to Isle of Man
Overseas teams played for: Gordon Districts CC, Sydney, Australia 1994-95; Taita CC, Wellington, New Zealand 1996-97
Cricketers particularly admired: Steve Waugh
Young players to look out for: Andy Kerr
Other sports followed: Bolton 'The Great' Wanderers
Injuries: Knee, missed six weeks
Relaxations: Playing golf, socialising, squash, television, swimming, sleeping, listening to music, spending time with friends and girlfriend Emma
Opinions on cricket: 'Pesh Naan!'
Best batting: 80 Somerset v West Indies, Taunton 1995
Best bowling: 5-82 Somerset v West Indies, Taunton 1995

1997 Season

	M	Inns	NO	Runs	HS	Avge	100s	50s	Ct	St	O	M	Runs	Wkts	Avge	Best	5wI	10wM
Test																		
All First	5	6	1	133	35	26.60	-	-	1	-	103	20	374	10	37.40	4-83	-	-
1-day Int																		
NatWest	2	1	0	0	0	0.00	-	-	-	-	15	0	73	5	14.60	3-32	-	
B & H	5	3	0	31	17	10.33	-	-	-	-	31	1	138	5	27.60	3-34	-	
Sunday	12	6	3	75	33	25.00	-	-	2	-	81.5	1	485	16	30.31	4-28	-	

50. Who was named Player of the Tournament in the 1997 Hong Kong Sixes?

 vodafone

Career Performances

	M	Inns	NO	Runs	HS	Avge	100s	50s	Ct	St	Balls	Runs	Wkts	Avge	Best	5wl	10wM
Test																	
All First	32	47	9	730	80	19.21	-	3	10	-	3866	2590	64	40.46	5-82	1	-
1-day Int																	
NatWest	4	3	0	3	3	1.00	-	-	-	-	156	147	7	21.00	3-32	-	
B & H	6	3	0	31	17	10.33	-	-	-	-	234	173	7	24.71	3-34	-	
Sunday	40	24	8	174	33	10.87	-	-	5	-	1597	1477	50	29.54	4-28	-	

KETTLEBOROUGH, R. A.   Middlesex

Name: Richard Allan Kettleborough
Role: Left-hand bat, right-arm medium bowler
Born: 15 March 1973, Sheffield
Height: 5ft 10in **Weight:** 12st
Nickname: Ketts
County debut: 1994
1st-Class 50s: 1
1st-Class 100s: 1
1st-Class catches: 9
Place in batting averages: (1996 121st av. 34.11)
Strike rate: 78.00 (career 66.00)
Parents: Allan and Pat
Marital status: Single
Family links with cricket: Father played for Yorkshire and is now coach at Worksop College
Education: Laughton All Saints Junior School; Worksop College; Airedale and Wharfdale College, Leeds
Qualifications: 5 GCSEs, BTEC in Recreational Management, senior coaching award
Career outside cricket: 'Would like to own my own pub'
Overseas tours: Worksop College to Australia 1988-89; England U18 to Canada 1991; Yorkshire CCC to South Africa 1995
Overseas teams played for: Somerset West, Cape Town 1993-94
Cricketers particularly admired: David Gower and 'all the Yorkshire team'
Young players to look out for: Anthony McGrath
Other sports followed: Football (Sheffield Wednesday FC)
Relaxations: 'Spending time with friends in Sheffield'
Extras: Won the Lord's Taverners U15 award for the Most Promising Young Cricketer in 1988. 2nd XI cap at Yorkshire. Has joined Middlesex for 1998

Opinions on cricket: 'Not enough time to practise during the season.'
Best batting: 108 Yorkshire v Essex, Headingley 1996
Best bowling: 2-26 Yorkshire v Nottinghamshire, Scarborough 1996

1997 Season

	M	Inns	NO	Runs	HS	Avge	100s	50s	Ct	St	O	M	Runs	Wkts	Avge	Best	5wI	10wM
Test																		
All First	3	5	0	22	10	4.40	-	-	2	-	13	3	74	1	74.00	1-74	-	-
1-day Int																		
NatWest																			
B & H																			
Sunday	1	1	0	9	9	9.00	-	-	-	-								

Career Performances

	M	Inns	NO	Runs	HS	Avge	100s	50s	Ct	St	Balls	Runs	Wkts	Avge	Best	5wI	10wM
Test																	
All First	13	19	2	446	108	26.23	1	2	9	-	198	153	3	51.00	2-26	-	-
1-day Int																	
NatWest																		
B & H																		
Sunday	10	6	3	71	28	23.66	-	-	4	-	66	72	3	24.00	2-43	-	

KEY, R. W. T.   Kent

Name: Robert William Trevor Key
Role: Right-hand bat, right-arm fast-medium
bowler, occasional wicket-keeper
Born: 12 May 1979, Dulwich
Height: 6ft 1in **Weight:** 13st 5lbs
Nickname: Keysy, Ronald, Builder
County debut: No first-team appearance
Parents: Trevor and Lynn
Marital status: Single
Family links with cricket: Mother played
for Kent Ladies. Father played club cricket in
Derby. Sister Elizabeth played for her junior
school side
Education: Worsley Bridge Primary School;
Langley Park Boys' School
Qualifications: 7 GCSEs, NCA coaching
award, GNVQ Business
Career outside cricket: Not decided

Overseas tours: Kent U13 to Holland
Overseas teams played for: Green Point CC, Cape Town 1996-97
Cricketers particularly admired: Eddy Stanford, Matt Walker, Jamie Rowe, Steve Rudduck, David Penfold, Jon Bond, Alan Ealham
Young players to look out for: Simon Evans, James Hockley, Jon Bond, Jamie Rowe, Ben Phillips, Will House
Other sports followed: Football (Newcastle United), hockey (plays for Beckenham), basketball (Chicago Bulls), squash, golf, tennis
Relaxations: Going out, socialising and 'playing indoor cricket with David Penfold and the greatest cheat Steve Rudduck'
Extras: Played for England U17 and England U19 Development XI. Also played for South England U14 and U19. County tennis player. Played for England U19 against Zimbabwe in 1997 and captained the England U17 side to victory in the international Under 19 tournament in Bermuda in July; played for the victorious England side in the U19 World Cup in South Africa
Opinions on cricket: 'There isn't a lack of talent in the English game, players just lack the mental toughness needed for the international game.'

KHAN, A. A. Sussex

Name: Amer Ali Khan
Role: Right-hand bat, leg-break bowler
Born: 5 November 1969, Lahore, Pakistan
Height: 5ft 9in **Weight:** 12st
Nickname: Agha
County debut: 1995 (Middlesex), 1997 (Suusex)
1st-Class 50s: 1
1st-Class 5 w. in innings: 1
1st-Class catches: 5
Place in batting averages: 256th av. 15.31
Place in bowling averages: 127th av. 42.33
Strike rate: 80.81 (career 76.17)
Parents: M. Haneef Khan and Shireen Haneef
Family links with cricket: Father used to play club cricket
Education: Muslim Model High School, Lahore, Pakistan; MAO College, Lahore, Pakistan
Career outside cricket: 'Don't know yet'
Off-season: 'I'd like to go overseas and play'
Overseas teams played for: Wakatu CC, Nelson, New Zealand 1994-95

Cricketers particularly admired: Mark Ramprakash, Steve Waugh, Mark Waugh
Young players to look out for: David Nash, James Hewitt, Owais Shah
Other sports followed: 'Touch rugby with my team mates'
Injuries: Hamstring, missed the last game of the season against Notts
Relaxations: Go to cinemas and listen to rap, swing, soul, hip-hop and a bit of reggae
Extras: Released by Middlesex at the end of the 1996 season and joined Sussex in 1997
Best batting: 52 Sussex v Hampshire, Southampton 1997
Best bowling: 5-137 Sussex v Middlesex, Lord's 1997

1997 Season

	M	Inns	NO	Runs	HS	Avge	100s	50s	Ct	St	O	M	Runs	Wkts	Avge	Best	5wI	10wM
Test																		
All First	15	24	5	291	52	15.31	-	1	4	-	444.3	100	1397	33	42.33	5-137	1	-
1-day Int																		
NatWest	4	1	0	4	4	4.00	-	-	1	-	40	4	196	2	98.00	1-13	-	
B & H	5	3	0	15	8	5.00	-	-	2	-	49	2	217	8	27.12	3-31	-	
Sunday	13	9	3	48	22 *	8.00	-	-	2	-	90.5	3	474	15	31.60	5-40	1	

Career Performances

	M	Inns	NO	Runs	HS	Avge	100s	50s	Ct	St	Balls	Runs	Wkts	Avge	Best	5wI	10wM
Test																	
All First	18	24	5	291	52	15.31	-	1	5	-	3123	1539	41	37.53	5-137	1	-
1-day Int																	
NatWest	4	1	0	4	4	4.00	-	-	1	-	240	196	2	98.00	1-13	-	
B & H	5	3	0	15	8	5.00	-	-	2	-	294	217	8	27.12	3-31	-	
Sunday	13	9	3	48	22 *	8.00	-	-	2	-	545	474	15	31.60	5-40	1	

KHAN, G. A.　　　　　　　　　　　　　Derbyshire

Name: Gul Abbass Khan
Role: Right-hand bat, leg-break bowler
Born: 31 December 1973, Gujrat, Pakistan
Height: 5ft 9in **Weight:** 12st
Nickname: Gullie
County debut: 1996
1st-Class 50s: 5
1st-Class 100s: 1
1st-Class catches: 7
Place in batting averages: 87th av. 38.00
Strike rate: (career 58.00)
Parents: Qufait and Shahnaz
Marital status: Single
Family links with cricket: Father played club
cricket in Pakistan
Education: Valentine High School; Ipswich
School; Swansea University; Keble College,
Oxford University
Qualifications: 8 GCSEs, 3 A-levels, BSc
(Hons) in Anthropology and Social Studies, Postgraduate Diploma in Social Studies
Overseas tours: Ipswich School to Australia 1991-92
Overseas teams played for: P&T Gymkhana, Lahore, Pakistan 1993-94
Cricketers particularly admired: Sunil Gavaskar, Javed Miandad, David Gower, Ayaz
Lodhi
Young players to look out for: Andrew Alexander, Russell Thompson, Pierre Du Prez
Other sports followed: Football (Manchester United), squash, badminton
Relaxations: Reading, travelling, going out to eat with friends
Extras: *Daily Telegraph* South of England Batting Award 1989 and 1991
Opinions on cricket: 'The issue of ball tampering should be conclusively dealt with by
the ICC.'
Best batting: 101* Oxford University v Kent, Canterbury 1996
Best bowling: 2-48 Oxford University v Hampshire, The Parks 1996

1997 Season

	M	Inns	NO	Runs	HS	Avge	100s	50s	Ct	St	O	M	Runs	Wkts	Avge	Best	5wI	10wM
Test																		
All First	3	5	1	95	62 *	23.75	-	1	-	-								
1-day Int																		
NatWest	2	2	0	19	19	9.50	-	-	1	-								
B & H	5	5	1	88	33	22.00	-	-	1	-								
Sunday	7	6	1	124	71 *	24.80	-	1	1	-								

302

Career Performances

	M	Inns	NO	Runs	HS	Avge	100s	50s	Ct	St	Balls	Runs	Wkts	Avge	Best	5wI	10wM
Test																	
All First	16	23	3	703	101 *	35.15	1	5	7	-	174	190	3	63.33	2-48	-	-
1-day Int																	
NatWest	3	3	0	34	19	11.33	-	-	2	-							
B & H	10	10	1	320	147	35.55	1	-	2	-							
Sunday	14	12	2	205	71 *	20.50	-	1	3	-							

KHAN, W. G. Sussex

Name: Wasim Gulzar Khan
Role: Left-hand bat, right-arm
leg-break bowler
Born: 26 February 1971, Birmingham
Height: 6ft 1in **Weight:** 11st 5lbs
Nickname: Wazby, Dog
County debut: 1992 (one-day,
Warwickshire),
1995 (first-class, Warwickshire)
1st-Class 50s: 8
1st-Class 100s: 4
1st-Class catches: 30
Place in batting averages: 180th av. 27.33
(1995 27th av. 49.82)
Parents: Gulzar Khan (deceased)
and Zarina Begum
Marital status: Single
Education: Small Heath Secondary School,
Birmingham; Josiah Mason Sixth Form
College, Birmingham
Qualifications: 6 O-levels, 1 A-level, NCA coaching award
Overseas tours: Warwickshire to Cape Town 1993 and 1995
Overseas teams played for: Western Suburbs, Sydney 1990-91; North Perth, Western
Australia 1991-93; Albion, Melbourne 1993-95; Petone Riverside, Wellington, New
Zealand 1996-97
Cricketers particularly admired: Graham Thorpe, Saeed Anwar, and 'all the
Warwickshire team for their competitiveness, desire to win and team spirit'
Young players to look out for: Anurag Singh, Darren Altree
Other sports followed: Football (Leeds United), golf, tennis, squash
Relaxations: Listening to music, spending time with family and friends
Extras: Most Promising Young Cricketer 1990. Scored four centuries in a row for

Warwickshire U19. Scored 171* v Northants in second trial game for Warwickshire 2nd XI. England Schools U19. Won Oxford/Cambridge U19 Festival 1989, 1990. Left Warwickshire at the end of the 1997 season to join Sussex
Best batting: 181 Warwickshire v Hampshire, Southampton 1995

1997 Season

	M	Inns	NO	Runs	HS	Avge	100s	50s	Ct	St	O	M	Runs	Wkts	Avge	Best	5wI	10wM
Test																		
All First	3	5	0	102	43	20.40	-	-	2	-	1	1	0	0	-	-	-	-
1-day Int																		
NatWest																			
B & H																			
Sunday	3	3	0	33	27	11.00	-	-	-	-								

Career Performances

	M	Inns	NO	Runs	HS	Avge	100s	50s	Ct	St	Balls	Runs	Wkts	Avge	Best	5wI	10wM
Test																	
All First	31	56	7	1687	181		34.42	4	8	30	-	61	24	0	-	-	-	-
1-day Int																	
NatWest																	
B & H	1	1	1	0	0 *	-	-	-	1	-							
Sunday	10	10	0	65	27	6.50	-	-	2	-							

KILLEEN, N.   Durham

Name: Neil Killeen
Role: Right-hand bat, right-arm
fast-medium bowler
Born: 17 October 1975, Shotley Bridge
Height: 6ft 2 in **Weight:** 14st 12lbs
Nickname: Killer, Squeaky, Quinny
County debut: 1995
1st-Class catches: 7
1st-Class 5 w. in innings: 1
Place in batting averages: 306th av. 6.66 (1995 260th av. 13.70)
Place in bowling averages: 102nd av. 36.16 (1995 132nd av. 45.11)
Strike rate: 54.85 (career 62.38)
Parents: Glen and Thora
Marital status: Single
Education: Greencroft Comprehensive School; Derwentside College, University of Teesside
Qualifications: 8 GCSEs, 2 A-levels, advanced coaching award

Off-season: Playing for Taiiangatta in Melbourne, Australia
Overseas tours: Durham CCC to Zimbabwe 1992; England U19 to West Indies 1994-95
Cricketers particularly admired: Ian Botham, Curtly Ambrose
Young players to look out for: Melvyn Betts
Other sports followed: Athletics (English Schools javelin) and football
Relaxations: 'Spending time with friends and going out. Listening to music and watching television'
Extras: First Durham bowler to take five wickets in a Sunday League game (5-26 against Northamptonshire in 1995)
Opinions on cricket: 'Too many overs in a day in the first-class game.'
Best batting: 48 Durham v Somerset, Chester-le-Street 1995
Best bowling: 5-118 Durham v Sussex, Hartlepool 1995

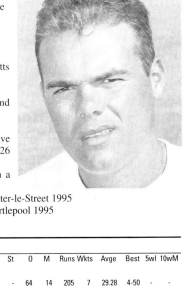

1997 Season

	M	Inns	NO	Runs	HS	Avge	100s	50s	Ct	St	O	M	Runs	Wkts	Avge	Best	5wI	10wM
Test																		
All First	3	3	2	24	15	24.00	-	-	2	-	64	14	205	7	29.28	4-50	-	-
1-day Int																		
NatWest																		
B & H	4	1	0	3	3	3.00	-	-	-	-	36	3	139	1	139.00	1-43	-	
Sunday	7	4	1	2	1 *	0.66	-	-	-	-	47.4	3	259	11	23.54	4-46	-	

Career Performances

	M	Inns	NO	Runs	HS	Avge	100s	50s	Ct	St	Balls	Runs	Wkts	Avge	Best	5wI	10wM
Test																	
All First	15	23	6	201	48	11.82	-	-	7	-	2246	1406	36	39.05	5-118	1	-
1-day Int																	
NatWest	1	0	0	0	0	-	-	-	1	-	72	46	1	46.00	1-46	-	
B & H	13	7	1	21	8	3.50	-	-	2	-	718	526	9	58.44	2-43	-	
Sunday	29	19	4	85	32	5.66	-	-	5	-	1247	1077	39	27.61	5-26	1	

KIRBY, S. P.   Leicestershire

Name: Stephen P. Kirby
Role: Right-hand bat, right-arm fast bowler
Born: 4 October 1977, Bury, Lancashire
Height: 6ft 3in **Weight:** 12st 4lbs
Nickname: 'There are more than a few'
County debut: No first-team appearance
Parents: Paul and Alison
Marital status: Single
Family links with cricket: None
Education: St Joseph's RC, Heywood,
Lancs; Elton High School, Bury; Bury
College, Lancs
Qualifications: 9 GCSEs, BTEC GNVQ
Advanced Leisure and Tourism
Career outside cricket: 'None at the
moment'
Off-season: Playing in New Zealand
Overseas teams played for: Taranaki,
Egmont Plains, New Zealand 1997-98

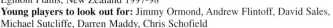

Young players to look out for: Jimmy Ormond, Andrew Flintoff, David Sales,
Michael Sutcliffe, Darren Maddy, Chris Schofield
Other sports followed: Football (Manchester United), rugby (Leicester Tigers),
basketball, tennis, golf, table tennis, squash, 'anything competitive'
Relaxations: Spending time with my girlfriend and friends
Opinions on cricket: 'I believe that we do not play on enough good pitches, therefore
not promoting enough good techniques with bat and ball from an early age. Also I do
not believe that we are producing enough world-class bowlers, because we are
expecting the pitch to do the work for us, instead of learning to do something with the
ball, which in turn goes back to the standard of the pitches.'

KIRTLEY, R. J.   Sussex

Name: Robert James Kirtley
Role: Right-hand bat, right-arm
fast-medium bowler
Born: 10 January 1975, Eastbourne
Height: 6ft **Weight:** 12st
Nickname: Ambi, Hurtler, Orange, Dufus
County debut: 1995

1st-Class 5 w. in innings: 4
1st-Class catches: 11
Place in batting averages: 304th av. 5.44
(1996 318th av. 2.75)
Place in bowling averages: 101st av. 35.29
(1996 44th av. 28.00)
Strike rate: 53.51 (career 46.97)
Parents: Bob and Pip
Marital status: Single
Family links with cricket: Brother plays
league cricket
Education: St Andrews School, Eastbourne;
Clifton College, Bristol
Qualifications: 9 GCSEs, 2 A-levels, NCA
coaching first level
Off-season: 'Enjoying'
Overseas tours: Sussex YC to Barbados
1993, to Sri Lanka 1995
Overseas teams played for: Mashonaland, Zimbabwe
Cricketers particularly admired: Curtly Ambrose, Jim Andrew and Darren Gough
Other sports followed: Hockey, golf and football (Brighton & Hove Albion)
Relaxations: Sleeping
Extras: Played in the Mashonaland side which defeated England on their 1996-97 tour
of Zimbabwe, taking seven wickets in the match
Opinions on cricket: 'With hard ground and indoor facilities, the workload of bowlers
should be lessened in order to prolong careers and keep bowlers fresh.'
Best batting: 15* Sussex v Surrey, Hove 1997
Best bowling: 6-60 Sussex v Glamorgan, Swansea 1997

1997 Season

	M	Inns	NO	Runs	HS	Avge	100s	50s	Ct	St	O	M	Runs	Wkts	Avge	Best	5wI	10wM
Test																		
All First	11	16	7	49	15*	5.44	-	-	4	-	276.3	48	1094	31	35.29	6-60	1	-
1-day Int																		
NatWest	2	0	0	0	0	-	-	-	-	-	24	3	100	7	14.28	5-39	1	
B & H																		
Sunday	7	4	2	14	7	7.00	-	-	2	-	48.1	0	300	7	42.85	2-36	-	

51. Who was voted the 1997 PCA Player of the Year?

O vodafone

Career Performances

	M	Inns	NO	Runs	HS	Avge	100s	50s	Ct	St	Balls	Runs	Wkts	Avge	Best	5wI	10wM
Test																	
All First	23	31	13	77	15 *	4.27	-	-	11	-	3476	2125	74	28.71	6-60	4	-
1-day Int																	
NatWest	2	0	0	0	0	-	-	-	-	-	144	100	7	14.28	5-39	1	
B & H																	
Sunday	16	7	4	17	7	5.66	-	-	2	-	571	554	12	46.16	2-36	-	

KNIGHT, N. V. Warwickshire

Name: Nicholas Verity Knight
Role: Left-hand bat, right-arm medium-fast bowler, close fielder, county vice-captain
Born: 28 November 1969, Watford
Height: 6ft **Weight:** 13st
Nickname: Stitch, Canvas, Fungus
County debut: 1991 (Essex),
1995 (Warwickshire)
County cap: 1994 (Essex),
1995 (Warwickshire)
Test debut: 1995
Tests: 11
One-Day Internationals: 12
1st-Class 50s: 31
1st-Class 100s: 16
1st-Class catches: 149
One-Day 100s: 6
Place in batting averages: 23rd av. 49.21
(1996 38th av. 47.84)
Strike rate: (career 148.00)
Parents: John and Rosemary
Marital status: Single
Family links with cricket: Father played for Cambridgeshire, brother plays club cricket for St Giles in Cambridge
Education: St John's School, Cambridge; Felsted Prep; Felsted School; Loughborough University
Qualifications: 9 O-levels, 3 A-levels, BSc (Hons) Sociology, coaching qualification
Off-season: Playing for England in Sharjah and then captaining England A in Kenya and Sri Lanka
Overseas tours: Felsted School to Australia 1986-87; England A to India 1994-95, to Pakistan 1995-96, to Kenya and Sri Lanka 1997-98; England to Zimbabwe and New

Zealand 1996-97, to Sharjah 1997-98, to West Indies (one-day series)
Overseas teams played for: Northern Districts, Sydney 1991-92; East Torrens, Adelaide 1992-94
Relaxations: 'Eating good food and painting'
Extras: Captained English Schools 1987 and 1988, England YC v New Zealand 1989 and Combined Universities 1991. Played hockey for Essex and Young England. Played rugby for Eastern Counties. Won *Daily Telegraph* award 1988; voted Gray-Nicolls Cricketer of the Year 1988, Cricket Society Cricketer of the Year 1989, Essex Young Player of the Year 1991 and Essex U19 Player of the Year. Left Essex at the end of 1994 season to join Warwickshire. Scored successive centuries in the Texaco Trophy against Pakistan in 1996
Opinions on cricket: 'Tea break not long enough and too many overs in a day.'
Best batting: 174 Warwickshire v Kent, Canterbury 1995
Best bowling: 1-61 Essex v Middlesex, Uxbridge 1994

1997 Season

	M	Inns	NO	Runs	HS	Avge	100s	50s	Ct	St	O	M	Runs	Wkts	Avge	Best	5wI	10wM
Test																		
All First	11	17	3	689	119 *	49.21	2	3	8	-	6	0	71	0	-	-	-	-
1-day Int	2	2	0	16	12	8.00	-	-	-	-								
NatWest	2	2	0	0	0	0.00	-	-	1	-								
B & H	2	2	0	74	69	37.00	-	1	-	-								
Sunday	8	8	0	252	102	31.50	1	-	3	-								

Career Performances

	M	Inns	NO	Runs	HS	Avge	100s	50s	Ct	St	Balls	Runs	Wkts	Avge	Best	5wI	10wM
Test	11	19	0	573	113	30.15	1	4	21	-							
All First	107	180	21	6412	174	40.32	16	31	149	-	148	176	1	176.00	1-61	-	-
1-day Int	12	12	3	428	125 *	47.55	2	1	3	-							
NatWest	12	12	1	419	151	38.09	1	3	5	-							
B & H	25	22	3	605	104	31.84	1	3	7	-	6	4	0	-	-	-	
Sunday	75	66	9	1667	134	29.24	2	5	30	-	84	85	2	42.50	1-14	-	

KNOTT, J. A.   Surrey

Name: James Alan Knott
Role: Right-hand bat, leg-spin bowler, wicket-keeper
Born: 14 June 1975
Height: 5ft 6in **Weight:** 11st 5lbs
Nickname: Billy Bunting ('Wolfey to ex-MCC team mates')
County debut: 1995
1st-Class catches: 11
1st-Class stumpings: 2
Place in batting averages: 217th av. 19.66
Parents: Alan and Janet
Marital status: Single
Family links with cricket: 'Dad played a bit'
Education: Herne Church of England Primary School; Dane Court Grammar School; City of Westminster College
Qualifications: 10 GCSEs, 2 A-levels, 2 GNVQ level 3s, basic basketball and cricket coach
Overseas tours: Canterbury District U15 to Holland
Overseas teams played for: Waverley, Sydney, Australia 1993-94
Cricketers particularly admired: Graham Gooch, David Boon, Mike Atherton and 'I guess my old man helped me out a bit'
Other sports followed: Football (West Ham United)
Relaxations: 'Enjoy movies, horror and science fiction novels, spending time with close friends and a good night out with the Surrey boys'
Extras: 'Shortest ever basketball captain at school.' Has never won a trophy through cricket but has won several through football
Opinions on cricket: 'Need to get youngsters playing a higher standard of cricket earlier. Need to start producing more players of Test calibre and introduce them early to it.'
Best batting: 49* Surrey v South Africa A, The Oval 1996

52. Who was voted the 1997 PCA Young Player of the Year?

 vodafone

310

1997 Season

	M	Inns	NO	Runs	HS	Avge	100s	50s	Ct	St	O	M	Runs	Wkts	Avge	Best	5wl	10wM
Test																		
All First	5	9	3	118	27 *	19.66	-	-	8	1								
1-day Int																		
NatWest																		
B & H	2	1	0	10	10	10.00	-	-	6	-								
Sunday	4	3	0	23	22	7.66	-	-	5	-								

Career Performances

	M	Inns	NO	Runs	HS	Avge	100s	50s	Ct	St	Balls	Runs	Wkts	Avge	Best	5wl	10wM
Test																	
All First	7	11	4	170	49 *	24.28	-	-	11	2							
1-day Int																	
NatWest																	
B & H	2	1	0	10	10	10.00	-	-	6	-							
Sunday	4	3	0	23	22	7.66	-	-	5	-							

KRIKKEN, K. M.   Derbyshire

Name: Karl Matthew Krikken
Role: Right-hand bat, wicket-keeper
Born: 9 April 1969, Bolton
Height: 5ft 10in **Weight:** 12st 7lbs
Nickname: Krikk
County debut: 1987 (one-day),
1989 (first-class)
County cap: 1992
1st-Class 50s: 15
1st-Class 100s: 1
1st-Class catches: 382
1st-Class stumpings: 25
Place in batting averages: 173rd av. 24.26
(1996 72nd av. 40.09)
Parents: Brian and Irene
Wife: Leesha
Children: 'At the time of going to press I
should have a little one'
Family links with cricket: Father played for
Lancashire and Worcestershire
Education: Horwich Church School; Rivington and Blackrod High School and Sixth
Form College

Qualifications: 6 O-levels, 3 A-levels, cricket coaching certificates
Overseas tours: Derbyshire to Bermuda 1993, to Torremolinos 1995
Overseas teams played for: CBC Old Boys, Kimberley, South Africa 1988-89; Green Island, Dunedin, New Zealand 1990-91; United, Cape Town 1992-93; Rivertonians, Cape Town 1993-94
Cricketers particularly admired: Bob Taylor, Derek Randall, Kim Barnett
Young players to look out for: Andrew Harris
Other sports followed: Football (Wigan FC, Bolton FC), rugby league (Wigan RLFC)
Relaxations: Relaxing at home with Leesha. Walking and good food
Extras: Derbyshire Supporters' Player of the Year 1991 and 1996, Derbyshire Clubman of the Year 1993. Appointed Derbyshire vice-captain for the 1998 season
Opinions on cricket: 'It's bloody good.'
Best batting: 104 Derbyshire v Lancashire, Old Trafford 1996

1997 Season

	M	Inns	NO	Runs	HS	Avge	100s	50s	Ct	St	O	M	Runs	Wkts	Avge	Best	5wI	10wM
Test																		
All First	19	27	4	558	72	24.26	-	3	53	2								
1-day Int																		
NatWest	3	2	0	39	38	19.50	-	-	1	-								
B & H	5	4	3	123	42 *	123.00	-	-	3	-								
Sunday	12	11	3	153	39	19.12	-	-	11	3								

Career Performances

	M	Inns	NO	Runs	HS	Avge	100s	50s	Ct	St	Balls	Runs	Wkts	Avge	Best	5wI	10wM
Test																	
All First	151	221	46	4057	104	23.18	1	15	382	25	36	40	0	-	-	-	-
1-day Int																	
NatWest	14	9	4	156	55	31.20	-	1	12	-							
B & H	23	16	7	252	42 *	28.00	-	-	25	2							
Sunday	91	61	21	719	44 *	17.97	-	-	98	13							

LACEY, S. J.   Derbyshire

Name: Simon James Lacey
Role: Right-hand bat, off-spin bowler
Born: 9 March 1975, Nottingham
Height: 5ft 11in **Weight:** 12st 7lbs
Nickname: Bone 'apparently I'm supposed to be bone idle'
County debut: 1997
1st-Class 50s: 1
1st-Class catches: 1

Strike rate: 80.57 (career 80.57)
Parents: Phil and Anne
Marital status: Single
Family links with cricket: None
Education: Mundy Street School, Heanor;
Aldercar Comprehensive School, Langley
Mill; Mill Hill Sixth Form, Ripley
Education: 6 GCSEs, NCA coaching award
(level 2)
Career outside cricket: Police force or PE
teacher
Cricketers particularly admired: Alec
Stewart, Kim Barnett
Young players to look out for: Andrew
Harris, Anurag Singh
Other sports followed: Football 'a very big
fan of the "Rams", Derby County. I also
follow Ilkeston Town who play in the Dr

Martens League', snooker, 'I play for South East Derbyshire Snooker Club'
Relaxations: Listening to music, 'Ocean Colour Scene, Bluetones and Oasis being
particular favourites, although I do listen to anything'
Extras: Was a member of the England Junior Volleyball squad in 1991. Captained the
NAYC at U19 level against ESCA at Lord's in 1994
Opinions on cricket: 'None in particular.'
Best batting: 50 Derbyshire v Somerset, Derby 1997
Best bowling: 3-97 Derbyshire v Essex, Southend 1997

1997 Season

	M	Inns	NO	Runs	HS	Avge	100s	50s	Ct	St	O	M	Runs	Wkts	Avge	Best	5wI	10wM
Test																		
All First	6	8	4	129	50	32.25	-	1	1	-	94	19	291	7	41.57	3-97	-	-
1-day Int																		
NatWest																		
B & H																		
Sunday	3	1	0	9	9	9.00	-	-	-	-	11	0	62	1	62.00	1-38	-	

Career Performances

	M	Inns	NO	Runs	HS	Avge	100s	50s	Ct	St	Balls	Runs	Wkts	Avge	Best	5wI	10wM
Test																	
All First	6	8	4	129	50	32.25	-	1	1	-	564	291	7	41.57	3-97	-	-
1-day Int																	
NatWest																	
B & H																	
Sunday	3	1	0	9	9	9.00	-	-	-	-	66	62	1	62.00	1-38	-	

LAMPITT, S. R.   Worcestershire

Name: Stuart Richard Lampitt
Role: Right-hand bat, right-arm
fast-medium bowler
Born: 29 July 1966, Wolverhampton
Height: 5ft 10in **Weight:** 13st 7lb
Nickname: Jed
County debut: 1985
County cap: 1989
50 wickets in a season: 5
1st-Class 50s: 17
1st-Class 100s: 1
1st-Class 5 w. in innings: 13
1st-Class catches: 118
One-Day 5 w. in innings: 3
Place in batting averages: 136th av. 27.70
(1996 159th av. 29.90)
Place in bowling averages: 108th av. 37.20
(1996 98th av. 35.53)
Strike rate: 57.37 (career 55.86)

Parents: Joseph Charles and Muriel Ann
Marital status: 'By time of printing hopefully engaged to Clare if she accepts'
Education: Kingswinford Secondary School; Dudley College of Technology
Qualifications: 7 O-levels; Diploma in Business Studies, NCA advanced coach
Career outside cricket: Coaching cricket
Off-season: Coaching
Overseas tours: NCA U19 to Bermuda; Worcestershire to Bahamas 1990, to
Zimbabwe 1990-91, to South Africa 1991-92, to Barbados 1996
Overseas teams played for: Mangere, Auckland 1986-88; University CC, Perth 1991-93
Cricketers particularly admired: All first-class cricketers
Young players to look out for: 'The good ones'
Other sports followed: Football (Wolves), golf, and most ball sports
Injuries: Back, missed two to three weeks
Relaxations: Golf and fishing
Extras: Took five wickets and made 42 for Stourbridge in final of the William Younger
Cup at Lord's in 1986. One of the Whittingdale Young Players of the Year 1990. 'Must
be the only bowler to be hit for six first ball by Adrian Jones and Phil Tufnell (two master
batsmen)'
Opinions on cricket: 'What a great game!'
Best batting: 122 Worcestershire v Middlesex, Lord's 1994
Best bowling: 5-32 Worcestershire v Kent, Worcester 1989

1997 Season

	M	Inns	NO	Runs	HS	Avge	100s	50s	Ct	St	O	M	Runs	Wkts	Avge	Best	5wI	10wM
Test																		
All First	15	17	7	277	52	27.70	-	1	16	-	334.4	70	1302	35	37.20	5-39	1	-
1-day Int																		
NatWest	2	2	1	28	28 *	28.00	-	-	1	-	12	0	72	0	-	-	-	-
B & H	4	4	2	57	23	28.50	-	-	-	-	29	4	109	3	36.33	2-17	-	
Sunday	15	8	5	130	38 *	43.33	-	-	5	-	92	0	460	21	21.90	4-49	-	

Career Performances

	M	Inns	NO	Runs	HS	Avge	100s	50s	Ct	St	Balls	Runs	Wkts	Avge	Best	5wI	10wM
Test																	
All First	176	224	49	4219	122	24.10	1	17	118	-	24133	13164	432	30.47	5-32	13	-
1-day Int																	
NatWest	22	15	4	163	29	14.81	-	-	7	-	1151	841	33	25.48	5-22	1	
B & H	35	19	7	242	41	20.16	-	-	10	-	1882	1230	60	20.50	6-26	1	
Sunday	138	79	30	1039	41 *	21.20	-	-	40	-	4788	3875	153	25.32	5-67	1	

LANEY, J. S.   Hampshire

Name: Jason Scott Laney
Role: Right-hand bat, right-arm off-spin bowler
Born: 24 April 1973, Winchester
Height: 5ft 10in **Weight:** 12st 10lbs
Nickname: Hurler, Chucky, Bing Bong, Hob Hob
County debut: 1993 (one-day), 1995 (first-class)
County cap: 1996
1000 runs in a season: 1
1st-Class 50s: 14
1st-Class 100s: 4
1st-Class catches: 28
One-Day 100s: 1
Place in batting averages: 11th av. 32.61 (1996 80th av. 38.76)
Parents: Geoff and Pam
Marital status: Single
Education: Pewsey Vale Comprehensive; St John's, Marlborough; Leeds Metropolitan University
Qualifications: 8 GCSEs, 2 A-levels, BA (Hons) in Human Movement Studies

Career outside cricket: 'Anything that pays'
Off-season: 'Decorating, coaching, drinking and belching'
Overseas tours: England U18 to Canada 1991
Overseas teams played for: Waikatu, New Zealand 1994-95; Matabeleland and Old Miltonians, Zimbabwe 1995-96; DHS Old Boys, South Africa 1996-97
Cricketers particularly admired: Rupert Cox, Robin Smith, Mark Garaway
Young players to look out for: Lee Savident, Andy Oram, Giles White
Other sports followed: Football (Swindon Town, Liverpool), golf, pool and snooker
Injuries: Broken finger ('thanks Sid'), missed three games
Relaxations: 'Television, videos, beer, golf, reading, porn (only educational of course), cricket – more or less in that order'
Extras: Hampshire Young Cricketer of the Year 1995. Awarded county cap in 1996. Only Hampshire cricketer to score a century before lunch on debut in the NatWest trophy
Opinions on cricket: 'Nice to see they are considering giving longer lunch and tea breaks – yesh mate! Less cricket, wider bats, bigger balls, smaller stumps, and something original – midget umpires.'
Best batting: 112 Hampshire v Oxford University, The Parks 1996

1997 Season

	M	Inns	NO	Runs	HS	Avge	100s	50s	Ct	St	O	M	Runs	Wkts	Avge	Best	5wI	10wM
Test																		
All First	15	27	1	848	95	32.61	-	6	6	-	5	2	19	0	-	-	-	-
1-day Int																		
NatWest	2	2	0	75	40	37.50	-	-	1	-								
B & H	4	4	0	39	17	9.75	-	-	1	-								
Sunday	14	14	0	371	69	26.50	-	2	4	-								

Career Performances

	M	Inns	NO	Runs	HS	Avge	100s	50s	Ct	St	Balls	Runs	Wkts	Avge	Best	5wI	10wM
Test																	
All First	43	78	2	2584	112	34.00	4	14	28	-	132	83	0	-	-	-	-
1-day Int																	
NatWest	5	5	0	340	153	68.00	1	1	2	-							
B & H	8	8	0	148	41	18.50	-	-	1	-							
Sunday	31	31	0	832	69	26.83	-	4	8	-							

LANGER, J. L.   Middlesex

Name: Justin Lee Langer
Role: Left-hand bat, right-arm medium
bowler
Born: 21 November 1970, Perth,
Western Australia
Height: 5ft 8in
County debut: No first-team appearance
Test debut: 1992-93
Tests: 8
One-Day Internationals: 8
1st-Class 50s: 23
1st-Class 100s: 17
1st-Class 200s: 3
1st-Class catches: 59
Place in batting averages: 37th av. 44.57
Education: Aquinas College, Perth;
University of Western Australia
Overseas tours: Australia to New Zealand
1992-93, to South Africa 1996-97, to England
1997; Young Australia to England 1995
Overseas teams played for: Western Australia 1990-98
Extras: A prolific run-scorer for Western Australia in recent years, Justin Langer was
drafted into the Australia in 1992-93 side after Damien Martyn suffered an injury
during the practice session for the match against the West Indies. He scored an heroic
54 in the face of some aggressive bowling by the West Indies but only played in
another five Tests over the next three years until he forced his way back into the Test
side in 1996-97 – ironically against the West Indies
Best batting: 274* Western Australia v South Australia, Perth 1996-97

1997 Season

	M	Inns	NO	Runs	HS	Avge	100s	50s	Ct	St	O	M	Runs	Wkts	Avge	Best	5wI	10wM
Test																		
All First	6	10	3	312	152*	44.57	1	1	5	-								
1-day Int	1	1	0	29	29	29.00	-	-	1	-								
NatWest																		
B & H																		
Sunday																		

Career Performances

	M	Inns	NO	Runs	HS	Avge	100s	50s	Ct	St	Balls	Runs	Wkts	Avge	Best	5wI	10wM
Test	8	12	0	272	69	22.66	-	3	2	-							
All First	77	134	16	5920	274 *	50.16	17	23	59	-	60	30	0	-	-	-	-
1-day Int	8	7	2	160	36	32.00	-	-	2	1							
NatWest																	
B & H																	
Sunday																	

LARA, B. C.   Warwickshire

Name: Brian Charles Lara
Role: Left-hand bat, leg-spin bowler, county captain
Born: 2 May 1969, Port of Spain, Trinidad
County debut: 1994
County cap: 1994
Test debut: 1990-91
Tests: 48
One-Day Internationals: 118
1000 runs in a season: 1
1st-Class 50s: 48
1st-Class 100s: 31
1st-Class 200s: 2
1st-Class 300s: 1
1st-Class 500s: 1
1st-Class catches: 161
One-Day 100s: 11
Overseas tours: West Indies to Pakistan
1990-91, to England 1991, to Australia 1992-
93, to Sri Lanka 1993-94, to India 1994-95, to New Zealand 1994-95, to England
1995, to Australia 1995-96, to India and Pakistan (World Cup) 1996-97, to Australia
1996-97, to Pakistan 1997-98
Overseas teams played for: Trinidad & Tobago
Extras: In an amazing few weeks in 1994, he broke the record for the highest Test score
(375) against England at Antigua, and the highest first-class score (501*) for
Warwickshire against Durham at Edgbaston. He also passed 1000 runs in an English
season in only seven innings, equalling the record held by Don Bradman, scoring a
record seven centuries in his first eight innings. He also created a record by scoring
centuries in his first four Championship innings. Has rejoined Warwickshire for the 1998
season after an absence of four years and has been appointed captain for the 1998
season. He replaced Courtney Walsh as West Indies captain for the series against

England in 1997-98
Best batting: 501* Warwickshire v Durham, Edgbaston 1994
Best bowling: 1-14 Trinidad & Tobago v Windward Islands, Dominica 1996-97

1997 Season (did not make any first-class or one-day appearances)

Career Performances

	M	Inns	NO	Runs	HS		Avge	100s	50s	Ct	St	Balls	Runs	Wkts	Avge	Best	5wI	10wM
Test	45	76	2	4004	375		54.10	10	20	59	-	60	28	0	-	-	-	-
All First	128	209	6	10978	501	*	54.07	31	48	161	-	383	306	2	153.00	1-14	-	-
1-day Int	118	116	12	4881	169		46.93	11	31	59	-	24	22	2	11.00	2-5	-	-
NatWest	5	5	0	158	81		31.60	-	1	3	-							
B & H	3	3	0	112	70		37.33	-	1	1	-							
Sunday	14	14	0	364	75		26.00	-	3	6	-							

LARAMAN, A. W.   Middlesex

Name: Aaron William Laraman
Role: Right-hand bat, right-arm fast bowler
Born: 10 January 1979, Enfield
Height: 6ft 5in **Weight:** 13st
Nickname: Lazza, Shanks
County debut: No first-team appearance
Parents: William and Lynda
Marital status: Single
Education: St Paul's C of E School; Enfield Grammar School
Qualifications: 8 GCSEs
Off-season: England U19 tour to South Africa 1997-98
Overseas tours: England U17 to Holland
Cricketers particularly admired: Viv Richards, Ian Botham
Young players to look out for: Robert Key, Stephen Peters
Other sports followed: Football (Arsenal)
Injuries: Left lower leg, was able to bat but not bowl for most of the season
Relaxations: Working out at the gym, watching football, playing golf
Extras: Middlesex Colts county cap. Enfield Grammar School cap at the age of 13
Opinions on cricket: 'In the game today, I feel that a high level of fitness is required. The game is becoming much more exciting and much more of a spectator sport.'

LATHWELL, M. N.   Somerset

Name: Mark Nicholas Lathwell
Role: Right-hand bat, right-arm medium and off-break bowler
Born: 26 December 1971, Bletchley, Bucks
Height: 5ft 8in **Weight:** 12st
Nickname: Lathers, Rowdy, Trough
County debut: 1991
County cap: 1992
Test debut: 1993
Tests: 2
1000 runs in a season: 4
1st-Class 50s: 43
1st-Class 100s: 11
1st-Class 200s: 1
1st-Class catches: 85
One-Day 100s: 4
Place in batting averages: 137th av. 27.63 (1996 59th av. 43.71)
Strike rate: 30.00 (career 84.76)
Parents: Derek Peter and Valerie
Wife: Lisa
Children: Jason, 16 January 1995
Family links with cricket: Brother plays local club cricket; father is a 'retired' club cricketer and now senior coach
Education: Overstone Primary, Wing, Bucks; Southmead Primary, Braunton, North Devon; Braunton Comprehensive
Qualifications: 5 GCSEs
Overseas tours: England A to Australia 1992-93, to South Africa 1993-94
Cricketers particularly admired: Ian Botham, Graham Gooch
Other sports followed: Snooker, darts
Relaxations: Cooking and eating
Extras: Spent one season on Lord's groundstaff. Played for England U19 v Australia U19 1991. Young Player of the Year and Somerset Player of the Year 1992. Cricket Writers' Club Young Cricketer of the Year 1993
Opinions on cricket: 'The size of the lunches at most grounds just cannot sustain you all day in the field.'
Best batting: 206 Somerset v Surrey, Bath 1994
Best bowling: 2-21 Somerset v Sussex, Hove 1994

1997 Season

	M	Inns	NO	Runs	HS	Avge	100s	50s	Ct	St	O	M	Runs	Wkts	Avge	Best	5wI	10wM
Test																		
All First	20	34	1	912	95	27.63	-	6	11	-	5	0	60	1	60.00	1-60	-	-
1-day Int																		
NatWest	2	2	0	43	42	21.50	-	-	1	-								
B & H	5	5	0	103	77	20.60	-	1	4	-								
Sunday	15	15	2	316	72	24.30	-	3	4	-								

Career Performances

	M	Inns	NO	Runs	HS	Avge	100s	50s	Ct	St	Balls	Runs	Wkts	Avge	Best	5wI	10wM
Test	2	4	0	78	33	19.50	-	-	-	-							
All First	122	218	9	7194	206	34.42	11	43	85	-	1102	684	13	52.61	2-21	-	-
1-day Int																	
NatWest	16	16	0	459	103	28.68	1	2	5	-	66	23	1	23.00	1-23	-	
B & H	21	21	0	821	121	39.09	2	6	7	-	25	50	0	-	-	-	-
Sunday	90	89	3	2300	117	26.74	1	14	22	-	102	85	0	-	-	-	-

LAW, D. R. C.   Essex

Name: Danny Richard Charles Law
Role: Right-hand bat, right-arm fast bowler
Born: 15 July 1975, Lambeth, London
Height: 6ft 5in **Weight:** 13st 7lbs
Nickname: Decas, Desperate
County debut: 1993 (Sussex), 1997 (Essex)
County cap: 1996 (Sussex), 1997 (Essex)
1st-Class 50s: 5
1st-Class 100s: 1
1st-Class 5 w. in innings: 3
1st-Class catches: 24
Place in batting averages: 237th av. 16.96
(1996 221st av. 22.10)
Place in bowling averages: 80th av. 31.25
(1996 52nd av. 29.07)
Strike rate: 52.35 (career 51.73)
Parents: Richard (deceased) and Claudette
Marital status: 'Attached'
Education: Wolverton Hall School; Steyning
Grammar School
Qualifications: Cricket coach
Overseas tours: Sussex Schools U16 to Jersey 1991; England U18 to South Africa

1992-93, to Denmark 1993; England U19 to Sri Lanka 1993-94
Cricketers particularly admired: Michael Holding, Allan Donald, Courtney Walsh, Franklyn Stephenson, John North, Chris Tugwell
Other sports followed: Most sports
Relaxations: Listening to music, spending time at home
Extras: Left Sussex during the 1996 off-season and joined Essex on a three-year contract for the 1997 season
Opinions on cricket: 'The 2nd XI Championship should be increased from a three-day game to a four-day game so that younger players are used to playing four-day cricket and are not thrown in at the deep end if they progress to first-class cricket.'
Best batting: 115 Sussex v Young Australia, Hove 1995
Best bowling: 5-33 Sussex v Durham, Hove 1996

1997 Season

	M	Inns	NO	Runs	HS	Avge	100s	50s	Ct	St	O	M	Runs	Wkts	Avge	Best	5wl	10wM
Test																		
All First	19	29	0	492	81	16.96	-	2	11	-	270.3	51	969	31	31.25	5-93	1	-
1-day Int																		
NatWest	5	3	0	40	17	13.33	-	-	2	-	3	0	18	0	-		-	-
B & H	4	3	0	38	28	12.66	-	-	1	-								
Sunday	15	14	3	339	82	30.81	-	3	4	-	22	0	139	2	69.50	2-29	-	

Career Performances

	M	Inns	NO	Runs	HS	Avge	100s	50s	Ct	St	Balls	Runs	Wkts	Avge	Best	5wl	10wM
Test																	
All First	47	72	0	1370	115	19.02	1	5	24	-	4346	2709	84	32.25	5-33	3	-
1-day Int																	
NatWest	9	6	0	65	18	10.83	-	-	3	-	81	80	1	80.00	1-2	-	
B & H	6	5	0	46	28	9.20	-	-	1	-	96	76	1	76.00	1-44	-	
Sunday	42	37	8	821	82	28.31	-	4	10	-	725	705	22	32.04	3-34	-	

LAW, S. G.   Essex

Name: Stuart Grant Law
Role: Right-hand bat, right-arm medium bowler
Born: 18 October 1968, Herston, Brisbane, Australia
Height: 6ft 2in
County debut: 1996
Test debut: 1995-96
Tests: 1
One-Day Internationals: 44
1000 runs in a season: 2

1st-Class 50s: 50
1st-Class 100s: 27
1st-Class 5 w. in innings: 1
1st-Class catches: 135
One-Day 100s: 9
Place in batting averages: 9th av. 57.00
(1996 12th av. 61.80)
Place in bowling averages: (1996 148th av.
54.28)
Strike rate: 139.20 (career 96.12)
Education: Craigslea State High School
Off-season: Playing for Queensland and
Australia
Overseas teams played for: Queensland
1988-1997
Overseas tours: Young Australia to England
1995; Australia to India and Pakistan (World
Cup) 1995-96

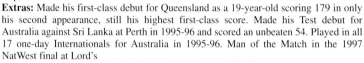

Extras: Made his first-class debut for Queensland as a 19-year-old scoring 179 in only his second appearance, still his highest first-class score. Made his Test debut for Australia against Sri Lanka at Perth in 1995-96 and scored an unbeaten 54. Played in all 17 one-day Internationals for Australia in 1995-96. Man of the Match in the 1997 NatWest final at Lord's
Best batting: 179 Queensland v Tasmania, Brisbane 1988-89
Best bowling: 5-39 Queensland v Tasmania, Brisbane 1995-96

1997 Season

	M	Inns	NO	Runs	HS	Avge	100s	50s	Ct	St	O	M	Runs	Wkts	Avge	Best	5wI	10wM
Test																		
All First	17	28	2	1482	175	57.00	5	8	19	-	116	30	356	5	71.20	3-27	-	-
1-day Int																		
NatWest	5	5	1	333	100	83.25	1	2	3	-	37.4	5	180	3	60.00	2-54	-	
B & H	4	4	0	181	88	45.25	-	2	3	-	12	0	58	0	-	-	-	-
Sunday	16	16	0	574	123	35.87	1	3	8	-	56.5	0	298	10	29.80	4-37	-	

Career Performances

	M	Inns	NO	Runs	HS	Avge	100s	50s	Ct	St	Balls	Runs	Wkts	Avge	Best	5wI	10wM
Test	1	1	1	54	54 *	-	-	1	1	-	18	9	0	-	-	-	-
All First	133	224	23	9522	179	47.37	27	50	135	-	6152	2963	64	46.29	5-39	1	-
1-day Int	44	42	3	1145	110	29.35	1	7	10	-	747	572	12	47.66	2-22	-	
NatWest	9	9	1	624	107	78.00	3	3	6	-	367	290	7	41.42	2-36	-	
B & H	9	9	0	406	116	45.11	1	2	3	-	262	241	4	60.25	2-57	-	
Sunday	29	29	1	1075	123	38.39	4	3	12	-	742	660	19	34.73	4-37	-	

LAW, W. L.   Glamorgan

Name: Wayne Lincoln Law
Role: Right-hand bat
Born: 4 September 1978, Swansea
Height: 5ft 10in **Weight:** 11st 7lbs
Nickname: Sods
County debut: 1997
Parents: Lincoln and Barbara
Marital status: Single
Education: Pentip Primary School; Graig
School
Qualifications: 1 GCSE, NCA coaching
award
Off-season: Coaching
Overseas tours: Dyfed U15 to Zimbabwe
1994
Cricketers particularly admired: 'The
Glamorgan 1st XI'
Young players to look out for: Michael
Powell, Ian Thomas

Other sports followed: Football (Manchester United), squash, running
Relaxations: Squash, running and reading
Best batting: 38* Glamorgan v Oxford University, The Parks 1997

1997 Season

	M	Inns	NO	Runs	HS	Avge	100s	50s	Ct	St	O	M	Runs	Wkts	Avge	Best	5wI	10wM
Test																		
All First	1	1	1	38	38 *	-	-	-	-	-								
1-day Int																		
NatWest																		
B & H																		
Sunday	2	2	0	23	15	11.50	-	-	1	-								

Career Performances

	M	Inns	NO	Runs	HS	Avge	100s	50s	Ct	St	Balls	Runs	Wkts	Avge	Best	5wI	10wM
Test																	
All First	1	1	1	38	38 *	-	-	-	-	-							
1-day Int																	
NatWest																	
B & H																	
Sunday	2	2	0	23	15	11.50	-	-	1	-							

LAWRENCE, D. V.   Gloucestershire

Name: David Valentine Lawrence
Role: Right-hand bat, right-arm fast bowler
Born: 28 January 1964, Gloucester
Height: 6ft 2in **Weight:** 16st 5lbs
Nickname: Syd
County debut: 1981
County cap: 1985
Benefit: 1993
Test debut: 1988
Tests: 5
One-Day Internationals: 1
50 wickets in a season: 5
1st-Class 50s: 2
1st-Class 5 w. in innings: 21
1st-Class 10 w. in match: 1
1st-Class catches: 45
One-Day 5 w. in innings: 4
Strike rate: 64.50 (career 52.31)
Parents: Joseph and Hilda Joyce
Marital status: Single
Children: Buster, November 1991
Family links with cricket: Father played club cricket in Jamaica
Education: Linden School, Gloucester
Qualifications: 3 CSEs
Overseas tours: England B to Sri Lanka 1985-86; England A to Zimbabwe 1989-90; England to New Zealand 1991-92
Overseas teams played for: Tasmania 1984; Scarborough, Perth, Western Australia 1984-85; Manly, Sydney 1987; Fremantle, Western Australia 1989; Randwyck, Sydney 1993-94
Extras: Was called up to join the England A tour in 1989-90 when Chris Lewis was promoted to join the senior squad in the West Indies. Was forced to retire from the game after shattering his knee cap during a Test match at Wellington on England's 1991-92 tour to New Zealand. Made his return to first-class cricket in 1997
Best batting: 66 Gloucestershire v Glamorgan, Abervagenny 1991
Best bowling: 7-47 Gloucestershire v Surrey, Cheltenham 1988

---

53. Who was voted the 1997 PCA Umpire of the Year?

1997 Season

	M	Inns	NO	Runs	HS	Avge	100s	50s	Ct	St	O	M	Runs	Wkts	Avge	Best	5wI	10wM
Test																		
All First	4	6	3	32	23 *	10.66	-	-	1	-	86	9	359	8	44.87	2-28	-	-
1-day Int																		
NatWest																		
B & H																		
Sunday																		

Career Performances

	M	Inns	NO	Runs	HS	Avge	100s	50s	Ct	St	Balls	Runs	Wkts	Avge	Best	5wI	10wM
Test	5	6	0	60	34	10.00	-	-	-	-	1089	676	18	37.55	5-106	1	-
All Firsts	185	211	38	1851	66	10.69	-	2	45	-	26942	16521	515	32.07	7-47	21	1
1-day Int	1	0	0	0	0	-	-	-	-	-	66	67	4	16.75	4-67	-	
NatWest	20	10	5	11	5 *	2.20	-	-	2	-	1108	763	28	27.25	5-17	1	
B & H	29	12	6	94	23	15.66	-	-	6	-	1614	1050	44	23.86	6-20	2	
Sunday	59	23	8	179	38 *	11.93	-	-	15	-	2430	2115	75	28.20	5-18	1	

LEATHERDALE, D. A. Worcestershire

Name: David Anthony Leatherdale
Role: Right-hand bat, right-arm medium bowler, cover fielder
Born: 26 November 1967, Bradford
Height: 5ft 10in **Weight:** 11st
Nickname: Lugsy, Spock
County debut: 1988
County cap: 1994
1st-Class 50s: 32
1st-Class 100s: 8
1st-Class 5 w. in innings: 1
1st-Class catches: 96
Place in batting averages: 17th av. 52.11
(1996 127th av. 33.68)
Place in bowling averages: 60th av. 28.53
(1996 92nd av. 34.90)
Strike rate: 50.65 (career 61.48)
Parents: Paul and Rosalyn
Wife's name: Vanessa
Children: Callum Edward, 6 July 1990
Family links with cricket: Father played local cricket; brother plays for East Bierley in Bradford League; brother-in-law played for England YC in 1979

Education: Bolton Royd Primary School; Pudsey Grangefield Secondary School
Qualifications: 8 O-levels, 2 A-levels; NCA coaching award (stage 1)
Overseas tours: England Indoor to Australia and New Zealand 1994-95
Overseas teams played for: Pretoria Police, South Africa 1987-88
Cricketers particularly admired: Mark Scott, George Batty, Peter Kippax
Other sports followed: Football, American football
Relaxations: Golf
Opinions on cricket: '2nd XI wickets need upgrading as many outgrounds are not up to standard, especially if four-day cricket is extended into the 2nd XI championship.'
Best batting: 157 Worcestershire v Somerset, Worcester 1991
Best bowling: 5-56 Worcestershire v Australia, Worcester 1997

1997 Season

	M	Inns	NO	Runs	HS	Avge	100s	50s	Ct	St	O	M	Runs	Wkts	Avge	Best	5wI	10wM
Test																		
All First	17	25	8	886	129	52.11	2	5	15	-	219.3	46	742	26	28.53	5-56	1	-
1-day Int																		
NatWest	2	2	0	51	42	25.50	-	-	-	-	12	0	61	0	-		-	-
B & H	5	5	1	51	25	12.75	-	-	-	-	35	2	126	9	14.00	4-13	-
Sunday	15	12	5	301	58 *	43.00	-	3	9	-	58.3	2	315	18	17.50	3-13	-

Career Performances

	M	Inns	NO	Runs	HS	Avge	100s	50s	Ct	St	Balls	Runs	Wkts	Avge	Best	5wI	10wM
Test																	
All First	125	193	24	5777	157	34.18	8	32	111	-	2890	1647	47	35.04	5-56	1	-
1-day Int																	
NatWest	19	16	1	297	43	19.80	-	-	5	-	136	106	3	35.33	3-14	-
B & H	24	19	4	267	66	17.80	-	1	4	-	282	188	9	20.88	4-13	-
Sunday	111	90	15	1395	62 *	18.60	-	6	56	-	611	517	29	17.82	4-31	-

LEHMANN, D. S. Yorkshire

Name: Darren Scott Lehmann
Role: Left-hand bat, slow left-arm bowler
Born: 5 February 1970, Gawler, Australia
County debut: 1997
One-Day International debut: 1996-97
One-Day Internationals: 3
1000 runs in a season: 1
1st-Class 50s: 48
1st-Class 100s: 29
1st-Class 200s: 4
1st-Class catches: 67
One-Day 100s: 1
Place in batting averages: 5th av. 63.00
Strike rate: 61.50 (career 121.16)
Off-season: Playing for South Australia
Overseas teams played for: South Australia
1987-1990; Victoria 1990-93; South Australia
1993-97

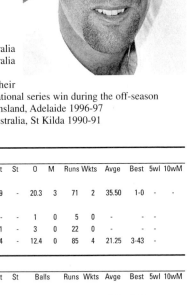

Extras: Played for Australia in their
successful Carlton Union One-Day International series win during the off-season
Best batting: 255 South Australia v Queensland, Adelaide 1996-97
Best bowling: 2-15 Victoria v Western Australia, St Kilda 1990-91

1997 Season

	M	Inns	NO	Runs	HS	Avge	100s	50s	Ct	St	O	M	Runs	Wkts	Avge	Best	5wl	10wM
Test																		
All First	17	27	2	1575	182	63.00	4	10	9	-	20.3	3	71	2	35.50	1-0	-	-
1-day Int																		
NatWest	3	3	0	132	105	44.00	1	-	-	-	1	0	5	0	-	-	-	-
B & H	5	5	0	166	67	33.20	-	1	1	-	3	0	22	0	-	-	-	-
Sunday	16	16	3	643	78 *	49.46	-	6	4	-	12.4	0	85	4	21.25	3-43	-	

Career Performances

	M	Inns	NO	Runs	HS	Avge	100s	50s	Ct	St	Balls	Runs	Wkts	Avge	Best	5wl	10wM
Test																	
All First	115	200	11	9792	255	51.80	29	48	67	-	1454	730	12	60.83	2-15	-	-
1-day Int	3	3	0	27	15	9.00	-	-	2	-	78	65	1	65.00	1-29	-	
NatWest	3	3	0	132	105	44.00	1	-	-	-	6	5	0	-	-	-	
B & H	5	5	0	166	67	33.20	-	1	1	-	18	22	0	-	-	-	
Sunday	16	16	3	643	78 *	49.46	-	6	4	-	76	85	4	21.25	3-43	-	

LENHAM, N. J.   Sussex

Name: Neil John Lenham
Role: Right-hand bat, right-arm
medium bowler
Born: 17 December 1965, Worthing
Height: 5ft 11in **Weight:** 11st
Nickname: Pin
County debut: 1984
County cap: 1990
1000 runs in a season: 3
1st-Class 50s: 49
1st-Class 100s: 20
1st-Class 200s: 1
1st-Class catches: 73
One-Day 100s: 1
One-Day 5 w. in innings: 1
Place in batting averages: 174th av. 24.16
(1996 101st av. 36.12)
Strike rate: (career 86.59)
Parents: Leslie John and Valerie Anne
Marital status: Single
Family links with cricket: Father played for Sussex and is now one of the NCA's
national coaches
Education: Broadwater Manor Prep School; Brighton College
Qualifications: 5 O-levels, 2 A-levels, advanced cricket coach
Career outside cricket: Marketing manager at Sussex CCC
Off-season: 'Retired from professional cricket due to injury and will take up the
position of marketing manager at the club as from October 1997'
Overseas tours: England YC to West Indies (as captain) 1985
Overseas teams played for: Port Elizabeth, South Africa 1987-88; Brighton,
Tasmania 1989-91; United, Namibia 1994-95
Cricketers particularly admired: Ken McEwan, Barry Richards
Young players to look out for: James Kirtley, Shaun Humphries
Other sports followed: Golf, horse racing, rugby and fishing
Injuries: Foot injury ended career in August 1997
Relaxations: Fishing, cooking and drinking wine
Extras: Made debut for England YC in 1983. Broke record for number of runs scored
in season at a public school in 1984 (1534 av. 80.74). Youngest player to appear for
Sussex 2nd XI at 14 years old. Appointed as Eastbourne's first Cricket Development
Officer in 1992. Retired from first-class cricket at the end of the 1997 season due to a
persistent foot injury
Best batting: 222* Sussex v Kent, Hove 1992
Best bowling: 4-13 Sussex v Durham, Durham University 1993

1997 Season

	M	Inns	NO	Runs	HS	Avge	100s	50s	Ct	St	O	M	Runs	Wkts	Avge	Best	5wI	10wM
Test																		
All First	7	12	0	290	93	24.16	-	2	2	-								
1-day Int																		
NatWest	1	1	1	28	28 *	-	-	-	-	-								
B & H	3	3	0	6	6	2.00	-	-	1	-								
Sunday	4	4	0	71	41	17.75	-	-	-	-	2	0	14	1	14.00	1-14	-	

Career Performances

	M	Inns	NO	Runs	HS	Avge	100s	50s	Ct	St	Balls	Runs	Wkts	Avge	Best	5wI	10wM
Test																	
All First	192	332	29	10135	222 *	33.44	20	49	73	-	3637	1847	42	43.97	4-13	-	-
1-day Int																	
NatWest	15	14	4	601	129 *	60.10	1	3	-	-	411	240	10	24.00	2-12	-	
B & H	28	26	6	606	82	30.30	-	4	4	-	264	223	4	55.75	1-3	-	
Sunday	98	85	16	1861	86	26.97	-	11	19	-	894	884	30	29.46	5-28	1	

LEWIS, C. C.   Leicestershire

Name: Christopher Clairmonte Lewis
Role: Right-hand bat, right-arm
fast-medium bowler
Born: 14 February 1968, Georgetown,
Guyana
Height: 6ft 2in **Weight:** 13st
Nickname: Carl
County debut: 1987 (Leics), 1992 (Notts),
1996 (Surrey)
County cap: 1990 (Leics), 1992 (Notts)
Test debut: 1990
Tests: 32
One-Day Internationals: 51
50 wickets in a season: 2
1st-Class 50s: 28
1st-Class 100s: 7
1st-Class 5w. in innings: 18
1st-Class 10 w. in match: 3
1st-Class catches: 131
One-Day 5 w. in innings: 1
Place in batting averages: 189th av. 22.88 (1996 147th av. 31.95)
Place in bowling averages: 66th av. 29.39 (1996 97th av. 35.48)

Strike rate: 53.03 (career 59.29)
Parents: Philip and Patricia
Marital status: Single
Education: Willesden High School
Qualifications: 2 O-levels
Overseas tours: England YC to Australia (Youth World Cup) 1987; England A to Kenya and Zimbabwe 1989-90; England to West Indies 1989-90, to Australia and New Zealand 1990-91, to New Zealand 1991-92, to India and Sri Lanka 1992-93, to West Indies 1993-94, to Australia 1994-95
Cricketers particularly admired: Graham Gooch, Robin Smith
Other sports followed: Snooker, football, darts, American football, basketball
Relaxations: Music, sleeping
Extras: Joined England's tour of West Indies in 1989-90 as a replacement for Ricky Ellcock. Suffers from Raynaud's disease, a problem of blood circulation, and has to spend one night in hospital every two months to have the disease treated. Left Leicestershire at the end of 1991 season and signed for Nottinghamshire. Hit first Test century v India at Madras on 1992-93 tour to India and Sri Lanka. Joined England tour party in Australia 1994-95 following injury to Darren Gough. Suffered a compressed fracture in the ball of his hip joint which prevented him from playing any Championship cricket in 1995. Left Nottinghamshire and joined Surrey for the 1996 season. Played for an England XI in the Cricket Max tournament in 1997. Has rejoined Leicestershire as vice-captain for the 1998 season
Best batting: 247 Nottinghamshire v Durham, Chester-le-Street 1993
Best bowling: 6-22 Leicestershire v Oxford University, The Parks 1988

1997 Season

	M	Inns	NO	Runs	HS	Avge	100s	50s	Ct	St	O	M	Runs	Wkts	Avge	Best	5wI	10wM
Test																		
All First	13	19	2	389	76	22.88	-	1	10~	-	291.4	66	970	33	29.39	5-42	1	-
1-day Int																		
NatWest	2	2	1	18	15	18.00	-	-	1	-	20	2	49	3	16.33	2-37	-	
B & H	7	4	1	102	35 *	34.00	-	-	3	-	57	12	217	12	18.08	3-39	-	
Sunday	12	11	5	182	68 *	30.33	-	1	8	-	79.3	1	345	16	21.56	4-21	-	

Career Performances

	M	Inns	NO	Runs	HS	Avge	100s	50s	Ct	St	Balls	Runs	Wkts	Avge	Best	5wI	10wM
Test	32	51	3	1105	117	23.02	1	4	25	-	6852	3490	93	37.52	6-111	3	-
All First	161	241	29	6439	247	30.37	7	28	131	-	28667	14366	481	29.86	6-22	18	3
1-day Int	51	38	13	348	33	13.92	-	-	20	-	2513	1854	65	28.52	4-30	-	
NatWest	19	17	2	361	89	24.06	-	2	11	-	1062	626	24	26.08	3-24	-	
B & H	35	26	10	494	48 *	30.87	-	-	13	-	1869	1245	53	23.49	5-46	1	
Sunday	101	86	21	1777	93 *	27.33	-	8	33	-	3932	2861	110	26.00	4-13	-	

LEWIS, J.   Gloucestershire

Name: Jonathan Lewis
Role: Right-hand bat,
right-arm medium-fast bowler
Born: 26 August 1975, Aylesbury
Height: 6ft 2in   **Weight:** 13st
Nickname: JJ, Nugget, Stupid
County debut: 1995
50 wickets in a season: 1
1st-Class 5 w. in innings: 1
1st-Class catches: 6
Place in batting averages: 233rd av. 17.54
(1996 299th av. 8.50)
Place in bowling averages: 37th av. 25.94
(1996 134th av. 47.00)
Strike rate: 46.53 (career 54.46)
Parents: John and Jane
Marital status: Single
Education: Lawn Junior School;

Churchfields Comprehensive School; Swindon College
Qualifications: 9 GCSEs, BTEC in Leisure and Hospitality
Career outside cricket: 'Sperm donor'
Off-season: 'Filling up those test tubes'
Overseas tours: Bath Schools to New South Wales, Australia 1993
Overseas teams played for: Marist, Christchurch, New Zealand 1994-95;
Richmond City, Melbourne 1995-96
Cricketers particularly admired: Dom Hewson, Jack Russell, Courtney Walsh, Jon
Summer, Alan Biggins, Paul Rignall
Young players to look out for: Monte Lynch
Other sports followed: Gurning
Injuries: 'Bang on the head, confused all season'
Extras: Was on Northamptonshire staff in 1994 but made no first-team appearance
Opinions on cricket: 'All overseas quick bowlers should be banned from English
cricket. They're not that good, not that fast, and they certainly don't scare me.'
Best batting: 30 Gloucestershire v Worcestershire, Bristol 1997
Best bowling: 6-50 Gloucestershire v Middlesex, Bristol 1997

---

54. Who scored the fastest first-class century of 1997?

1997 Season

	M	Inns	NO	Runs	HS	Avge	100s	50s	Ct	St	O	M	Runs	Wkts	Avge	Best	5wI	10wM
Test																		
All First	15	19	8	193	30	17.54	-	-	2	-	418.5	98	1401	54	25.94	6-50	3	-
1-day Int																		
NatWest	1	0	0	0	0	-	-	-	1	-	9	0	38	0	-	-	-	-
B & H	1	0	0	0	0	-	-	-	-	-	9	0	74	1	74.00	1-74	-	
Sunday	12	5	3	16	8	8.00	-	-	2	-	83	3	389	14	27.78	3-39	-	

Career Performances

	M	Inns	NO	Runs	HS	Avge	100s	50s	Ct	St	Balls	Runs	Wkts	Avge	Best	5wI	10wM
Test																	
All First	28	38	10	315	30	11.25	-	-	6	-	4575	2456	84	29.23	6-50	3	-
1-day Int																	
NatWest	3	2	1	7	6 *	7.00	-	-	1	-	152	84	5	16.80	3-27	-	
B & H	2	0	0	0	0	-	-	-	-	-	114	105	4	26.25	3-31	-	
Sunday	29	14	10	47	9 *	11.75	-	-	5	-	1173	979	29	33.75	3-27	-	

LEWIS, J. J. B.　　　　　　　Durham

Name: Jonathan James Benjamin Lewis
Role: Right-hand bat, right-arm
slow-medium net bowler
Born: 21 May 1970, Middlesex
Height: 5ft 9in **Weight:** 11st 5lbs
Nickname: Judge, Mouse
County debut: 1990 (Essex), 1997 (Durham)
County cap: 1994 (Essex)
1000 runs in a season: 1
1st-Class 50s: 25
1st-Class 100s: 7
1st-Class 200s: 1
1st-Class catches: 59
One-Day 100s: 1
Place in batting averages: 35th av. 44.71
(1996 190th av. 26.44)
Parents: Graham Edward and Regina Mary
Marital status: Single
Family links with cricket: Father played

county schools. Uncle is a lifelong Somerset supporter. Sister is right-arm medium-fast
bowler for NorTel
Education: King Edward VI School, Chelmsford; Roehampton Institute of Higher

Education
Qualifications: 5 O-levels, 3 A-levels, BSc (Hons) Sports Science, NCA Senior Coach
Off-season: Playing and coaching in South Africa
Overseas teams played for: Old Hararians, Zimbabwe 1991-92; Taita District, New Zealand 1992-93; Eshoue and Zululand 1994-95; Richards Bay 1996-97; Empangeni, Natal 1997-98
Cricketers particularly admired: John Childs, Greg Matthews, Alan Walker
Young players to look out for: Melvyn Betts, Paul Collingwood
Other sports followed: Soccer (West Ham United), rugby, basketball, 'most sports really'
Injuries: Rotated collarbone, but no time missed
Relaxations: 'Pubs with real ale and Trotters Wine Bar'
Extras: Hit century on first-class debut in Essex's final Championship match of the 1990 season. Joined Durham for the 1997 season – 'I am slowly learning the local dialect'. Scored a double century on his debut for Durham (210* v Oxford University), placing him in a unique club, alongside Peter Bowler and Neil Taylor, of players who have scored centuries on debut for two different counties
Opinions on cricket: 'In the interest of Durham players, the A1 needs to be improved.'
Best batting: 210* Durham v Oxford University, The Parks 1997

1997 Season

	M	Inns	NO	Runs	HS	Avge	100s	50s	Ct	St	O	M	Runs	Wkts	Avge	Best	5wl	10wM
Test																		
All First	18	32	4	1252	210 *	44.71	3	5	10	-								
1-day Int																		
NatWest	1	1	0	1	1	1.00	-	-	-	-								
B & H	4	4	0	119	47	29.75	-	-	1	-								
Sunday	16	15	4	469	102	42.63	1	3	5	-								

Career Performances

	M	Inns	NO	Runs	HS	Avge	100s	50s	Ct	St	Balls	Runs	Wkts	Avge	Best	5wl	10wM
Test																	
All First	76	133	18	4211	210 *	36.61	7	25	59	-	72	48	0	-	-	-	-
1-day Int																	
NatWest	7	7	1	76	24 *	12.66	-	-	1	-							
B & H	9	9	1	171	47	21.37	-	-	3	-							
Sunday	58	48	12	915	102	25.41	1	5	14	-	2	4	0	-	-	-

LEWRY, J. D. Sussex

Name: Jason David Lewry
Role: Left-hand bat, left-arm
fast-medium bowler
Born: 2 April 1971, Worthing, West Sussex
Height: 6ft 3in **Weight:** 14st 6lbs
Nickname: Urco ('thanks Ath')
County debut: 1994
County cap: 1996
1st-Class 5 w. in innings: 7
1st-Class 10 w. in match: 1
1st-Class catches: 7
Place in batting averages:
(1996 284th av. 11.50)
Place in bowling averages:
(1996 15th av. 22.97)
Strike rate: (career 47.25)
Parents: David and Veronica
Wife and date of marriage: Naomi
Madeleine, 18 August 1997

Children: 'A baby due on 16 February 1998'
Family links with cricket: Father coaches
Education: Durrington High School, Worthing; Sixth Form College, Worthing
Qualifications: 6 O-levels, 3 GCSEs, City & Guilds, NCA Award Course
Career outside cricket: 'Still looking'
Off-season: 'Getting fit, recovering from year out!'
Cricketers particularly admired: The Sussex staff, David Gower, Wasim Akram,
Martin Andrews
Young players to look out for: Swing bowlers
Other sports followed: Football (West Ham United), golf, squash, 'kicking on … zzz'
Injuries: Stress fracture pars articularis L5, out for the whole season. 'Trapped nerve
was diagnosed as a stress fracture in January 1997. Had surgery in March 1997'
Relaxations: Golf, eating out, 'kicking on with Stan and annoying the wife''
Extras: Selected in a 15-man England indoor cricket squad for the series against South
Africa in England, alongside Mike Gatting and Asif Din, and for the tour of New
Zealand and Australia during 1991-92. The tour was cancelled due to a lack of funds of
the UKICF (UK Indoor Cricket Federation). Diagnosed with a stress fracture of the back
which caused him to miss the whole of the 1997 season
Opinions on cricket: 'Play every game as though it is your last.'
Best batting: 34 Sussex v Kent, Hove 1995
Best bowling: 6-43 Sussex v Worcestershire, Eastbourne 1995

1997 Season (did not make any first-class or one-day appearances)

Career Performances

	M	Inns	NO	Runs	HS	Avge	100s	50s	Ct	St	Balls	Runs	Wkts	Avge	Best	5wI	10wM
Test																	
All First	26	40	11	302	34	10.41	-	-	2	-	4489	2504	95	26.35	6-43	7	1
1-day Int																	
NatWest	4	3	3	10	5 *	-	-	-	-	-	252	182	7	26.00	3-45	-	
B & H	4	2	2	22	14 *	-	-	-	-	-	192	174	0	-	-	-	
Sunday	22	9	3	22	7 *	3.66	-	-	4	-	868	694	29	23.93	4-29	-	

LLONG, N. J.   Kent

Name: Nigel James Llong
Role: Left-hand bat, off-spin bowler
Born: 11 February 1969, Ashford, Kent
Height: 6ft **Weight:** 11st 6lbs
Nickname: Nidge, Lloydie
County debut: 1991
County cap: 1993
1st-Class 50s: 16
1st-Class 100s: 6
1st-Class 5 w. in innings: 2
1st-Class catches: 57
One-Day 100s: 1
Place in batting averages: 226th av. 18.28 (1996 84th av. 38.15)
Place in bowling averages: (1996 13th av. 22.63)
Strike rate: 78.75 (career 64.94)
Parents: Richard and Peggy (deceased)
Wife and date of marriage: Rosemary Ann, 29 February 1996
Family links with cricket: Father and brother play club cricket
Education: Newtown County Primary; North School for Boys
Qualifications: 6 CSEs, NCA coaching award
Career outside cricket: Snooker table technician and groundsman
Off-season: Playing and coaching in Cape Town, South Africa
Overseas tours: Kent to Zimbabwe 1992-93
Overseas teams played for: Ashburton, Melbourne 1988-90, 1996-97; Green Point, Cape Town 1990-95
Cricketers particularly admired: David Gower

Other sports followed: Golf, football, Aussie rules and fishing
Injuries: Ankle ligaments, but missed no cricket
Relaxations: 'Watching any sport'
Extras: Kent Supporters Club Young Player of the Year Award 1993
Opinions on cricket: 'All teams prepare pitches to suit their own strengths and the situation of pitches being reported could be stopped if the ECB took full control of all pitch conditions (i.e. by employing groundsmen). This would ensure that good quality pitches are played on. Test match pitches are prepared as well as possible so why not first-class games? All 2nd XI cricket should be played on first-class grounds, with practice facilities so that young, up-and-coming players have the facilities to work at their skills.'
Best batting: 130 Kent v Hampshire, Canterbury 1996
Best bowling: 5-21 Kent v Middlesex, Canterbury 1996

1997 Season

	M	Inns	NO	Runs	HS	Avge	100s	50s	Ct	St	O	M	Runs	Wkts	Avge	Best	5wl	10wM
Test																		
All First	8	14	0	256	99	18.28	-	2	9	-	52.3	11	200	4	50.00	2-33	-	-
1-day Int																		
NatWest	1	1	0	68	68	68.00	-	1	-	-	9.2	0	49	2	24.50	2-49	-	
B & H	8	7	0	266	75	38.00	-	2	3	-	19	0	106	0	-	-	-	-
Sunday	15	9	0	123	52	13.66	-	1	4	-	26.4	0	162	5	32.40	1-1	-	

Career Performances

	M	Inns	NO	Runs	HS	Avge	100s	50s	Ct	St	Balls	Runs	Wkts	Avge	Best	5wl	10wM
Test																	
All First	66	104	10	2992	130	31.82	6	16	57	-	2273	1259	35	35.97	5-21	2	-
1-day Int																	
NatWest	6	6	3	261	115 *	87.00	1	1	3	-	134	96	6	16.00	3-36	-	
B & H	17	14	1	320	75	24.61	-	2	4	-	204	175	3	58.33	2-38	-	
Sunday	87	71	15	1126	70	20.10	-	5	26	-	619	611	23	26.56	4-24	-	

55. Who won the 1997 2nd XI Championship?

LLOYD, G. D.   Lancashire

Name: Graham David Lloyd
Role: Right-hand bat, right-arm
medium bowler
Born: 1 July 1969, Accrington
Height: 5ft 7in **Weight:** 13st
Nickname: Bumble
County debut: 1988
County cap: 1992
One-Day Internationals: 5
1000 runs in a season: 4
1st-Class 50s: 48
1st-Class 100s: 18
1st-Class 200s: 2
1st-Class catches: 95
One-Day 100s: 3
Place in batting averages: 24th av. 48.77
(1996 31st av. 49.75)
Strike rate: (career 117.00)
Parents: David and Susan
Marital status: Single

Family links with cricket:
Father played for Lancashire and England
Education: Hollins County High School, Accrington
Qualifications: 3 O-levels, NCA coaching certificate
Overseas tours: England A to Australia 1992-93; Lancashire CCC to Guernsey 1995
Overseas teams played for: Maroochydore, Queensland 1988-89 and 1991-95
Cricketers particularly admired: Gordon Parsons, David Millns, Nigel Briers
Other sports followed: Football (Manchester United)
Relaxations: 'Eating out and racing'
Extras: His school did not play cricket, so he learnt at Accrington, playing in the same team as his father. Won the Walter Lawrence Trophy for the fastest century of the year (for the second year running) – 100 off 73 balls against Leicestershire on 2 June 1997. Played for England in the 1997 Hong Kong Sixes tournament in which England were runners-up to Pakistan
Opinions on cricket: 'Bring back timeless cricket (i.e. Test and Championship). Everybody wants to see someone win.'
Best batting: 241 Lancashire v Essex, Chelmsford 1996
Best bowling: 1-4 Lancashire v Warwickshire, Edgbaston 1996

1997 Season

	M	Inns	NO	Runs	HS	Avge	100s	50s	Ct	St	O	M	Runs	Wkts	Avge	Best	5wI	10wM
Test																		
All First	16	24	2	1073	225	48.77	4	5	17	-	11.5	0	101	0	-	-	-	-
1-day Int	3	2	0	22	22	11.00	-	-	1	-								
NatWest	2	2	0	100	96	50.00	-	1	-	-	2	0	12	0	-	-	-	
B & H	5	5	0	91	36	18.20	-	-	1	-	2	0	8	0	-	-	-	
Sunday	15	14	0	461	134	32.92	1	1	4	-								

Career Performances

	M	Inns	NO	Runs	HS	Avge	100s	50s	Ct	St	Balls	Runs	Wkts	Avge	Best	5wI	10wM
Test																	
All First	145	236	24	8306	241	39.17	18	48	95	-	234	291	2	145.50	1-4	-	-
1-day Int	5	4	1	39	22	13.00	-	-	2	-							
NatWest	16	15	0	428	96	28.53	-	3	3	-	30	35	1	35.00	1-23	-	
B & H	35	29	9	612	81 *	30.60	-	3	5	-	30	50	0	-	-	-	
Sunday	126	116	16	3222	134	32.22	3	19	27	-	12	18	0	-	-	-	

LOGAN, R. J.   Northamptonshire

Name: Richard James Logan
Role: Right-hand bat, right-arm bowler
Born: 28 January 1980, Stone
Height: 6ft 1in **Weight:** 12st 10lbs
Nickname: Logie, Gus
County debut: No first-team appearance
Parents: Robert and Margaret
Marital status: Girlfriend Sarah
Family links with cricket: Father plays club cricket for Cannock CC
Education: Walhouse C of E School, Cannock; Wolverhampton Grammar School
Qualifications: 10 GCSEs and studying for A-levels
Off-season: England U19 to South Africa
Overseas tours: England U17 to Bermuda for International Youth Tournament 1997
Cricketers particularly admired: Michael Atherton
Young players to look out for: David Sales, Graham Napier, John Blain, Graeme Swann, Michael Davies
Other sports followed: Hockey (Cannock – 'also played for Staffordshire from age 9

to present day. Played for Midlands U14 but had to decline Midlands training due to commitment to cricket'), football (Wolverhampton Wanderers)

Relaxations: Music, relaxing with girlfriend

Extras: Played for Staffordshire at every level from U11 to U19, and as captain from U13 to U17. Played for Midlands U14 and U15 (both as captain), HMC Schools U15. 1995 *Daily Telegraph*/Lombard U15 Midlands Bowler and Batsman of the Year. Played for Northamptonshire U17 and U19 national champions in 1997. Has played for England U15, U17 and U19

LOUDON, H. J. H. Hampshire

Name: Hugo John Hope Loudon
Role: Right-hand opening bat, slow left-arm bowler
Born: 11 December 1978, London
Height: 6ft 2in **Weight:** 12st 3lbs
County debut: No first-team appearance
Parents: James and Jane
Marital status: Single
Family links with cricket: Grandfather played for Berkshire. Father played for Cambridge 2nd XI and Eton. Brother is the captain of England U15
Education: Wellesley House; Eton College; Durham University
Qualifications: 9 GCSEs and 3 A-levels
Career outside cricket: Student
Off-season: 'At university, working and relaxing'
Overseas tours: Kent U11 to Holland 1991; Eton College to South Africa 1996-97
Cricketers particularly admired: Mike Atherton, Matthew Fleming, Aravinda De Silva
Young players to look out for: James Fulton
Other sports followed: Rugby, football (Manchester United), rackets (won Public Schoolboys Doubles in 1997), tennis, golf and squash
Relaxations: Playing golf, socialising, travelling, shooting, watching Sky television
Extras: Captain of HMC South in 1997
Opinions on cricket: 'There are far too many matches played and we need more time to practice. We should have a two-divisional championship.'

LOYE, M. B. Northamptonshire

Name: Malachy Bernard Loye
Role: Right-hand bat, off-spin bowler
Born: 27 September 1972, Northampton
Height: 6ft 2in **Weight:** 13st 7lbs
Nickname: Mal, Mad Jack, Fruit Bat, Slugs
County debut: 1991
County cap: 1994
1st-Class 50s: 21
1st-Class 100s: 7
1st-Class 200s: 1
1st-Class catches: 48
One-Day 100s: 1
Place in batting averages: 99th av. 34.33
(1996 47th av. 45.56)
Parents: Patrick and Anne
Marital status: Single
Family links with cricket: Father and
brother both played for Cogenhoe CC in
Northampton

Education: Brixworth Primary School; Moulton Comprehensive School
Qualifications: GCSEs and senior coaching certificate
Overseas tours: England U18 to Canada 1991; England U19 to Pakistan 1991-92;
England A to South Africa 1993-94
Overseas teams played for: Riccarton, New Zealand and Canterbury B 1992-93;
Onslow, Wellington, New Zealand 1995-96
Cricketers particularly admired: Gordon Greenidge, Wayne Larkins, Curtly Ambrose
Young players to look out for: David Roberts, David Sales, Alec Swann, Kevin
Innes, Tobin Bailey
Other sports followed: Football (Liverpool and Northampton Town), golf, basketball
and boxing
Relaxations: Watching films, listening to music, singing and having a good night out
with friends
Extras: Played for England U19 in the home series against Australia U19 in 1991 and
against Sri Lanka U19 1992. Voted Professional Cricket Association's Young Player of
the Year 1993 and Whittingdale Young Player of the Year 1993. Shared a record opening
stand of 375 with Richard Montgomerie versus Yorkshire in 1996
Opinions on cricket: 'Tea time is too short. For such a great game it is so poorly
marketed, which is why we are so far behind other sports. Cricketers should have nine-
month contracts beginning January: this I'm sure will encourage better preparation and
commitment before a season.'
Best batting: 205 Northamptonshire v Yorkshire, Northampton 1996

1997 Season

	M	Inns	NO	Runs	HS	Avge	100s	50s	Ct	St	O	M	Runs	Wkts	Avge	Best	5wI	10wM
Test																		
All First	8	15	3	412	86	34.33	-	2	2	-								
1-day Int																		
NatWest	2	2	0	21	19	10.50	-	-	3	-								
B & H	5	5	1	120	47	30.00	-	-	-	-								
Sunday	6	6	0	151	68	25.16	-	1	1	-								

Career Performances

	M	Inns	NO	Runs	HS	Avge	100s	50s	Ct	St	Balls	Runs	Wkts	Avge	Best	5wI	10wM
Test																		
All First	82	133	15	4107	205	34.80	7	21	48	-	1	1	0	-	-	-	-
1-day Int																		
NatWest	12	11	3	218	65	27.25	-	1	4	-								
B & H	17	17	4	406	68 *	31.23	-	2	6	-								
Sunday	61	57	6	1500	122	29.41	1	8	12	-								

LUGSDEN, S.   Durham

Name: Steven Lugsden
Role: Right-hand bat, right-arm fast bowler
Born: 10 July 1976, Gateshead
Height: 6ft 3in **Weight:** 13st
Nickname: 8-ball, Lugsy, Dime Bar, Bluntest tool in the box
County debut: 1993
1st-Class catches: 1
Place in bowling averages:
(1996 18th av. 23.81)
Strike rate: 101.00 (career 77.52)
Parents: William and Nora
Wife and date of marriage: Janette, 19 December 1997
Children: John James, 21 December 1997
Education: St Edmund Campion RC School, Wrekenton, Gateshead
Qualifications: 7 GCSEs, BTEC Business and Finance
Career outside cricket: Landscape gardener and model ('clothed')
Off-season: 'Socialising in New Zealand'
Overseas tours: England U19 to West Indies 1994-95

Cricketers particularly admired: Geoff Cook, Allan Donald
Young players to look out for: Myself and Jason Searle
Other sports followed: 'Boxed to amateur county level' and snooker
Injuries: 'Sore body at frequent points through the year'
Extras: Youngest player (17 years 27 days) to make first-class debut for Durham. Played against India for England U19 in home series 1994. 'Daftest cricketer in the North East'
Opinions on cricket: 'David Boon is too short to be a fast bowler.'
Best batting: 9 Durham v Gloucestershire, Chester-le-Street 1996
Best bowling: 3-45 Durham v Lancashire, Chester-le-Street 1996

1997 Season

	M	Inns	NO	Runs	HS	Avge	100s	50s	Ct	St	O	M	Runs	Wkts	Avge	Best	5wI	10wM
Test																		
All First	1	2	1	4	4	4.00	-	-	-	-	16.5	2	88	1	88.00	1-88	-	-
1-day Int																		
NatWest																			
B & H																			
Sunday																			

Career Performances

	M	Inns	NO	Runs	HS	Avge	100s	50s	Ct	St	Balls	Runs	Wkts	Avge	Best	5wI	10wM
Test																	
All First	10	13	5	30	9	3.75	-	-	1	-	1318	847	17	49.82	3-45	-	-
1-day Int																	
NatWest																		
B & H																		
Sunday	1	0	0	0	0	-	-	-	-	-	48	55	1	55.00	1-55	-	

> 56. Who was voted the 1997 Wombwell Cricket
> Lovers' Society Young Player of the Year?

 vodafone

LYE, D.　　　　　　　　　　　　　　　　Middlesex

Name: David Lye
Role: Right-hand bat
Born: 11 April 1979
Height: 5ft 8in　**Weight:** 12st 7lbs
County debut: No first-team appearance
Parents: Gerald and Marilyn
Marital status: Single
Family links with cricket: Dad plays
cricket locally
Education: Stockland Primary School;
Honiton Secondary School
Qualifications: 'Going through the stages to
become a coach'
Career outside cricket: 'Left school to play
cricket'
Cricketers particularly admired: Ian
Botham, Graham Gooch, Allan Border
Other sports followed: Football (Manchester
United) and indoor cricket (Honiton)
Relaxations: Field sports
Extras: Devon Young Cricketer of the Year in 1996. Devon U17 Player of the Season
in 1995 and 1996

LYNCH, M. A.　　　　　　　　　Gloucestershire

Name: Monte Allan Lynch
Role: Right-hand bat, right-arm medium and off-spin bowler
Born: 21 May 1958, Georgetown, Guyana
Height: 5ft 9in **Weight:** 13st 3lbs
Nickname: Mont
County debut: 1977 (Surrey), 1994 (Glos)
County cap: 1982 (Surrey), 1995 (Glos)
Benefit: 1991 (£107,000)
One-Day Internationals: 3
1000 runs in a season: 10
1st-Class 50s: 88
1st-Class 100s: 39
1st-Class catches: 367
One-Day 100s: 6

Place in batting averages: 153rd av. 25.83
(1996 155th av. 30.72)
Strike rate: (career 84.42)
Parents: Lawrence and Doreen Austin
Marital status: Single
Children: Lours, 31 September 1983;
Marissa, 30 July 1989
Family links with cricket: 'Father and most of
family played at some time or another'
Education: Ryden's School, Walton-on-
Thames
Overseas tours: Unofficial West Indies XI to
South Africa 1983-84
Overseas teams played for: Guyana 1982-
83
Other sports followed: Football, table tennis
Extras: When he made 141* for Surrey v
Glamorgan at Guildford in August 1982, off

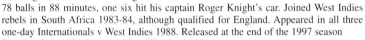

78 balls in 88 minutes, one six hit his captain Roger Knight's car. Joined West Indies
rebels in South Africa 1983-84, although qualified for England. Appeared in all three
one-day Internationals v West Indies 1988. Released at the end of the 1997 season
Best batting: 172* Surrey v Kent, The Oval 1989
Best bowling: 3-6 Surrey v Glamorgan, Swansea 1981

1997 Season

	M	Inns	NO	Runs	HS	Avge	100s	50s	Ct	St	O	M	Runs	Wkts	Avge	Best	5wl	10wM
Test																		
All First	12	19	1	465	64	25.83	-	3	9	-								
1-day Int																		
NatWest	2	2	1	100	100	100.00	1	-	1	-								
B & H	5	5	1	133	87	33.25	-	1	2	-								
Sunday	14	13	2	356	88 *	32.36	-	3	5	-								

Career Performances

	M	Inns	NO	Runs	HS	Avge	100s	50s	Ct	St	Balls	Runs	Wkts	Avge	Best	5wl	10wM
Test																	
All First	359	585	64	18325	172 *	35.17	39	88	367	-	2195	1398	26	53.76	3-6	-	-
1-day Int	3	3	0	8	6	2.66	-	-	1	-							
NatWest	43	38	6	989	129	30.90	2	4	20	-	304	179	7	25.57	2-28	-	
B & H	68	63	4	1521	112 *	25.77	2	8	34	-	132	121	0	-	-	-	
Sunday	248	228	29	5593	136	28.10	2	34	85	-	167	205	8	25.62	2-2	-	

MACMILLAN, G. I.   Leicestershire

Name: Gregor Innes Macmillan
Role: Right-hand bat, off-spin bowler
Born: 7 August 1969, Guildford
Height: 6ft 5in **Weight:** 13st 2lbs
County debut: 1994 (one-day),
1995 (first-class)
1st-Class 50s: 9
1st-Class 100s: 3
1st-Class catches: 51
Place in batting averages: 242nd av. 16.60
(1996 242nd av. 18.27)
Strike rate: (career 90.47)
Parents: Angus and Evelyn
Marital status: Single
Family links with cricket: 'Father plays club
cricket at Odiham and Greywell and
Hampshire Maniacs. Mother takes a mean
video. Her mother makes a great tea. Great-
uncle played a match at Kroonstad on Queen
Victoria's Jubilee Day'
Education: Guildford County School; Charterhouse; Southampton University; Keble
College, Oxford University
Qualifications: 'A few O- and A-levels', BA (Hons) Philosophy and Politics (Soton),
Dip.Soc Admin (Oxon), M Litt in Politics at Oxford
Overseas teams played for: Harvinia, Orange Free State 1988-89, 1993-94 'plus the
odd game whenever they ask me'
Cricketers particularly admired: 'Those like Jim Bovill who put up with me without
often complaining. Mickey Carr. Gordon Parsons for being tidy and Richard
Montgomerie for being less tidy than I am'
Other sports followed: Football (Liverpool FC) and 'Scotland at anything except
rugby union and curling'
Extras: Captained Southampton University to the UAU final 1991. Played for Surrey
from U11 to U19. Captain of Oxford University for 1995 season. Played in Oxford's last
two Varsity match victories, plus the winning first one-day match between the two
Universities in 1995. Captained both Oxford and Combined Universities ('a good way
to stay thin'). Scored a century on his championship debut for Leicestershire in 1995.
Released at the end of the 1997 season
Opinions on cricket: 'You'll have to give me time before I become judgmental. That's
not something you lightly ask a philosopher to do.'
Best batting: 122 Leicestershire v Surrey, Leicester 1995
Best bowling: 3-13 Oxford University v Cambridge University, Lord's 1993

1997 Season

	M	Inns	NO	Runs	HS	Avge	100s	50s	Ct	St	O	M	Runs	Wkts	Avge	Best	5wI	10wM
Test																		
All First	5	7	1	99	34	16.50	-	-	3	-	11	1	41	0	-	-	-	-
1-day Int																		
NatWest																		
B & H	4	3	1	43	16 *	21.50	-	-	1	-	3	0	28	0	-	-	-	
Sunday	4	4	0	33	15	8.25	-	-	3	-								

Career Performances

	M	Inns	NO	Runs	HS	Avge	100s	50s	Ct	St	Balls	Runs	Wkts	Avge	Best	5wI	10wM
Test																	
All First	48	76	9	1848	122	27.58	3	9	51	-	2081	1203	23	52.30	3-13	-	-
1-day Int																	
NatWest	1	1	0	9	9	9.00	-	-	-	-	18	13	1	13.00	1-13	-	
B & H	15	14	2	339	77	28.25	-	2	4	-	107	109	2	54.50	1-18	-	
Sunday	23	22	2	378	58	18.90	-	1	7	-	96	76	3	25.33	2-37	-	

MADDY, D. L.   Leicestershire

Name: Darren Lee Maddy
Role: Right-hand bat, right-arm
medium bowler
Born: 23 May 1974, Leicester
Height: 5ft 9in ('One inch taller than
Dominic Williamson, two inches taller than
Tim Mason') **Weight:** 11st
Nickname: Roaster, Stompie, St George
County debut: 1993 (one-day),
1994 (first-class)
County cap: 1996
1000 runs in a season: 1
1st-Class 50s: 10
1st-Class 100s: 5
1st-Class catches: 53
One-Day 100s: 2
Place in batting averages: 84th av. 36.10
(1996 120th av. 34.21)
Strike rate: 142.00 (career 96.33)
Parents: William Arthur and Hilary Jean
Marital status: Single
Family links with cricket: Father and younger brother, Greg, play club cricket

Education: Herrick Junior School, Leicester; Roundhills, Thurmaston; Wreake Valley, Syston
Qualifications: 8 GCSEs
Off-season: Touring Kenya and Sri Lanka with England A
Overseas tours: Leicestershire to Bloemfontein 1995, to Western Transvaal 1996, to Durban 1997; England A to Kenya and Sri Lanka
Overseas teams played for: Wanderers, Johannesburg 1992-93; Northern Free State, Orange Free State 1993-95; Rhodes University, South Africa 1995-97
Cricketers particularly admired: Brian Lara, Michael Atherton, Richard Hadlee, Viv Richards, 'Babe Ruth' Dakin
Young players to look out for: Iain Sutcliffe, Darren Stevens, Jimmy Ormond
Other sports followed: 'Six-a-side football in the morning before a game – hold the record for the number of goals scored past Neil Johnson this season.' Rugby union (Leicester Tigers), golf, American football, baseball, football (Leicester City and Manchester United)
Relaxations: Scuba diving, bungee jumping, listening to music
Extras: 'Voted having the biggest thighs in Leicester by team-mates.' Set a new 2nd XI Championship run aggregate record (1498) beating the previous one which had stood since 1961. Rapid Cricketline 2nd XI Player of the Year 1994. Scored his maiden first-class double century against Kenya at Nairobi on England A's 1997-98 tour and finished up as the leading run-scorer on the tour
Opinions on cricket: 'Counties should employ players on a nine-month basis. NatWest should be reduced to 50 overs … 60 overs is too long. The over-rate fine system is still too severe. The third umpire should be used in all one-day competitions.'
Best batting: 131 Leicestershire v Oxford University, The Parks 1995
Best bowling: 2-21 Leicestershire v Lancashire, Old Trafford 1996

1997 Season

	M	Inns	NO	Runs	HS	Avge	100s	50s	Ct	St	O	M	Runs	Wkts	Avge	Best	5wI	10wM
Test																		
All First	19	30	1	1047	103	36.10	3	5	18	-	47.2	10	122	2	61.00	1-2	-	-
1-day Int																		
NatWest	2	2	0	15	15	7.50	-	-	1	-	4	0	15	0	-		-	-
B & H	6	6	0	253	101	42.16	1	1	3	-	8	1	31	1	31.00	1-23	-	
Sunday	15	15	0	515	85	34.33	-	5	4	-	30.4	0	184	9	20.44	3-11	-	

Career Performances

	M	Inns	NO	Runs	HS	Avge	100s	50s	Ct	St	Balls	Runs	Wkts	Avge	Best	5wI	10wM
Test																	
All First-	52	85	4	2401	131	29.64	5	10	53	-	578	298	6	49.66	2-21	-	-
1-day Int																	
NatWest	5	5	0	62	34	12.40	-	-	1	-	132	109	4	27.25	2-38	-	
B & H	14	14	1	497	101	38.23	1	3	4	-	126	112	5	22.40	3-32	-	
Sunday	58	50	5	1414	106 *	31.42	1	12	23	-	738	739	24	30.79	3-11	-	

MALCOLM, D. E. Northamptonshire

Name: Devon Eugene Malcolm
Role: Right-hand bat, right-arm fast bowler
Born: 22 February 1963, Kingston, Jamaica
Height: 6ft 2in **Weight:** 15st
Nickname: Dude
County debut: 1984
County cap: 1989
Benefit: 1995
Test debut: 1989
Tests: 40
One-Day Internationals: 10
50 wickets in a season: 6
1st-Class 50s: 1
1st-Class 5 w. in innings: 31
1st-Class 10 w. in innings: 7
1st-Class catches: 33
One-Day 5 w. in innings: 2
Place in batting averages: 302nd av. 6.13
(1996 305th av. 7.43)

Place in bowling averages: 27th av. 23.48 (1996 71st av. 31.67)
Strike rate: 42.09 (career 51.14)
Parents: Albert and Brendalee (deceased)
Wife and date of marriage: Jennifer, October 1989
Children: Erica Cian, 11 June 1991; Natile Jade, 25 June 1993
Education: St Elizabeth Technical High School; Richmond College; Derby College of Higher Education
Qualifications: College certificates, O-levels, coaching certificate
Overseas tours: England to West Indies 1989-90, to Australia 1990-91, to India and Sri Lanka 1992-93, to West Indies 1993-94, to Australia 1994-95, to South Africa 1995-96; England A to Bermuda and West Indies 1991-92
Overseas teams played for: Ellerslie, Auckland 1985-87
Cricketers particularly admired: Michael Holding, Richard Hadlee, Malcolm Marshall, Alan Warner, Viv Richards
Other sports followed: Football, boxing
Relaxations: Music and movies, eating
Extras: Played league cricket for Sheffield Works and Sheffield United. Became eligible to play for England in 1987. Took 10 for 137 v West Indies in Port-of-Spain Test, 1989-90. Struck down with chickenpox early in the England tour to Australia 1994-95. Left Derbyshire during the off-season to join Northamptonshire for 1998
Best batting: 51 Derbyshire v Surrey, Derby 1989
Best bowling: 9-57 England v South Africa, The Oval 1994

1997 Season

	M	Inns	NO	Runs	HS	Avge	100s	50s	Ct	St	O	M	Runs	Wkts	Avge	Best	5wI	10wM
Test	4	5	1	12	12	3.00	-	-	2	-	93	19	307	6	51.16	3-100	-	-
All First	19	24	9	92	21 *	6.13	-	-	2	-	526.1	81	1761	75	23.48	6-23	5	2
1-day Int																		
NatWest	3	0	0	0	0	-	-	-	-	-	28.1	3	95	10	9.50	7-35	1	
B & H	3	3	0	16	13	5.33	-	-	-	-	26.5	3	116	5	23.20	2-38	-	
Sunday	1	1	0	3	3	3.00	-	-	-	-	8	0	51	1	51.00	1-51	-	

Career Performances

	M	Inns	NO	Runs	HS	Avge	100s	50s	Ct	St	Balls	Runs	Wkts	Avge	Best	5wI	10wM
Test	40	58	19	236	29	6.05	-	-	7	-	8480	4748	128	37.09	9-57	5	2
All First	232	277	86	1524	51	7.97	-	1	33	-	40561	24247	793	30.57	9-57	31	7
1-day Int	10	5	2	9	4	3.00	-	-	1	-	526	404	16	25.25	3-40	-	
NatWest	21	10	1	29	10 *	3.22	-	-	1	-	1307	847	33	25.66	7-35	1	
B & H	32	17	4	88	15	6.76	-	-	3	-	1799	1320	50	26.40	5-27	1	
Sunday	64	25	10	134	42	8.93	-	-	7	-	2827	2428	87	27.90	4-21	-	

MARSH, S. A. Kent

Name: Steven Andrew Marsh
Role: Right-hand bat, wicket-keeper,
county captain
Born: 27 January 1961, Westminster
Height: 5ft 11in **Weight:** 13st
Nickname: Marshy
County debut: 1982
County cap: 1986
Benefit: 1995
1st-Class 50s: 48
1st-Class 100s: 9
1st-Class catches: 618
1st-Class stumpings: 50
Place in batting averages: 65th av. 39.85
(1996 228th av. 20.78)
Strike rate: (career 101.00)
Parents: Melvyn Graham and Valerie Ann
Wife and date of marriage: Julie, 27
September 1986
Children: Hayley Ann, 15 May 1987; Christian James Robert, 20 November 1990
Family links with cricket: Father played local cricket for Lordswood. Father-in-law,
Bob Wilson, played for Kent 1954-66

Education: Walderslade Secondary School for Boys; Mid-Kent College of Higher and Further Education
Qualifications: 6 O-levels, 2 A-levels, OND in Business Studies
Off-season: Working for South East Telecom
Overseas tours: Fred Rumsey XI to Barbados 1986-87
Overseas teams played for: Avendale CC, Cape Town 1985-86
Cricketers particularly admired: Robin Smith, Graham Cowdrey, Ian Botham, Colin Johns, Mark Bradley
Young players to look out for: Ben Phillips
Other sports followed: Golf, football (Chelsea FC)
Extras: Appointed Kent vice-captain in 1991. In the match v Middlesex at Lord's in 1991 he held a world record eight catches in an innings and scored 113*. 'Cycling proficiency'
Opinions on cricket: 'The majority of county cricketers know and believe that our game needs change. Why don't they listen to us?'
Best batting: 142 Kent v Sussex, Horsham 1997
Best bowling: 2-20 Kent v Warwickshire, Edgbaston 1990

1997 Season

	M	Inns	NO	Runs	HS	Avge	100s	50s	Ct	St	O	M	Runs	Wkts	Avge	Best	5wl	10wM
Test																		
All First	18	27	6	837	142	39.85	1	3	61	2								
1-day Int																		
NatWest	1	1	0	0	0	0.00	-	-	-	-								
B & H	8	4	2	79	27 *	39.50	-	-	6	1								
Sunday	16	12	6	107	39 *	17.83	-	-	10	1								

Career Performances

	M	Inns	NO	Runs	HS	Avge	100s	50s	Ct	St	Balls	Runs	Wkts	Avge	Best	5wl	10wM
Test																	
All First	260	379	63	9012	142	28.51	9	48	618	50	202	240	2	120.00	2-20	-	-
1-day Int																	
NatWest	23	16	3	209	55	16.07	-	1	33	4	3	3	1	3.00	1-3	-	
B & H	59	44	11	584	71	17.69	-	1	67	4							
Sunday	178	129	39	1763	59	19.58	-	4	168	22							

MARTIN, N. D.   Middlesex

Name: Neil Donald Martin
Role: Right-hand bat, right-arm
fast-medium bowler
Born: 19 August 1979, Enfield
Height: 5ft 10in **Weight:** 13st
Nickname: Nelly
County debut: 1997 (one-day)
Parents: Cliff and Jill
Marital status: Single
Family links with cricket: Father plays local
club cricket for North Mymms and is a
playing member of the MCC
Education: Wheatfields, St Albans; Verulam,
St Albans
Qualifications: 9 GCSEs, NCA coaching award
Career outside cricket: 'Various'
Off-season: 'Any offers are gratefully
received'
Overseas tours: England U19 to Pakistan 1996-97
Cricketers particularly admired: Allan Donald, Darren Gough
Other sports followed: Football (Tottenham Hotspur)
Injuries: Stress fracture of the back, missed four months at the close of the season and
four weeks at the start of the season. Groin strain put him out for two weeks
Relaxations: Socialising with friends, 'winding up team mates, talking breeze to
anyone who will listen'
Opinions on cricket: 'Lunch and tea breaks should be longer. Extra-hour rule should be
abolished in 2nd XI cricket. Overs should be reduced from 110 to 104, i.e. quality not
quantity. The Sunday League should be used to bring younger players through who are
doing well in 2nd XI cricket. Players' wages should at least be doubled!'

1997 Season

	M	Inns	NO	Runs	HS	Avge	100s	50s	Ct	St	O	M	Runs	Wkts	Avge	Best	5wI	10wM
Test																		
All First																		
1-day Int																		
NatWest																		
B & H																		
Sunday	1	0	0	0	0	-	-	-	-	-	6	0	29	1	29.00	1-29	-	

Career Performances

	M	Inns	NO	Runs	HS	Avge	100s	50s	Ct	St	Balls	Runs	Wkts	Avge	Best	5wI	10wM
Test																	
All First																	
1-day Int																	
NatWest																	
B & H																	
Sunday	1	0	0	0	0	-	-	-	-	-	36	29	1	29.00	1-29	-	

MARTIN, P. J. Lancashire

Name: Peter James Martin
Role: Right-hand bat, right-arm
fast-medium bowler
Born: 15 November 1968, Accrington
Height: 6ft 5in **Weight:** 15st 4lbs
Nickname: Digger, Long John
County debut: 1989
County cap: 1994
Test debut: 1995
Tests: 8
One-Day Internationals: 16
50 wickets in a season: 1
1st-Class 50s: 5
1st-Class 100s: 1
1st-Class 5 w. in innings: 7
1st-Class 10 w. in match: 1
1st-Class catches: 33
One-Day 5 w. in innings: 3
Place in batting averages: 223rd av. 18.73
(1996 235th av. 19.85)
Place in bowling averages: 22nd av. 23.13 (1996 33rd av. 26.38)
Strike rate: 49.06 (career 65.70)
Parents: Keith and Catherine Lina
Marital status: Single
Education: Danum School, Doncaster
Qualifications: 6 O-levels, 2 A-levels
Off-season: With England to Sharjah
Overseas tours: England YC to Australia (Youth World Cup) 1988; 'and various other tours with English Schools and NAYC'; England to South Africa 1995-96, to India and Pakistan (World Cup) 1995-96, to Sharjah 1997-98
Overseas teams played for: Southern Districts, Queensland 1988-89; South

Launceston, Tasmania 1989-90; South Canberra, ACT 1990-92
Cricketers particularly admired: 'Too many to mention'
Other sports followed: Football (Manchester United), rugby league (St Helens), golf
Relaxations: Music, painting, golf, cooking, walking, rugby league
Extras: Plays district football and basketball for Doncaster. Played for England A v Sri Lankans 1991. Was originally selected for the England A tour to Pakistan in 1995-96, but was drafted on to the senior tour after the withdrawal of Richard Johnson
Opinions on cricket: 'Should only be six-hour days with 100 overs a day.'
Best batting: 133 Lancashire v Durham, Gateshead Fell 1992
Best bowling: 7-50 Lancashire v Nottinghamshire, Trent Bridge 1996

1997 Season

	M	Inns	NO	Runs	HS	Avge	100s	50s	Ct	St	O	M	Runs	Wkts	Avge	Best	5wI	10wM
Test	1	2	0	23	20	11.50	-	-	1	-	19	5	51	0	-	-	-	-
All First	17	19	4	281	78 *	18.73	-	1	3	-	474.2	136	1342	58	23.13	8-32	3	1
1-day Int																		
NatWest	2	0	0	0	0	-	-	-	-	-	21.3	5	60	1	60.00	1-14	-	
B & H	5	2	1	10	10 *	10.00	-	-	1	-	48.3	7	197	11	17.90	3-31	-	
Sunday	16	5	2	17	11 *	5.66	-	-	3	-	96.2	8	392	31	12.64	5-21	2	

Career Performances

	M	Inns	NO	Runs	HS	Avge	100s	50s	Ct	St	Balls	Runs	Wkts	Avge	Best	5wI	10wM
Test	8	13	0	115	29	8.84	-	-	6	-	1452	580	17	34.11	4-60	-	-
All First	134	154	39	2316	133	20.13	1	5	33	-	22405	10414	341	30.53	8-32	7	1
1-day Int	16	10	6	33	6	8.25	-	-	1	-	838	610	25	24.40	4-44	-	
NatWest	14	4	3	27	16	27.00	-	-	1	-	825	443	23	19.26	4-36	-	
B & H	19	6	5	28	10 *	28.00	-	-	5	-	1053	719	25	28.76	3-31	-	
Sunday	81	25	15	149	35 *	14.90	-	-	12	-	3120	2341	102	22.95	5-21	3	

MARTIN-JENKINS, R. S. C.   Sussex

Name: Robin Simon Christopher Martin-Jenkins
Role: Right-hand bat, right-arm medium-fast bowler
Born: 28 October 1975, Guildford
Height: 6ft 6in   **Weight:** 13st 7lbs
Nickname: Tucker, Cérise, Crazy MF
County debut: 1995
1st-Class 50s: 1
1st-Class catches: 2
Strike rate: 68.40 (career 118.00)
Parents: Christopher and Judy
Marital status: Single

Family links with cricket: Father is *Daily Telegraph* cricket correspondent
Education: Cranleigh Prep School, Surrey; Radley College, Oxon; Durham University
Qualifications: 10 GCSEs, 3 A-levels, 1 AS-level, Grade 3 bassoon
Overseas tours: Radley College to Barbados 1992
Overseas teams played for: Lima, Peru 1995
Cricketers particularly admired: Robin Smith, Angus Fraser, Steve Waugh·
Young players to look out for: Raj Rao, Jim Chaplin
Other sports followed: Fives, hockey, tennis, skiing, football (Liverpool FC)
Relaxations: Watching television ('Pink Panther, James Bond'), listening to music

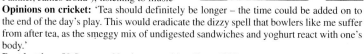

Opinions on cricket: 'Tea should definitely be longer – the time could be added on to the end of the day's play. This would eradicate the dizzy spell that bowlers like me suffer from after tea, as the smeggy mix of undigested sandwiches and yoghurt react with one's body.'

Best batting: 50 Sussex v Northamptonshire, Hove 1995
Best bowling: 3-26 Sussex v Pakistan A, Hove 1997

1997 Season

	M	Inns	NO	Runs	HS	Avge	100s	50s	Ct	St	O	M	Runs	Wkts	Avge	Best	5wI	10wM
Test																		
All First	3	6	1	77	36 *	15.40	-	-	2	-	57	10	184	5	36.80	3-26	-	-
1-day Int																		
NatWest																			
B & H	3	2	0	20	10	10.00	-	-	-	-	23	0	140	5	28.00	4-57	-	
Sunday	2	2	0	5	3	2.50	-	-	-	-	16	0	90	1	90.00	1-32	-	

Career Performances

	M	Inns	NO	Runs	HS	Avge	100s	50s	Ct	St	Balls	Runs	Wkts	Avge	Best	5wI	10wM
Test																	
All First	7	9	2	147	50	21.00	-	1	2	-	708	353	6	58.83	3-26	-	-
1-day Int																	
NatWest																		
B & H	6	5	0	36	12	7.20	-	-	-	-	304	276	9	30.66	4-57	-	
Sunday	12	8	1	17	10	2.42	-	-	-	-	420	382	6	63.66	2-41	-	

MARU, R. J.   Hampshire

Name: Rajesh Jamnadass Maru
Role: Right-hand bat, slow left-arm bowler, part-time wicket-keeper
Born: 28 October 1962, Nairobi, Kenya
Height: 5ft 6in **Weight:** 11st
Nickname: Raj, Rat
County debut: 1980 (Middlesex), 1984 (Hampshire)
County cap: 1986 (Hampshire)
50 wickets in a season: 4
1st-Class 50s: 7
1st-Class 5 w. in innings: 15
1st-Class 10 w. in match: 1
1st-Class catches: 252
Place in batting averages:
(1996 198th av. 25.25)
Place in bowling averages:
(1996 116th av. 40.77)
Strike rate: 254.00 (career 75.71)
Parents: Jamnadass and Prabhavati
Wife and date of marriage: Amanda Jane, 21 September 1991
Children: Christopher Patrick, 21 January 1993; Daniel James, 7 January 1996
Family links with cricket: Father played in Kenya and in England for North London Polytechnic. Brother Pradip played for Wembley in the Middlesex League and has played for Middlesex 2nd XI, Middlesex U19 and for Middlesex Colts & Schools
Education: Rooks Heath High School, Harrow; Pinner Sixth Form College
Qualifications: NCA advanced coach
Off-season: Coaching for Hampshire CCC and planning a benefit for 1998
Overseas tours: England YC South to Canada 1979; England YC to West Indies 1979-80; Middlesex to Zimbabwe 1980; Hampshire to Barbados 1987,1988,1990, to Anguilla 1997; Hampshire to Dubai 1989; Barbican International XI to Dubai 1981; MCC to Leeward Islands 1992, to Far East 1995
Overseas teams played for: Marlborough CA, Blenheim, New Zealand 1985-87
Cricketers particularly admired: Bishan Bedi, Phil Edmonds, Malcolm Marshall, Brian Lara, Shane Warne
Young players to look out for: Jason Laney
Other sports followed: Football, rugby (Wasps and England), 'would watch any sport'
Injuries: 'Not being selected – only played four or five first-class games'
Relaxations: 'Spending time with my family'
Extras: Played for Middlesex 1980-83; reached 500 first-class wickets in 1995. Awarded benefit for 1998
Opinions on cricket: 'Leave the same structure in four-day cricket. The same structure

in one-day cricket but without the 40-over game.'
Best batting: 74 Hampshire v Gloucestershire, Gloucester 1988
Best bowling: 8-41 Hampshire v Kent, Southampton 1989

1997 Season

	M	Inns	NO	Runs	HS	Avge	100s	50s	Ct	St	O	M	Runs	Wkts	Avge	Best	5wI	10wM
Test																		
All First	4	4	1	67	36 *	22.33	-	-	6	-	127	35	336	3	112.00	2-60	-	-
1-day Int																		
NatWest	2	0	0	0	0	-	-	-	-	-	11	0	55	0	-		-	-
B & H	3	2	2	19	10 *	-	-	-	1	-	30	2	114	3	38.00	2-51	-	
Sunday	7	4	2	15	6 *	7.50	-	-	5	-	45	0	231	7	33.00	4-29	-	

Career Performances

	M	Inns	NO	Runs	HS	Avge	100s	50s	Ct	St	Balls	Runs	Wkts	Avge	Best	5wI	10wM
Test																	
All First	227	229	57	2938	74	17.08	-	7	252	-	39750	17547	525	33.42	8-41	15	1
1-day Int																	
NatWest	16	6	2	44	22	11.00	-	-	12	-	948	586	13	45.07	3-30	-	
B & H	15	6	3	38	10 *	12.66	-	-	6	-	771	511	15	34.06	3-46	-	
Sunday	71	32	19	184	33 *	14.15	-	-	27	-	2527	2192	55	39.85	4-29	-	

MASCARENHAS, D. A.   Hampshire

Name: Dimitri Adrian Mascarenhas
Role: Right-hand bat, right-arm
medium bowler
Born: 30 October 1977, Chiswick, London
Height: 6ft 2in **Weight:** 11st 7lbs
Nickname: Dimmie, Genii, Gibson
County debut: 1996
1st-Class 5 w. in innings: 2
Place in batting averages: 292nd av. 8.33
Place in bowling averages: (1996 8th av.
18.56)
Strike rate: 95.00 (career 54.66)
Parents: Malik and Pauline
Marital status: Single
Family links with cricket: Uncle played in
Sri Lanka and brothers both play for Melville
CC in Perth, WA
Education: Our Lady's Primary, Melbourne;

Trinity College, Perth
Off-season: Playing club cricket in Perth, Western Australia
Overseas teams played for: Melville CC, Perth 1991-97
Cricketers particularly admired: Viv Richards, Malcolm Marshall, the Waugh twins
Young players to look out for: Ben Hollioake
Other sports followed: Aussie rules (Collingwood)
Injuries: Back injury, out for seven weeks
Relaxations: Aussie rules, tennis, golf, 'occasional scenario'
Extras: Played for Western Australia at U17 and U19 level as captain
Opinions on cricket: 'Great game'
Best batting: 21 Hampshire v Gloucestershire, Bristol 1997
Best bowling: 6-88 Hampshire v Glamorgan, Southampton 1996

1997 Season

	M	Inns	NO	Runs	HS	Avge	100s	50s	Ct	St	O	M	Runs	Wkts	Avge	Best	5wI	10wM
Test																		
All First	6	7	1	50	21	8.33	-	-	-	-	126.4	22	417	8	52.12	5-63	1	-
1-day Int																		
NatWest																			
B & H	2	2	0	21	20	10.50	-	-	-	-	17	1	92	0	-		-	-
Sunday	3	2	0	17	10	8.50	-	-	1	-	11	0	96	0	-		-	-

Career Performances

	M	Inns	NO	Runs	HS	Avge	100s	50s	Ct	St	Balls	Runs	Wkts	Avge	Best	5wI	10wM
Test																	
All First	8	10	1	74	21	8.22	-	-	-	-	1312	714	24	29.75	6-88	2	-
1-day Int																	
NatWest																		
B & H	2	2	0	21	20	10.50	-	-	-	-	102	92	0	-		-	-
Sunday	6	4	1	24	10	8.00	-	-	2	-	194	220	5	44.00	2-34	-	

MASON, T. J.   Leicestershire

Name: Timothy James Mason
Role: Right-hand bat, right-arm
off-spin bowler
Born: 12 April 1975, Leicester
Height: 5ft 8in **Weight:** 10st 4lbs
Nickname: Perry, Biffa, Stone
County debut: 1994
1st-Class catches: 4
Strike rate: 17.00 (career 75.33)

Parents: Phillip John and Anthea Jane
Marital status: Single
Family links with cricket: Father plays club cricket and is manager of Leicestershire Schools U11
Education: Brookvale High School, Leicester; Denstone College
Qualifications: 9 GCSEs, 3 A-levels
Career outside cricket: Undecided
Overseas tours: Denstone College to South Africa 1993; England U19 to Sri Lanka 1993-94; Westgold CC to Northern Transvaal 1996
Overseas teams played for: Eastern Freestate, South Africa 1994-95; Westgold CC, Western Transvaal 1995-97
Cricketers particularly admired: Allan Lamb, Malcolm Marshall, Jon Dakin, Darren 'Roasting' Maddy
Young players to look out for: Darren Maddy, Jon Dakin 'and of course myself'
Other sports followed: Rugby union (Leicester Tigers), football (Leicester City)
Relaxations: Going out with friends and girlfriend, Nicole. Listening to music
Extras: Captained Leicestershire Schools at all age levels. 1992 *Daily Telegraph* U19 Midlands Bowler of the Year; 1993 *Daily Telegraph* U19 National Bowler of the Year; 1993 Gray-Nicolls Outstanding Schoolboy Player of the Year. Dislocated shoulder prevented him from going on England U18 tour to South Africa 1992-93. Played in the winning Bain Hogg team in 1996
Opinions on cricket: 'Great game, but 2nd XI grounds have to be better. This will definitely make young players better – especially young bowlers.'
Best batting: 4 Leicestershire v Australia, Leicester 1997
Best bowling: 2-21 Leicestershire v Australia, Leicester 1997

1997 Season

	M	Inns	NO	Runs	HS	Avge	100s	50s	Ct	St	O	M	Runs	Wkts	Avge	Best	5wI	10wM
Test																		
All First	1	1	0	4	4	4.00	-	-	1	-	5.4	0	22	2	11.00	2-21	-	-
1-day Int																		
NatWest	2	2	0	66	36	33.00	-	-	-	-	24	1	92	3	30.66	3-29	-	
B & H	1	1	0	30	30	30.00	-	-	-	-	10	0	55	1	55.00	1-55	-	
Sunday	10	9	4	56	17 *	11.20	-	-	2	-	43.4	0	247	8	30.87	2-15	-	

Career Performances

	M	Inns	NO	Runs	HS	Avge	100s	50s	Ct	St	Balls	Runs	Wkts	Avge	Best	5wI	10wM
Test																	
All First	3	2	0	7	4	3.50	-	-	4	-	226	123	3	41.00	2-21	-	-
1-day Int																	
NatWest	4	3	0	71	36	23.66	-	-	3	-	288	164	3	54.66	3-29	-	
B & H	5	4	2	61	30	30.50	-	-	1	-	264	186	5	37.20	2-35	-	
Sunday	22	13	5	85	17 *	10.62	-	-	3	-	700	635	14	45.35	2-15	-	

MASTERS, D. D.   Kent

Name: Daniel D. Masters
Role: Right-hand bat, right-arm
medium-fast bowler
Born: 22 April 1978
Height: 6ft 4ins **Weight:** 12st
County debut: No first-team appearance
Parents: Kevin and Tracey
Marital status: Single
Family links with cricket:
Father played for Kent and Surrey
Education: Luton Primary School; Fort
Luton High School; Mid-Kent College
Qualifications: 6 GCSEs, qualified
football coach
Career outside cricket: Builder
Off-season: 'Work hard at my game and do
as well for Kent as I possibly can'
Young players to look out for: Daniel
Masters, Buster Gibbons, Peter Stock

Other sports followed: Football (Manchester United)
Relaxations: Football and going out with friends
Opinions on cricket: 'The game is getting bigger and more entertaining, but it's still a batsman's game.'

MAUNDERS, J. K.   Middlesex

Name: John Kenneth Maunders
Role: Left-hand bat
Born: 4 April 1981, Ashford, Middlesex
Height: 5ft 10in **Weight:** 12st 7lbs
Nickname: Johnny, Johnboy
County debut: No first-team appearance
Parents: Kenny and Lynn
Marital status: Single
Family links with cricket: 'Grandad is No. 1 supporter and two uncles play club cricket'
Education: Ashford Parl Primary School; Ashford High Secondary School; Speltthorpe College of Further Education
Qualifications: 9 GCSEs, Duke of Edinburgh Bronze and Silver Award
Career outside cricket: Student
Off-season: Studying PE A-level, keepiung fit, playing hockey and football and training with England U17s and Middlesex
Cricketers particularly admired: Neil Fairbrother, Graham Thorpe, Angus Fraser and Alec Stewart
Young players to look out for: Huw Jones, Mark Wright
Other sports followed: Football (Liverpool FC)
Relaxations: 'Socialising with friends, playing sports, listening to music, making a few bob here and there'
Extras: Awarded junior county cap at the age of 12. Ruled out of the Lombard World Challenge Trophy through injury (broken thumb) and currently training with England U17
Opinions on cricket: 'Tea should be extended so that players have more time to recoup and get ready for the last session's play.'

---

59. Glamorgan were crowned 1997 County Champions, but when was the last time they won the crown and who led them to victory?

MAY, M. R.   Derbyshire

Name: Michael Robert May
Role: Right-hand bat, off-spin bowler
Born: 22 July 1971, Chesterfield
Height: 5ft 9in **Weight:** 14st
Nickname: Hazey, Boonie, Maggie
County debut: 1996
1st-Class 50s: 4
1st-Class 100s: 2
1st-Class catches: 3
Place in batting averages: 69th av. 39.20
Parents: Mick and Christine
Wife and date of marriage: Sasha May, 14
January 1996
Family links with cricket: Brother Paul
plays for 2nd XI and Colts for Derbyshire
Education: Duckmanton Primary School;
The Bolsover School; North East Derbyshire
College
Qualifications: City and Guilds in
Recreation and Leisure, NCA cricket coach
Overseas teams played for: Marist, New Zealand 1988-89; Johannesburg Municipals
1990-92; Sandringham CC, Melbourne 1994-96; St Kilda CC 1996-97
Cricketers particularly admired: Steve Waugh, Ian Botham, Peter Kirsten, Allan
Border
Young players to look out for: Andrew Harris, Shawn Craig
Other sports followed: Aussie rules (Essendon) and football (Nottingham Forest)
Relaxations: Watching most sports, reading, music, specnding time with my wife and
family
Opinions on cricket: 'Far too much emphasis on one-day cricket in domestic and
international cricket.'
Best batting: 116 Derbyshire v Glamorgan, Chesterfield 1997

1997 Season

	M	Inns	NO	Runs	HS	Avge	100s	50s	Ct	St	O	M	Runs	Wkts	Avge	Best	5wI	10wM
Test																		
All First	9	17	2	588	116	39.20	2	3	2	-	4.1	0	50	0	-	-	-	-
1-day Int																		
NatWest	1	1	0	5	5	5.00	-	-	-	-								
B & H																		
Sunday																		

Career Performances

	M	Inns	NO	Runs	HS	Avge	100s	50s	Ct	St	Balls	Runs	Wkts	Avge	Best	5wl	10wM
Test																	
All First	12	21	4	748	116	44.00	2	4	3	-	43	69	0	-	-	-	-
1-day Int																	
NatWest	1	1	0	5	5	5.00	-	-	-	-							
B & H																	
Sunday																	

MAYNARD, M. P.   Glamorgan

Name: Matthew Peter Maynard
Role: Right-hand bat, right-arm medium
'declaration' bowler, cover fielder, county
captain
Born: 21 March 1966, Oldham, Lancashire
Height: 5ft 11in **Weight:** 13st
Nickname: Ollie
County debut: 1985
County cap: 1987
Benefit: 1996
Test debut: 1988
Tests: 4
One-Day Internationals: 10
1000 runs in a season: 10
1st-Class 50s: 101
1st-Class 100s: 43
1st-Class 200s: 3
1st-Class catches: 274
1st-Class stumpings: 5
One-Day 100s: 10
Place in batting averages: 3rd av. 65.00 (1996 10th av. 61.92)
Strike rate: (career 161.00)
Parents: Ken (deceased) and Pat
Wife and date of marriage: Susan, 27 September 1986
Children: Tom, 25 March 1989; Ceri Lloyd, 5 August 1993
Family links with cricket: Father played for many years for Duckinfield. Brother
Charles plays for St Fagans
Education: Ysgol David Hughes, Menai Bridge, Anglesey
Qualifications: Cricket coach
Off-season: Player/coach for Otago in New Zealand
Overseas tours: North Wales XI to Barbados 1982; Glamorgan to Barbados 1982, to

South Africa 1993; unofficial England XI to South Africa 1989-90; HKCC (Australia) to Bangkok and Hong Kong, 1990; England VI to Hong Kong Sixes 1992 and 1994; England to West Indies 1993-94

Overseas teams played for: St Joseph's, Whakatane, New Zealand 1986-88; Gosnells, Perth, Western Australia 1988-89; Papakura and Northern Districts, New Zealand 1990-92; Morrinsville College and Northern Districts 1991-92; Otago, New Zealand 1996-97

Cricketers particularly admired: Ian Botham, Viv Richards, David Gower

Young players to look out for: Dean Cosker, Simon Jones ('when fit')

Other sports followed: Football (Manchester City), golf and squash

Injuries: Dislocated finger, missed one Sunday League game

Relaxations: Spending time with my wife and family and relaxing

Extras: Scored century on first-class debut v Yorkshire at Swansea in 1985, when he became the youngest centurion for Glamorgan, and scored 1000 runs in first full season. In 1987 scored the fastest ever 50 for Glamorgan (14 mins) v Yorkshire and was youngest player to be awarded Glamorgan cap. Voted Young Cricketer of the Year 1988 by the Cricket Writers' Club. Banned from Test cricket for five years for joining 1989-90 tour of South Africa, ban remitted 1992. Scored 987 runs in July 1991, including a century in each innings v Gloucestershire at Cheltenham. Captained Glamorgan for most of 1992 in Alan Butcher's absence. Second child was born on the morning of the fifth Test against Australia at Edgbaston 1993 – he had a daughter and a duck on the same day. Glamorgan's captain for the 1996 season. Awarded benefit for 1996. Voted Wombwell Cricket Lovers' Society captain of the year for 1997. He captained an England XI in the Cricket Max tournament in New Zealand in 1997-98

Opinions on cricket: 'Good to see four-day cricket starting on a Wednesday to lose the Sunday sandwich. Counties should reduce the size of playing staffs, but increase the salaries of the retained players.'

Best batting: 243 Glamorgan v Hampshire, Southampton 1991

Best bowling: 3-21 Glamorgan v Oxford University, The Parks 1987

1997 Season

	M	Inns	NO	Runs	HS	Avge	100s	50s	Ct	St	O	M	Runs	Wkts	Avge	Best	5wl	10wM
Test																		
All First	18	25	7	1170	161 *	65.00	3	7	21	-	13.5	0	66	0	-	-	-	-
1-day Int																		
NatWest	4	4	1	159	62	53.00	-	1	3	-	3	0	8	0	-		-	-
B & H	4	4	0	106	50	26.50	-	1	4	-	1	0	6	0	-		-	-
Sunday	12	12	2	426	132	42.60	1	1	7	-	0.4	0	2	0	-		-	-

58. Who finished top of the 1997 first-class batting averages?

O vodafone

Career Performances

	M	Inns	NO	Runs	HS	Avge	100s	50s	Ct	St	Balls	Runs	Wkts	Avge	Best	5wI	10wM
Test	4	8	0	87	35	10.87	-	-	3	-							
All First	288	473	52	18516	243	43.98	43	101	274	5	966	783	6	130.50	3-21	-	-
1-day Int	10	10	1	153	41	17.00	-	-	2	-							
NatWest	34	33	3	1374	151 *	45.80	2	11	13	-	18	8	0	-		-	-
B & H	46	46	6	1737	151 *	43.42	4	8	17	-	30	38	0	-		-	-
Sunday	175	167	13	4727	132	30.69	4	30	67	-	22	31	0	-		-	-

McCAGUE, M. J. Kent

Name: Martin John McCague
Role: Right-hand bat, right-arm fast bowler
Born: 24 May 1969, Larne, Northern Ireland
Height: 6ft 5in **Weight:** 17st
Nickname: Pigsy, Macca, Mad Mick
County debut: 1991
County cap: 1992
Test debut: 1993
Tests: 3
50 wickets in a season: 4
1st-Class 50s: 4
1st-Class 5 w. in innings: 24
1st-Class 10 w. in match: 2
1st-Class catches: 58
One-Day 5 w. in innings: 3
Place in batting averages: 234th av. 17.27
(1996 239th av. 18.78)
Place in bowling averages: 26th av. 23.43
(1996 23rd av. 24.96)
Strike rate: 39.08 (career 48.88)
Parents: Mal and Mary
Wife and date of marriage: Leigh-Anne, 8 February 1997
Education: Hedland Senior High School
Qualifications: Electrician
Off-season: Coaching
Overseas tours: England A to South Africa 1993-94; England to Australia 1994-95
Overseas teams played for: Western Australia 1990-91
Cricketers particularly admired: Paul Strang, Courtney Walsh
Young players to look out for: Ben Phillips, David Sales
Other sports followed: Football (Crystal Palace FC), golf and snooker
Injuries: Ligament strain on facet joint, out for five weeks

Relaxations: Playing golf
Extras: Kent Player of the Year in 1996
Opinions on cricket: 'Players let the counties know their opinion on the changes Lord MacLaurin advised and they didn't seem to listen, so why bother?'
Best batting: 63* Kent v Surrey, The Oval 1996
Best bowling: 9-86 Kent v Derbyshire, Derby 1994

1997 Season

	M	Inns	NO	Runs	HS	Avge	100s	50s	Ct	St	O	M	Runs	Wkts	Avge	Best	5wI	10wM
Test																		
All First	11	17	6	190	53 *	17.27	-	1	3	-	312.4	55	1125	48	23.43	7-50	4	-
1-day Int																		
NatWest	1	1	1	4	4 *	-	-	-	1	-	2	0	8	0	-		-	-
B & H	8	4	3	24	12 *	24.00	-	-	-	-	67	4	326	10	32.60	4-41	-	
Sunday	12	8	1	41	11	5.85	-	-	3	-	72.2	1	377	14	26.92	3-50	-	

Career Performances

	M	Inns	NO	Runs	HS	Avge	100s	50s	Ct	St	Balls	Runs	Wkts	Avge	Best	5wI	10wM
Test	3	5	0	21	11	4.20	-	-	1	-	593	390	6	65.00	4-121	-	-
All First	106	146	36	1691	63 *	15.37	-	4	58	-	19163	10369	392	26.45	9-86	24	2
1-day Int																	
NatWest	12	10	6	100	31 *	25.00	-	-	3	-	654	437	21	20.80	5-26	1	
B & H	30	19	8	169	30	15.36	-	-	7	-	1532	1186	39	30.41	5-43	1	
Sunday	77	42	13	252	22 *	8.68	-	-	15	-	3000	2634	109	24.16	5-40	1	

McGRATH, A.   Yorkshire

Name: Anthony McGrath
Role: Right-hand bat, off-spin bowler
Born: 6 October 1975, Bradford
Height: 6ft 2in **Weight:** 13st 6lbs
Nickname: Mags, Gripper
County debut: 1995
1st-Class 50s: 9
1st-Class 100s: 5
1st-Class catches: 29
One-Day 100s: 1
Place in batting averages: 95th av. 34.66 (1996 144th av. 32.22)
Strike rate: 77.00 (career 101.50)
Parents: Terry and Kathleen
Marital status: Single
Family links with cricket: Brother plays local league cricket

Education: St Winefrides; St Blaise; Yorkshire Martyrs Collegiate School
Qualifications: 9 GCSEs, BTEC in Leisure Studies
Off-season: Getting fit
Overseas tours: England U19 to West Indies 1994-95; England A to Pakistan 1995-96, to Australia 1996-97
Cricketers particularly admired: Robin Smith, Nasser Hussain, Ronnie Irani, Darren Lehmann
Young players to look out for: Alex Morris, Ian Fisher
Other sports followed: Football (Manchester United)
Injuries: Lower back, missed one game
Relaxations: 'Spending time with my friends outside cricket, playing and watching other sports'

Extras: Captained Yorkshire Schools U13, U14, U15 and U16; captained English Schools U17. Bradford League Young Cricketer of the Year 1992 and 1993. Played for England U17, and for England U19 in home series against India 1994. Appeared as 12th man for England in the First Test against West Indies at Headingley in 1995. Scored his maiden first-class century on the England A tour to Pakistan
Opinions on cricket: 'Too many games are played during the county season. A two division system would eradicate the problem – less games would be played allowing more time between games. Also, with promotion and relegation, there would be interest till the end of the season.'
Best batting: 141 Yorkshire v Worcestershire, Headingley 1997
Best bowling: 1-6 England A v Queensland, Brisbane 1996-97

1997 Season

	M	Inns	NO	Runs	HS	Avge	100s	50s	Ct	St	O	M	Runs	Wkts	Avge	Best	5wI	10wM
Test																		
All First	15	25	1	832	141	34.66	2	3	5	-	12.5	0	59	1	59.00	1-19	-	-
1-day Int																		
NatWest	3	3	0	35	24	11.66	-	-	-	-								
B & H	6	6	1	223	109 *	44.60	1	-	2	-								
Sunday	13	11	3	281	63	35.12	-	2	5	-								

Career Performances

	M	Inns	NO	Runs	HS	Avge	100s	50s	Ct	St	Balls	Runs	Wkts	Avge	Best	5wl	10wM
Test																	
All First	49	84	4	2436	141	30.45	5	9	29	-	203	129	2	64.50	1-6	-	-
1-day Int																	
NatWest	7	7	1	115	34	19.16	-	-	3	-							
B & H	13	12	1	331	109 *	30.09	1	-	2	-	12	10	2	5.00	2-10	-	
Sunday	31	27	6	608	72	28.95	-	4	10	-							

McKEOWN, P. C. Lancashire

Name: Patrick Christopher McKeown
Role: Right-hand bat
Born: 1 June 1976, Liverpool
Height: 6ft 3in **Weight:** 13st
Nickname: Paddy
County debut: 1996
1st-Class 50s: 1
1st-Class catches: 3
Place in batting averages: 191st av. 22.50
Parents: Paddy and Cathy
Marital status: Single
Education: St Mary's College, Crosby;
Rossall School (Blackpool)
Qualifications: 7 GCSEs, 3 A-levels
Overseas tours: Rossall School to Australia
1994-95
Overseas teams played for: Subiaco-Floriat,
Perth, Australia 1995-96
Cricketers particularly admired: Graeme
Hick and Neil Fairbrother
Other sports followed: Football (Liverpool)
Relaxations: 'Playing most sports, especially football and rugby. I enjoy spending time on the golf course.'
Extras: Represented England Schools U19, and U18 versus India. Played for Development of Excellence U19, National Cricket Association U19, Headmasters' Conference U19. Awarded 2nd XI cap in 1996
Opinions on cricket: 'Tea should be 30 minutes. Players should be on 12-month contracts to give them more security during the winter.'
Best batting: 64 Lancashire v Warwickshire, Edgbaston 1996

1997 Season

	M	Inns	NO	Runs	HS	Avge	100s	50s	Ct	St	O	M	Runs	Wkts	Avge	Best	5wI	10wM
Test																		
All First	4	6	0	135	46	22.50	-	-	2	-								.
1-day Int																		
NatWest	1	1	0	42	42	42.00	-	-	-	-	10	0	51	0	-		-	-
B & H	1	1	0	10	10	10.00	-	-	-	-								
Sunday	4	4	0	39	37	9.75	-	-	2	-								

Career Performances

	M	Inns	NO	Runs	HS	Avge	100s	50s	Ct	St	Balls	Runs	Wkts	Avge	Best	5wI	10wM
Test																	
All First	6	8	0	208	64	26.00	-	1	3	-							
1-day Int																	
NatWest	1	1	0	42	42	42.00	-	-	-	-	60	51	0	-		-	-
B & H	1	1	0	10	10	10.00	-	-	-	-							
Sunday	9	9	0	156	69	17.33	-	1	5	-							

METCALFE, A. A. Nottinghamshire

Name: Ashley Anthony Metcalfe
Role: Right-hand opening bat,
off-spin bowler
Born: 25 December 1963, Horsforth, Leeds
Height: 5ft 9½in **Weight:** 11st 7lbs
County debut: 1983 (Yorkshire), 1996
(Nottinghamshire)
County cap: 1986 (Yorkshire)
Benefit: 1995
1000 runs in a season: 6
1st-Class 50s: 57
1st-Class 100s: 26
1st-Class 200s: 1
1st-Class catches: 82
One-Day 100s: 4
Place in batting averages: 178th av. 23.81
(1996 114th av. 35.04)
Strike rate: (career 107.00)
Parents: Tony and Ann
Wife and date of marriage: Diane, 20 April 1986
Children: Zoë, 18 July 1990; Amy, 22 August 1993
Family links with cricket: Father played in local league; father-in-law Ray

Illingworth (Yorkshire and England)

Education: Ladderbanks Middle School; Bradford Grammar School; University College, London

Qualifications: 9 O-levels, 3 A-levels, NCA coaching certificate

Career outside cricket: 'Metcalfe & Sidebottom Associates – sports promotion company'

Overseas teams played for: Orange Free State 1988-89

Cricketers particularly admired: Barry Richards, Doug Padgett, Don Wilson, Arnie Sidebottom, Pete Hartley, Paul Jarvis

Other sports followed: Most, particularly golf

Relaxations: 'Relaxing at home with my family'

Extras: Making 122 on first-class debut v Nottinghamshire at Park Avenue in 1983 he became the youngest Yorkshire player to achieve the feat and recorded the highest debut score by a Yorkshireman. Reached 2000 runs for the season in the last match of 1990 with 194* and 107 v Nottinghamshire at Trent Bridge. Left Yorkshire at the end of the 1995 season and signed for Nottinghamshire for the 1996 season. Retired from first-class cricket at the end of the 1997 season and has taken up a coaching job with Cumbria

Best batting: 216* Yorkshire v Middlesex, Headingley 1988

Best bowling: 2-18 Yorkshire v Warwickshire, Scarborough 1987

1997 Season

	M	Inns	NO	Runs	HS	Avge	100s	50s	Ct	St	O	M	Runs	Wkts	Avge	Best	5wI	10wM
Test																		
All First	9	12	1	262	79	23.81	-	2	4	-								
1-day Int																		
NatWest	1	0	0	0	0	-	-	-	-	-								
B & H																		
Sunday	5	5	1	133	70 *	33.25	-	1	-	-								

Career Performances

	M	Inns	NO	Runs	HS	Avge	100s	50s	Ct	St	Balls	Runs	Wkts	Avge	Best	5wI	10wM
Test																	
All First	216	369	21	11938	216 *	34.30	26	57	82	-	428	362	4	90.50	2-18	-	-
1-day Int																	
NatWest	22	21	3	742	127 *	41.22	1	5	5	-	42	44	2	22.00	2-44	-	
B & H	35	35	4	1438	114	46.38	1	10	11	-							
Sunday	157	149	11	3887	116	28.16	2	25	37	-							

METSON, C. P. — Glamorgan

Name: Colin Peter Metson
Role: Right-hand bat, wicket-keeper
Born: 2 July 1963, Cuffley, Herts
Height: 5ft 5in **Weight:** 10st 10lbs
Nickname: Meto, Stumpie
County debut: 1981 (Middlesex),
1987 (Glamorgan)
County cap: 1987 (Glamorgan)
1st-Class 50s: 7
1st-Class catches: 560
1st-Class stumpings: 51
Place in batting averages:
(1996 304th av. 7.57)
Parents: Denis Alwyn and Jean Mary
Wife and date of marriage:
Stephanie Leslie Astrid, 13 October 1991
Family links with cricket: Father captained
Winchmore Hill
Education: Stanborough School, Welwyn
Garden City; Enfield Grammar School; Durham University
Qualifications: 10 O-levels, 5 A-levels, BA (Hons) Economic History, advanced
cricket coach
Career outside cricket: Project co-ordinator with Castle Services
Overseas tours: MCC to Bangladesh 1996
Overseas teams played for: Payneham, Adelaide 1986-88; Rostrevor Old Boys,
Adelaide 1987-91
Cricketers particularly admired: Bob Taylor, Rod Marsh, Ian Botham, Mike Gatting
Other sports followed: Football (Tottenham Hotspur FC), golf, rugby (Ebbw Vale
RFC)
Relaxations: Watching sport, videos, good wine, port
Extras: Played for England YC v India YC 1981 and was voted Young Wicket-keeper
of the Year. In 1984 captained Durham University, losing finalists in UAU competition.
Left Middlesex at end of 1986 season. Holds the Glamorgan record for most catches in
an innings (7) and match (9). Played 160 consecutive Championship matches for
Glamorgan, 1987-94. Wombwell Cricket Lovers' Society Wicket-keeper of the Year
1993. Received Man of the Match Award for the first time in his career in the NatWest
quarter-final against Middlesex in 1995, after nine years in the game. Retired from first-
class cricket at the end of the 1997 season
Opinions on cricket: 'Cricket must find ways to market itself better, and must give the
sponsors value for money. The 25-point deduction regarding "unfit" pitches should be
more widely used so that the counties will prepare the best possible pitches. Counties

should take more interest in the winter and future careers of its players (regarding placements, qualifications, etc). Use of the third umpire in semi-finals as well as the finals. All players should fully support the Professional Cricketers' Association and work together to improve playing standards. The County Championship should be split into two equal divisions, similar to American football with the top two teams playing off for the title.'

Best batting: 96 Middlesex v Gloucestershire, Uxbridge 1984

1997 Season

	M	Inns	NO	Runs	HS	Avge	100s	50s	Ct	St	O	M	Runs	Wkts	Avge	Best	5wI	10wM
Test																		
All First	1	1	0	0	0	0.00	-	-	3	1								
1-day Int																		
NatWest																		
B & H																		
Sunday																		

Career Performances

	M	Inns	NO	Runs	HS	Avge	100s	50s	Ct	St	Balls	Runs	Wkts	Avge	Best	5wI	10wM
Test																	
All First	231	302	71	4059	96	17.57	-	7	560	51	6	0	0	-	-	-	-
1-day Int																	
NatWest	28	16	2	90	21	6.42	-	-	27	2							
B & H	38	22	4	189	23	10.50	-	-	31	5							
Sunday	156	87	42	647	30 *	14.37	-	-	153	47							

MILBURN, S. M.   Hampshire

Name: Stuart Mark Milburn
Role: Right-hand bat, right-arm
medium-fast bowler
Born: 29 September 1972, Harrogate
Height: 6ft 1in **Weight:** 13st
Nickname: Miller, Mick
County debut: 1992 (Yorkshire), 1996 (Hampshire)
1st-Class 50s: 1
1st-Class catches: 1
Place in batting averages: 259th av. 15.00 (1996 245th av. 18.00)
Place in bowling averages: 136th av. 51.22 (1996 149th av. 55.23)
Strike rate: 90.54 (career 82.43)
Parents: Ken and Pam
Wife and date of marriage: Emily, 9 May 1997

Education: Upper Nidderdale High School, Pateley Bridge, Harrogate
Qualifications: 7 GCSEs, Diploma in Catering
Off-season: Staying in England
Overseas teams played for: Somerset West, South Africa 1992-93
Cricketers particularly admired: Ian Botham, Richard Hadlee, Malcolm Marshall
Other sports followed: Golf, snooker
Injuries: Calf strain, out for ten days
Relaxations: Going to gym, 'staying at home watching a video with a nice cold beer'
Extras: Retired from first-class cricket at the end of the 1997 season
Opinions on cricket: 'No comment!'
Best batting:
54* Hampshire v India, Southampton 1996
Best bowling: 4-38 Hampshire v Sussex, Southampton 1997

1997 Season

	M	Inns	NO	Runs	HS	Avge	100s	50s	Ct	St	O	M	Runs	Wkts	Avge	Best	5wI	10wM
Test																		
All First	11	8	2	90	23	15.00	-	-	1	-	332	56	1127	22	51.22	4-38	-	-
1-day Int																		
NatWest																			
B & H	1	1	0	1	1	1.00	-	-	-	-	5.4	1	32	1	32.00	1-32	-	
Sunday	4	3	1	1	1	0.50	-	-	-	-	27	0	137	4	34.25	1-27	-	

Career Performances

	M	Inns	NO	Runs	HS	Avge	100s	50s	Ct	St	Balls	Runs	Wkts	Avge	Best	5wI	10wM
Test																	
All First	27	28	6	292	54 *	13.27	-	1	1		4369	2497	53	47.11	4-38	-	-
1-day Int																	
NatWest	2	1	0	27	27	27.00	-	-	-	-	120	108	0	-		-	-
B & H	3	2	0	3	2	1.50	-	-	1	-	119'	93	3	31.00	2-7	-	
Sunday	13	7	3	24	13 *	6.00	-	-	3	-	546	454	11	41.27	2-18	-	

MILLNS, D. J.   Leicestershire

Name: David James Millns
Role: Left-hand bat, right-arm fast bowler, slip fielder
Born: 27 February 1965, Clipstone, Nottinghamshire
Height: 6ft 3in **Weight:** 15st
Nickname: Rocket Man, Double D
County debut: 1988 (Nottinghamshire), 1990 (Leicestershire)
County cap: 1991
50 wickets in a season: 4
1st-Class 50s: 6
1st-Class 100s: 3
1st-Class 5 w. in innings: 21
1st-Class 10 w. in match: 4
1st-Class catches: 64
Place in batting averages: 96th av. 34.53 (1996 219th av. 22.31)
Place in bowling averages: 50th av. 27.36 (1996 17th av. 23.04)

Strike rate: 50.04 (career 48.91)
Parents: Bernard and Brenda
Wife and date of marriage: Wanda, 25 September 1993
Family links with cricket: Andy Pick, former Notts CCC player is brother-in-law. Brother Paul and his son Matthew play for Clipstone MWCC
Education: Samuel Barlow Junior; Garibaldi Comprehensive; North Notts College of Further Education; Nottingham Trent Polytechnic
Qualifications: Advanced coach
Career outside cricket: 'Working on it. Golf maybe!'
Off-season: 'Staying fit on the golf course and taking as much money off J.J. Whitaker as possible'
Overseas tours: England A to Australia 1992-93; Leicestershire to South Africa 1994 and 1995, to Holland 1994 and 1996
Overseas teams played for: Uitenhage, Port Elizabeth, South Africa 1988-89; Birkenhead, Auckland 1989-91; Tasmania, Australia 1994-95; Boland, South Africa 1996-97
Cricketers particularly admired: Gordon Parsons, Vince Wells, 'anyone who takes a catch off my bowling – usually at cover!'
Young players to look out for: 'A lot of good young players at Leicester'
Other sports followed: Football (Leicester City), rugby union (Leicester Tigers), golf ('taking money off J.J. Whitaker on the golf course gives me great pleasure')

Injuries: 'Sore knee, out for one week and a sore back through having to bowl Mullally's overs'

Relaxations: Computers and property development

Extras: Harold Larwood Bowling Award 1984. Asked to be released by Nottinghamshire at the end of 1989 season and joined Leicestershire in 1990. Finished third in national bowling averages in 1990. Britannic Assurance Player of the Month in August 1991 after taking 9-37 v Derbyshire, the best Leicestershire figures since George Geary's 10-18 v Glamorgan in 1929. Players' representative on Cricketers' Association Executive for Leicestershire. Leicestershire Cricketer of the Year 1992. Leicestershire Bowling Award 1990, 1991, 1992 and 1994

Opinions on cricket: 'Leave the four-day competition alone. Kiwi Max cricket looked good. Play as much day/night cricket as possible and all one-day games should be played between Monday and Friday.'

Best batting: 121 Leicestershire v Northamptonshire, Northampton 1997

Best bowling: 9-37 Leicestershire v Derbyshire, Derby 1991

1997 Season

	M	Inns	NO	Runs	HS	Avge	100s	50s	Ct	St	O	M	Runs	Wkts	Avge	Best	5wI	10wM
Test																		
All First	15	15	2	449	121	34.53	2	1	2	-	408.4	87	1341	49	27.36	6-61	2	1
1-day Int																		
NatWest	2	2	1	9	6 *	9.00	-	-	-	-	19	5	81	1	81.00	1-25	
B & H	6	4	2	23	12	11.50	-	-	3	-	51	8	216	6	36.00	3-36	-
Sunday	3	2	2	6	3 *	-	-	-	-	-	18	1	67	2	33.50	1-9	-

Career Performances

	M	Inns	NO	Runs	HS	Avge	100s	50s	Ct	St	Balls	Runs	Wkts	Avge	Best	5wI	10wM
Test																	
All First	145	171	51	2455	121	20.45	3	6	64	-	22747	12973	465	27.89	9-37	21	4
1-day Int																	
NatWest	11	5	3	49	29 *	24.50	-	-	2	-	648	423	12	35.25	3-22	-
B & H	22	13	7	100	39 *	16.66	-	-	5	-	1064	756	27	28.00	4-26	-
Sunday	40	19	10	104	20 *	11.55	-	-	9	-	1512	1323	31	42.67	2-11	-

59. Who scored the most first-class centuries during the 1997 season?

O vodafone

MIRZA, M. M.   Worcestershire

Name: Maneer Mohammed Mirza
Role: Right-hand bat, right-arm fast bowler
Born: 1 April 1978, Birmingham
Height: 5ft 10in **Weight:** 11st 9lbs
Nickname: Mo
County debut: 1997
1st-Class catches: 1
Place in bowling averages: 85th av. 32.63
Strike rate: 48.21 (career 48.21)
Parents: Mirza Sherbaz (deceased) and
Zarda Bi
Marital status: Single
Family links with cricket: 'My brother
Parvaz played for Worcestershire CCC 1993-
1995'

Education: Wyndcliffe Primary School;
Sheldon Heath Secondary School;
Bourneville College of Further Education
Qualifications: 5 GCSEs and 2 A-levels
Career outside cricket: About to start a degree in Business Management and Sports
Studies
Off-season: Working hard on my studies and training
Overseas tours: England U15 to South Africa 1993; Birmingham Schools to India and
Pakistan 1996
Cricketers particularly admired: Parvaz, Imran Khan, Wasim Akram, Malcolm
Marshall, Ian Botham
Other sports followed: Boxing and basketball
Relaxations: Sleeping and spending time with friends and family
Opinions on cricket: 'The standard of wickets could be improved to produce better
players. Contracts should be extended to nine months instead of six.'
Best batting: 10* Worcestershire v Warwickshire, Edgbaston 1997
Best bowling: 4-51 Worcestershire v Warwickshire, Edgbaston 1997

60. Who recorded the highest first-class score of 1997?

1997 Season

	M	Inns	NO	Runs	HS	Avge	100s	50s	Ct	St	O	M	Runs	Wkts	Avge	Best	5wI	10wM
Test																		
All First	6	7	4	17	10 *	5.66	-	-	1	-	152.4	25	620	19	32.63	4-51	-	-
1-day Int																		
NatWest																		
B & H																		
Sunday	4	0	0	0	0	-	-	-	1	-	16	0	113	1	113.00	1-31	-	

Career Performances

	M	Inns	NO	Runs	HS	Avge	100s	50s	Ct	St	Balls	Runs	Wkts	Avge	Best	5wI	10wM
Test																	
All First	6	7	4	17	10 *	5.66	-	-	1	-	916	620	19	32.63	4-51	-	-
1-day Int																	
NatWest																	
B & H																	
Sunday	4	0	0	0	0	-	-	-	1	-	96	113	1	113.00	1-31	-	

MOFFAT, S. P. Middlesex

Name: Scott Park Moffat
Role: Right-hand bat, off-spin bowler
Born: 1 February 1973, Germiston, South Africa
Height: 6ft **Weight:** 13st 7lbs
Nickname: Access, Fraz
County debut: 1996
1st-Class catches: 2
Parents: Duncan and Dagny
Marital status: Single
Family links with cricket: Father played league cricket in the Transvaal
Education: Bedfordview, South Africa; Aldenham School, Hertfordshire; Swansea University
Qualifications: 8 GCSEs, 3 A-levels, BSc in Economics, senior coaching award
Career outside cricket: Sports promotion
Overseas tours: Radlett to India 1995
Overseas teams played for: RAU, Transvaal, South Africa
Cricketers particularly admired: Mike Atherton, Graeme Hick, Angus Fraser, Nick Bothas

Young players to look out for: Owais Shah, Steven Peters
Other sports followed: Golf, football (Tottenham Hotspur)
Relaxations: Socialising, eating out, reading and fishing
Extras: Played for Hertfordshire since 1992. Represented NAYC in 1992. Won the UAU with Swansea University
Opinions on cricket: 'The 2nd XI team one-day competition (Bain Hogg), should be changed to come in line with the 1st XI one-day i.e. Benson and Hedges format. The present 55-over system seems pointless as it doesn't prepare you properly.'
Best batting: 47 Middlesex v Warwickshire, Edgbaston 1997

1997 Season

	M	Inns	NO	Runs	HS	Avge	100s	50s	Ct	St	O	M	Runs	Wkts	Avge	Best	5wl	10wM
Test																		
All First	4	6	1	122	47	24.40	-	-	2	-								
1-day Int																		
NatWest																		
B & H	2	2	0	62	60	31.00	-	1	1	-								
Sunday	6	5	0	77	29	15.40	-	-	1	-								

Career Performances

	M	Inns	NO	Runs	HS	Avge	100s	50s	Ct	St	Balls	Runs	Wkts	Avge	Best	5wl	10wM
Test																	
All First	5	7	1	122	47	20.33	-	-	2	-							
1-day Int																	
NatWest																	
B & H	2	2	0	62	60	31.00	-	1	1	-							
Sunday	6	5	0	77	29	15.40	-	-	1	-							

MOHAMMED AKRAM   Northamptonshire

Name: Mohammed Akram Awan
Role: Right-hand bat, right-arm fast bowler
Born: 10 September 1972, Islamabad, Pakistan
Height: 6ft 2in   **Weight:** 13st 5lbs
Nickname: Haji, Akee
County debut: 1997
Test debut: 1996
One-Day Internationals: 7
1st-Class 5 w. in innings: 7
1st-Class catches: 13
Place in batting averages: 288th av. 9.66
Place in bowling averages: 111th av. 37.83 (1996 86th av. 33.78)

Strike rate: 57.40 (career 51.12)
Parents: Mohammed Akber Awan and Zaria Awan
Marital status: Single
Education: Gordon College, Rawalpindi
Career outside cricket: Business and investment
Overseas teams played for: Rawalpindi 1992-97
Cricketers particularly admired: Michael Holding, Wasim Akram, Martin Crowe
Young players to look out for: Zahir Ali, Shoaib Akhter, Rob Cunliffe, Shadab Kabir and Mal Loye
Other sports followed: Football (Brazil), squash (Pakistan)
Relaxations: Hunting, music. 'Visit to Swat Valley with my friends or any part of the world with natural scenery. Being with my mother and father'

Opinions on cricket: 'Today's game is very fast and anyone who wants to play has to be super fit. We play too much one-day cricket – Test cricket is the real cricket. I do not agree with the bouncer rule in one-day and Test cricket, it favours the batsman – the bouncer is one of the beauties of the game.'
Best batting: 28 Northampton v Durham, Northampton 1997
Best bowling: 7-51 Pakistan v Leicestershire, Leicester 1996

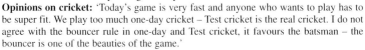

1997 Season

	M	Inns	NO	Runs	HS	Avge	100s	50s	Ct	St	O	M	Runs	Wkts	Avge	Best	5wl	10wM
Test																		
All First	11	14	2	116	28	9.66	-	-	1	-	287	43	1135	30	37.83	5-72	2	-
1-day Int																		
NatWest	1	1	1	0	0*	-	-	-	-	-	12	2	42	1	42.00	1-42	-	
B & H	4	2	1	4	4	4.00	-	-	-	-	37	4	158	6	26.33	4-47	-	
Sunday	5	3	3	3	2*	-	-	-	1	-	34	3	141	6	23.50	4-19	-	

Career Performances

	M	Inns	NO	Runs	HS	Avge	100s	50s	Ct	St	Balls	Runs	Wkts	Avge	Best	5wl	10wM
Test	6	9	2	29	11	4.14	-	-	4	-	1033	522	10	52.20	3-39	-	-
All First	37	47	11	279	28	7.75	-	-	13	-	5777	3294	113	29.15	7-51	7	-
1-day Int	7	5	3	11	7*	5.50	-	-	2	-	342	307	9	34.11	2-36	-	
NatWest	1	1	1	0	0*	-	-	-	-	-	72	42	1	42.00	1-42	-	
B & H	4	2	1	4	4	4.00	-	-	-	-	222	158	6	26.33	4-47	-	
Sunday	5	3	3	3	2*	-	-	-	1	-	204	141	6	23.50	4-19	-	

MOLES, A. J.   Warwickshire

Name: Andrew James Moles
Role: Right-hand opening bat, right-arm
medium bowler
Born: 12 February 1961, Solihull
Height: 5ft 10in **Weight:** 'Above average'
Nickname: Moler
County debut: 1986
County cap: 1987
1000 runs in a season: 6
1st-Class 50s: 89
1st-Class 100s: 29
1st-Class 200s: 4
1st-Class catches: 146
One-Day 100s: 2
Place in batting averages: 107th av. 33.42
(1996 102nd av. 36.12)
Strike rate: (career 84.90)
Parents: Stuart Francis and Gillian Margaret
Wife and date of marriage:
Jacquie, 17 December 1988
Children: Daniel
Family links with cricket: Brother plays club cricket
Education: Finham Park Comprehensive, Coventry; Henley College of Further
Education; Butts College of Further Education
Qualifications: 3 O-levels, 4 CSEs, Toolmaker/Standard Room Inspector City & Guilds
Career outside cricket: Selling corporate hospitality
Overseas teams played for: Griqualand West, South Africa 1986-88
Cricketers particularly admired: Dennis Amiss, Fred Gardner, Tom Moody
Other sports followed: Football, golf
Relaxations: Playing golf and spending time with family
Best batting: 230* Griqualand West v Northern Transvaal B, Verwoerdburg 1988-89
Best bowling: 3-21 Warwickshire v Oxford University, The Parks 1987

---

61. Who finished top of the 1997 first-class bowling averages?

1997 Season

	M	Inns	NO	Runs	HS	Avge	100s	50s	Ct	St	O	M	Runs	Wkts	Avge	Best	5wI	10wM
Test																		
All First	12	22	3	635	168	33.42	1	2	10	-								
1-day Int																		
NatWest	4	4	0	159	64	39.75	-	2	1	-								
B & H	4	4	0	72	60	18.00	-	1	1	-								
Sunday	1	1	0	19	19	19.00	-	-	-	-								

Career Performances

	M	Inns	NO	Runs	HS	Avge	100s	50s	Ct	St	Balls	Runs	Wkts	Avge	Best	5wI	10wM
Test																	
All First	230	416	40	15305	230 *	40.70	29	89	146	-	3396	1882	40	47.05	3-21	-	-
1-day Int																	
NatWest	35	35	3	1155	127	36.09	2	7	6	-	90	81	0	-		-	-
B & H	36	34	0	1036	89	30.47	-	12	11	-	300	224	4	56.00	1-11	-
Sunday	100	95	5	2268	96 *	25.20	-	15	26	-	446	415	7	59.28	2-24	-

MONTGOMERIE, R. R.　　Northamptonshire

Name: Richard Robert Montgomerie
Role: Right-hand opening bat, right-arm
off-spin bowler
Born: 3 July 1971, Rugby
Height: 5ft 10in **Weight:** 12st 7lbs
Nickname: Monty, Sheep's Head
County debut: 1991
County cap: 1995
1000 runs in a season: 2
1st-Class 50s: 26
1st-Class 100s: 9
1st-Class catches: 80
One-Day 100s: 1
Place in batting averages: 105th av. 33.60
(1996 86th av. 38.00)
Parents: Robert and Gillian
Marital status: Single
Family links with cricket: Father captained
Oxfordshire
Education: Rugby School; Worcester College, Oxford University
Qualifications: 12 O-levels, 4 A-levels, BA (Chemistry)
Career outside cricket: Ernst & Young

Off-season: Working for Ernst & Young in Luton
Overseas tours: Oxford University to Namibia 1991
Overseas teams played for: Sydney University CC 1995-96
Cricketers particularly admired: Many
Other sports followed: Golf, rackets, real tennis and many others
Relaxations: Any sport, good television, reading and 'occasionally testing my brain'
Extras: Scored unbeaten 50 in each innings of 1991 Varsity match and was Oxford captain in 1994. Oxford rackets Blue 1990. Captain Combined Universities 1994
Opinions on cricket: 'Four-day cricket is in its infancy. It produces good quality matches and deserves time to mature in the present structure. An Under-21 first-class side should be considered and paid for by the ECB.'
Best batting: 192 Northamptonshire v Kent, Canterbury 1995

1997 Season

	M	Inns	NO	Runs	HS	Avge	100s	50s	Ct	St	O	M	Runs	Wkts	Avge	Best	5wl	10wM
Test																		
All First	10	18	3	504	73	33.60	-	4	7	-	1	0	1	0	-	-	-	-
1-day Int																		
NatWest																		
B & H	1	1	0	39	39	39.00	-	-	-	-								
Sunday	5	5	1	204	86 *	51.00	-	2	2	-								

Career Performances

	M	Inns	NO	Runs	HS	Avge	100s	50s	Ct	St	Balls	Runs	Wkts	Avge	Best	5wl	10wM
Test																	
All First	88	154	16	4675	192	33.87	9	26	80	-	102	66	0	-	-	-	-
1-day Int																	
NatWest	7	7	1	300	109	50.00	1	2	3	-							
B & H	15	14	2	412	75	34.33	-	2	2	-	6	0	0	-	-	-	
Sunday	35	34	1	1040	86 *	31.51	-	10	10	-							

MOODY, T. M.   Worcestershire

Name: Thomas Masson Moody
Role: Right-hand bat, right-arm medium bowler, county captain
Born: 2 October 1965, Adelaide
Height: 6ft 7in **Weight:** 16st
Nickname: Moods, Tex
County debut: 1990 (Warwickshire), 1991 (Worcestershire)
County cap: 1990 (Warwickshire), 1991 (Worcestershire)
Test debut: 1989-90
Tests: 8

One-Day Internationals: 40
1000 runs in a season: 5
1st-Class 50s: 84
1st-Class 100s: 56
1st-Class 200s: 4
1st-Class 5 w. in innings: 7
1st-Class 10 w. in match: 2
1st-Class catches: 258
One-Day 100s: 15
Place in batting averages: 25th av. 48.65
(1996 26th av. 50.96)
Place in bowling averages: 128th av. 43.63
(1996 30th av. 25.83)
Strike rate: 67.47 (career 67.98)
Parents: John and Janet
Wife and date of marriage: Helen, 3 March
1993
Children: Jackson, 5 March 1995
Family links with cricket: Father played A Grade cricket in South Australia
Education: Guildford Grammar School, Western Australia
Qualifications: HSE
Career outside cricket: Sports shop owner
Overseas tours: Australia to India/Pakistan (World Cup) 1987, to England 1989, to
India 1989-90, to Sri Lanka 1992
Overseas teams played for: Western Australia 1985-98; Midland Guildford, Perth,
Western Australia
Cricketers particularly admired: Dennis Lillee, Allan Border, Viv Richards, Rod
Marsh
Other sports followed: Aussie rules football (West Coast Eagles), football, golf,
tennis
Relaxations: Golf, sleeping and films
Extras: Scored 150s in both innings of 1988-89 Sheffield Shield final for Western
Australia v Queensland. Hit a century against Warwickshire during Australia's 1989 tour
and signed a one-year contract with them for 1990. Hit centuries in first three first-class
matches for Warwickshire, and seven in first eight matches – a unique achievement.
Scored the (then) fastest ever first-class century v Glamorgan in 26 minutes – taking
advantage of declaration bowling. Reached 1000 first-class runs in first season of county
cricket in only 12 innings – another record. Released by Warwickshire at the end of the
1990 season after they had chosen Allan Donald as their one overseas player and was
signed by Worcestershire for 1991 when Graeme Hick was no longer considered an
overseas player. Not re-signed for 1993 season because he was expected to be touring
with the Australian team, although in the event he was not selected. Re-turned for 1994
season. Scored 180* and shared record unbeaten partnership with Tim Curtis in the
semi-final of the NatWest Trophy 1994. Appointed Worcestershire's captain in 1996
after replacing Tim Curtis halfway through the 1995 season. Reclaimed a place in the

Australian one-day side for the World Series against West Indies and Pakistan in 1996-97. Became the fastest player to score 4000 runs in the Sunday League, achieving the feat in only 100 innings. Represented Australia in the World Series against South Africa and New Zealand in 1997-98

Opinions on cricket: 'We need more quality not quantity.'
Best batting: 272 Western Australia v Tasmania, Hobart 1994-95
Best bowling: 7-38 Western Australia v Tasmania, Hobart 1995-96

1997 Season

	M	Inns	NO	Runs	HS	Avge	100s	50s	Ct	St	O	M	Runs	Wkts	Avge	Best	5wI	10wM
Test																		
All First	14	21	1	973	180 *	48.65	3		4	14	-	213.4	42	829	19	43.63	5-148	1	-
1-day Int																		
NatWest	2	2	0	114	108	57.00	1	-	-	-	-	8	0	35	0	-	-	-	-
B & H	5	5	0	259	92	51.80	-	3	6	-								
Sunday	15	15	0	529	112	35.26	1	3	7	-	53	3	241	8	30.12	2-29	-	

Career Performances

	M	Inns	NO	Runs	HS	Avge	100s	50s	Ct	St	Balls	Runs	Wkts	Avge	Best	5wI	10wM
Test	8	14	0	456	106	32.57	2	3	9	-	432	147	2	73.50	1-17	-	-
All First	258	429	35	18555	272	47.09	56	84	258	-	18288	8424	269	31.31	7-38	7	2
1-day Int	40	36	4	766	89	23.93	-	7	11	-	1163	854	21	40.66	3-56	-	
NatWest	15	15	3	856	180 *	71.33	3	3	10	-	559	308	9	34.22	2-33	-	
B & H	34	32	7	1459	110 *	58.36	2	13	17	-	786	460	15	30.66	4-59	-	
Sunday	106	104	10	4222	160	44.91	10	28	33	-	2331	1648	59	27.93	4-46	-	

MOORES, P.   Sussex

Name: Peter Moores
Role: Right-hand bat, wicket-keeper
Born: 18 December 1962, Macclesfield, Cheshire
Height: 6ft **Weight:** 13st
Nickname: Billy
County debut: 1983 (Worcestershire), 1985 (Sussex)
County cap: 1989
1st-Class 50s: 31
1st-Class 100s: 7
1st-Class catches: 499
1st-Class stumpings: 44
Place in batting averages: 203rd av. 21.14 (1996 175th av. 27.92)
Parents: Bernard and Winifred
Wife and date of marriage: Karen Jane, 28 September 1989

Children: Natalie Marie, 4 August 1993
Family links with cricket: Brothers, Anthony, Stephen and Robert, all play club cricket
Education: King Edward VI School, Macclesfield
Qualifications: 7 O-levels, 3 A-levels, advanced cricket coach
Career outside cricket: Coach for Sussex in off-season
Overseas tours: Christians in Sport to India 1989-90; MCC to Namibia 1990-91, to Leeward Islands 1991-92, to Bahrain 1994-95
Overseas teams played for: Orange Free State, South Africa 1988-89
Cricketers particularly admired: Bob Taylor, Alan Knott, Clive Lloyd
Other sports followed: Football, golf
Relaxations: Golf, wine and old films

Extras: On MCC groundstaff in 1982 before joining Worcestershire in latter half of 1982 season. Joined Sussex in 1985 and has been appointed captain for the 1997 season
Best batting: 185 Sussex v Cambridge University, Hove 1996

1997 Season

	M	Inns	NO	Runs	HS	Avge	100s	50s	Ct	St	O	M	Runs	Wkts	Avge	Best	5wI	10wM
Test																		
All First	17	31	4	571	102 *	21.14	1	2	36	-								
1-day Int																		
NatWest	4	2	1	64	45	64.00	-	-	4	1								
B & H	5	5	1	54	21 *	13.50	-	-	7	1								
Sunday	15	15	1	182	32	13.00	-	-	10	1								

Career Performances

	M	Inns	NO	Runs	HS	Avge	100s	50s	Ct	St	Balls	Runs	Wkts	Avge	Best	5wI	10wM
Test																	
All First	228	342	41	7295	185	24.23	7	31	499	44	18	16	0	-	-	-	-
1-day Int																	
NatWest	28	19	4	231	45	15.40	-	-	36	3							
B & H	34	27	4	329	76	14.30	-	1	30	4							
Sunday	168	136	37	1927	89 *	19.46	-	7	144	23							

MORRIS, A. C.   Hampshire

Name: Alexander Corfield Morris
Role: Left-hand bat, right-arm
medium bowler
Born: 4 October 1976, Barnsley
Height: 6ft 4in **Weight:** 12st 7lbs
County debut: 1995 (Yorkshire)
1st-Class 50s: 1
1st-Class catches: 12
Place in batting averages: 290th av. 13.00
(1996 226th av. 21.00)
Strike rate: 117.00 (career 94.00)
Parents: Chris and Janet
Marital status: Single
Education: Wilthorpe Primary School;
Holgate School, Barnsley; Barnsley College
Qualifications: 4 GCSEs, BTEC National
Diploma in Sports Science, NCA coaching
award
Off-season: Playing club cricket in South
Africa
Overseas tours: England U19 to West Indies 1994-95, to Zimbabwe 1995-96;
England VI to Hong Kong 1996
Cricketers particularly admired: Ian Botham, Martyn Moxon
Young players to look out for: Anthony McGrath, Michael Vaughan
Other sports followed: Football (Barnsley FC)
Injuries: Broken hand, missed one month
Relaxations: Listening to music, relaxing with mates
Extras: Played for Yorkshire U11-U19. Played for England U15 against Barbados and
in 1994 for both England U17 and U19 against India. Played junior football with both
Barnsley and Rotherham and had trials for Nottingham Forest and Leeds. Left Yorkshire
and has signed for Hampshire along with his brother Zac for the 1998 season
Opinions on cricket: 'More coloured clothing cricket.'
Best batting: 60 Yorkshire v Lancashire, Old Trafford 1996
Best bowling: 2-62 Yorkshire v Surrey, The Oval 1997

---

62. Who ended the 1997 season as the leading first-class wicket-taker?

 vodafone

1997 Season

	M	Inns	NO	Runs	HS	Avge	100s	50s	Ct	St	O	M	Runs	Wkts	Avge	Best	5wI	10wM
Test																		
All First	7	9	0	117	37	13.00	-	-	4	-	78	17	289	4	72.25	2-62	-	-
1-day Int																		
NatWest																		
B & H																		
Sunday	10	7	2	102	35	20.40	-	-	3	-	34	0	209	9	23.22	4-49	-	

Career Performances

	M	Inns	NO	Runs	HS	Avge	100s	50s	Ct	St	Balls	Runs	Wkts	Avge	Best	5wI	10wM
Test																	
All First	16	23	2	362	60	17.23	-	1	12	-	846	508	9	56.44	2-62	-	-
1-day Int																	
NatWest	1	1	1	1	1 *	-	-	-	-	-	48	43	1	43.00	1-43	-	
B & H	1	0	0	0	0	-	-	-	1	-	6	4	0	-	-	-	
Sunday	23	15	3	208	48 *	17.33	-	-	5	-	402	362	15	24.13	4-49	-	

MORRIS, H.   Glamorgan

Name: Hugh Morris
Role: Left-hand bat, right-arm
medium bowler
Born: 5 October 1963, Cardiff
Height: 5ft 8in **Weight:** 12st 9lbs
Nickname: Banners
County debut: 1981
County cap: 1986
Benefit: 1994 (£118,837)
Test debut: 1991
Tests: 3
1000 runs in a season: 10
1st-Class 50s: 98
1st-Class 100s: 53
1st-Class 200s: 2
1st-Class catches: 197
One-Day 100s: 13
Place in batting averages: 16th av. 52.58
(1996 17th av. 55.53)
Parents: Roger and Anne
Wife: Debra Jane
Children: Bethan Louise; Emily Charlotte

Family links with cricket: Father played club cricket. Brother played junior representative cricket

Education: Llanfair County Primary School; Blundells School; University of Wales Institute, Cardiff

Qualifications: 9 O-levels, 2 A-levels, 1 AO-level, BA (Hons) in Physical Education, advanced cricket coach

Off-season: Doing some television presenting and media work. Working with cricket development officer – coaching in schools

Overseas tours: English Public Schoolboys to West Indies 1980-81, to Sri Lanka 1982-83; England A to Pakistan 1990-91 (called up to join England tour party in Australia), to Bermuda and West Indies 1991-92, to South Africa 1993-94; England to Australia 1990-91; Glamorgan to Holland and Zimbabwe

Overseas teams played for: CBC Old Boys, Pretoria 1985-87

Cricketers particularly admired: Viv Richards, Ian Botham

Young players to look out for: Dean Cosker

Other sports followed: Rugby ('played first-class rugby for Aberavon and Cardiff Institute and gained a Wales Student cap versus France in 1984'), golf (handicap 11)

Injuries: Tennis elbow all season but missed no cricket. Sprained ankle, out for one game

Relaxations: Spending time at home with family

Extras: Highest schoolboy cricket average in 1979 (89.71), 1981 (184.60) and 1982 (149.20). Captain of English Schools U19 in 1981 and 1982; played for England YC v West Indies 1982, and captain v Australia 1983. Appointed youngest ever Glamorgan captain 1986, but resigned in 1989 to concentrate on batting. In 1990 scored most runs in a season by a Glamorgan player (2276) and hit most centuries (10). After missing selection for the tour of Australia, appointed captain for England A tour of Pakistan in 1990-91; then, after Gooch had required a hand operation and England had lost the First Test to Australia, he flew out to join the senior tour until the England captain recovered. Glamorgan Player of the Year. Captained the England A tour to South Africa 1993-94 and Wombwell Cricket Lovers' Society Captain of the Year 1993. Played first-class rugby for Aberavon 1984-85 and South Glamorgan Institute, scoring over 150 points. Stood down as Glamorgan captain at the end of the 1995 season. Retired from first-class cricket at the end of the 1997 season to take up a full-time position as the technical director of the ECB

Opinions on cricket: 'The championship should be split into two equal divisions and run along the lines of American football. Each team would play everyone in their division once and four teams from the other division – i.e. 12 games per season and the top two in each group would go into the play-offs with the top two teams playing a five-day final. This system would keep the best players at their clubs.'

Best batting: 233* Glamorgan v Warwickshire, Cardiff 1997

Best bowling: 1-6 Glamorgan v Oxford University, The Parks 1987

1997 Season

	M	Inns	NO	Runs	HS	Avge	100s	50s	Ct	St	O	M	Runs	Wkts	Avge	Best	5wI	10wM
Test																		
All First	17	28	4	1262	233 *	52.58	4	3	14	-								
1-day Int																		
NatWest	4	4	0	79	53	19.75	-	1	3	-								
B & H	4	4	0	169	76	42.25	-	2	-	-								
Sunday	10	10	1	180	66 *	20.00	-	1	4	-								

Career Performances

	M	Inns	NO	Runs	HS	Avge	100s	50s	Ct	St	Balls	Runs	Wkts	Avge	Best	5wI	10wM
Test	3	6	0	115	44	19.16	-	-	3	-							
All First	314	544	53	19785	233 *	40.29	53	98	197	-	348	380	2	190.00	1-6	-	-
1-day Int																	
NatWest	36	35	4	1361	154 *	43.90	4	5	13	-	12	12	0	-	-	-	
B & H	45	45	3	1361	143 *	32.40	4	5	15	-	18	15	1	15.00	1-14	-	
Sunday	182	176	19	5447	127 *	34.69	5	36	62	-							

MORRIS, J. E. — Durham

Name: John Edward Morris
Role: Right-hand bat, right-arm
medium bowler
Born: 1 April 1964, Crewe
Height: 5ft 10in **Weight:** 13st 6lbs
Nickname: Animal
County debut: 1982 (Derbyshire),
1994 (Durham)
County cap: 1986 (Derbyshire)
Test debut: 1990
Tests: 3
One-Day Internationals: 8
1000 runs in a season: 11
1st-Class 50s: 92
1st-Class 100s: 44
1st-Class 200s: 2
1st-Class catches: 134
One-Day 100s: 9
Place in batting averages: 94th av. 34.79
(1996 271st av. 14.30)
Strike rate: (career 142.57)
Parents: George (Eddie) and Jean

Wife and date of marriage: Sally, 30 September 1990
Children: Thomas Edward, 27 June 1991
Family links with cricket: Father played for Crewe for many years as an opening bowler
Education: Shavington Comprehensive School; Dane Bank College of Further Education
Qualifications: O-levels
Overseas tours: England to Australia 1990-91; Romany to South Africa 1993: MCC to Bahrain 1994-95
Overseas teams played for: Umbilo, Durban, South Africa 1982-84; Alex Old Boys, Pietermaritzburg, South Africa 1984-85; Subiaco-Floriat, Western Australia 1986-87; Griqualand West, South Africa 1988-89, 1993-94; Protea, Johannesburg, South Africa 1993
Other sports followed: Golf, football (Derby County)
Relaxations: The golf course and home life
Extras: Youngest player to score a Sunday League century.
Best batting: 229 Derbyshire v Gloucestershire, Cheltenham 1993
Best bowling: 1-6 Derbyshire v Cambridge University, Fenner's 1993

1997 Season

	M	Inns	NO	Runs	HS	Avge	100s	50s	Ct	St	O	M	Runs	Wkts	Avge	Best	5wI	10wM
Test																		
All First	17	30	1	1009	149	34.79	2	4	7	-	1	0	1	0	-	-	-	-
1-day Int																		
NatWest	1	1	0	75	75	75.00	-	1	1	-								
B & H	1	1	0	62	62	62.00	-	1	-	-								
Sunday	15	15	0	376	110	25.06	1	-	4	-	1	0	1	0	-	-	-	

Career Performances

	M	Inns	NO	Runs	HS	Avge	100s	50s	Ct	St	Balls	Runs	Wkts	Avge	Best	5wI	10wM
Test	3	5	2	71	32	23.66	-	-	3	-							
All First	313	527	31	18739	229	37.78	44	92	134	-	998	913	7	130.42	1-6	-	-
1-day Int	8	8	1	167	63 *	23.85	-	1	2	-							
NatWest	27	26	3	812	109	35.30	1	5	9	-							
B & H	55	51	6	1441	145	32.02	3	7	12	-	24	14	0	-	-	-	
Sunday	197	188	12	4530	134	25.73	5	19	44	-	9	8	0	-	-	-	

MORRIS, Z. C.   Hampshire

Name: Zachary Clegg Morris
Role: Right-hand bat, slow left-arm bowler
Born: 4 September 1978, Barnsley
Height: 6ft **Weight:** 12st 7lbs
Nickname: Cleggy
County debut: No first-team appearance
Parents: Lance and Janet
Marital status: Single
Family links with cricket: 'Lance runs local junior team and Janet is a cricket nut'
Education: Wilthorpe Primary School; Holgate Secondary School; 'The University of Life'
Qualifications: NCA coaching award
Career outside cricket: 'Master baker and handy man'
Off-season: Travelling
Overseas tours: England U19 to Pakistan 1997
Cricketers particularly admired: Alex Wharf, Gareth Batty, Craig Dudley, Dave Lyons
Young players to look out for: Ben Spendlove, Stephen Peters, Robert Key
Other sports followed: 'Coinidje, three man Chinese off-spin, Barnsley FC'
Relaxations: 'Visiting commercial places. Watching Keysi and Ralph dance. Black jack. The *Jerry Springer Show*'
Extras: 'Pretty useful groundsman!' Moved to Hampshire in the close season along with his brother, Alex
Opinions on cricket: 'Enjoyable but could also do with a bit more pzazz.'

---

63. Which wicket-keeper recorded the most
dismissals in the 1997 season?

MOXON, M. D.   Yorkshire

Name: Martyn Douglas Moxon
Role: Right-hand bat, right-arm
medium bowler
Born: 4 May 1960, Barnsley
Height: 6ft 1in **Weight:** 14st
Nickname: Frog
County debut: 1981
County cap: 1984
Benefit: 1993
Test debut: 1986
Tests: 10
One-Day Internationals: 8
1000 runs in a season: 12
1st-Class 50s: 116
1st-Class 100s: 45
1st-Class 200s: 5
1st-Class catches: 218
One-Day 100s: 7
One-Day 5 w. in innings: 1
Place in batting averages: 110th av. 32.72 (1996 61st av. 43.68)
Strike rate: (career 94.64)
Parents: Audrey and Derek (deceased)
Wife and date of marriage: Sue, October 1985
Children: Charlotte Louise, 13 March 1990; Jonathan James, 6 May 1993
Family links with cricket: Father and grandfather played local league cricket
Education: Holgate Grammar School, Barnsley
Qualifications: 8 O-levels, 3 A-levels, HNC in Business Studies, advanced cricket
coach
Off-season: 'Not sure yet'
Overseas tours: England to India and Australia 1984-85, to Australia and New
Zealand 1987-88; England B to Sri Lanka 1985-86; England A to Bermuda and West
Indies 1991-92, to Australia 1992-93
Overseas teams played for: Griqualand West, South Africa 1982-83 and 1983-84
Cricketers particularly admired: Viv Richards
Young players to look out for: Anthony McGrath, Michael Vaughan, Chris
Silverwood, Matthew Dowman, Vikram Solanki
Other sports followed: Football (supporter of Barnsley FC) and golf
Injuries: Prolapsed disc, out for five weeks
Relaxations: Listening to most types of music, having a drink with friends
Extras: Captained Yorkshire Schools U15, North of England U15 and Yorkshire Senior
Schools. Played for Wombwell Cricket Lovers' Society U18 side. First Yorkshire player

to make centuries in his first two Championship games in Yorkshire, 116 v Essex at Headingley (on debut) and 111 v Derbyshire at Sheffield, and scored 153 in his first innings in a Roses match. Picked for Lord's Test of 1984 v West Indies, but withdrew through injury and had to wait until 1986 to make Test debut. Appointed Yorkshire captain in 1990. Appointed captain of England A team to tour Bermuda and West Indies 1991-92, but played no first-class cricket owing to injury. Wombwell Cricket Lovers' Society Cricketer of the Year 1991. Scored 274* against Worcester which is the highest individual score for Yorkshire since the war. Stood down as Yorkshire captain at the end of the 1995 season

Best batting: 274* Yorkshire v Worcestershire, Worcester 1994
Best bowling: 3-24 Yorkshire v Hampshire, Southampton 1989

1997 Season

	M	Inns	NO	Runs	HS	Avge	100s	50s	Ct	St	O	M	Runs	Wkts	Avge	Best	5wI	10wM
Test																		
All First	12	18	0	589	155	32.72	1	5	3	-								
1-day Int																		
NatWest	3	3	0	108	74	36.00	-	1	-	-								
B & H	3	3	0	97	52	32.33	-	1	-	-								
Sunday	2	2	0	14	13	7.00	-	-	-	-								

Career Performances

	M	Inns	NO	Runs	HS	Avge	100s	50s	Ct	St	Balls	Runs	Wkts	Avge	Best	5wI	10wM
Test	10	17	1	455	99	28.43	-	3	10	-	48	30	0	-	-	-	-
All First	317	541	47	21161	274 *	42.83	45	116	218	-	2650	1481	28	52.89	3-24	-	-
1-day Int	8	8	0	174	70	21.75	-	1	5	-							
NatWest	34	34	6	1316	137	47.00	2	10	12	-	156	85	5	17.00	2-19	-	
B & H	50	50	7	1863	141 *	43.32	2	14	19	-	342	242	9	26.88	5-31	1	
Sunday	151	143	8	4128	129 *	30.57	3	24	46	-	984	868	21	41.33	3-29	-	

MULLALLY, A. D.   Leicestershire

Name: Alan David Mullally
Role: Right-hand bat, left-arm fast bowler
Born: 12 July 1969, Southend
Height: 6ft 5in **Weight:** 14st
Nickname: Bob, Bryan, Eric, Spider, 'too
many to mention'
County debut: 1988 (Hampshire), 1990
(Leicestershire)
County cap: 1993
Test debut: 1996
Tests: 9
One-Day Internationals: 8
50 wickets in a season: 3
1st-Class 50s: 2
1st-Class 5 w. in innings: 13
1st-Class 10 w. in match: 2
1st-Class catches: 28
Place in batting averages: 295th av. 7.16
(1996 229th av. 20.75)
Place in bowling averages: 100th av. 35.18 (1996 28th av. 25.34)
Strike rate: 62.13 (career 66.74)
Parents: Michael and Ann
Marital status: Single
Family links with cricket: 'Sister fancied David Gower'
Education: Cannington High School and Primary, Perth, Australia; Wembley and
Carlisle Technical College
Qualifications: 'This and that'
Career outside cricket: Musician
Overseas tours: Western Australia to India 1990-91; Leicestershire to Jamaica 1992-93;
England to Zimbabwe and New Zealand 1996-97
Overseas teams played for: Western Australia; Victoria; Australian YC
Cricketers particularly admired: Geoff Marsh, Dermot Reeve
Young players to look out for: Darren Maddy
Other sports followed: Australian rules football, basketball, most sports
Relaxations: Music
Extras: English-qualified as he was born in Southend, he made his first-class debut for
Western Australia in the 1987-88 Sheffield Shield final, and played for Australian YC
1988-89. Played one match for Hampshire in 1988 before joining Leicestershire
Opinions on cricket: 'Good fun.'
Best batting: 75 Leicestershire v Middlesex, Leicester 1996
Best bowling: 7-72 Leicestershire v Gloucestershire, Leicester 1993

1997 Season

	M	Inns	NO	Runs	HS	Avge	100s	50s	Ct	St	O	M	Runs	Wkts	Avge	Best	5wI	10wM
Test																		
All First	13	12	6	43	13 *	7.16	-	-	2	-	383.1	89	1302	37	35.18	5-52	4	-
1-day Int																		
NatWest	1	1	1	0	0 *	-	-	-	-	-	12	0	59	0	-		-	-
B & H	6	4	2	6	4	3.00	-	-	-	-	55	5	235	10	23.50	3-33	-	
Sunday	6	1	0	6	6	6.00	-	-	1	-	38	0	207	7	29.57	3-36	-	

Career Performances

	M	Inns	NO	Runs	HS	Avge	100s	50s	Ct	St	Balls	Runs	Wkts	Avge	Best	5wI	10wM
Test	9	12	4	79	24	9.87	-	-	1	-	2379	927	28	33.10	3-44	-	-
All First	142	159	42	1034	75	8.83	-	2	28	-	26229	12608	393	32.08	7-72	13	2
1-day Int	8	3	0	22	20	7.33	-	-	3	-	396	276	10	27.60	3-29	-	
NatWest	14	8	5	42	19 *	14.00	-	-	2	-	864	497	18	27.61	2-22	-	
B & H	32	14	5	33	11	3.66	-	-	-	-	1780	1131	28	40.39	3-33	-	
Sunday	80	34	16	181	38	10.05	-	-	16	-	3491	2663	83	32.08	5-15	1	

MUNTON, T. A.   Warwickshire

Name: Timothy Alan Munton
Role: Right-hand bat, right-arm
fast-medium bowler
Born: 30 July 1965, Melton Mowbray
Height: 6ft 6in **Weight:** 15st 7lbs
Nickname: Harry, Captain Sensible
County debut: 1985
County cap: 1990
Test debut: 1991
Tests: 2
50 wickets in a season: 5
1st-Class 50s: 2
1st-Class 5 w. in innings: 26
1st-Class 10 w. in match: 6
1st-Class catches: 68
One-Day 5 w. in innings: 2
Place in batting averages: 163rd av. 29.50
Place in bowling averages: 66th av. 31.20
(1995 7th av. 19.83)
Strike rate: 69.25 (career 60.02)
Parents: Alan and Brenda
Wife and date of marriage: Helen, 20 September 1986

Children: Camilla Dallas, 13 August 1988; Harrison George Samuel, 17 February 1992
Family links with cricket: Father played for Buckminster CC
Education: Sarson High School; King Edward VII Upper School, Melton Mowbray
Qualifications: CSE grade 1, 9 O-levels, 1 A-level
Overseas tours: England A to Pakistan 1990-91, to Bermuda and West Indies 1991-92, to Pakistan 1995-96
Overseas teams played for: Victoria University, Wellington, New Zealand 1985-86; Witwatersrand University, Johannesburg, South Africa 1986-87
Cricketers particularly admired: Richard Hadlee, David Gower
Other sports followed: Basketball, soccer, golf
Injuries: Missed the whole of the 1997 season through injury
Relaxations: 'Playing golf, spending time with my family'
Extras: Appeared for Leicestershire 2nd XI 1982-84. Second highest wicket-taker in 1990 with 78. Called into England A squad to tour Bermuda and West Indies 1991-92 when Dermot Reeve replaced the injured Angus Fraser on the senior tour. Was voted Warwickshire Player of the Season 1990, 1991 and 1994. Missed the first six months of the 1995 season recovering from a back operation. He was flown out to Pakistan as a replacement for the injured Mike Smith on the England A tour to Pakistan in 1995-96, and played in the second 'Test' less than a week after his arrival. Assumed the Warwickshire captaincy after the retirement of Dermot Reeve in 1996 but replaced by Brian Lara for the 1998 season after missing the whole of the 1997 season through injury
Best batting: 54 Warwickshire v Worcestershire, Worcester 1992
Best bowling: 8-89 Warwickshire v Middlesex, Edgbaston 1991

1997 Season (did not make any first-class or one-day appearances)

Career Performances

	M	Inns	NO	Runs	HS	Avge	100s	50s	Ct	St	Balls	Runs	Wkts	Avge	Best	5wI	10wM
Test	2	2	1	25	25 *	25.00	-	-	-	-	405	200	4	50.00	2-22	-	-
All First	205	207	86	1339	54 *	11.06	-	2	68	-	35655	15577	594	26.22	8-89	26	6
1-day Int																	
NatWest	32	10	6	11	5	2.75	-	-	5	-	1972	950	35	27.14	3-36	-	
B & H	31	14	9	58	13	11.60	-	-	6	-	1894	1094	36	30.38	4-35	-	
Sunday	142	35	25	128	15 *	12.80	-	-	28	-	6119	3969	141	28.14	5-23	2	

MUSHTAQ AHMED   Somerset

Name: Mushtaq Ahmed
Role: Right-hand bat, leg-break bowler
Born: 28 June 1970, Sahiwal, Pakistan
Height: 5ft 4in **Weight:** 13st
Nickname: Mushy
County debut: 1993
County cap: 1993
Test debut: 1991-92
Tests: 28
One-Day Internationals: 124
50 wickets in a season: 3
1st-Class 50s: 7
1st-Class 5w. in innings: 47
1st-Class 10w. in match: 13
1st-Class catches: 72
One-Day 5 w. in innings: 2
Place in batting averages: 273rd av. 12.42
(1996 270th av. 14.75)
Place in bowling averages: 56th av. 28.14
(1996 8th av. 21.00)
Strike rate: 61.56 (career 52.43)
Marital status: Married
Career outside cricket: Banking
Overseas tours: Pakistan to Australia 1989-90, to New Zealand and Australia (World Cup) 1991-92, to England 1992, Australia and South Africa 1992-93, to New Zealand 1993-94, 1995-96, to Sri Lanka 1994, to Australia 1995-96, to New Zealand 1995-96, to India and Sri Lanka (World Cup) 1995-96, to New Zealand and Australia 1996-97
Overseas teams played for: United Bank, Pakistan
Cricketers particularly admired: Viv Richards, Waqar Younis
Other sports followed: Football (Brazil), hockey
Relaxations: Watching videos, eating, spending time with family
Extras: Took 6-81 against England for Punjab Chief Minister's XI 1987. Finished second to Wasim Akram as Pakistan's highest wicket-taker in the World Cup 1991-92 with 16 wickets. Received specialist coaching from Intikhab Alam. Named Somerset Player of the Year 1993. Replaced as overseas player by Shane Lee for the 1996 season due to Pakistan's tour of England, but returned for the 1997 season
Opinions on cricket: 'I like the four-day county championship because it gives spin bowlers a good chance to bowl long spells. One-day cricket is exciting to watch and play in. A good cricketer can play all types of cricket successfully. Most of those against that view have never played it.'
Best batting: 90 Somerset v Sussex, Taunton 1993
Best bowling: 9-93 Multan v Peshawar, Sahiwal 1986-87

1997 Season

	M	Inns	NO	Runs	HS	Avge	100s	50s	Ct	St	O	M	Runs	Wkts	Avge	Best	5wI	10wM
Test																		
All First	14	16	2	174	33	12.42	-	-	3	-	513	146	1407	50	28.14	6-70	3	-
1-day Int																		
NatWest	2	1	1	10	10 *	-	-	-	1	-	24	3	61	6	10.16	4-27	-	
B & H	3	2	0	41	31	20.50	-	-	-	-	22.2	3	81	7	11.57	7-24	1	
Sunday	12	5	2	15	7 *	5.00	-	-	3	-	89.1	8	348	12	29.00	3-36	-	

Career Performances

	M	Inns	NO	Runs	HS	Avge	100s	50s	Ct	St	Balls	Runs	Wkts	Avge	Best	5wI	10wM
Test	28	42	7	355	42	10.14	-	-	10	-	7172	3309	117	28.28	7-56	7	2
All First	150	189	22	2345	90	14.04	-	7	72	-	35186	17052	671	25.41	9-93	47	13
1-day Int	124	64	27	332	26	8.97	-	-	27	-	6431	4638	141	32.89	5-36	1	
NatWest	9	6	2	92	35	23.00	-	-	2	-	610	313	15	20.86	4-27	-	
B & H	11	8	0	87	31	10.87	-	-	-	-	606	324	17	19.05	7-24	1	
Sunday	46	35	10	251	32	10.04	-	-	5	-	2057	1428	45	31.73	3-17	-	

NAPIER, G. R. Essex

Name: Graham Richard Napier
Role: Right-hand bat, medium pace bowler
Born: 6 January 1978, Colchester
Height: 5ft 9in **Weight:** 11st 7lbs
Nickname: Napes, Mensa
County debut: 1997
Strike rate: 34.00 (career 34.00)
Parents: Roger and Carol
Marital status: Single
Family links with cricket: Father played for
Palmers Boys School 1st XI (1965-68), Essex
Police divisional teams, and Harwich
Immigration CC. 'Now makes guest
appearances on Walton beach'
Education: Myland School, Colchester;
Gilberd School, Colchester
Qualifications: NCA coaching award
Off-season: Touring South Africa with
England U19
Overseas tours: England U17 to Bermuda; England U19 to South Africa 1997-98
Cricketers particularly admired: Graham Gooch, Stuart Law, Viv Richards, Barry
Richards

Young players to look out for: Richard Logan, Michael Gough
Other sports followed: Football (Ipswich Town and Wimbledon FC)
Relaxations: 'Fishing, although I haven't been keen for a couple of years. Going out with my mates outside cricket when I'm not playing'
Opinions on cricket: 'I have only played two first-class games and I would hesitate to make any comment about the game until I have had more experience.'
Best batting: 35* Essex v Nottinghamshire, Worksop 1997
Best bowling: 2-25 Essex v Cambridge University, Fenner's 1997

1997 Season

	M	Inns	NO	Runs	HS	Avge	100s	50s	Ct	St	O	M	Runs	Wkts	Avge	Best	5wI	10wM
Test																		
All First	2	2	2	39	35 *	-	-	-	-	-	17	6	65	3	21.66	2-25	-	-
1-day Int																		
NatWest																			
B & H																			
Sunday	3	2	0	17	12	8.50	-	-	1	-	11	0	79	0	-		-	-

Career Performances

	M	Inns	NO	Runs	HS	Avge	100s	50s	Ct	St	Balls	Runs	Wkts	Avge	Best	5wI	10wM
Test																	
All First	2	2	2	39	35 *	-	-	-	-	-	102	65	3	21.66	2-25	-	-
1-day Int																	
NatWest																	
B & H																	
Sunday	3	2	0	17	12	8.50	-	-	1	-	66	79	0	-		-	-

64. Who was the fielder with the most catches in the 1997 season?

◐ vodafone

NASH, D. C.   Middlesex

Name: David Charles Nash
Role: Right-hand bat, wicket-keeper
Born: 19 January 1978, Chertsey, Surrey
Height: 5ft 8in **Weight:** 11st 3lbs
Nickname: Nashy
County debut: 1995 (one-day),
1997 (first-class)
1st-Class 50s: 1
1st-Class 100s: 1
1st-Class catches: 4
Place in batting averages: 11th av. 55.33
Strike rate: 18.00 (career 18.00)
Parents: David and Christine
Marital status: Single
Family links with cricket: 'Father played
club cricket, and brother Glen is a very
talented left-hand bat and off-spin bowler.
Mother is an avid watcher and tea lady'
Education: Sunbury Manor; Malvern
College, Worcestershire

Qualifications: 10 GCSEs, 1 A-level, NCA coaching award, qualified football referee
Career outside cricket: 'Any ideas are welcome'
Off-season: Working hard on game and fitness, touring Kenya and Sri Lanka with
England A
Overseas tours: England U15 to South Africa 1993; British Airways Youth Team to
West Indies 1993-94; England U19 to Zimbabwe 1995-96, to Pakistan 1996-97;
England A to Kenya and Sri Lanka 1997-98
Cricketers particularly admired: Mark Ramprakash, George Simons and Gareth
Rees 'for their big hearts', Simon Puritt 'for his avoidance of buying a beer', Angus
Fraser 'for always smiling and enjoying his cricket, however unlucky he is!'
Young players to look out for: Owais Shah, David Sales
Other sports followed: Football (Brentford) and rugby union (London Irish)
Injuries: Earache listening to Messrs Shah, Martin, Wellings, Fraser, Johnson and
Pooley all season
Relaxations: 'I enjoy playing golf, listening to music, going out for a beer with my
mates, and visiting Legends household, Gary, Stan and Tanny'
Extras: A qualified referee. Represented Middlesex at all ages. Played for England U14,
U15, U17 and U18. Once took six wickets in six balls when aged 11 – 'when I could
bowl!'. *Daily Telegraph* Southern England Batting Award 1993. Seaxe Young Player of
the Year 1993
Opinions on cricket: '2nd XI cricket should mirror the first-class game i.e. four-day

games, decent wickets and facilities. Two divisional cricket is a good idea and floodlit cricket should be introduced. At least four players under the age of 23 should play on Sundays to give youngsters some experience. The rain rule of 2nd XI cricket of a 7.30 finish should be abolished. Please read the entries of Angus Fraser, Owais Shah, Richard Johnson and Peter Wellings as these will be 100 per cent correct!!'

Best batting: 100 Middlesex v Essex, Chelmsford 1997
Best bowling: 1-8 Middlesex v Essex, Chelmsford 1997

1997 Season

	M	Inns	NO	Runs	HS	Avge	100s	50s	Ct	St	O	M	Runs	Wkts	Avge	Best	5wI	10wM
Test																		
All First	6	8	2	332	100	55.33	1	1	4	-	3	0	19	1	19.00	1-8	-	-
1-day Int																		
NatWest																			
B & H																			
Sunday	6	5	0	69	23	13.80	-	-	5	-								

Career Performances

	M	Inns	NO	Runs	HS	Avge	100s	50s	Ct	St	Balls	Runs	Wkts	Avge	Best	5wI	10wM
Test																	
All First	6	8	2	332	100	55.33	1	1	4	-	18	19	1	19.00	1-8	-	-
1-day Int																	
NatWest																		
B & H																		
Sunday	7	5	0	69	23	13.80	-	-	7	1							

65. Who recorded the best bowling analysis in an innings in 1997?

O vodafone

NEWELL, K.   Sussex

Name: Keith Newell
Role: Right-hand bat, occasional
medium-pace bowler
Born: 25 March 1972, Crawley
Height: 6ft **Weight:** 12st
Nickname: Ede, Wheely
County debut: 1993 (one-day),
1995 (first-class)
1st-Class 50s: 6
1st-Class 100s: 4
1st-Class catches: 6
Place in batting averages: 132nd av. 28.51
(1996 166th av. 29.25)
Place in bowling averages: 120th av. 39.63
Strike rate: 75.36 (career 99.58)
Parents: Peter Charles and Julie Anne
Marital status: Single
Family links with cricket: Brother Mark is
on the Sussex staff. My other brother,
Jonathan, plays for Sussex U17 and U19
Education: Gossops Green Junior School; Ifield Community College
Qualifications: 'A few GCSEs', coaching certificate
Career outside cricket: Cricket coach
Overseas teams played for: Zimbabwe Universals 1989-90; Bulawayo Athletic Club
1991-92, 1995-96; Riverside CC, Wellington 1993-94
Cricketers particularly admired: Ian Botham
Young players to look out for: James Kirtley
Other sports followed: Table tennis, football, motor sport
Relaxations: Going to the cinema, music
Opinions on cricket: 'Still too much cricket played. Slightly less cricket would help
guarantee the players' enthusiasm to get out there and play.'
Best batting: 135 Sussex v West Indies, Hove 1995
Best bowling: 4-61 Sussex v Kent, Horsham 1997

66. Who recorded the best match figures in 1997?

1997 Season

	M	Inns	NO	Runs	HS	Avge	100s	50s	Ct	St	O	M	Runs	Wkts	Avge	Best	5wI	10wM
Test																		
All First	17	31	2	827	112	28.51	2	3	2	-	138.1	35	436	11	39.63	4-61	-	-
1-day Int																		
NatWest	4	2	1	52	29 *	52.00	-	-	1	-	35	4	148	2	74.00	1-61	-	
B & H	3	3	0	45	34	15.00	-	-	1	-	11	0	58	1	58.00	1-35	-	
Sunday	13	12	0	152	35	12.66	-	-	4	-	53	2	222	7	31.71	2-22	-	

Career Performances

	M	Inns	NO	Runs	HS	Avge	100s	50s	Ct	St	Balls	Runs	Wkts	Avge	Best	5wI	10wM
Test																	
All First	33	61	5	1625	135	29.01	4	6	6	-	1195	647	12	53.91	4-61	-	-
1-day Int																	
NatWest	6	4	1	152	52	50.66	-	1	1	-	210	148	2	74.00	1-61	-	
B & H	7	6	0	126	46	21.00	-	-	1	-	145	115	2	57.50	1-25	-	
Sunday	34	29	2	449	76 *	16.62	-	1	8	-	474	418	8	52.25	2-22	-	

NEWELL, M.   Sussex

Name: Mark Newell
Role: Right-hand bat, right-arm
fast-medium bowler
Born: 19 December 1973, Crawley
Height: 6ft 1in **Weight:** 12st
Nickname: Little Ede
County debut: 1996
1st-Class 50s: 3
1st-Class 100s: 1
1st-Class catches: 10
Place in batting averages: 192nd av. 22.42
Parents: Peter Charles and Julie Anne
Marital status: Single
Family links with cricket: Brother Keith
also on the Sussex staff, younger brother
Jonathan plays for Sussex Young Cricketers
Education: Hazelwick Comprehensive; City
of Westminster College
Qualifications: 9 GCSEs, GNVQ Advanced
Leisure and Tourism, NCA senior coaching award
Career outside cricket: None as yet
Overseas tours: Sussex U18 to India 1990-91; Sussex U19 to Barbados (as captain)

1993-94

Overseas teams played for: Bulawayo Athletic Club, Zimbabwe 1991-92; Marist CC, Whangerei, New Zealand 1996-97
Cricketers particularly admired: Curtly Ambrose, Allan Donald, Allan Border, Graham Gooch
Other sports followed: 'A bit of football every now and then (support West Ham)'
Relaxations: 'Building a nest in the changing-room and sleeping in it.' Films and the film industry
Extras: MCC Young Cricketer in 1994. Was on a sponsored scholarship at Arundel Castle which enabled him and two others to work, play and coach all over Sussex for two years. Played Sussex youth cricket since the age of nine. 'Bagged them, first-class debut versus Worcestershire – thanks "G"'
Opinions on cricket: 'Four-day cricket in 2nd XI.'
Best batting: 100 Sussex v Nottinghamshire, Hove 1997

1997 Season

	M	Inns	NO	Runs	HS	Avge	100s	50s	Ct	St	O	M	Runs	Wkts	Avge	Best	5wI	10wM
Test																		
All First	12	22	1	471	100	22.42	1	3	9	-								
1-day Int																		
NatWest	4	3	1	186	79	93.00	-	2	-	-								
B & H	2	2	0	147	87	73.50	-	2	-	-								
Sunday	13	13	1	258	60	21.50	-	1	4	-								

Career Performances

	M	Inns	NO	Runs	HS	Avge	100s	50s	Ct	St	Balls	Runs	Wkts	Avge	Best	5wI	10wM
Test																	
All First	13	24	1	471	100	20.47	1	3	10	-							
1-day Int																	
NatWest	4	3	1	186	79	93.00	-	2	-	-							
B & H	2	2	0	147	87	73.50	-	2	-	-							
Sunday	18	18	2	423	69	26.43	-	2	7	-							

NEWELL, M.   Nottinghamshire

Name: Michael Newell
Role: Right-hand opening bat, leg-break bowler, occasional wicket-keeper
Born: 25 February 1965, Blackburn
Height: 5ft 10in **Weight:** 11st
Nickname: Mugly, Tricky, Animal
County debut: 1984
County cap: 1987
1000 runs in a season: 1
1st-Class 50s: 24
1st-Class 100s: 6
1st-Class 200s: 1
1st-Class catches: 93
1st-Class stumpings: 1
One-Day 100s: 1
Parents: Barry and Janet
Wife and date of marriage: Jayne, 23 September 1989
Children: Elizabeth Rose, 1 September 1993
Family links with cricket: Father chairman of Notts Unity CC and brother, Paul, is the captain
Education: West Bridgford Comprehensive
Qualifications: 8 O-levels, 3 A-levels, NCA advanced coach
Off-season: Working for Notts full time
Cricketers particularly admired: Matthew Dowman, Dominic Cork, James Hindson
Young players to look out for: Paul Franks, Andy Oram, Guy Welton
Other sports followed: Rugby union, football, darts
Relaxations: Football, studying, being at home
Opinions on cricket: 'Why do players who become journalists forget all that is good and just criticise? For some reason they change opinions and moan about things that they never criticised whilst they were playing. We should be playing in two divisions and four-day cricket should be played in the 2nd XI. Smaller staffs of a minimum of 20 would be more competitive.'
Best batting: 203* Nottinghamshire v Derbyshire, Derby 1987
Best bowling: 2-38 Nottinghamshire v Sri Lankans, Trent Bridge 1988

67. Who has recorded the most 5-wicket hauls in one-day Internationals?

1997 Season (did not make any first-class or one-day appearances)

Career Performances

	M	Inns	NO	Runs	HS	Avge	100s	50s	Ct	St	Balls	Runs	Wkts	Avge	Best	5wI	10wM
Test																	
All First	102	178	26	4636	203 *	30.50	6	24	93	1	363	282	7	40.28	2-38	-	-
1-day Int																	
NatWest	5	5	0	136	60	27.20	-	1	3	-	6	10	0	-		-	-
B & H	10	10	1	205	39	22.77	-	-	2	-							
Sunday	24	21	4	611	109 *	35.94	1	3	8	-							

NEWPORT, P. J. Worcestershire

Name: Philip John Newport
Role: Right-hand bat, right-arm
fast-medium bowler, outfielder
Born: 11 October 1962, High Wycombe
Height: 6ft 2in **Weight:** 13st 7lbs
Nickname: Schnozz, Newps
County debut: 1982
County cap: 1986
Test debut: 1988
Tests: 3
50 wickets in a season: 8
1st-Class 50s: 20
1st-Class 5 w. in innings: 35
1st-Class 10 w. in match: 3
1st-Class catches: 72
One-Day 5 w. in innings: 3
Place in batting averages: 258th av. 15.16
(1996 208th av. 23.66)
Place in bowling averages: 24th av. 23.36
(1996 95th av. 35.26)
Strike rate: 56.00 (career 52.57)
Parents: John and Sheila Diana (deceased)
Wife and date of marriage: Christine Anne, 26 October 1985
Children: Nathan Alexander, 10 May 1989
Family links with cricket: Brother Stewart is captain of Octopus CC in North London
Education: Royal Grammar School, High Wycombe; Portsmouth University
Qualifications: 8 O-levels, 3 A-levels, BA (Hons) Geography, advanced coaching
qualification
Off-season: Coaching in the Worcester area

Overseas tours: NCA to Denmark 1981; England A to Pakistan 1990-91; England to Australia 1990-91

Overseas teams played for: Vogeltown, New Plymouth, New Zealand 1986; Boland, South Africa 1987-88; Ginnenderra and ACT, Australia 1991; Northern Transvaal, South Africa 1992-93

Other sports followed: American football, basketball, golf, football (QPR)

Injuries: Achilles tendon 'again!', missed two months

Extras: Had trial as schoolboy for Southampton FC. Played cricket for NAYC England Schoolboys 1981 and for Buckinghamshire in Minor Counties Championship in 1981 and 1982. Selected for cancelled England tour to India 1988-89 and selected as a replacement for England's tour to Australia in 1990-91. Winner of Worcestershire's Dick Lygon Award 1992 and voted Worcestershire Player of the Year 1992 and 1993. Finished 3rd in the Whyte and Mackay bowling ratings in 1995. Awarded a benefit in 1998

Opinions on cricket: 'How long must England suffer in the Test series before the counties put their self-interest to one side and back changes to our domestic structure that will produce quality Test cricketers? You won't attract youngsters to our game unless we generate enthusiasm through a winning England team and the associated production of cricketing heroes that children want to emulate.'

Best batting: 98 Worcestershire v New Zealanders, Worcester 1990

Best bowling: 8-52 Worcestershire v Middlesex, Lord's 1988

1997 Season

	M	Inns	NO	Runs	HS	Avge	100s	50s	Ct	St	O	M	Runs	Wkts	Avge	Best	5wI	10wM
Test																		
All First	8	6	0	91	45	15.16	-	-	-	-	177.2	56	444	19	23.36	7-37	1	-
1-day Int																		
NatWest	2	1	0	2	2	2.00	-	-	1	-	18	0	84	3	28.00	2-52	-	
B & H	5	4	1	42	15 *	14.00	-	-	1	-	47	10	161	11	14.63	4-37	-	
Sunday	5	1	0	7	7	7.00	-	-	-	-	30	3	107	8	13.37	3-18	-	

Career Performances

	M	Inns	NO	Runs	HS	Avge	100s	50s	Ct	St	Balls	Runs	Wkts	Avge	Best	5wI	10wM
Test	3	5	1	110	40 *	27.50	-	-	1	-	669	417	10	41.70	4-87	-	-
All First	266	307	87	5445	98	24.75	-	20	72	-	42693	22097	813	27.17	8-52	35	3
1-day Int																	
NatWest	31	16	5	134	25	12.18	-	-	4	-	1665	1040	41	25.36	4-30	-	
B & H	52	26	7	206	28	10.84	-	-	10	-	3275	1675	79	21.20	5-22	2	
Sunday	161	68	25	440	26 *	10.23	-	-	32	-	6310	4436	170	26.09	5-32	1	

NIXON, P. A.   Leicestershire

Name: Paul Andrew Nixon
Role: Left-hand bat, wicket-keeper
Born: 21 October 1970, Carlisle
Height: 5ft 11in **Weight:** 12st 5lbs
Nickname: Nico, Nobbler
County debut: 1989
1000 runs in a season: 1
1st-Class 50s: 19
1st-Class 100s: 8
1st-Class catches: 382
1st-Class stumpings: 31
Place in batting averages: 40th av. 44.25
(1996 74th av. 40.00)
Parents: Brian and Sylvia
Marital status: Single
Family links with cricket: 'Grandad and
father played local league cricket. Mom made
the teas for Edenhall CC, Penrith'
Education: Langwathby Primary; Ullswater High
Qualifications: Coaching certificates
Career outside cricket: 'A bit of coaching here and there'
Off-season: Holiday and fitness
Overseas tours: Cumbria U16 to Denmark 1985; Leicestershire to Holland 1991, to
Montego Bay 1992, to Bloemfontein 1994 and 1995; England A to India 1994-95
Overseas teams played for: Melville and North Fremantle, Perth, Western Australia
1989-92; Mitchells Rain, Cape Town 1993; Primrose CC, Cape Town, South Africa
1995-96
Cricketers particularly admired: Darren Maddy, Phil Simmons, Ian Healy
Young players to look out for: Darren Maddy, Ian Sutcliffe, Ben Smith, Jim Ormond,
Graeme Welch, David Hemp, Alex Tudor, Jon Dakin
Other sports followed: Football (Carlisle United, Newcastle United and Liverpool FC)
Injuries: Burns to hands but missed no cricket
Relaxations: 'Walking with Our Jen in Lake District and Scotland'
Extras: Youngest person to score a century against Yorkshire (at U15). Played for
England U15 and played in Minor Counties Championship for Cumberland at 16, MCC
Young Pro in 1988. Took eight catches in debut match v Warwickshire at Hinckley in
1989. Played for Carlisle United and 'once got lost in South African township at
3.30am'. Leicester Young Player of the Year two years running. Second Leicester
wicket-keeper to score 1000 runs in a season. Voted Cumbrian Sports Personality of the
Year 1994-95. Has signed a contract that will keep him at Grace Road until the year 2000
Opinions on cricket: 'Hierarchy needs to listen to players. England should stick to 30
players for a few years. First-class wickets should be the same as Test wickets, which

should be the same across the country.'
Best batting: 131 Leicestershire v Hampshire, Leicester 1994

1997 Season

	M	Inns	NO	Runs	HS	Avge	100s	50s	Ct	St	O	M	Runs	Wkts	Avge	Best	5wI	10wM
Test																		
All First	19	25	9	708	96	44.25	-	4	57	4	2	0	4	0	-	-	-	-
1-day Int																		
NatWest	2	2	0	15	14	7.50	-	-	2	1								
B & H	6	5	1	98	53	24.50	-	1	11	2								
Sunday	15	14	2	181	33	15.08	-	-	11	3								

Career Performances

	M	Inns	NO	Runs	HS	Avge	100s	50s	Ct	St	Balls	Runs	Wkts	Avge	Best	5wI	10wM
Test																	
All First	144	206	48	4803	131	30.39	8	19	382	31	12	4	0	-	-	-	-
1-day Int																	
NatWest	16	14	4	219	39	21.90	-	-	18	5							
B & H	18	16	2	223	53	15.92	-	1	17	4							
Sunday	109	91	15	1498	84	19.71	-	6	83	21							

NOON, W. M. Nottinghamshire

Name: Wayne Michael Noon
Role: Right-hand bat, wicket-keeper
Born: 5 February 1971, Grimsby
Height: 5ft 9in **Weight:** 11st 7lbs
Nickname: Noonie, Spain Boon
County debut: 1988 (one-day),
1989 (first-class) (Northamptonshire),
1994 (Nottinghamshire)
County cap: 1995 (Nottinghamshire)
1st-Class 50s: 12
1st-Class catches: 168
1st-Class stumpings: 20
Place in batting averages: 154th av. 25.80
(1996 241st av. 18.44)
Parents: Trafford and Rosemary
Marital status: Engaged
Education: Caistor Grammar School
Qualifications: 5 O-levels
Career outside cricket: Manager of G.

Atkins (bookmakers)

Overseas tours: Lincolnshire U15 to Pakistan 1984; England YC to Australia 1989-90; Rutland tourists to South Africa 1988; Northamptonshire to Durban 1992, to Cape Town 1993

Overseas teams played for: Burnside West, Christchurch, New Zealand 1989-90 and 1993-96; Rivertonians, Cape Town 1993-94; Canterbury, Christchurch 1994-95

Cricketers particularly admired: Ian Botham

Young players to look out for: Guy Welton

Other sports followed: Football (Lincoln City), horse racing (flat)

Relaxations: Having a bet. Eating out and having a pint

Extras: Played for England YC v New Zealand YC 1989; captain v Australian YC 1989-90 and Pakistan YC 1990. Was the 1000th player to appear in the Sunday League competition. Broke the Northants record for most 2nd XI hundreds in one season in 1993

Opinions on cricket: 'I think that two divisions is a must. Longer contracts should be introduced i.e. nine or 12 months.'

Best batting: 83 Nottinghamshire v Northamptonshire, Northampton 1997

1997 Season

	M	Inns	NO	Runs	HS	Avge	100s	50s	Ct	St	O	M	Runs	Wkts	Avge	Best	5wI	10wM
Test																		
All First	18	25	4	542	83	25.80	-	3	34	4	1	0	12	0	-	-	-	-
1-day Int																		
NatWest	3	2	1	32	19	32.00	-	-	2	-								
B & H	3	2	1	31	24	31.00	-	-	1	1								
Sunday	13	10	5	89	31	17.80	-	-	10	4								

Career Performances

	M	Inns	NO	Runs	HS	Avge	100s	50s	Ct	St	Balls	Runs	Wkts	Avge	Best	5wI	10wM
Test																	
All First	81	128	21	2423	83	22.64	-	12	168	20	30	34	0	-	-	-	-
1-day Int																	
NatWest	7	4	1	73	34	24.33	-	-	4	2							
B & H	13	8	2	94	24	15.66	-	-	7	4							
Sunday	74	46	14	421	38	13.15	-	-	55	13							

ORAM, A. R. Nottinghamshire

Name: Andrew Richard Oram
Role: Right-hand bat, right-arm medium-fast bowler
Born: 7 March 1975, Northampton
Height: 6ft 2in **Weight:** 12st
Nickname: Tonto, Rustler, Dick, Maro
County debut: 1997
1st-Class catches: 6
Place in bowling averages: 40th av. 26.30
Strike rate: 52.30 (career 52.30)
Parents: Richard and Anne
Marital status: Single
Family links with cricket: Father played cricket for local club sides in Northampton leagues and is now groundsman for Horton House CC

Education: Hackleton Primary School; Roade Comprehensive
Qualifications: 10 GCSEs, 4 A-levels, 1 AS-level, NCA coaching award
Off-season: Travelling to Perth, WA for three months from December playing for Wanneroo Districts CC
Overseas teams played for: Wanneroo Districts CC 1993-94, 1997-98
Cricketers particularly admired: Allan Donald, Glen McGrath, Paul Taylor
Young players to look out for: Graeme Swann, David Sales, Steven Randall
Other sports followed: Hockey, golf, football (Northampton Town, Liverpool FC) and rugby union (Northampton Saints)
Injuries: Bruised knee, out for one week
Relaxations: Eating out, playing golf, travelling, socialising with friends, wine tasting and watching sport
Opinions on cricket: 'With only the 1997 season to comment on I feel that enough was talked about throughout the season. I would have preferred to have seen further changes to the structure of competitions, but at least people are now aware of the need to change. Floodlit games were a big bonus for last season and more of these should be seen in domestic games.'
Best batting: 5* Nottinghamshire v Leicestershire, Leicester 1997
Best bowling: 4-53 Nottinghamshire v Somerset, Trent Bridge 1997

1997 Season

	M	Inns	NO	Runs	HS	Avge	100s	50s	Ct	St	O	M	Runs	Wkts	Avge	Best	5wI	10wM
Test																		
All First	8	9	5	14	5 *	3.50	-	-	6	-	226.4	55	684	26	26.30	4-53	-	-
1-day Int																		
NatWest	1	0	0	0	0	-	-	-	-	-	11	2	51	1	51.00	1-51	-	
B & H																		
Sunday	9	2	2	0	0 *	-	-	-	-	-	58.5	0	283	10	28.30	4-45	-	

Career Performances

	M	Inns	NO	Runs	HS	Avge	100s	50s	Ct	St	Balls	Runs	Wkts	Avge	Best	5wI	10wM
Test																	
All First	8	9	5	14	5 *	3.50	-	-	6	-	1360	684	26	26.30	4-53	-	-
1-day Int																	
NatWest	1	0	0	0	0	-	-	-	-	-	66	51	1	51.00	1-51	-	
B & H																	
Sunday	9	2	2	0	0 *	-	-	-	-	-	353	283	10	28.30	4-45	-	

ORMOND, J.　　　　　　　　Leicestershire

Name: James Ormond
Role: Right-hand bat, right-arm
fast bowler
Born: 20 August 1977, Walsgrave, Coventry
Height: 6ft 3in **Weight:** 14st 7lbs
Nickname: Stavros, Horse, Fred, Del, Bob
County debut: 1995
1st-Class 5 w. in innings: 3
1st-Class catches: 3
Place in batting averages: 297th av. 6.90
Place in bowling averages: 43rd av. 26.40
Strike rate: 47.11 (career 47.28)
Parents: Richard and Margaret
Marital status: Single
Family links with cricket: Dad plays local
club cricket
Education: St Anthony's, Bedworth; St
Thomas More, Nuneaton; North
Warwickshire College of Further Education
Qualifications: 6 GCSEs
Off-season: Training and touring Kenya and Sri Lanka with England A
Overseas tours: England U19 to Zimbabwe 1995-96; England A to Kenya and Sri

Lanka 1997-98
Overseas teams played for: Sydney University CC 1996-97
Cricketers particularly admired: Allan Donald, Ian Botham, Richard Hadlee
Young players to look out for: Darren Maddy, Lee Westwood
Other sports followed: Football (Coventry City)
Injuries: Side strain, out for one week
Relaxations: Music and seeing my friends
Extras: Played for the Development of Excellence side and England U19 against South Africa U19 in 1995. Was forced to return home after one day of the England U19 tour to Zimbabwe in 1995-96 through injury. Played for England U19 in the summer series against New Zealand U19. Won Leicestershire's 2nd XI bowling award
Opinions on cricket: 'I would like to see the championship split into two divisions.'
Best batting: 35 Leicestershire v Gloucestershire, Leicester 1997
Best bowling: 6-54 Leicestershire v Australia, Leicester 1997

1997 Season

	M	Inns	NO	Runs	HS	Avge	100s	50s	Ct	St	O	M	Runs	Wkts	Avge	Best	5wI	10wM
Test																		
All First	13	12	2	69	35	6.90	-	-	2	-	345.3	72	1162	44	26.40	6-54	3	-
1-day Int																		
NatWest																		
B & H																		
Sunday	8	7	4	70	18	23.33	-	-	1	-	39	1	167	9	18.55	3-30	-	

Career Performances

	M	Inns	NO	Runs	HS	Avge	100s	50s	Ct	St	Balls	Runs	Wkts	Avge	Best	5wI	10wM
Test																	
All First	14	12	2	69	35	6.90	-	-	3	-	2175	1227	46	26.67	6-54	3	-
1-day Int																	
NatWest																	
B & H																	
Sunday	12	8	5	72	18	24.00	-	-	1	-	336	271	10	27.10	3-30	-	

68. Who was voted the Coopers and Lybrand
International Test Player of the Year?

OSTLER, D. P. Warwickshire

Name: Dominic Piers Ostler
Role: Right-hand bat, right-arm medium bowler
Born: 15 July 1970, Solihull
Height: 6ft 2in **Weight:** 14st
Nickname: Ossie, Blondie
County debut: 1990
County cap: 1991
1000 runs in a season: 4
1st-Class 50s: 50
1st-Class 100s: 9
1st-Class 200s: 1
1st-Class catches: 178
One-Day 100s: 1
Place in batting averages: 213th av. 19.95 (1996 160th av. 29.75)
Parents: Mike and Ann
Marital status: Single
Family links with cricket: Brother plays for Knowle and Dorridge

Education: Our Lady of the Wayside; Princethorpe College; Solihull Technical College
Qualifications: 4 O-levels, City and Guilds Recreation Course
Overseas tours: Gladstone Small's Benefit Tour to Barbados, 1992; England A to Pakistan 1995-96
Overseas teams played for: Avendale CC, South Africa 1991-92
Cricketers particularly admired: Trevor Penney, Gladstone Small, Graeme Welch, Jason Radcliffe
Young players to look out for: Ashley Giles
Other sports followed: Football (Birmingham City)
Relaxations: Taking the dog for a walk
Extras: Played club cricket for Moseley in the Birmingham League; made his Warwickshire 2nd XI debut in 1989 and was a member of Warwickshire U19 side that won Esso U19 County Festivals in 1988 and 1989. Has collected winner's medals for B&H Cup, Britannic Assurance County Championship, NatWest Trophy and Sunday League. Played for an England XI in the Cricket Max tournament in New Zealand in 1997
Opinions on cricket: 'The wickets aren't up to standard.'
Best batting: 208 Warwickshire v Surrey, Edgbaston 1995

	M	Inns	NO	Runs	HS	Avge	100s	50s	Ct	St	O	M	Runs	Wkts	Avge	Best	5wI	10wM
Test																		
All First	15	22	1	419	65	19.95	-	3	29	-	7	0	75	0	-	-	-	-
1-day Int																		
NatWest	4	4	0	197	58	49.25	-	3	3	-								
B & H	6	6	1	132	44	26.40	-	-	4	-								
Sunday	17	16	4	466	70	38.83	-	4	3	-								

Career Performances

	M	Inns	NO	Runs	HS	Avge	100s	50s	Ct	St	Balls	Runs	Wkts	Avge	Best	5wI	10wM
Test																	
All First	147	246	20	7659	208	33.88	9	50	178	-	185	197	0	-	-	-	-
1-day Int																	
NatWest	30	29	3	848	104	32.61	1	6	16	-	9	4	1	4.00	1-4	-	
B & H	30	29	4	1055	87	42.20	-	9	16	-							
Sunday	118	110	15	3012	91 *	31.70	-	22	30	-	6	4	0	-	-	-	

OWEN, J. E.   Derbyshire

Name: John Edward Owen
Role: Right-hand bat
Born: 7 August 1971, Derby
Height: 5ft 10in **Weight:** 12st
Nickname: Horts 'after grandfather Horton Owen'
County debut: 1995
1st-Class 50s: 4
1st-Class 100s: 2
1st-Class catches: 6
Place in batting averages: 267th av. 13.83 (1996 133rd av. 33.26)
Parents: David Horton and Carole
Marital status: Single
Family links with cricket: Father played in Derbyshire League for Alvaston, Boulton and Spondon and a few times for Derbyshire 2nd XI. Grandfather played for Crewe in the North Staffs South Cheshire league
Education: Springfield Primary School; Spondon School, Derby; Broomfield College
Qualifications: NCA coach, qualified green-keeper
Career outside cricket: 'Don't know yet'

Cricketers particularly admired: Viv Richards, Brian Lara, Dean Jones, Chris Adams, Kim Barnett
Young players to look out for: Andrew Harris, David Sales
Other sports followed: Football (Derby County), golf, rugby union
Relaxations: Cinema, reading, spending time with family and friends
Opinions on cricket: 'I think we should cut out one of the one-day competitions. The Sunday League is fun and popular with the public so maybe one of the others should go.'
Best batting: 105 Derbyshire v Glamorgan, Cardiff 1996

1997 Season

	M	Inns	NO	Runs	HS	Avge	100s	50s	Ct	St	O	M	Runs	Wkts	Avge	Best	5wI	10wM
Test																		
All First	4	6	0	83	22	13.83	-	-	3	-								
1-day Int																		
NatWest	1	1	0	10	10	10.00	-	-	-	-								
B & H																		
Sunday	2	1	0	5	5	5.00	-	-	-	-								

Career Performances

	M	Inns	NO	Runs	HS	Avge	100s	50s	Ct	St	Balls	Runs	Wkts	Avge	Best	5wI	10wM
Test																	
All First	17	29	0	782	105	26.96	2	4	6	-							
1-day Int																	
NatWest	3	3	0	20	10	6.66	-	-	1	-							
B & H	2	2	0	70	49	35.00	-	-	-	-							
Sunday	13	11	1	191	45	19.10	-	-	2	-							

PARKER, B. — Yorkshire

Name: Bradley Parker
Role: Right-hand bat, right-arm medium bowler, cover point fielder
Born: 23 June 1970, Mirfield
Height: 5ft 10in **Weight:** 12st 7lbs
Nickname: Nesty, Ceefax, Floyd
County debut: 1992
1st-Class 50s: 9
1st-Class 100s: 2
1st-Class catches: 16
Place in batting averages: 115th av. 32.24 (1996 178th av. 23.00)
Parents: Diane and David
Marital status: Single
Family links with cricket: Father played club cricket and Lincolnshire U23
Education: Bingley Grammar School
Qualifications: 'None worth mentioning from school.' Cricket coaching awards

Overseas teams played for: Ellerslie, Auckland 1988-90
Cricketers particularly admired: Chris Spence, Alec Stewart, Graham Thorpe
Other sports followed: Rugby league, boxing
Relaxations: Films, eating out, drinking and socialising
Opinions on cricket: 'Far too much cricket played in too short a time.'
Best batting: 138* Yorkshire v Oxford University, The Parks 1997

1997 Season

	M	Inns	NO	Runs	HS	Avge	100s	50s	Ct	St	O	M	Runs	Wkts	Avge	Best	5wl	10wM
Test																		
All First	19	30	5	806	138 *	32.24	1	4	6	-	1	0	3	0	-	-	-	-
1-day Int																		
NatWest	2	2	0	69	69	34.50	-	1	-	-								
B & H	4	2	0	73	58	36.50	-	1	-	-								
Sunday	16	14	2	193	42	16.08	-	-	1	-								

69. Who equalled the Test record for a fielder of five catches in an innings in 1997?

Career Performances

	M	Inns	NO	Runs	HS	Avge	100s	50s	Ct	St	Balls	Runs	Wkts	Avge	Best	5wl	10wM
Test																	
All First	36	61	8	1659	138 *	31.30	2	9	16	-	6	3	0	-	-	-	-
1-day Int																	
NatWest	3	2	0	69	69	34.50	-	1	-	-							
B & H	4	2	0	73	58	36.50	-	1	-	-							
Sunday	38	33	5	480	42	17.14	-	-	6	-							

PARKIN, O. T. Glamorgan

Name: Owen Thomas Parkin
Role: Right-hand bat, right-arm medium-fast bowler
Born: 24 August 1972, Coventry
Height: 6ft 3in **Weight:** 11st 10lbs
Nickname: Buddy, Residential
County debut: 1994
1st-Class catches: 5
One-Day 5 w. in innings: 1
Place in bowling averages:
(1996 126th av. 43.26)
Strike rate: 68.00 (career 78.16)
Parents: Vernon Cyrus and Sarah Patricia
Marital status: Single
Family links with cricket: Younger brother Morgan plays for the county in his age group and took a hat-trick last year
Education: Bournemouth Grammar School; Bath University
Qualifications: 9 GCSEs, 4 A-levels, 1 S-level, BSc (Hons) in Mathematics
Career outside cricket: Teacher
Off-season: Playing in Sydney
Overseas tours: Dorset Youth to Denmark
Overseas teams played for: Kew, Melbourne 1992-93; North Balwyn, Melbourne 1993-94
Cricketers particularly admired: Malcolm Marshall, Richard Hadlee
Other sports followed: Rugby, football (Nottingham Forest), golf
Injuries: Hamstring, out for one month
Relaxations: General socialising and listening to 'Green Day'
Extras: Played for Dorset in the NatWest Trophy 1992 and 1993. ASW Young Player of the Month July 1994. Took 5 for 28 on debut in Sunday League at Hove – a club record

Opinions on cricket: 'The reverse sweep should be banned – as bowlers you have to tell the batsman which hand you are going to use and which side of the wicket you are going to bowl, yet as a right-handed batsman you play this shot and become a left-handed player whenever you like – it would be a refreshing change to have a rule brought in that was not in favour of the batsman.'

Best batting: 14 Glamorgan v Warwickshire, Edgbaston 1996
Best bowling: 3-22 Glamorgan v Durham, Chester-le-Street 1996

1997 Season

	M	Inns	NO	Runs	HS	Avge	100s	50s	Ct	St	O	M	Runs	Wkts	Avge	Best	5wI	10wM
Test																		
All First	1	1	1	0	0 *	-	-	-	1	-	34	7	116	3	38.66	3-38	-	-
1-day Int																		
NatWest																		
B & H	4	2	0	15	8	7.50	-	-	1	-	32	2	149	5	29.80	3-42	-	
Sunday	8	5	3	2	1 *	1.00	-	-	1	-	46	3	262	7	37.42	4-45	-	

Career Performances

	M	Inns	NO	Runs	HS	Avge	100s	50s	Ct	St	Balls	Runs	Wkts	Avge	Best	5wI	10wM
Test																	
All First	13	15	10	67	14	13.40	-	-	5	-	1876	1030	24	42.91	3-22	-	-
1-day Int																	
NatWest	3	2	1	1	1 *	1.00	-	-	2	-	120	77	3	25.66	3-23	-	
B & H	4	2	0	15	8	7.50	-	-	1	-	192	149	5	29.80	3-42	-	
Sunday	13	5	3	2	1 *	1.00	-	-	1	-	504	435	16	27.18	5-28	1	

70. Who holds the record for the latest century in an English season – a record which has now stood for 75 years?

O vodafone

PARSONS, G. J.   Leicestershire

Name: Gordon James Parsons
Role: Left-hand bat, right-arm
medium-fast bowler
Born: 17 October 1959, Slough
Height: 6ft **Weight:** 13st ('April') – 14st
('September')
Nickname: Bullhead, Taz
County debut: 1978 (Leicestershire),
1986 (Warwickshire)
County cap: 1984 (Leicestershire),
1987 (Warwickshire)
Benefit: 1994
50 wickets in a season: 3
1st-Class 50s: 29
1st-Class 5 w. in innings: 19
1st-Class 10 w. in match: 1
1st-Class catches: 147
Place in batting averages: (1996 260th av.
16.11)
Place in bowling averages: 113th av. 38.46 (1996 75th av. 32.68)
Strike rate: 84.15 (career 61.70)
Parents: David and Evelyn
Wife and date of marriage: Hester Sophia, 8 February 1991
Children: Alexandra Suzanna, 5 June 1992; James Gordon, 12 December 1995
Family links with cricket: Brothers-in-law, Hansie and Frans Cronje, both play first-class cricket in South Africa. Dad played club cricket 'in the days when bowlers hit a sixpence five balls in six'
Education: Wexham Primary School; Woodside County Secondary School, Slough
Qualifications: 5 O-levels
Career outside cricket: Coaching North-West Province in South Africa
Overseas tours: ESCA to India 1977-78; Derrick Robins XI to Australasia 1980;
Leicestershire to Zimbabwe 1981, to Jamaica 1993
Overseas teams played for: Maharaja's, Sri Lanka 1979,1987; Boland, South Africa
1982-83; Griqualand West, South Africa 1984-85; Orange Free State, South Africa 1986-92
Cricketers particularly admired: Viv Richards, Andy Roberts, David Gower,
Graham Lloyd
Young players to look out for: Iain Sutcliffe, Darren Maddy, Darren Stevens
Other sports followed: Golf 'very occasionally', football (Reading FC)
Injuries: Chicken pox, out for two weeks
Relaxations: Family, videos and music
Extras: Played for Leicester 2nd XI from 1976 and for Buckinghamshire in 1977. Left

Leicestershire after 1985 season and joined Warwickshire. Capped by Warwickshire while in plaster and on crutches. Released at end of 1988 season and returned to his old county. Justin Benson was best man at his wedding, 'contradiction in terms, though it is!' Released by Leicestershire at the end of the 1997 season

Opinions on cricket: 'I think that two leagues would be good for the game. 2nd XI cricket needs to improve. Maybe less games on proper wickets. Need more experienced players!'

Best batting: 76 Boland v Western Province B, Cape Town 1984-85

Best bowling: 9-72 Boland v Transvaal B, Johannesburg 1984-85

1997 Season

	M	Inns	NO	Runs	HS		Avge	100s	50s	Ct	St	O	M	Runs	Wkts	Avge	Best	5wI	10wM
Test																			
All First	6	6	1	113	69	*	22.60	-	1	1	-	182.2	48	500	13	38.46	4-22	-	-
1-day Int																			
NatWest	2	2	0	17	9		8.50	-	-	-	-	24	4	102	3	34.00	3-68	-	
B & H	1	1	0	4	4		4.00	-	-	2	-	10	0	39	1	39.00	1-39	-	
Sunday	11	6	4	70	41	*	35.00	-	-	3	-	76	3	345	8	43.12	2-9	-	

Career Performances

	M	Inns	NO	Runs	HS		Avge	100s	50s	Ct	St	Balls		Runs	Wkts	Avge	Best	5wI	10wM
Test																			
All First	338	449	100	6767	76		19.38	-	29	147	-	49923		24509	809	30.29	9-72	19	1
1-day Int																			
NatWest	34	23	6	189	25	*	11.11	-	-	7	-	1928		1199	28	42.82	3-68	-	
B & H	61	35	14	357	63	*	17.00	-	1	13	-	3300		1985	72	27.56	4-12	-	
Sunday	207	129	55	1183	41	*	15.98	-	-	31	-	8545		6332	203	31.19	4-19	-	

71. Who were the 1997 BUSA Champions?

PARSONS, K. A.   Somerset

Name: Keith Alan Parsons
Role: Right-hand bat, right-arm
medium bowler
Born: 2 May 1973, Taunton
Height: 6ft 1in **Weight:** 13st 4lbs
Nickname: Pilot, Pars, Orv
County debut: 1992
1st-Class 50s: 14
1st-Class 100s: 1
1st-Class catches: 32
Place in batting averages: 82nd av. 36.41
(1996 117th av. 31.57)
Strike rate: 67.57 (career 90.73)
Parents: Alan and Lynne
Marital status: Single
Family links with cricket: Identical twin
brother, Kevin, was on the Somerset staff
1992-94 and now plays Minor Counties for
Wiltshire. Father played six seasons for

Somerset 2nd XI and captained National Civil Service XI
Education: Bishop Henderson Primary School; The Castle School, Taunton; Richard
Huish Sixth Form College, Taunton
Qualifications: 8 GCSEs, 3 A-levels, NCA coaching award
Career outside cricket: Unknown
Off-season: Coaching and working in the Clerical Medical indoor school in Taunton
until Christmas and then off to Perth for two months training and practising
Overseas tours: Castle School to Barbados 1989
Overseas teams played for: Kapiti Old Boys, New Zealand 1992-93; Harowhenera,
New Zealand 1992-93; Taita District, Wellington, New Zealand 1993-96
Cricketers particularly admired: Viv Richards, Richard Hadlee, Robin Smith
Other sports followed: Rugby union (Bath RFC), football (Nottingham Forest FC),
golf
Injuries: Broken hand, missed the last two games of the season
Relaxations: Playing golf, going to the cinema, listening to music 'and the occasional
pint of beer'
Extras: Captained two National Cup winning sides – Taunton St Andrews in National
U15 Club Championship and Richard Huish College in National U17 School
Championship. Represented English Schools at U15 and U19 level. Somerset Young
Player of the Year 1993
Opinions on cricket: 'Having played in the first day/night game at Edgbaston in 1997
in front of 18,000 people, it is important that all first-class cricketers experience such an
occasion. All counties should be encouraged to play day/night games in the future if at

all possible.'
Best batting: 105 Somerset v Young Australia, Taunton 1995
Best bowling: 2-4 Somerset v Oxford University, Taunton 1997

1997 Season

	M	Inns	NO	Runs	HS	Avge	100s	50s	Ct	St	O	M	Runs	Wkts	Avge	Best	5wI	10wM
Test																		
All First	10	15	3	437	74	36.41	-	3	12	-	78.5	18	204	7	29.14	2-4	-	-
1-day Int																		
NatWest	2	2	1	1	1	1.00	-	-	-	-	11	1	34	3	11.33	3-34	-	
B & H	3	3	2	32	22 *	32.00	-	-	1	-	10	0	74	1	74.00	1-74	-	
Sunday	11	7	3	125	52 *	31.25	-	1	7	-	64	0	301	7	43.00	2-18	-	

Career Performances

	M	Inns	NO	Runs	HS	Avge	100s	50s	Ct	St	Balls	Runs	Wkts	Avge	Best	5wI	10wM
Test																	
All First	43	74	8	1839	105	27.86	1	14	32	-	1361	851	15	56.73	2-4	-	-
1-day Int																	
NatWest	8	8	3	158	51	31.60	-	1	1	-	264	190	8	23.75	3-34		
B & H	6	5	3	68	33 *	34.00	-	-	3	-	138	171	3	57.00	2-60		
Sunday	43	32	6	548	56	21.07	-	3	20	-	936	764	22	34.72	3-36		

PATEL, C.   Hampshire

Name: Chetan Patel
Role: Left-hand bat, right-arm
medium-fast bowler
Born: 12 April 1972, Islington, London
Height: 6ft 2in **Weight:** 13st 12lbs
Nickname: Shabba, Ranks, Snout
County debut: 1997
1st-Class 50s: 3
1st-Class 5 w. in innings: 1
1st-Class catches: 2
Place in batting averages: 166th av. 24.70
Place in bowling averages: 133rd 49.11
Strike rate: 72.66 (career 72.66)
Parents: Morar and Jasoo
Marital status: Single
Family links with cricket: 'Father played
club cricket in Kenya. Younger brother
Sanjay plays for Hornsey CC and has played

for Middlesex, Worcestershire and Gloucestershire 2nd XIs. Mum does the teas at my old club, Calthorpe'

Education: Rokesly Junior School; Fortismere School; Loughborough University; Keble College, Oxford University

Qualifications: 7 GCSEs, 2 A-levels, BSc (Hons) Computing, Dip. Soc (Oxon), NCA coaching award

Career outside cricket: IT consultant

Off-season: 'Training and looking for suitable employment'

Overseas teams played for: St Albans CC, Christchurch, New Zealand 1995-96

Cricketers particularly admired: Andy Flower, Mark Ramprakash, Sachin Tendulkar, Allan Donald, Richard Hadlee, Robin Smith

Young players to look out for: Owais Shah, Mark Wagh

Other sports followed: 'Used to play hockey and football at school'

Injuries: Side strain and sore calf, missed a total of two weeks

Relaxations: Spending time at home, going out with friends, eating out, music

Extras: Played for Middlesex from U15 to U19 and also for the 2nd XI as well as playing 2nd XI cricket for Warwickshire, Essex, Glamorgan and Surrey. Captained Loughborough University to the national indoor final. Scored a half century in only his second innings of first-class cricket. Completed a hat-trick for Oxford University in their game against Warwickshire in 1997 (his victims being Powell, Welch and Brown). Was released by Hampshire at the end of the 1997 season

Opinions on cricket: 'Not been in the game long enough to make any valid comment. However tea breaks pass far too quickly when you are the fielding side. A great game – a true test of courage, character, ability and fitness. Oxbridge should keep its first-class status – what harm does it do?'

Best batting: 63* Oxford University v Glamorgan, The Parks 1997

Best bowling: 6-110 Oxford University v Cambridge University, Lord's 1997

1997 Season

	M	Inns	NO	Runs	HS	Avge	100s	50s	Ct	St	O	M	Runs	Wkts	Avge	Best	5wl	10wM
Test																		
All First	12	22	5	420	63 *	24.70	-	3	2	-	327	51	1326	27	49.11	6-110	1	-
1-day Int																		
NatWest																		
B & H																		
Sunday	1	0	0	0	0	-	-	-	1	-	4	0	25	0	-	-	-	-

72. Who captained England U19 to success
in the 1997 Youth World Cup?

Career Performances

	M	Inns	NO	Runs	HS	Avge	100s	50s	Ct	St	Balls	Runs	Wkts	Avge	Best	5wl	10wM
Test																	
All First	12	22	5	420	63 *	24.70	-	3	2	-	1962	1326	27	49.11	6-110	1	-
1-day Int																	
NatWest																	
B & H																	
Sunday	1	0	0	0	0	-	-	-	1	-	24	25	0	-	-	-	

PATEL, D. Worcestershire

Name: Depesh Patel
Role: Right-hand bat, right-arm fast bowler
Born: 23 September 1981, Wolverhampton
Height: 6ft 3in   **Weight:** 11st
Nickname: Dip, Dippy, Petal
County debut: No first-team appearance
Parents: Balvant and Mena
Marital status: Single
Family links with cricket: 'Dad has played for Thompsons CC since the age of 18'
Education: Wilkinson Park Primary School; Mosely Park GM School
Qualifications: GCSEs
Off-season: Studying, keeping fit, Saturday job, learning to drive
Cricketers particularly admired: Allan Donald, Sachin Tendulkar, Glenn McGrath
Young players to look out for: Vikram Solanki
Other sports followed: Football (Wolverhampton Wanderers), badminton, basketball, table tennis
Injuries: Groin, out for two weeks
Relaxations: Keeping fit, jogging, computers, listening to music, watching television
Extras: Scored 120 aged 15 against Cheshire playing for Staffordshire. Has best bowling of 7 for 1 playing against Glamorgan U11 for Staffordshire U11
Opinions on cricket: 'Cricket today is played at a faster pace than ten years ago, especially in the one-day game.'

PATEL, M. M.   Kent

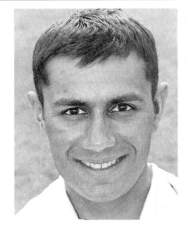

Name: Minal Mahesh Patel
Role: Right-hand bat, slow left-arm bowler
Born: 7 August 1970, Bombay, India
Height: 5ft 9in **Weight:** 9st 10lbs
Nickname: Spin, Geezer, Diamond, Ho-Chi
County debut: 1989
County cap: 1994
Test debut: 1996
Tests: 2
50 wickets in a season: 2
1st-Class 50s: 2
1st-Class 5 w. in innings: 15
1st-Class 10 w. in match: 7
1st-Class catches: 43
Place in batting averages:
(1996 267th av. 15.44)
Place in bowling averages:
(1996 135th av. 47.15)
Strike rate: (career 72.76)
Parents: Mahesh and Aruna
Wife and date of marriage: Karuna, 8 October 1995
Education: Dartford GS; Erith College of Technology; Manchester Polytechnic
Qualifications: 6 O-levels, 3 A-levels, BA (Hons) in Economics
Off-season: Playing for Alberton CC in Johannesburg
Overseas tours: Dartford GS to Barbados 1988; England A to India 1994-95; MCC to Malta 1996, to Fiji, Sydney and Hong Kong 1997
Cricketers particularly admired: Derek Underwood, Sachin Tendulkar, Aravinda De Silva
Young players to look out for: Ed Smith, Rob Key
Other sports followed: Football (Tottenham Hotspur), American football and basketball
Injuries: Torn anterior cruciate ligament in right knee, out for almost the whole season
Relaxations: Music, D-Jing
Extras: Played for English Schools 1988, 1989 and NCA England South 1989. Was voted Kent League Young Player of the Year 1987 while playing for Blackheath. First six overs in NatWest Trophy were all maidens. Whittingdale Young Player of the Year 1994
Opinions on cricket: 'Domestic cricket is in need of change – quality not quantity.'
Best batting: 56 Kent v Leicestershire, Canterbury 1995
Best bowling: 8-96 Kent v Lancashire, Canterbury 1994

1997 Season

	M	Inns	NO	Runs	HS	Avge	100s	50s	Ct	St	O	M	Runs	Wkts	Avge	Best	5wI	10wM
Test																		
All First	1	2	0	38	30	19.00	-	-	1	-	3	0	12	0	-		-	-
1-day Int																		
NatWest																		
B & H																		
Sunday																		

Career Performances

	M	Inns	NO	Runs	HS	Avge	100s	50s	Ct	St	Balls	Runs	Wkts	Avge	Best	5wI	10wM
Test	2	2	0	45	27	22.50	-	-	2	-	276	180	1	180.00	1-101	-	-
All First	80	114	25	1231	56	13.83	-	2	43	-	18191	8118	250	32.47	8-96	15	7
1-day Int																	
NatWest	6	2	1	9	5 *	9.00	-	-	5	-	386	200	7	28.57	2-29	-	
B & H	10	6	5	39	18 *	39.00	-	-	3	-	456	327	6	54.50	2-29	-	
Sunday	6	2	0	6	5	3.00	-	-	1	-	176	191	6	31.83	3-50	-	

PATTERSON, M. W.   Surrey

Name: Mark William Patterson
Role: Right-hand bat, right-arm
fast-medium bowler
Born: 2 February 1974, Belfast
Height: 6ft 1in **Weight:** 12st 4lbs
Nickname: Paddy, Pato, Irish
County debut: 1996
1st-Class 5 w. in innings: 1
Strike rate: (career 23.57)
Parents: Billy and Phyllis
Marital status: Single
Family links with cricket: Dad has always
played club cricket. Younger brother plays for
Ireland as a wicket-keeper batsman and has
ambitions to play county cricket
Education: Carnmoney Primary School;
Belfast Royal Academy; University of Ulster
Qualifications: 9 GCSEs, 3 A-levels, BA
(Hons) in Sport and Leisure Studies
Career outside cricket: Qualified coach in soccer, cricket, rugby, hockey, basketball,
swimming and squash
Overseas tours: Ireland U19 to Denmark for International Youth Tournament 1993;

Ireland to Denmark for European Championships 1996
Overseas teams played for: Mount Maunganui, Bay of Plenty, New Zealand 1994-95
Cricketers particularly admired: Malcolm Marshall, John Solanky 'our first club professional in Ireland'
Young players to look out for: Alex Tudor, Ben Hollioake
Other sports followed: Soccer (Lingfield, Rangers and Manchester United)
Relaxations: Drinking with friends, clubbing, dance music, watching Lingfield with my dad and horse racing
Extras: 1993 Irish Young Cricketer of the Year. In 1996 took 6 for 80 against South Africa A – the best ever figures by a Surrey bowler on debut
Opinions on cricket: 'The County Championship needs a new image and structure that will make it more appealing to spectators, sponsors and television.'
Best batting: 4 Surrey v South Africa A, The Oval 1996
Best bowling: 6-80 Surrey v South Africa A, The Oval 1996

1997 Season (did not make any first-class or one-day appearances)

Career Performances

	M	Inns	NO	Runs	HS	Avge	100s	50s	Ct	St	Balls	Runs	Wkts	Avge	Best	5wI	10wM
Test																	
All First	1	2	0	6	4	3.00	-	-	-	-	165	124	7	17.71	6-80	1	-
1-day Int																	
NatWest	2	1	0	1	1	1.00	-	-	-	-	138	154	4	38.50	3-66	-	
B & H	7	5	1	23	9	5.75	-	-	-	-	342	330	10	33.00	3-48	-	
Sunday																	

PEARSON, R. M.   Surrey

Name: Richard Michael Pearson
Role: Right-hand bat, right arm off-spin bowler
Born: 27 January 1972, Batley, Yorkshire
Height: 6ft 3in **Weight:** 13st 7lbs
Nickname: Batley, Pancho
County debut: 1992 (Northamptonshire), 1994 (Essex), 1996 (Surrey)
1st-Class 5 w. in innings: 2
1st-Class catches: 15
Place in bowling averages: (1996 137th av. 48.67)
Strike rate: 78.00 (career 103.60)
Parents: Mike and Carol
Marital status: Single
Family links with cricket: 'Dad played for Birstall in the Central Yorkshire League. Mum was a highly esteemed tea lady'

Education: Batley Grammar School; St John's College, Cambridge
Qualifications: 2 O-levels, 9 GCSEs, 4 A-levels, BA (Hons) in History
Career outside cricket: Starting my own property business in Harrogate
Overseas teams played for: Bulawayo Athletic Club, Zimbabwe 1995-96
Cricketers particularly admired: John Childs, Peter Such, Graham Gooch
Other sports followed: Football (Leeds), rugby league (Batley)
Relaxations: Eating out, music, reading
Extras: Made first-class debut for Cambridge University in 1991 and has played for Combined Universities in the Benson & Hedges Cup since 1991. Football and cricket Blues at Cambridge. Moved to Essex for the 1994 season and joined Surrey for the 1996 season

Opinions on cricket: 'Players should be able to move between clubs more freely. If a contract has expired a player should be a free agent.'
Best batting: 37 Surrey v Sussex, Guildford 1996
Best bowling: 5-108 Cambridge University v Warwickshire, Fenner's 1992

1997 Season

	M	Inns	NO	Runs	HS	Avge	100s	50s	Ct	St	O	M	Runs	Wkts	Avge	Best	5wl	10wM
Test																		
All Firsts	1	1	0	1	1	1.00	-	-	1	-	26	4	90	2	45.00	2-90	-	-
1-day Int																		
NatWest																		
B & H																		
Sunday																		

Career Performances

	M	Inns	NO	Runs	HS	Avge	100s	50s	Ct	St	Balls	Runs	Wkts	Avge	Best	5wl	10wM
Test																	
All First	51	56	16	475	37	11.87	-	-	15	-	10360	5516	100	55.16	5-108	2	-
1-day Int																	
NatWest	5	1	0	11	11	11.00	-	-	-	-	276	188	3	62.66	1-39	-	
B & H	13	3	2	22	12 *	22.00	-	-	1	-	749	556	11	50.54	3-46	-	
Sunday	29	13	10	46	9 *	15.33	-	-	3	-	901	828	23	36.00	3-33	-	

PEIRCE, M. T. E.   Sussex

Name: Michael Toby Edward Peirce
Role: Left-hand bat, slow left-arm bowler
Born: 14 June 1973, Maidenhead
Height: 5ft 11in **Weight:** 11st 11lbs
Nickname: Carrot, Juice
County debut: 1994 (one-day),
1995 (first-class)
1st-Class 50s: 4
1st-Class 100s: 1
1st-Class catches: 16
Place in batting averages: 164th av. 25.04
(1996 193rd av. 21.90)
Parents: Mike and Kate
Marital status: Single
Education: Ardingly College; Durham
University
Qualifications: GCSEs and A-levels, BA
(Dunelm)
Career outside cricket: 'None at present, but
mucked about in the City once'
Off-season: Playing and coaching in Stellenbosch, South Africa
Overseas tours: Sussex Schools U14 to Barbados 1987; Sussex Schools U18 to India
1990-91; Ardingly College to India 1988-89
Overseas teams played for: Kilbirnie, Wellington, New Zealand 1991-92; Wellington
B, New Zealand 1991-92; Van der Stel CC, Stellenbosch, South Africa 1996-98
Cricketers particularly admired: David Smith, David Gower, Phil Edmonds,
Desmond Haynes
Young players to look out for: 'All the Sussex lot'
Other sports followed: Rugby, football, golf
Relaxations: 'Aviation, dining out and wine by the bottle'
Extras: 'Am I the only retired cricketer still playing?'
Opinions on cricket: 'Bloody hard work but worth it. Despise anyone who says that
cricket was better in their day.'
Best batting: 104 Sussex v Hampshire, Southampton 1997

---

73. Who has assumed the Northamptonshire
captaincy for the 1998 season?

O vodafone

430

1997 Season

	M	Inns	NO	Runs	HS	Avge	100s	50s	Ct	St	O	M	Runs	Wkts	Avge	Best	5wI	10wM
Test																		
All First	12	23	0	576	104	25.04	1	3	10	-	20.1	2	76	0	-		-	-	-
1-day Int																		
NatWest																		
B & H																		
Sunday	1	1	0	7	7	7.00	-	-	-	-								

Career Performances

	M	Inns	NO	Runs	HS	Avge	100s	50s	Ct	St	Balls	Runs	Wkts	Avge	Best	5wI	10wM
Test																	
All First	19	35	0	819	104	23.40	1	4	16	-	175	106	0	-		-	-	-
1-day Int																	
NatWest																	
B & H	5	5	0	134	44	26.80	-	-	1	-							
Sunday	3	3	0	20	7	6.66	-	-	2	-							

PENBERTHY, A. L.   Northamptonshire

Name: Anthony Leonard Penberthy
Role: Left-hand bat, right-arm medium bowler
Born: 1 September 1969, Troon, Cornwall
Height: 6ft 1in **Weight:** 12st
Nickname: Berth, Penbers, Lennie, Denzil
County debut: 1989
County cap: 1994
1st-Class 50s: 17
1st-Class 100s: 1
1st-Class 5 w. in innings: 3
1st-Class catches: 58
One-Day 5 w. in innings: 1
Place in batting averages: 149th av. 26.26
(1996 196th av. 25.40)
Place in bowling averages:
(1996 72nd av. 31.67)
Strike rate: 126.66 (career 68.35)
Parents: Gerald and Wendy
Wife and date of marriage: Rebecca, 9 November 1996
Family links with cricket: Father played in local leagues in Cornwall and is now a qualified umpire instructor

Education: Troon County Primary; Camborne Comprehensive
Qualifications: 3 O-levels, 3 CSEs, coaching certificate
Overseas tours: Druids to Zimbabwe 1988; Northants to Durban 1992, to Cape Town 1993, to Zimbabwe 1995, to Johannesburg 1996
Cricketers particularly admired: Ian Botham, David Gower, Dennis Lillee, Viv Richards, Eldine Baptiste
Young players to look out for: David Sales, David Roberts
Other sports followed: Football (West Ham United), snooker, rugby, golf
Relaxations: Listening to music ('especially Luther Vandross'), watching videos and comedy programmes, 'walking my Irish setter'
Extras: Had football trials for Plymouth Argyle but came to Northampton for cricket trials instead. Took wicket with first ball in first-class cricket – Mark Taylor caught behind, June 1989. Played for England YC v New Zealand YC 1989
Opinions on cricket: 'Short run-ups on Sunday. Lunch and tea intervals are too short. All international one-day cricket should be with a white ball and coloured clothing.'
Best batting: 101* Northamptonshire v Cambridge University, Fenner's 1990
Best bowling: 5-37 Northamptonshire v Glamorgan, Swansea 1993

1997 Season

	M	Inns	NO	Runs	HS	Avge	100s	50s	Ct	St	O	M	Runs	Wkts	Avge	Best	5wI	10wM
Test																		
All First	13	19	0	499	96	26.26	-	3	8	-	190	29	722	9	80.22	2-52	-	-
1-day Int																		
NatWest	2	2	0	119	62	59.50	-	2	2	-	13	2	79	5	15.80	5-56	1	
B & H	6	5	1	102	38	25.50	-	-	-	-	23	1	112	1	112.00	1-34	-	
Sunday	14	14	2	317	81*	26.41	-	3	3	-	69	1	307	16	19.18	3-32	-	

Career Performances

	M	Inns	NO	Runs	HS	Avge	100s	50s	Ct	St	Balls	Runs	Wkts	Avge	Best	5wI	10wM
Test																	
All First	101	151	19	3010	101*	22.80	1	17	58	-	10527	5848	154	37.97	5-37	3	-
1-day Int																	
NatWest	19	12	1	320	79	29.09	-	3	7	-	817	583	17	34.29	5-56	1	
B & H	24	18	3	315	41	21.00	-	-	6	-	996	725	18	40.27	3-38	-	
Sunday	95	73	13	1261	81*	21.01	-	6	18	-	3015	2673	88	30.37	5-36	1	

PENNEY, T. L. — Warwickshire

Name: Trevor Lionel Penney
Role: Right-hand bat, right-arm
leg-break bowler
Born: 12 June 1968, Salisbury, Rhodesia
Height: 6ft **Weight:** 11st
Nickname: TP, Lemon Kop
County debut: 1992
County cap: 1994
1000 runs in a season: 2
1st-Class 50s: 29
1st-Class 100s: 13
1st-Class catches: 67
Place in batting averages: 55th av. 41.26
(1996 63rd av. 43.16)
Strike rate: (career 41.16)
Parents: George and Bets
Wife and date of marriage: Deborah Anne,
19 December 1992
Children: Samantha Anne, 20 August 1995
Family links with cricket: Brother Stephen played for Zimbabwe U25
Education: Blakiston Primary; Prince Edward Boys High School, Zimbabwe
Qualifications: 3 O-levels
Career outside cricket: Tobacco buyer
Overseas tours: Zimbabwe to Sri Lanka 1987; ICC Associates to Australia (Youth World Cup) 1987-88; Zimbabwe U20 to England 1984
Overseas teams played for: Old Hararians, Zimbabwe 1983-89 and 1993-94; Scarborough, Australia 1989-90; Boland, South Africa 1991-92; Avendale, South Africa 1992-93
Cricketers particularly admired: Colin Bland, Ian Botham, Graeme Hick, Allan Donald
Other sports followed: Football (Liverpool FC), American football (San Francisco 49ers), golf and tennis
Relaxations: Playing golf and drinking Castle on Lake Kariba. Spending time with my wife and daughter
Extras: Captained the ICC Associates team at the Youth World Cup in 1987-88. Played for Zimbabwe against Sri Lanka in 1987. Played hockey for Zimbabwe from 1984-87 and also made the African team who played Asia in 1987. Qualified to play for England in 1992
Best batting: 151 Warwickshire v Middlesex, Lord's 1992
Best bowling: 3-18 Mashonaland v Mashonaland U24, Harare 1993-94

1997 Season

	M	Inns	NO	Runs	HS	Avge	100s	50s	Ct	St	O	M	Runs	Wkts	Avge	Best	5wI	10wM
Test																		
All First	16	24	5	784	99	41.26	-	6	11	-								
1-day Int																		
NatWest	5	5	1	100	45	25.00	-	-	2	-	0.3	0	4	0	-		-	-
B & H	6	6	1	182	55	36.40	-	1	3	-								
Sunday	17	15	3	268	57	22.33	-	1	4	-								

Career Performances

	M	Inns	NO	Runs	HS	Avge	100s	50s	Ct	St	Balls	Runs	Wkts	Avge	Best	5wI	10wM
Test																	
All First	114	180	26	6268	151	40.70	13	29	67	-	247	183	6	30.50	3-18	-	-
1-day Int																	
NatWest	24	22	5	459	90	27.00	-	2	13	-	13	16	1	16.00	1-8	-	
B & H	23	20	4	443	55	27.68	-	2	8	1							
Sunday	92	79	27	1499	83 *	28.82	-	6	36	-	6	2	0	-		-	-

PETERS, S. D.   Essex

Name: Stephen David Peters
Role: Right-hand bat
Born: 10 December 1976, Harold Wood
Height: 5ft 10in   **Weight:** 10st 7lbs
Nickname: Geezer, Pedro, Hot Rod, Rodders
County debut: 1996
1st-Class 100s: 2
1st-Class catches: 8
Place in batting averages: 209th av. 23.66
Parents: Brian and Lesley
Marital status: Single
Family links with cricket: 'Father plays for Upminster. Mother scores and is a keen follower of cricket. Sister organises social events at Upminster CC. Brother-in-law claims he's quick!'
Education: Upminster Junior School; Coopers Coburn and Company School
Qualifications: 9 GCSEs
Overseas tours: Essex U14 to Hong Kong; Essex U15 to Barbados; England U19 to Pakistan 1996-97, to South Africa 1997-98
Cricketers particularly admired: Graham Gooch and Nasser Hussain 'strange bloke'

Young players to look out for: Ben Hollioake, Alex Tudor
Other sports followed: Football (West Ham United), golf
Relaxations: Music round at DJ Hibbert's and television
Extras: The Sir John Hobbs Jubilee Memorial Prize 1994, a *Daily Telegraph* regional batting award 1994, represented England at U14, U15, U17 and U19. Essex Young Player of the Year 1996. Scored a century in the U19 World Cup final in South Africa
Opinions on cricket: 'All 2nd XI games should be played on 1st XI grounds.'
Best batting: 110 Essex v Cambridge University, Fenner's 1996

1997 Season

	M	Inns	NO	Runs	HS	Avge	100s	50s	Ct	St	O	M	Runs	Wkts	Avge	Best	5wl	10wM
Test																		
All First	3	3	1	135	102 *	67.50	1	-	3	-								
1-day Int																		
NatWest																		
B & H																		
Sunday	3	2	0	17	15	8.50	-	-	-	-								

Career Performances

	M	Inns	NO	Runs	HS	Avge	100s	50s	Ct	St	Balls	Runs	Wkts	Avge	Best	5wl	10wM
Test																	
All First	7	10	2	277	110	34.62	2	-	8	-							
1-day Int																	
NatWest																	
B & H																	
Sunday	4	3	0	18	15	6.00	-	-	-	-							

74. Who has taken over the Hampshire captaincy for 1998?

 vodafone

PHILLIPS, B. J.   Kent

Name: Ben James Phillips
Role: Right-hand bat, right-arm
fast-medium bowler
Born: 30 September 1974, Lewisham
Height: 6ft 6in **Weight:** 15st 7lbs
Nickname: BGS, Action Spice, Bomb,
Golden Arm
County debut: 1996
1st-Class 50s: 1
1st-Class 100s: 1
1st-Class 5 w. in innings: 2
1st-Class catches: 7
Place in batting averages: 163rd av. 25.06
Place in bowling averages: 9th av. 19.93
Strike rate: 38.47 (career 40.27)
Parents: Trevor and Glynnis
Marital status: Single
Family links with cricket: Father and
brother keen club cricketers

Education: St Joseph's Primary, Bromley; Langley Park School for Boys,
Beckenham; Langley Park Sixth Form
Qualifications: 9 GCSEs and 3 A-levels
Career outside cricket: 'Keeping my options open, but hopefully something sports
related'
Off-season: Playing and coaching in Cape Town, South Africa
Overseas teams played for: University of Queensland, Australia 1993-94; Cape
Technikon, Cape Town, South Africa 1994-95, 1996-98
Cricketers particularly admired: Jason Gillespie, Brian Macmillan, Carl Hooper and
'Kent team-mates'
Young players to look out for: Steve Marsh, Alan Wells
Other sports followed: Football (West Ham United) and basketball (Chicago Bulls)
Injuries: Sore shins, missed one week
Relaxations: 'Enjoy watching a decent film or listening to music. Slothing it on a
beach somewhere sunny in the off-season'
Extras: Represented England U19 Schools in 1993-94. Holds Langley Park School
record for the fastest half century off 11 balls
Opinions on cricket: 'The problem with English cricket is the lack of adequate off-
season structure in place to improve playing standards. I would like to see 12-month
contracts therefore allowing players to develop aspects of their game during the off-
season.'
Best batting: 100* Kent v Lancashire, Old Trafford 1997
Best bowling: 5-47 Kent v Sussex, Horsham 1997

1997 Season

	M	Inns	NO	Runs	HS	Avge	100s	50s	Ct	St	O	M	Runs	Wkts	Avge	Best	5wI	10wM
Test																		
All First	13	19	4	376	100 *	25.06	1	1	6	-	282.1	73	877	44	19.93	5-47	2	-
1-day Int																		
NatWest																		
B & H																		
Sunday	2	1	1	1	1 *	-	-	-	2	-	10	1	34	2	17.00	1-17	-	

Career Performances

	M	Inns	NO	Runs	HS	Avge	100s	50s	Ct	St	Balls	Runs	Wkts	Avge	Best	5wI	10wM
Test																	
All First	16	22	4	381	100 *	21.16	1	1	7	-	1933	986	48	20.54	5-47	2	-
1-day Int																	
NatWest																	
B & H																	
Sunday	6	5	2	34	29	11.33	-	-	5	-	185	146	5	29.20	2-42	-	

PHILLIPS, N. C. Sussex

Name: Nicholas Charles Phillips
Role: Right-hand bat, off-spin bowler
Born: 10 May 1974, Pembury, Kent
Height: 6ft **Weight:** 11st 4lbs
Nickname: Milky, Spoons, Beastie, Nicky P
County debut: 1994
1st-Class 50s: 3
1st-Class catches: 9
Place in bowling averages: (1996 154th av. 59.84)
Strike rate: 156.00 (career 107.51)
Parents: Robert and Joan
Marital status: Single
Family links with cricket: Father plays club cricket for Hastings. Represents Sussex Over 50s and has represented Kent 2nd XI, Kent League XI and has scored over 100 club centuries
Education: Hilden Grange School, Tonbridge; St Thomas's School, Winchelsea; William Parker School, Hastings
Qualifications: 8 GCSEs, NCA coaching award
Overseas tours: Sussex U18 to India 1990-91

Overseas teams played for: Maris CC, Auckland 1996-97
Cricketers particularly admired: Eddie Hemmings, Derek Randall
Other sports followed: Hockey, football
Relaxations: Spending time with friends and girlfriend. Listening to music. Eating out and socialising with fellow players
Extras: Represented England U19 in home series against West Indies U19 in 1993. Has played hockey for Sussex U14 and U16. Released by Sussex at the end of the 1997 season
Opinions on cricket: 'It is a good thing that four-day games are being brought into 2nd XI cricket, but this means that the wicket standards should be reviewed as many 2nd XI wickets would not last four days. The NatWest should be scrapped because all one-day cricket around the world is now the 50-over format. Why should we be different?'
Best batting: 53 Sussex v Young Australia, Hove 1995
Best bowling: 3-39 Sussex v Cambridge University 1995

1997 Season

	M	Inns	NO	Runs	HS	Avge	100s	50s	Ct	St	O	M	Runs	Wkts	Avge	Best	5wI	10wM
Test																		
All First	3	2	1	7	6	7.00	-	-	-	-	26	3	114	1	114.00	1-47	-	-
1-day Int																		
NatWest																		
B & H	5	4	1	11	11	3.66	-	-	2	-	34.1	1	161	5	32.20	3-48	-	
Sunday	5	4	0	31	21	7.75	-	-	-	-	16	1	79	1	79.00	1-17	-	

Career Performances

	M	Inns	NO	Runs	HS	Avge	100s	50s	Ct	St	Balls	Runs	Wkts	Avge	Best	5wI	10wM
Test																	
All First	19	26	10	450	53	28.12	-	3	9	-	2903	1643	27	60.85	3-39	-	-
1-day Int																	
NatWest																	
B & H	6	5	1	21	11	5.25	-	-	2	-	235	210	5	42.00	3-48	-	
Sunday	19	13	5	110	38 *	13.75	-	-	3	-	521	464	7	66.28	2-19	-	

PICK, R. A.   Nottinghamshire

Name: Robert Andrew Pick
Role: Left-hand bat, right-arm fast-medium bowler
Born: 19 November 1963, Nottingham
Height: 5ft 10in **Weight:** 13st
Nickname: Dad
County debut: 1983
County cap: 1987

50 wickets in a season: 4
1st-Class 50s: 5
1st-Class 5 w. in innings: 16
1st-Class 10 w. in match: 3
1st-Class catches: 50
One-Day 5 w. in innings: 2
Place in batting averages:
(1996 300th av. 8.25)
Strike rate: 116.80 (career 61.08)
Parents: Bob and Lillian
Wife and date of marriage: Jennie Ruth,
8 April 1989
Family links with cricket: Father, uncles
and cousins all play local cricket; David
Millns (Leicestershire) is brother-in-law
Education: Alderman Derbyshire
Comprehensive; High Pavement College
Qualifications: 7 O-levels, 1 A-level, senior
cricket coach

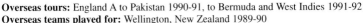

Overseas tours: England A to Pakistan 1990-91, to Bermuda and West Indies 1991-92
Overseas teams played for: Wellington, New Zealand 1989-90
Cricketers particularly admired: Bob White, Mike Hendrick, Mike Harris, Franklyn
Stephenson, Wayne Noon
Other sports followed: Ice hockey (Nottingham Panthers), soccer and American football
Relaxations: 'Spending time with family, fishing, a good pint and a nice feed'
Extras: Played for England YC v Australia YC 1983. Played football for Nottingham
Schoolboys. Took Nottinghamshire's only ever hat-trick in the NatWest against Scotland
in 1995. Awarded benefit for 1996. Released by Nottinghamshire at the end of the 1997
season
Opinions on cricket: 'Plenty but no-one who can do anything about them listens.'
Best batting: 65* Nottinghamshire v Northamptonshire, Trent Bridge 1994
Best bowling: 7-128 Nottinghamshire v Leicestershire, Leicester 1990

1997 Season

	M	Inns	NO	Runs	HS	Avge	100s	50s	Ct	St	O	M	Runs	Wkts	Avge	Best	5wI	10wM
Test																		
All First	4	2	1	15	8 *	15.00	-	-	-	-	97.2	22	307	5	61.40	2-23	-	-
1-day Int																		
NatWest	1	0	0	0	0	-	-	-	-	-	9	1	17	3	5.66	3-17	-	
B & H	3	2	1	3	2	3.00	-	-	-	-	25	1	153	1	153.00	1-43	-	
Sunday	3	1	0	8	8	8.00	-	-	1	-	17.5	1	67	1	67.00	1-30	-	

Career Performances

	M	Inns	NO	Runs	HS	Avge	100s	50s	Ct	St	Balls	Runs	Wkts	Avge	Best	5wI	10wM
Test																	
All First	195	206	55	2259	65 *	14.96	-	5	50	-	30238	16454	495	33.24	7-128	16	3
1-day Int																	
NatWest	29	16	11	121	34 *	24.20	-	-	5	-	1867	1186	50	23.72	5-22	2	
B & H	44	19	12	117	25 *	16.71	-	-	5	-	2593	1861	48	38.77	4-42	-	
Sunday	121	43	19	370	58 *	15.41	-	1	28	-	5258	4375	128	34.17	4-32	-	

PIERSON, A. R. K. Somerset

Name: Adrian Roger Kirshaw Pierson
Role: Right-hand bat, right-arm
off-spin bowler
Born: 21 July 1963, Enfield, Middlesex
Height: 6ft 4in **Weight:** 12st
Nickname: Stick, Skirlogue, Bunny, Bun
County debut: 1985 (Warwickshire), 1993
(Leicestershire)
County cap: 1995 (Leicestershire)
50 wickets in a season: 1
1st-Class 50s: 2
1st-Class 5 w. in innings: 13
1st-Class catches: 72
One-Day 5 w. in innings: 1
Place in batting averages: 241st av. 16.62
(1996 232nd av. 20.23)
Place in bowling averages: 117th av. 38.89
(1996 99th av. 35.62)
Strike rate: 78.81 (career 72.40)
Parents: Patrick and Patricia
Wife and date of marriage: Helen Majella, 29 September 1990
Education: Lochinver House Primary School; Kent College, Canterbury; Hatfield
Polytechnic
Qualifications: 8 O-levels, 2 A-levels, senior coaching award
Career outside cricket: Entrepreneur
Overseas teams played for: Walmer, South Africa; Manicaland, Zimbabwe
Cricketers particularly admired: John Emburey, Phil Edmonds, Tony Greig, Clive Rice
Young players to look out for: Darren Maddy, Aftab Habib, Matt Brimson
Other sports followed: All sports except horse racing, but especially golf
Relaxations: Gardening, music, chess, reading, driving
Extras: On Lord's groundstaff 1984-85 and on Warwickshire staff from 1985-91. First
Championship wicket was Viv Richards. Won two Gold Awards in the Benson and

Hedges. 'Literally ruffled John Major in an embarrassing encounter...!?' Released by Leicestershire at the end of the 1997 season and has joined Somerset for 1998

Opinions on cricket: 'Scheduled finish time should not be re-adjusted after an innings closes. Generally the pace of the wickets should be improved – bland wickets lead to bland cricket and cricketers. The media should try to talk the game up and find something positive to say – after all, they are earning a living from it.'

Best batting: 59 Leicestershire v Durham, Leicester 1997

Best bowling: 8-42 Leicestershire v Warwickshire, Edgbaston 1994

1997 Season

	M	Inns	NO	Runs	HS	Avge	100s	50s	Ct	St	O	M	Runs	Wkts	Avge	Best	5wI	10wM
Test																		
All First	16	16	0	266	59	16.62	-	1	8	-	499.1	104	1478	38	38.89	6-56	1	-
1-day Int																		
NatWest																		
B & H																		
Sunday	1	0	0	0	0	-	-	-	1	-	1	0	11	0	-	-	-	

Career Performances

	M	Inns	NO	Runs	HS	Avge	100s	50s	Ct	St	Balls	Runs	Wkts	Avge	Best	5wI	10wM
Test																		
All First	147	180	60	1948	59	16.23	-	3	72	-	23313	11815	322	36.69	8-42	13	-
1-day Int																		
NatWest	11	6	2	33	20 *	8.25	-	-	2	-	668	345	9	38.33	3-20	-	
B & H	17	12	8	47	11	11.75	-	-	5	-	866	530	12	44.16	3-34	-	
Sunday	68	35	14	202	29 *	9.61	-	-	31	-	2547	2094	61	34.32	5-36	1	

PIPER, K. J.   Warwickshire

Name: Keith John Piper
Role: Right-hand bat, wicket-keeper
Born: 18 December 1969, Leicester
Height: 5ft 7in   **Weight:** 10st 8lbs
Nickname: Tubbsy, Garden Boy
County debut: 1989
County cap: 1992
1st-Class 50s: 9
1st-Class 100s: 2
1st-Class catches: 372
1st-Class stumpings: 24
Place in batting averages: 264th av. 13.87
(1996 223rd av. 21.45)
Strike rate: (career 28.00)
Parents: John and Charlotte
Marital status: Single
Family links with cricket: Father plays club
cricket in Leicester
Education: Seven Sisters Junior; Somerset
Senior
Qualifications: Senior coaching award, basketball coaching award, volleyball
coaching award
Overseas tours: Haringey Cricket College to Barbados 1986, to Trinidad 1987, to
Jamaica 1988; Warwickshire to La Manga 1989, to St Lucia 1990; England A to India
1994-95, to Pakistan 1995-96
Overseas teams played for: Desmond Haynes's XI, Barbados v Haringey Cricket College
Cricketers particularly admired: Jack Russell, Alec Stewart, Dermot Reeve, Colin
Metson
Other sports followed: Snooker, football, tennis
Relaxations: Music, eating
Extras: London Young Cricketer of the Year 1989 and in the last five 1992. Played for
England YC 1989. Was batting partner (116*) to Brian Lara when he reached his 501*
Best batting: 116* Warwickshire v Durham, Edgbaston 1994
Best bowling: 1-57 Warwickshire v Nottinghamshire, Edgbaston 1992

---

75. Who has replaced Mike Watkinson as Lancashire
captain for the 1998 season?

O vodafone

1997 Season

	M	Inns	NO	Runs	HS	Avge	100s	50s	Ct	St	O	M	Runs	Wkts	Avge	Best	5wI	10wM
Test																		
All First	8	11	3	111	34 *	13.87	-	-	24	1								
1-day Int																		
NatWest	4	2	1	28	15 *	28.00	-	-	4	-								
B & H	4	3	0	8	7	2.66	-	-	3	-								
Sunday	10	4	1	53	29 *	17.66	-	-	13	1								

Career Performances

	M	Inns	NO	Runs	HS	Avge	100s	50s	Ct	St	Balls	Runs	Wkts	Avge	Best	5wI	10wM
Test																	
All First	138	191	29	3197	116 *	19.73	2	9	372	24	28	57	1	57.00	1-57	-	-
1-day Int																	
NatWest	25	12	6	104	16 *	17.33	-	-	36	2							
B & H	19	13	4	62	11 *	6.88	-	-	23	1							
Sunday	77	42	20	302	30	13.72	-	-	77	18							

POLLARD, P. R.   Nottinghamshire

Name: Paul Raymond Pollard
Role: Left-hand opening bat, right-arm medium bowler
Born: 24 September 1968, Carlton, Nottinghamshire
Height: 5ft 11in **Weight:** 12st
Nickname: Polly, Sugar Ray
County debut: 1987
County cap: 1992
1000 runs in a season: 3
1st-Class 50s: 39
1st-Class 100s: 13
1st-Class catches: 137
One-Day 100s: 5
Place in batting averages: 63rd av. 40.00 (1996 146th av. 32.04)
Strike rate: (career 68.50)
Parents: Eric (deceased) and Mary
Wife's name and date of marriage: Kate, 14 March 1992
Education: Gedling Comprehensive
Overseas teams played for: Southern Districts, Brisbane 1988; North Perth 1990

Cricketers particularly admired: David Gower, Derek Randall, Ian Botham, Graham Gooch

Other sports followed: Football, golf, ice hockey

Relaxations: Watching videos, playing golf and music

Extras: Made debut for Nottinghamshire 2nd XI in 1985. Worked in Nottinghamshire CCC office on a Youth Training Scheme. Shared stands of 222 and 282 with Tim Robinson in the same game v Kent 1989. Youngest player to reach 1000 runs for Nottinghamshire

Opinions on cricket: 'The one bouncer rule should be abolished.'

Best batting: 180 Nottinghamshire v Derbyshire, Trent Bridge 1993

Best bowling: 2-79 Nottinghamshire v Gloucestershire, Bristol 1993

1997 Season

	M	Inns	NO	Runs	HS	Avge	100s	50s	Ct	St	O	M	Runs	Wkts	Avge	Best	5wl	10wM
Test																		
All First	10	17	5	480	115 *	40.00	1	1	8	-								
1-day Int																		
NatWest	2	2	1	44	42 *	44.00	-	-	1	-								
B & H	3	3	0	70	38	23.33	-	-	-	-								
Sunday	6	5	0	129	87	25.80	-	1	4	-								

Career Performances

	M	Inns	NO	Runs	HS	Avge	100s	50s	Ct	St	Balls	Runs	Wkts	Avge	Best	5wl	10wM
Test																	
All First	153	268	20	8226	180	33.16	13	39	146	-	274	268	4	67.00	2-79	-	-
1-day Int																	
NatWest	13	13	2	369	96	33.54	-	2	4	-	18	9	0	-	-	-	
B & H	27	26	2	746	104	31.08	1	6	9	-							
Sunday	95	85	9	2666	132 *	35.07	4	13	38	-							

POOLEY, J. C.   Middlesex

Name: Jason Calvin Pooley

Role: Left-hand bat, right-arm slow bowler

Born: 8 August 1969, Hammersmith

Height: 6ft **Weight:** 13st

County debut: 1989

County cap: 1995

1000 runs in a season: 1

1st-Class 50s: 17

1st-Class 100s: 8

1st-Class catches: 81

One-Day 100s: 1
Place in batting averages: 187th av. 22.92
(1996 179th av. 27.53)
Parents: Dave and Kath
Wife and date of marriage: Justine, 30
September 1995
Children: Jake Aaron, 29 March 1997
Family links with cricket: Father and older
brother play club cricket. Younger brother
Gregg has played for Middlesex YC,
Middlesex 2nd XI and Derbyshire 2nd XI
Education: Acton High School
Overseas tours: England A to Pakistan 1995-
96
Overseas teams played for: St George's, Sydney
1988-89; Western Suburbs, Sydney 1991-92
Cricketers particularly admired: David
Gower, Desmond Haynes, Mark Ramprakash
Other sports followed: 'All sports, support Portsmouth FC'
Relaxations: 'Eating out with my wife Justine'
Extras: Voted Rapid Cricketline 2nd XI Player of the Year in 1989, his first year on the
Middlesex staff. Called up as a late replacement on the England A tour to Pakistan after
the withdrawal of Andrew Symonds
Opinions on cricket: 'Ask Angus Fraser. He will be able to tell you all you need to
know.'
Best batting: 138* Middlesex v Cambridge University, Fenner's 1996

1997 Season

	M	Inns	NO	Runs	HS	Avge	100s	50s	Ct	St	O	M	Runs	Wkts	Avge	Best	5wI	10wM
Test																		
All First	18	28	1	619	98	22.92	-	3	21	-								
1-day Int																		
NatWest	3	3	1	125	79 *	62.50	-	1	-	-								
B & H	4	4	1	82	50 *	27.33	-	1	-	-								
Sunday	13	12	3	438	94 *	48.66	-	5	5	-								

Career Performances

	M	Inns	NO	Runs	HS	Avge	100s	50s	Ct	St	Balls		Runs	Wkts	Avge	Best	5wI	10wM
Test																		
All First	81	137	12	3811	138 *	30.48	8	17	81	-	60		68	0	-	-	-	-
1-day Int																		
NatWest	8	8	1	204	79 *	29.14	-	1	1	-								
B & H	18	18	1	351	50 *	20.64	-	2	5	-								
Sunday	57	54	6	1354	109	28.20	1	10	18	-								

POWELL, J. C.   Essex

Name: Jonathan Christopher Powell
Role: Right-hand bat, off-spin bowler
Born: 13 June 1979, Harold Wood
Height: 5ft 11in **Weight:** 11st
Nickname: Powelly, Ralphy, Cyril
County debut: 1996 (one-day),
1997 (first-class)
Strike rate: 234.00 (career 234.00)
Parents: Geoff and Joan
Marital status: Single
Family links with cricket: Brother Mark
was on the Essex staff for two years and now
plays Minor Counties cricket for Norfolk.
Father plays local cricket
Education: St Peter's C of E Primary School,
Brentwood; Brentwood County High;
Chelmsford College
Qualifications: 9 GCSEs, NCA coaching
award (level 2)
Off-season: Touring South Africa with England U19 and Kenya and Sri Lanka with
England A
Overseas tours: Essex U14 to Barbados, to Hong Kong; England U19 to Pakistan
1996-97, to South Africa 1997-98; England A to Kenya and Sri Lanka 1997-98
Cricketers particularly admired: Graham Gooch, Ronnie Irani, Nasser Hussain
Young players to look out for: Stephen Peters, David Nash, Chris Read
Other sports followed: Football (Arsenal FC) and golf
Injuries: 'None, because I lost my ladder!'
Relaxations: Watching television and going out
Extras: Winner of the *Daily Telegraph* U15 Bowling Award in 1994
Opinions on cricket: '2nd XI games should be played on first-class grounds. Lunch and
tea should be longer.'
Best batting: 4* Essex v Leicestershire, Leicester 1997
Best batting: 1-109 Essex v Leicestershire, Leicester 1997

76. Who in October 1997 became the youngest player to score a first-class
double century – beating Ijaz Ahmed's 13-year record?

O vodafone

1997 Season

	M	Inns	NO	Runs	HS	Avge	100s	50s	Ct	St	O	M	Runs	Wkts	Avge	Best	5wI	10wM
Test																		
All First	1	1	1	4	4 *	-	-	-	-	-	39	5	109	1	109.00	1-109	-	-
1-day Int																		
NatWest																		
B & H																		
Sunday	5	3	1	4	2	2.00	-	-	1	-	11	1	63	2	31.50	2-10	-	

Career Performances

	M	Inns	NO	Runs	HS	Avge	100s	50s	Ct	St	Balls	Runs	Wkts	Avge	Best	5wI	10wM
Test																	
All First	1	1	1	4	4 *	-	-	-	-	-	234	109	1	109.00	1-109	-	-
1-day Int																	
NatWest																	
B & H																	
Sunday	6	3	1	4	2	2.00	-	-	1	-	114	125	4	31.25	2-10	-	

POWELL, M. J.   Warwickshire

Name: Michael James Powell
Role: Right-hand bat, right-arm medium bowler
Born: 5 April 1975, Bolton
Height: 5ft 11in **Weight:** 11st 3lbs
Nickname: Arthur
County debut: 1996
1st-Class catches: 4
Place in batting averages: 216th av. 22.75
Strike rate: (career 24.00)
Parents: Terry and Pat
Wife and date of marriage: Sarah, 26 October 1996
Education: Rivington and Blackrod High School, Horwich; Lawrence Sheriff School, Rugby
Qualifications: 6 GCSEs, 2 A-levels, basic coaching award
Career outside cricket: Part-time PE teacher
Off-season: Playing in Cape Town, South Africa
Overseas tours: England U18 (captain) to South Africa 1992-93, to Denmark (captain) 1993; England U19 to Sri Lanka 1993-94

Overseas teams played for: Avendale CC, Cape Town, 1994-95, 1996-97
Cricketers particularly admired: Ian Botham, Graham Gooch, Nick Knight, Andy Moles, Dermot Reeve
Other sports followed: Rugby, football (Manchester United), golf
Relaxations: Golf, spending time with my wife, Sarah
Extras: 2nd XI Player of the Month June 1996. Made his first-class debut against Durham in July 1996. Scored a career-best 210 against Somerset 2nd XI in July 1996
Opinions on cricket: 'Too much cricket.'
Best batting: 39 Warwickshire v Worcestershire, Worcester 1996
Best bowling: 1-18 Warwickshire v Surrey, The Oval 1996

1997 Season

	M	Inns	NO	Runs	HS	Avge	100s	50s	Ct	St	O	M	Runs	Wkts	Avge	Best	5wI	10wM
Test																		
All First	1	1	0	20	20	20.00	-	-	2	-								
1-day Int																		
NatWest																		
B & H																		
Sunday																		

Career Performances

	M	Inns	NO	Runs	HS	Avge	100s	50s	Ct	St	Balls	Runs	Wkts	Avge	Best	5wI	10wM
Test																	
All First	5	9	0	202	39	22.44	-	-	4	-	24	18	1	18.00	1-18	-	-
1-day Int									~								
NatWest																	
B & H																	
Sunday																	

77. Which county had the highest average innings total in 1997?

O vodafone

POWELL, M. J.   Glamorgan

Name: Michael John Powell
Role: Right-hand bat
Born: 3 February 1977, Abergavenny,
South Wales
Height: 6ft 1in **Weight:** 14st 4lbs
Nickname: Powelly
County debut: 1997
1st-Class 200s: 1
1st-Class catches: 1
Parents: John and Linda
Family links with cricket: 'My dad played
for Abergavenny CC and my uncle played for
Glamorgan 2nd XI'
Education: Crickhowell Primary School;
Crickhowell Secondary School; Pontypool
College

Qualifications: 5 GCSEs, BTEC National
Sports Science, NCA coaching award
Off-season: Playing for Western Suburbs in
Brisbane
Overseas teams played for: Western Suburbs, Brisbane 1997-98
Cricketers particularly admired: Stuart Law, Gareth Meredith
Young players to look out for: Dean Cosker, Mark Wagh
Relaxations: Going out with my girlfriend Emma and my friends
Extras: Scored 200 not out on his first-class debut
Opinions on cricket: 'Play more day/night cricket.'
Best batting: 200* Glamorgan v Oxford University, The Parks 1997

1997 Season

	M	Inns	NO	Runs	HS	Avge	100s	50s	Ct	St	O	M	Runs	Wkts	Avge	Best	5wI	10wM
Test																		
All First	5	8	3	286	200 *	57.20	1	-	1	-	1	0	3	0	-	-	-	-
1-day Int																		
NatWest																		
B & H																		
Sunday	3	3	0	85	42	28.33	-	-	-	-								

Career Performances

	M	Inns	NO	Runs	HS	Avge	100s	50s	Ct	St	Balls	Runs	Wkts	Avge	Best	5wI	10wM
Test																	
All Firs	5	8	3	286	200 *	57.20	1	-	1	-		6	3	0	-		-	-	-
1-day Int																	
NatWest																	
B & H																	
Sunday	3	3	0	85	42	28.33	-	-	-	-							

PRATT, A.   Durham

Name: Andrew Pratt
Role: Left-hand bat, wicket-keeper
Born: 4 March 1975, Bishop Auckland
Height: 6ft **Weight:** 11st 3lbs
County debut: 1997
Parents: Gordon and Brenda
Marital status: Single
Family links with cricket: Brother was with
MCC Young Cricketers for four years.
Younger brother plays for Durham County
Schools and father played in local leagues
Education: Parkside Comprehensive School;
Durham New College
Qualications: 9 GCSEs, Advanced Diploma
in Information Technology, cricket coaching
certificate
Cricketers particularly admired: Alan
Knott, Jack Russell

Young players to look out for: Jimmy Daley
Other sports followed: Golf and football (Middlesbrough FC)
Extras: Played for Durham County Schools at all levels and for the North of England
U15. Played for MCC Young Cricketers for three years
Opinions on cricket: 'I think that the English game is very demanding both physically
and mentally. England should take note of Australia and play less matches, especially
one-day games. I also think that the better young English players should be given more
of a chance to play for their country.'

1997 Season

	M	Inns	NO	Runs	HS	Avge	100s	50s	Ct	St	O	M	Runs	Wkts	Avge	Best	5wI	10wM
Test																		
All First	1	0	0	0	0	-	-	-	-	-	-							
1-day Int																		
NatWest																		
B & H																		
Sunday																		

Career Performances

	M	Inns	NO	Runs	HS	Avge	100s	50s	Ct	St	Balls	Runs	Wkts	Avge	Best	5wI	10wM
Test																	
All First	1	0	0	0	0	-	-	-	-	-							
1-day Int																	
NatWest																	
B & H																	
Sunday																	

PRESTON, N. W. — Kent

Name: Nicholas William Preston
Role: Right-hand bat, right-arm medium-fast bowler
Born: 22 January 1972, Dartford
Height: 6ft 1in **Weight:** 11st 5lbs
Nickname: North End, Jagback
County debut: 1996
1st-Class catches: 3
Place in batting averages:
(1996 297th av. 9.00)
Place in bowling averages:
(1996 74th av. 32.00)
Strike rate: 48.00 (career 69.41)
Parents: Susan and Geoffrey
Marital status: Single
Family links with cricket: Grandfather played for Leicestershire. Brother plays for Kent youth teams
Education: Gravesend Grammar School; Exeter University
Qualifications: BSc (Hons) Biology/Geography
Overseas teams played for: Avendale, Cape Town 1993-94; Green Point, Cape Town 1994-95

Cricketers particularly admired: Richard Hadlee, Allan Donald, Carl Hooper
Other sports followed: Rugby, tennis, football, golf
Relaxations: Golf, listening to music, watching movies, spending time with close friends
Extras: Kent League record of five wickets in five balls for Sevenoaks Vine v Midland Bank, 1994. Released by Kent at the end of the 1997 season
Opinions on cricket: 'All 2nd XI cricket should be played on first-class grounds. Four-day cricket is good, but pitches need to last four days, not two or three. The structure of league cricket needs to be improved, as does the quality of pitches played on.'
Best batting: 17* Kent v Derbyshire, Derby 1996
Best bowling: 4-68 Kent v Yorkshire, Canterbury 1996

1997 Season

	M	Inns	NO	Runs	HS	Avge	100s	50s	Ct	St	O	M	Runs	Wkts	Avge	Best	5wI	10wM
Test																		
All First	1	1	0	8	8	8.00	-	-	-	-	8	2	21	1	21.00	1-21	-	-
1-day Int																		
NatWest																		
B & H																		
Sunday																		

Career Performances

	M	Inns	NO	Runs	HS	Avge	100s	50s	Ct	St	Balls	Runs	Wkts	Avge	Best	5wI	10wM
Test																	
All First	9	12	4	71	17 *	8.87	-	-	3	-	833	373	12	31.08	4-68	-	-
1-day Int																	
NatWest	1	0	0	0	0	-	-	-	1	-	36	6	0	-		-	-
B & H																	
Sunday	5	2	1	11	7 *	11.00	-	-	-	-	78	83	0	-		-	-

PRICHARD, P. J.   Essex

Name: Paul John Prichard
Role: Right-hand bat, cover/mid-wicket fielder, county captain
Born: 7 January 1965, Brentwood, Essex
Height: 5ft 10in **Weight:** 13st
Nickname: Pablo
County debut: 1984
County cap: 1986
1000 runs in a season: 8
1st-Class 50s: 86
1st-Class 100s: 29

1st-Class 200s: 3
1st-Class catches: 178
One-Day 100s: 6
Place in batting averages: 27th av. 47.36
(1996 154th av. 30.93)
Strike rate: (career 144.50)
Parents: John and Margaret
Wife's name and date of marriage:
Separated
Children: Danielle Jade, 23 April 1993;
Alexander James, 16 August 1995
Family links with cricket: Father played
club cricket in Essex
Education: Warley Primary School;
Brentwood County High School
Qualifications: NCA coaching certificate
Off-season: Sales PR with Ridleys Brewery
Overseas tours: England A to Australia
1992-93
Overseas teams played for: VOB Cavaliers, Cape Town 1981-82; Sutherland,
Sydney 1984-87; Waverley, Sydney 1987-92
Cricketers particularly admired: Malcolm Marshall, Allan Border, David Gower,
Mark Waugh, Greg Matthews
Young players to look out for: Ashley Cowan, Owais Shah
Other sports followed: Football (West Ham), rugby union (London Irish) and rugby
league (London Broncos)
Injuries: Groin strain and hamstring, missed a total of six weeks
Relaxations: Sleeping, being with family, watching West Ham
Extras: Shared county record second wicket partnership of 403 with Graham Gooch v
Leicestershire in 1990. Britannic Assurance Cricketer of the Year 1992. Essex joint
Player of the Year 1993. Appointed Essex captain for 1995. Awarded benefit for 1996
Best batting: 245 Essex v Leicestershire, Chelmsford 1990
Best bowling: 1-28 Essex v Hampshire, Chelmsford 1991

1997 Season

	M	Inns	NO	Runs	HS	Avge	100s	50s	Ct	St	O	M	Runs	Wkts	Avge	Best	5wI	10wM
Test																		
All First	17	27	2	1184	224	47.36	3	9	10	-								
1-day Int																		
NatWest	4	4	0	156	58	39.00	-	2	1	-								
B & H	4	4	0	173	114	43.25	1	-	3	-								
Sunday	12	12	0	349	103	29.08	1	1	3	-								

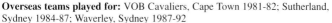

Career Performances

	M	Inns	NO	Runs	HS	Avge	100s	50s	Ct	St	Balls	Runs	Wkts	Avge	Best	5wI	10wM
Test																	
All First	280	454	46	14769	245	36.19	29	86	178	-	289	497	2	248.50	1-28	-	-
1-day Int																	
NatWest	32	31	4	1057	94	39.14	-	8	12	-							
B & H	55	52	8	1388	114	31.54	2	7	14	-							
Sunday	169	151	9	3742	107	26.35	4	17	49	-							

PYEMONT, J. P.   Sussex

Name: James Patrick Pyemont
Role: Right-hand bat, occasional off-spin bowler
Born: 10 April 1978, Eastbourne
Height: 6ft **Weight:** 12st
Nickname: Chucker, Pumper, Piggy, Pye, Pie Man, Cheggers, Martha
County debut: 1997
1st-Class catches: 2
Parents: Christopher and Christina
Marital status: Single
Family links with cricket: Father played for Cambridge University (1967) and Sussex 2nd XI
Education: St Bede's Prep School, Eastbourne; Tonbridge School; Trinity Hall, Cambridge University
Qualifications: 9 GCSEs, 3 A-levels, NCA coaching award
Career outside cricket: Student
Off-season: 'Mildly inebriated'
Overseas tours: Sussex U19 to Barbados 1993
Cricketers particularly admired: Mark Robinson, Sachin Tendulkar, Shaun Humphries
Young players to look out for: R. Allen, T. Greenwood, D. Forster, D. Smith, C. Nkonde and R. Kowenicki Esq
Other sports followed: 'Anything except horse racing and show jumping. Support Brighton and Hove Albion and am the goal-keeping coach for Trinity Hall WAFC'
Relaxations: 'Trinity Hall bar, The Pilot, Playstation, greek culture – ancient (Homer) and modern (kebabs)'
Extras: Schools Cricketer of the Year for 1996. Played for England U18 against New Zealand U19 in 1996. Sussex 2nd XI Fielder of the Year in 1997

Opinions on cricket: 'We do play too much. Second-class cricket must mirror the first-class game.'

Best batting: 22 Sussex v Oxford University, The Parks 1997

1997 Season

	M	Inns	NO	Runs	HS	Avge	100s	50s	Ct	St	O	M	Runs	Wkts	Avge	Best	5wI	10wM
Test																		
All First	1	1	0	22	22	22.00	-	-	2	-								
1-day Int																		
NatWest																		
B & H																		
Sunday	4	4	1	23	18 *	7.66	-	-	1	-								

Career Performances

	M	Inns	NO	Runs	HS	Avge	100s	50s	Ct	St	Balls	Runs	Wkts	Avge	Best	5wI	10wM
Test																	
All First	1	1	0	22	22	22.00	-	-	2	-							
1-day Int																	
NatWest																	
B & H																	
Sunday	4	4	1	23	18 *	7.66	-	-	1	-							

RADFORD, T. A.   Sussex

Name: Toby Alexander Radford
Role: Right-hand bat, 'very occasional right-arm off-spin bowler'
Born: 3 December 1971, Caerphilly, Mid Glamorgan
Height: 5ft 10in **Weight:** 10st 4lbs
Nickname: Ronnie, Jockey, Radders
County debut: 1993 (one-day, Middlesex), 1994 (first-class, Middlesex), 1996 (Sussex)
1st-Class 50s: 5
1st-Class catches: 13
Place in batting averages: (1996 281st av. 12.12)
Strike rate: (career 6.00)
Parents: Brian and Gillian
Marital status: Single
Family links with cricket: 'Dad is a senior coach and has written articles on cricket in

the national press and the book *From the Nursery End* in which he interviewed the county coaches'

Education: Park House School, Newbury; St Bartholomew's School, Newbury; City University, London

Qualifications: 9 O-levels, 3 A-levels, BA (Hons) in Journalism, senior coaching certificate

Career outside cricket: Journalism and coaching

Overseas tours: England YC to Australia 1989-90, to New Zealand 1990-91

Cricketers particularly admired: Desmond Haynes, Dean Jones, Geoff Boycott

Young players to look out for: Anurag Singh, Umer Rashid

Other sports followed: Football, snooker, speedway, ice hockey, 'boomerang throwing'

Relaxations: Cinema, videos, music (U2), crosswords, eating out, current affairs, writing

Extras: *Daily Telegraph* U15 Batsman of the Year 1987; MCC/Lord's Taverners' Player of the Year at U13, U15 and U19 age-groups. Middlesex Uncapped Player of the Year 1995. Left Middlesex at the end of the 1995 season and joined Sussex in 1996. Released by Sussex at the end of the 1997 season

Opinions on cricket: 'Standard of 2nd XI wickets is generally poor and could be improved.'

Best batting: 69* Sussex v Oxford University, The Parks 1997

Best bowling: 1-0 Middlesex v Oxford University, The Parks 1995

1997 Season

	M	Inns	NO	Runs	HS	Avge	100s	50s	Ct	St	O	M	Runs	Wkts	Avge	Best	5wI	10wM
Test																		
All First	2	4	2	131	69 *	65.50	-	2	3	-								
1-day Int																		
NatWest																		
B & H																		
Sunday																		

Career Performances

	M	Inns	NO	Runs	HS	Avge	100s	50s	Ct	St	Balls	Runs	Wkts	Avge	Best	5wI	10wM
Test										\							
All First	14	24	6	476	69 *	26.44	-	5	13	-		6	0	1	0.00	1-0	-	-
1-day Int																	
NatWest	1	1	0	82	82	82.00	-	1	-	-							
B & H																	
Sunday	4	4	1	73	38	24.33	-	-	-	-							

RAMPRAKASH, M. R. Middlesex

Name: Mark Ravindra Ramprakash
Role: Right-hand bat, right-arm
off-spin bowler
Born: 5 September 1969, Bushey, Herts
Height: 5ft 10in **Weight:** 12st 4lbs
Nickname: Ramps, Bloodaxe
County debut: 1987
County cap: 1990
Test debut: 1991
Tests: 20
One-Day Internationals: 10
1000 runs in a season: 8
1st-Class 50s: 72
1st-Class 100s: 39
1st-Class 200s: 4
1st-Class catches: 120
One-Day 100s: 7
One-Day 5 w. in innings: 1
Place in batting averages: 10th av. 55.88
(1996 33rd av. 49.68)
Strike rate: 106.00 (career 106.94)
Parents: Deonarine and Jennifer
Date of marriage: 24 September 1993
Family links with cricket: Father played club cricket in Guyana
Education: Gayton High School; Harrow Weald Sixth Form College
Qualifications: 6 O-levels, 2 A-levels
Career outside cricket: 'Any ideas welcome'
Off-season: Touring West Indies with England
Overseas tours: England YC to Sri Lanka 1986-87, to Australia (Youth World Cup) 1987-88; England A to Pakistan 1990-91; to West Indies 1991-92, to India (vice-captain) 1994-95; England to New Zealand 1991-92, to West Indies 1993-94, to Australia 1994-95, to South Africa 1995-96, to West Indies 1997-98; Lion Cubs to Barbados 1993
Overseas teams played for: Nairobi Jafferys, Kenya 1988; North Melbourne 1989
Cricketers particularly admired: 'All the great all-rounders'
Other sports followed: Snooker, football
Relaxations: 'Being at home with the family, going to movies, eating out'
Extras: Did not begin to play cricket until he was nine years old; played for Bessborough CC at age 13, played for Middlesex 2nd XI aged 16 and made first-team debut for Middlesex aged 17. Scored 204* in NCA Guernsey Festival Tournament and in 1987 made 186* on his debut for Stanmore CC. Voted Best U15 Schoolboy of 1985

by Cricket Society, Best Young Cricketer of 1986 and Most Promising Player of the Year in 1988. Played for England YC v New Zealand YC in 1989. Man of the Match in Middlesex's NatWest Trophy final win in 1988, on his debut in the competition. While on tour with England A in India was called up as replacement for Graeme Hick on the senior tour to Australia 1994-95. Finished top of the Whyte and Mackay batting ratings in 1995 and again in 1997

Opinions on cricket: 'To lose overseas players would lower playing standards greatly. People should think about the positive things that 99 per cent of them bring to county cricket. Why do the powers-that-be feel that they must constantly tamper with the rules, i.e. bouncers etc?'

Best batting: 235 Middlesex v Yorkshire, Headingley 1995
Best bowling: 3-91 Middlesex v Somerset, Taunton 1995

1997 Season

	M	Inns	NO	Runs	HS	Avge	100s	50s	Ct	St	O	M	Runs	Wkts	Avge	Best	5wI	10wM
Test	1	2	0	52	48	26.00	-	-	-	-								
All First	19	30	4	1453	190	55.88	6	7	9	-	35.2	10	126	2	63.00	1-30	-	-
1-day Int																		
NatWest	3	3	0	212	98	70.66	-	2	3	-	13	0	45	0	-		-	-
B & H	3	3	0	155	77	51.66	-	1	4	-								
Sunday	12	11	1	329	90	32.90	-	3	3	-	4.3	0	28	1	28.00	1-26	-	-

Career Performances

	M	Inns	NO	Runs	HS	Avge	100s	50s	Ct	St	Balls	Runs	Wkts	Avge	Best	5wI	10wM
Test	20	35	1	585	72	17.20	-	2	13	-	265	149	0	-	-	-	-
All First	224	364	47	14596	235	46.04	39	72	120	-	1925	1151	18	63.94	3-91	-	-
1-day Int	10	10	3	184	32	26.28	-	-	5	-	12	14	0	-		-	
NatWest	24	23	1	734	104	33.36	1	3	9	-	282	169	6	28.16	2-15	-	
B & H	35	34	7	1130	119 *	41.85	2	6	14	-	126	94	3	31.33	3-35	-	
Sunday	130	123	23	4289	147 *	42.89	4	30	39	-	289	309	13	23.76	5-38	1	

RAO, R. K.   Sussex

Name: Rajesh Krishnakant Rao
Role: Right-hand bat, right-arm leg-spin bowler
Born: 9 December 1974, London
Height: 5ft 10in **Weight:** 12st 7lbs
Nickname: Harry, Mayo, Chairman
County debut: 1996
1st-Class 50s: 3
1st-Class catches: 6
One-Day 100s: 1

Place in batting averages: 215th av. 19.73
Strike rate: 84.00 (career 99.00)
Parents: Krishnakant and Meena
Marital status: Single
Family links with cricket: Dad played for Ugandan national side. Brother Rishi has represented Middlesex regional sides. All uncles and cousins are cricket fanatics
Education: Lyon Park Primary School; Alperton High School; City of Westminster College; University of Brighton
Qualifications: 5 GCSEs, GNVQ Advanced Leisure and Tourism, BSc Sports Science, basic coaching award
Career outside cricket: Student
Overseas tours: Sussex to Portugal 1996
Cricketers particularly admired: My Dad, Sachin Tendulkar, Shane Warne, Sunil Gavaskar, Kapil Dev
Young players to look out for: 'Too many to mention'
Other sports followed: Football (Liverpool and Bedmont Eagles), tennis, snooker, badminton
Relaxations: Spending time with family and friends. Listening to music (soul, swing and rap), going on holiday
Extras: Played for England at all youth levels up to age 18. MCC Lord's Taverners Player of the Year 1989 (at Under 14)
Opinions on cricket: 'Standards of 2nd XI grounds and pitches must improve in order for younger players to be better prepared to first team introduction. All second team Championship matches should be four days instead of three. The golden hour rule should be abolished.'
Best batting: 89 Sussex v Essex, Hove 1997
Best bowling: 1-14 Sussex v Middlesex, Lord's 1997

1997 Season

	M	Inns	NO	Runs	HS	Avge	100s	50s	Ct	St	O	M	Runs	Wkts	Avge	Best	5wl	10wM
Test																		
All First	11	20	1	375	89	19.73	-	3	6	-	28	3	100	2	50.00	1-14	-	-
1-day Int																		
NatWest	2	2	0	158	158	79.00	1	-	2	-								
B & H	2	2	0	76	61	38.00	-	1	1	-								
Sunday	12	12	0	266	60	22.16	-	2	5	-	5	0	34	0	-		-	-

Career Performances

	M	Inns	NO	Runs	HS	Avge	100s	50s	Ct	St	Balls	Runs	Wkts	Avge	Best	5wI	10wM
Test																	
All First	13	23	2	462	89	22.00	-	3	6	-	198	107	2	53.50	1-14	-	-
1-day Int																	
NatWest	2	2	0	158	158	79.00	1	-	2	-							
B & H	2	2	0	76	61	38.00	-	1	1	-							
Sunday	23	23	1	559	91	25.40	-	5	9	-	84	82	3	27.33	3-31	-	

RASHID, U. B. A.   Middlesex

Name: Umer Bin Abdul Rashid
Role: Left-hand bat, slow left-arm bowler
Born: 6 February 1976, Southampton
Height: 6ft 3in **Weight:** 12st 7lbs
Nickname: Umie, Looney, Bin
County debut: 1995 (one-day), 1996 (first-class)
Parents: Mirza and Sebea
Marital status: Single
Education: Southfield Combined First and
Middle School; Ealing Green High; Ealing
Tertiary College; South Bank University
Qualifications: 7 GCSEs, 2 A-levels,
'currently studying for BA (Hons) in
Business Studies'
Cricketers particularly admired: Carl
Hooper, Aamir Sohail
Young players to look out for: Vikram
Solanki, Owais Shah, David Nash, David
Sales, Anurag Singh

Other sports followed: Football (Southampton FC), Formula One
Relaxations: 'Chilling out with family and friends, playing Nintendo and computer
games. A keen reader of books by John Grisham'
Extras: Lord's Taverners' Cricketer of the Year 1994-95. Played England U19 against
South Africa in 1995. Played for the Combined Universities side in the B & H Cup
Opinions on cricket: 'I think that a two-tier league system should be introduced to
improve the intensity and the standard of cricket. This will allow all of the best players
to play with each other and thus prepare them for international cricket.'
Best batting: 9 Middlesex v Gloucestershire, Lord's 1996

1997 Season

	M	Inns	NO	Runs	HS	Avge	100s	50s	Ct	St	O	M	Runs	Wkts	Avge	Best	5wI	10wM
Test																		
All First																		
1-day Int																		
NatWest																		
B & H	5	5	0	150	82	30.00	-	1	2	-	43	0	243	4	60.75	1-33	-	
Sunday																		

Career Performances

	M	Inns	NO	Runs	HS	Avge	100s	50s	Ct	St	Balls	Runs	Wkts	Avge	Best	5wI	10wM
Test																		
All First	1	2	0	15	9	7.50	-	-	-	-	36	17	0	-	-	-	-
1-day Int																		
NatWest																		
B & H	12	11	2	246	82	27.33	-	1	3	-	663	543	9	60.33	2-57	-	
Sunday	7	4	0	14	8	3.50	-	-	-	-	240	235	7	33.57	2-34	-	

RATCLIFFE, J. D.   Surrey

Name: Jason David Ratcliffe
Role: Right-hand opening bat, right-arm
medium/off-spin bowler, slip fielder
Born: 19 June 1969, Solihull
Height: 6ft 4in **Weight:** 14st 7lbs
Nickname: Ratters, Fridge
County debut: 1988 (Warwickshire),
1995 (Surrey)
1st-Class 50s: 34
1st-Class 100s: 4
1st-Class catches: 58
One-Day 100s: 1
Place in batting averages: 117th av. 31.62
(1996 136th av. 32.93)
Strike rate: 348.00 (career 94.30)
Parents: David and Sheila
Wife and date of marriage: Andrea, 7
January 1995
Family links with cricket: Father (D.P.
Ratcliffe) played for Warwickshire 1956-62
Education: Meadow Green Primary School; Sharmans Cross Secondary School;
Solihull Sixth Form College

Qualifications: 6 O-levels; NCA staff coach
Career outside cricket: Sports PR and marketing
Overseas tours: NCA (South) to Ireland 1988; Warwickshire to South Africa 1991-92
Overseas teams played for: West End, Kimberley, South Africa 1987-88; Belmont, Newcastle, NSW 1990-91; Penrith, Sydney 1992-94
Cricketers particularly admired: Nadeem Shahid
Young players to look out for: Ben Hollioake
Other sports followed: Football, tennis, golf
Relaxations: Music, reading, eating out
Extras: Scored a century against Boland on Warwickshire tour to South Africa 1991-92.
Best batting: 135 Surrey v Worcestershire, Worcester 1997
Best bowling: 2-26 Surrey v Yorkshire, Middlesbrough 1996

1997 Season

	M	Inns	NO	Runs	HS	Avge	100s	50s	Ct	St	O	M	Runs	Wkts	Avge	Best	5wI	10wM
Test																		
All First	15	26	2	759	135	31.62	1	4	3	-	58	10	177	1	177.00	1-14	-	-
1-day Int																		
NatWest	2	2	0	42	39	21.00	-	-	-	-								
B & H	3	2	1	13	13 *	13.00	-	-	1	-	8	0	42	2	21.00	2-42	-	
Sunday	13	10	0	290	82	29.00	-	3	5	-	19	0	92	2	46.00	1-16	-	

Career Performances

	M	Inns	NO	Runs	HS	Avge	100s	50s	Ct	St	Balls		Runs	Wkts	Avge	Best	5wI	10wM
Test																		
All First	111	203	11	5666	135	29.51	4	34	58	-	943		578	10	57.80	2-26	-	-
1-day Int																		
NatWest	11	11	1	379	105	37.90	1	2	1	-	30		20	0	-		-	-
B & H	5	4	1	56	29	18.66	-	-	1	-	48		42	2	21.00	2-42	-	
Sunday	34	30	3	567	82	21.00	-	3	11	-	277		271	7	38.71	2-11	-	

RAWNSLEY, M. J.   Worcestershire

Name: Matthew James Rawnsley
Role: Right-hand bat, slow left-arm bowler
Born: 8 June 1976, Birmingham
Height: 6ft 4in **Weight:** 12st
County debut: 1996
1st-Class catches: 1
Strike rate: 86.50 (career 88.63)
Parents: Christopher (deceased) and June
Marital status: Single

Education: Northfield Manor Primary School; Bourneville Secondary School, Birmingham; Brynteg Comprehensive, Bridgend
Qualifications: 9 GCSEs and 4 A-levels, NCA coaching award, qualified canoe instructor
Overseas tours: Worcestershire CCC to Zimbabwe 1997
Overseas teams played for: Kumeu, Auckland 1995-96; Sunrise Sports Club, Harare, Zimbabwe 1996-97
Cricketers particularly admired: Phil Tufnell, Richard Illingworth
Young players to look out for: 'None that I rate higher than myself'
Other sports followed: Rugby union and canoeing
Injuries: Sprained ankle and sore finger, out for a total of five weeks
Relaxations: 'Scouring Teletext (what an interesting life I lead) and, of course, drinking'
Extras: Holds the record for the most wickets at the Oxford festival (27). Warwickshire U19 Player of the Year in 1995. Got ten wickets and scored 133 not out against Gloucestershire 2nd XI in 1997
Opinions on cricket: 'I have faith in the ECB's new proposals. We need to come round to a more Australian way of thinking, i.e. less cricket but of a higher quality, thus putting more pressure on players to perform.'
Best batting: 26 Worcestershire v Essex, Chelmsford 1997
Best bowling: 3-67 Worcestershire v Pakistan A, Worcester 1997

1997 Season

	M	Inns	NO	Runs	HS	Avge	100s	50s	Ct	St	O	M	Runs	Wkts	Avge	Best	5wI	10wM
Test																		
All First	4	5	2	71	26	23.66	-	-	-	-	86.3	23	218	6	36.33	3-67	-	-
1-day Int																		
NatWest	1	0	0	0	0	-	-	-	-	-	11	2	50	2	25.00	2-50	-	
B & H																			
Sunday	2	1	1	1	1 *	-	-	-	-	-	15	0	83	4	20.75	2-29	-	

Career Performances

	M	Inns	NO	Runs	HS	Avge	100s	50s	Ct	St		Balls	Runs	Wkts	Avge	Best	5wI	10wM
Test																		
All First	8	6	3	75	26	25.00	-	-	1	-		975	437	11	39.72	3-67	-	-
1-day Int																		
NatWest	1	0	0	0	0	-	-	-	-	-		66	50	2	25.00	2-50	-	
B & H																		
Sunday	5	4	1	12	7	4.00	-	-	-	-		167	152	4	38.00	2-29	-	

READ, C. M. W. Gloucestershire

Name: Christopher Mark Wells Read
Role: Right-hand bat, wicket-keeper
Born: 10 August 1978, Paignton, Devon
Height: 5ft 8in **Weight:** 10st 7lbs
Nickname: Readie
County debut: 1997 (one-day)
Parents: Geoffrey and Caroline
Family links with cricket: Father played club cricket and is a very keen supporter
Education: Roselands Primary School; Torquay Boys' Grammar School; University of Bath
Qualifications: 9 GCSEs, 4 A-levels, NCA coaching award
Off-season: England A tour to Kenya and Sri Lanka
Overseas tours: West of England U13 to Holland 1991; West of England U15 to West Indies 1992-93; England U17 to Holland (International Youth tournament) 1995; England U19 to Pakistan 1996-97; England A to Kenya and Sri Lanka 1997-98
Cricketers particularly admired: Alan Knott, Jack Russell, Graham Thorpe
Young players to look out for: David Sales
Other sports followed: Football (Everton), rugby union (Bath), hockey
Relaxations: Listening to music, sleeping, going out with friends
Extras: Represented Devon in Minor Counties Championship and NatWest in 1995, 1996 and 1997. Played for England U18 against New Zealand U19 in 1996. Has also played hockey for Devon U18 and U21 and for West of England U17. Played for England U19 in the series against Zimbabwe U19. He was selected for the England A tour to Kenya and Sri Lanka without having played a first-class game. Asked to be released by Gloucestershire whilst still on tour with England A

Opinions on cricket: '2nd XI games should be extended to four days to prepare players better for the jump to the 1st XI. More 2nd XI games should be played on county pitches. Tea should last 30 minutes.'

1997 Season

	M	Inns	NO	Runs	HS	Avge	100s	50s	Ct	St	O	M	Runs	Wkts	Avge	Best	5wI	10wM
Test																		
All First																		
1-day Int																		
NatWest	1	1	0	3	3	3.00	-	-	1	1								
B & H																		
Sunday	1	1	0	0	0	0.00	-	-	-	-								

Career Performances

	M	Inns	NO	Runs	HS	Avge	100s	50s	Ct	St	Balls		Runs	Wkts	Avge	Best	5wI	10wM
Test																		
All First																		
1-day Int																		
NatWest	3	2	0	40	37	20.00	-	-	1	1								
B & H																		
Sunday	1	1	0	0	0	0.00	-	-	-	-								

REIFFEL, P. R.   Northamptonshire

Name: Paul Ronald Reiffel
Role: Right-hand bat, right-arm
fast-medium bowler
Born: 19 April 1966, Box Hill,
Victoria, Australia
Height: 6ft 2in
County debut: No first-team appearance
Test debut: 1991-92
Tests: 29
One-Day Internationals: 75
1st-Class 50s: 8
1st-Class 5 w. in innings: 14
1st-Class 10 w. in match: 2
Place in bowling averages: 4th av. 18.57
Strike rate: 40.42 (career 60.48)
Education: Jordanville Technical School
Overseas teams played for:
Victoria 1987-1998

Overseas tours: Australia XI to Zimbabwe 1991-92; Australia to New Zealand 1992-93, to England 1993, to South Africa 1993-94, to Sharjah 1993-94, to West Indies 1994-95, to India and Pakistan (World Cup) 1995-96, to Sri Lanka and India 1996-97, to South Africa 1996-97, to England 1998
Extras: Was called up to replace the injured Andy Bichel in the 1998 Ashes tour and remained in the side for the rest of the series, until missing the last Test at The Oval. Will be Northamptonshire's overseas player for the 1998 season
Best batting: 86 Victoria v Tasmania, St Kilda 1990-91
Best bowling: 6-57 Victoria v Tasmania, St Kilda 1990-91

1997 Season

	M	Inns	NO	Runs	HS	Avge	100s	50s	Ct	St	O	M	Runs	Wkts	Avge	Best	5wl	10wM
Test	4	6	3	179	54 *	59.66	-	1	1	-	112.1	28	293	11	26.63	5-49	1	-
All First	8	9	4	242	56	48.40	-	2	2	-	188.4	49	520	28	18.57	5-49	2	-
1-day Int																		
NatWest																			
B & H																			
Sunday																			

Career Performances

	M	Inns	NO	Runs	HS	Avge	100s	50s	Ct	St	Balls	Runs	Wkts	Avge	Best	5wl	10wM
Test	29	41	12	648	56	22.34	-	3	14	-	5293	2401	91	26.38	6-71	5	-
All First	115	137	42	2137	86	22.49	-	8	58	-	22623	10349	374	27.67	6-57	14	2
1-day Int	75	48	19	441	58	15.20	-	1	23	-	3898	2526	90	28.06	4-13	-	
NatWest																	
B & H																	
Sunday																	

RENSHAW, S. J.   Hampshire

Name: Simon John Renshaw
Role: Right-hand bat, right-arm fast bowler
Born: 6 March 1974, Bebington, Wirral
Height: 6ft 3in **Weight:** 14st 6lbs
Nickname: Rennie Arnoux, Toady
County debut: 1996
1st-Class 50s: 1
1st-Class 5 w. in innings: 1
One-Day 5 w. in innings: 1
1st-Class catches: 3
Place in batting averages: 193rd av. 22.41
Place in bowling averages: 99th av. 34.54 (1996 143rd av. 49.53)

Strike rate: 57.81 (career 67.03)
Parents: Michael and Barbara
Marital status: Engaged
Family links with cricket: Father and brother play in local league competitions
Education: Birkenhead Prep School; Birkenhead; Leeds University
Qualifications: 9 GCSEs, 4 A-levels, BSc in Microbiology
Career outside cricket: 'None yet but expected to be in microbiology'
Off-season: Coaching and working in Southampton
Overseas teams played for: Mulgrave, Melbourne 1995-96; Ashwood, Melbourne 1996-97
Cricketers particularly admired: Ian Botham, Viv Richards

Young players to look out for: David Sales, Alex Tudor
Other sports followed: Football (Everton FC)
Relaxations: Music, films and reading
Extras: Was captain of the Birkenhead U17 side that won the Barclays Knock-out Cup in 1991. Captain of Birkenhead 1st XI in 1992. Represented North of England Schools and MCC Schools. Played for Cheshire in the Minor Counties and for Cheshire U25 in the Bain Hogg Trophy in 1995. Captain of Cheshire U19 at the Cambridge Festival and was voted Cheshire Young Player of the Year. Best performance in the Minor Counties was 7 for 19 against Shropshire. Played for the Combined Universities in the Benson and Hedges Cup and against West Indies at The Parks. Priestley Cup Final Winner with Farsley in 1995. Took six for 25 against Surrey in the Benson & Hedges Cup – the best bowling by a Hampshire bowler in that competition
Opinions on cricket: 'Current County Championship is stagnating. Two divisions with promotion and relegation would increase interest. There should be a greater liaison between minor counties and major ones. There is no structured development plan for any boy who lives outside the major county catchment area, which means that many players of county standard are ignored.'
Best batting: 56 Hampshire v Surrey, Guildford 1997
Best bowling: 5-110 Hampshire v Derbyshire, Chesterfield 1997

---

78. Which county had the lowest average innings total in 1997 ?

 vodafone

1997 Season

	M	Inns	NO	Runs	HS	Avge	100s	50s	Ct	St	O	M	Runs	Wkts	Avge	Best	5wl	10wM
Test																		
All First	13	19	7	269	56	22.41	-	1	3	-	356.3	62	1278	37	34.54	5-110	1	-
1-day Int																		
NatWest	2	0	0	0	0	-	-	-	1	-	19	2	88	2	44.00	2-71	-	
B & H	5	4	1	3	2 *	1.00	-	-	1	-	49	6	202	13	15.53	6-25	1	
Sunday	17	12	7	104	25	20.80	-	-	1	-	115	1	621	22	28.22	3-45	-	

Career Performances

	M	Inns	NO	Runs	HS	Avge	100s	50s	Ct	St	Balls	Runs	Wkts	Avge	Best	5wl	10wM
Test																	
All First	21	27	12	279	56	18.60	-	1	6	-	3620	2212	54	40.96	5-110	1	-
1-day Int																	
NatWest	4	2	0	5	4	2.50	-	-	1	-	186	133	4	33.25	2-20	-	
B & H	10	6	2	3	2 *	0.75	-	-	2	-	588	412	18	22.88	6-25	1	
Sunday	22	14	9	111	25	22.20	-	-	1	-	828	730	25	29.20	3-45	-	

RHODES, S. J.   Worcestershire

Name: Steven John Rhodes
Role: Right-hand bat, wicket-keeper, county vice-captain
Born: 17 June 1964, Bradford
Height: 5ft 8in **Weight:** 12st
Nickname: Bumpy
County debut: 1981 (Yorkshire), 1985 (Worcestershire)
County cap: 1986 (Worcestershire)
Benefit: 1996
Test debut: 1994
Tests: 11
One-Day Internationals: 9
1000 runs in a season: 1
1st-Class 50s: 57
1st-Class 100s: 9
1st-Class catches: 882
1st-Class stumpings: 108
Place in batting averages: 98th av. 34.35 (1996 79th av. 39.12)
Parents: William Ernest and Norma Kathleen
Wife and date of marriage: Judy Ann, 6 March 1993

Children: Holly Jade, 20 August 1985; George Harry, 26 October 1993; Lily Amber, 3 March 1995
Family links with cricket: Father played for Nottinghamshire 1959-64
Education: Bradford Moor Junior School; Lapage St Middle; Carlton-Bolling Comprehensive, Bradford
Qualifications: 4 O-levels, coaching certificate
Career outside cricket: Labourer; trainee sports shop manager
Overseas tours: England A to Sri Lanka 1986-86; England A to Zimbabwe and Kenya 1989-90, to Pakistan 1990-91, to West Indies 1991-92, to South Africa 1993-94; England to Australia 1994-95
Overseas teams played for: Past Bros, Bundaberg, Queensland; Avis Vogeltown, New Plymouth, New Zealand; Melville, Perth, Australia
Cricketers particularly admired: Graeme Hick, Richard Hadlee
Other sports followed: Horse racing and golf
Relaxations: Horse racing
Extras: Played for England YC v Australia YC in 1983 and holds record for most victims in an innings for England YC. Youngest wicket-keeper to play for Yorkshire. Released by Yorkshire to join Worcestershire at end of 1984 season. Selected for cancelled England tour to India 1988-89 and was one of four players put on stand-by as reserves for 1992 World Cup squad. Writes a weekly cricket column for a Birmingham newspaper. One of the *Wisden* Cricketers of the Year for 1994. Awarded benefit for 1996. Overtook David Bairstow as the wicket-keeper with the most dismissals in the Sunday League
Opinions on cricket: 'As long as English cricket is tough and competitive I see no reason why England shouldn't be one of the top two Test-playing cricketing nations. To be this, we must remain fresh with the right balance between rest and competition.'
Best batting: 122* Worcestershire v Young Australia, Worcester 1995

1997 Season

	M	Inns	NO	Runs	HS	Avge	100s	50s	Ct	St	O	M	Runs	Wkts	Avge	Best	5wI	10wM
Test																		
All First	18	23	6	584	78	34.35	-	4	44	3								
1-day Int																		
NatWest	2	2	2	7	7 *	-	-	-	2	-								
B & H	5	4	0	44	37	11.00	-	-	6	-								
Sunday	16	7	4	38	19	12.66	-	-	20	4								

Career Performances

	M	Inns	NO	Runs	HS	Avge	100s	50s	Ct	St	Balls	Runs	Wkts	Avge	Best	5wI	10wM
Test	11	17	5	294	65 *	24.50	-	1	46	3							
All First	328	450	126	10837	122 *	33.44	9	57	822	108	6	30	0	-	-	-	-
1-day Int	9	8	2	107	56	17.83	-	1	9	2							
NatWest	39	30	11	394	61	20.73	-	2	47	7							
B & H	62	44	7	525	51 *	14.18	-	1	85	9							
Sunday	198	119	31	1612	48 *	18.31	-	-	206	59							

RIDGWAY, P. M.   Lancashire

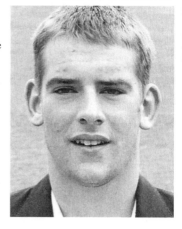

Name: Paul Matthew Ridgway
Role: Right-hand bat, right-arm
fast-medium bowler
Born: 13 February 1977, Keighley, Yorkshire
Height: 6ft 4in **Weight:** 16st 5lbs
Nickname: Ridgeback, Balloon
County debut: 1997
Strike rate: 117.00 (career 117.00)
Parents: Peter and Judith
Marital status: Single
Family links with cricket: Father is first
cousin to Don Wilson (Yorkshire and
England)
Education: Hellifield Primary School;
Settle High School
Qualifications: GCSEs, BTEC Business and
Finance
Career outside cricket: Dump truck driver
Off-season: 'Getting ready for the season'
Cricketers particularly admired: Ian Austin, Steve Titchard
Young players to look out for: Tim Green
Other sports followed: Rugby league, superbikes
Injuries: Shin, out for two weeks
Relaxations: Music
Opinions on cricket: 'Not a long enough time to have lunch and tea.'
Best bowling: 2-46 Lancashire v Kent, Old Trafford 1997

1997 Season

	M	Inns	NO	Runs	HS	Avge	100s	50s	Ct	St	O	M	Runs	Wkts	Avge	Best	5wI	10wM
Test																		
All First	2	2	1	0	0*	0.00	-	-	-	-	39	6	163	2	81.50	2-46	-	-
1-day Int																		
NatWest																		
B & H																		
Sunday																		

---

79. Which county had the highest average of runs
conceded per innings in 1997?

Career Performances

	M	Inns	NO	Runs	HS	Avge	100s	50s	Ct	St	Balls	Runs	Wkts	Avge	Best	5wI	10wM
Test																	
All First	2	2	1	0	0 *	0.00	-	-	-	-	234	163	2	81.50	2-46	-	-
1-day Int																	
NatWest	2	1	1	47	47 *	-	-	-	-	1	-	120	103	5	20.60	4-62	-
B & H																	
Sunday																	

RIPLEY, D.　　　　Northamptonshire

Name: David Ripley
Role: Right-hand bat, wicket-keeper
Born: 13 September 1966, Leeds
Height: 5ft 11in **Weight:** 12st
Nickname: Rips, Spud
County debut: 1984
County cap: 1987
1st-Class 50s: 21
1st-Class 100s: 6
1st-Class catches: 526
1st-Class stumpings: 74
Place in batting averages: 48th av. 42.88
(1996 30th av. 49.77)
Strike rate: (career 30.00)
Parents: Arthur and Brenda
Wife and date of marriage: Jackie, 24
September 1988

Children: Joe David, 11 October 1989;
George William, 5 March 1994
Education: Woodlesford Primary; Royds High, Leeds
Qualifications: 5 O-levels, NCA advanced coach
Career outside cricket: Youth development coaching for Northants
Off-season: Coaching and working on benefit
Overseas tours: England YC to West Indies 1984-85; Northants to Durban, South
Africa 1991-92, to Cape Town 1992-93, to Zimbabwe 1994-95, to Johannesburg 1996
Overseas teams played for: Marists and Poverty Bay, New Zealand 1985-87
Cricketers particularly admired: Alan Knott, Bob Taylor 'and many other keepers',
Clive Radley, Ian Botham, Geoff Boycott, Dennis Lillee
Young players to look out for: David Sales, Michael Davies
Other sports followed: Football (Leeds United), rugby league (Castleford), golf
Relaxations: 'Eating out, and sampling different bitters'

Extras: Finished top of wicket-keepers' dismissals list for 1988 and 1992 and was voted Wombwell Cricket Lovers' Society Best Wicket-keeper 1992. Played for England YC v Sri Lanka 1986. Northamptonshire Player of the Year in 1997
Opinions on cricket: 'I think we should have taken the opportunity for two divisions in the championship.'
Best batting: 134* Northamptonshire v Yorkshire, Scarborough 1986
Best bowling: 2-89 Northamptonshire v Essex, Ilford 1987

1997 Season

	M	Inns	NO	Runs	HS	Avge	100s	50s	Ct	St	O	M	Runs	Wkts	Avge	Best	5wI	10wM
Test																		
All First	17	24	6	772	92	42.88	-	6	30	7								
1-day Int																		
NatWest																		
B & H	5	2	1	20	11 *	20.00	-	-	7	2								
Sunday	3	3	0	35	20	11.66	-	-	1	-								

Career Performances

	M	Inns	NO	Runs	HS	Avge	100s	50s	Ct	St	Balls	Runs	Wkts	Avge	Best	5wI	10wM
Test																	
All First	247	323	87	6249	134 *	26.47	6	21	526	74	60	103	2	51.50	2-89	-	-
1-day Int																	
NatWest	35	20	9	130	27 *	11.81	-	-	36	3							
B & H	42	27	10	325	36 *	19.11	-	-	44	6							
Sunday	137	83	36	867	52 *	18.44	-	1	96	13							

ROBERTS, D. J.   Northamptonshire

Name: David James Roberts
Role: Right-hand bat
Born: 29 December 1976, Truro, Cornwall
Height: 5ft 11in **Weight:** 12st 7lbs
Nickname: Robbo, Chips, Maverick
County debut: 1996
1st-Class 50s: 2
1st-Class 100s: 1
1st-Class catches: 1
Place in batting averages: 125th av. 29.61 (1996 99th av. 36.28)
Parents: Dennis and Pam
Marital status: Single
Family links with cricket: Cousin, Chris Bullen, played for Surrey. Father played cricket for local club and is also a youth coach. Mother is a keen supporter!

Education: Mullion County Primary; Mullion Comprehensive
Qualifications: 9 GCSEs, senior cricket coach
Career outside cricket: Coaching
Off-season: Coaching in Bedford schools
Overseas tours: West of England to Barbados, Trinidad and Tobago 1990-91 and 1991-92 (captain)
Cricketers particularly admired: Graeme Hick, Mal Loye, David Gower
Young players to look out for: John Blain, Graeme Swann, Richard Logan
Other sports followed: Football (Manchester United), NBA basketball and all sports
Injuries: Tendonitis in left wrist, out for seven weeks
Relaxations: Watching television, listening to music, playing football
Extras: Played for English Schools since the age of 14, including matches against South Africa in 1992. Represented England U17 against India U17 in 1994
Opinions on cricket: 'Tea is too short, should be increased from 10 minutes to 30 minutes. 2nd XI cricket should be played at first-class grounds instead of club grounds.'
Best batting: 117 Northamptonshire v Essex, Northampton 1997

1997 Season

	M	Inns	NO	Runs	HS	Avge	100s	50s	Ct	St	O	M	Runs	Wkts	Avge	Best	5wI	10wM
Test																		
All First	7	13	0	385	117	29.61	1	-	1	-								
1-day Int																		
NatWest																		
B & H																		
Sunday																		

Career Performances

	M	Inns	NO	Runs	HS	Avge	100s	50s	Ct	St	Balls	Runs	Wkts	Avge	Best	5wI	10wM
Test																	
All First	11	20	0	639	117	31.95	1	2	1	-							
1-day Int																	
NatWest																	
B & H																	
Sunday																	

ROBERTS, G. M.   Derbyshire

Name: Glenn Martin Roberts
Role: Left-hand bat, slow left-arm bowler
Born: 4 November 1973, Huddersfield
Height: 5ft 11in **Weight:** 12st
Nickname: Glenda, Robbo
County debut: 1996
1st-Class 50s: 1
1st-Class catches: 1
Strike rate: (career 252.00)
Parents: Tony and Margaret
Marital status: Single
Family links with cricket: 'Major influence
was my grandfather who played Huddersfield
League cricket. My parents took me
everywhere to play and support me'
Education: King James's School; Greenhead
College, Huddersfield; Carnegie College,
Leeds Metropolitan University
Qualifications: 8 GCSEs, 4 A-levels, BEd
(Hons) Physical Education, FA Teaching Certificate, NCA advanced coach
Off-season: Playing district cricket in Australia
Cricketers particularly admired: Phil Carrick, Phil Tufnell, Kim Barnett
Young players to look out for: Andrew Harris, Kevin Dean, Steve Griffiths
Other sports followed: Rugby league (Huddersfield) and football
Relaxations: Jogging, fitness, gym work, 'socialising with Mark Vincent'
Extras: Played for Yorkshire from U14 to U19 and captained the U16s and the U19s.
Was a member of the Yorkshire Academy for two years. Scored 50 batting at No.9 on
his Championship debut for Derbyshire and featured in a Derbyshire record eighth-
wicket stand of 118 with Karl Krikken
Opinions on cricket: 'Introduce fitness trainers, sports psychologists, dieticians,
nutritionists and other support systems to maintain and enhance the performance of
county and international players. Optional schemes for players to obtain professional
qualifications during the off-season e.g. sports coaching, PE teaching, etc.'
Best batting: 52 Derbyshire v Somerset, Taunton 1996
Best bowling: 1-55 Derbyshire v Somerset, Taunton 1996

---

80. Which county had the lowest average of runs
conceded per innings in 1997?

1997 Season

	M	Inns	NO	Runs	HS	Avge	100s	50s	Ct	St	O	M	Runs	Wkts	Avge	Best	5wI	10wM
Test																		
All First	2	3	1	45	30 *	22.50	-	-	-	-	6	1	8	0	-	-	-	-
1-day Int																		
NatWest																		
B & H	5	3	1	15	12	7.50	-	-	2	-	46	1	228	9	25.33	3-45	-	
Sunday	6	5	2	19	9	6.33	-	-	1	-	32.3	0	195	0	-	-	-	

Career Performances

	M	Inns	NO	Runs	HS	Avge	100s	50s	Ct	St	Balls	Runs	Wkts	Avge	Best	5wI	10wM
Test																	
All First	3	4	1	97	52	32.33	-	1	1	-	252	81	1	81.00	1-55	-	-
1-day Int																	
NatWest																	
B & H	5	3	1	15	12	7.50	-	-	2	-	276	228	9	25.33	3-45	-	
Sunday	11	7	4	25	9	8.33	-	-	3	-	423	393	6	65.50	2-28	-	

ROBINSON, D. D. J.   Essex

Name: Darren David John Robinson
Role: Right-hand opening bat, occasional right-arm medium bowler
Born: 2 March 1973, Braintree, Essex
Height: 5ft 11in **Weight:** 14st
Nickname: Pie shop 'or any other name that Fletch might call me'
County debut: 1993
County cap: 1997
1st-Class 50s: 13
1st-Class 100s: 4
1st-Class catches: 34
Place in batting averages: 92nd av. 35.00 (1996 113th av. 35.14)
Parents: David and Dorothy
Marital status: Engaged to Alyssa Jarvi ('she's bloody lovely'), date set in September 1998
Family links with cricket: Father plays club cricket for Halstead
Education: Tabor High School, Braintree; Chelmsford College of Further Education
Qualifications: 5 GCSEs, BTEC National Diploma in Building and Construction

Career outside cricket: Civil engineering and surveying
Overseas tours: England U18 to Canada 1991; England U19 to Pakistan 1991-92
Overseas teams played for: Waverley, Sydney 1992-94; Eden Roshill CC, Auckland 1995-96
Cricketers particularly admired: Stuart Law ('drinking ability'), Graham Gooch
Young players to look out for: Stephen Peters, Jonathan Powell
Other sports followed: Golf, football, rugby, swimming
Relaxations: Reading crime novels, music, eating out, pubs
Extras: *Daily Telegraph* batting award 1988 and International Youth Tournament in Canada batting award 1991
Opinions on cricket: 'Cricket's a great game when everything is going well, but a pain in the arse when it's not.'
Best batting: 148 Essex v Worcestershire, Chelmsford 1997

1997 Season

	M	Inns	NO	Runs	HS	Avge	100s	50s	Ct	St	O	M	Runs	Wkts	Avge	Best	5wl	10wM
Test																		
All First	14	22	1	735	148	35.00	2	3	13	-								
1-day Int																		
NatWest	5	3	0	74	62	24.66	-	1	1	-								
B & H	1	1	0	8	8	8.00	-	-	-	-								
Sunday	14	14	2	300	38	25.00	-	-	7	-	0.5	0	7	1	7.00	1-7	-	

Career Performances

	M	Inns	NO	Runs	HS	Avge	100s	50s	Ct	St	Balls	Runs	Wkts	Avge	Best	5wl	10wM
Test																	
All First	46	82	3	2335	148	29.55	4	13	47	-	36	31	0	-	-	-	-
1-day Int																	
NatWest	12	10	0	202	62	20.20	-	2	4	-							
B & H	11	10	2	200	36	25.00	-	-	2	-							
Sunday	46	46	6	973	80	24.32	-	3	14	-	17	26	1	26.00	1-7	-	

ROBINSON, M. A.   Sussex

Name: Mark Andrew Robinson
Role: Right-hand bat, right-arm medium-fast bowler
Born: 23 November 1966, Hull
Height: 6ft 3in **Weight:** 13st 3lbs
Nickname: Jessy, Coddy, Scoope, Tiger, Stormy, Storm
County debut: 1987 (Northamptonshire), 1991 (Yorkshire), 1996 (Sussex)
County cap: 1990 (Northamptonshire), 1992 (Yorkshire)
1st-Class 5 w. in innings: 9

1st-Class 10 w. in match: 2
1st-Class catches: 35
Place in batting averages: 296th av. 7.12
Place in bowling averages: 67th av. 29.70
Strike rate: 56.04 (career 67.06)
Parents: Malcolm and Joan
Wife and date of marriage: Julia, 8 October 1994
Children: Samuel Lewis, 11 January 1996
Family links with cricket: Grandfather a prominent local cricketer and 'father was hostile bowler in the back garden'
Education: Fifth Avenue Primary; Endike Junior High; Hull Grammar School
Qualifications: 6 O-levels, 2 A-levels, advanced cricket coach, badminton coach, rugby union coach
Career outside cricket: Self-employed cricket coach

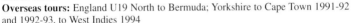

Overseas tours: England U19 North to Bermuda; Yorkshire to Cape Town 1991-92 and 1992-93, to West Indies 1994
Overseas teams played for: East Shirley, Canterbury, New Zealand 1987-89; Canterbury, New Zealand 1989-98
Cricketers particularly admired: Dennis Lillee
Young players to look out for: 'The boys from Joe Duffy's junior set up at Hull CC'
Injuries: 'General wear and tear, especially in the back'
Extras: Took hat-trick with first three balls of innings in Yorkshire League playing for Hull v Doncaster. First player to win Yorkshire U19 Bowler of the Season in two successive years. Northamptonshire Uncapped Player of the Year in 1989. Endured a world record 11 innings without scoring a run in 1990. Currently trying to open an eight-lane indoor cricket stadium
Opinions on cricket: 'What goes around comes around. Beware the wolf in sheep's clothing.'
Best batting: 27 Sussex v Lancashire, Old Trafford 1997
Best bowling: 9-37 Yorkshire v Northamptonshire, Harrogate 1993

1997 Season

	M	Inns	NO	Runs	HS	Avge	100s	50s	Ct	St	O	M	Runs	Wkts	Avge	Best	5wl	10wM
Test																		
All First	17	25	9	114	27	7.12	-	-	4	-	448.2	87	1426	48	29.70	6-78	2	
1-day Int																		
NatWest	4	1	1	3	3 *	-	-	-	1	-	46.5	6	175	6	29.16	3-59	-	
B & H	5	3	2	0	0 *	0.00	-	-	2	-	46	1	173	4	43.25	2-34	-	
Sunday	14	10	5	39	9 *	7.80	-	-	2	-	90	3	365	9	40.55	1-15	-	

Career Performances

	M	Inns	NO	Runs	HS	Avge	100s	50s	Ct	St	Balls	Runs	Wkts	Avge	Best	5wI	10wM
Test																	
All First	172	186	77	426	27	3.90	-	-	35	-	27966	13485	417	32.33	9-37	9	2
1-day Int																	
NatWest	22	8	6	7	3 *	3.50	-	-	3	-	1500	833	32	26.03	4-32	-	
B & H	24	11	6	6	3 *	1.20	-	-	2	3	1336	764	27	28.29	3-20	-	
Sunday	111	42	19	77	9 *	3.34	-	-	13	-	4718	3512	94	37.36	4-23	-	

ROBINSON, P. E. Leicestershire

Name: Phillip Edward Robinson
Role: Right-hand bat, left-arm 'declaration' bowler
Born: 3 August 1963, Keighley, West Yorkshire
Height: 5ft 9in **Weight:** 13st 10lbs
Nickname: Roundbat, Brigadier, F.B., Skip, Robbo, Red
County debut: 1984 (Yorkshire), 1992 (Leicestershire)
County cap: 1988 (Yorkshire)
1000 runs in a season: 3
1st-Class 50s: 51
1st-Class 100s: 7
1st-Class catches: 130
One-Day 100s: 1
Place in batting averages:
(1994 40th av. 43.57)
Parents: Keith and Lesley
Wife and date of marriage: Jane, 19 September 1986
Family links with cricket: Father and brother played in Bradford League. Dad now an umpire
Education: Long Lee Primary; Hartington Middle; Greenhead Comprehensive
Qualifications: 2 O-levels
Overseas tours: Southland CC to Tasmania 1987; Yorkshire to St Lucia and Barbados 1988; Leicestershire to Jamaica 1993, to South Africa 1994-95
Overseas teams played for: Southland, New Zealand 1987; Eastern Southland cricket coach 1987; Eden Roskill, Auckland 1989-90; Riverside, Wellington 1990-91
Cricketers particularly admired: Geoff Boycott, Richard Hadlee, Michael Holding
Other sports followed: Football (Manchester United), rugby league (Keighley Cougars)

Relaxations: War-gaming, eating out

Extras: Made the highest score by a Yorkshire 2nd XI player with 233 in 1983. Scored most runs by an overseas player in the Auckland Cricket League for Eden Roskill 1989-90 (1200 runs). Hit the fastest televised 50 in the Sunday League (19 balls) v Derbyshire at Chesterfield 1991. Released by Yorkshire at his own request at the end of the 1991 season. Played for Cumberland in 1992 and could play only limited-overs for Leicestershire in 1992 (apart from one match) but on full contract from 1993. Captain of Leicestershire 2nd XI. Led the team to Bain Hogg win in 1995

Opinions on cricket: 'Cricket should be played on uncovered pitches over three days. Alternatively, four-day games should be played Wednesday to Saturday, with the Sunday League game after. Also, second-class cricket should be played Wednesday to Friday to allow the younger players to work with the senior players during the season.'

Best batting: 189 Yorkshire v Lancashire, Scarborough 1991

Best bowling: 1-10 Yorkshire v Somerset, Scarborough 1990

1997 Season (did not make any first-class or one-day appearances)

Career Performances

	M	Inns	NO	Runs	HS	Avge	100s	50s	Ct	St	Balls	Runs	Wkts	Avge	Best	5wI	10wM
Test																	
All First	159	261	35	7617	189	33.70	7	51	130	-	296	329	3	109.66	1-10	-	-
1-day Int																	
NatWest	17	13	0	421	73	32.38	-	3	5	-							
B & H	33	29	4	684	73 *	27.36	-	4	12	-							
Sunday	145	140	14	3111	104	24.69	1	14	59	-							

---

81. Who has scored the most runs in the County Championship since 1993?

479

ROBINSON, R. T.   Nottinghamshire

Name: Robert Timothy Robinson
Role: Right-hand opening bat, right-arm
medium bowler
Born: 21 November 1958, Sutton-in-
Ashfield, Nottinghamshire
Height: 6ft **Weight:** 12st 7lbs
Nickname: Robbo
County debut: 1978
County cap: 1983
Benefit: 1992 (£90,040)
Test debut: 1984-85
Tests: 29
One-Day Internationals: 26
1000 runs in a season: 14
1st-Class 50s: 133
1st-Class 100s: 62
1st-Class 200s: 3
1st-Class catches: 241
One-Day 100s: 9

Place in batting averages: 112th av. 32.48 (1996 50th av. 44.89)
Strike rate: (career 64.75)
Parents: Eddy and Christine
Wife and date of marriage: Separated
Children: Philip Thomas; Alex James
Family links with cricket: Father, uncle, cousin and brother all played local cricket
Education: Dunstable Grammar School; High Pavement College, Nottingham;
Sheffield University
Qualifications: BA (Hons) in Accountancy and Financial Management
Career outside cricket: Director of sports retailer
Overseas tours: England to India and Australia 1984-85, to West Indies 1985-86, to
India and Pakistan (World Cup) 1987-88, to New Zealand 1987-88; unofficial English
XI to South Africa 1989-90
Cricketers particularly admired: Clive Rice, Geoffrey Boycott
Other sports followed: Golf, squash, football and rugby
Injuries: Broken hand, out for one month
Extras: Played for Northamptonshire 2nd XI in 1974-75 and for Nottinghamshire 2nd
XI in 1977. Had soccer trials with Portsmouth, Chelsea and QPR. One of *Wisden*'s Five
Cricketers of the Year 1985. Banned from Test cricket for joining 1989-90 tour of South
Africa, remitted in 1992. Handed over captaincy to Paul Johnson in 1995 to give more
time to business
Best batting: 220* Nottinghamshire v Yorkshire, Trent Bridge 1990
Best bowling: 1-22 Nottinghamshire v Northamptonshire, Northampton 1982

1997 Season

	M	Inns	NO	Runs	HS	Avge	100s	50s	Ct	St	O	M	Runs	Wkts	Avge	Best	5wI	10wM
Test																		
All First	17	29	4	812	143 *	32.48	1	5	7	-								
1-day Int																		
NatWest	3	3	1	94	52	47.00	-	1	1	-								
B & H	3	3	0	36	25	12.00	-	-	-	-								
Sunday	7	7	1	240	58	40.00	-	2	2	-								

Career Performances

	M	Inns	NO	Runs	HS	Avge	100s	50s	Ct	St	Balls	Runs	Wkts	Avge	Best	5wI	10wM
Test	29	49	5	1601	175	36.38	4	6	8	-	6	0	0	-	-	-	-
All First	402	699	82	26493	220 *	42.93	62	133	241	-	259	289	4	72.25	1-22	-	-
1-day Int	26	26	0	597	83	22.96	-	3	6	-							
NatWest	41	41	3	1595	139	41.97	2	8	17	-							
B & H	74	72	9	2531	120	40.17	3	18	16	-							
Sunday	229	223	27	6568	119 *	33.51	4	44	72	-							

ROLLINS, A. S. Derbyshire

Name: Adrian Stewart Rollins
Role: Right-hand bat, right-arm medium bowler, occasional wicket-keeper
Born: 8 February 1972, Barking, Essex
Height: 6ft 5in **Weight:** 16st 7lbs
Nickname: Rollie
County debut: 1993
County cap: 1995
1000 runs in a season: 3
1st-Class 50s: 24
1st-Class 100s: 8
1st-Class 200s: 1
1st-Class catches: 61
1st-Class stumpings: 1
One-Day 100s: 1
Place in batting averages: 41st av. 43.92 (1996 110th av. 35.51)
Strike rate: (career 90.00)
Parents: Marva
Marital status: Engaged to Debbie
Family links with cricket: Brother Robert on Essex staff. Brother Gary is trialling for various counties
Education: Little Ilford Comprehensive School, Manor Park, London

Qualifications: 10 GCSEs, 4 A-levels, NCA coaching award, Diploma in Sports Psychology
Overseas tours: London Federation of Boys Clubs to Barbados 1987
Overseas teams played for: Kaponga, New Zealand 1993-94
Cricketers particularly admired: Gordon Greenidge, Kim Barnett, Desmond Haynes, Phillip DeFreitas, Viv Richards, Michael Holding
Young players to look out for: Robert Rollins, Vikram Solanki
Other sports followed: Basketball and football (West Ham United)
Relaxations: Listening to music
Extras: Made Championship debut on same day as brother. Became 500th first-class player for Derbyshire, for whom he was named Young Player of the Year 1993. Was the 100th Derbyshire player to score a hundred. Holds record for the highest score by a Derbyshire opener to carry his bat and his 200 not out against Gloucestershire was the longest innings by a Derbyshire player. He became the youngest English qualified Derbyshire double centurion. Voted Derbyshire Player of the Year for 1995
Opinions on cricket: 'Something is not right in the professional cricket game today. Rugby union turns professional and players are on £50,000 to £200,000-a-year contracts. The crowds are no greater in rugby than in cricket, so where is our money? Pay the players.'
Best batting: 210 Derbyshire v Hampshire, Chesterfield 1997
Best bowling: 1-19 Derbyshire v Essex, Chelmsford 1995

1997 Season

	M	Inns	NO	Runs	HS	Avge	100s	50s	Ct	St	O	M	Runs	Wkts	Avge	Best	5wI	10wM
Test																		
All First	17	29	3	1142	210	43.92	3	6	11	-	3	0	21	0	-	-	-	-
1-day Int																		
NatWest	3	3	0	67	40	22.33	-	-	-	-								
B & H	1	1	0	0	0	0.00	-	-	-	-								
Sunday	8	8	2	212	36	35.33	-	-	3	-	2	0	15	0	-		-	-

Career Performances

	M	Inns	NO	Runs	HS	Avge	100s	50s	Ct	St	Balls	Runs	Wkts	Avge	Best	5wI	10wM
Test																	
All First	76	140	15	4438	210	35.50	8	24	61	1	90	122	1	122.00	1-19	-	-
1-day Int																	
NatWest	7	7	0	131	56	18.71	-	1	3	-							
B & H	7	7	0	159	70	22.71	-	1	2	-							
Sunday	45	39	4	739	126 *	21.11	1	1	21	-	12	15	0	-		-	-

ROLLINS, R. J. Essex

Name: Robert John Rollins
Role: Right-hand bat, wicket-keeper
Born: 30 January 1974, Plaistow, London
Height: 5ft 9in **Weight:** 13st 10lbs
Nickname: Walter, Rollie
County debut: 1992
County cap: 1995
1st-Class 50s: 11
1st-Class 100s: 1
1st-Class catches: 139
1st-Class stumpings: 20
Place in batting averages: 161st av. 25.11
(1996 205th av. 23.96)
Parents: Marva
Family links with cricket: 'Big brother
(Adrian) plays for Derbyshire, middle brother
(Gary) is an aspiring professional, little
cousins just starting the game (Ryan, Carl,
Benjamin and Dominic)'
Education: Avenue Primary School; Little Ilford Comprehensive School
Qualifications: 6 GCSEs, NCA coaching award
Off-season: 'Enjoying myself with the Barmy Army'
Overseas tours: England U18 to Canada 1991; England U19 to Pakistan 1991-92, to
India 1992-93
Overseas teams played for: MOB Pietermaritzburg, South Africa 1995-96; Shell
Harbour, New South Wales 1996-97
Cricketers particularly admired: Keith Hurst, Alan Knott, Keith Fletcher
Other sports followed: 'West Ham United and Tiger Woods'
Injuries: Broken left index finger, out for three weeks
Relaxations: Reading and money
Extras: Named Essex Young Player of the Year 1992 and awarded his 2nd XI cap in
September of that year. Made Championship debut on the same day as his brother
Adrian. Both kept wicket in the same Sunday League game
Opinions on cricket: 'Four-day cricket is enjoyable.'
Best batting: 133* Essex v Glamorgan, Swansea 1995

---

82. Who has taken the most County Championship
wickets since 1993?

1997 Season

	M	Inns	NO	Runs	HS	Avge	100s	50s	Ct	St	O	M	Runs	Wkts	Avge	Best	5wI	10wM
Test																		
All First	13	19	1	452	82	25.11	-	4	24	2								
1-day Int																		
NatWest	5	3	1	85	67 *	42.50	-	1	2	-								
B & H	4	3	1	43	18 *	21.50	-	-	5	2								
Sunday	12	9	0	124	38	13.77	-	-	9	7								

Career Performances

	M	Inns	NO	Runs	HS	Avge	100s	50s	Ct	St	Balls	Runs	Wkts	Avge	Best	5wI	10wM
Test																	
All First	58	95	9	2022	133 *	23.51	1	11	139	20							
1-day Int																	
NatWest	12	10	4	248	67 *	41.33	-	3	4	3							
B & H	12	6	2	46	18 *	11.50	-	-	12	2							
Sunday	55	44	9	443	38	12.65	-	-	51	13							

ROSE, G. D. Somerset

Name: Graham David Rose
Role: Right-hand bat, right-arm
fast-medium bowler, first slip
Born: 12 April 1964, Tottenham
Height: 6ft 4in **Weight:** 15st
Nickname: Hagar
County debut: 1985 (Middlesex),
1987 (Somerset)
County cap: 1988 (Somerset)
Benefit: 1996
1000 runs in a season: 1
50 wickets in a season: 4
1st-Class 50s: 35
1st-Class 100s: 8
1st-Class 5 w. in innings: 12
1st-Class 10 w. in match: 1
1st-Class catches: 107
One-Day 100s: 2
Place in batting averages: 20th av. 50.11
(1996 193rd av. 25.50)
Place in bowling averages: 31st av. 24.80 (1996 19th av. 24.36)
Strike rate: 46.55 (career 54.99)

Parents: William and Edna
Wife and date of marriage: Teresa Julie, 19 September 1987
Children: Georgina Charlotte, 6 December 1990; Felix William Michael, 11 August 1997
Family links with cricket: Father and brothers have played club cricket
Education: Northumberland Park School, Tottenham
Qualifications: 6 O-levels, 4 A-levels, NCA coaching certificate
Off-season: 'The usual chestnut – to be decided'
Overseas teams played for: Carey Park, Bunbury, Western Australia 1984-85; Fremantle, Perth 1986-87; Paarl, Cape Town 1988-89
Cricketers particularly admired: Richard Hadlee, Jimmy Cook, Mushtaq Ahmed
Young players to look out for: James Ormond
Other sports followed: Football, rugby, golf
Injuries: 'Amazingly, none!'
Relaxations: Wine, music, gardening, playing golf and 'my daughter, Georgina'
Extras: Played for England YC v Australia YC 1983. Took 6-41 on Middlesex debut in 1985, then scored 95 on debut for Somerset in 1987. Completed double of 1000 runs and 50 wickets in first-class cricket in 1990 and scored fastest recorded centuries in NatWest Trophy (v Devon) and Sunday League (v Glamorgan)
Opinions on cricket: 'Not sure that a two-divisional split at county level will produce a better Test team – didn't the all-play-all format produce the likes of Gower, Gatting, Gooch, Botham et al? Surely haven't we got to focus on the bottom half of the pyramid – school and club cricket – to produce a better product at the apex?'
Best batting: 191 Somerset v Sussex, Taunton 1997
Best bowling: 7-47 Somerset v Nottinghamshire, Taunton 1996

1997 Season

	M	Inns	NO	Runs	HS	Avge	100s	50s	Ct	St	O	M	Runs	Wkts	Avge	Best	5wI	10wM
Test																		
All First	18	26	9	852	191	50.11	2	3	7	-	488.5	124	1563	63	24.80	5-53	1	-
1-day Int																		
NatWest	2	1	0	18	18	18.00	-	-	1	-	21	1	88	4	22.00	2-43	-	
B & H	5	5	0	46	24	9.20	-	-	2	-	40.4	2	214	9	23.77	3-31	-	
Sunday	15	13	5	181	37 *	22.62	-	-	5	-	113.4	5	436	24	18.16	3-15	-	

Career Performances

	M	Inns	NO	Runs	HS	Avge	100s	50s	Ct	St	Balls	Runs	Wkts	Avge	Best	5wI	10wM
Test																	
All First	204	284	54	7170	191	31.17	8	35	107	-	27664	14749	503	29.32	7-47	12	1
1-day Int																	
NatWest	22	19	3	347	110	21.68	1	1	4	-	1187	786	25	31.44	3-11	-	
B & H	50	44	4	814	79	20.35	-	4	11	-	2740	1830	64	28.59	4-21	-	
Sunday	165	144	28	3230	148	27.84	1	17	44	-	6402	4803	164	29.28	4-26	-	

ROSEBERRY, M. A. Durham

Name: Michael Anthony Roseberry
Role: Right-hand bat, right-arm
medium-fast bowler
Born: 28 November 1966,
Houghton-le-Spring, Sunderland
Height: 6ft 2in **Weight:** 14st 7lbs
Nickname: Micky
County debut: 1985 (Middlesex),
1995 (Durham)
County cap: 1990 (Middlesex)
1000 runs in a season: 4
1st-Class 50s: 51
1st-Class 100s: 19
1st-Class catches: 144
One-Day 100s: 6
Place in batting averages: 265th av. 13.83
(1996 186th av. 26.57)
Strike rate: (career 127.75)
Parents: Matthew and Jean
Wife and date of marriage: Helen Louise, 22 February 1991
Children: Jordan Louise, 29 May 1992; Lauren Ella, 19 February 1994
Family links with cricket: Brother Andrew played for Glamorgan and Leicestershire;
father is director of Durham CCC
Education: Tonstall Preparatory School, Sunderland; Durham School
Qualifications: 5 O-levels, 1 A-level, advanced cricket coach
Career outside cricket: 'Coaching cricket. Director in our business'
Overseas tours: England YC to West Indies 1984-85; England A to Australia 1992-93;
England XI and Lord's Taverners to Hong Kong 'on numerous occasions'; MCC to
West Africa 1993-94; Durham CCC to South Africa 1994-95
Overseas teams played for: Fremantle, Western Australia 1986; Melville, Perth 1988;
Alberton, Johannesburg 1994-96
Cricketers particularly admired: 'Desmond Haynes for the obvious and his
generosity on the golf course'
Other sports followed: 'Played rugby union at a good level when at school,
representing Durham County at all levels except the senior side. Follow golf and very
loyal supporter of Sunderland FC'
Relaxations: 'Eating out and spending time with my family which is limited during
the summer'
Extras: Won Lord's Taverners/MCC Cricketer of the Year 1983, Cricket Society award
for Best Young Cricketer of the Year 1984 and twice won Cricket Society award for best
all-rounder in schools cricket. Played in Durham League as a professional while still at

school. At age 16, playing for Durham School v St Bees, he hit 216 in 160 minutes. In 1992 scored 2044 runs in 1992 – joint highest in first-class cricket with Peter Bowler and was named Middlesex Player of the Year and Lucozade Player of the Year. Left Middlesex at end of 1994 to return to his native Durham as captain for the 1995 season but relinquished the captaincy during the 1996 season

Best batting: 185 Middlesex v Leicestershire, Lord's 1993
Best bowling: 1-1 Middlesex v Sussex, Hove 1988

1997 Season

	M	Inns	NO	Runs	HS	Avge	100s	50s	Ct	St	O	M	Runs	Wkts	Avge	Best	5wI	10wM
Test																		
All First	4	8	1	97	45	13.85	-	-	3	-								
1-day Int																		
NatWest																		
B & H	3	3	1	50	27 *	25.00	-	-	-	-								
Sunday	7	6	4	202	91 *	101.00	-	2	3	-								

Career Performances

	M	Inns	NO	Runs	HS	Avge	100s	50s	Ct	St	Balls	Runs	Wkts	Avge	Best	5wI	10wM
Test																	
All First	196	332	37	10203	185	34.58	19	51	144	-	511	406	4	101.50	1-1	-	-
1-day Int																	
NatWest	16	16	0	680	121	42.50	3	1	7	-	36	42	1	42.00	1-22	-	
B & H	30	28	3	688	84	27.52	-	6	7	-	6	2	0	-	-	-	
Sunday	118	112	14	3226	119 *	32.91	3	23	45	-	4	7	0	-	-	-	

RUSSELL, R. C.   Gloucestershire

Name: Robert Charles Russell
Role: Left-hand bat, wicket-keeper,
county captain
Born: 15 August 1963, Stroud
Height: 5ft 8¼in **Weight:** 9st 9lbs
Nickname: Jack
County debut: 1981
County cap: 1985
Benefit: 1994
Test debut: 1988
Tests: 49
One-Day Internationals: 38
1000 runs in a season: 1
1st-Class 50s: 70
1st-Class 100s: 7
1st-Class catches: 893
1st-Class stumpings: 109
One-Day 100s: 1
Place in batting averages: 30th av. 45.60
(1996 118th av. 34.82)

Strike rate: (career 56.00)
Parents: John and Jennifer
Wife and date of marriage: Aileen Ann, 6 March 1985
Children: Stepson, Marcus Anthony 1980; Elizabeth Ann, March 1988; Victoria,
1989; Charles David, 1991; Katherine Jane, 1996
Education: Uplands County Primary School; Archway Comprehensive School; Bristol
Polytechnic ('walked out after two months of accountancy course. Couldn't
understand the sociology and economics – wanted to play cricket instead')
Qualifications: 7 O-levels, 2 A-levels
Career outside cricket: Professional artist
Off-season: Touring West Indies with England
Overseas tours: England to Pakistan 1987-88, to India and West Indies 1989-90, to
Australia 1990-91, to New Zealand 1991-92, to West Indies 1993-94, to Australia
1994-95, to South Africa 1995-96, to Pakistan and India (World Cup) 1995-96, to
Zimbabwe and New Zealand 1996-97, to West Indies 1997-98; England A to Australia
1992-93
Cricketers particularly admired: Alan Knott, Bob Taylor, Ian Botham, Rodney
Marsh 'and other greats'
Other sports followed: Football (Tottenham Hotspur), rugby (England), snooker,
'anything competitive'
Relaxations: Playing cricket and painting pictures. 'I love comedians and comedies.
Life is too short, you need to laugh as much as you can'

Extras: Spotted at age nine by Gloucestershire coach, Graham Wiltshire. Youngest Gloucestershire wicket-keeper (17 years 307 days) and set record for most dismissals in a match on first-class debut: 8 (7 caught, 1 stumped) for Gloucestershire v Sri Lankans at Bristol, 1981. Hat-trick of catches v Surrey at The Oval 1986. Represented England YC v West Indies YC in 1982. Was chosen as England's Man of the Test Series, England v Australia 1989 and was one of *Wisden*'s Five Cricketers of the Year 1990. Appointed vice-captain to Martyn Moxon on the England A tour to Australia 1992-93. Called up as stand-by wicket-keeper for the England tour to Australia 1994-95 when Alec Stewart broke his finger for the second time on the tour. Opened Jack Russell Gallery in Chipping Sodbury, South Gloucestershire in 1995 where he displays original oil paintings and limited edition prints of cricketing scenes, landscapes, wildlife etc. Books of his that have been published include *A Cricketer's Art – Sketches by Jack Russell* (1988), *Sketches of a Season – illustrated by Jack Russell* (1989), *Jack Russell's Sketch Book* (1996) and *Jack Russell – Unleashed*, an autobiography which made the top ten bestsellers in 1997. Commissioned by Dean of Gloucester to do a drawing of Gloucester Cathedral to raise funds for 900th Anniversary. Still turns out for his original club, Stroud CC, whenever he can. Runs six miles a day to keep fit and drinks up to 20 cups of tea a day. Keen military enthusiast, 'We must never forget'. His paintings are sold and displayed in museums and private collections all around the world. Loves England, 'To me, it's the greatest place of all to play and paint.' Broke Bob Taylor's long-standing world record for the number of dismissals in a Test match with 11 in the second Test v South Africa at Johannesburg 1995-96. Awarded MBE in 1996 for his services to cricket. Has been the Whyte and Mackay wicket-keeper/batsman of the year for the last three years. He also has his own website: http://www.jackrussell.co.uk
Best batting: 128* England v Australia, Old Trafford 1989
Best bowling: 1-4 Gloucestershire v West Indians, Bristol 1991

1997 Season

	M	Inns	NO	Runs	HS	Avge	100s	50s	Ct	St	O	M	Runs	Wkts	Avge	Best	5wI	10wM
Test																		
All First	19	29	6	1049	103 *	45.60	1	8	52	5	3	0	15	0	-		-	-
1-day Int																		
NatWest	2	1	0	20	20	20.00	-	-	5	1								
B & H	5	4	1	143	66	47.66	-	1	4	2								
Sunday	13	10	1	156	59 *	17.33	-	1	13	1								

Career Performances

	M	Inns	NO	Runs	HS	Avge	100s	50s	Ct	St	Balls	Runs	Wkts	Avge	Best	5wI	10wM
Test	49	77	15	1807	128 *	29.14	2	6	141	11							
All First	367	536	118	12934	129 *	30.94	7	70	893	109	56	68	1	68.00	1-4	-	-
1-day Int	38	29	7	383	50	17.40	-	1	41	6							
NatWest	38	26	7	454	59 *	23.89	-	1	52	9							
B & H	61	44	16	776	66	27.71	-	2	58	12							
Sunday	195	148	34	2599	108	22.79	1	10	159	28							

SAEED ANWAR   Derbyshire

Name: Saeed Anwar
Role: Left-hand bat, slow left-arm bowler
Born: 6 September 1968, Karachi, Pakistan
County debut: No first-team appearance
Test debut: 1990-91
Tests: 21
One-Day Internationals: 122
1st-Class 50s: 35
1st-Class 100s: 21
1st-Class 200s: 1
1st-Class catches: 54
One-Day 100s: 12
Overseas tours: Pakistan to Australia 1988-89, to Australia 1988-89, to Sharjah 1988-89, to Sharjah 1990-91, to Australia and New Zealand 1992-93, to Sharjah 1992-93, to South Africa 1992-93, to Sharjah 1993-94, to New Zealand 1993-94, to Sri Lanka 1994-95, to South Africa and Zimbabwe 1994-95, to

Sharjah 1994-95, to Sharjah 1995-96, to Singapore 1995-96, to England 1996, to Toronto and Nairobi, to Sharjah and India 1996-97
Extras: Holds the record for the highest score in a one-day International with 194 against India at Madras in 1996-97. Has captained Pakistan in a one-day International
Best batting: 221 Karachi Whites v Multan, Karachi 1989-90
Best bowling: 3-83 for ADPB, 1990-91

1997 Season (did not make any first-class or one-day appearances)

Career Performances

	M	Inns	NO	Runs	HS	Avge	100s	50s	Ct	St	Balls	Runs	Wkts	Avge	Best	5wI	10wM
Test	21	37	1	1739	176	48.30	4	13	12	-	18	4	0	-	-	-	-
All First	97	155	6	6961	221	46.71	21	35	54	-	623	393	9	43.66	3-83	-	-
1-day Int	122	121	11	4399	194	39.99	12	17	25	-	174	154	3	51.33	1-9	-	
NatWest																	
B & H																	
Sunday																	

SAGGERS, M. J.   Durham

Name: Martin John Saggers
Role: Right-hand bat, right-arm
fast-medium bowler
Born: 23 May 1972, King's Lynn
Height: 6ft 2in **Weight:** 14st
Nickname: Saggs, Pony
County debut: 1996
1st-Class 5 w. in innings: 2
1st-Class catches: 2
Place in batting averages:
(1996 229th av. 11.12)
Place in bowling averages:
(1996 90th av. 34.07)
Strike rate: 54.85 (career 49.50)
Parents: Brian and Edna
Marital status: Single
Education: Roseberry Avenue Primary
School; Springwood High School; University
of Huddersfield

Qualifications: BA (Hons) Architectural Studies
Career outside cricket: Architectural technician/consultant
Off-season: 'Going to sunnier climes'
Overseas teams played for: Randburg CC, Johannesburg, South Africa 1996-97
Cricketers particularly admired: Neil Foster, Richard Hadlee
Young players to look out for: Robert Ferley, Richard Saddleton
Other sports followed: Football (Tottenham Hotspur), golf, tiddlywinks, seven-card
stud poker
Injuries: Golfer's elbow, three to four weeks
Relaxations: Egyptology, sleeping
Opinions on cricket: 'Batsmen should not be allowed to play attacking shots. Catches
should be allowed with one hand one bounce. The old back foot law should be brought
.back for bowlers.'
Best batting: 18 Durham v Somerset, Weston-super-Mare 1996
Best bowling: 6-65 Durham v Glamorgan, Chester-le-Street 1996

---

83. Who is the leading all-rounder in County
Championship cricket since 1993?

1997 Season

	M	Inns	NO	Runs	HS	Avge	100s	50s	Ct	St	O	M	Runs	Wkts	Avge	Best	5wI	10wM
Test																		
All First	3	4	2	14	10 *	7.00	-	-	2	-	64	15	177	7	25.28	5-57	1	-
1-day Int																		
NatWest																		
B & H																		
Sunday	4	1	1	5	5 *	-	-	-	1	-	28	0	141	6	23.50	4-35	-	

Career Performances

	M	Inns	NO	Runs	HS	Avge	100s	50s	Ct	St	Balls	Runs	Wkts	Avge	Best	5wI	10wM
Test																	
All First	8	13	3	103	18	10.30	-	-	2	-	990	620	20	31.00	6-65	2	-
1-day Int																	
NatWest	1	1	0	0	0	0.00	-	-	-	-	60	56	0	-		-	-
B & H	5	5	3	58	34 *	29.00	-	-	2	-	246	247	5	49.40	2-49	-	
Sunday	7	2	1	18	13	18.00	-	-	1	-	288	200	9	22.22	4-35	-	

SALES, D. J.   Northamptonshire

Name: David John Sales
Role: Right-hand bat, right-arm
occasional bowler
Born: 3 December 1977, Carshalton, Surrey
Height: 6ft   **Weight:** 13st
Nickname: Jumble
County debut: 1994 (one-day),
1996 (first-class)
1st-Class 50s: 2
1st-Class 100s: 1
1st-Class 200s: 1
1st-Class catches: 8
Place in batting averages: 139th av. 27.40
(1996 75th av. 40.00)
Parents: John and Daphne
Marital status: Single
Family links with cricket: Father played
club cricket
Education: Cumnor House Prep School,
Croydon; Caterham Boys' School
Qualifications: 7 GCSEs, cricket coach
Off-season: Touring Kenya and Sri Lanka with England A

Overseas tours: England U15 to South Africa 1993; England U19 to West Indies 1994-95, to Zimbabwe 1995-96, to Pakistan 1996-97; England A to Kenya and Sri Lanka 1997-98
Cricketers particularly admired: Graham Gooch
Young players to look out for: Owais Shah
Other sports followed: Football (Crystal Palace), golf
Relaxations: Golf and fishing
Extras: Youngest batsman to score a 50 in the Sunday League. The first Englishman to score a double century on his Championship debut and the youngest ever to score a double century
Best batting: 210* Northamptonshire v Worcestershire, Kidderminster 1996

1997 Season

	M	Inns	NO	Runs	HS	Avge	100s	50s	Ct	St	O	M	Runs	Wkts	Avge	Best	5wI	10wM
Test																		
All First	14	21	1	548	103	27.40	1	2	4	-	8	2	28	0	-	-	-	-
1-day Int																		
NatWest	2	2	0	53	53	26.50	-	1	1	-								
B & H	1	1	0	15	15	15.00	-	-	-	-								
Sunday	10	10	1	168	42 *	18.66	-	-	2	-								

Career Performances

	M	Inns	NO	Runs	HS	Avge	100s	50s	Ct	St	Balls	Runs	Wkts	Avge	Best	5wI	10wM
Test																	
All First	18	29	2	828	210 *	30.66	2	2	8	-	48	28	0	-	-	-	-
1-day Int																	
NatWest	2	2	0	53	53	26.50	-	1	1	-							
B & H	1	1	0	15	15	15.00	-	-	-	-							
Sunday	18	16	4	284	70 *	23.66	-	1	4	-							

SALISBURY, I. D. K. Surrey

Name: Ian David Kenneth Salisbury
Role: Right-hand bat, leg-break bowler
Born: 21 January 1970, Northampton
Height: 5ft 11in **Weight:** 12st
Nickname: Sals
County debut: 1989 (Sussex), 1997 (Surrey)
County cap: 1991 (Sussex)
Test debut: 1992
Tests: 9
One-Day Internationals: 4
50 wickets in a season: 4
1st-Class 50s: 10
1st-Class 5 w. in innings: 26
1st-Class 10 w. in match: 4
1st-Class catches: 131
One-Day 5 w. in innings: 1
Place in batting averages: 283rd av. 10.60
(1996 227th av. 20.81)
Place in bowling averages: 79th av. 31.20
(1996 51st av. 28.96)

Strike rate: 62.83 (career 64.60)
Parents: Dave and Margaret
Wife and date of marriage: Emma Louise, 25 September 1993
Family links with cricket: 'Dad is vice-president of my first club, Brixworth'
Education: Moulton Comprehensive, Northampton
Qualifications: 7 O-levels, NCA coaching certificate
Overseas tours: England A to Pakistan 1990-91, to Bermuda and West Indies 1991-92, to India 1994-95, to Pakistan 1995-96; England to India and Sri Lanka 1992-93, to West Indies 1993-94; World Masters XI v Indian Masters XI November 1996 ('Masters aged 26?')
Cricketers particularly admired: 'Any that keep performing day in, day out, for both country and county'
Young players to look out for: Ben Hollioake, Owais Shah, Vasbert Drakes
Other sports followed: Most sports
Relaxations: 'Spending time with wife, Emma, meeting friends and relaxing with them and eating out – with good wine'
Extras: Picked to play two Tests for England against Pakistan in 1992, 'proudest moments of my career'. Originally selected for England A tour to Australia 1992-93 but was asked to stay on in India and played in the first two Tests of the series. In 1992 was named Young Player of the Year by both the Wombwell Cricket Lovers and the Cricket Writers. One of *Wisden*'s Five Cricketers of the Year 1993. Left Sussex during the 1996-

97 off-season to join Surrey

Opinions on cricket: 'Players should be asked for their opinion on changes in the game, before authorities make the changes themselves.'

Best batting: 83 Sussex v Glamorgan, Hove 1996

Best bowling: 8-75 Sussex v Essex, Chelmsford 1996

1997 Season

	M	Inns	NO	Runs	HS	Avge	100s	50s	Ct	St	O	M	Runs	Wkts	Avge	Best	5wl	10wM
Test																		
All First	13	17	2	159	30 *	10.60	-	-	7	-	314.1	65	936	30	31.20	6-19	2	-
1-day Int																		
NatWest	2	1	0	5	5	5.00	-	-	-	-	24	1	68	5	13.60	3-36	-	
B & H	8	5	1	31	14	7.75	-	-	4	-	63.5	1	292	8	36.50	4-53	-	
Sunday	10	5	4	43	23 *	43.00	-	-	5	-	56	0	310	10	31.00	3-56	-	

Career Performances

	M	Inns	NO	Runs	HS	Avge	100s	50s	Ct	St	Balls	Runs	Wkts	Avge	Best	5wl	10wM
Test	9	17	2	255	50	17.00	-	1	3	-	1773	1154	18	64.11	4-163	-	-
All First	178	234	50	3335	86	18.12	-	10	131	-	32883	17285	509	33.95	8-75	26	4
1-day Int	4	2	1	7	5	7.00	-	-	1	-	186	177	5	35.40	3-41	-	
NatWest	19	13	3	102	33	10.20	-	-	5	-	1212	662	23	28.78	3-28	-	
B & H	26	16	5	129	19	11.72	-	-	12	-	1448	1027	31	33.12	4-53	-	
Sunday	102	65	20	623	48 *	13.84	-	-	32	-	3894	3224	94	34.29	5-30	1	

84. Who won the Wills Quadrangular Tournament in Lahore in November 1997 and whom did they beat in the final?

O vodafone

SAQLAIN MUSHTAQ   Surrey

Name: Saqlain Mushtaq
Role: Right-hand bat, off-spin bowler
Born: 27 November 1976, Lahore, Pakistan
County debut: 1997
Test debut: 1995-96
Tests: 9
One-Day Internationals: 56
1st-Class 50s: 4
1st-Class 5 w. in innings: 13
1st-Class 10 w. in match: 3
1st-Class catches: 21
One-Day 5 w. in innings: 2
Place in batting averages: 165th av. 24.85
Place in bowling averages: 7th av. 19.28
Strike rate: 47.78 (career 54.68)
Overseas teams played for: PIA, Islamabad
1994-1998

Overseas tours: Pakistan to Australia 1994-
95, to Sharjah 1995-96, to Singapore 1995-
96, to England 1996, to Sri Lanka 1996-97, to Toronto and Nairobi 1996-97, to
Sharjah 1996-97, to Australia 1996-97, to India 1996-97
Best batting: 79 Pakistan v Zimbabwe, Sheikhupura 1996-97
Best bowling: 7-66 PIA v Railways, Lahore 1994-95

1997 Season

	M	Inns	NO	Runs	HS	Avge	100s	50s	Ct	St	O	M	Runs	Wkts	Avge	Best	5wI	10wM
Test																		
All First	8	10	4	149	41 *	24.83	-	-	1	-	254.5	75	617	32	19.28	5-17	4	2
1-day Int																		
NatWest	2	1	1	6	6 *	-	-	-	-	-	20.1	1	93	4	23.25	3-30	-	
B & H	2	0	0	0	0	-	-	-	-	-	17	2	54	2	27.00	2-33	-	
Sunday	9	4	1	61	29 *	20.33	-	-	2	-	55.3	1	276	12	23.00	3-31	-	

85. Who captained the England Lions in the first
Max International Series in New Zealand?

O vodafone

Career Performances

	M	Inns	NO	Runs	HS	Avge	100s	50s	Ct	St	Balls	Runs	Wkts	Avge	Best	5wI	10wM
Test	9	14	4	256	79	25.60	-	2	4		3045	1387	38	36.50	5-89	1	-
All First	41	61	17	716	79	16.27	-	4	21		9405	4011	172	23.31	7-66	13	3
1-day Int	56	37	10	255	30 *	9.44	-	-	17		2971	2116	109	19.41	5-29	2	
NatWest	2	1	1	6	6 *	-	-	-	-		121	93	4	23.25	3-30	-	
B & H	2	0	0	0	0	-	-	-	-		102	54	2	27.00	2-33	-	
Sunday	9	4	1	61	29 *	20.33	-	-	2		333	276	12	23.00	3-31	-	

SAVIDENT, L.   Hampshire

Name: Lee Savident
Role: Right-hand bat, right-arm
medium bowler
Born: 22 October 1976, Guernsey
Height: 6ft 5in **Weight:** 15st 4lbs
Nickname: Sav, Eiffel, Frenchman
County debut: 1997
1st-Class catches: 1
Strike rate: 84.00 (career 84.00)
Parents: Nev and Sue
Marital status: Single
Family links with cricket: None
Education: Castel Primary School;
Guernsey Grammar School; Guernsey
College of Further Education
Qualifications: 5 GCSEs and 1 A-level
Off-season: Playing cricket in South Africa
Overseas teams played for: Glenwood Old
Boys, Durban, South Africa 1997-98
Cricketers particularly admired: Malcolm Marshall, Robin Smith, Allan Donald
Young players to look out for: Andy Oram, Paul Hutchison
Other sports followed: Football (Tottenham Hotspur), basketball
Injuries: Arthroscopy on left knee to remove piece of cartilage and shin splints, out
for a total of seven weeks
Relaxations: 'Beating Terry Brewer at golf, shopping and watching television'
Extras: First person from the Channel Islands to play first-class cricket
Opinions on cricket: 'I would like to see two divisions as sides have more to play for
at the end of the season.'
Best batting: 6 Hampshire v Yorkshire, Portsmouth 1997
Best bowling: 2-86 Hampshire v Yorkshire, Portsmouth 1997

1997 Season

	M	Inns	NO	Runs	HS	Avge	100s	50s	Ct	St	O	M	Runs	Wkts	Avge	Best	5wI	10wM
Test																		
All First	3	4	1	15	6	5.00	-	-	1	-	56	9	247	4	61.75	2-86	-	-
1-day Int																		
NatWest																		
B & H																		
Sunday	3	2	2	8	7 *	-	-	-	1	-	19.1	0	104	6	17.33	3-41	-	

Career Performances

	M	Inns	NO	Runs	HS	Avge	100s	50s	Ct	St	Balls		Runs	Wkts	Avge	Best	5wI	10wM
Test																		
All First	3	4	1	15	6	5.00	-	-	1	-	336		247	4	61.75	2-86	-	-
1-day Int																		
NatWest																		
B & H																		
Sunday	3	2	2	8	7 *	-	-	-	1	-	115		104	6	17.33	3-41	-	

SCHOFIELD, C. J.   Yorkshire

Name: Christopher John Schofield
Role: Right-hand bat, leg-break bowler
Born: 21 March 1976, Barnsley
Height: 5ft 7in **Weight:** 10st 3lbs
Nickname: Scoff, Linford, Munchkin
County debut: 1996
Parents: John and Pat
Marital status: Single
Family links with cricket: Father played
local league cricket
Education: Kingstone School
Qualifications: 6 GCSEs, City and Guilds
Sport and Leisure
Off-season: Training and relaxing
Overseas tours: England U19 to Sri Lanka
1993-94, to West Indies 1994-95
Cricketers particularly admired: Carlisle
Best, Desmond Haynes, Viv Richards, Brian
Lara, Richie Richardson
Other sports followed: Football, rugby league
Extras: Played Yorkshire U11 to U15, Yorkshire Cricket Association U16 and U19,
Yorkshire Cricket Academy and England U19 in home series against India 1994

Opinions on cricket: 'Cricket needs to be made more attractive to the public, e.g. televised county cricket leading to more sponsorship.'
Best batting: 25 Yorkshire v Lancashire, Old Trafford 1996

1997 Season (did not make any first-class or one-day appearances)

Career Performances

	M	Inns	NO	Runs	HS	Avge	100s	50s	Ct	St	Balls	Runs	Wkts	Avge	Best	5wI	10wM
Test																	
All First	1	1	0	25	25	25.00	-	-	-	-							
1-day Int																	
NatWest																	
B & H																	
Sunday																	

SEARLE, J. P.   Durham

Name: Jason Paul Searle
Role: Right-hand bat, off-spin bowler
Born: 16 May 1976, Chittenham
Height: 5ft 8in **Weight:** 11st
Nickname: Shaggy, Village, Dumb, Elf
County debut: 1994
Parents: Paul and Chris
Marital status: Single
Family links with cricket: Father played for Chippenham and Wiltshire
Education: John Bentley School, Calne; Wiltshire and Swindon Building College
Qualifications: Bricklayer, farmer, 'gigolo'
Overseas tours: England U19 to West Indies 1994-95; Durham to South Africa
Cricketers particularly admired: Steve Lugsden, Martin Robinson
Young players to look out for: 'Me'
Other sports followed: Football (Manchester United)
Relaxations: 'Music and the fairer sex'
Opinions on cricket: 'Teams should have to play two spinners. Change it to a winter sport.'
Best batting: 5* Durham v Lancashire, Stockton 1994
Best bowling: 2-126 Durham v Surrey, The Oval 1995

1997 Season (did not make any first-class or one-day appearances)

Career Performances

	M	Inns	NO	Runs	HS	Avge	100s	50s	Ct	St	Balls	Runs	Wkts	Avge	Best	5wI	10wM
Test																	
All First	2	4	3	7	5 *	7.00	-	-	-	-	222	133	2	66.50	2-126	-	-
1-day Int																	
NatWest																	
B & H	1	0	0	0	0	-	-	-	-	-							
Sunday	1	0	0	0	0	-	-	-	-	-	12	19	0	-		-	-

SHADFORD, D. J.   Lancashire

Name: Darren James Shadford
Role: Right-hand bat, right-arm
medium fast bowler
Born: 4 March 1975, Oldham, Lancashire
Height: 6ft 1in **Weight:** 14st
Nickname: Shaddy, Shed Head
County debut: 1994 (one-day),
1995 (first-class)
1st-Class 5 w. in innings: 1
1st-Class catches: 1
Place in batting averages: 258th av. 15.14
Place in bowling averages: 125th av. 41.36
Strike rate: 47.05 (career 48.77)
Parents: Ken and Susan
Marital status: Single
Family links with cricket: Father and
brother play club cricket for Oldham CC.
Andrew plays with LSCA U19
Education: Roundthorn Primary School;
Breeze Hill High School; Oldham College of Technology
Career outside cricket: Travelling the world
Off-season: 'Taking it easy, relaxing, playing lots of golf, training for the 1998
season'
Overseas tours: Lancashire to Jamaica 1995-96, to South Africa 1997
Overseas teams played for: Sandgate CC, Brisbane 1993-94
Cricketers particularly admired: Jamie Haynes 'for his wicket-keeping abilities and
for being the biggest lead balloon in the game today'
Young players to look out for: Mark Chilton
Other sports followed: Football (Manchester United), squash, golf, snooker, 'the lot

really'

Injuries: 'None this season, I've been lucky – touch wood'

Relaxations: Socialising, shopping, listening to music, playing on my Sony PlayStation and going for a couple of curries every now and then'

Extras: 'Coaching award in cricket and canoeing first star'

Opinions on cricket: 'Second team should play four-day cricket to prepare the players for first-class cricket. Tea should be extended by ten to 15 minutes.'

Best batting: 30 Lancashire v Hampshire, Southampton 1997

Best bowling: 5-80 Lancashire v Warwickshire, Blackpool 1997

1997 Season

	M	Inns	NO	Runs	HS	Avge	100s	50s	Ct	St	O	M	Runs	Wkts	Avge	Best	5wI	10wM
Test																		
All First	8	10	3	106	30	15.14	-	-	6	-	149	8	786	19	41.36	5-80	1	-
1-day Int																		
NatWest	1	0	0	0	0	-	-	-	-	-	7	0	31	0	-		-	-
B & H																		
Sunday	7	3	2	3	2	3.00	-	-	3	-	42	2	246	11	22.36	3-30	-	

Career Performances

	M	Inns	NO	Runs	HS	Avge	100s	50s	Ct	St	Balls	Runs	Wkts	Avge	Best	5wI	10wM
Test																	
All First	10	12	4	107	30	13.37	-	-	6	-	1073	893	22	40.59	5-80	1	-
1-day Int																	
NatWest	1	0	0	0	0	-	-	-	-	-	42	31	0	-		-	-
B & H																	
Sunday	10	3	2	3	2	3.00	-	-	4	-	300	288	11	26.18	3-30	-	

SHAH, O. A.   Middlesex

Name: Owais Alam Shah
Role: Right-hand bat, off-spin bowler
Born: 22 October 1978, Karachi, Pakistan
Height: 6ft 1in **Weight:** 12st
Nickname: Ace
County debut: 1995 (one-day),
1996 (first-class)
1st-Class 50s: 4
1st-Class 100s: 1
1st-Class catches: 16
Place in batting averages: 70th av. 39.14
(1996 189th av. 26.50)
Strike rate: (career 42.00)
Parents: Jamshed and Mehjabeen
Marital status: Single
Family links with cricket: Father played for
his college side

Education: Berkley's Junior School;
Isleworth and Syon School; Lampton School;
National Westminster University
Qualifications: 7 GCSEs, 2 A-levels, starting Business Administration degree
Off-season: 'Captain of England U19 World Cup squad and then joining England A in
Sri Lanka'
Overseas tours: England U19 to Zimbabwe 1995-96, to South Africa 1997-98;
England A to Australia 1996-97, to Kenya and Sri Lanka 1997-98
Cricketers particularly admired: Viv Richards, Mark Waugh
Young players to look out for: Ian Blanchett, Stephen Peters, David Sales, James
Hewitt, Dean Cosker, Usman Afzaal, David Nash
Other sports followed: Football ('I like to see Manchester United do well'), table
tennis, snooker
Relaxations: 'Relaxing and hanging out with best friends.' Music, films, ten-pin
bowling
Extras: Middlesex Sports Federation Award winner. Man of the Series in U17 Test
series against India 1994. Played for Middlesex U13, Ken Barrington Trophy (National
Champions) and Middlesex U15, county competition winners, as captain. Scored record
232 for England U15 against England U16. Man of the Series for England U17 against
India U17. Awarded 2nd XI cap in 1996. Captained the England U19 side to success in
the U19 World Cup in South Africa scoring 53 not out in the final in 1997-98
Opinions on cricket: 'We need to play more competitive cricket. Too many people are
worried about doing well personally and instead should play and work as a team.'
Best batting: 104* Middlesex v Nottinghamshire, Lord's 1997
Best bowling: 1-24 Middlesex v Somerset, Uxbridge 1996

1997 Season

	M	Inns	NO	Runs	HS	Avge	100s	50s	Ct	St	O	M	Runs	Wkts	Avge	Best	5wI	10wM
Test																		
All First	11	16	2	548	104 *	39.14	1	2	14	-	2	0	19	0	-	-	-	-
1-day Int																		
NatWest	3	3	1	46	27 *	23.00	-	-	1	-								
B & H																		
Sunday	7	7	2	201	66 *	40.20	-	2	1	-	2	0	29	0	-	-	-	

Career Performances

	M	Inns	NO	Runs	HS	Avge	100s	50s	Ct	St	Balls	Runs	Wkts	Avge	Best	5wI	10wM
Test																	
All First	18	28	3	813	104 *	32.52	1	4	16	-	42	43	1	43.00	1-24	-	-
1-day Int																	
NatWest	4	4	1	57	27 *	19.00	-	-	1	-							
B & H	3	3	1	52	42 *	26.00	-	-	-	-							
Sunday	23	20	5	448	66 *	29.86	-	3	6	-	19	33	1	33.00	1-4	-	

SHAHID, N.   Surrey

Name: Nadeem Shahid
Role: Right-hand bat, leg-spin bowler
Born: 23 April 1969, Karachi
Height: 6ft **Weight:** 12st
Nickname: Nad, Gonads, National Hero, Maggie, 'far too many to mention'
County debut: 1989 (Essex), 1995 (Surrey)
1000 runs in a season: 1
1st-Class 50s: 23
1st-Class 100s: 5
1st-Class catches: 89
One-Day 100s: 1
Place in batting averages: 228th av. 18.00 (1996 131st av. 33.43)
Strike rate: (career 71.07)
Parents: Ahmed and Salma
Marital status: Single
Family links with cricket: Brother plays in the local Two Counties League for Felixstowe
Education: Stoke High; Northgate High; Ipswich School; Plymouth Polytechnic
Qualifications: 6 O-levels, 1 A-level, coaching certificate
Overseas tours: Ipswich School to Barbados (Sir Garfield Sobers Trophy) 1987;

England (South) to N Ireland (Youth World Tournament) 1988

Overseas teams played for: Gosnells, Perth, Western Australia 1989-91; Fairfield, Sydney 1992-93

Cricketers particularly admired: Ian Botham, Shane Warne, Graham Thorpe and Nasser Hussain

Young players to look out for: Ben Hollioake, Alex Tudor

Other sports followed: Golf, tennis, badminton, squash, most ball sports

Extras: Youngest Suffolk player aged 17. Played for HMC, MCC Schools, ESCA U19, NCA Young Cricketers (Lord's and International Youth tournament in Belfast), England U25 and at every level for Suffolk. TSB Young Player of the Year 1987, winner of the *Daily Telegraph* Bowling Award 1987 and 1988, Cricket Society's All-rounder of the Year 1988 and Laidlaw Young Player of the Year for Essex 1993. Essex Society Player of the Year 1993. Released by Essex at end of 1994 season and signed for Surrey. Member of the Surrey Sunday League-winning side of 1996

Opinions on cricket: 'Players should be allowed to have fun on the field, and be allowed to express themselves in order to bring the best out of them. Players can and should work a lot harder at their game. I favour the two-divisional system in order to improve the standard of English cricket. It would allow players more time off the field and more time to work on skills, fitness etc. All first-class cricketers should be presented with a gold card which would allow them into any night club.'

Best batting: 139 Surrey v Yorkshire, The Oval 1995

Best bowling: 3-91 Essex v Surrey, The Oval 1990

1997 Season

	M	Inns	NO	Runs	HS	Avge	100s	50s	Ct	St	O	M	Runs	Wkts	Avge	Best	5wI	10wM
Test																		
All First	7	11	0	198	34	18.00	-	-	4	-	5	0	14	0	-	-	-	-
1-day Int																		
NatWest																			
B & H	6	6	3	122	52	40.66	-	1	1	-								
Sunday	9	8	2	97	34 *	16.16	-	-	1	-								

Career Performances

	M	Inns	NO	Runs	HS	Avge	100s	50s	Ct	St	Balls	Runs	Wkts	Avge	Best	5wI	10wM
Test																	
All First	98	154	21	4195	139	31.54	5	23	89	-	2914	1927	41	47.00	3-91	-	-
1-day Int																	
NatWest	7	5	1	151	85 *	37.75	-	1	5	-	18	0	1	0.00	1-0	-	
B & H	18	12	4	238	65 *	29.75	-	2	2	-	150	131	1	131.00	1-59	-	
Sunday	77	65	11	1307	101	24.20	1	2	24	-	36	43	0	-	-	-	

SHAW, A. D. Glamorgan

Name: Adrian David Shaw
Role: Right-hand bat, wicket-keeper
Born: 17 February 1972, Neath
Height: 5ft 11in **Weight:** 12st 10lbs
Nickname: Shawsy, Gloves, Teflon, Cymbals, Dale, Barrymore
County debut: 1992 (one-day), 1994 (first-class)
1st-Class 50s: 3
1st-Class catches: 89
1st-Class stumpings: 9
Place in batting averages: 171st av. 2431 (1996 258th av. 16.52)
Parents: David Colin and Christina
Marital status: Single
Family links with cricket: 'Mum thinks Mark Ramprakash is "handsome". Apart from that absolutely none … Grandad saw a game once'
Education: Llangatwe Comprehensive; Neath Tertiary College, 'Wallabies, Market Tavern and very often on Saturday nights. Very enlightening!'
Qualifications: 9 O-levels, 3 A-levels, cricket coaching awards
Career outside cricket: 'Currently making a living from the government i.e. unemployed'
Overseas tours: Welsh Schools to Barbados 1988; England YC to New Zealand 1990-91
Overseas teams played for: Welkom, Orange Free State 1995-96
Young players to look out for: Matthew Condé, Scott Bater, Lyndon Joshua. 'Watch this space'
Other sports followed: Rugby (played for Neath RFC, Welsh Youth and Wales U21 squads), football (Leeds), rugby league (Warrington) 'and contrary to what Anthony Cottey and Robert Croft may believe, I do actually support Wales'
Relaxations: 'There is nothing like a good chat on a rainy day with Cotts and Crofty. They always value my moderate opinions on things very highly. Thanks boys!'
Extras: One of youngest players (18 years 7 days) to play first-class rugby for Neath. Played for Neath against Swansea six days after playing against Zimbabwe for Glamorgan, and had the 'pleasure' of marking Scott Gibbs. Neath RFC Back of the Year 1993-94. Hopes to become the first player for a number of years to play against South Africa in two sports when Neath play them. 'Hoping to be awarded Glamorgan 2nd XI's first benefit after 10 years in the "Stiffs"!' Voted Glamorgan 2nd XI Player of the Year and Glamorgan Young Player of the Year in 1995. 2nd XI Player of the Month, June 1996
Best batting: 74 Glamorgan v Surrey, Cardiff 1996

1997 Season

	M	Inns	NO	Runs	HS	Avge	100s	50s	Ct	St	O	M	Runs	Wkts	Avge	Best	5wI	10wM
Test																		
All First	18	21	5	389	53 *	24.31	-	1	52	2								
1-day Int																		
NatWest	4	4	1	64	34 *	21.33	-	-	4	-								
B & H	4	3	0	26	15	8.66	-	-	5	1								
Sunday	14	9	2	73	48	10.42	-	-	7	1								

Career Performances

	M	Inns	NO	Runs	HS	Avge	100s	50s	Ct	St	Balls	Runs	Wkts	Avge	Best	5wI	10wM
Test																		
All First	36	46	8	708	74	18.63	-	3	89	9								
1-day Int																		
NatWest	4	4	1	64	34 *	21.33	-	-	4	-								
B & H	4	3	0	26	15	8.66	-	-	5	1								
Sunday	26	16	5	178	48	16.18	-	-	10	5								

SHEERAZ, K. P. Gloucestershire

Name: Kamran Pashah Sheeraz
Role: Right-hand bat, right-arm medium-fast bowler
Born: 28 December 1973, Wellington, Shropshire
Height: 5ft 11in **Weight:** 13st 7lbs
County debut: 1994
1st-Class 5 w. in innings: 2
1st-Class 10 w. in match: 1
1st-Class catches: 4
Strike rate: (career 63.59)
Parents: Mohammed and Shamim
Wife and date of marriage: Shamim, 25 March 1996
Family links with cricket: Brother, Humeran, a county youth player. Cousin, Ali, plays for Berkshire Colts
Education: Licensed Victuallers School, Ascot; East Berks College of Further Education; University of East London
Qualifications: GCSEs and BTEC National Diploma (Business and Finance), advanced cricket coach

Overseas teams played for: RDCA Rawalpindi, Pakistan
Cricketers particularly admired: Imran Khan, Dennis Lillee, Courtney Walsh
Young players to look out for: Rob Cunliffe, Matt Windows, Dom Hewson
Other sports followed: Football (Liverpool and Slough Town)
Relaxations: Reading, music, working out and spending time with family and loved ones
Extras: Toured Australia 1991-92 with Berkshire Youth XI and attended Bull Development of Excellence at Lilleshall 1992. Received Texaco (U16) outstanding bowling award (seven wickets in innings) from Ted Dexter. Represented Bedfordshire in Minor Counties Championship. Senior NABC 67kg Boxing Champion. England Amateur Boxing International
Opinions on cricket: 'Too much cricket is played in the first-class season. Players should be given more time to recover to prevent injuries.'
Best batting: 12* Gloucestershire v Glamorgan, Swansea 1997
Best bowling: 6-67 Gloucestershire v West Indies, Bristol 1995

1997 Season

	M	Inns	NO	Runs	HS	Avge	100s	50s	Ct	St	O	M	Runs	Wkts	Avge	Best	5wI	10wM
Test																		
All First	2	2	2	15	12 *	-	-	-	-	-	7	0	40	0	-	-	-	-
1-day Int																		
NatWest	1	0	0	0	0	-	-	-	-	-	10	1	30	0	-	-	-	
B & H																		
Sunday	5	3	2	9	7 *	9.00	-	-	-	-	19.5	1	87	3	29.00	2-34	-	

Career Performances

	M	Inns	NO	Runs	HS	Avge	100s	50s	Ct	St	Balls	Runs	Wkts	Avge	Best	5wI	10wM
Test																	
All First	13	16	9	27	12 *	3.85	-	-	4	-	1717	1104	27	40.88	6-67	2	1
1-day Int																	
NatWest	1	0	0	0	0	-	-	-	-	-	60	30	0	-	-	-	
B & H																	
Sunday	17	8	5	35	14 *	11.66	-	-	2	-	611	486	12	40.50	2-20	-	

SHEIKH, M. A.   Warwickshire

Name: Mohammed Avez Sheikh
Born: 2 July 1973, Birmingham
Role: Left-hand bat, right-arm
medium bowler
Nickname: Sheikhy
Education: Broadway School
County debut: 1997
Strike rate: 29.00 (career 29.00)
Off-season: Playing in South Africa
Overseas teams played for: Western
Province CC 1997-98
Extras: Has also played for
Warwickshire U19 and played for both
Worcestershire and Essex 2nd XIs in 1995
Best batting: 24 Warwickshire v Middlesex,
Edgbaston 1997
Best bowling: 2-14 Warwickshire v
Middlesex, Edgbaston 1997

1997 Season

	M	Inns	NO	Runs	HS	Avge	100s	50s	Ct	St	O	M	Runs	Wkts	Avge	Best	5wI	10wM
Test																		
All First	1	1	0	24	24	24.00	-	-	-	-	14.3	7	24	3	8.00	2-14	-	-
1-day Int																		
NatWest																		
B & H																		
Sunday	2	1	0	1	1	1.00	-	-	-	-								

Career Performances

	M	Inns	NO	Runs	HS	Avge	100s	50s	Ct	St	Balls	Runs	Wkts	Avge	Best	5wI	10wM
Test																	
All First	1	1	0	24	24	24.00	-	-	-	-	87	24	3	8.00	2-14	-	-
1-day Int																	
NatWest																	
B & H																	
Sunday	2	1	0	1	1	1.00	-	-	-	-							

SHERIYAR, A.   Worcestershire

Name: Alamgir Sheriyar
Role: Right-hand bat, left-arm fast bowler
Born: 15 November 1973, Birmingham
Height: 6ft 1in **Weight:** 13st
Nickname: Sheri
County debut: 1993 (one-day, Leics),
1994 (first-class, Leics),
1996 (Worcestershire)
50 wickets in a season: 1
1st-Class 5 w. in innings: 6
1st-Class 10 w. in match: 2
1st-Class catches: 5
Place in batting averages: 284th av. 10.44
(1996 311th av. 6.33)
Place in bowling averages: 33rd av. 25.40
(1996 129th av. 44.89)
Strike rate: 43.14 (career 51.48)
Parents: Mohammed Zaman (deceased) and
Safia Sultana
Marital status: Single
Family links with cricket: Brothers play a bit
Education: George Dixon Secondary School, Birmingham; Joseph Chamberlain Sixth
Form College, Birmingham; Oxford Brookes University
Qualifications: 6 O-levels, studying for BEng (Hons) Combined Engineering
Overseas tours: Leicestershire to South Africa 1995; Worcestershire to
Barbados 1996
Cricketers particularly admired: Wasim Akram
Other sports followed: Football, basketball
Relaxations: Time at home, music
Extras: Played for English Schools U17 and has also played in the Indoor National
League. Became only the second player to take a hat-trick on his first-class debut. Asked
to be released by Leicestershire at the end of the 1995 season and joined Worcestershire
for 1996
Opinions on cricket: 'It's a batsman's game.'
Best batting: 21 Worcestershire v Pakistan A, Worcester 1997
Best bowling: 6-19 Worcestershire v Sussex, Arundel 1997

---

86. Who was voted as England's Man of the Tournament during
their victorious Sharjah campaign in December 1997?

1997 Season

	M	Inns	NO	Runs	HS	Avge	100s	50s	Ct	St	O	M	Runs	Wkts	Avge	Best	5wI	10wM
Test																		
All First	18	13	4	94	21	10.44	-	-	4	-	445.5	94	1575	62	25.40	6-19	3	1
1-day Int																		
NatWest	2	1	0	0	0	0.00	-	-	-	-	15	0	74	2	37.00	1-35	-	
B & H	1	0	0	0	0	-	-	-	-	-	10	0	65	1	65.00	1-65	-	
Sunday	12	2	1	1	1	1.00	-	-	1	-	49.5	2	272	11	24.72	4-18	-	

Career Performances

	M	Inns	NO	Runs	HS	Avge	100s	50s	Ct	St	Balls	Runs	Wkts	Avge	Best	5wI	10wM
Test																	
All First	46	43	16	219	21	8.11	-	-	11	-	7157	4435	139	31.90	6-19	6	2
1-day Int																	
NatWest	3	2	0	10	10	5.00	-	-	-	-	120	109	2	54.50	1-35	-	
B & H	4	1	1	1	1*	-	-	-	-	-	211	173	6	28.83	3-40	-	
Sunday	29	8	6	36	19	18.00	-	-	3	-	767	718	20	35.90	4-18	-	

SHINE, K. J. Somerset

Name: Kevin James Shine
Role: Right-hand bat, right-arm fast bowler
Born: 22 February 1969, Bracknell, Berks
Height: 6ft 3in **Weight:** 15st
Nickname: Kenny, Shiney, Wookie, Polish ('courtesy of Robbo')
County debut: 1989 (Hampshire), 1994 (Middlesex), 1996 (Somerset)
50 wickets in a season: 1
1st-Class 5 w. in innings: 12
1st-Class 10 w. in match: 2
1st-Class catches: 21
Place in batting averages: 300th av. 6.40 (1996 289th av. 11.00)
Place in bowling averages: 72nd av. 30.50 (1996 91st av. 34.54)
Strike rate: 48.38 (career 55.31)
Parents: Joe and Clair
Marital status: Single
Education: Winnersh County Primary; Maiden Erlegh Comprehensive
Qualifications: 5 O-levels, 'gave up A-levels to pursue a cricket career', NCA advanced coach, qualified free weight training instructor

Career outside cricket: Cricket coach. Director of Coaching for Berkshire Indoor Cricket Centre
Overseas teams played for: Merewether, Newcastle, NSW 1990
Cricketers particularly admired: Malcolm Marshall, Bob Cottam ('great bowling coach'), Adi Aymes, SS, CCM, Paul Farbrace ('for his continued commitment to diet and fitness even after retirement')
Young players to look out for: Jason Laney
Other sports followed: Football (Reading)
Relaxations: 'Constructive arguments with the "Posh Boy", and also watching him display his boxing skills'
Extras: Took 8-47 including a hat-trick against Lancashire at Old Trafford in May 1992. Has written (with Jason Harris) a weekly column for the *Reading Chronicle*. 'Told I was released by Middlesex four days before major surgery on left ankle.' Joined Somerset for the 1996 season
Opinions on cricket: 'It's still too easy for the batters.'
Best batting: 40 Somerset v Surrey, Taunton 1996
Best bowling: 8-47 Hampshire v Lancashire, Old Trafford 1992

1997 Season

	M	Inns	NO	Runs	HS	Avge	100s	50s	Ct	St	O	M	Runs	Wkts	Avge	Best	5wI	10wM
Test																		
All First	18	20	5	96	18	6.40	-	-	5	-	443.3	89	1678	55	30.50	7-43	3	1
1-day Int																		
NatWest																		
B & H																		
Sunday	5	1	0	3	3	3.00	-	-	-	-	30.2	0	182	6	30.33	2-25	-	

Career Performances

	M	Inns	NO	Runs	HS	Avge	100s	50s	Ct	St	Balls	Runs	Wkts	Avge	Best	5wI	10wM
Test																	
All First	99	91	35	520	40	9.28	-	-	21	-	13551	8772	245	35.80	8-47	12	2
1-day Int																	
NatWest	2	0	0	0	0	-	-	-	-	-	129	92	3	30.66	3-31	-	
B & H	7	2	1	38	38 *	38.00	-	-	-	-	308	329	6	54.83	4-68	-	
Sunday	23	5	4	8	3	8.00	-	-	2	-	913	846	26	32.53	4-31	-	

SIDEBOTTOM, R. J. — Yorkshire

Name: Ryan Jay Sidebottom
Role: Left-hand bat, left-arm
fast-medium bowler
Born: 15 January 1978, Huddersfield
Height: 6ft 3in **Weight:** 12st 7lbs
Nickname: Red Pup, Gigsy, Medusa
County debut: 1997
Strike rate: 33.33 (career 33.33)
Parents: Arnie and Gillian
Marital status: Single
Family links with cricket: Father played for
Yorkshire and England
Education: Almondbury Primary,
Huddersfield; King James Grammar School,
Huddersfield
Qualifications: 5 GCSEs
Off-season: Coaching at the Yorkshire
Cricket School and promoting the game at
schools around the county
Overseas tours: England U17 to Holland 1995
Cricketers particularly admired: Allan Donald, Darren Gough, Craig White, Bradley
Parker
Young players to look out for: Chris Silverwood, Matthew Thewlis, John Inglis
Other sports followed: Football (Huddersfield Town FC), rugby league (Leeds)
Relaxations: Listening to music, sleeping, watching videos
Best batting: 2* Yorkshire v Leicestershire, Leicester 1997
Best bowling: 3-71 Yorkshire v Leicestershire, Leicester 1997

1997 Season

	M	Inns	NO	Runs	HS	Avge	100s	50s	Ct	St	O	M	Runs	Wkts	Avge	Best	5wI	10wM
Test																		
All First	1	1	1	2	2 *	-	-	-	-	-	16.4	4	71	3	23.66	3-71	-	-
1-day Int																		
NatWest																		
B & H																		
Sunday	3	0	0	0	0	-	-	-	1	-	19	2	103	1	103.00	1-41	-	

Career Performances

	M	Inns	NO	Runs	HS	Avge	100s	50s	Ct	St	Balls	Runs	Wkts	Avge	Best	5wI	10wM
Test																	
All First	1	1	1	2	2 *	-	-	-	-	-	100	71	3	23.66	3-71	-	-
1-day Int																	
NatWest																	
B & H																	
Sunday	3	0	0	0	0	-	-	-	1	-	114	103	1	103.00	1-41	-	

SILVERWOOD, C. E. W. Yorkshire

Name: Christopher Eric Wilfred Silverwood
Role: Right-hand bat, right-arm
fast-medium bowler
Born: 5 March 1975, Pontefract
Height: 6ft 1in **Weight:** 12st 9lbs
Nickname: Spoons, Silvers, Chubby
County debut: 1993
Test debut: 1996-97
Tests: 1
One-Day Internationals: 6
1st-Class 50s: 2
1st-Class 5 w. in innings: 4
1st-Class 10 w. in match: 1
1st-Class catches: 11
One-Day 5 w. in innings: 1
Place in batting averages: 202nd av. 21.47
(1996 290th av. 11.00)
Place in bowling averages: 42nd av. 26.39
(1996 63rd av. 30.68)
Strike rate: 49.51 (career 50.23)
Parents: Brenda
Wife and date of marriage: Emma, 3 October 1997
Family links with cricket: 'Dad played a bit'
Education: Gibson Lane School, Kippax; Garforth Comprehensive
Qualifications: 8 GCSEs, City and Guilds in Leisure and Recreation
Off-season: Touring Kenya and Sri Lanka with England A
Overseas tours: England to Zimbabwe and New Zealand 1996-97, to West Indies
1997-98; England A to Kenya and Sri Lanka 1997-98
Overseas teams played for: Wellington, Cape Town 1993-94, 1995-96
Cricketers particularly admired: Ian Botham, Allan Donald
Other sports followed: Rugby league (Castleford), karate

Relaxations: Listening to music, watching videos, 'riding my motorbike'
Extras: Black belt in karate. Attended the Yorkshire Cricket Academy. Represented Yorkshire at athletics. Played for England U19 in the home series against India in 1994. Made his Test debut against Zimbabwe in the first Test at Bulawayo in 1996-97. Called up to the England tour of West Indies after the withdrawal of Darren Gough through injury
Best batting: 58 Yorkshire v Lancashire, Old Trafford 1997
Best bowling: 7-93 Yorkshire v Kent, Headingley 1997

1997 Season

	M	Inns	NO	Runs	HS	Avge	100s	50s	Ct	St	O	M	Runs	Wkts	Avge	Best	5wI	10wM
Test																		
All First	18	23	6	365	58	21.47	-	1	-	-	478.4	108	1531	58	26.39	7-93	4	1
1-day Int	1	0	0	0	0	-	-	-	-	-	6	0	44	0	-	-	-	
NatWest	3	1	0	3	3	3.00	-	-	-	-	22.2	4	95	4	23.75	3-24	-	
B & H	6	2	0	8	8	4.00	-	-	-	-	50	3	225	10	22.50	3-22	-	
Sunday	14	8	4	21	7 *	5.25	-	-	2	-	89.3	4	452	14	32.28	3-12	-	

Career Performances

	M	Inns	NO	Runs	HS	Avge	100s	50s	Ct	St	Balls	Runs	Wkts	Avge	Best	5wI	10wM
Test	1	1	0	0	0	0.00	-	-	1	-	150	71	4	17.75	3-63	-	-
All First	55	77	18	829	58	14.05	-	2	14	-	8440	4849	168	28.86	7-93	8	1
1-day Int	6	4	0	17	12	4.25	-	-	-	-	252	201	3	67.00	2-27	-	
NatWest	8	3	2	11	8 *	11.00	-	-	3	-	416	264	8	33.00	3-24	-	
B & H	11	4	0	11	8	2.75	-	-	2	-	568	402	22	18.27	5-28	1	
Sunday	47	22	13	86	14 *	9.55	-	-	4	-	1860	1449	57	25.42	4-26	-	

SIMMONS, P. V.   Leicestershire

Name: Philip Verant Simmons
Role: Right-hand bat, right-arm
medium bowler, county vice-captain
Born: 18 April 1963, Port-of-Spain, Trinidad
County debut: 1994
Test debut: 1988
Tests: 25
One-Day Internationals: 119
1000 runs in a season: 1
50 wickets in a season: 1
1st-Class 50s: 54
1st-Class 100s: 20
1st-Class 200s: 2

1st-Class 5 w. in innings: 4
1st-Class catches: 196
One-Day 100s: 8
One-Day 5 w. in innings: 1
Place in batting averages: 16th av. 56.54
Place in bowling averages: 5th av. 18.23
Strike rate: 39.07 (career 62.38)
Overseas tours: West Indies YC to England 1982; West Indies B to Zimbabwe 1983 and 1986; West Indies to India and Pakistan (World Cup) 1987-88, to England 1988, to Sharjah and India (Nehru Cup) 1989-90, to Sharjah 1991-92, to Australia and South Africa 1992-93, to Sharjah, India (Hero Cup) and Sri Lanka 1993-94, to India 1994-95, to England 1995, to Australia 1995-95, to India and Pakistan (World Cup) 1995-96, to Australia 1996-97, to Pakistan 1997-98

Overseas teams played for: Crompton, Trinidad; Trinidad and Tobago 1983-98; Eastern Transvaal 1996-97
Extras: Suffered a bad head injury on West Indies tour to England in 1988. Appointed captain of Trinidad in 1989. Scored record 261 on his debut for Leicestershire in 1994. Returns to Leicestershire in 1998 as their overseas player after a year's absence
Best batting: 261 Leicestershire v Northamptonshire, Leicester 1994
Best bowling: 6-14 Leicestershire v Durham, Chester-le-Street 1996

1997 Season (did not make any first-class or one-day appearances)

Career Performances

	M	Inns	NO	Runs	HS	Avge	100s	50s	Ct	St	Balls	Runs	Wkts	Avge	Best	5wI	10wM
Test	25	45	2	1000	110	23.25	1	4	26	-	612	248	4	62.00	2-34	-	-
All First	169	289	13	10297	261	37.30	22	55	196	-	10309	4779	161	29.68	6-14	4	-
1-day Int	119	117	7	3242	122	29.47	5	17	51	-	3034	2185	62	35.24	4-3	-	
NatWest	6	6	0	193	82	32.16	-	1	3	-	312	243	8	30.37	3-31	-	
B & H	4	4	0	136	64	34.00	-	2	2	-	162	134	1	134.00	1-29	-	
Sunday	33	33	1	1475	140	46.09	3	10	15	-	1103	924	31	29.80	5-37	1	

SINGH, A.   Warwickshire

Name: Anurag Singh
Role: Right-hand bat, off-spin bowler
Born: 9 September 1975, Kanpur, India
Height: 5ft 10in **Weight:** 11st
Nickname: Ragga, Ragi, Ragstar, Rood
County debut: 1995
1st-Class 50s: 2
1st-Class 100s: 3
1st-Class catches: 12
One-Day 100s: 1
Place in batting averages: 140th av. 27.30
(1996 106th av. 35.90)
Parents: Vijay and Rajul
Marital status: Single
Education: King Edward's School,
Birmingham; Gonville and Caius College,
Cambridge
Qualifications: 12 GCSEs, 4 A-levels
Overseas tours: England U19 to West Indies
1994-95; Warwickshire U21 to South Africa; Warwickshire CCC to South Africa
Cricketers particularly admired: Trevor Penney, Graeme Welch, Brian Lara, Allan
Donald, Mohammed Azharuddin
Young players to look out for: Darren Altree, Vikram Solanki
Other sports followed: Football (Wimbledon FC and Aston Villa)
Relaxations: 'Spending time with my family. Going out with friends and girlfriend,
Louise'
Extras: Broke school record for number of runs in a season (1102). *Daily Telegraph*
regional award for batting (twice) and bowling (once). Tiger Smith Memorial Award for
Warwickshire Most Promising Young Cricketer 1994, Coney Edmonds Trophy for
Warwickshire Best U19 Cricketer 1994, Lord's Taverners Trophy for Best Young
Cricketer 1994, Gray-Nicolls Len Newberry Award for ESCA U19 Best Player 1994.
Scored two centuries for England U19 against India U19 in 1994. Scored one century
against West Indies U20 and was Man of the Series 1994-95. Scored 128 for
Warwickshire 2nd XI v Gloucestershire 2nd XI in 1994. Awarded 2nd XI cap in 1995
Opinions on cricket: 'Have not played enough to give any valued judged opinions.'
Best batting: 157 Cambridge University v Sussex, Hove 1996

---

87. Who was voted the Player of the Tournament in Sharjah 1997?

O vodafone

1997 Season

	M	Inns	NO	Runs	HS	Avge	100s	50s	Ct	St	O	M	Runs	Wkts	Avge	Best	5wI	10wM
Test																		
All First	10	14	1	355	134	27.30	1	1	5	-	3	1	10	0	-	-	-	-
1-day Int																		
NatWest																		
B & H	5	5	1	78	53 *	19.50	-	1	-	-								
Sunday	5	5	0	112	86	22.40	-	1	1	-								

Career Performances

	M	Inns	NO	Runs	HS	Avge	100s	50s	Ct	St	Balls	Runs	Wkts	Avge	Best	5wI	10wM
Test																	
All First	23	38	3	1085	157	31.00	3	2	12	-	42	24	0	-	-	-	-
1-day Int																	
NatWest																	
B & H	10	10	1	338	123	37.55	1	2	1	-							
Sunday	6	6	0	114	86	19.00	-	1	1	-							

SMALL, G. C.   Warwickshire

Name: Gladstone Cleophas Small
Role: Right-hand bat, right-arm
fast-medium bowler
Born: 18 October 1961, St George, Barbados
Height: 5ft 11in **Weight:** 12st
Nickname: Gladys, Glad, Stoney
County debut: 1980
County cap: 1982
Benefit: 1992 (£129,500)
Test debut: 1986
Tests: 17
One-Day Internationals: 53
50 wickets in a season: 6
1st-Class 50s: 7
1st-Class 5 w. in innings: 29
1st-Class 10 w. in match: 2
1st-Class catches: 95
One-Day 5 w. in innings: 4
Place in bowling averages:
(1996 47th av. 28.21)
Strike rate: 100.00 (career 58.17)
Parents: Chelston and Gladys
Wife and date of marriage: Lois, 19 September 1987

Children: Zak, Marcus and Zoe
Family links with cricket: Cousin Milton Small toured England with West Indies in 1988
Education: Moseley School; Hall Green Technical College, Birmingham
Qualifications: 2 O-levels, NCA senior coaching award
Career outside cricket: Sports marketing consultant
Overseas tours: England YC to New Zealand 1979-80; England to Australia 1986-87, to India and Pakistan (World Cup) 1987-88, to India and West Indies 1989-90, to Australia 1990-91, to Australia and New Zealand (World Cup) 1991-92; Warwickshire to Cape Town, to Zimbabwe, to Trinidad
Overseas teams played for: Balwyn, Melbourne 1982-83, 1984-85; West Torrens, Adelaide 1985-86; South Australia 1985-86
Cricketers particularly admired: Malcolm Marshall, Richard Hadlee, Allan Donald, Brian Lara, Robin Smith
Other sports followed: Golf, tennis, football (Aston Villa FC)
Relaxations: 'Home with family, tending my vegetable garden, wining and dining with friends'
Extras: Was called up for England Test squad v Pakistan at Edgbaston, July 1982, but did not play. Bowled 18-ball over v Middlesex in August 1982, with 11 no-balls. Grandfather watched him take eight wickets in the Barbados Test v West Indies in 1989-90 on his return to the land of his birth. Was Andy Lloyd's best man
Opinions on cricket: 'Counties having to bowl more than 18 overs per hour is one of the major reasons why we can't produce any bowler able to bowl fast consistently. By the time that they have reached fast bowling maturity they have long become line and length medium pacers. Please install a law to assist the bowlers.'
Best batting: 70 Warwickshire v Lancashire, Old Trafford 1988
Best bowling: 7-15 Warwickshire v Nottinghamshire, Edgbaston 1988

1997 Season

	M	Inns	NO	Runs	HS	Avge	100s	50s	Ct	St	O	M	Runs	Wkts	Avge	Best	5wI	10wM
Test																		
All First	3	4	1	13	11	4.33	-	-	1	-	50	12	158	3	52.66	3-51	-	-
1-day Int																		
NatWest	5	2	1	36	32 *	36.00	-	-	-	-	37.2	1	121	5	24.20	3-22	-	
B & H	6	2	1	15	14 *	15.00	-	-	-	-	47	7	195	15	13.00	5-23	1	
Sunday	15	3	2	11	9 *	11.00	-	-	3	-	95.5	5	462	21	22.00	5-26	1	

Career Performances

	M	Inns	NO	Runs	HS	Avge	100s	50s	Ct	St	Balls	Runs	Wkts	Avge	Best	5wI	10wM
Test	17	24	7	263	59	15.47	-	1	9	-	3927	1871	55	34.01	5-48	2	-
All First	315	404	97	4409	70	14.36	-	7	95	-	49567	24392	852	28.62	7-15	29	2
1-day Int	53	24	9	98	18 *	6.53	-	-	7	-	2793	1942	58	33.48	4-31	-	
NatWest	48	30	9	256	33	12.19	-	-	8	-	2828	1491	53	28.13	3-22	-	
B & H	64	37	10	184	22	6.81	-	-	11	-	3572	2084	79	26.37	5-23	1	
Sunday	191	85	31	429	40 *	7.94	-	-	40	-	8006	5924	240	24.68	5-26	3	

SMITH, A. M.   Gloucestershire

Name: Andrew Michael Smith
Role: Right-hand bat, left-arm
medium bowler
Born: 1 October 1967, Dewsbury,
West Yorks
Height: 5ft 9in **Weight:** 12st
Nickname: Smudge, Ronnie, Piano Man
County debut: 1991
Test debut: 1997
Tests: 1
50 wickets in a season: 3
1st-Class 50s: 2
1st-Class 5 w. in innings: 13
1st-Class 10 w. in match: 5
1st-Class catches: 15
Place in batting averages: 287th av. 9.70
(1996 257th av. 16.54)
Place in bowling averages: 3rd av. 17.63
(1996 38th av. 26.91)

Strike rate: 37.03 (career 50.18)
Parents: Hugh and Margaret
Wife and date of marriage: Sarah, 2 October 1993
Children: William James, 9 October 1994
Family links with cricket: Father, uncle and brother all play or played club cricket in Yorkshire
Education: Queen Elizabeth Grammar School, Wakefield; Exeter University
Qualification: 10 O-levels, 4 A-levels, BA (Hons) French and German
Overseas tours: Queen Elizabeth Grammar School to Holland 1985; Bradford Junior Cricket League to Barbados 1986; Exeter University to Barbados 1987; Gloucestershire to Kenya 1990, to Sri Lanka 1992-93, to Zimbabwe 1996; England A to Pakistan 1995-96
Overseas teams played for: Waimea, New Zealand 1990; WTTU, New Zealand 1991
Cricketers particularly admired: Richard Hadlee, Allan Lamb, Wasim Akram
Young players to look out for: Rob Cunliffe
Other sports followed: Football (Leeds United)
Relaxations: Crosswords, reading
Extras: Played for English Schools U19, NAYC and represented Combined Universities in the B&H Cup in 1988 and 1990. Persistent side strain forced him to fly home from the England A tour of Pakistan in 1995-96. Finished the 1997 season as leading wicket-taker with 83 first-class wickets
Opinions on cricket: 'Why, at international level, do we produce pitches that suit our

opposition? Why do we give them a choice of balls if they win the toss? Why do we chop and change players so much? Our opposition are bewildered at our team selection. We should make it hard for teams to play here instead of pampering them. We get few favours when we go overseas. Time to get tough.'

Best batting: 55* Gloucestershire v Nottinghamshire, Trent Bridge 1996
Best bowling: 8-73 Gloucestershire v Middlesex, Lord's 1996

1997 Season

	M	Inns	NO	Runs	HS	Avge	100s	50s	Ct	St	O	M	Runs	Wkts	Avge	Best	5wl	10wM
Test	1	2	1	4	4 *	4.00	-	-	-	-	23	2	89	0	-	-	-	-
All First	18	26	9	165	41 *	9.70	-	-	4	-	512.2	125	1464	83	17.63	6-45	5	3
1-day Int																		
NatWest	1	1	0	4	4	4.00	-	-	-	-	12	0	62	2	31.00	2-62	-	
B & H	5	2	1	5	3 *	5.00	-	-	-	-	50	10	180	8	22.50	3-24	-	
Sunday	14	8	4	46	10	11.50	-	-	1	-	89	13	386	16	24.12	2-14	-	

Career Performances

	M	Inns	NO	Runs	HS	Avge	100s	50s	Ct	St	Balls	Runs	Wkts	Avge	Best	5wl	10wM
Test	1	2	1	4	4 *	4.00	-	-	-	-	138	89	0	-	-	-	-
All First	92	115	24	1044	55 *	11.47	-	2	15	-	15006	7916	299	26.47	8-73	13	5
1-day Int																	
NatWest	14	7	4	44	13	14.66	-	-	3	-	775	490	16	30.62	3-21	-	
B & H	32	20	10	81	15 *	8.10	-	-	7	-	1838	1247	43	29.00	6-39	1	
Sunday	94	48	28	261	26 *	13.05	-	-	13	-	3645	2914	101	28.85	4-38	-	

SMITH, B. F.   Leicestershire

Name: Benjamin Francis Smith
Role: Right-hand bat, right-arm medium bowler
Born: 3 April 1972, Corby
Height: 5ft 9in **Weight:** 11st
Nickname: Smudge, Ferret, Gadget
County debut: 1990
County cap: 1995
1000 runs in a season: 1
1st-Class 50s: 23
1st-Class 100s: 7
1st-Class catches: 41
One-Day 100s: 1
Place in batting averages: 36th av. 44.57 (1996 39th av. 47.80)
Strike rate: (career 115.00)
Parents: Keith and Janet

Marital status: Engaged to Lisa
Family links with cricket: Father, grandfather and uncles all played
Education: Tugby Primary; Kibworth High; Robert Smyth, Market Harborough
Qualifications: 5 O-levels, NCA coaching certificate
Off-season: Playing club cricket in New Zealand
Overseas tours: England YC to New Zealand 1990-91; Rutland Tourists to South Africa 1992
Overseas teams played for: Alexandria, Zimbabwe 1990; Bankstown Canterbury, Sydney 1993-96
Cricketers particularly admired: David Gower, Viv Richards
Young players to look out for: Michael Jones
Other sports followed: Football (Leicester City), rugby union (Leicester Tigers), tennis and golf
Injuries: Broken little finger on left hand, missed six first-class games, five Sunday League games and three Benson & Hedges matches
Relaxations: Music, family, eating out and cinema
Extras: Played tennis for Leicestershire aged 12. Cricket Society Young Player of the Year 1991
Best batting: 190 Leicestershire v Glamorgan, Swansea 1996
Best bowling: 1-5 Leicestershire v Essex, Ilford 1991

1997 Season

	M	Inns	NO	Runs	HS	Avge	100s	50s	Ct	St	O	M	Runs	Wkts	Avge	Best	5wI	10wM
Test																		
All First	13	19	5	624	131 *	44.57	2	2	3	-	1	0	4	0	-	-	-	-
1-day Int																		
NatWest	1	1	0	4	4	4.00	-	-	1	-								
B & H	2	2	0	72	61	36.00	-	1	1	-								
Sunday	12	12	1	275	71	25.00	-	2	4	-								

88. Prior to Pakistan in 1997-98, when was the last time the West Indies suffered a 3-0 series whitewash and against whom?

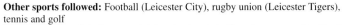

O vodafone

Career Performances

	M	Inns	NO	Runs	HS	Avge	100s	50s	Ct	St	Balls	Runs	Wkts	Avge	Best	5wl	10wM
Test																	
All First	109	167	25	4726	190	33.28	7	23	41	-	231	194	2	97.00	1-5	-	-
1-day Int																	
NatWest	9	8	1	170	63 *	24.28	-	1	3	-							
B & H	19	17	0	418	61	24.58	-	3	9	-							
Sunday	96	94	11	2197	115	26.46	1	8	23	-	18	15	0	-		-	-

SMITH, E. T.   Kent

Name: Edward Thomas Smith
Role: Right-hand bat, right-arm medium bowler
Born: 19 July 1977, Pembury, Kent
Height: 6ft 2in **Weight:** 13st
Nickname: Jazzer
County debut: 1996
1000 runs in a season: 1
1st-Class 50s: 10
1st-Class 100s: 4
1st-Class catches: 8
Place in batting averages: 47th av. 43.07 (1996 37th av. 48.00)
Parents: Jonathan and Gillie
Marital status: Single
Family links with cricket: Father Jonathan wrote *Good Enough?* with Chris Cowdrey
Education: Tonbridge School; Peterhouse, Cambridge University
Qualifications: 11 GCSEs, 3 A-levels
Cricketers particularly admired: Greg Chappell, Martin Crowe, Graham Cowdrey amd Michael Slater
Young players to look out for: Will House, Anurag Singh, Owais Shah
Other sports followed: Football (Arsenal FC)
Relaxations: Reading, theatre, cinema, socialising
Extras: Scored a century on his first-class debut against Glamorgan (101) and in doing so became the youngest player to score a century on debut for Cambridge University. He is also the first person to score 50 or more in each of his first five first-class games. Cambridge Blue in 1996. Played for England U19 against New Zealand U19 in 1996
Opinions on cricket: 'Cricket is not 50 per cent head, 50 per cent heart and nothing to do with technique. English players should have greater ambition in their own

performance – technical and temperamental. The system encourages them to settle for enough; which is not enough at the highest level.'

Best batting: 190 Cambridge University v Leicestershire, Fenner's 1997

1997 Season

	M	Inns	NO	Runs	HS	Avge	100s	50s	Ct	St	O	M	Runs	Wkts	Avge	Best	5wI	10wM
Test																		
All First	18	30	3	1163	190	43.07	2	6	7	-	2	0	22	0	-	-	-	-
1-day Int																		
NatWest																		
B & H	4	4	0	61	43	15.25	-	-	3	-								
Sunday	4	3	2	146	72 *	146.00	-	2	2	-								

Career Performances

	M	Inns	NO	Runs	HS	Avge	100s	50s	Ct	St	Balls	Runs	Wkts	Avge	Best	5wI	10wM
Test																	
All First	25	42	3	1739	190	44.58	4	10	8	-	12	22	0	-	-	-	-
1-day Int																	
NatWest																	
B & H	4	4	0	61	43	15.25	-	-	3	-							
Sunday	4	3	2	146	72 *	146.00	-	2	2	-							

SMITH, N. M. K.   Warwickshire

Name: Neil Michael Knight Smith
Role: Right-hand bat, off-spin bowler
Born: 27 July 1967, Solihull
Height: 6ft **Weight:** 13st 7lbs
Nickname: Gurt
County debut: 1987
County cap: 1993
One-Day Internationals: 7
1st-Class 50s: 18
1st-Class 100s: 2
1st-Class 5 w. in innings: 15
1st-Class catches: 44
One-Day 5 w. in innings: 3
Place in batting averages: 104th av. 33.78 (1996 181st av. 27.21)
Place in bowling averages: 123rd av. 40.23 (1996 77th av. 32.95)
Strike rate: 83.04 (career 75.21)

Parents: Mike (M.J.K.) and Diana
Wife and date of marriage: Rachel, 4 December 1993
Family links with cricket: Father captained Warwickshire and England
Education: Warwick School
Qualifications: 3 O-levels (Maths, English, French), cricket coach Grade 1
Career outside cricket: Sports teacher
Overseas tours: England to South Africa 1995-96, to India and Pakistan (World Cup) 1995-96
Overseas teams played for: Phoenix, Perth, Western Australia 1988-89
Cricketers particularly admired: David Gower, Ian Botham, Allan Donald
Other sports followed: Golf, rugby and football
Relaxations: Sport, family and music
Extras: Played for England in the one-day series against South Africa in 1995-96 and was then selected for the squad to play in the World Cup in India and Pakistan. Followed in his father's footsteps when he led his side out against Northamptonshire in the Sunday League – the first time both father and son have captained Warwickshire. Played for an England XI in the Cricket Max tournament in New Zealand in 1997-98
Opinions on cricket: 'Visiting teams should be given the option of batting or bowling to try to stop doctoring of pitches by the home side.'
Best batting: 161 Warwickshire v Yorkshire, Headingley 1989
Best bowling: 7-42 Warwickshire v Lancashire, Edgbaston 1994

1997 Season

	M	Inns	NO	Runs	HS	Avge	100s	50s	Ct	St	O	M	Runs	Wkts	Avge	Best	5wI	10wM
Test																		
All First	15	22	3	642	148	33.78	1	3	7	-	318.2	77	930	23	40.43	4-32	-	-
1-day Int																		
NatWest	5	5	0	85	72	17.00	-	1	2	-	13	0	57	1	57.00	1-30	-	
B & H	6	6	0	212	125	35.33	1	1	-	-	36.1	1	181	3	60.33	2-42	-	
Sunday	17	17	0	532	60	31.29	-	5	10	-	70	2	329	10	32.90	3-20	-	

Career Performances

	M	Inns	NO	Runs	HS	Avge	100s	50s	Ct	St	Balls	Runs	Wkts	Avge	Best	5wI	10wM
Test																	
All First	127	182	25	4084	161	26.01	2	18	44	-	19933	9964	265	37.60	7-42	15	-
1-day Int	7	6	1	100	31	20.00	-	-	1	-	261	190	6	31.66	3-29	-	
NatWest	32	28	6	479	72	21.77	-	3	11	-	1342	813	36	22.58	5-17	1	
B & H	30	24	2	548	125	24.90	1	3	5	-	1112	863	27	31.96	3-29	-	
Sunday	139	113	18	2428	111 *	25.55	1	15	50	-	4536	3520	130	27.07	6-33	2	

SMITH, R. A.   Hampshire

Name: Robin Arnold Smith
Role: Right-hand bat, slip fielder,
county captain
Born: 13 September 1963, Durban,
South Africa
Height: 6ft **Weight:** 15st
Nickname: The Judge
County debut: 1982
County cap: 1985
Benefit: 1996
Test debut: 1988
Tests: 62
One-Day Internationals: 71
1000 runs in a season: 10
1st-Class 50s: 103
1st-Class 100s: 51
1st-Class 200s: 1
1st-Class catches: 188
One-Day 100s: 23
Place in batting averages: 52nd av. 41.72 (1996 36th av. 48.13)
Strike rate: (career 79.58)
Parents: John and Joy
Wife and date of marriage: Katherine, 21 September 1988
Children: Harrison Arnold, 4 December 1991; Margaux Elizabeth, 28 July 1994
Family links with cricket: Grandfather played for Natal in Currie Cup. Brother Chris played for Natal, Hampshire and England
Education: Northlands Boys High, Durban
Qualifications: Matriculation, '62 England caps'
Career outside cricket: Director of Masuri Helmets and Judge Tours
Overseas tours: England to India and West Indies 1989-90, to Australia 1990-91, to Australia and New Zealand (World Cup) 1991-92, to India and Sri Lanka 1992-93, to West Indies 1993-94, to South Africa 1995-96, to India and Pakistan (World Cup) 1995-96
Overseas teams played for: Natal, South Africa 1980-84; Perth, Western Australia 1984-85 (grade cricket)
Cricketers particularly admired: Malcolm Marshall, Brian Lara, Graeme Hick, Graham Gooch, Allan Lamb
Other sports followed: Soccer, athletics, rugby, golf, racing
Relaxations: 'Reading (Leslie Thomas in particular), trout fishing, assembling a good wine cellar, keeping fit and spending as much time as possible with my lovely wife Katherine and my children'

Extras: Played rugby for Natal Schools and for Romsey RFC as a full-back. Held 19 school athletics records and two South African schools records in shot putt and 100-metre hurdles. One of *Wisden*'s Five Cricketers of the Year 1990. First child was born while he was on tour in Australia. Played for an England XI in the Cricket Max tournament in New Zealand in 1997-98. Has been appointed Hampshire captain for the 1998 season

Opinions on cricket: 'I enjoy playing cricket for Hampshire and particularly enjoy the camaraderie of the county circuit.'

Best batting: 209* Hampshire v Essex, Southampton 1987

Best bowling: 2-11 Hampshire v Surrey, Southampton 1985

1997 Season

	M	Inns	NO	Runs	HS	Avge	100s	50s	Ct	St	O	M	Runs	Wkts	Avge	Best	5wI	10wM
Test																		
All First	14	23	1	918	154	41.72	2	4	4	-	5.1	0	75	0	-		-	-	-
1-day Int																		
NatWest	2	2	0	245	126	122.50	2	-	-	-								
B & H	5	5	0	166	92	33.20	-	1	-	-								
Sunday	14	13	0	229	49	17.61	-	-	4	-								

Career Performances

	M	Inns	NO	Runs	HS	Avge	100s	50s	Ct	St	Balls	Runs	Wkts	Avge	Best	5wI	10wM
Test	62	112	15	4236	175	43.67	9	28	39	-	24	6	0	-	-	-	-
All First	333	568	78	21645	209 *	44.17	53	107	192	-	955	768	12	64.00	2-11	-	-
1-day Int	71	70	8	2419	167 *	39.01	4	15	26	-							
NatWest	35	35	10	1954	158	78.16	7	8	20	-	17	13	2	6.50	2-13	-	
B & H	52	49	8	2105	155 *	51.34	5	9	21	-	6	2	0	-	-	-	
Sunday	154	147	16	5231	131	39.93	9	32	64	-	2	0	1	0.00	1-0	-	

SMITH, T. M.   Derbyshire

Name: Trevor Mark Smith
Role: Left-hand bat, right-arm
medium-fast bowler
Born: 18 January 1977
Height: 6ft 3in **Weight:** 14st
Nickname: Tricky
County debut: No first-team appearance
Parents: Graham and Marilyn
Marital status: Single
Family links with cricket: Brothers all play
for Sandiacre Town CC
Education: Cloudside Junior School,
Sandiacre; Friesland School, Sandiacre;
Broxtowe College of Further Education,
Chilwell
Qualifications: 4 GCSEs, BTEC National
Diploma in Business and Finance
Off-season: Working and training
Cricketers particularly admired: Ian
Botham

Young players to look out for: Ben Spendlove
Other sports followed: Football
Relaxations: Music, football and golf
Opinions on cricket: 'The idea of Sunday League matches being played under lights is
brilliant. More things like that should be done to create more interest in the first-class
game.'

SNAPE, J. N. — Northamptonshire

Name: Jeremy Nicholas Snape
Role: Right-hand bat, off-spin bowler
Born: 27 April 1973, Stoke-on-Trent, Staffordshire
Height: 5ft 8in **Weight:** 12st
Nickname: Snapey, Coot, Jez
County debut: 1992
1st-Class 50s: 7
1st-Class 5 w. in innings: 1
1st-Class catches: 34
Place in batting averages: 182nd av. 23.53 (1996 224th av. 21.30)
Place in bowling averages: 131st av. 48.26 (1996 127th av. 44.04)
Strike rate: 101.26 (career 84.58)
Parents: Keith and Barbara
Marital status: Single

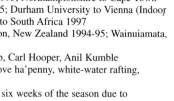

Family links with cricket: Brother Jonathan plays local club cricket in North Staffs and South Cheshire League for Kidsgrove, 'Dad only umpired once as he was the only person to appeal for a caught behind – off my bowling in the U13'
Education: Denstone College; Durham University
Qualifications: 8 GCSEs, 3 A-levels, studying for BSc (Hons) Natural Science
Career outside cricket: 'Open to suggestions'
Off-season: Two months working in sports marketing and then four months playing club cricket in Cape Town, South Africa
Overseas tours: England U18 to Canada 1991 (captain); England U19 to Pakistan 1991-92; Durham University to South Africa 1993; Northamptonshire to Cape Town 1993; Christians in Sport to Zimbabwe 1994-95; Durham University to Vienna (Indoor European Championships) 1994; Troubadours to South Africa 1997
Overseas teams played for: Petone, Wellington, New Zealand 1994-95; Wainuiamata, Wellington, New Zealand 1995-96
Cricketers particularly admired: Allan Lamb, Carl Hooper, Anil Kumble
Other sports followed: Golf, rugby union, shove ha'penny, white-water rafting, Bangalore kabadi team, yarding
Injuries: Badly broken thumb, missed the last six weeks of the season due to operation on hand where thumb was plated and pinned
Relaxations: Good food and drink, listening to music, travelling
Extras: Sir Jack Hobbs award (U15 Schoolboy 1988), Gold Award winner for Combined Universities v Worcestershire 1992 (3-34) at The Parks. Player of the Tournament at European Indoor 6-a-side Championships in 1994
Opinions on cricket: 'Definitely in favour of four-day cricket as it induces a more

disciplined approach, although I equally enjoy the challenges of one-day cricket. Counties should work harder to maximise the potential of their individual players while encouraging the teamwork essential to competition.'

Best batting: 87 Northamptonshire v Mashonaland Select XI, Harare 1994-95
Best bowling: 5-65 Northamptonshire v Durham, Northampton 1995

1997 Season

	M	Inns	NO	Runs	HS	Avge	100s	50s	Ct	St	O	M	Runs	Wkts	Avge	Best	5wI	10wM
Test																		
All First	11	16	3	306	66	23.53	-	3	9	-	253.1	60	724	15	48.26	4-46	-	-
1-day Int																		
NatWest	2	2	0	59	54	29.50	-	1	1	-	24	4	72	1	72.00	1-22	-	
B & H	6	4	1	45	27 *	15.00	-	-	4	-	42	2	163	8	20.37	5-32	1	
Sunday	9	6	2	95	33	23.75	-	-	2	-	52	3	261	9	29.00	4-31	-	

Career Performances

	M	Inns	NO	Runs	HS	Avge	100s	50s	Ct	St	Balls	Runs	Wkts	Avge	Best	5wI	10wM
Test																	
All First	39	56	11	1139	87	25.31	-	7	34	-	5498	2931	65	45.09	5-65	1	-
1-day Int																	
NatWest	7	6	2	99	54	24.75	-	1	3	-	289	189	5	37.80	2-44	-	
B & H	15	12	4	210	52	26.25	-	1	7	-	798	521	18	28.94	5-32	1	
Sunday	39	23	10	242	33	18.61	-	-	11	-	1182	968	34	28.47	4-31	-	

SOLANKI, V. S. — Worcestershire

Name: Vikram Singh Solanki
Role: Right-hand bat, off-spin bowler
Born: 1 April 1976, Udaipur, India
Height: 6ft **Weight:** 11st 7lbs
County debut: 1993 (one-day),
1995 (first-class)
1st-Class 50s: 9
1st-Class 100s: 1
1st-Class 5 w. in innings: 3
1st-Class 10 w. in match: 1
1st-Class catches: 29
Place in batting averages: 133rd av. 28.11
(1996 77th av. 39.42)
Place in bowling averages:
(1996 73rd av. 31.96)
Strike rate: 267.00 (career 73.93)
Parents: Vijay and Florabell
Marital status: Single
Family links with cricket: Father played in India
Education: Regis School, Wolverhampton
Qualifications: 9 GCSEs, 3 A-levels
Overseas tours: England U18 to South Africa 1992-93, to Denmark 1993; England U19 to West Indies 1994-95
Cricketers particularly admired: Sachin Tendulkar, Graeme Hick, Anthony McGrath and 'anyone who has made the grade at Test level'
Other sports followed: 'Enjoy playing most sports'
Relaxations: 'Spending time with friends and family'
Opinions on cricket: 'Four-day cricket seems to be working. However, there may be an argument for a two-league system as this would improve the standard of the game in general and also provide players with more time to practise.'
Best batting: 128* Worcestershire v Oxford University, The Parks 1997
Best bowling: 5-69 Worcestershire v Middlesex, Lord's 1996

1997 Season

	M	Inns	NO	Runs	HS	Avge	100s	50s	Ct	St	O	M	Runs	Wkts	Avge	Best	5wI	10wM
Test																		
All First	14	18	1	478	128*	28.11	1	2	10	-	89	21	309	2	154.50	1-33	-	-
1-day Int																		
NatWest	1	1	0	6	6	6.00	-	-	-	-	10.3	0	51	1	51.00	1-51	-	
B & H	5	5	0	90	21	18.00	-	-	1	-	3	0	17	1	17.00	1-17	-	
Sunday	16	13	1	239	58	19.91	-	1	5	-	4	0	18	1	18.00	1-9	-	

Career Performances

	M	Inns	NO	Runs	HS	Avge	100s	50s	Ct	St	Balls	Runs	Wkts	Avge	Best	5wl	10wM
Test																	
All First	35	53	5	1517	128 *	31.60	1	9	29	-	2366	1550	32	48.43	5-69	3	1
1-day Int																	
NatWest	5	4	0	94	50	23.50	-	1	1	-	183	142	2	71.00	1-48	-	
B & H	5	5	0	90	21	18.00	-	-	1	-	18	17	1	17.00	1-17	-	
Sunday	40	28	5	418	58	18.17	-	2	12	-	132	141	4	35.25	1-9	-	

SPEAK, N. J. Durham

Name: Nicholas Jason Speak
Role: Right-hand opening bat,
off-spin bowler
Born: 21 October 1966, Manchester
Height: 6ft **Weight:** 12st 7lbs
Nickname: Judge, Pod
County debut: 1986-87 (Lancashire),
1997 (Durham)
County cap: 1992 (Lancashire)
1000 runs in a season: 3
1st-Class 50s: 44
1st-Class 100s: 13
1st-Class 200s: 1
1st-Class catches: 90
One-Day 100s: 1
Place in batting averages: 181st av. 23.66
(1996 122nd av. 34.05)
Strike rate: (career 84.50)
Parents: John and Irene

Wife and date of marriage: Michelle, 11 March 1993
Children: Kenneth John, 24 September 1995; Ella Frances, 13 July 1997
Family links with cricket: Father and uncle were league professionals in Lancashire
and Yorkshire
Education: Parrs Wood High School; Sixth Form College, Didsbury, Manchester
Qualifications: 5 O-levels, NCA coaching certificate
Career outside cricket: Yarra Leisure, coaching in Melbourne
Off-season: Playing for Hawthorne in Melbourne
Overseas tours: Lancashire to Jamaica 1986-87, to Zimbabwe 1989, to Perth
1990-91, to Johannesburg 1992
Overseas teams played for: South Canberra 1988-89; North Canberra 1991-93;
Hawthorne, Melbourne 1994-98

Cricketers particularly admired: Mark Waugh, Shane Warne
Other sports followed: Most sports – Manchester City FC
Relaxations: Chardonnay, cold lager, Indian food, spending time at home with our children
Extras: Scored century for Australian Capital Territories v England A at Canberra 1992-93. Released by Lancashire at the end of the 1996 season and joined Durham for 1997
Opinions on cricket: 'Tea should be ten minutes longer.'
Best batting: 232 Lancashire v Leicestershire, Leicester 1992
Best bowling: 1-0 Lancashire v Warwickshire, Old Trafford 1991

1997 Season

	M	Inns	NO	Runs	HS	Avge	100s	50s	Ct	St	O	M	Runs	Wkts	Avge	Best	5wI	10wM
Test																		
All First	12	21	3	426	124 *	23.66	1	1	6	-	4	0	14	0	-		-	-
1-day Int																		
NatWest	1	1	0	4	4	4.00	-	-	-	-								
B & H	4	3	0	90	59	30.00	-	1	1	-								
Sunday	9	9	1	192	74 *	24.00	-	1	3	-								

Career Performances

	M	Inns	NO	Runs	HS	Avge	100s	50s	Ct	St	Balls	Runs	Wkts	Avge	Best	5wI	10wM
Test																	
All First	135	234	24	7826	232	37.26	13	44	90	-	169	178	2	89.00	1-0	-	-
1-day Int																	
NatWest	8	8	0	223	83	27.87	-	2	2	-	24	31	0	-		-	-
B & H	20	18	2	516	82	32.25	-	4	1	-							
Sunday	77	71	8	1675	102 *	26.58	1	7	16	-							

SPEIGHT, M. P.   Durham

Name: Martin Peter Speight
Role: Right-hand bat, wicket-keeper
Born: 24 October 1967, Walsall
Height: 5ft 10in **Weight:** 12st 7lbs
Nickname: Gordon, Dougie
County debut: 1986 (Sussex), 1997 (Durham)
County cap: 1991 (Sussex)
1000 runs in a season: 2
1st-Class 50s: 38
1st-Class 100s: 13
1st-Class catches: 154
One-Day 100s: 3

Place in batting averages: 188th av. 22.92 (1996 182nd av. 27.05)

Strike rate: (career 10.50)

Parents: Peter John and Valerie

Wife and date of marriage: Lisa, 27 September 1997

Education: The Windmills School, Hassocks; Hurstpierpoint College Junior and Senior Schools; Durham University (St Chad's College)

Qualifications: 13 O-levels, 3 A-levels, BA (Hons) Archaeology/Ancient History

Career outside cricket: Artist, coach, painter and decorator

Off-season: Honeymoon in Cape Town and Mauritius then painting a commission, coaching, training and decorating the house

Overseas tours: NCA U19 to Bermuda 1984; Hurstpierpoint to India 1986; England YC to Sri Lanka 1986-87

Overseas teams played for: Karori, Wellington, New Zealand 1989-90; University CC, Wellington 1990-93; North City, Wellington 1995-96; Wellington CA 1989-90, 1992-93, 1995-96

Cricketers particularly admired: Martin Crowe, James Boiling, Ian Salisbury

Young players to look out for: Melvyn Betts

Other sports followed: Golf, rugby, hockey

Relaxations: Wine and food

Extras: Member of Durham University UAU winning side 1987; played for Combined Universities in B&H Cup 1987 and 1988; Sussex Most Promising Player 1989. Fastest first-class 100 in 1993 against Lancashire and fastest 50-overs 100 v Somerset at Taunton 1993 (off 48 balls) which still stands as the second fastest Sunday League 100 ever. Has won two Gold Awards in the Benson and Hedges competition. Painted an oil painting of the maiden first-class game at Arundel Castle between Sussex and Hampshire which was later auctioned to raise £1200 for the Sussex YC tour to India 1990-91, and of which a limited edition has also been printed and sold. Has done paintings of Hove, Southampton and The Oval for the benefits of Messrs Pigott, Parks and Greig. Member of Durham University's men's hockey team to Barbados 1988. Book of his paintings, *A Cricketer's View*, a collection of 54 paintings and commentary, published in 1995. Various commissions and a print of Abergavenny CC to be published in 1997. Joined Durham from Sussex for the 1997 season

Opinions on cricket: 'The A1(M) should be made into three lanes all the way!'

Best batting: 184 Sussex v Nottinghamshire, Eastbourne 1993

Best bowling: 1-2 Sussex v Middlesex, Hove 1988

	M	Inns	NO	Runs	HS	Avge	100s	50s	Ct	St	O	M	Runs	Wkts	Avge	Best	5wI	10wM
Test																		
All First	17	28	3	573	73 *	22.92	-	3	54	-								
1-day Int																		
NatWest	1	1	0	9	9	9.00	-	-	2	-								
B & H	4	3	1	82	42 *	41.00	-	-	4	-								
Sunday	16	16	1	407	64 *	27.13	-	3	10	1								

Career Performances

	M	Inns	NO	Runs	HS	Avge	100s	50s	Ct	St	Balls	Runs	Wkts	Avge	Best	5wI	10wM
Test																	
All First	140	234	18	7387	184	34.19	13	38	154	-	21	32	2	16.00	1-2	-	-
1-day Int																	
NatWest	17	16	1	359	50	23.93	-	1	6	-							
B & H	35	32	1	738	83	23.80	-	3	24	1							
Sunday	112	103	6	2882	126	29.71	3	15	39	2							

SPENDLOVE, B. L. Derbyshire

Name: Benjamin Lee Spendlove
Role: Right-hand bat, right-arm medium bowler, occasional wicket-keeper
Born: 4 October 1978, Derby
Height: 6ft 2in **Weight:** 13st
County debut: 1997
1st-Class catches: 2
Nickname: Dylan
Parents: Lee and Chris
Marital status: Single
Family links with cricket: Father ex-cricket professional for Trent College
Education: Harrington Primary School; Trent College
Overseas tours: England U17 to Holland (International Youth Tournament)
Overseas teams played for: Gold Coast CC, Queensland, Australia 1996-97
Cricketers particularly admired: David Gower, Robin Smith, Alec Stewart
Young players to look out for: Stephen Peters, Jeff Pfaff (Queensland)
Other sports followed: Rugby union (Leicester Tigers), football (Derby County)
Opinions on cricket: 'More money and support should be given to schools cricket.

Schools cricket should have a more competitive format. Maybe a little more faith should be shown in selections at international level.'

Best batting: 15* Derbyshire v Yorkshire, Derby 1997

1997 Season

	M	Inns	NO	Runs	HS	Avge	100s	50s	Ct	St	O	M	Runs	Wkts	Avge	Best	5wl	10wM
Test																		
All First	2	3	1	27	15 *	13.50	-	-	2	-								
1-day Int																		
NatWest																		
B & H																		
Sunday	1	1	0	4	4	4.00	-	-	-	-								

Career Performances

	M	Inns	NO	Runs	HS	Avge	100s	50s	Ct	St	Balls	Runs	Wkts	Avge	Best	5wl	10wM
Test																	
All First	2	3	1	27	15 *	13.50	-	-	2	-							
1-day Int																	
NatWest																	
B & H																	
Sunday	1	1	0	4	4	4.00	-	-	-	-							

SPIRING, K. R.   Worcestershire

Name: Karl Reuben Spiring
Role: Right-hand opening bat
Born: 13 November 1974, Southport
Height: 5ft 10in **Weight:** 12st
Nickname: Ginga
County debut: 1993 (one-day), 1994 (first-class)
1000 runs in a season: 1
1st-Class 50s: 13
1st-Class 100s: 4
1st-Class catches: 19
Place in batting averages: 91st av. 35.04 (1996 66th av. 41.69)
Parents: Peter and June
Marital status: Single
Education: Monmouth School; Durham University
Qualifications: 9 GCSEs, 3 A-levels, NCA

Senior Coach
Off-season: Playing and coaching in Perth, Australia
Overseas tours: Worcestershire to Barbados 1996
Overseas teams played for: Fremantle/Mosman Park Pirates, Perth, Western Australia 1995-97
Cricketers particularly admired: 'Phil Weston's off-field activities'
Young players to look out for: Peter 'Zecamel' Cambden
Other sports followed: 'Frisby with Raggy and Zig'
Injuries: Tonsillitis, pulled hamstring, out for one week
Relaxations: 'Spending time away from cricket'
Extras: Father was a professional footballer. Rapid Cricketline 2nd XI Player of the Month June 1994. Worcestershire Uncapped Player of the Year 1994
Opinions on cricket: 'Far too much cricket played.'
Best batting: 150 Worcestershire v Essex, Chelmsford 1997

1997 Season

	M	Inns	NO	Runs	HS	Avge	100s	50s	Ct	St	O	M	Runs	Wkts	Avge	Best	5wl	10wM
Test																		
All First	17	28	3	876	150	35.04	1	4	7	-	2	0	10	0	-	-	-	-
1-day Int																		
NatWest	2	2	0	100	53	50.00	-	1	2	-								
B & H	5	5	1	82	33	20.50	-	-	1	-								
Sunday	13	12	6	235	58 *	39.16	-	1	5	-								

Career Performances

	M	Inns	NO	Runs	HS	Avge	100s	50s	Ct	St	Balls	Runs	Wkts	Avge	Best	5wl	10wM
Test																	
All First	37	64	9	2072	150	37.67	4	13	19	-	12	10	0	-	-	-	-
1-day Int																	
NatWest	4	4	0	141	53	35.25	-	1	2	-							
B & H	12	10	1	202	35	22.44	-	-	4	-							
Sunday	29	25	10	518	58 *	34.53	-	1	9	-							

STANFORD, E. J.   Kent

Name: Edward John Stanford
Role: Left-hand bat, left-arm spinner
Born: 21 January 1971, Dartford
Height: 5ft 10in **Weight:** 12st
Nickname: Teddy, Oist
County debut: 1995
1st-Class catches: 2

Strike rate: 30.00 (career 100.22)
Parents: Paul and Pam
Family links with cricket: Father played club cricket for Dartford CC
Education: Downs Secondary School, Dartford
Qualifications: 'Too many to mention at school'
Career outside cricket: 'Had several. Banker. Groundsman'
Overseas tours: Kent Schools U17 to Singapore and New Zealand 1988
Overseas teams played for: Petersham, Sydney 1990-91
Cricketers particularly admired: Graham Cowdrey ('lot of time'), Matthew Walker ('the greatest')
Young players to look out for: Matthew Walker 'the greatest man to walk the planet'
Other sports followed: Golf, snooker ('Min Patel complete bandit at both!'), football (Charlton Athletic)
Relaxations: Jack Daniels and Coke, William Hill, Corals
Extras: Headed a ball for six in debut against Essex in the Bain Clarkson Championship 1993 ('Totally misjudged a top edge whilst fielding at fine leg, the ball struck me on the forehead and carried a further 20 yards to go for six!'). 'Once got Matt Walker out in the nets'
Best batting: 32 Kent v Cambridge University, Canterbury 1997
Best bowling: 3-84 Kent v Leicestershire, Leicester 1996

1997 Season

	M	Inns	NO	Runs	HS	Avge	100s	50s	Ct	St	O	M	Runs	Wkts	Avge	Best	5wl	10wM
Test																		
All First	1	1	0	32	32	32.00	-	-	-	-	5	2	10	1	10.00	1-10	-	-
1-day Int																		
NatWest																		
B & H																		
Sunday																		

---

89. Who won the 1997 Women's World Cup and whom did they defeat in the final?

Career Performances

	M	Inns	NO	Runs	HS	Avge	100s	50s	Ct	St	Balls	Runs	Wkts	Avge	Best	5wI	10wM
Test																	
All First	5	6	4	48	32	24.00	-	-	2	-	902	388	9	43.11	3-84	-	-
1-day Int																	
NatWest																	
B & H																	
Sunday																	

STEELE, M. V. Northamptonshire

Name: Mark Vincent Steele
Role: Left-hand bat, right-arm
fast-medium bowler
Born: 13 November 1976, Kettering
Height: 6ft **Weight:** 13st 5lbs
Nickname: Stan
County debut: No first-team appearance
Parents: David and Carol
Marital status: Single
Family links with cricket: Father played
cricket for Northants and England. Father's
brother, J.F. Steele, played for Leicestershire
and managed Glamorgan, father's cousin,
Brian Crump, played for Northants
Education: Wellingborough School; Tresham
College, Kettering
Qualifications: 6 GCSEs, GNVQ in
Advanced Business

Cricketers particularly admired: Dennis
Lillee
Other sports followed: Football, table tennis
Relaxations: 'Having a couple of sherbets with friends'
Extras: MCC U13 Young Cricketer of the Year 1984. Played for Midlands Schools from
U15 upwards and played for England U16 in 1993. Wellingborough scholarship in 1991.
Public School Batsman of the Year 1993

STEMP, R. D. Yorkshire

Name: Richard David Stemp
Role: Right-hand bat, slow left-arm bowler
Born: 11 December 1967, Erdington,
Birmingham
Height: 6ft **Weight:** 12st 4lbs
Nickname: Stempy, Sherriff, Badger
County debut: 1990 (Worcestershire),
1993 (Yorkshire)
County cap: 1996 (Yorkshire)
1st-Class 50s: 2
1st-Class 5 w. in innings: 12
1st-Class 10 w. in match: 1
1st-Class catches: 53
Place in batting averages: 281st av. 11.00
(1996 250th av. 11.00)
Place in bowling averages: 87th av. 32.83
(1996 103rd av. 36.59)
Strike rate: 67.57 (career 79.08)
Parents: Arnold and Rita Homer
Marital status: Single

Family links with cricket: Father played Birmingham League cricket for Old Hill
Education: Britannia High School, Rowley Regis
Qualifications: NCA coaching award
Overseas tours: England A to India 1994-95, to Pakistan 1995-96
Overseas teams played for: Pretoria Technikon 1988-89
Cricketers particularly admired: Ian Botham, Phil Tufnell
Other sports followed: Indoor cricket, American football (New England Patriots)
Relaxations: Ornithology, music, driving
Extras: Played for England indoor cricket team v Australia in ManuLife 'Test' series 1990. Moved to Yorkshire at end of 1992 season (first English non-Yorkshireman to be signed for the county). Included in England Test squad against New Zealand in 1994
Opinions on cricket: 'Groundsmen should prepare cricket wickets, not wickets made for corporate hospitality. Is not being given run out as much human judgement as LBW or caught behind? If we are using television to check and decide on run out, why not all decisions?'
Best batting: 65 Yorkshire v Durham, Chester-le-Street 1996
Best bowling: 6-37 Yorkshire v Durham, Durham University 1994

1997 Season

	M	Inns	NO	Runs	HS	Avge	100s	50s	Ct	St	O	M	Runs	Wkts	Avge	Best	5wI	10wM
Test																		
All First	17	20	6	154	33 *	11.00	-	-	7	-	473	111	1379	42	32.83	6-77	1	-
1-day Int																		
NatWest	3	1	1	0	0 *	-	-	-	-	-	24	4	89	4	22.25	4-54	-	
B & H	6	1	0	2	2	2.00	-	-	-	-	55	5	195	9	21.66	3-22	-	
Sunday	13	6	2	13	9 *	3.25	-	-	3	-	88	1	437	18	24.27	3-29	-	

Career Performances

	M	Inns	NO	Runs	HS	Avge	100s	50s	Ct	St	Balls	Runs	Wkts	Avge	Best	5wI	10wM
Test																	
All First	124	145	44	1292	65	12.79	-	2	53	-	23094	9867	292	33.79	6-37	12	1
1-day Int																	
NatWest	10	2	2	1	1 *	-	-	-	1	-	606	369	14	26.35	4-45	-	
B & H	19	4	1	3	2	1.00	-	-	-	-	1062	679	19	35.73	3-22	-	
Sunday	59	19	6	108	23 *	8.30	-	-	15	-	2271	1848	64	28.87	4-25	-	

STEPHENSON, J. P. Hampshire

Name: John Patrick Stephenson
Role: Right-hand opening bat,
right-arm medium bowler
Born: 14 March 1965, Stebbing, Essex
Height: 6ft 1in **Weight:** 12st 7lbs
Nickname: Stan
County debut: 1985 (Essex), 1995 (Hants)
County cap: 1989 (Essex)
Test debut: 1989
Tests: 1
1000 runs in a season: 5
1st-Class 50s: 66
1st-Class 100s: 21
1st-Class 200s: 1
1st-Class 5 w. in innings: 9
1st-Class catches: 135
One-Day 100s: 7
One-Day 5 w. in innings: 3
Place in batting averages: 101st av. 34.08
(1996 187th av. 26.56)
Place in bowling averages: 121st av. 40.00 (1996 62nd av. 30.50)
Strike rate: 69.54 (career 61.74)

Parents: Pat and Eve
Wife and date of marriage: Fiona Maria, 24 September 1994
Children: Emma-Lydia, 19 May 1997
Family links with cricket: Father was member of Rugby Meteors Cricketer Cup-winning side in 1973. Three brothers played in Felsted 1st XI; Guy played for Essex 2nd XI and now plays for Teddington
Education: Felsted Prep School; Felsted Senior School; Durham University
Qualifications: 7 O-levels, 3 A-levels, BA General Arts (Dunelm)
Career outside cricket: Writing on cricket for *Southern Telegraph* and the *Observer*
Off-season: 'Working in England until Christmas then possibly going abroad after'
Overseas tours: English Schools U19 to Zimbabwe 1982-83; England A to Kenya and Zimbabwe 1989-90, to Bermuda and West Indies 1991-92
Overseas teams played for: Fitzroy, Melbourne 1982-83, 1987-88; Boland, South Africa 1988-89; Gold Coast Dolphins and Bond University, Australia 1990-91; St George's, Argentina 1994-95; Belgrano, Argentina 1994-95; Victoria CC, South Africa 1995-96
Cricketers particularly admired: Brian Hardie
Relaxations: Watching cricket, reading (*Sunday Telegraph*, *Wisden*, *The Cricketer*), alternative music
Extras: Awarded 2nd XI cap in 1984 when leading run-scorer with Essex 2nd XI. Essex Young Player of the Year, 1985. Captained Durham University to victory in UAU Championship 1986 and captain of Combined Universities team 1987 in the first year that it was drawn from all universities. Called up to replace the injured Michael Atherton on England A tour to Bermuda and West Indies 1991-92 and was leading wicket-taker. Scored two not out centuries v Somerset at Taunton in 1992 and was on the field for the whole game (the first Essex player to achieve this). First Essex player to achieve 500 runs and 20 wickets in Sunday League season 1993. Took over the captaincy of Hampshire in 1996, but relinquished it at the end of the 1997 season. Founded the One Test Wonder Club in 1996
Opinions on cricket: 'Leave the Championship as it is and change the structure of one-day cricket if change has to happen.'
Best batting: 202* Essex v Somerset, Bath 1990
Best bowling: 7-51 Hampshire v Middlesex, Lord's 1995

1997 Season

	M	Inns	NO	Runs	HS	Avge	100s	50s	Ct	St	O	M	Runs	Wkts	Avge	Best	5wI	10wM
Test																		
All First	17	26	3	784	140	34.08	2	1	7	-	428.5	68	1480	37	40.00	6-54	1	-
1-day Int																		
NatWest	2	1	0	1	1	1.00	-	-	2	-	23.2	4	83	8	10.37	5-34	1	
B & H	5	5	1	124	65	31.00	-	1	2	-	49	1	252	8	31.50	2-34	-	
Sunday	16	13	4	251	38 *	27.88	-	-	7	-	100.5	3	544	24	22.66	6-33	1	

Career Performances

	M	Inns	NO	Runs	HS	Avge	100s	50s	Ct	St	Balls	Runs	Wkts	Avge	Best	5wI	10wM
Test	1	2	0	36	25	18.00	-	-	-	-							
All First	237	405	41	12517	202 *	34.38	21	66	135	-	15682	8771	254	34.53	7-51	9	-
1-day Int																	
NatWest	23	21	1	770	107	38.50	1	7	9	-	829	681	20	34.05	5-34	1	
B & H	42	37	5	1398	142	43.68	2	10	9	-	1342	965	38	25.39	3-22	-	
Sunday	148	130	18	3218	110 *	28.73	4	13	63	-	4328	3389	137	24.73	6-33	2	

STEVENS, D. I.   Leicestershire

Name: Darren Ian Stevens
Role: Right-hand bat, right-arm medium bowler
Born: 30 April 1976, Leicester
Height: 5ft 11in **Weight:** 12st 7lbs
Nickname: Beetroot, JJ Junior
County debut: 1997
1st-Class catches: 1
Strike rate: 12.00 (career 12.00)
Parents: Robert and Madeleine
Marital status: Single
Family links with cricket: Father and grandfather played club cricket in local leagues **Education:** Richmond Primary School; Mount Grace High School; John Cleavland College, Hinckley
Qualifications: 4 GCSEs, BTEC in National Sports Studies
Off-season: Player/coach at Rhodes University, Grahamstown in South Africa
Overseas tours: Leicestershire U19 to South Africa 1994-95
Overseas teams played for: Wanderers CC, Johannesburg, South Africa 1995-97; Rhodes University, Grahamstown, South Africa 1997-98
Cricketers particularly admired: Ian Botham, Graham Thorpe, David Gower
Young players to look out for: Darren Maddy, Tim 'Biffa' Mason, Jon 'Babe Ruth' Dakin, Dominic 'Yoda' Williamson
Other sports followed: Football (Leicester City), rugby (Leicester Tigers), golf, squash
Relaxations: Socialising, going out with friends, clubbing, spending time with girlfriend Clare. 'Having a round of golf – not walking around but on a buggy'
Opinions on cricket: 'Great game.'

Best batting: 27 Leicestershire v Cambridge University, Fenner's 1997
Best bowling: 1-5 Leicestershire v Sussex, Eastbourne 1997

1997 Season

	M	Inns	NO	Runs	HS	Avge	100s	50s	Ct	St	O	M	Runs	Wkts	Avge	Best	5wI	10wM
Test																		
All First	2	2	0	35	27	17.50	-	-	1	-	2	1	5	1	5.00	1-5	-	-
1-day Int																		
NatWest																		
B & H																		
Sunday	2	2	0	7	6	3.50	-	-	1	-								

Career Performances

	M	Inns	NO	Runs	HS	Avge	100s	50s	Ct	St	Balls	Runs	Wkts	Avge	Best	5wI	10wM
Test																	
All First	2	2	0	35	27	17.50	-	-	1	-	12	5	1	5.00	1-5	-	-
1-day Int																	
NatWest																	
B & H																	
Sunday	2	2	0	7	6	3.50	-	-	1	-							

STEWART, A. J. Surrey

Name: Alec James Stewart
Role: Right-hand bat, wicket-keeper
Born: 8 April 1963, Merton
Nickname: Stewie, Ming
Height: 5ft 11in **Weight:** 12st 10lbs
County debut: 1981
County cap: 1985
Benefit: 1994 (£202,187)
Test debut: 1989-90
Tests: 69
One-Day Internationals: 90
1000 runs in a season: 8
1st-Class 50s: 110
1st-Class 100s: 41
1st-Class 200s: 2
1st-Class catches: 456
1st-Class stumpings: 17
One-Day 100s: 14
Place in batting averages: 54th av. 41.41

(1996 64th av. 42.00)
Strike rate: (career 156.33)
Parents: Michael and Sheila
Wife and date of marriage: Lynn, 28 September 1991
Children: Andrew James, 21 May 1993; Emily Elizabeth, 6 September 1996
Family links with cricket: Father played for England (1962-64), Surrey (1954 -72) and Malden Wanderers. Brother Neil captains Malden Wanderers
Education: Tiffin Boys School
Qualifications: 'Streetwise'
Off-season: Touring Sharjah and West Indies with England
Overseas tours: England to India (Nehru Cup) 1989-90, to West Indies 1989-90, to Australia 1990-91, to Australia and New Zealand (World Cup) 1991-92, to India and Sri Lanka 1992-93, to West Indies 1993-94, to Australia 1994-95; to South Africa 1995-96, to Pakistan and India (World Cup) 1996, to Zimbabwe and New Zealand 1996-97, to Sharjah 1997-98, to West Indies 1997-98
Overseas teams played for: Midland Guildford, Perth, Western Australia 1981-89
Cricketers particularly admired: Graham Monkhouse, Graham Gooch, Alan Knott, Geoff Arnold, K Gartrell
Young players to look out for: Ben Hollioake
Other sports followed: Football (Chelsea)
Relaxations: 'Spending as much time with my family as possible'
Extras: Captained England in a Test match for the first time v India at Madras 1992-93 and has acted as vice-captain to both Graham Gooch and Mike Atherton. First Englishman to score a century in each innings against West Indies, at Barbados 1994. He was the leading scorer in Test cricket in the 1996 calendar year (with 793 runs) ahead of Saeed Anwar (701)
Opinions on cricket: 'England players, especially bowlers, should be rested from county cricket when it is needed.'
Best batting: 271 Surrey v Yorkshire, The Oval 1997
Best bowling: 1-7 Surrey v Lancashire, Old Trafford 1989

1997 Season

	M	Inns	NO	Runs	HS	Avge	100s	50s	Ct	St	O	M	Runs	Wkts	Avge	Best	5wl	10wM
Test	6	12	1	268	87	24.36	-	1	23	-								
All First	15	26	2	994	271 *	41.41	2	3	39	-								
1-day Int	3	3	0	126	79	42.00	-	1	2	1								
NatWest	2	2	1	116	90 *	116.00	-	1	3	-								
B & H	8	8	2	384	87	64.00	-	5	10	-								
Sunday	8	8	1	141	67 *	20.14	-	1	7	2								

Career Performances

	M	Inns	NO	Runs	HS	Avge	100s	50s	Ct	St	Balls	Runs	Wkts	Avge	Best	5wl	10wM
Test	69	123	8	4701	190	40.87	10	23	112	7	20	13	0	-	-	-	-
All First	333	551	62	19965	271 *	40.82	41	110	456	17	469	417	3	139.00	1-7	-	-
1-day Int	90	85	7	2452	103	31.43	1	14	77	8							
NatWest	36	33	6	1356	125 *	50.22	3	9	40	2							
B & H	58	58	10	2321	167 *	48.35	3	18	44	4							
Sunday	162	146	16	4093	125	31.48	7	23	126	10	4	8	0	-	-	-	-

STRANG, P. A.   Nottinghamshire

Name: Paul Andrew Strang
Role: Right-hand bat, leg-spin bowler
Born: 28 July 1970, Bulawayo, Zimbabwe
Height: 5ft 9in **Weight:** 11st 7lbs
Nickname: Stump
County debut: 1997 (Kent)
50 wickets in a season: 1
1st-Class 50s: 11
1st-Class 100s: 2
1st-Class 5 w. in innings: 15
1st-Class 10 w. in match: 2
1st-Class catches: 49
One-Day 5 w. in innings: 1
Place in batting averages: 168th av. 24.58
Place in bowling averages: 74th av. 30.61
Strike rate: 69.82 (career 69.78)
Parents: Ronald Charles and Jennifer Joan
Marital status: Single

Family links with cricket: Father is a first-
class umpire. Brother Bryan plays for Zimbabwe
Education: Falcon College, Esigodini, Zimbabwe; University of Cape Town,
South Africa
Qualifications: A-levels, BSoc Sc (Econ), advanced coach
Overseas tours: Zimbabwe U19 to New Zealand 1989; Zimbabwe to India and
Pakistan (World Cup) 1995-96, to Pakistan 1996-97
Cricketers particularly admired: David Houghton and John Traicos
Young players to look out for: Brian Murphy ('a young leg-spinner currently playing
for Zimbabwe B')
Other sports followed: Most international sport. 'Liverpool FC. I always keep an eye
on Nick Price (golf) and Byron Black (tennis).' Played hockey for Zimbabwe U19
Relaxations: 'I like to relax with mates watching sport'

Extras: Captained Zimbabwe U19 (1989-90). Shared all ten wickets with brother Bryan in a local game. Played in the Birmingham league for Aston Manor (1989) and Barnt Green (1996). Became only the 18th player to score a century and take five wickets in an innings in a Test match against Pakistan at Sheikhupura. Made his first-class debut in Zimbabwe against Kent. Has signed a two-year contract as overseas player for Nottinghamshire starting from 1998

Opinions on cricket: 'LBWs for balls pitching outside leg would be nice!'

Best batting: 106* Zimbabwe v Pakistan, Sheikhupura 1996-97

Best bowling: 7-75 Mashonaland Country Districts v Mashonaland U24, Harare South 1994-95

1997 Season

	M	Inns	NO	Runs	HS	Avge	100s	50s	Ct	St	O	M	Runs	Wkts	Avge	Best	5wl	10wM
Test																		
All First	17	26	2	590	82	24.58	-	5	17	-	733.1	211	1929	63	30.61	7-118	4	1
1-day Int																		
NatWest	1	1	0	6	6	6.00	-	-	-	-	12	0	62	0	-		-	-
B & H	8	7	5	86	38 *	43.00	-	-	4	-	68.3	12	222	12	18.50	4-27	-	
Sunday	17	12	1	165	40	15.00	-	-	5	-	111.3	5	531	16	33.18	3-31	-	

Career Performances

	M	Inns	NO	Runs	HS	Avge	100s	50s	Ct	St	Balls	Runs	Wkts	Avge	Best	5wl	10wM
Test	13	21	5	505	106 *	31.56	1	1	6	-	2894	1278	32	39.93	5-106	3	-
All First	60	90	19	2037	106 *	28.69	2	11	49	-	13399	6203	192	32.30	7-75	15	2
1-day Int	38	34	10	603	47	25.12	-	-	12	-	1872	1355	37	36.62	5-21	1	
NatWest	1	1	0	6	6	6.00	-	-	-	-	72	62	0	-		-	-
B & H	8	7	5	86	38 *	43.00	-	-	4	-	411	222	12	18.50	4-27	-	
Sunday	17	12	1	165	40	15.00	-	-	5	-	669	531	16	33.18	3-31	-	

STRAUSS, A. J.   Middlesex

Name: Andrew John Strauss
Role: Left-hand bat
Born: 2 March 1977, Johannesburg,
South Africa
Height: 5ft 11in **Weight:** 12st 7lbs
Nickname: Johann, Mousey
County debut: 1997 (one-day)
Parents: David and Dawn
Marital status: Single
Education: Caldicott Prep School; Radley
College; University of Durham
Qualifications: 4 A-levels
Career outside cricket: Student
Off-season: Studying hard for my degree,
and going on a cricket tour to Zimbabwe with
Durham University
Cricketers particularly admired: Brian
Lara, Allan Donald
Young players to look out for: Luke Sutton
Other sports followed: Rugby (plays for Durham University), golf
Injuries: Pulled hamstring, out for one month
Relaxations: Macroeconomics
Opinions on cricket: 'Turning down the opportunity for a two-divisional championship
was a real missed opportunity.'

1997 Season

	M	Inns	NO	Runs	HS	Avge	100s	50s	Ct	St	O	M	Runs	Wkts	Avge	Best	5wl	10wM
Test																		
All First																		
1-day Int																		
NatWest																		
B & H	1	1	0	1	1	1.00	-	-	-	-								
Sunday	2	2	0	7	4	3.50	-	-	1	-								

90. Who replaced Wasim Akram as the Pakistan captain
for the tour of South Africa in 1997-98?

Career Performances

	M	Inns	NO	Runs	HS	Avge	100s	50s	Ct	St	Balls	Runs	Wkts	Avge	Best	5wl	10wM
Test																	
All First																	
1-day Int																	
NatWest																	
B & H	1	1	0	1	1	1.00	-	-	-	-							
Sunday	2	2	0	7	4	3.50	-	-	1	-							

STRONG, M. Sussex

Name: Michael Strong
Role: Left-hand bat, right-arm
fast-medium bowler
Born: 28 June 1974, Cuckfield, West Sussex
Height: 6ft 1in **Weight:** 13st 5lbs
Nickname: Stella, Strongy
County debut: 1997
Parents: David and Gillian
Marital status: Single
Family links with cricket: 'Father and
brother have both played locally. Father is
still managing to play (just!)'
Education: St Peter's School, Burgess Hill;
Brighton College; Brunel University College
Qualifications: 9 GCSEs, 3 A-levels,
BA/BSc (QTS) PE and Geography
Career outside cricket: Physical education
and geography teacher
Off-season: Playing cricket in South Africa
Overseas tours: Brighton College to India 1991-92
Overseas teams played for: Multiquip Umbilo CC, Durban, South Africa 1992-93,
1997-98
Cricketers particularly admired: 'Any bowler who manages to bowl at the speed of
light and any batsmen who enjoy playing it'
Young players to look out for: 'Too many to mention'
Other sports followed: Football (Chelsea and Brighton), hockey and golf
Injuries: Inflamed back ligament, out for three weeks
Relaxations: Socialising with friends, 'playing the odd round of golf'
Extras: 'Would like to thank the master in charge of cricket at Brighton College, John
Spencer, for all the time he spent coaching me from the age of ten'
Opinions on cricket: 'Uncertain as the game is going through a transition. I haven't
been in the game long enough to say anything worthwhile.'

1997 Season

	M	Inns	NO	Runs	HS	Avge	100s	50s	Ct	St	O	M	Runs	Wkts	Avge	Best	5wI	10wM
Test																		
All First																		
1-day Int																		
NatWest																		
B & H																		
Sunday	1	1	0	1	1	1.00	-	-	-	-	3	0	23	0	-		-	-

Career Performances

	M	Inns	NO	Runs	HS	Avge	100s	50s	Ct	St	Balls	Runs	Wkts	Avge	Best	5wI	10wM
Test																	
All First																	
1-day Int																	
NatWest																	
B & H																	
Sunday	3	3	1	4	2 *	2.00	-	-	-	-	92	97	0	-		-	-

STUBBINGS, S. D.   Derbyshire

Name: Stephen David Stubbings
Role: Left-hand bat
Born: 31 March 1978, Huddersfield
Height: 6ft 4in   **Weight:** 14st 1lb
Nickname: Stubbo
County debut: 1997
Parents: David and Marie-Anne
Marital status: Single
Family links with cricket: 'Father played the odd game'
Education: Frankston High School, Victoria
Qualifications: Completed Year 12
Career outside cricket: Student
Off-season: Playing in Australia
Overseas teams played for: Frankston-Finchley CC, Victoria 1993-1998
Cricketers particularly admired: Mark Taylor, Ricky Ponting, Steve Waugh, Michael Atherton
Young players to look out for: Ian Blackwell, Kevin Dean, Ben Spendlove
Other sports followed: Aussie rules (Essendon Bombers), football (Cambridge United)

Relaxations: Golf, eating, drinking and television
Extras: Has also played for Victoria at U17, Colts and U21 level
Best batting: 22 Derbyshire v Worcestershire, Worcester 1997

1997 Season

	M	Inns	NO	Runs	HS	Avge	100s	50s	Ct	St	O	M	Runs	Wkts	Avge	Best	5wI	10wM
Test																		
All First	1	2	0	27	22	13.50	-	-	-	-								
1-day Int																		
NatWest																		
B & H																		
Sunday																		

Career Performances

	M	Inns	NO	Runs	HS	Avge	100s	50s	Ct	St	Balls	Runs	Wkts	Avge	Best	5wI	10wM
Test																	
All First	1	2	0	27	22	13.50	-	-	-	-							
1-day Int																	
NatWest																	
B & H																	
Sunday																	

SUCH, P. M.   Essex

Name: Peter Mark Such
Role: Right-hand bat, off-spin bowler
Born: 12 June 1964, Helensburgh, Scotland
Height: 6ft **Weight:** 11st 7lbs
Nickname: Suchy
County debut: 1982 (Nottinghamshire),
1987 (Leicestershire), 1990 (Essex)
County cap: 1991 (Essex)
Test debut: 1993
Tests: 8
50 wickets in a season: 5
1st-Class 50s: 2
1st-Class 5 w. in innings: 39
1st-Class 10 w. in innings: 7
1st-Class catches: 98
One-Day 5 w. in innings: 3
Place in batting averages: 303rd av. 5.72
(1996 262nd av. 16.00)

Place in bowling averages: 41st av. 26.34 (1996 34th av. 26.39)
Strike rate: 65.92 (career 65.67)
Parents: John and Margaret
Marital status: Engaged
Family links with cricket: Father and brother both village cricketers
Education: Lantern Lane Primary; Harry Carlton Comprehensive, East Leake, Notts
Qualifications: 9 O-levels, 3 A-levels, advanced cricket coach
Overseas tours: England A to Australia 1992-93, to South Africa 1993-94, to Australia 1996-97
Overseas teams played for: Kempton Park, South Africa 1982-83; Bathurst, Australia 1985-86; Matabeleland, Zimbabwe 1989-92
Cricketers particularly admired: Bob White, Eddie Hemmings, Graham Gooch, John Childs
Young players to look out for: Ashley Cowan, Robert Rollins, Andrew Harris
Relaxations: Gardening
Extras: Played for England YC v Australian YC 1983 and for TCCB XI v New Zealand, 1985. Left Nottinghamshire at end of 1986 season; joined Leicestershire in 1987 and released at end of 1989; signed by Essex for 1990. Played in one-day games for England A v Sri Lanka 1991. Joint winner with J.H. Childs of the Essex Player of the Year Award 1992 and shared the award again in 1993. Took 6-67 on Test debut v Australia 1993 – best figures by England Test debutant since John Lever in India 1976-77. Holds the record for the most overs bowled in a County Championship innings when he bowled 86 overs against Leicestershire in August 1997 – he ended up with figures of 4 for 96
Opinions on cricket: 'Present balance of one-day and four-day cricket is about right. NatWest should be 55 overs, B&H 50 overs, Sunday League 40 overs. Over rates in Championship are too high, 102 overs per day would be better. The quality of the pitches has improved this year but needs to be maintained. The TCCB needs to be very strict when monitoring the situation.'
Best batting: 54 Essex v Worcestershire, Chelmsford 1993
                54 Essex v Nottinghamshire, Chelmsford 1996
Best bowling: 8-93 Essex v Hampshire, Colchester 1995

1997 Season

	M	Inns	NO	Runs	HS	Avge	100s	50s	Ct	St	O	M	Runs	Wkts	Avge	Best	5wI	10wM
Test																		
All First	21	22	11	63	14	5.72	-	-	5	-	725.1	218	1739	66	26.34	6-55	6	1
1-day Int																		
NatWest	5	1	1	4	4 *	-	-	-	1	-	58	4	211	3	70.33	1-27	-	
B & H	4	2	1	3	3	3.00	-	-	1	-	34	2	126	3	42.00	2-34	-	
Sunday	16	7	6	25	15 *	25.00	-	-	3	-	99.2	0	459	21	21.85	5-29	1	

Career Performances

	M	Inns	NO	Runs	HS	Avge	100s	50s	Ct	St	Balls	Runs	Wkts	Avge	Best	5wl	10wM
Test	8	11	4	65	14 *	9.28	-	-	2	-	2177	805	22	36.59	6-67	1	-
All First	239	240	81	1206	54	7.58	-	2	98	-	44922	19800	684	28.94	8-93	39	7
1-day Int																	
NatWest	22	8	4	18	8 *	4.50	-	-	3	-	1422	806	23	35.04	3-56	-	
B & H	31	12	6	31	10 *	5.16	-	-	4	-	1632	999	30	33.30	4-43	-	
Sunday	114	45	27	167	19 *	9.27	-	-	31	-	4511	3522	114	30.89	5-29	3	

SUTCLIFFE, I. J.   Leicestershire

Name: Iain John Sutcliffe
Role: Left-hand bat, leg-spin bowler
Born: 20 December 1974, Leeds
Height: 6ft 1in **Weight:** 12st
Nickname: Sooty, Bertie, Ripper
County debut: 1995
1st-Class 50s: 13
1st-Class 100s: 3
1st-Class catches: 18
One-Day 100s: 1
Place in batting averages: 59th av. 40.38
(1996 94th av. 36.91)
Strike rate: (career 49.50)
Parents: John and Valerie
Marital status: Single
Education: Leeds Grammar School;
Oxford University
Qualifications: 10 GCSEs, 4 A-levels,
2:1 PPE degree
Overseas tours: Leeds GS to Kenya
Cricketers particularly admired: David Gower, Brian Lara, Saeed Anwar
Young players to look out for: Gul Khan
Other sports followed: Boxing (Mike Tyson), football (Liverpool)
Relaxations: Listening to music, eating out
Extras: Played NCA England U14 and NCA Development Team U18/U19. Oxford boxing Blue 1994 and 1995, British Universities Light-middleweight Champion 1993. Highest partnership (283) with C. Gupte for Oxford University against a first-class county in which he scored 163 not out
Best batting: 163* Oxford University v Hampshire, The Parks 1995
Best bowling: 2-21 Oxford University v Cambridge University, Lord's 1996

1997 Season

	M	Inns	NO	Runs	HS	Avge	100s	50s	Ct	St	O	M	Runs	Wkts	Avge	Best	5wI	10wM
Test																		
All First	13	20	2	727	130	40.38	2	3	6	-	1	0	12	0	-	-	-	-
1-day Int																		
NatWest	2	2	1	193	103 *	193.00	1	1	-	-								
B & H	3	3	0	85	59	28.33	-	1	-	-								
Sunday	7	7	1	182	96	30.33	-	1	2	-								

Career Performances

	M	Inns	NO	Runs	HS	Avge	100s	50s	Ct	St	Balls	Runs	Wkts	Avge	Best	5wI	10wM
Test																	
All First	41	62	7	2036	163 *	37.01	3	13	18	-	198	149	4	37.25	2-21	-	-
1-day Int																	
NatWest	4	4	1	276	103 *	92.00	1	2	1	-							
B & H	6	6	0	155	59	25.83	-	1	-	-							
Sunday	8	8	1	196	96	28.00	-	1	4	-							

SUTTON, L. D. Somerset

Name: Luke David Sutton
Role: Right-hand bat, 'deceptive' off-spin bowler, wicket-keeper
Born: 4 October 1976, Keynsham
Height: 5ft 11in **Weight:** 12st 10lbs
Nickname: Donkey, Monster
County debut: 1997
1st-Class catches: 5
Parents: David and Molly
Marital status: 'Single at the moment – I'm working on it'
Family links with cricket: 'Grandfather kept wicket, and one of my cousins was arrested for streaking at Lord's in 1987'
Education: Edgarley Hall; Millfield School; Warrington Technical College
Qualifications: Qualified fitter and turner
Career outside cricket: Art collector and furniture restorer
Off-season: 'I plan to visit several art galleries. I have a particular interest in tapestries'
Overseas tours: Millfield School to Zimbabwe 1993; West of England U15 to West

Indies 1991

Cricketers particularly admired: Ian Healy, Steve Waugh, Jack Russell, Richard Arbuthnot, Graham Thorpe

Young players to look out for: Alex Tudor, Owais Shah, Lance Thompson

Other sports followed: 'Follow most sports, particularly Aussie rules and kabadi'

Injuries: Minor haemorrhoid problem, out for two weeks

Relaxations: Art exhibitions, amateur theatricals, cake decorating, embroidery

Extras: Captain of the England U15 side that played against South Africa and also played for England U18 and U19. Won John Hobbs Award for the U16 Cricketer of the Year in 1992 and the Gray Nicolls Award for the English Schools Cricketer of the Year in 1995

Opinions on cricket: 'Too much cricket played. The success of the Australians cannot be ignored. We need to take a leaf out of their book to become tougher and more professional cricketers.'

Best batting: 11* Somerset v Pakistan A, Taunton 1997

1997 Season

	M	Inns	NO	Runs	HS	Avge	100s	50s	Ct	St	O	M	Runs	Wkts	Avge	Best	5wl	10wM
Test																		
All First	1	2	1	17	11 *	17.00	-	-	5	-								
1-day Int																		
NatWest																		
B & H																		
Sunday																		

Career Performances

	M	Inns	NO	Runs	HS	Avge	100s	50s	Ct	St	Balls	Runs	Wkts	Avge	Best	5wl	10wM
Test																	
All First	1	2	1	17	11 *	17.00	-	-	5	-							
1-day Int																	
NatWest																	
B & H																	
Sunday																	

SWANN, A. J.   Northamptonshire

Name: Alec James Swann
Role: Right-hand opening bat, occasional
off-spin bowler
Born: 26 October 1976, Northampton
Height: 6ft 2in **Weight:** 12st
Nickname: Swanny, Ron
County debut: 1996
1st-Class 50s: 1
1st-Class 100s: 1
1st-Class catches: 1
Parents: Raymond and Mavis
Marital status: Single
Family links with cricket: Father played for
Northumberland, Bedfordshire,
Northamptonshire 2nd XI and England
Amateurs. Brother Graeme has played for
England U14 and U15 and Northamptonshire
2nd XI and some 1st XI games

Education: Sponne Comprehensive,
Towcester
Qualifications: 9 GCSEs, 4 A-levels, NCA coaching award
Career outside cricket: Have worked for Nationwide Building Society
Off-season: Playing club cricket in Australia
Overseas teams played for: Wallsend, NSW, Australia 1995-96, 1997-98
Cricketers particularly admired: Mark and Steve Waugh, Robin Smith, Russell
Warren
Young players to look out for: Graeme Swann, Ben Hollioake, James Ormond,
Darren Altree
Other sports followed: Football (Newcastle) and most other sports except athletics
Relaxations: 'I enjoy gambling on horses and sometimes on football or cricket,'
reading political thrillers, watching films
Extras: Played for England Schools U15 and U19. Opened batting for Bedfordshire
(with father in Minor Counties game). *Daily Telegraph* U15 Young Cricketer of the Year
1992. Midlands Club Cricket Conference Young Cricketer of the Year 1992. Played for
England U19 against New Zealand in 1996
Opinions on cricket: 'I like the idea of a national one-day league, one cup competition
and a two-divisional championship. County cricket is not as soft or as uncompetitive as
people seem to believe, but some slight adjustments to the system could improve county
cricket for the better. Day/night cricket should be given an increased priority.'
Best batting: 136 Northamptonshire v Warwickshire, Edgbaston 1997

1997 Season

	M	Inns	NO	Runs	HS	Avge	100s	50s	Ct	St	O	M	Runs	Wkts	Avge	Best	5wl	10wM
Test																		
All First	2	3	0	162	136	54.00	1	-	-	-								
1-day Int																		
NatWest																		
B & H																		
Sunday																		

Career Performances

	M	Inns	NO	Runs	HS	Avge	100s	50s	Ct	St	Balls	Runs	Wkts	Avge	Best	5wl	10wM
Test																	
All First	5	8	1	262	136	37.42	1	1	1	-	30	15	0	-	-	-	-
1-day Int																	
NatWest																	
B & H																	
Sunday																	

SWANN, G. P.   Northamptonshire

Name: Graeme Peter Swann
Role: Right-hand bat, off-spin bowler
Born: 24 March 1979, Northampton
Height: 6ft **Weight:** 11st 7lbs
Nickname: Swanny, Reeme
County debut: 1997 (one-day)
Parents: Raymond and Mavis
Marital status: Single
Family links with cricket: Dad has played
Minor Counties cricket for Bedfordshire and
Northumberland and also for England
Amateurs. Brother is contracted to
Northamptonshire
Education: Abington Vale Lower School;
Sponne School, Towcester
Qualifications: 10 GCSEs, 4 A-levels, NCA
coaching award
Cricketers particularly admired: Mark and
Steve Waugh, Matthew Elliott, Graham
Thorpe, Ian Botham, Don Bradman, Neil Foster
Young players to look out for: Alec Swann, Michael Davies, Tim Walton, Andy
Oram, John Blain

Other sports followed: Football (Newcastle United), rugby (Northampton Saints), golf and baseball

Injuries: 'Stitches in the back of the head, only missed four hours of play but couldn't wear a helmet for two weeks'

Relaxations: Listening to music, spending time with girlfriend Natalie, spending money

Extras: Played for England U14, U15 and U17. Dual registered with Bedfordshire Minor County. *Daily Telegraph* regional bowling award winner in 1994. Gray Nicolls/Len Newbury Schools Cricketer of the Year in 1996

Opinions on cricket: 'Hopefully second team cricket will not be amended as proposed in the *Blueprint for the Future*, as this would only lead to a wider gulf between second- and first-class cricket. Also clubs should do more to find employment for players during the winter.'

1997 Season

	M	Inns	NO	Runs	HS	Avge	100s	50s	Ct	St	O	M	Runs	Wkts	Avge	Best	5wI	10wM
Test																		
All First																		
1-day Int																		
NatWest																		
B & H																		
Sunday	4	2	1	0	0 *	0.00	-	-	-	-	32	1	128	5	25.60	2-28	-	

Career Performances

	M	Inns	NO	Runs	HS	Avge	100s	50s	Ct	St	Balls	Runs	Wkts	Avge	Best	5wI	10wM
Test																	
All First																	
1-day Int																	
NatWest																	
B & H																	
Sunday	4	2	1	0	0 *	0.00	-	-	-	-	192	128	5	25.60	2-28	-	

TAYLOR, J. P.   Northamptonshire

Name: Jonathan Paul Taylor
Role: Left-hand bat, left-arm
fast-medium bowler
Born: 8 August 1964, Ashby-de-la-Zouch,
Leicestershire
Height: 6ft 2in **Weight:** 13st 10lbs
Nickname: Roadie, PT
County debut: 1988 (Derbyshire), 1991
(Northamptonshire)
County cap: 1992 (Northamptonshire)
Test debut: 1992-93
Tests: 2
One-Day Internationals: 1
50 wickets in a season: 5
1st-Class 50s: 4
1st-Class 5 w. in innings: 16
1st-Class 10 w. in match: 3
1st-Class catches: 45
Place in batting averages: 272nd av. 12.70
(1996 252nd av. 17.28)
Place in bowling averages: 58th av. 28.37 (1996 42nd av. 27.59)
Strike rate: 50.62 (career 56.49)
Parents: Derek and Janet
Wife and date of marriage: Elaine Mary, 30 July 1993
Children: Christopher Paul, 8 July 1994
Family links with cricket: Father and brother played local league cricket
Education: Pingle School, Swadlincote, Derbyshire
Qualifications: 6 O-levels, NCA coaching certificate
Overseas tours: Midland Club Cricket Conference to Australia 1990-91; England to
India and Sri Lanka 1992-93; Northamptonshire to Natal 1993, to Zimbabwe 1995, to
Johannesburg 1996; England A to South Africa 1993-94
Overseas teams played for: Papakura, New Zealand 1984-85; Napier High School
Old Boys, New Zealand 1985-86; North Kalgoorlie, Western Australia 1990-91; Great
Boulder, Western Australia 1991-92
Cricketers particularly admired: Dennis Lillee, Bob Taylor, John Lever
Young players to look out for: Anthony McGrath, David Sales, Kevin Innes
Other sports followed: Soccer, rugby, basketball
Relaxations: Watching videos, eating out, 'looking after hyperactive little boy, if you
can call that relaxing!'
Extras: Spent four seasons on the staff at Derbyshire 1984-87 and played Minor
Counties cricket for Staffordshire 1989-90. Won Man of the Match in the Bain Clarkson

Final in 1987 for Derbyshire, after being released. Played first game at Lord's in NatWest Trophy final 1992. Was voted Northamptonshire's Player of the Year in 1992. Called up as replacement during England A tour to South Africa 1993-94. Selected for England Indoor World Cup squad 1995

Opinions on cricket: 'More quality, less quantity.'
Best batting: 86 Northamptonshire v Durham, Northampton 1995
Best bowling: 7-23 Northamptonshire v Hampshire, Bournemouth 1992

1997 Season

	M	Inns	NO	Runs	HS	Avge	100s	50s	Ct	St	O	M	Runs	Wkts	Avge	Best	5wI	10wM
Test																		
All First	16	21	4	216	36	12.70	-	-	7	-	455.4	81	1532	54	28.37	7-87	3	1
1-day Int																		
NatWest	2	2	1	9	6	9.00	-	-	-	-	19	1	98	2	49.00	2-58	-	
B & H	6	2	0	13	7	6.50	-	-	1	-	57	4	195	7	27.85	2-31	-	
Sunday	13	4	3	33	20	33.00	-	-	2	-	86	5	369	9	41.00	2-13	-	

Career Performances

	M	Inns	NO	Runs	HS	Avge	100s	50s	Ct	St	Balls	Runs	Wkts	Avge	Best	5wI	10wM
Test	2	4	2	34	17 *	17.00	-	-	-	-	288	156	3	52.00	1-18	-	-
All First	132	145	56	1197	86	13.44	-	4	45	-	22822	11969	404	29.62	7-23	16	3
1-day Int	1	1	0	1	1	1.00	-	-	-	-	18	20	0	-	-	-	-
NatWest	26	10	5	31	9	6.20	-	-	6	-	1581	1016	35	29.02	4-34	-	
B & H	29	11	7	36	7 *	9.00	-	-	5	-	1617	931	39	23.87	5-45	1	
Sunday	96	32	16	160	24	10.00	-	-	17	-	4176	3241	108	30.00	3-14	-	

TAYLOR, N. R. Sussex

Name: Neil Royston Taylor
Role: Right-hand bat, occasional
off-spin bowler
Born: 21 July 1959, Farnborough, Kent
Height: 6ft 1in **Weight:** 15st
Nickname: Map
County debut: 1979 (Kent), 1997 (Sussex)
County cap: 1982 (Kent)
Benefit: 1992 (£131,000)
1000 runs in a season: 11
1st-Class 50s: 89
1st-Class 100s: 45
1st-Class 200s: 2
1st-Class catches: 154
One-Day 100s: 6
Place in batting averages: 74th av. 38.25
(1996 58th av. 42.10)
Strike rate: (career 98.43)
Parents: Leonard and Audrey
Wife and date of marriage: Jane Claire, 25 September 1982
Children: Amy Louise, 7 November 1985; Lauren, 21 July 1988
Family links with cricket: Brother Colin played for Kent U19. Father played club cricket
Education: Cray Valley Technical High School
Qualifications: 8 O-levels, 2 A-levels, advanced cricket coach
Overseas tours: English Schools to India 1977-78; Kent to Canada 1978, to
Zimbabwe 1992-93; Fred Rumsey XI to West Indies 1988
Overseas teams played for: Randburg, Johannesburg 1979-85; St Stithian's College,
Johannesburg (as coach) 1980-85
Cricketers particularly admired: Chris Tavaré, Mark Benson, Mike Gatting, Robin
Smith
Other sports followed: Rugby union, golf
Relaxations: Music and reading (mainly biographies)
Extras: Made 110 on debut for Kent v Sri Lankans, 1979. Won four Man of the Match
awards in his first five matches and scored three successive centuries in the B&H.
Played for England B v Pakistan, 1982 and twice fielded as 12th man for England – v
India in 1982 and v West Indies in 1988, both matches at The Oval. Holds Kent first and
second wicket record partnerships with Mark Benson (300 v Derbyshire) and Simon
Hinks (366 v Middlesex). Only Kent player to score 200 and 100 in a match twice (204
and 142 v Surrey, 111 and 203* v Sussex). Has scored 13 centuries at Canterbury,
beating Frank Woolley and Colin Cowdrey. Provides a weekly contribution to Radio
Kent through the summer. Joined Sussex for the 1997 season and scored a century on
debut, placing him in a unique club alongside Peter Bowler (Somerset) and Jon Lewis

(Durham) of players who have scored centuries on debut for two different counties
Best batting: 204 Kent v Surrey, Canterbury 1990
Best bowling: 2-20 Kent v Somerset, Canterbury 1985

1997 Season

	M	Inns	NO	Runs	HS	Avge	100s	50s	Ct	St	O	M	Runs	Wkts	Avge	Best	5wI	10wM
Test																		
All First	16	28	1	1033	127	38.25	3	5	3	-								
1-day Int																		
NatWest	4	3	0	68	48	22.66	-	-	1	-								
B & H	5	5	0	250	116	50.00	1	1	3	-								
Sunday	8	8	1	139	47	19.85	-	-	3	-								

Career Performances

	M	Inns	NO	Runs	HS	Avge	100s	50s	Ct	St	Balls	Runs	Wkts	Avge	Best	5wI	10wM
Test																	
All First	319	543	69	18804	204	39.67	45	89	154	-	1575	891	16	55.68	2-20	-	-
1-day Int																	
NatWest	35	34	1	870	86	26.36	-	5	7	-	143	86	6	14.33	3-29	-	
B & H	56	53	2	2122	137	41.60	6	8	14	-	12	5	0	-	-	-	
Sunday	155	149	15	4026	95	30.04	-	24	40	-							

THOMAS, P. A. Worcestershire

Name: Paul Anthony Thomas
Role: Right-hand bat, right-arm fast bowler
Height: 5ft 9in **Weight:** 11st 8lbs
Born: 3 June 1971, Dudley
Nickname: Thommo
County debut: 1995
1st-Class 5 w. in innings: 1
1st-Class catches: 1
Place in batting averages:
(1996 310th av. 6.57)
Place in bowling averages:
(1996 136th av. 47.91)
Strike rate: 64.50 (career 67.42)
Parents: Clifford and Myrtle
Marital status: Single
Family links with cricket: Father is a great
fan of the game. Brothers play
Education: Broadway School

Off-season: Playing club cricket in Australia
Extras: Awarded 2nd XI cap in 1995 and was released by Worcestershire at the end of the 1997 season
Best batting: 25 Worcestershire v Warwickshire, Edgbaston 1995
Best bowling: 5-70 Worcestershire v West Indies, Worcester 1995

1997 Season

	M	Inns	NO	Runs	HS	Avge	100s	50s	Ct	St	O	M	Runs	Wkts	Avge	Best	5wI	10wM
Test																		
All First	2	2	1	16	16 *	16.00	-	-	-	-	43	6	166	4	41.50	3-43	-	-
1-day Int																		
NatWest																		
B & H																		
Sunday																		

Career Performances

	M	Inns	NO	Runs	HS	Avge	100s	50s	Ct	St	Balls	Runs	Wkts	Avge	Best	5wI	10wM
Test																	
All First	21	24	5	119	25	6.26	-	-	1	-	3304	2295	49	46.83	5-70	1	-
1-day Int																	
NatWest	1	0	0	0	0	-	-	-	-	-	60	30	2	15.00	2-30	-	
B & H	2	1	0	3	3	3.00	-	-	-	-	112	85	1	85.00	1-34	-	
Sunday	1	0	0	0	0	-	-	-	-	-	36	30	0	-	-	-	

THOMAS, S. D.   Glamorgan

Name: Stuart Darren Thomas
Role: Left-hand bat, right-arm medium-fast bowler
Born: 25 January 1975, Morriston
Height: 6ft **Weight:** 12st 9lbs
Nickname: Teddy, Tedrick, Thomo
County debut: 1992
50 wickets in a season: 1
1st-Class 50s: 4
1st-Class 5 w. in innings: 8
1st-Class catches: 17
One-Day 5 w. in innings: 2
Place in batting averages: 212th av. 20.00 (1996 269th av. 15.30)
Place in bowling averages: 49th av. 27.24 (1996 153rd av. 58.75)
Strike rate: 45.90 (career 54.33)
Parents: Stuart and Anne
Marital status: 'Courting Clare very strongly'

Family links with cricket: Dad played local cricket
Education: Craig Comprehensive; Neath Tertiary College
Qualifications: 4 GCSEs, BTEC National Diploma in Sports Science, NCA coaching certificate
Off-season: 'Drinking lots of beer in the Bahamas on holiday'
Overseas tours: England U18 to South Africa 1992-93; Glamorgan to South Africa 1992-93, to Portugal 1994, to Zimbabwe 1995; England U19 to Sri Lanka 1993-94
Cricketers particularly admired: Dean Cosker 'for his natural length'
Young players to look out for: Alun 'face like a clock' Evans 'for his pulling ability'
Other sports followed: Rugby union and league (Warrington)

Injuries: Anal disorder, missed one Sunday League match
Relaxations: 'Talking smut with Dean Cosker. Spending a lot of time horseriding with my girlfriend. Surfing off the Gower coastline. Socialising with a few pints.'
Extras: Youngest player to take five wickets on debut v Derbyshire in 1992 and finished eighth in national bowling averages. BBC Welsh Young Sports Personality 1992. Played last U19 Test against India at Edgbaston 1994. Broke Alan Wilkins' (Glamorgan) best Benson and Hedges bowling record on his debut in the competition with six for 20 in 1995
Opinions on cricket: 'Best game in the world.'
Best batting: 78* Glamorgan v Gloucestershire, Abergavenny 1995
Best bowling: 5-24 Glamorgan v Sussex, Swansea 1997

1997 Season

	M	Inns	NO	Runs	HS	Avge	100s	50s	Ct	St	O	M	Runs	Wkts	Avge	Best	5wI	10wM
Test																		
All First	18	19	4	300	75 *	20.00	-	1	8	-	405.3	58	1444	53	27.24	5-24	3	-
1-day Int																		
NatWest	4	3	0	15	13	5.00	-	-	-	-	43	1	226	8	28.25	5-74	1	
B & H	2	2	2	14	13 *	-	-	-	-	-	16	0	107	4	26.75	2-47	-	
Sunday	10	7	0	53	15	7.57	-	-	3	-	62.1	2	307	10	30.70	3-30	-	

Career Performances

	M	Inns	NO	Runs	HS	Avge	100s	50s	Ct	St	Balls	Runs	Wkts	Avge	Best	5wI	10wM
Test																	
All First	53	69	19	928	78 *	18.56	-	4	17	-	8096	5252	149	35.24	5-24	8	-
1-day Int																	
NatWest	5	3	0	15	13	5.00	-	-	-	-	312	262	8	32.75	5-74	1	
B & H	9	5	3	41	27 *	20.50	-	-	5	-	428	371	17	21.82	6-20	1	
Sunday	21	12	3	102	20 *	11.33	-	-	4	-	669	585	15	39.00	3-30	-	

THOMPSON, J. B. de C.   Kent

Name: Julian Barton de Courcy Thompson
Role: Right-hand bat, right-arm
fast-medium bowler
Born: 28 October 1968, Cape Town,
South Africa
Height: 6ft 5in **Weight:** 13st 7lbs
Nickname: Thommo, Doc, Bambi
County debut: 1994
1st-Class 50s: 1
1st-Class 5 w. in innings: 2
1st-Class catches: 4
Place in batting averages: 258th av. 15.14
Place in bowling averages: 62nd av. 28.70
Strike rate: 43.22 (career 49.23)
Parents: John and Joyce
Wife and date of marriage: Tanya,
4 October 1997

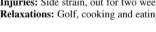

Family links with cricket: 'Wife hates it.
Father and brother play locally'
Education: The Judd School, Tonbridge, Kent; Guy's Hospital Medical School,
London
Qualifications: MBBS, NCA coaching award
Career outside cricket: Doctor
Off-season: Senior House Officer in Obstetrics and Gynaecology, Kent and
Canterbury Hospital
Overseas tours: University of London to India 1991
Overseas teams played for: Northern Districts, Sydney 1987-88
Cricketers particularly admired: Steve Waugh, Glen McGrath, Steve Marsh
Young players to look out for: Ben Phillips, James Hockley, Robert Key
Other sports followed: Golf, football (Liverpool), squash
Injuries: Side strain, out for two weeks
Relaxations: Golf, cooking and eating food

Extras: Dismissed Brian Lara twice for a duck in Kent's game against the West Indies in 1995 – Brian Lara's only pair in first-class cricket. Dismissed three England captains in first month of the 1996 season – Atherton, Gatting and Gooch

Opinions on cricket: 'The counties missed a great opportunity for a two-divisional championship in August. The sooner that club chairmen/secretaries start to see beyond the end of their noses the better. Good to see the PCA improving services for the players.'

Best batting: 59* Kent v Warwickshire, Tunbridge Wells 1997
Best bowling: 5-72 Kent v Surrey, The Oval 1996

1997 Season

	M	Inns	NO	Runs	HS	Avge	100s	50s	Ct	St	O	M	Runs	Wkts	Avge	Best	5wl	10wM
Test																		
All First	9	10	3	106	59 *	15.14	-	1	3	-	223.2	30	890	31	28.70	5-89	1	-
1-day Int																		
NatWest																			
B & H																			
Sunday	11	5	3	27	18 *	13.50	-	-	1	-	70.4	2	322	11	29.27	3-17	-	

Career Performances

	M	Inns	NO	Runs	HS	Avge	100s	50s	Ct	St	Balls	Runs	Wkts	Avge	Best	5wl	10wM
Test																	
All First	18	23	6	281	59 *	16.52	-	1	4	-	2314	1503	47	31.97	5-72	2	-
1-day Int																	
NatWest																		
B & H	4	3	2	17	12 *	17.00	-	-	-	-	180	114	6	19.00	3-29	-	
Sunday	27	15	8	74	30	10.57	-	-	3	-	862	696	20	34.80	3-17	-	

THORPE, G. P.   Surrey

Name: Graham Paul Thorpe
Role: Left-hand bat, occasional right-arm
medium bowler
Born: 1 August 1969, Farnham
Height: 5ft 10in **Weight:** 12st
Nickname: Chalky
County debut: 1988
County cap: 1991
Test debut: 1993
Tests: 43
One-Day Internationals: 39
1000 runs in a season: 8
1st-Class 50s: 82
1st-Class 100s: 30
1st-Class 200s: 2
1st-Class catches: 167
One-Day 100s: 6
Place in batting averages: 7th av. 61.05
(1996 9th av. 62.76)
Strike rate: (career 88.76)
Parents: 'Mr and Mrs Thorpe'
Wife: Nicola

Family links with cricket: Both brothers play for Farnham, father also plays cricket
and mother is 'professional scorer'
Education: Weydon Comprehensive; Farnham Sixth Form College
Qualifications: 7 O-levels, PE Diploma
Off-season: Going to Sharjah and West Indies with England
Overseas tours: England A to Zimbabwe and Kenya 1989-90, to Pakistan 1990-91, to
Bermuda and West Indies 1991-92, to Australia 1992-93; England to West Indies
1993-94, to Australia 1994-95, to South Africa 1995-96, to India and Pakistan (World
Cup) 1996, to Zimbabwe and New Zealand 1996-97, to Sharjah 1997-98, to West
Indies 1997-98
Cricketers particularly admired: Viv Richards, Grahame Clinton, David Gower
Young players to look out for: Ben Hollioake
Other sports followed: Football (Chelsea FC), golf
Relaxations: Sleeping
Extras: Played for English Schools cricket U15 and U19 and England Schools football
U18. Scored a century against Australia on his Test debut at Trent Bridge 1993. Arrived
a few days late for the Zimbabwe leg of England's tour to attend the birth of his son. He
scored hundreds in successive Tests during the winter tour to New Zealand. England's
Player of the Series and leading run scorer in the 1997 Ashes campaign with 453 runs at

an average of 50.33
Best batting: 222 Surrey v Glamorgan, The Oval 1997
Best bowling: 4-40 Surrey v Australians, The Oval 1993

1997 Season

	M	Inns	NO	Runs	HS	Avge	100s	50s	Ct	St	O	M	Runs	Wkts	Avge	Best	5wI	10wM
Test	6	11	2	453	138	50.33	1	3	8	-								
All First	14	23	4	1160	222	61.05	3	6	17	-	4	0	13	0	-	-	-	-
1-day Int	3	3	2	127	75 *	127.00	-	1	3	-								
NatWest	2	2	0	0	0	0.00	-	-	3	-								
B & H	8	8	1	327	79	46.71	-	3	7	-								
Sunday	6	6	1	225	100 *	45.00	1	-	2	-								

Career Performances

	M	Inns	NO	Runs	HS	Avge	100s	50s	Ct	St	Balls	Runs	Wkts	Avge	Best	5wI	10wM
Test	43	78	8	2964	138	42.34	5	22	39	-	138	37	0	-	-	-	-
All First	215	362	49	14048	222	44.88	30	82	167	-	2219	1235	25	49.40	4-40	-	-
1-day Int	39	39	6	1349	89	40.87	-	12	22	-	120	97	2	48.50	2-15	-	
NatWest	23	22	4	807	145 *	44.83	1	6	13	-	13	12	0	-	-	-	-
B & H	37	36	3	1239	103	37.54	1	8	19	-	168	131	4	32.75	3-35	-	
Sunday	108	99	14	3088	115 *	36.32	4	21	41	-	318	307	8	38.37	3-21	-	

THURSFIELD, M. J.   Sussex

Name: Martin John Thursfield
Role: Right-hand bat, right-arm
medium-fast bowler
Born: 14 December 1971, South Shields
Height: 6ft 4in **Weight:** 14st
Nickname: Thursy
County debut: 1990 (Middlesex),
Hampshire (1992), Sussex (1997)
1st-Class 5 w. in innings: 1
1st-Class catches: 2
Strike rate: 59.00 (career 78.84)
Parents: Anthony John and Maureen
Marital status: Single
Family links with cricket: Great-grandfather
played for Yorkshire, and father is a keen
club cricketer
Education: Boldon Comprehensive
Qualifications: GCSEs, NCA coaching

certificate
Overseas tours: England YC to New Zealand 1990-91
Cricketers particularly admired: Robin Smith, Malcolm Marshall, Allan Donald
Other sports followed: Football, golf
Relaxations: Playing golf, watching football and sleeping
Extras: Bowled two balls with broken leg in first England YC One-Day International v New Zealand 1990-91. One of the youngest golfers in the country to achieve a hole in one, aged ten. Released by Hampshire at the end of the 1996 season, played for Sussex during 1997 and was released at the end of the season
Best batting: 47 Hampshire v Glamorgan, Southampton 1994
Best bowling: 6-130 Hampshire v Middlesex, Southampton 1994

1997 Season

	M	Inns	NO	Runs	HS	Avge	100s	50s	Ct	St	O	M	Runs	Wkts	Avge	Best	5wI	10wM
Test																		
All First	2	2	1	32	32 *	32.00	-	-	1	-	29.3	5	108	3	36.00	2-36	-	-
1-day Int																		
NatWest	1	0	0	0	0	-	-	-	-	-								
B & H	1	1	0	2	2	2.00	-	-	1	-	8	0	49	2	24.50	2-49	-	
Sunday																		

Career Performances

	M	Inns	NO	Runs	HS	Avge	100s	50s	Ct	St	Balls	Runs	Wkts	Avge	Best	5wI	10wM
Test																	
All First	24	26	6	309	47	15.45	-	-	2	-	2844	1539	38	40.50	6-130	1	-
1-day Int																	
NatWest	2	0	0	0	0	-	-	-	-	-	60	34	1	34.00	1-34	-	
B & H	7	5	3	26	19	13.00	-	-	2	-	360	291	8	36.37	2-33	-	
Sunday	23	11	3	34	9	4.25	-	-	4	-	948	805	16	50.31	3-31	-	

TITCHARD, S. P.   Lancashire

Name: Stephen Paul Titchard
Role: Right-hand bat, right-arm medium bowler
Born: 17 December 1967, Warrington, Cheshire
Height: 6ft 3in **Weight:** 15st
Nickname: Titch, Stainy, Tyrone
County debut: 1990
1st-Class 50s: 25
1st-Class 100s: 4
1st-Class catches: 52
Place in batting averages: 211th av. 20.00 (1996 51st av. 44.71)

Strike rate: 30.00 (career 78.00)
Parents: Alan and Margaret
Marital status: Single
Family links with cricket: Father, uncle and two brothers have played for Grappenhall 1st XI in the Manchester Association League. Father also represented the Army
Education: Lymm County High School; Priestley College
Qualifications: 3 O-levels, NCA senior coaching award
Career outside cricket: Coach
Overseas tours: Lancashire to Tasmania and Western Australia 1990, to Western Australia 1991, to Johannesburg 1992
Overseas teams played for: South Canberra, Australia 1991-92
Cricketers particularly admired: Graham Gooch, Malcolm Marshall
Other sports followed: Football (Manchester City) and rugby league (Warrington)
Relaxations: Snooker, golf, 'most sports'
Extras: Played for England U19. Made record scores for Manchester Association U18 (200*) and Cheshire Schools U19 (203*)
Opinions on cricket: 'In Championship games, the day should comprise of three two-hour sessions, with an extended tea break of at least ten minutes!'
Best batting: 163 Lancashire v Essex, Chelmsford 1996
Best bowling: 1-11 Lancashire v Northamptonshire, Old Trafford 1997
1-11 Lancashire v Kent, Old Trafford 1997

1997 Season

	M	Inns	NO	Runs	HS	Avge	100s	50s	Ct	St	O	M	Runs	Wkts	Avge	Best	5wI	10wM
Test																		
All First	6	9	0	180	79	20.00	-	1	2	-	15	1	47	3	15.66	1-11	-	-
1-day Int																		
NatWest																			
B & H																			
Sunday																			

91. Angus Fraser's 8 for 53 in the second Test against the West Indies at Trinidad were the best-ever bowling figures by an Englishman in the West Indies. Whose record did he beat?

○ **vodafone**

569

Career Performances

	M	Inns	NO	Runs	HS	Avge	100s	50s	Ct	St	Balls	Runs	Wkts	Avge	Best	5wI	10wM
Test																	
All First	75	131	8	3945	163	32.07	4	25	52	-	312	171	4	42.75	1-11	-	-
1-day Int																	
NatWest	3	3	0	116	92	38.66	-	1	1	-							
B & H	3	3	0	101	82	33.66	-	1	1	-							
Sunday	29	29	3	705	96	27.11	-	3	4	-							

TOLLEY, C. M.   Nottinghamshire

Name: Christopher Mark Tolley
Role: Right-hand bat, left-arm
medium bowler
Born: 30 December 1967, Kidderminster
Height: 5ft 9in **Weight:** 11st 12lbs
Nickname: Red Dog, Red'uns, Ginger
Warrior
County debut: 1989 (Worcestershire),
1996 (Nottinghamshire)
County cap: 1993 (Worcestershire)
1st-Class 50s: 8
1st-Class 5 w. in innings: 2
1st-Class catches: 35
Place in batting averages: 146th av. 26.61
(1996 194th av. 25.50)
Place in bowling averages: 63rd av. 28.71
(1996 151st av. 57.42)
Strike rate: 62.22 (career 74.74)
Parents: Ray and Liz
Marital status: Single
Family links with cricket: Brother Richard plays in the Birmingham League for
Stourbridge
Education: Oldswinford Primary School; Redhill Comprehensive School; King
Edward VI College, Stourbridge; Loughborough University
Qualifications: 9 O-levels, 3 A-levels, BSc (Hons) PE, Sports Science & Recreation
Management. Qualified teacher and level 2 hockey coach
Career outside cricket: PE teacher
Off-season: Coaching around Nottingham and training for a sports massage therapy
diploma
Overseas tours: British Universities Sports Federation tour to Barbados, October
1989; Worcestershire to Zimbabwe and South Africa

Overseas teams played for: Lancaster Park, Christchurch, New Zealand 1996-97
Cricketers particularly admired: Ian Botham, Graeme Hick
Young players to look out for: Andy Oram, Jamie Hart
Other sports followed: Hockey
Injuries: Shoulder and torn adductor, out for a total of five weeks
Relaxations: Food and wine
Extras: Played for English Schools U19 in 1986 and for the Combined Universities in B&H Cup. Asked to be released by Worcestershire at the end of the 1995 season and joined Nottinghamshire for the 1996 season. Took first-class hat-trick against Leicestershire in 1997
Best batting: 84 Worcestershire v Derbyshire, Derby 1994
Best bowling: 6-61 Nottinghamshire v Leicestershire, Leicester 1997

1997 Season

	M	Inns	NO	Runs	HS		Avge	100s	50s	Ct	St	O	M	Runs	Wkts	Avge	Best	5wI	10wM
Test																			
All First	12	22	4	479	73	*	26.61	-	3	6	-	363	87	1005	35	28.71	6-61	1	-
1-day Int																			
NatWest	2	2	1	30	18		30.00	-	-	-	-	21	1	55	4	13.75	3-21	-	
B & H	3	3	1	62	23	*	31.00	-	-	-	-	26	2	104	1	104.00	1-33	-	
Sunday	11	10	2	196	43		24.50	-	-	4	-	64	1	328	15	21.86	4-24	-	

Career Performances

	M	Inns	NO	Runs	HS	Avge	100s	50s	Ct	St	Balls	Runs	Wkts	Avge	Best	5wI	10wM
Test																	
All First	85	112	28	1963	84	23.36	-	8	35	-	10913	5357	146	36.69	6-61	2	-
1-day Int																	
NatWest	8	5	3	67	18	33.50	-	-	-	-	432	258	11	23.45	3-21	-	
B & H	20	17	2	355	77	23.66	-	3	3	-	978	633	9	70.33	1-12	-	
Sunday	60	34	10	368	43	15.33	-	-	20	-	1960	1616	62	26.06	5-16	1	

TRAINOR, N. J.   Gloucestershire

Name: Nicholas James Trainor
Role: Right-hand bat, off-spin bowler
Born: 29 June 1975, Gateshead
Height: 6ft 2in **Weight:** 13st 10lbs
Nickname: Big Red, Geordie
County debut: 1996
1st-Class 50s: 3
1st-Class 100s: 1
1st-Class catches: 8
One-Day 100s: 1
Place in batting averages: 208th av. 20.16
(1996 234th av. 20.07)
Parents: Eric and Anna-Maria
Marital status: Single
Family links with cricket: 'Father played
club cricket for Gateshead Fell CC in the
Durham Senior League until a knock on his
head finished his career!'
Education: St Peters Primary School; St
Edmund Campion Secondary School
Qualifications: 9 GCSEs, BTEC in Business and Finance, NCA coaching award
Off-season: Playing for Zoo Lake in the Jo'burg Premier League in South Africa
Overseas teams played for: Triangle Rovers CC, South Africa 1994-95; Zoo Lake
CC, South Africa 1995-98
Cricketers particularly admired: Geoff Boycott, Jack Russell, Robin Smith, Mark
Ramprakash, Mike Atherton, Eric Trainor, Ian Botham
Young players to look out for: Kamran Sheeraz, Jon Lewis, J. Coetzee, B. Gannon
Other sports followed: Golf, football (Newcastle United), squash, tennis,
synchronised swimming, gurning, morris dancing, bungee jumping
Injuries: Knee, out for two weeks
Relaxations: 'Spending time with friends and team-mates on the strip. Eating out at
Boom wine bar, Clifton, with the proprietor'
Extras: Holds the record with Tony Wright for the highest partnership in the NatWest
competition with 311 against Scotland in 1997
Opinions on cricket: 'Leave first- and second-class cricket as it is.'
Best batting: 121 Gloucestershire v Australia, Bristol 1997

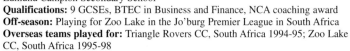

92. Who, on 16 January 1998, became the first black player to
represent South Africa in an International match?

1997 Season

	M	Inns	NO	Runs	HS	Avge	100s	50s	Ct	St	O	M	Runs	Wkts	Avge	Best	5wI	10wM
Test																		
All First	14	25	1	484	121	20.16	1	1	3	-	21	7	89	0	-	-	-	-
1-day Int					ᵧ													
NatWest	2	2	0	172	143	86.00	1	-	1	-	8	0	49	2	24.50	2-25	-	
B & H	3	3	0	98	62	32.66	-	1	1	-	6	0	26	0	-	-	-	
Sunday	3	2	0	26	22	13.00	-	-	1	-	4	0	12	0	-	-	-	

Career Performances

	M	Inns	NO	Runs	HS	Avge	100s	50s	Ct	St	Balls	Runs	Wkts	Avge	Best	5wI	10wM
Test																	
All First	22	39	2	745	121	20.13	1	3	8	-	132	93	0	-	-	-	-
1-day Int																	
NatWest	3	3	0	186	143	62.00	1	-	1	-	48	49	2	24.50	2-25	-
B & H	4	4	0	123	62	30.75	-	1	1	-	36	26	0	-	-	-
Sunday	4	3	0	46	22	15.33	-	-	1	-	24	12	0	-	-	-

TRESCOTHICK, M. E.   Somerset

Name: Marcus Edward Trescothick
Role: Left-hand bat, right-arm swing bowler, reserve wicket-keeper
Born: 25 December 1975, Keynsham, Bristol
Height: 6ft 3in **Weight:** 14st 7lbs
Nickname: Banger
County debut: 1993
1st-Class 50s: 15
1st-Class 100s: 4
1st-Class catches: 48
One-Day 100s: 2
Place in batting averages: 199th av. 21.66 (1996 178th av. 27.69)
Strike rate: 90.00 (career 71.00)
Parents: Martyn and Lin
Marital status: Single
Family links with cricket: Father played for Somerset 2nd XI; uncle played club cricket
Education: Sir Bernard Lovell School
Qualifications: 7 GCSEs
Overseas tours: England U18 to South Africa 1992-93; England U19 to Sri Lanka 1993-94, to West Indies (captain) 1994-95

Cricketers particularly admired: Neil Fairbrother, Graham Gooch, Mark Lathwell
Young players to look out for: Stephen Peters
Other sports followed: Golf, football
Relaxations: Playing golf, repairing and renovating cricket bats and listening to music
Extras: Member of England U19 squad for home series against West Indies 1993. Man of the Series against India U19 in 1994, scoring most runs in the series. Whittingdale Young Player of the Month, August 1994. Took a hat-trick against Young Australia in 1995. Scored more than 1000 runs for England U19. Scored 322 in the second innings of a 2nd XI game against Warwickshire in 1997 – Somerset were chasing a target of 612 and Trescothick was the last man out with the score on 605!
Opinions on cricket: 'There should be some sort of retainer contract.'
Best batting: 178 Somerset v Hampshire, Taunton 1996
Best bowling: 4-36 Somerset v Young Australia, Taunton 1995

1997 Season

	M	Inns	NO	Runs	HS	Avge	100s	50s	Ct	St	O	M	Runs	Wkts	Avge	Best	5wI	10wM
Test																		
All First	13	19	1	390	83 *	21.66	-	4	6	-	15	3	69	1	69.00	1-18	-	-
1-day Int																		
NatWest																		
B & H																		
Sunday	5	4	1	50	28	16.66	-	-	2	-	7	0	52	0	-		-	-

Career Performances

	M	Inns	NO	Runs	HS	Avge	100s	50s	Ct	St	Balls	Runs	Wkts	Avge	Best	5wI	10wM
Test																	
All First	54	93	2	2465	178	27.08	4	15	48	-	426	309	6	51.50	4-36	-	-
1-day Int																	
NatWest	4	4	0	189	116	47.25	1	-	2	-	18	28	0	-		-	-
B & H	7	7	1	266	122	44.33	1	2	5	-							
Sunday	41	37	2	705	74	20.14	-	3	13	-	96	107	2	53.50	1-13	-	

TROTT, B. J.   Somerset

Name: Benjamin James Trott
Role: Right-hand bat, right-arm fast bowler
Born: 14 March 1975, Wellington, Somerset
Height: 6ft 5in **Weight:** 14st
Nickname: Trotty, Gallop
County debut: 1997
1st-Class catches: 1
Strike rate: 32.40 (career 32.40)

Parents: Alan Robert and Jane Elizabeth
Marital status: Single
Family links with cricket: Younger brother, Thomas, plays for Somerset youth teams
Education: Wellesley Park Primary School, Wellington; Court Fields Community School, Wellington; Richard Huish College, South Road, Taunton; University College of St Mark and St John, Plymouth
Qualifications: GCSEs, 3 A-levels, 'working towards a teaching degree'
Career outside cricket: Primary school teacher
Off-season: 'Teaching or playing cricket abroad'
Cricketers particularly admired: Ian Botham, Waqar Younis, Graham Rose
Young players to look out for: Joe Tucker
Other sports followed: Football (Manchester United), rugby and basketball
Relaxations: Music, socialising, driving
Extras: Wellington Young Player of the Year in 1993. Wellington Players' Player of the Year in 1996
Opinions on cricket: 'I feel that fitness plays a very important part in today's game. You need a lot of physical and mental strength to play the amount of games required today.'
Best batting: 1* Somerset v Glamorgan, Taunton 1997
Best bowling: 3-74 Somerset v Glamorgan, Taunton 1997

1997 Season

	M	Inns	NO	Runs	HS	Avge	100s	50s	Ct	St	O	M	Runs	Wkts	Avge	Best	5wI	10wM
Test																		
All First	2	2	1	1	1*	1.00	-	-	1	-	27	3	128	5	25.60	3-74	-	-
1-day Int																		
NatWest																		
B & H																		
Sunday	1	0	0	0	0	-	-	-	-	-	4	0	29	1	29.00	1-29	-	

Career Performances

	M	Inns	NO	Runs	HS	Avge	100s	50s	Ct	St	Balls	Runs	Wkts	Avge	Best	5wI	10wM
Test																	
All First	2	2	1	1	1*	1.00	-	-	1	-	162	128	5	25.60	3-74	-	-
1-day Int																	
NatWest																	
B & H																	
Sunday	1	0	0	0	0	-	-	-	-	-	24	29	1	29.00	1-29	-	

TRUMP, H. R. J.   Somerset

Name: Harvey Russell John Trump
Role: Right-hand bat, off-spin bowler, gully/slip fielder
Born: 11 October 1968, Taunton
Height: 6ft 1in **Weight:** 14st
Nickname: Trumpy, Club Foot
County debut: 1988
County cap: 1994
50 wickets in a season: 1
1st-Class 5 w. in innings: 9
1st-Class 10 w. in match: 2
1st-Class catches: 76
Place in batting averages: 233rd av. 17.25 (1994 223rd av. 17.25)
Place in bowling averages: 129th av. 43.62 (1994 87th av. 33.57)
Strike rate: 64.50 (career 78.79)
Parents: Gerald and Jackie
Marital status: Single
Family links with cricket: Father played for Somerset 2nd XI and captained Devon
Education: Millfield School; Chester College of Higher Education
Qualifications: 7 O-levels, 2 A-levels, BA (Hons)
Career outside cricket: Teaching at Stamford School, Lincolnshire
Overseas tours: England YC to Sri Lanka 1986-87, to Australia (Youth World Cup) 1987-88
Cricketers particularly admired: David Graveney, John Emburey, Viv Richards
Other sports followed: Hockey, rugby and most other sports
Relaxations: Theatre, cinema, crosswords, reading
Extras: Played county hockey for Somerset U19. Qualified lifeguard, attaining bronze medallion life-saving award, and is preliminary teacher of disabled swimming certificate. 'He's the best fielder off his own bowling I've ever seen' – David Graveney 1991
Best batting: 48 Somerset v Hampshire, Taunton 1988
Best bowling: 7-52 Somerset v Gloucestershire, Gloucester 1992

---

93. Which Australian Test player has announced that he will play for Ireland in 1998?

1997 Season

	M	Inns	NO	Runs	HS	Avge	100s	50s	Ct	St	O	M	Runs	Wkts	Avge	Best	5wI	10wM
Test																		
All First																		
1-day Int																		
NatWest																		
B & H	3	2	2	3	2 *	-	-	-	2	-	14	0	80	4	20.00	4-51	-	
Sunday	2	1	0	0	0	0.00	-	-	1	-	10	0	70	0	-	-	-	

Career Performances

	M	Inns	NO	Runs	HS	Avge	100s	50s	Ct	St	Balls	Runs	Wkts	Avge	Best	5wI	10wM
Test																	
All First	107	121	41	991	48	12.38	-	-	76	-	19146	9424	243	38.78	7-52	9	2
1-day Int																	
NatWest	10	6	2	19	10 *	4.75	-	-	4	-	547	342	7	48.85	3-15	-	
B & H	21	9	3	27	11	4.50	-	-	9	-	984	668	22	30.36	4-51	-	
Sunday	90	28	14	131	19	9.35	-	-	33	-	3608	2837	78	36.37	3-19	-	

TUCKER, J. Somerset

Name: Joe Tucker
Role: Right-hand bat, right-arm
fast-medium bowler
Born: 14 September 1979, Bath
Height: 6ft 3in **Weight:** 13st
Nickname: Tucks, Smokey, Hugo, Farmer
County debut: No first-team appearance
Parents: Geoff and Chris
Marital status: Single
Family links with cricket: Father, brother
and grandfather all played good club cricket
Education: Pensford Primary School,
Bristol; Chew Valley and Colston Collegiate
School, Bristol; Richard Huish College,
Taunton
Qualifications: 9 GCSEs, NCA coaching
award
Career outside cricket: Cricket coach
Overseas tours: England U19 to South Africa
(World Cup) 1997-98; England U17 to Bermuda 1997; West of England U16 to West
Indies 1996
Young players to look out for: Stephen Peters, Paul Franks, Graham Napier, Owais

Shah

Other sports followed: Football (Manchester United and Bristol City), squash, rugby (Bath RFC), basketball (Taunton Tigers) and 'my cousin, Martin, at motorcross'

Relaxations: Going to the gym. Going to the cinema and ten-pin bowling, listening to music. Spending time with my family, girlfriend and friends, eating out

Extras: Recorded the best bowling for Somerset 2nd XI last season with 5 for 41 in the Bain Hogg Trophy against Worcestershire. Recorded the best bowling figures for England U17 in the International Youth tournament in Bermuda in 1997 with 4 for 41 against Holland. Made his 2nd XI debut for Somerset at the age of 15

Opinions on cricket: 'It's great that more and more youngsters are now getting into the game earlier and the game is becoming more competitive for places. It's also good to hear that we are trying to cut down on the number of games in the English summer so more people are more hungry for runs and wickets.'

TUDOR, A. J.   Surrey

Name: Alexander Jeremy Tudor
Role: Right-hand bat, right-arm fast bowler
Born: 23 October 1977,
West Brompton, London
Height: 6ft 4in **Weight:** 13st 7lbs
Nickname: Big Al, Bambi, Tudes
County debut: 1995
1st-Class 50s: 1
1st-Class 5 w. in innings: 2
1st-Class catches: 1
Place in bowling averages: 103rd av. 35.70
Strike rate: 56.64 (career 47.22)
Parents: Daryll and Jennifer
Marital status: Single
Family links with cricket: Brother was on the staff at The Oval
Education: Wandle Primary, Earlsfield; St Mark's C of E, Fulham; City of Westminster College
Overseas tours: England U15 to South Africa 1992-93; England U19 to Zimbabwe 1995-96, to Pakistan 1996-97
Cricketers particularly admired: Curtly Ambrose, Brian Lara
Other sports followed: Basketball, football (QPR)
Relaxations: Listening to music
Extras: Played for London Schools at all ages from U8. Played for England U17 against India in 1994. MCC Young Cricketer. Had to return home from the England U19 tour to Zimbabwe in 1995-96 through injury and subsequently missed the majority of the 1996

season through injury. He toured Pakistan with England U19 in 1996-97
Best batting: 56 Surrey v Leicestershire, Leicester 1995
Best bowling : 6-101 Surrey v Gloucestershire, Gloucester 1997

1997 Season

	M	Inns	NO	Runs	HS	Avge	100s	50s	Ct	St	O	M	Runs	Wkts	Avge	Best	5wI	10wM
Test																		
All First	9	11	6	109	35 *	21.80	-	-	-	-	160.3	27	607	17	35.70	6-101	1	-
1-day Int																		
NatWest																		
B & H																		
Sunday	2	0	0	0	0	-	-	-	-	2	-	9	0	49	2	24.50	1-23	-

Career Performances

	M	Inns	NO	Runs	HS	Avge	100s	50s	Ct	St	Balls	Runs	Wkts	Avge	Best	5wI	10wM
Test																	
All First	14	20	6	232	56	16.57	-	1	1	-	1464	927	31	29.90	6-101	2	-
1-day Int																	
NatWest	1	0	0	0	0	-	-	-	-	-	60	27	1	27.00	1-27	-
B & H																	
Sunday	4	2	1	40	29 *	40.00	-	-	4	-	96	97	3	32.33	1-19	-

TUFNELL, P. C. R.   Middlesex

Name: Philip Clive Roderick Tufnell
Role: Right-hand bat, slow left-arm spinner
Born: 29 April 1966, Hadley Wood,
Hertfordshire
Height: 6ft **Weight:** 12st 7lbs
Nickname: The Cat
County debut: 1986
County cap: 1990
Test debut: 1990-91
Tests: 28
One-Day Internationals: 19
50 wickets in a season: 7
1st-Class 50s: 1
1st-Class 5 w. in innings: 40
1st-Class 10 w. in match: 5
1st-Class catches: 92
One-Day 5 w. in innings: 1
Place in batting averages: 298th av. 6.73

(1996 243rd av. 18.12)
Place in bowling averages: 15th av. 21.90 (1996 12th av. 21.94)
Strike rate: 61.29 (career 70.99)
Parents: Sylvia and Alan
Marital status: Divorced
Education: Highgate School; Southgate School
Qualifications: O-level in Art; City & Guilds Silversmithing
Off-season: Touring West Indies with England
Overseas tours: England YC to West Indies 1984-85; England to Australia 1990-91, to New Zealand and Australia (World Cup) 1991-92, to India and Sri Lanka 1992-93, to West Indies 1993-94, to Australia 1994-95, to Zimbabwe and New Zealand 1996-97, to West Indies 1997-98
Overseas teams played for: Queensland University, Australia
Cricketers particularly admired: Jason Pooley
Other sports followed: American football
Relaxations: Sleeping
Extras: MCC Young Cricketer of the Year 1984 and Middlesex Uncapped Bowler of the Year 1987. Was originally a seam bowler and gave up cricket for three years in his mid-teens. Recalled to the England squad for winter tours to Zimbabwe and New Zealand in 1996-97 after an absence of two years and ensured himself a place on England's tour to West Indies with match figures of 11 for 93 in the final Test against Australia at The Oval in 1997 – picking up the Man of the Match award in the process
Best batting: 67* Middlesex v Worcestershire, Lord's 1996
Best bowling: 8-29 Middlesex v Glamorgan, Cardiff 1993

1997 Season

	M	Inns	NO	Runs	HS	Avge	100s	50s	Ct	St	O	M	Runs	Wkts	Avge	Best	5wI	10wM
Test	1	2	0	1	1	0.50	-	-	-	-	47.4	22	93	11	8.45	7-66	1	1
All First	17	21	6	101	21	6.73	-	-	4	-	560.5	174	1205	55	21.90	7-66	3	1
1-day Int																		
NatWest																		
B & H	2	2	0	12	10	6.00	-	-	-	-	16	0	72	2	36.00	1-35	-	
Sunday	2	1	0	7	7	7.00	-	-	-	-	16	0	103	1	103.00	1-56	-	

Career Performances

	M	Inns	NO	Runs	HS	Avge	100s	50s	Ct	St	Balls	Runs	Wkts	Avge	Best	5wI	10wM
Test	28	39	20	112	22 *	5.89	-	-	11	-	7953	3198	93	34.38	7-47	5	2
All First	222	235	95	1445	67 *	10.32	-	1	92	-	54450	22265	767	29.02	8-29	40	5
1-day Int	20	10	9	15	5 *	15.00	-	-	4	-	1020	699	19	36.78	4-22	-	
NatWest	8	1	0	8	8	8.00	-	-	4	-	570	323	10	32.30	3-29	-	
B & H	15	8	4	56	18	14.00	-	-	2	-	809	591	15	39.40	3-32	-	
Sunday	33	10	5	30	13 *	6.00	-	-	3	-	1392	1064	41	25.95	5-28	1	

TURNER, R. J.   Somerset

Name: Robert Julian Turner
Role: Right-hand bat, wicket-keeper
Born: 25 November 1967, Worcestershire
Height: 6ft 2in **Weight:** 13st 4lbs
Nickname: Noddy, Kingo, Turns
County debut: 1991
County cap: 1994
1000 runs in a season: 1
1st-Class 50s: 21
1st-Class 100s: 5
1st-Class catches: 272
1st-Class stumpings: 36
Place in batting averages: 18th av. 50.90
(1996 148th av. 31.80)
Parents: Derek Edward and Doris Lilian
Marital status: Single
Family links with cricket: Father is
chairman of Weston-Super-Mare CC.
Brothers Simon and Richard play for and
have both captained the club and Simon is the current captain. Simon played for
Somerset 1st XI as a wicket-keeper
Education: Uphill Primary School; Broadoak School, Weston-Super-Mare; Millfield
School; Magdalene College, Cambridge University
Qualifications: B Eng (Hons) in Engineering, Diploma in Computer Science, NCA
coaching award
Career outside cricket: Stockbroker
Off-season: Working with stockbrokers Rowan Dartington in Bristol
Overseas tours: Millfield School to Barbados, 1985; Combined Universities to
Barbados 1989, to Kuala Lumpur, Malaysia 1992, to Qantas, Western Australia 1993
Overseas teams played for: Claremont-Nedlands, Perth, Western Australia 1991-93
Cricketers particularly admired: Mushtaq Ahmed, Ian Healy, Alec Stewart
Young players to look out for: Owais Shah
Other sports followed: Football ('The Villa'), hockey (Taunton Vale Ladies), rugby
(Bath and Bristol)
Relaxations: Reading, eating out, painting and decorating
Extras: Captain of Cambridge University (Blue 1988-91) and Combined Universities
1991. Capped at end of 1994 season. Equalled Somerset record of six catches in an
innings in 1995 against West Indies and eight dismissals in a match against West Indies
and Durham. Holds the Somerset record seventh wicket partnership with Shane Lee of
278 against Worcestershire in 1996. Played for an England XI in the Cricket Max
tournament in New Zealand in 1997-98
Opinions on cricket: 'Overseas players bring excitement, charisma and quality to the

English game, as well as inspiring their team-mates. I would be very reluctant to stop them playing county cricket.'

Best batting: 144 Somerset v Kent, Taunton 1997

1997 Season

	M	Inns	NO	Runs	HS	Avge	100s	50s	Ct	St	O	M	Runs	Wkts	Avge	Best	5wI	10wM
Test																		
All First	17	28	7	1069	144	50.90	1	7	51	2								
1-day Int																		
NatWest	2	2	1	15	14 *	15.00	-	-	3	-								
B & H	5	5	2	129	42	43.00	-	-	7	-								
Sunday	14	12	1	220	67	20.00	-	1	13	1								

Career Performances

	M	Inns	NO	Runs	HS	Avge	100s	50s	Ct	St	Balls	Runs	Wkts	Avge	Best	5wI	10wM
Test																	
All First	119	186	40	4431	144	30.34	5	21	272	36	19	29	0	-	-	-	-
1-day Int																	
NatWest	9	7	2	100	40	20.00	-	-	17	1							
B & H	21	19	9	475	70	47.50	-	1	22	1							
Sunday	63	52	17	738	67	21.08	-	1	57	10							

TWEATS, T. A.   Derbyshire

Name: Timothy Andrew Tweats
Role: Right-hand bat, off-spin bowler
Born: 18 April 1974, Stoke-on-Trent
Height: 6ft 3in **Weight:** 13st
County debut: 1992
1st-Class 50s: 4
1st-Class 100s: 1
1st-Class catches: 19
Place in batting averages: 13th av. 53.63
Strike rate: (career 70.00)
Parents: Malcolm and Linda
Marital status: Single
Family links with cricket: Father and two
brothers, Jon and Simon, play for the local
club, Leek, for whom he played before
joining Derbyshire
Education: Endon High School; Stoke-on-
Trent Sixth Form College; Staffordshire

University
Qualifications: 5 GCSEs, 2 A-levels
Career outside cricket: Student
Overseas tours: Kidsgrove and District Junior Cricket League to Australia 1991
Cricketers particularly admired: Robin Smith, Phil Tufnell
Other sports followed: Football
Best batting: 189 Derbyshire v Yorkshire, Derby 1997
Best bowling: 1-23 Derbyshire v Surrey, Derby 1995

1997 Season

	M	Inns	NO	Runs	HS	Avge	100s	50s	Ct	St	O	M	Runs	Wkts	Avge	Best	5wI	10wM
Test																		
All First	7	13	2	590	189	53.63	1	1	7	-								
1-day Int																		
NatWest	1	1	1	5	5 *	-	-	-	-	-								
B & H																		
Sunday	4	4	1	40	19	13.33	-	-	2	-								

Career Performances

	M	Inns	NO	Runs	HS	Avge	100s	50s	Ct	St	Balls	Runs	Wkts	Avge	Best	5wI	10wM
Test																	
All First	20	37	5	1052	189	32.87	1	4	19	-	280	208	4	52.00	1-23	-	-
1-day Int																	
NatWest	2	2	1	21	16	21.00	-	-	1	-							
B & H	2	1	0	10	10	10.00	-	-	-	-							
Sunday	14	10	2	100	19	12.50	-	-	9	-	24	27	0	-	-	-	-

UDAL, S. D. Hampshire

Name: Shaun David Udal
Role: Right-hand bat, off-spin bowler, 'field in the deep', county vice-captain
Born: 18 March 1969, Farnborough
Height: 6ft 3in **Weight:** 13st 8lbs
Nickname: Shaggy
County debut: 1989
County cap: 1992
One-Day Internationals: 10
50 wickets in a season: 4
1st-Class 50s: 16
1st-Class 100s: 1
1st-Class 5 w. in innings: 20
1st-Class 10 w. in match: 4
1st-Class catches: 60
Place in batting averages: 131st av. 28.57 (1996 225th av. 21.28)
Place in bowling averages:
139th av. 53.23 (1996 132nd av. 46.52)
Strike rate: 110.64 (career 72.57)
Parents: Robin and Mary

Wife and date of marriage: Emma Jane, 5 October 1991
Children: Katherine Mary, 26 August 1992; Rebecca Jane, 17 November 1995
Family links with cricket: Father played for Surrey Colts and Camberley for 42 years; brother plays for Camberley 1st XI. Grandfather played for Leicestershire and Middlesex
Education: Tower Hill Infant and Junior Schools; Cove Comprehensive School
Qualifications: 8 CSEs, qualified print finisher
Career outside cricket: Director of Omega Print Finishers
Off-season: Running my business
Overseas tours: England to Australia 1994-95; England A to Pakistan 1995-96
Overseas teams played for: Hamilton Wickham, Newcastle, NSW 1990-91
Cricketers particularly admired: Ian Botham, Robin Smith, Malcolm Marshall, John Emburey
Young players to look out for: Ashley Cowan, Owais Shah
Other sports followed: Football ('Aldershot Town in their quest for the ICIS championship') and golf (handicap of 14)
Injuries: Back and side, but continued playing
Relaxations: Good food and spending time with family
Extras: Has taken two hat-tricks in club cricket, scored a double hundred in a 40-over club game and took 8-50 v Sussex in the first game of 1992 season, his seventh Championship match. Man of the Match on NatWest debut against Berkshire 1991 and

named Hampshire Cricket Association Player of the Year 1993. Scored his maiden first-class century in 1997 against Warwickshire. Played for an England XI in the Cricket Max tournament in New Zealand in 1997-98. Appointed county vice-captain for the 1998 season

Opinions on cricket: 'Whatever the powers that be decide on our game, let's get on with it and just play the game.'

Best batting: 117* Hampshire v Warwickshire, Southampton 1997

Best bowling: 8-50 Hampshire v Sussex, Southampton 1992

1997 Season

	M	Inns	NO	Runs	HS	Avge	100s	50s	Ct	St	O	M	Runs	Wkts	Avge	Best	5wl	10wM
Test																		
All First	18	24	3	600	117 *	28.57	1	4	3	-	627	156	1810	34	53.23	4-17	-	-
1-day Int																		
NatWest	2	2	2	45	39 *	-	-	-	1	-	24	7	69	3	23.00	3-13	-	
B & H	5	4	0	40	34	10.00	-	-	5	-	48	2	199	7	28.42	2-28	-	
Sunday	17	14	3	342	78	31.09	-	4	5	-	126	4	590	29	20.34	3-26	-	

Career Performances

	M	Inns	NO	Runs	HS	Avge	100s	50s	Ct	St	Balls	Runs	Wkts	Avge	Best	5wl	10wM
Test																	
All First	126	180	30	3352	117 *	22.34	1	16	60	-	25836	12934	356	36.33	8-50	20	4
1-day Int	10	6	4	35	11 *	17.50	-	-	1	-	570	372	8	46.50	2-37	-	
NatWest	17	8	4	102	39 *	25.50	-	-	7	-	1134	621	22	28.22	3-13	-	
B & H	30	15	4	142	34	12.90	-	-	9	-	1848	1181	40	29.52	4-40	-	
Sunday	111	69	23	797	78	17.32	-	5	33	-	4805	4017	131	30.66	4-51	-	

VANDRAU, M. J. — Derbyshire

Name: Matthew James Vandrau
Role: Right-hand bat, off-spin bowler
Born: 22 July 1969, Epsom, Surrey
Height: 6ft 4in **Weight:** 12st 8lbs
Nickname: Cat, Luther
County debut: 1993
1st-Class 50s: 5
1st-Class 5 w. in innings: 7
1st-Class 10 w. in match: 2
1st-Class catches: 28
Place in batting averages: 147th av. 26.57
(1996 249th av. 17.50)
Place in bowling averages:
(1996 142nd av. 49.31)
Strike rate: 67.50 (career 63.78)
Parents: Bruce and Maureen
Marital status: Single
Family links with cricket: Father played for
Transvaal in 1963, was Director of Cricket
between 1976 and 1991 and is now Vice President. Brother Kevin plays for Durham
University
Education: Craighall Primary School, Johannesburg; St Stithians College; St Johns
College; University of Witwatersrand, Johannesburg
Qualifications: JMB Matriculation, 3 A-levels, Bachelor of Commerce degree
Overseas teams played for: South African Schools 1986; South African Universities
1990; Transvaal 1991-95
Cricketers particularly admired: Clive Rice, Kim Barnett
Young players to look out for: Zander Debruin
Other sports followed: Golf, rugby (Transvaal), football (West Ham)
Relaxations: Golf, game parks, red wine, music, braaiis
Best batting: 66 Derbyshire v Kent, Derby 1994
Best bowling: 6-34 Derbyshire v Hampshire, Southampton 1996

1997 Season

	M	Inns	NO	Runs	HS	Avge	100s	50s	Ct	St	O	M	Runs	Wkts	Avge	Best	5wl	10wM
Test																		
All First	5	8	1	186	54	26.57	-	1	1	-	45	7	182	4	45.50	3-78	-	-
1-day Int																		
NatWest																		
B & H																		
Sunday	3	2	0	16	10	8.00	-	-	1	-	10	0	63	2	31.50	2-32	-	

Career Performances

	M	Inns	NO	Runs	HS	Avge	100s	50s	Ct	St	Balls	Runs	Wkts	Avge	Best	5wI	10wM
Test																	
All First	59	94	18	1567	66	20.61	-	5	29	-	8420	4440	132	33.63	6-34	7	2
1-day Int																	
NatWest	7	5	1	55	27	13.75	-	-	-	-	294	163	7	23.28	2-36	-	
B & H	4	3	1	23	12 *	11.50	-	-	1	-	186	158	3	52.66	1-46	-	
Sunday	26	12	4	175	32 *	21.87	-	-	11	-	855	800	22	36.36	3-25	-	

VAN TROOST, A. P. Somerset

Name: Adrianus Pelrus van Troost
Role: Right-hand bat, right-arm fast bowler
Born: 2 October 1972, Schiedam, Holland
Height: 6ft 7in **Weight:** 16st 7lbs
Nickname: Flappie, Rooster
County debut: 1991
1st-Class 5 w. in innings: 4
1st-Class catches: 10
One-Day 5 w. in innings: 1
Place in batting averages:
(1996 316th av. 4.50)
Strike rate: 67.57 (career 59.08)
Parents: Aad and Anneke
Marital status: Single
Family links with cricket: Father plays for
Excelsior in Holland; brother plays for
Excelsior and Holland U23; grandfather
played for Excelsior and Holland
Education: Spieringshoek College, Schiedam
Qualifications: Finished Havo schooling – specialised in languages
Career outside cricket: Works in a bank
Off-season: Playing and training in Perth, Western Australia
Overseas tours: Holland to Zimbabwe 1989, to Namibia 1990, to Dubai 1991, to
Canada, New Zealand and South Africa 1992
Overseas teams played for: Excelsior, Holland 1979-91; Alma Marist, Cape Town
1992-93; Griqualand West, South Africa 1994-96
Cricketers particularly admired: James 'batmaker' Parkhouse, Erik 'mac-attack'
van 't Zelfde, Jacob Jan Esmeyer, Wim 'the Skip' Bruning
Young players to look out for: Bas Zuiderent, Koos Oosterholt, JP
Other sports followed: Football, tennis and most other sports
Injuries: Hamstring injury, out for three weeks and rib injury ('I have to stop ducking

into half volleys')

Relaxations: Reading, listening to 80s music, cinema and having the odd lager

Extras: Played for Holland at age 15 and became third Dutch national to play professional cricket. Took 6-3 v Durham 2nd XI in 1992 season

Opinions on cricket: 'Stop slagging it off, it's too good a game for that. It only takes one Shane Warne to become a top-three Test-playing nation.'

Best batting: 35 Somerset v Lancashire, Taunton 1993

Best bowling: 6-48 Somerset v Essex, Taunton 1992

1997 Season

	M	Inns	NO	Runs	HS	Avge	100s	50s	Ct	St	O	M	Runs	Wkts	Avge	Best	5wI	10wM
Test																		
All First	6	8	3	20	12 *	4.00	-	-	1	-	78.5	5	496	7	70.85	3-79	-	-
1-day Int																		
NatWest																			
B & H																			
Sunday																			

Career Performances

	M	Inns	NO	Runs	HS	Avge	100s	50s	Ct	St	Balls	Runs	Wkts	Avge	Best	5wI	10wM
Test																	
All First	66	78	26	400	35	7.69	-	-	10	-	7740	5199	131	39.68	6-48	4	-
1-day Int																	
NatWest	7	3	1	27	17 *	13.50	-	-	-	-	366	274	12	22.83	5-22	1	
B & H	3	3	1	19	9 *	9.50	-	-	-	-	172	172	4	43.00	2-38	-	
Sunday	17	6	3	29	9 *	9.66	-	-	2	-	639	532	17	31.29	4-23	-	

VAUGHAN, M. P.   Yorkshire

Name: Michael Paul Vaughan

Role: Right-hand bat, off-spin bowler

Born: 29 October 1974, Eccles, Manchester

Height: 6ft 2in **Weight:** 11st 7lbs

Nickname: Virgil, Frankie

County debut: 1993

County cap: 1995

1000 runs in a season: 3

1st-Class 50s: 22

1st-Class 100s: 10

1st-Class catches: 31

Place in batting averages: 106th av. 33.56 (1996 81st av. 38.70)

Place in bowling averages: (1996 125th av. 42.82)

Strike rate: 176.60 (career 87.42)
Parents: Graham John and Dee
Marital status: Single
Family links with cricket: Dad played for Worsley CC and mother is related to the famous Tyldesley family (Lancashire and England)
Education: St Marks, Worsley; Dore Juniors, Sheffield; Silverdale Comprehensive, Sheffield
Qualifications: 4 GCSEs
Overseas tours: England U19 to India 1992-93, to Sri Lanka 1993-94; Yorkshire to West Indies 1994, to South Africa 1995, to Zimbabwe 1996; England A to India 1994-95, to Australia 1996-97
Cricketers particularly admired: Peter Hartley, Michael Slater, Alex Morris, Glenn Chapple

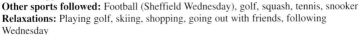

Other sports followed: Football (Sheffield Wednesday), golf, squash, tennis, snooker
Relaxations: Playing golf, skiing, shopping, going out with friends, following Wednesday
Extras: Played club cricket for Sheffield Collegiate in the Yorkshire League. *Daily Telegraph* U15 Batsman of the Year, 1990. Maurice Leyland Batting Award 1990. Rapid Cricketline Player of the Month, June 1993. The Cricket Society's Most Promising Young Cricketer 1993. AA Thompson Memorial Trophy – The Roses Cricketer of the Year 1993. Whittingdale Cricketer of the Month, July 1994. Scored 1066 runs in first full season of first-class cricket in 1994. Captained England U19 in home series against India 1994. Awarded county cap at the end of the 1995 season
Best batting: 183 Yorkshire v Glamorgan, Cardiff 1996
Best bowling: 4-39 Yorkshire v Oxford University, The Parks 1994

1997 Season

	M	Inns	NO	Runs	HS	Avge	100s	50s	Ct	St	O	M	Runs	Wkts	Avge	Best	5wI	10wM
Test																		
All First	15	27	2	839	161	33.56	3	2	3	-	147.1	17	619	5	123.80	2-3	-	-
1-day Int																		
NatWest	1	1	0	22	22	22.00	-	-	-	-	5	0	17	1	17.00	1-17	-	
B & H	6	6	0	325	88	54.16	-	2	-	-	12.3	0	57	3	19.00	1-0	-	
Sunday	9	9	0	309	66	34.33	-	2	1	-	35	0	229	7	32.71	3-48	-	

Career Performances

	M	Inns	NO	Runs	HS	Avge	100s	50s	Ct	St	Balls	Runs	Wkts	Avge	Best	5wI	10wM
Test																	
All First	80	146	6	4679	183	33.42	10	22	31	-	5333	3121	61	51.16	4-39	-	-
1-day Int																	
NatWest	11	11	0	185	64	16.81	-	1	2	-	30	17	1	17.00	1-17	-	
B & H	16	16	1	623	88	41.53	-	5	4	-	141	104	4	26.00	1-0	-	
Sunday	45	44	3	1027	71 *	25.04	-	4	8	-	252	273	7	39.00	3-48	-	

WAGH, M. A. Warwickshire

Name: Mark Anant Wagh
Role: Right-hand bat, off-spin bowler
Born: 20 October 1976, Birmingham
Height: 6ft 2in **Weight:** 12st 7lbs
Nickname: Waggy
County debut: 1997
1st-Class 50s: 5
1st-Class 100s: 4
1st-Class catches: 18
Place in batting averages: 64th av. 39.86
(1996 236th av. 19.80)
Place in bowling averages:
(1996 155th av. 63.20)
Strike rate: 197.00 (career 144.18)
Parents: Mohan and Rita
Marital status: Single
Education: Harborne Junior School; King
Edward's School, Birmingham; Keble
College, Oxford
Qualifications: 12 GCSEs, 4 A-levels, basic coaching
Overseas tours: Warwickshire U19 to South Africa 1992
Cricketers particularly admired: Carl Hooper, Brian Lara, David Gower, Daryll
Cullinan
Other sports followed: Hockey, snooker, football
Relaxations: Snooker and going out with friends
Best batting: 125* Oxford University v Somerset, Taunton 1997
Best bowling: 3-82 Oxford University v Glamorgan, The Parks 1996

1997 Season

	M	Inns	NO	Runs	HS	Avge	100s	50s	Ct	St	O	M	Runs	Wkts	Avge	Best	5wI	10wM
Test																		
All First	18	31	2	1156	125 *	39.86	4	5	14	-	197	39	669	6	111.50	2-45	-	-
1-day Int																		
NatWest																		
B & H	1	1	1	7	7 *	-	-	-	-	-	9	0	39	1	39.00	1-39	-	
Sunday																		

Career Performances

	M	Inns	NO	Runs	HS	Avge	100s	50s	Ct	St	Balls	Runs	Wkts	Avge	Best	5wI	10wM
Test																	
All First	29	44	5	1354	125 *	34.71	4	5	18	-	2307	1301	16	81.31	3-82	-	-
1-day Int																	
NatWest																	
B & H	3	3	1	36	23	18.00	-	-	-	-	174	119	3	39.66	1-39	-	
Sunday																	

WALKER, A. Durham

Name: Alan Walker
Role: Left-hand bat, right-arm
medium-fast bowler
Born: 7 July 1962, Emley, near Huddersfield
Height: 5ft 11in **Weight:** 13st 7lbs
Nickname: Wacky, Walks
County debut: 1983 (Northants),
1994 (Durham)
County cap: 1987 (Northants)
1st-Class 5 w. in innings: 6
1st-Class 10 w. in match: 1
1st-Class catches: 39
Place in batting averages: 294th av. 7.66
Place in bowling averages: 82nd av. 32.21
Strike rate: 62.03 (career 62.24)
Parents: Malcolm and Enid
Wife and date of marriage:
Nicky, 2 October 1994

Children: Jessica, 3 March 1988
Family links with cricket: Grandfather played in local league
Education: Emley Junior School; Kirkburton Middle School; Shelley High School
Qualifications: 2 O-levels, 4 CSEs, qualified coal-face worker

Career outside cricket: Mining, building, coaching
Overseas tours: NCA North U19 to Denmark; Northamptonshire to Durban
Overseas teams played for: Uitenhage, South Africa 1984-85 and 1987-88; Sunshine, Melbourne 1994-95
Cricketers particularly admired: Dennis Lillee, Richard Hadlee, Jeremy Snape 'for his ability to see the funny side of things when things are not going well'
Other sports followed: Football (Huddersfield Town and Emley), rugby league (Wakefield Trinity)
Relaxations: DIY, drinking, gardening
Extras: Recorded best bowling and match figures by a Durham bowler in 1995 (8 for 118 and 14 for 177)
Best batting: 41* Northamptonshire v Warwickshire, Edgbaston 1987
Best bowling: 8-118 Durham v Essex, Chester-le-Street 1995

1997 Season

	M	Inns	NO	Runs	HS	Avge	100s	50s	Ct	St	O	M	Runs	Wkts	Avge	Best	5wI	10wM
Test																		
All First	12	20	8	92	16	7.66	-	-	-	-	341.1	87	1063	33	32.21	7-56	2	-
1-day Int																		
NatWest	1	0	0	0	0	-	-	-	-	-	9.5	1	32	0	-		-	-
B & H	4	1	1	3	3 *	-	-	-	-	-	37	2	159	5	31.80	2-32	-	
Sunday	16	5	3	25	11	12.50	-	-	5	-	103	5	538	14	38.42	4-18	-	

Career Performances

	M	Inns	NO	Runs	HS	Avge	100s	50s	Ct	St	Balls	Runs	Wkts	Avge	Best	5wI	10wM
Test																	
All First	127	140	61	917	41 *	11.60	-	-	43	-	18550	9616	298	32.26	8-118	6	1
1-day Int																	
NatWest	22	7	1	52	13	8.66	-	-	5	-	1311	770	24	32.08	4-7	-	
B & H	37	16	11	55	15 *	11.00	-	-	7	-	1955	1418	44	32.22	4-42	-	
Sunday	150	44	19	278	30	11.12	-	-	35	-	6138	4885	168	29.07	4-18	-	

WALKER, L. N.   Nottinghamshire

Name: Lyndsay Nicholas Walker
Role: Right-hand bat, wicket-keeper
Born: 22 June 1974, Armidale, Australia
Height: 6ft 1in **Weight:** 12st 9lbs
Nickname: Max
County debut: 1994
1st-Class catches: 19
1st-Class stumpings: 3

Parents: Graham (deceased) and Barbara
Wife and date of marriage: Laurie, 17 June 1994
Children: Guy Lyndsay, 12 September 1995; Chloe Ellen, 20 April 1997
Family links with cricket: 'Dad and brother played good level of grade cricket in Australia. Mum was a great encouragement. My dog turns out in benefit games'
Education: Garden Suburb Primary School; Cardiff High School, New South Wales, Australia
Qualifications: High School Certificate, senior coaching certificate
Career outside cricket: 'Building, coaching, learning more in my journey for the Lord Jesus'
Off-season: Coaching and training at Trent Bridge. 'Going into schools and churches and sharing the experience of my faith in Jesus'
Overseas teams played for: Wallsend, Newcastle, Australia 1987-93; Johore, Malaysia 1993-94
Cricketers particularly admired: Ian Healy, Bruce French, Dick Faulk, Chris Johnson 'and Wadey'
Young players to look out for: Glynn Isaacs, Bill White
Other sports followed: Rugby league (Newcastle Knights), golf
Relaxations: 'Anything to do with the Lord Jesus. Relaxing and spending time with my wife, children and dog'
Extras: Equalled the record for Nottinghamshire's most dismissals in an innings in 1996
Opinions on cricket: 'The game is in great need of a Kerry Packer-type figure to come in, invest millions and shake things up. We have to start entertaining the crowds. Ground attendances will prove that the game today does not do this.'
Best batting: 42* Nottinghamshire v Oxford University, The Parks 1997

1997 Season

	M	Inns	NO	Runs	HS	Avge	100s	50s	Ct	St	O	M	Runs	Wkts	Avge	Best	5wl	10wM
Test																		
All First	4	5	2	97	42 *	32.33	-	-	1	-								
1-day Int																		
NatWest																		
B & H																		
Sunday	2	2	0	24	22	12.00	-	-	-	-								

Career Performances

	M	Inns	NO	Runs	HS	Avge	100s	50s	Ct	St	Balls	Runs	Wkts	Avge	Best	5wl	10wM
Test																	
All First	12	15	3	233	42 *	19.41	-	-	19	3							
1-day Int																	
NatWest	1	1	0	1	1	1.00	-	-	-	-							
B & H																	
Sunday	2	2	0	24	22	12.00	-	-	-	-							

WALKER, M. J. Kent

Name: Matthew Jonathan Walker
Role: Left-hand bat, occasional right-arm medium bowler
Born: 2 January 1974, Gravesend, Kent
Height: 5ft 6in **Weight:** 13st
Nickname: Walkdog
County debut: 1992-93
1st-Class 50s: 5
1st-Class 100s: 2
1st-Class 200s: 1
1st-Class catches: 10
One-Day 100s: 1
Place in batting averages: 218th av. 19.42 (1996 13th av. 60.60)
Parents: Richard and June
Marital status: Single
Family links with cricket: Grandfather played for Kent as a wicket-keeper and father was on Lord's groundstaff, having played for Middlesex and Kent 2nd XI
Education: Shorne Primary School; King's School, Rochester
Qualifications: 9 GCSEs, 2 A-levels, coaching certificates
Career outside cricket: 'Yet to be decided'
Overseas tours: Kent U17 to New Zealand 1991; England U19 to Pakistan 1991-92, to India 1992-93; Kent to Zimbabwe 1992-93
Cricketers particularly admired: Aravinda De Silva, Carl Hooper
Young players to look out for: Eddie Stanford, Robert Key
Other sports followed: Rugby, hockey, skiing, football
Relaxations: Music, watching films; 'like old pubs'
Extras: Captained England U15, U16 and U17 at hockey; represented Kent U18 at rugby; had football trials with Chelsea and Gillingham. Captained England U19 tour to

India 1992-93 and v West Indies in 1993 home series which England U19 won 2-0 in one-day matches and 1-0 in 'Test' series. Received Sir Jack Hobbs award for best young cricketer 1989, and *Daily Telegraph* U15 batting award 1989. Selected for Kent U21 hockey team in 1993 and 1994. Woolwich Kent League's Young Cricketer of the Year 1994. Scored 275 not out against Somerset in 1996 – the highest ever individual score by a Kent batsman at Canterbury

Opinions on cricket: 'It's magnificent. I love the game and everything that goes with it.'

Best batting: 275* Kent v Somerset, Canterbury 1996

1997 Season

	M	Inns	NO	Runs	HS	Avge	100s	50s	Ct	St	O	M	Runs	Wkts	Avge	Best	5wI	10wM
Test																		
All First	10	19	0	369	62	19.42	-	2	4	-								
1-day Int																		
NatWest	1	1	0	13	13	13.00	-	-	-	-								
B & H	7	7	1	335	117	55.83	1	3	3	-								
Sunday	13	13	0	374	80	28.76	-	3	2	-								

Career Performances

	M	Inns	NO	Runs	HS	Avge	100s	50s	Ct	St	Balls	Runs	Wkts	Avge	Best	5wI	10wM
Test																	
All First	33	55	5	1415	275 *	28.30	2	5	16	-	6	19	0	-	-	-	-
1-day Int																	
NatWest	3	3	1	105	51	52.50	-	1	-	-							
B & H	18	17	3	611	117	43.64	1	4	8	-							
Sunday	47	45	6	807	80	20.69	-	4	12	-							

94. Who won the 1997-98 Carlton and United limited-over series?

WALSH, C. A.   Gloucestershire

Name: Courtney Andrew Walsh
Role: Right-hand bat, right-arm fast bowler
Born: 30 October 1962, Kingston, Jamaica
Height: 6ft 5¹/₂in **Weight:** 14st 7lbs
Nickname: Mark, Walshy, Cuddy, RP
County debut: 1984
County cap: 1985
Test debut: 1984-85
Tests: 93
One-Day Internationals: 176
50 wickets in a season: 9
100 wickets in a season: 1
1st-Class 50s: 8
1st-Class 5 w. in innings: 86
1st-Class 10 w. in match: 16
1st-Class catches: 98
One-Day 5 w. in innings: 3
Place in batting averages:
(1996 272nd av. 14.00)

Place in bowling averages: (1996 4th av. 16.84)
Strike rate: 37.16 (career 46.55)
Parents: Eric and Joan
Marital status: Single
Education: Excelsior High School
Qualifications: GCE and CXL
Overseas tours: West Indies YC to England 1982; West Indies B to Zimbabwe 1983-84; West Indies to England 1984, to Australia 1984-85, to Pakistan, Australia and New Zealand 1986-87, to India and Pakistan (World Cup) 1987-88, to England 1988, to Australia 1988-89, to Pakistan 1990-91, to England 1991, to Australia and South Africa 1992-93, to Sharjah, India (Hero Cup) and Sri Lanka 1993-94, to India and New Zealand 1994-95, to Australia 1995-96, to India and Pakistan (World Cup) 1996, to Australia 1996-97
Overseas teams played for: Jamaica 1981-97
Relaxations: Swimming, reading and listening to music
Extras: Took record 10-43 in Jamaican school cricket in 1979. On tour, he has a reputation as an insatiable collector of souvenirs. David Graveney, when captaining Gloucestershire, reckoned Walsh was the 'best old-ball bowler in the world'. One of *Wisden*'s Five Cricketers of the Year 1986. Took hat-trick for West Indies v Australia in 1988-89. Captain of Jamaica 1991-92 and 1993-94. Cricketers' Association Player of the Year and Wombwell Cricket Lovers' Cricketer of the Year 1993. Took over captaincy of West Indies from Richie Richardson for Test series against India and New Zealand in 1994-95 and took full control in 1996. Was the leading wicket-taker in first-class cricket

in 1996 with 85 wickets. Commitments with the West Indies side prevented him from playing for Gloucestershire in the 1997 season but returns in 1998. Surpassed Danny Morrison's unenviable record of the most ducks (25) in Test cricket on 24 June against Sri Lanka. Was replaced as West Indies captain by Brian Lara for the series against England in 1997-98

Opinions on cricket: 'Watch the changes.'

Best batting: 66 Gloucestershire v Kent, Cheltenham 1994

Best bowling: 9-72 Gloucestershire v Somerset, Bristol 1986

1997 Season (did not make any first-class or one-day appearances)

Career Performances

	M	Inns	NO	Runs	HS	Avge	100s	50s	Ct	St	Balls	Runs	Wkts	Avge	Best	5wl	10wM
Test	93	122	37	769	30 *	9.04	-	-	18	-	19857	8798	339	25.95	7-37	13	2
All First	357	452	115	4148	66	12.30	-	8	98	-	68871	32593	1465	22.24	9-72	86	16
1-day Int	176	66	28	291	30	7.94	-	-	18	-	9288	5936	196	30.28	5-1	1	
NatWest	21	14	3	136	37	12.36	-	-	2	-	1314	712	42	16.95	6-21	2	
B & H	23	15	5	114	28	11.40	-	-	1	-	1367	819	26	31.50	2-19	-	
Sunday	109	69	11	545	38	9.39	-	-	23	-	4436	3003	143	21.00	4-19	-	

WALSH, C. D.   Kent

Name: Christopher David Walsh
Role: Right-hand bat, leg-spin bowler
Born: 6 November 1975
Height: 6ft 1in **Weight:** 12st 7lbs
Nickname: Courtney, Spaceman
County debut: 1996
1st-Class 50s: 1
1st-Class catches: 2
Parents: David Robert and Carol Susan
Family links with cricket: Father played for Oxford University 1967-69
Education: Yardley Court Prep School; Tonbridge School; Exeter University
Qualifications: 11 GCSEs, 4 A-levels, 2AO-levels, 2 S-levels
Overseas tours: Tonbridge School to South Africa 1992-93
Overseas teams played for: Swanbourne CC, Perth, Australia

Cricketers particularly admired: David Gower, Trevor Ward, Michael Atherton
Other sports followed: Hockey (University XI), rackets (British U21 finalist), squash, football (Tottenham Hotspur), Aussie rules (West Coast Eagles)
Relaxations: Cinema, skiing, listening to music, travelling
Extras: Scored three centuries in first 2nd XI championship season in 1995. *Daily Telegraph* Batting Award in 1994. Woolwich Kent League Young Player of the Year in 1995. Kent CCC Blue Circle Award for The Most Improved Uncapped Player in 1995. Member of the Kent U19 side which won the Hilda Overy Trophy at the Oxford/Cambridge Festival in 1995
Opinions on cricket: 'Too much reluctance in the English game to throw young players into high-pressure situations or matches. University cricket is in great need of re-structuring (especially a need for better facilities) and more financial support needed.'
Best batting: 56* Kent v Oxford University, Canterbury 1996

1997 Season (did not make any first-class or one-day appearances)

Career Performances

	M	Inns	NO	Runs	HS	Avge	100s	50s	Ct	St	Balls	Runs	Wkts	Avge	Best	5wl	10wM
Test																	
All First	1	1	1	56	56 *	-	-	1	2	-	72	64	0	-	-	-	-
1-day Int																	
NatWest																	
B & H																	
Sunday	1	1	0	0	0	0.00	-	-	-	-	48	20	1	20.00	1-20	-	

WALTON, T. C. Northamptonshire

Name: Timothy Charles Walton
Role: Right-hand bat, right-arm medium bowler
Born: 8 November 1972, Low Lead, North Yorkshire
Height: 6ft **Weight:** 12st 10lbs
Nickname: TC, Spadge
County debut: 1992 (one-day), 1994 (first-class)
1st-Class 50s: 7
1st-Class catches: 5
Place in batting averages: 155th av. 25.66 (1996 128th av. 33.55)
Strike rate: (career 97.50)
Parents: Alan Michael and Sally Ann
Marital status: Single
Family links with cricket: Younger brother Adam (16) played Yorkshire Schools

cricket and is a good prospect
Education: Leeds Grammar School;
University of Northumbria, Newcastle
Qualifications: 7 GCSEs, 3 A-levels
Off-season: Playing and coaching in
Christchurch, New Zealand
Overseas tours: England U19 to Pakistan
1991-92
Overseas teams played for: Woolston
Workingmens CC, New Zealand
Cricketers particularly admired:
Viv Richards, Greg Blewett
Young players to look out for: David Sales,
Jason Brown
Other sports followed: Rugby union ('long
ago I played for England U16 at full-back')
and league
Relaxations: Sketching and impersonating
Opinions on cricket: 'Still too stiff. Needs loosening to make it interesting for all
people i.e. Cricket Max in New Zealand.'
Best batting: 71 Northamptonshire v Somerset, Taunton 1995
Best bowling: 1-26 Northamptonshire v Kent, Northampton 1994

1997 Season

	M	Inns	NO	Runs	HS	Avge	100s	50s	Ct	St	O	M	Runs	Wkts	Avge	Best	5wI	10wM
Test																		
All First	7	10	1	231	60	25.66	-	2	1	-	8	0	45	0	-	-	-	-
1-day Int																		
NatWest	2	2	0	6	6	3.00	-	-	1	-								
B & H	6	4	1	105	35 *	35.00	-	-	4	-								
Sunday	13	11	1	163	42	16.30	-	-	1	-								

Career Performances

	M	Inns	NO	Runs	HS	Avge	100s	50s	Ct	St	Balls	Runs	Wkts	Avge	Best	5wI	10wM
Test																	
All First	19	29	3	653	71	25.11	-	7	5	-	390	282	4	70.50	1-26	-	-
1-day Int																	
NatWest	3	2	0	6	6	3.00	-	-	1	-							
B & H	11	8	2	238	70 *	39.66	-	1	5	-	36	27	1	27.00	1-27	-	
Sunday	47	40	6	821	72	24.14	-	4	12	-	240	197	6	32.83	2-27	-	

WAQAR YOUNIS Glamorgan

Name: Waqar Younis
Role: Right-hand bat, right-arm fast bowler
Born: 16 November 1971, Vehari, Pakistan
Height: 5ft 11in **Weight:** 12st
Nickname: Wicky
County debut: 1990 (Surrey)
County cap: 1990 (Surrey)
Test debut: 1989-90
Tests: 44
One-Day Internationals: 156
50 wickets in a season: 4
1st-Class 50s: 2
1st-Class 5 w. in innings: 54
1st-Class 10 w. in match: 13
1st-Class catches: 37
One-Day 5 w. in innings: 11
Place in batting averages: 221st av. 19.33
Place in bowling averages: 18th av. 22.80
(1996 10th av. 21.80)
Strike rate: 38.97 (career 39.41)
Marital status: Single
Education: Pakistani College, Sharjah; Government College, Vehari
Off-season: Playing for Pakistan
Overseas tours: Pakistan to India, Australia and Sharjah 1989-90, to England 1992, to New Zealand, Australia, South Africa and West Indies 1992-93, to Sharjah 1993-94, to New Zealand 1993-94, to South Africa 1994-95, to Pakistan and India (World Cup) 1995-96, to England 1996, to Australia 1996-97
Overseas teams played for: United Bank, Pakistan
Cricketers particularly admired: Imran Khan, Wasim Akram, Geoff Arnold, Alec Stewart
Other sports followed: Football, badminton, squash
Relaxations: 'Sleeping and family get-togethers'
Extras: Made Test debut for Pakistan against India aged 17, taking 4 for 80 at Karachi. Signed by Surrey during the 1990 season on recommendation of Imran Khan who had first seen him bowling on television, and made his county debut in the quarter-final of the B&H Cup. Martin Crowe described his bowling during Pakistan's series with New Zealand as the best display of fast bowling he had ever seen. Named Cricketers' Association Cricketer of the Year 1991 and one of *Wisden*'s Cricketers of the Year in 1992. Joined Glamorgan on a two-year contract from 1997. Took a hat-trick against Lancashire on 21 June – the first Glamorgan player to do so since Ossie Wheatley achieved the feat in 1968
Opinions on cricket: 'There should be no over-rate fines.'

Best batting: 55 Pakistan v Natal, Durban 1994-95
Best bowling: 8-17 Glamorgan v Sussex, Swansea 1997

1997 Season

	M	Inns	NO	Runs	HS	Avge	100s	50s	Ct	St	O	M	Runs	Wkts	Avge	Best	5wI	10wM
Test																		
All First	16	17	2	290	47	19.33	-	-	3	-	441.4	83	1551	68	22.80	8-17	3	1
1-day Int																		
NatWest	4	2	2	42	34 *	-	-	-	1	-	43	5	203	4	50.75	2-35	-	
B & H	1	0	0	0	0	-	-	-	-	-	10	0	42	1	42.00	1-42	-	
Sunday	9	4	2	12	11 *	6.00	-	-	-	-	58	3	285	14	20.35	4-14	-	

Career Performances

	M	Inns	NO	Runs	HS	Avge	100s	50s	Ct	St	Balls	Runs	Wkts	Avge	Best	5wI	10wM
Test	44	57	11	429	34	9.32	-	-	6	-	9071	4844	227	21.33	7-76	19	4
All First	151	168	42	1684	55	13.36	-	2	37	-	27115	14501	688	21.07	8-17	54	13
1-day Int	156	78	29	463	37	9.44	-	-	18	-	7707	5762	265	21.74	8-26	9	
NatWest	13	5	2	75	34 *	25.00	-	-	2	-	859	557	29	19.20	5-40	1	
B & H	7	5	2	15	5 *	5.00	-	-	1	-	401	264	9	29.33	3-29	-	
Sunday	49	20	6	116	39	8.28	-	-	7	-	2202	1583	92	17.20	5-26	1	

WARD, I. J.   Surrey

Name: Ian Jerome Ward
Role: Left-hand bat, right-arm
medium bowler
Born: 20 September 1973, Guildford
Height: 5ft 8in **Weight:** 14st
Nickname: Stumpy, The Chimp, The Gnome,
Son of the Baboon, The All-American Kid
County debut: 1996
1st-Class 50s: 1
1st-Class catches: 7
Parents: Tony and Mary
Marital status: Single
Family links with cricket: Dad was a good
umpire and wicket-keeper
Education: Ripley Primary School; Millfield
School; 'Ben Hollioake's School of Life'
Qualifications: NCA coaching award and
'some A-levels'
Career outside cricket: 'Sloane No.1 of

White Horse'
Overseas tours: Surrey U19 to Barbados 1990; Millfield to Barbados 1991; Malden Wanderers to Jersey 1994
Overseas teams played for: North Perth CC, Western Australia 1996-97
Cricketers particularly admired: Gregor Kennis, Ben Hollioake, Graham Thorpe
Young players to look out for: Ben Hollioake, Gregor Kennis, Richard Nowell
Other sports followed: Rugby, basketball, three-day eventing (the Olympic equestrian squad)
Relaxations: Doing lunch
Extras: Surrey 2nd XI cap at the age of 23
Opinions on cricket: 'I'm just glad to be getting a second bite of the cherry. Better filling in of footholes by groundsmen should be monitored.'
Best batting: 56 Surrey v Durham, The Oval 1997

1997 Season

	M	Inns	NO	Runs	HS	Avge	100s	50s	Ct	St	O	M	Runs	Wkts	Avge	Best	5wI	10wM
Test																		
All First	3	4	0	102	56	25.50	-	1	6	-								
1-day Int																		
NatWest																		
B & H																		
Sunday	10	9	3	81	31	13.50	-	-	1	-								

Career Performances

	M	Inns	NO	Runs	HS	Avge	100s	50s	Ct	St	Balls	Runs	Wkts	Avge	Best	5wI	10wM
Test																	
All First	5	7	0	121	56	17.28	-	1	7	-	102	84	0	-	-	-	-
1-day Int																	
NatWest	1	1	0	14	14	14.00	-	-	-	-							
B & H																	
Sunday	13	11	4	83	31	11.85	-	-	2	-	23	41	0	-	-	-

WARD, T. R. Kent

Name: Trevor Robert Ward
Role: Right-hand bat, occasional off-spin bowler
Born: 18 January 1968, Farningham, Kent
Height: 5ft 11in **Weight:** 13st
Nickname: Wardy, Chikka
County debut: 1986
County cap: 1989

1000 runs in a season: 6
1st-Class 50s: 69
1st-Class 100s: 23
1st-Class 200s: 1
1st-Class catches: 180
One-Day 100s: 6
Place in batting averages: 102nd av. 33.93
(1996 65th av. 41.73)
Strike rate: (career 133.87)
Parents: Robert Henry and Hazel Ann
Wife and date of marriage: Sarah Ann, 29
September 1990
Children: Holly Ann, 23 October 1995
Family links with cricket: Father played
club cricket
Education: Anthony Roper County Primary;
Hextable Comprehensive
Qualifications: 7 O-levels, NCA coaching
award
Overseas tours: NCA to Bermuda 1985; England YC to Sri Lanka 1986-87, to
Australia (Youth World Cup) 1987-88
Overseas teams played for: Scarborough, Perth, Western Australia 1985; Gosnells,
Perth 1993
Cricketers particularly admired: Ian Botham, Graham Gooch, Robin Smith
Other sports followed: Most sports
Relaxations: Fishing, watching television, golf
Extras: Was awarded £1000 for becoming the first player to score 400 runs in the
Benson and Hedges Cup in 1995
Best batting: 235* Kent v Middlesex, Canterbury 1991
Best bowling: 2-10 Kent v Yorkshire, Canterbury 1996

1997 Season

	M	Inns	NO	Runs	HS	Avge	100s	50s	Ct	St	O	M	Runs	Wkts	Avge	Best	5wI	10wM
Test																		
All First	18	32	2	1018	161 *	33.93	1	8	30	-	5	0	34	0	-	-	-	-
1-day Int																		
NatWest	1	1	0	0	0	0.00	-	-	-	-								
B & H	8	8	0	182	78	22.75	-	1	3	-								
Sunday	17	16	1	566	68 *	37.73	-	4	5	-								

Career Performances

	M	Inns	NO	Runs	HS	Avge	100s	50s	Ct	St	Balls	Runs	Wkts	Avge	Best	5wI	10wM
Test																	
All First	186	320	19	11241	235 *	37.34	23	69	180	-	1071	643	8	80.37	2-10	-	-
1-day Int																	
NatWest	20	20	0	845	120	42.25	1	7	2	-	156	129	2	64.50	1-28	-	
B & H	45	45	3	1522	125	36.23	2	10	11	-	12	10	0	-	-	-	-
Sunday	144	142	6	4150	131	30.51	3	26	33	-	228	187	6	31.16	3-20	-	

WARREN, R. J.   Northamptonshire

Name: Russell John Warren
Role: Right-hand bat, wicket-keeper
Born: 10 September 1971, Northampton
Height: 6ft 2in **Weight:** 13st
Nickname: Rabb
County debut: 1992
County cap: 1995
1st-Class 50s: 15
1st-Class 100s: 2
1st-Class 200s: 1
1st-Class catches: 75
1st-Class stumpings: 3
One-Day 100s: 1
Place in batting averages: 39th av. 44.26
(1996 171st av. 28.58)
Parents: John and Sally
Marital status: Single
Education: Whitehills Lower School;
Kingsthorpe Middle and Upper Schools
Qualifications: 8 O-levels, 2 A-levels
Off-season: Playing for Alma Marist CC in Cape Town, South Africa
Overseas tours: England YC to New Zealand 1990-91; Northamptonshire to Cape
Town 1993, to Zimbabwe 1995, to Johannesburg 1996
Overseas teams played for: Lancaster Park, Christchurch, and Canterbury B, New
Zealand 1991-93; Riverside CC, Lower Hutt, New Zealand 1994-95; Petone CC,
Wellington, New Zealand 1995-96; Alma Marist CC, Cape Town, South Africa 1997-
98
Cricketers particularly admired: Allan Lamb, Wayne Larkins
Young players to look out for: John Blain
Other sports followed: Football (Manchester United and Northampton Town), rugby
(Northampton Saints), golf, snooker and horse racing 'mostly Nick Cook and John

Hughes tips!'

Injuries: Broken index finger, damaged wrist tendons, out for a total of seven weeks

Relaxations: Sky television, PlayStation and girlfriend

Opinions on cricket: 'Fewer games, smaller staffs and increased wages. Too many "ra-ras" in the game.'

Best batting: 201* Northamptonshire v Glamorgan, Northampton 1996

1997 Season

	M	Inns	NO	Runs	HS	Avge	100s	50s	Ct	St	O	M	Runs	Wkts	Avge	Best	5wI	10wM
Test																		
All First	10	17	2	664	174 *	44.26	1	4	12	1								
1-day Int																		
NatWest	2	2	0	3	3	1.50	-	-	3	1								
B & H	1	1	0	4	4	4.00	-	-	2	-								
Sunday	9	8	3	144	44	28.80	-	-	9	2								

Career Performances

	M	Inns	NO	Runs	HS	Avge	100s	50s	Ct	St	Balls	Runs	Wkts	Avge	Best	5wI	10wM
Test																	
All Firsts	56	92	12	2713	201 *	33.91	3	15	75	3							
1-day Int																	
NatWest	12	10	2	251	100 *	31.37	1	-	17	1							
B & H	12	11	1	95	23	9.50	-	-	11	-							
Sunday	52	42	9	689	71 *	20.87	-	3	44	8							

WASIM AKRAM Lancashire

Name: Wasim Akram
Role: Left-hand bat, left-arm
fast-medium bowler, county captain
Born: 3 June 1966, Lahore, Pakistan
Height: 6ft 3in **Weight:** 12st 7lbs
County debut: 1988
County cap: 1989
Test debut: 1984-85
Tests: 72
One-Day Internationals: 232
50 wickets in a season: 5
1st-Class 50s: 18
1st-Class 100s: 5
1st-Class 200s: 1
1st-Class 5 w. in innings: 63
1st-Class 10 w. in match: 15
1st-Class catches: 67
One-Day 5 w. in innings: 8
Place in batting averages:
(1996 191st av. 26.37)
Place in bowling averages: (1996 21st av. 24.59)
Strike rate: 72.00 (career 47.92)
Education: Islamia College, Pakistan
Off-season: Playing for Pakistan

Overseas tours: Pakistan U23 to Sri Lanka 1984-85; Pakistan to New Zealand
1984-85, to Sri Lanka 1985-86, to India 1986-87, to England 1987, to West Indies
1987-88, to Australia 1989-90, to Australia and New Zealand (World Cup) 1991-92,
to England 1992, to New Zealand, Australia, South Africa and West Indies 1992-93,
to New Zealand 1993-94, to South Africa 1994-95, to Australia 1995-96, to India and
Sri Lanka (World Cup) 1995-96, to England 1996, to Australia 1996-97, to Sharjah
1997-98
Overseas teams played for: PACO 1984-86; Lahore Whites 1985-86
Extras: His second first-class match was playing for Pakistan on tour in New Zealand.
Imran Khan wrote of him: 'I have great faith in Wasim Akram. I think he will become a
great all-rounder, as long as he realises how much hard work is required. As a bowler he
is extremely gifted, and has it in him to be the best left-armer since Alan Davidson.' Hit
maiden Test 100 v Australia 1989-90 during stand of 191 with Imran Khan. Signed a
new four-year contract with Lancashire in 1992. Appointed captain of Pakistan 1992-93
and replaced by Salim Malik on tour to New Zealand 1993-94 but captained the tour to
England in 1996. Alan Mullally became his 300th Test victim as the final wicket fell in
the third Test at The Oval in 1996. Scored a career best 257 not out for Pakistan against
Zimbabwe at Sheikhupura in 1996-97 – the highest score batting at No.8 in Test history.

Awarded a benefit for 1998 and appointed Lancashire captain for the forthcoming season
Best batting: 257* Pakistan v Zimbabwe, Sheikhupura 1996-97
Best bowling: 8-30 Lancashire v Somerset, Southport 1994

1997 Season

	M	Inns	NO	Runs	HS	Avge	100s	50s	Ct	St	O	M	Runs	Wkts	Avge	Best	5wI	10wM
Test																		
All First	1	2	0	16	13	8.00	-	-	1	-	36	10	86	3	28.66	3-74	-	-
1-day Int																		
NatWest																			
B & H	3	3	1	84	52 *	42.00	-	1	-	-	28	2	120	5	24.00	2-31	-	
Sunday	3	2	0	29	28	14.50	-	-	2	-	23	1	89	6	14.83	3-39	-	

Career Performances

	M	Inns	NO	Runs	HS	Avge	100s	50s	Ct	St	Balls	Runs	Wkts	Avge	Best	5wI	10wM
Test	72	100	13	1944	257 *	22.34	2	4	28	-	16464	7054	311	22.68	7-119	21	4
All First	197	271	31	5380	257 *	22.41	5	18	67	-	39728	17731	829	21.38	8-30	63	15
1-day Int	232	181	33	2180	86	14.72	-	4	56	-	11954	7518	333	22.57	5-15	5	
NatWest	17	14	3	192	50	17.45	-	1	5	-	1090	681	23	29.60	4-27	-	
B & H	31	24	5	538	64	28.31	-	3	2	-	1841	1208	59	20.47	5-10	2	
Sunday	94	75	19	1250	51 *	22.32	-	2	20	-	4060	2914	151	19.29	5-41	1	

WATKIN, S. L. Glamorgan

Name: Steven Llewellyn Watkin
Role: Right-hand bat, right-arm
fast-medium bowler
Born: 15 September 1964, Maesteg
Height: 6ft 3in **Weight:** 12st 8lbs
Nickname: Watty, Banger
County debut: 1986
County cap: 1989
Test debut: 1991
Tests: 3
One-Day Internationals: 4
50 wickets in a season: 9
1st-Class 5 w. in innings: 24
1st-Class 10 w. in match: 4
1st-Class catches: 54
One-Day 5 w. in innings: 1
Place in batting averages: 282nd av. 10.61
(1996 291st av. 10.92)

Place in bowling averages: 19th av. 22.83 (1996 36th av. 26.82)
Strike rate: 50.00 (career 58.00)
Parents: John and Sandra
Marital status: Single
Family links with cricket: One brother plays local cricket; 'older brother a good watcher'
Education: Cymer Afan Comprehensive; Swansea College of Further Education; South Glamorgan Institute of Higher Education
Qualifications: 8 O-levels, 2 A-levels, BA (Hons) in Human Movement Studies
Off-season: Cricket development officer for Cricket Board of Wales
Overseas tours: British Colleges to West Indies 1987; England A to Kenya and Zimbabwe 1989-90, to Pakistan and Sri Lanka 1990-91, to Bermuda and West Indies 1991-92; England to West Indies 1993-94
Overseas teams played for: Potchefstroom University, South Africa 1987-88; Aurora, Durban, South Africa 1991-92
Cricketers particularly admired: Richard Hadlee, Dennis Lillee, Ian Botham
Young players to look out for: Dean Cosker, David Sales
Other sports followed: All sports except horse racing
Relaxations: Watching television, music, DIY, motor mechanics, 'a quiet pint'
Extras: Joint highest wicket-taker in 1989 with 94 wickets and took most (92) in 1993. Sister Lynda has played for Great Britain at hockey. Players' Player of the Year and Glamorgan Player of the Year 1993
Opinions on cricket: 'The amount of cricket must be reduced. It's not possible for players to perform at 100 per cent with present format. This surely affects Test performances as well.'
Best batting: 41 Glamorgan v Worcestershire, Worcester 1992
Best bowling: 8-59 Glamorgan v Warwickshire, Edgbaston 1988

1997 Season

	M	Inns	NO	Runs	HS	Avge	100s	50s	Ct	St	O	M	Runs	Wkts	Avge	Best	5wl	10wM
Test																		
All First	17	16	3	138	39	10.61	-	-	3	-	508.2	143	1393	61	22.83	7-41	2	-
1-day Int																		
NatWest	4	1	0	1	1	1.00	-	-	-	-	47	7	169	7	24.14	3-23	-	
B & H	4	2	1	11	10*	11.00	-	-	2	-	40	4	134	8	16.75	3-26	-	
Sunday	11	4	1	22	15	7.33	-	-	3	-	77	3	348	10	34.80	4-15	-	

Career Performances

	M	Inns	NO	Runs	HS	Avge	100s	50s	Ct	St	Balls	Runs	Wkts	Avge	Best	5wl	10wM
Test	3	5	0	25	13	5.00	-	-	1	-	534	305	11	27.72	4-65	-	-
All First	210	232	74	1531	41	9.68	-	-	54	-	42108	20720	726	28.53	8-59	24	4
1-day Int	4	2	0	4	4	2.00	-	-	-	-	221	193	7	27.57	4-49	-	
NatWest	27	12	4	53	13	6.62	-	-	2	-	1740	904	37	24.43	4-26	-	
B & H	33	18	9	72	15	8.00	-	-	8	-	1971	1278	46	27.78	4-31	-	
Sunday	124	46	15	239	31*	7.70	-	-	20	-	5420	3912	148	26.43	5-23	1	

WATKINSON, M.   Lancashire

Name: Michael Watkinson
Role: Right-hand bat, right-arm medium or
off-spin bowler
Born: 1 August 1961, Westhoughton
Height: 6ft 1½in **Weight:** 13st
Nickname: Winker
County debut: 1982
County cap: 1987
Test debut: 1995
Tests: 4
One-Day Internationals: 1
1000 runs in a season: 1
50 wickets in a season: 7
1st-Class 50s: 48
1st-Class 100s: 10
1st-Class 5 w. in innings: 26
1st-Class 10 w. in match: 3
1st-Class catches: 146
One-Day 100s: 1
One-Day 5 w. in innings: 3

Place in batting averages: 130th av. 28.88 (1996 206th av. 23.88)
Place in bowling averages: 122nd av. 40.25 (1996 115th av. 40.56)
Strike rate: 69.50 (career 64.78)
Parents: Albert and Marian
Wife and date of marriage: Susan, 12 April 1986
Children: Charlotte, 24 February 1989; Liam, 27 July 1991
Education: Rivington and Blackrod High School, Horwich
Qualifications: 8 O-levels, HTC Civil Engineering
Career outside cricket: Draughtsman
Overseas tours: England to South Africa 1995-96
Cricketers particularly admired: Clive Lloyd, Imran Khan
Other sports followed: Football
Relaxations: Watching Bolton Wanderers
Extras: Played for Cheshire in Minor Counties Championship and in NatWest Trophy
(v Middlesex) 1982. Man of the Match in the first Refuge Assurance Cup final 1988 and
in B&H Cup final 1990. Resigned the Lancashire captaincy during the off-season
Best batting: 161 Lancashire v Essex, Old Trafford 1995
Best bowling: 8-30 Lancashire v Hampshire, Old Trafford 1994

1997 Season

	M	Inns	NO	Runs	HS	Avge	100s	50s	Ct	St	O	M	Runs	Wkts	Avge	Best	5wI	10wM
Test																		
All First	12	19	1	520	135	28.88	1	2	5	-	231.4	41	805	20	40.25	3-35	-	-
1-day Int																		
NatWest	1	1	0	36	36	36.00	-	-	-	-	7	0	41	1	41.00	1-41	-	
B & H																		
Sunday	12	11	0	162	66	14.72	-	1	6	-	38	0	224	8	28.00	3-23	-	

Career Performances

	M	Inns	NO	Runs	HS	Avge	100s	50s	Ct	St	Balls	Runs	Wkts	Avge	Best	5wI	10wM
Test	4	6	1	167	82 *	33.40	-	1	1	-	672	348	10	34.80	3-64	-	-
All First	290	434	47	10277	161	26.55	10	48	146	-	45930	23940	709	33.76	8-30	26	3
1-day Int	1	0	0	0	0	-	-	-	-	-	54	43	0	-	-	-	
NatWest	40	34	7	891	90	33.00	-	7	11	-	2411	1581	42	37.64	3-14	-	
B & H	70	50	12	785	76	20.65	-	4	21	-	3656	2565	86	29.82	5-44	2	
Sunday	214	169	37	2865	121	21.70	1	8	55	-	8208	6744	212	31.81	5-46	1	

WEEKES, P. N.   Middlesex

Name: Paul Nicholas Weekes
Role: Left-hand bat, off-spin bowler
Born: 8 July 1969, Hackney, London
Height: 5ft 11in **Weight:** 13st
Nickname: Weekesy, Twiddles
County debut: 1990
County cap: 1993
1000 runs in a season: 1
1st-Class 50s: 18
1st-Class 100s: 8
1st-Class 5 w. in innings: 3
1st-Class catches: 84
One-Day 100s: 3
Place in batting averages: 225th av. 18.29
(1996 95th av. 36.90)
Place in bowling averages:
(1996 87th av. 33.81)
Strike rate: 143.00 (career 85.95)
Parents: Robert and Carol
Marital status: 'Partner Christine'
Children: Cheri, 4 September 1993
Family links with cricket: Father played club cricket
Education: Homerton House Secondary School, Hackney; Hackney College

Qualifications: NCA cricket coach
Career outside cricket: Coaching for Middlesex CYT
Overseas tours: England A to India 1994-95
Overseas teams played for: Newcastle University, NSW, 1989; Sunrise, Zimbabwe 1990
Cricketers particularly admired: David Gower, Richie Richardson
Other sports followed: Boxing – 'middle and heavyweight especially'
Relaxations: 'Listening to music – ragga, soca. Chilling with the family'
Extras: Scored 50 in first innings for both 2nd and 1st teams. Took two catches whilst appearing as 12th man for England in the second Test against West Indies at Lord's in 1995
Opinions on cricket: 'Lunch and tea intervals should be longer.'
Best batting: 171* Middlesex v Somerset, Uxbridge 1996
Best bowling: 8-39 Middlesex v Glamorgan, Lord's 1996

1997 Season

	M	Inns	NO	Runs	HS	Avge	100s	50s	Ct	St	O	M	Runs	Wkts	Avge	Best	5wI	10wM
Test																		
All First	15	24	0	439	101	18.29	1	-	18	-	143	21	432	6	72.00	2-35	-	-
1-day Int																		
NatWest	3	3	0	46	34	15.33	-	-	1	-	28	1	136	3	45.33	1-35	-	
B & H	4	4	0	158	77	39.50	-	1	2	-	27	1	143	1	143.00	1-47	-	
Sunday	15	14	1	306	53 *	23.53	-	2	4	-	73	2	369	17	21.70	4-38	-	

Career Performances

	M	Inns	NO	Runs	HS	Avge	100s	50s	Ct	St	Balls	Runs	Wkts	Avge	Best	5wI	10wM
Test																	
All First	103	157	15	4425	171 *	31.16	8	18	84	-	10314	4905	120	40.87	8-39	3	-
1-day Int																	
NatWest	12	12	1	380	143 *	34.54	2	1	4	-	701	494	14	35.28	3-35	-	
B & H	26	23	3	588	77	29.40	-	4	6	-	1118	817	21	38.90	3-32	-	
Sunday	108	87	12	2004	119 *	26.72	1	10	43	-	3776	3206	119	26.94	4-29	-	

WELCH, G.   Warwickshire

Name: Graeme Welch
Role: Right-hand bat, right-arm medium-fast bowler
Born: 21 March 1972, Tyne and Wear
Height: 6ft **Weight:** 13st
Nickname: Pop, Red Beard, Lalas
County debut: 1992 (one-day), 1994 (first-class)
50 wickets in a season: 1
1st-Class 50s: 6
1st-Class 5 w. in innings: 3
1st-Class 10 w. in match: 1
1st-Class catches: 18
Place in batting averages: 190th av. 22.75 (1996 276th av. 13.12)
Place in bowling averages: 32nd av. 25.00 (1996 61st av. 30.44)
Strike rate: 49.92 (career 53.60)
Parents: Robert and Jean
Marital status: Engaged to Emma
Family links with cricket: Dad plays club cricket in Durham. Brother Barrie plays club cricket for Olton in Birmingham
Education: Hetton Lyons Junior School; Hetton Comprehensive
Qualifications: 9 GCSEs, City & Guilds in Sports and Leisure, coaching certificate
Career outside cricket: 'Everything and anything'
Overseas tours: Warwickshire to Cape Town 1992 and 1993
Overseas teams played for: Avendale, Cape Town 1991-93; Johnsonville CC, New Zealand 1995-96
Cricketers particularly admired: Allan Donald, Dean Jones, Steve Waugh, Gladstone Small, Mike Burns, Dominic Ostler
Young players to look out for: Darren Altree, Tony Frost, Ashley Giles, Anurag Singh
Other sports followed: Football (Newcastle United)
Relaxations: 'Eating out with my fiancée Emma, playing Mortal Combat on Sega with brother Barrie'
Extras: Played for England YC v Australian YC 1991. Has taken two hat-tricks in the 2nd XI against Durham in 1992 and against Worcestershire. Axa Equity and Law Winners Medal 1994. Britannic Assurance Winners Medal 1994. Warwickshire's most improved player in 1994. Played for an England XI in the Cricket Max tournament in New Zealand in 1997-98
Opinions on cricket: 'Lunch and tea should be extended by ten minutes. Third umpire is a good idea. 2nd XI facilities should be improved. 12-month contracts

should be introduced.'
Best batting: 84* Warwickshire v Nottinghamshire, Edgbaston 1994
Best bowling: 6-115 Warwickshire v Lancashire, Blackpool 1997

1997 Season

	M	Inns	NO	Runs	HS	Avge	100s	50s	Ct	St	O	M	Runs	Wkts	Avge	Best	5wI	10wM
Test																		
All First	18	26	6	455	75	22.75	-	2	3	-	540.5	151	1625	65	25.00	6-115	3	1
1-day Int																		
NatWest	5	4	1	38	20	12.66	-	-	-	-	47	4	191	3	63.66	1-18	-	
B & H	6	5	2	129	55 *	43.00	-	1	-	-	34	4	156	2	78.00	1-18	-	
Sunday	17	15	8	195	32 *	27.85	-	-	3	-	97.5	0	439	12	36.58	2-18	-	

Career Performances

	M	Inns	NO	Runs	HS	Avge	100s	50s	Ct	St	Balls	Runs	Wkts	Avge	Best	5wI	10wM
Test																	
All First	45	62	10	1121	84 *	21.55	-	6	18	-	6700	3749	125	29.99	6-115	3	1
1-day Int																	
NatWest	8	6	2	52	20	13.00	-	-	-	-	408	243	4	60.75	1-11	-	
B & H	14	10	3	190	55 *	27.14	-	1	-	-	612	524	8	65.50	2-43	-	
Sunday	39	30	14	421	54	26.31	-	1	7	-	1347	1097	28	39.17	3-37	-	

WELLINGS, P. E.   Middlesex

Name: Peter Edward Wellings
Role: Right-hand bat, right-arm
medium bowler
Born: 5 March 1970, Wolverhampton
Height: 6ft 1in **Weight:** 13st 7lbs
Nickname: Wello, Action, Jarv
County debut: 1996
1st-Class 100s: 1
1st-Class catches: 2
Place in batting averages:
(1996 125th av. 33.85)
Parents: John and Sandra
Marital status: Single
Family links with cricket: 'Uncle Keith
Worrall gave me bags of encouragement –
and still is. Dad has developed an interest.
Also big thanks to James While – the
infamous Goochie'

Education: Smeston Comprehensive, Wolverhampton; Wulfrew College of Further Education; Thames Valley University

Qualifications: 7 O-levels, 2 A-levels, BA (Hons) in Leisure Management, basic coaching award

Career outside cricket: Sports development, coaching and club management

Overseas tours: Harrow Chequers to South Africa 1993-94

Overseas teams played for: Pingrup, Western Australia 1991-92; Ongerup Green Range, Western Australia 1991-92; Coronations, Stellenbosch, South Africa 1993-94

Cricketers particularly admired: Keith Brown, Graham Gooch, Angus Fraser, Michael Bevan, Chris Cooper

Young players to look out for: Ian Blanchett, David Nash, Andy Strauss, Darren Altree, Tim Walton

Other sports followed: Rugby union (Wolverhampton RFC), football (Wolves)

Relaxations: 'Science fiction, watching sport, reading, keeping fit, joining The Nighttrain'

Extras: Scored 1,000 2nd XI runs on debut in 1996. Retired from first-class cricket at the end of the 1997 season

Opinions on cricket: 'There is plenty of talent in British cricket but unlike Australia, our system does not maximise its development. 2nd XI cricket must become more competitive – not the middle practice it often is. We play too much cricket at the expense of practice and preparation. Unless we gear our system into producing top-class Test cricketers, we may, quite seriously, not regain the Ashes for decades.'

Best batting: 128* Middlesex v Cambridge University, Fenner's 1997

1997 Season

	M	Inns	NO	Runs	HS	Avge	100s	50s	Ct	St	O	M	Runs	Wkts	Avge	Best	5wI	10wM
Test																		
All First	2	2	1	141	128 *	141.00	1	-	1	-	3	0	18	0	-		-	-	-
1-day Int																		
NatWest																		
B & H	1	1	0	23	23	23.00	-	-	-	-								
Sunday	1	1	0	12	12	12.00	-	-	1	-	1	0	9	0	-		-	-

Career Performances

	M	Inns	NO	Runs	HS	Avge	100s	50s	Ct	St	Balls	Runs	Wkts	Avge	Best	5wI	10wM
Test																	
All First	6	10	2	378	128 *	47.25	1	-	2	-	18	18	0	-		-	-	-
1-day Int																	
NatWest	1	1	1	9	9 *	-	-	-	-	-	35	20	1	20.00	1-20	-
B & H	2	2	1	37	23	37.00	-	-	1	-	35	45	1	45.00	1-45	-
Sunday	9	8	1	82	42	11.71	-	-	4	-	48	81	2	40.50	1-22	-

WELLS, A. P.   Kent

Name: Alan Peter Wells
Role: Right-hand bat, right-arm
medium bowler
Born: 2 October 1961, Newhaven
Height: 6ft **Weight:** 'Going up'
Nickname: Morph, Bomber
County debut: 1981 (Sussex), 1997 (Kent)
County cap: 1986 (Sussex)
Benefit: 1995
Test debut: 1995
Tests: 1
1000 runs in a season: 11
1st-Class 50s: 93
1st-Class 100s: 44
1st-Class 200s: 1
1st-Class catches: 220
One-Day 100s: 6
Place in batting averages: 77th av. 37.33
(1996 97th av. 36.54)
Strike rate: (career 115.30)
Parents: Ernest William Charles and Eunice Mae
Wife and date of marriage: Melanie Elizabeth, 26 September 1987
Children: Luke William Peter, 29 December 1990; Daniel Allan Christian, 24 June 1995
Family links with cricket: Father, Billy, played for many years for local club and had
trial for Sussex. Eldest brother Ray plays club cricket; brother Colin played for Sussex
and then joined Derbyshire and is now with Somerset
Education: Tideway Comprehensive, Newhaven
Qualifications: 5 O-levels, NCA coaching certificate
Career outside cricket: Family packaging business
Off-season: 'Relaxing with wife and family, coaching and trying to find a career
outside of cricket'
Overseas tours: Unofficial England XI to South Africa 1989-90; England A to South
Africa 1993-94, to India (captain) 1994-95
Overseas teams played for: Border, South Africa 1981-82
Cricketers particularly admired: Graham Gooch
Young players to look out for: Giles Haywood
Other sports followed: Football (Tottenham Hotspur)
Relaxations: Good wine, cooking, spending time with family, reading books and
articles on wine
Extras: Played for England YC v India 1981. Banned from Test cricket for five years in
1990 for joining tour of South Africa, suspension remitted in 1992. Scored a century in
each of his first two matches as acting-captain of Sussex and won both matches. Won

top batting award for Sussex 1989-93, 'much to David Smith's annoyance'. Vice-captain on England A tour to South Africa 1993-94 and captain for the highly successful tour to India 1994-95. Scored a century in both innings against Kent at Hove in 1995, the first Sussex player to do so since C.B. Fry. This was followed by a pair against Glamorgan at Swansea ('Funny old game!'). Left Sussex after 15 years during the off-season and joined Kent in 1997

Opinions on cricket: 'The Super 8s is a complete waste of time and cannot possibly improve county cricket and therefore will do no better to help us compete better at Test level. Until counties have a broader view that Test cricket is paramount then we will always struggle to keep up with the likes of Australia and South Africa.'

Best batting: 253* Sussex v Yorkshire, Middlesbrough 1991
Best bowling: 3-67 Sussex v Worcestershire, Worcester 1987

1997 Season

	M	Inns	NO	Runs	HS	Avge	100s	50s	Ct	St	O	M	Runs	Wkts	Avge	Best	5wI	10wM
Test																		
All First	18	31	1	1120	109	37.33	1	9	16	-	18	6	55	0	-	-	-	-
1-day Int																		
NatWest	1	1	0	9	9	9.00	-	-	-	-								
B & H	8	8	0	110	40	13.75	-	-	5	-								
Sunday	16	15	2	321	56 *	24.69	-	2	10	-								

Career Performances

	M	Inns	NO	Runs	HS	Avge	100s	50s	Ct	St	Balls	Runs	Wkts	Avge	Best	5wI	10wM
Test	1	2	1	3	3 *	3.00	-	-	-	-							
All First	339	568	78	19628	253 *	40.05	44	93	220	-	1153	820	10	82.00	3-67	-	-
1-day Int	1	1	0	15	15	15.00	-	-	-	-							
NatWest	35	32	6	961	119	36.96	3	4	13	-	6	1	0	-	-	-	-
B & H	62	59	7	1528	74	29.38	-	14	15	-	60	72	3	24.00	1-17	-	
Sunday	234	216	24	5803	127	30.22	3	36	70	-	62	69	4	17.25	1-0	-	

WELLS, C. M. Somerset

Name: Colin Mark Wells
Role: Right-hand bat, right-arm medium bowler
Born: 3 March 1960, Newhaven
Height: 6ft **Weight:** 13st
Nickname: Bomber, Dougie
County debut: 1979 (Sussex), 1994 (Derbyshire)
County cap: 1982 (Sussex)
Benefit: 1993 (£50,353)
One-Day Internationals: 2

1000 runs in a season: 6
50 wickets in a season: 2
1st-Class 50s: 67
1st-Class 100s: 24
1st-Class 200s: 1
1st-Class 5 w. in innings: 7
1st-Class catches: 110
One-Day 100s: 4
Place in batting averages:
(1996 85th av. 38.06)
Place in bowling averages: (1996 av. 48.88)
Strike rate: 109.33 (career 73.03)
Parents: Ernest William Charles and
Eunice Mae
Wife and date of marriage: Divorced
Children: Jessica Louise, 2 October 1987
Family links with cricket: Father, Billy, had
trials for Sussex and played for Sussex

Cricket Association. Elder brother Ray plays club cricket and younger brother Alan
was captain of Sussex and has now joined Kent
Education: Tideway Comprehensive School, Newhaven
Qualifications: 9 O-levels, 2 CSEs, 1 A-level, senior coaching award
Overseas tours: England to Sharjah 1984-85
Overseas teams played for: Border, South Africa 1980-81; Western Province, South
Africa 1984-85
Other sports followed: Football, rugby, hockey, basketball, tennis, table tennis
Relaxations: Sea-angling, philately, listening to music
Extras: Played in three John Player League matches in 1978. Was recommended to
Sussex by former Sussex player, Ian Thomson. Appointed vice-captain of Sussex in
1988 and captain in 1992. Joined Derbyshire in 1994 but left at the end of the 1996
season to become the 2nd XI coach at Somerset
Opinions on cricket: 'Test players play far too much cricket to achieve optimum
performances at either Test or county level. 2nd XI cricket should totally mirror the first-
class format i.e. four-day cricket on county grounds whenever possible.'
Best batting: 203 Sussex v Hampshire, Hove 1984
Best bowling: 7-42 Sussex v Derbyshire, Derby 1991

---

95. Who was voted Man of the Series in the 1997-98
Carlton and United limited-over series?

1997 Season (did not make any first-class or one-day appearances)

Career Performances

	M	Inns	NO	Runs	HS	Avge	100s	50s	Ct	St	Balls	Runs	Wkts	Avge	Best	5wI	10wM
Test																	
All First	318	510	78	14289	203	33.07	24	67	110	-	31257	14748	428	34.45	7-42	7	-
1-day Int	2	2	0	22	17	11.00	-	-	-	-							
NatWest	37	30	4	545	76	20.96	-	2	8	-	1737	855	22	38.86	3-16	-	
B & H	60	57	8	1442	117	29.42	3	5	13	-	2148	1390	44	31.59	4-21	-	
Sunday	216	188	30	4102	104 *	25.96	1	21	51	-	7305	4805	156	30.80	4-15	-	

WELLS, V. J. Leicestershire

Name: Vincent John Wells
Role: Right-hand bat, right-arm medium
bowler, occasional wicket-keeper
Born: 6 August 1965, Dartford
Height: 6ft **Weight:** 13st
Nickname: Vinny, Both
County debut: 1987 (Kent),
1992 (Leicestershire)
1000 runs in a season: 2
1st-Class 50s: 29
1st-Class 100s: 9
1st-Class 200s: 3
1st-Class 5 w. in innings: 2
1st-Class catches: 75
One-Day 100s: 4
One-Day 200s: 1
One-Day 5 w. in innings: 1
Place in batting averages: 38th av. 44.44
(1996 56th av. 44.36)
Place in bowling averages: 119th av. 39.47 (1996 56th av. 29.42)
Strike rate: 72.00 (career 54.95)
Parents: Pat and Jack
Wife and date of marriage: Deborah Louise, 14 October 1989
Children: Harrison John, 25 January 1995; Molly Louise, 2 June 1996
Family links with cricket: Brother plays Kent league cricket
Education: Downs School, Dartford; Sir William Nottidge School, Whitstable
Qualifications: 1 O-level, 8 CSEs, junior and senior coaching certificates
Off-season: Coaching
Overseas tours: Leicestershire to Jamaica 1993, to Bloemfontein 1994 and 1995, to

Western Transvaal 1996, to Durban 1997
Overseas teams played for: Parnell, Auckland 1986; Avendale, Cape Town 1986-89, 1990-91; Potchefstroom University, North West Transvaal 1996-97
Cricketers particularly admired: Phil Simmons, Gordon Parsons, James Whitaker, Robin Smith
Young players to look out for: Darren Maddy, James Ormond
Other sports followed: Most sports especially football
Injuries: Slight thigh strain, missed one Benson & Hedges game
Relaxations: Spending time with family, pint of Guinness and good food
Extras: Was a schoolboy footballer with Leyton Orient. Scored 100 not out on NatWest debut v Oxfordshire. Left Kent at the end of 1991 season to join Leicestershire. Missed 1992 NatWest final owing to viral infection. Hat-trick against Durham, 1994. Scored 201 not out against Berkshire in the 1996 NatWest Trophy
Opinions on cricket: 'Would have liked to have seen the introduction of a two-divisional championship. The NatWest competition is still too long at 60 overs a side.'
Best batting: 224 Leicestershire v Middlesex, Lord's 1997
Best bowling: 5-43 Kent v Leicestershire, Leicester 1990

1997 Season

	M	Inns	NO	Runs	HS	Avge	100s	50s	Ct	St	O	M	Runs	Wkts	Avge	Best	5wI	10wM
Test																		
All First	18	27	0	1200	224	44.44	3	6	10	-	204	47	671	17	39.47	2-8	-	-
1-day Int																		
NatWest	2	2	0	0	0	0.00	-	-	-	-	22	2	70	4	17.50	3-30	-	
B & H	5	5	0	211	90	42.20	-	2	-	-	41.4	4	170	8	21.25	3-35	-	
Sunday	15	15	0	376	69	25.06	-	2	3	-	69.5	4	366	12	30.50	3-33	-	

Career Performances

	M	Inns	NO	Runs	HS	Avge	100s	50s	Ct	St	Balls	Runs	Wkts	Avge	Best	5wI	10wM
Test																	
All First	115	182	14	5735	224	34.13	9	29	75	-	9563	4851	174	27.87	5-43	2	-
1-day Int																	
NatWest	13	13	3	427	201	42.70	2	-	-	-	521	314	14	22.42	3-30	-	
B & H	29	26	3	609	90	26.47	-	3	8	-	1126	867	28	30.96	4-37	-	
Sunday	93	87	12	2046	101	27.28	2	9	22	-	2922	2416	86	28.09	5-10	1	

WELTON, G. E.   Nottinghamshire

Name: Guy Edward Welton
Role: Right-hand bat
Born: 4 May 1978, Grimsby
Height: 6ft 1in **Weight:** 13st 4lbs
Nickname: Trigger, Giggs
County debut: 1997
1st-Class 50s: 1
1st-Class catches: 1
Place in batting averages: 141st av. 26.81
Parents: Robert and Diana
Marital status: Single
Family links with cricket: Father a qualified
coach and club cricketer in Lincolnshire
Education: Healing Comprehensive;
Grimsby College of Technology
Qualifications: 9 GCSEs, BTEC in Business
and Finance, NCA coaching award
Off-season: Playing club cricket in Perth,
Western Australia
Overseas tours: England U17 to Holland 1995
Overseas teams played for: Randfontein CC, South Africa 1996-97; Willoughton CC,
Perth, Western Australia 1997-98
Cricketers particularly admired: David Gower, Viv Richards, Sachin Tendulkar
Young players to look out for: Usman Afzaal, Noel Gie, Phil Hudson
Other sports followed: Football (Grimsby Town and Liverpool)
Relaxations: Music, shopping, going to the gym
Extras: Completed a two-year YTS with Grimsby Town Football Club where he made
one first-team appearance as a substitute. Played cricket for England U14, U15 and U17.
Won the Lord's Taverners Young Player Award in 1993 and MCC Young Cricketer from
1994-95. Was 12th man for England at Lord's and The Oval against West Indies in 1995
Opinions on cricket: 'Precious few are born with it, even fewer know how to use it.'
Best batting: 95 Nottinghamshire v Sussex, Hove 1997

1997 Season

	M	Inns	NO	Runs	HS	Avge	100s	50s	Ct	St	O	M	Runs	Wkts	Avge	Best	5wI	10wM
Test																		
All First	6	11	0	295	95	26.81	-	1	1	-								
1-day Int																		
NatWest																		
B & H																		
Sunday	5	5	0	96	68	19.20	-	1	2	-								

Career Performances

	M	Inns	NO	Runs	HS	Avge	100s	50s	Ct	St	Balls	Runs	Wkts	Avge	Best	5wI	10wM
Test																	
All First	6	11	0	295	95	26.81	-	1	1	-							
1-day Int																	
NatWest																	
B & H																	
Sunday	5	5	0	96	68	19.20	-	1	2	-							

WESTON, R. M. S.   Durham

Name: Robin Michael Swann Weston
Role: Right-hand bat, leg-break bowler
Born: 7 June 1975, Durham
Height: 6ft **Weight:** 12st 7lbs
County debut: 1995
1st-Class catches: 11
Place in batting averages: 236th av. 17.12
Strike rate: (career 151.00)
Parents: Michael Philip and Kathleen Mary
Marital status: Single
Family links with cricket: Father played for
Durham; brother Philip plays for
Worcestershire

Education: Bow School; Durham School;
Loughborough University
Qualifications: 10 GCSEs, 4 A-levels, basic
cricket coaching certificate
Career outside cricket: Student at
Loughborough
Overseas tours: England U18 to South Africa 1992-93, to Denmark 1993; England
U19 to Sri Lanka 1993-94
Cricketers particularly admired: Graeme Hick and Wayne Larkins
Other sports followed: Rugby and golf
Relaxations: Most sports, listening to music and socialising with friends
Extras: Youngest to play for Durham 1st XI, in Minor Counties competition, aged 15 in
1991. Played rugby for England U18. Released by Durham at the end of the 1997 season
Opinions on cricket: '30 minutes for tea. Lower over-rate per hour.'
Best batting: 36 Durham v Middlesex, Chester-le-Street 1997
Best bowling: 1-41 Durham v Somerset, Chester-le-Street 1995

1997 Season

	M	Inns	NO	Runs	HS	Avge	100s	50s	Ct	St	O	M	Runs	Wkts	Avge	Best	5wI	10wM
Test																		
All First	5	8	0	137	36	17.12	-	-	5	-	1	0	5	0	-		-	-	-
1-day Int																		
NatWest																		
B & H																		
Sunday	2	2	0	19	13	9.50	-	-	1	-								

Career Performances

	M	Inns	NO	Runs	HS	Avge	100s	50s	Ct	St	Balls	Runs	Wkts	Avge	Best	5wI	10wM
Test																	
All First	11	19	0	181	36	9.52	-	-	11	-	151	81	1	81.00	1-41	-	-
1-day Int																	
NatWest																	
B & H																	
Sunday	3	3	0	32	13	10.66	-	-	1	-							

WESTON, W. P. C.   Worcestershire

Name: William Philip Christopher Weston
Role: Left-hand bat, left-arm medium bowler
Born: 16 June 1973, Durham
Height: 6ft 4in **Weight:** 14st
Nickname: Sven, Junior, Reverend
County debut: 1991
County cap: 1995
1000 runs in a season: 3
1st-Class 50s: 29
1st-Class 100s: 13
1st-Class 200s: 1
1st-Class catches: 59
Place in batting averages: 22nd av. 49.58
(1996 62nd av. 43.40)
Strike rate: (career 226.75)
Parents: Michael Philip and Kathleen Mary
Marital status: Single
Family links with cricket: Father played
Minor Counties cricket, brother played for
England U19 and Durham CCC
Education: Bow School, Durham; Durham School
Qualifications: 9 GCSEs, 4 A-levels, NCA coaching award

Career outside cricket: 'None as yet'
Off-season: 'Taking a break from cricket until Christmas and then playing and training in Perth, Western Australia '
Overseas tours: England U18 to Canada; England YC to New Zealand 1990-91, to Pakistan 1991-92 (captain); Worcestershire to Zimbabwe 1996
Overseas teams played for: Melville, Perth 1992-94 and 1996-97; Swanbourne, Perth 1995-96
Cricketers particularly admired: 'Everyone who makes the most of their talent'
Other sports followed: Rugby union and football (Sunderland AFC)
Injuries: Bruised foot, out for one week
Relaxations: Travelling. Beach life, hanging out with friends and family
Extras: Scored century for England YC v Australian YC 1991. Was appointed captain of England U19 for their tour to Pakistan 1991-92 and told by Keble College, Oxford, that he would not be accepted if he decided to tour; he chose to sacrifice his place at Oxford. Downing College, Cambridge, offered him a place the following year, but by then he was so disillusioned with universities that he turned down the offer and decided to concentrate on his cricket. Played for Northamptonshire 2nd XI and Worcestershire 2nd XI in 1989. Cricket Society's Most Promising Young Cricketer 1992. Worcestershire Uncapped Player of the Year, 1992. Member of Whittingdale Fringe Squad 1993
Opinions on cricket: 'Four-day cricket is good, better pitches are still needed and a two-division championship would surely produce a more competitive finish to the season. I cannot see the logic in rewarding four-day success with a one-day tournament (two separate games now almost).'
Best batting: 205 Worcestershire v Northamptonshire, Northampton 1997
Best bowling: 2-39 Worcestershire v Pakistanis, Worcester 1992

1997 Season

	M	Inns	NO	Runs	HS	Avge	100s	50s	Ct	St	O	M	Runs	Wkts	Avge	Best	5wI	10wM
Test																		
All First	17	29	5	1190	205	49.58	4	3	7	-	9	0	63	0	-	-	-	-
1-day Int																		
NatWest																			
B & H	5	5	0	37	16	7.40	-	-	3	-								
Sunday	14	11	1	93	28	9.30	-	-	2	-								

Career Performances

	M	Inns	NO	Runs	HS	Avge	100s	50s	Ct	St	Balls	Runs	Wkts	Avge	Best	5wI	10wM
Test																	
All First	106	182	20	6033	205	37.24	13	29	58	-	907	579	4	144.75	2-39	-	-
1-day Int																	
NatWest	7	7	0	97	31	13.85	-	-	1	-							
B & H	17	16	2	201	54 *	14.35	-	1	7	-							
Sunday	50	42	7	872	80 *	24.91	-	4	9	-	6	2	1	2.00	1-2	-

WHARF, A. G.   Nottinghamshire

Name: Alexander George Wharf
Role: Right-hand bat, right-arm
fast-medium bowler
Born: 4 June 1975, Bradford
Height: 6ft 4in **Weight:** 15st 10lbs
Nickname: Gangster, River
County debut: 1994 (Yorks)
1st-Class 50s: 1
1st-Class catches: 2
Strike rate: 64.50 (career 68.54)
Parents: Derek and Jane
Marital status: Lives with girlfriend Shelley
Children: 'Baby due 24 November 1997'
Family links with cricket: Father played
local league cricket
Education: Marshfields First School;
Preistman Middle School; Buttershaw Upper
School; Thomas Danby College

Qualifications: 6 GCSEs, City and Guilds in
Sports Management, NCA coaching award, junior football coaching award
Career outside cricket: Anything
Off-season: 'Changing nappies'
Overseas tours: Yorkshire to Cape Town 1994-95, to Guernsey 1996
Overseas teams played for: Somerset West, Cape Town 1993-95; Johnsonville CC,
Wellington, New Zealand 1996-97
Cricketers particularly admired: Ian Botham, Wasim Akram, Curtly Ambrose,
Anthony McGrath, Bradley Parker, Chris Burns, 'King Ray!'
Young players to look out for: Alex and Zac Morris, Guy Welton, Ian Fisher
Other sports followed: Football (Manchester United)
Injuries: 'Ribs, didn't miss any games just didn't bowl for four weeks'
Relaxations: Watching movies, eating out, spending time with friends outside cricket,
clothes shopping
Opinions on cricket: 'Two divisions should be brought into the first-class game. 2nd XI
cricket should be changed to four days and should be played on first-class grounds.
Bring in some sort of transfer system.'
Best batting: 62 Yorkshire v Glamorgan, Cardiff 1996
Best bowling: 4-29 Yorkshire v Lancashire, Old Trafford 1996

1997 Season

	M	Inns	NO	Runs	HS	Avge	100s	50s	Ct	St	O	M	Runs	Wkts	Avge	Best	5wI	10wM
Test																		
All First	2	3	0	19	14	6.33	-	-	1	-	43	5	155	4	38.75	2-37	-	-
1-day Int																		
NatWest																		
B & H																		
Sunday	1	0	0	0	0	-	-	-	-	-	3	0	34	0	-		-	-

Career Performances

	M	Inns	NO	Runs	HS	Avge	100s	50s	Ct	St	Balls	Runs	Wkts	Avge	Best	5wI	10wM
Test																	
All First	7	9	1	186	62	23.25	-	1	2	-	754	454	11	41.27	4-29	-	-
1-day Int																	
NatWest																	
B & H	2	0	0	0	0	-	-	-	-	-	114	89	5	17.80	4-29	-	
Sunday	4	1	1	2	2 *	-	-	-	1	-	84	87	3	29.00	3-39	-	

WHITAKER, J. J.   Leicestershire

Name: John James Whitaker
Role: Right-hand bat, off-spin bowler,
county captain
Born: 5 May 1962, Skipton, Yorkshire
Height: 6ft **Weight:** 13st
Nickname: Jimmy
County debut: 1983
County cap: 1986
Benefit: 1993
Test debut: 1986-87
Tests: 1
One-Day Internationals: 2
1000 runs in a season: 10
1st-Class 50s: 80
1st-Class 100s: 38
1st-Class 200s: 2
1st-Class catches: 171
One-Day 100s: 6
Place in batting averages: 45th av. 43.76
(1996 19th av. 54.65)
Strike rate: (career 89.00)
Parents: John and Ann

Family links with cricket: Father is a local league player
Education: Malsis Hall Prep School; Uppingham School
Qualifications: 7 O-levels
Overseas tours: Uppingham to Australia 1980-81; England to Australia 1986-87, to Sharjah 1987; England A to Zimbabwe and Kenya 1990-91; Hong Kong Sixes 1991, 1992
Overseas teams played for: Glenelg, Australia 1982-83; Old Scotch, Tasmania 1983-84; Somerset West, Cape Town 1984-85
Cricketers particularly admired: Geoff Boycott, Dennis Amiss, Brian Davison, Maurice Hallam
Other sports followed: Football (Leicester City), golf, rugby (Leicester Tigers)
Relaxations: Eating out, movies, watching sport
Extras: One of *Wisden*'s Five Cricketers of the Year 1986. Second in batting averages in 1986. Young Cricketer Award jointly in 1986. Voted the Brian Sellars County Captain of the Year by the Wombwell Cricket Lovers' Society in 1996. His 218 v Yorkshire in 1996 at Bradford was the highest score by a Yorkshireman against his native county
Best batting: 218 Leicestershire v Yorkshire, Bradford 1996
Best bowling: 1-29 Leicestershire v Somerset, Leicester 1992

1997 Season

	M	Inns	NO	Runs	HS	Avge	100s	50s	Ct	St	O	M	Runs	Wkts	Avge	Best	5wI	10wM
Test																		
All First	16	23	2	919	133 *	43.76	3	4	5	-	0.2	0	0	0	-		-	-	-
1-day Int																		
NatWest	2	2	0	17	12	8.50	-	-	-	-								
B & H	5	5	1	115	51	28.75	-	2	1	-								
Sunday	14	14	0	400	74	28.57	-	4	8	-								

Career Performances

	M	Inns	NO	Runs	HS	Avge	100s	50s	Ct	St	Balls	Runs	Wkts	Avge	Best	5wI	10wM
Test	1	1	0	11	11	11.00	-	-	1	-							
All First	309	490	51	17068	218	38.87	38	80	171	-	178	268	2	134.00	1-29	-	-
1-day Int	2	2	1	48	44 *	48.00	-	-	1	-							
NatWest	30	29	2	1077	155	39.88	1	6	1	-	24	9	0	-		-	-
B & H	58	53	3	1490	100	29.80	1	10	10	-							
Sunday	183	171	18	5025	132	32.84	4	31	52	-	2	4	0	-		-	-

WHITAKER, P. R. Hampshire

Name: Paul Robert Whitaker
Role: Left-hand opening bat, right-arm off-spin bowler
Born: 28 June 1973, Keighley, West Yorkshire
Height: 5ft 10in **Weight:** 12st 4lbs 'and still rising'
Nickname: Tika, Pudsey Bear, Yorkie Bar, Big Boy
County debut: 1994
1st-Class 50s: 9
1st-Class 100s: 1
1st-Class catches: 8
Place in batting averages:
(1996 174th av. 28.15)
Place in bowling averages:
(1996 123rd av. 42.30)
Strike rate: 148.00 (career 76.58)
Parents: Robert and Maureen
Marital status: Single
Family links with cricket: Father coaches at Yorkshire School of Excellence and played in Bradford League for Bingley for over 20 years. Mother used to make nice cricket teas for Bingley U12s
Education: 8 GCSEs, 2 A-levels, NCA coaching award
Career outside cricket: Part-time cricket coach
Off-season: Playing and coaching in Nelson, New Zealand
Overseas tours: Represented England U17, U18 and U19
Overseas teams played for: Bedford, Perth, Australia 1992-93; Southern Hawkes Bay, New Zealand 1993-97
Cricketers particularly admired: Ian Botham, Malcolm Marshall, Robin Smith, Phil Tufnell, Ramanesh Kaluwitharana
Young players to look out for: Daniel Vettori, Shahid Afridi, Alan Bigglewaite
Other sports followed: Rugby league (Bradford Bulls), football (Leeds United), horse racing
Relaxations: 'A quiet meal and a nice bottle of Liebfraumilch and then feeding the horse'
Extras: Hampshire Exiles Cricketer of the Year 1994-95
Opinions on cricket: 'Leave cricket alone! Keep a full 2nd XI programme as this is the nearest thing we have and the smallest stepping stone to county cricket. England players and groundsmen should be contracted to the Board. Lunch should be 45 minutes and tea 30 minutes in order for a full three-course meal and a light snooze.'

Best batting: 119 Hampshire v Worcestershire, Southampton 1995
Best bowling: 3-36 Hampshire v Oxford University, The Parks 1996

1997 Season

	M	Inns	NO	Runs	HS	Avge	100s	50s	Ct	St	O	M	Runs	Wkts	Avge	Best	5wI	10wM
Test																		
All First	3	5	1	132	73	33.00	-	1	1	-	24.4	4	89	1	89.00	1-31	-	-
1-day Int																		
NatWest																			
B & H	3	2	0	28	28	14.00	-	-	1	-	8	0	50	0	-		-	-
Sunday	3	2	0	6	6	3.00	-	-	1	-	12	0	54	1	54.00	1-37	-	

Career Performances

	M	Inns	NO	Runs	HS	Avge	100s	50s	Ct	St	Balls	Runs	Wkts	Avge	Best	5wI	10wM
Test																	
All First	30	51	4	1425	119	30.31	1	9	8	-	919	546	12	45.50	3-36	-	-
1-day Int																	
NatWest	4	4	1	23	13	7.66	-	-	-	-	120	99	3	33.00	3-48	-	
B & H	9	8	0	149	53	18.62	-	1	1	-	216	155	4	38.75	2-33	-	
Sunday	29	27	2	460	97	18.40	-	2	8	-	332	303	10	30.30	3-44	-	

WHITE, C. Yorkshire

Name: Craig White
Role: Right-hand bat, off-spin bowler, cover fielder
Born: 16 December 1969, Morley, Yorkshire
Height: 6ft 1in **Weight:** 11st 11lbs
Nickname: Chalky, Bassey
County debut: 1990
County cap: 1993
Test debut: 1994
Tests: 8
One-Day Internationals: 15
1st-Class 50s: 30
1st-Class 100s: 7
1st-Class 5 w. in innings: 5
1st-Class catches: 87
One-Day 100s: 2
Place in batting averages: 129th av. 29.04
(1996 139th av. 32.72)
Place in bowling averages: 71st av. 30.14

(1996 59th av. 29.72)
Strike rate: 51.75 (career 30.14)
Parents: Fred Emsley and Cynthia Anne
Wife and date of marriage: Elizabeth Anne, 19 September 1992
Family links with cricket: Father played for Pudsey St Lawrence
Education: Kennington Primary; Flora Hill High School; Bendigo Senior High School (all Victoria, Australia)
Overseas tours: Australian YC to West Indies 1989-90; England to Australia 1994-95, to South Africa 1995-96, to India and Pakistan (World Cup) 1995-96, to Zimbabwe and New Zealand 1996-97; England A to Pakistan 1995-96, to Australia 1996-97
Overseas teams played for: Victoria, Australia 1990-94
Cricketers particularly admired: Graeme Hick, Mark Waugh, Brian Lara
Other sports followed: Leeds RFC, motocross, golf, tennis
Relaxations: Playing guitar, reading, gardening and socialising
Extras: Recommended to Yorkshire by Victorian Cricket Academy, being eligible to play for Yorkshire as he was born in the county. 'Fred Trueman and I are the only Yorkshire players to debut in the 1st XI before the 2nd XI.' Had to fly home from the World Cup in 1995-96 with a side strain and was replaced by Dermot Reeve. Called up to England's tour to Zimbabwe and New Zealand in 1996-97 after a successful A tour to Australia as cover for the injured Ronnie Irani
Best batting: 181 Yorkshire v Lancashire, Headingley 1996
Best bowling: 5-31 Yorkshire v Northamptonshire, Headingley 1997

1997 Season

	M	Inns	NO	Runs	HS	Avge	100s	50s	Ct	St	O	M	Runs	Wkts	Avge	Best	5wI	10wM
Test																		
All First	17	24	2	639	172 *	29.04	1	2	17	-	353.4	58	1236	41	30.14	5-31	1	-
1-day Int																		
NatWest	3	3	1	180	96 *	90.00	-	2	1	-	20	0	79	1	79.00	1-43	-	
B & H	6	6	2	111	36 *	27.75	-	-	2	-	52	6	226	7	32.28	3-22	-	
Sunday	15	13	0	408	148	31.38	1	2	9	-	90	0	462	20	23.10	4-18	-	

Career Performances

	M	Inns	NO	Runs	HS	Avge	100s	50s	Ct	St	Balls	Runs	Wkts	Avge	Best	5wI	10wM
Test	8	12	0	166	51	13.83	-	1	3	-	811	452	11	41.09	3-18	-	-
All First	135	204	30	5582	181	32.08	7	30	87	-	10628	5902	205	28.79	6-66	5	-
1-day Int	15	13	0	187	38	14.38	-	-	-	-	608	446	15	29.73	4-37	-	
NatWest	18	15	5	569	113	56.90	1	4	8	-	845	511	17	30.05	3-38	-	
B & H	22	19	5	329	57 *	23.50	-	1	5	-	906	716	19	37.68	3-22	-	
Sunday	90	77	14	1758	148	27.90	1	6	33	-	2546	2011	73	27.54	4-18	-	

WHITE, G. W.   Hampshire

Name: Giles William White
Role: Right-hand bat, leg-break bowler
Born: 23 March 1972, Barnstaple
Height: 6ft **Weight:** 12st
Nickname: Chalky, Giler
County debut: 1991 (Somerset), 1994 (Hampshire)
1st-Class 50s: 15
1st-Class 100s: 2
1st-Class catches: 47
Place in batting averages: 32nd av. 45.40 (1996 153rd av. 31.04)
Strike rate: (career 257.00)
Parents: John and Tina
Marital status: Single
Family links with cricket: Father played club cricket for Exeter CC
Education: Exeter Cathedral School; Millfield School; Loughborough University
Qualifications: 10 O-levels, 3 A-levels, BA (Hons) in Sports Management
Off-season: UK before Christmas in hope of some work. Then to Perth, Western Australia
Overseas tours: Millfield School to Australia 1989; Hampshire to Anguilla, Cork and Guernsey
Overseas teams played for: Waverley, Sydney 1990-91; Tigers Parrow, Cape Town 1994-95; Techs Mutual, Cape Town 1995-96; Rygersdaal, Cape Town 1996-97
Cricketers particularly admired: Wayne Larkins, Paul Terry, Cardigan Connor
Young players to look out for: Derek Kenway, Jason Laney
Other sports followed: Rugby (Bath RFC), football (Leeds United), tennis, golf, squash
Relaxations: Pubs, restaurants, travelling, painting, money-making schemes
Best batting: 145 Hampshire v Yorkshire, Portsmouth 1997
Best bowling: 1-30 Somerset v Sri Lanka, Taunton 1991

---

96. Who was voted Man of the Series in the 1997-98 Test series between Australia and South Africa?

1997 Season

	M	Inns	NO	Runs	HS	Avge	100s	50s	Ct	St	O	M	Runs	Wkts	Avge	Best	5wl	10wM
Test																		
All First	10	17	2	681	145	45.40	1	4	8	-	10.5	0	49	0	-		-	-
1-day Int																		
NatWest																		
B & H	1	1	0	56	56	56.00	-	1	-	-								
Sunday	7	7	0	154	67	22.00	-	1	-	-	2	0	14	0	-		-	-

Career Performances

	M	Inns	NO	Runs	HS	Avge	100s	50s	Ct	St	Balls	Runs	Wkts	Avge	Best	5wl	10wM
Test																	
All First	50	86	8	2396	145	30.71	2	15	47	-	257	189	1	189.00	1-30	-	-
1-day Int																	
NatWest	3	3	0	12	11	4.00	-	-	2	-	72	45	1	45.00	1-45	-	
B & H	7	6	0	125	56	20.83	-	1	-	-							
Sunday	35	33	3	754	67	25.13	-	4	8	-	12	14	0	-		-	-

WHITTICASE, P.   Leicestershire

Name: Philip Whitticase
Role: Right-hand bat, wicket-keeper
Born: 15 March 1965, Wythall, Birmingham
Height: 5ft 8in **Weight:** 11st
Nickname: Jasper, Tracy, Boggy, Rat
County debut: 1984
County cap: 1987
Benefit: 1997
1st-Class 50s: 17
1st-Class 100s: 1
1st-Class catches: 309
1st-Class stumpings: 14
Parents: Larry Gordon and Ann
Marital status: Single
Family links with cricket: Grandfather and father played local club cricket (both were wicket-keepers)
Education: Belle Vue Junior and Middle School; Buckpool Secondary; Crestwood Comprehensive
Qualifications: 5 O-levels, 4 CSEs, senior coaching certificate
Overseas teams played for: South Bunbury, Western Australia 1983-85
Cricketers particularly admired: Bob Taylor, Alan Knott, Dennis Amiss

Other sports followed: Football, rugby
Relaxations: Playing soccer, watching rugby and 'a good night out'
Extras: Played schoolboy football for Birmingham City. Was Derek Underwood's last first-class victim. Lost seven teeth after being struck in the mouth by a bouncer from Neil Williams in Leicestershire's game against Essex in April 1995
Best batting: 114* Leicestershire v Hampshire, Bournemouth 1991

1997 (did not make any first-class or one-day appearances)

Career Performances

	M	Inns	NO	Runs	HS	Avge	100s	50s	Ct	St	Balls	Runs	Wkts	Avge	Best	5wI	10wM
Test																	
All First	132	174	40	3113	114 *	23.23	1	17	309	14	5	7	0	-		-	-	-
1-day Int																	
NatWest	13	6	1	67	32	13.40	-		-	14	-
B & H	29	19	7	313	45	26.08	-		-	29	4
Sunday	69	45	9	413	38	11.47	-		-	56	4

WILLIAMS, N. F.   Essex

Name: Neil FitzGerald Williams
Role: Right-hand bat, right-arm
fast-medium bowler
Born: 2 July 1962, Hope Well, St Vincent,
West Indies
Height: 5ft 10in **Weight:** 11st 7lbs
Nickname: Joe
County debut: 1982 (Middlesex),
1995 (Essex)
County cap: 1984 (Middlesex), 1996 (Essex)
Benefit: 1994
Test debut: 1990
Tests: 1
50 wickets in a season: 3
1st-Class 50s: 13
1st-Class 5 w. in innings: 22
1st-Class 10 w. in match: 2
1st-Class catches: 65
Place in batting averages: (1996 255th av.
17.00)
Place in bowling averages: 35th av. 25.84 (1996 78th av. 33.14)
Strike rate: 46.61 (career 55.47)

Parents: Alexander and Aldreta

Marital status: Single

Family links with cricket: 'Uncle Joe plays first division cricket in St Vincent and the Grenadines'

Education: Cane End Primary School, St Vincent; Acland Burghley School, Tufnell Park

Qualifications: School Leaver's Certificate, 6 O-levels, 1 A-level

Overseas tours: English Counties to Zimbabwe 1984-85; MCC to Leeward Islands 1992

Overseas teams played for: St Vincent 1982-92; Windward Islands 1982-92; Tasmania 1983-84

Cricketers particularly admired: Viv Richards, Desmond Haynes, David Gower

Other sports followed: Athletics

Relaxations: Music, 'useful DJ', cinema

Extras: Was on stand-by for England in New Zealand and Pakistan 1983-84. Joined Essex for the 1995 season

Best batting: 77 Middlesex v Warwickshire, Edgbaston 1991

Best bowling: 8-75 Middlesex v Gloucestershire, Lord's 1992

1997 Season

	M	Inns	NO	Runs	HS	Avge	100s	50s	Ct	St	O	M	Runs	Wkts	Avge	Best	5wI	10wM
Test																		
All First	4	5	1	66	23	16.50	-	-	3	-	101	16	336	13	25.84	5-55	1	-
1-day Int																		
NatWest	1	0	0	0	0	-	-	-	1	-	12	4	41	1	41.00	1-41	-	
B & H																		
Sunday																		

Career Performances

	M	Inns	NO	Runs	HS	Avge	100s	50s	Ct	St	Balls	Runs	Wkts	Avge	Best	5wI	10wM
Test	1	1	0	38	38	38.00	-	-	-	-	246	148	2	74.00	2-148	-	-
All First	246	286	57	4286	77	18.71	-	13	65	-	36004	19599	649	30.19	8-75	22	2
1-day Int																	
NatWest	23	12	5	66	11 *	9.42	-	-	5	-	1151	778	18	43.22	4-36	-	
B & H	56	31	7	259	29 *	10.79	-	-	7	-	2940	1879	58	32.39	3-16	-	
Sunday	125	55	20	455	43	13.00	-	-	31	-	5159	3860	137	28.17	4-39	-	

WILLIAMS, R. C. J. 　　　　Gloucestershire

Name: Richard Charles James Williams
Role: Left-hand bat, wicket-keeper
Born: 8 August 1969, Bristol
Height: 5ft 10in **Weight:** 11st
Nickname: Reg
County debut: 1990
County cap: 1996
1st-Class 50s: 4
1st-Class catches: 93
1st-Class stumpings: 14
Place in batting averages: 256th av. 16.62
(1995 166th av. 24.77)
Parents: Michael (deceased) and Angela
Marital status: Single
Family links with cricket: Father played
local club cricket
Education: Clifton College Preparatory
School; Millfield School
Qualifications: PE Diploma, NCA junior
coaching award

Overseas tours: Gloucestershire to Namibia 1990, to Kenya 1991, to Sri Lanka 1992-93; Romany CC to Durban & Cape Town 1993; Gloucestershire Gypsies to Zimbabwe 1994-95, to South Africa 1995-96
Overseas teams played for: Manicaland, Zimbabwe 1990-91
Cricketers particularly admired: Andy Brassington, Jack Russell, David Gower
Other sports followed: Football, hockey, squash, snooker
Relaxations: 'Eating out, pubs and clubs, strutting my funky stuff'
Best batting: 90 Gloucestershire v Oxford University, Bristol 1995

1997 Season

	M	Inns	NO	Runs	HS	Avge	100s	50s	Ct	St	O	M	Runs	Wkts	Avge	Best	5wI	10wM
Test																		
All First																		
1-day Int																		
NatWest																		
B & H																		
Sunday	1	1	0	0	0	0.00	-	-	-	-		-						

Career Performances

	M	Inns	NO	Runs	HS	Avge	100s	50s	Ct	St	Balls	Runs	Wkts	Avge	Best	5wl	10wM
Test																	
All First	35	44	8	640	90	17.77	-	4	93	14							
1-day Int																	
NatWest																	
B & H																	
Sunday	18	7	2	76	19	15.20	-	-	19	4							

WILLIAMSON, D.   Leicestershire

Name: Dominic Williamson
Role: Right-hand bat, right-arm
medium-fast bowler
Born: 15 November 1975, Durham City
Height: 5ft 10in **Weight:** 11st
Nickname: Ewok, Yoda, Big Fella
County debut: 1996
Strike rate: 26.75 (career 56.20)
Parents: Ged and Dorothy
Marital status: Single, 'but if interested
contact Leics CCC'
Family links with cricket: Father Ged and
brother Mark both play for Kimblesworth CC
Education: Easington C of E Primary
School, Co. Durham; St Leonards RC
Comprehensive, Co. Durham; Durham Sixth
Form Centre
Qualifications: 7 GCSEs, 3 A-levels
Career outside cricket: Accountant
Overseas tours: Leicestershire CCC to Holland 1996, to Guernsey 1997
Overseas teams played for: Ashburton CC, Australia 1993-95; Klerksdorp CC, South
Africa 1996-97
Cricketers particularly admired: Brian McMillan, Ian Botham
Young players to look out for: Phil Smith, Davey 'Big Bird' Showler
Other sports followed: Football (Newcastle United – 'they are a far superior team to
Leicester'), tennis and golf
Injuries: Side strain, out for one month
Relaxations: Playing cricket and visiting Simpkins on a regular basis
Extras: Winner of the Leicestershire 2nd XI Bowler of the Year award in 1997
Opinions on cricket: 'Top drawer.'
Best batting: 3 Leicestershire v Glamorgan, Leicester 1997
Best bowling: 3-19 Leicestershire v Glamorgan, Leicester 1997

1997 Season

	M	Inns	NO	Runs	HS	Avge	100s	50s	Ct	St	O	M	Runs	Wkts	Avge	Best	5wI	10wM
Test																		
All First	1	1	0	3	3	3.00	-	-	-	-	17.5	5	40	4	10.00	3-19	-	-
1-day Int																		
NatWest																		
B & H																		
Sunday	5	4	2	28	17	14.00	-	-	3	-	32.4	0	147	8	18.37	5-32	1	

Career Performances

	M	Inns	NO	Runs	HS	Avge	100s	50s	Ct	St	Balls	Runs	Wkts	Avge	Best	5wI	10wM
Test																	
All First	2	1	0	3	3	3.00	-	-	-	-	281	135	5	27.00	3-19	-	-
1-day Int																	
NatWest																	
B & H	2	1	0	6	6	6.00	-	-	-	-	84	91	1	91.00	1-64	-	
Sunday	18	12	7	53	17	10.60	-	-	6	-	531	442	15	29.46	5-32	1	

WILLIS, S. C.   Kent

Name: Simon Charles Willis
Role: Right-hand bat, wicket-keeper
Born: 19 March 1974, Greenwich, London
Height: 5ft 8in **Weight:** 12st 7lbs
Nickname: Wilco
County debut: 1993
1st-Class 50s: 3
1st-Class catches: 24
Parents: Ray and Janet
Wife and date of marriage: Louise Clare, 12 October 1996
Family links with cricket: Father played in Kent League. Father-in-law Alan Ealham played for Kent 1962-82. Brother-in-law Mark Ealham plays for Kent and England
Education: Fleetdown Primary School; Wilmington Grammar School
Qualifications: 9 GCSEs, coaching award
Off-season: Coaching
Overseas tours: Kent U17 to New Zealand 1990-91; Kent to Zimbabwe 1993
Overseas teams played for: Scarborough, Western Australia 1992-93
Cricketers particularly admired: Alan Knott, Robin Smith, Carl Hooper, Jack Russell
Young players to look out for: Robert Key, Ed Smith, Will House

Other sports followed: Golf, soccer (Arsenal FC), horse racing, squash
Relaxations: 'Playing golf, spending time with my wife'
Best batting: 82 Kent v Cambridge University, Folkestone 1995

1997 Season

	M	Inns	NO	Runs	HS	Avge	100s	50s	Ct	St	O	M	Runs	Wkts	Avge	Best	5wI	10wM
Test																		
All First	1	2	1	37	19	37.00	-	-	1	-								
1-day Int																		
NatWest																		
B & H																		
Sunday	1	0	0	0	0	-	-	-	-	-	1							

Career Performances

	M	Inns	NO	Runs	HS	Avge	100s	50s	Ct	St	Balls	Runs	Wkts	Avge	Best	5wI	10wM
Test																	
All First	10	13	3	331	82	33.10	-	3	24	-							
1-day Int																	
NatWest	1	1	1	19	19 *	-	-	-	1	-							
B & H	1	0	0	0	0	-	-	-	-	-							
Sunday	8	6	2	80	31 *	20.00	-	-	11	1							

WILSON, D. G.   Essex

Name: Daniel Graeme Wilson
Role: Right-hand bat, right-arm
medium-fast bowler
Born: 18 February 1977, Paddington
Height: 6ft 2in **Weight:** 13st
Nickname: OJ, Juice, Juicy, Stan
County debut: 1996 (one-day),
1997 (first-class)
1st-Class catches: 1
Strike rate: 46.50 (career 46.50)
Parents: Tony and Margaret
Marital status: Single
Family links with cricket: 'Dad played for
Trinidad Colts. Stepbrother Nick, brother Rob
and stepdad John give it licks for the local
village. Mum plays fantasy cricket'
Education: The Firs Primary School,
Bishop's Stortford; St Mary's RC School;

Cheltenham and Gloucester College of Higher Education (currently deferred course)

Qualifications: 10 GCSEs, 3 A-levels, certificate of higher education

Off-season: Recovering from back operation then playing for Queen's Park CC in Trinidad

Overseas teams played for: Queen's Park CC, Trinidad 1997-98

Cricketers particularly admired: Stuart Law, Rob Wilson, Nick Malay, 'anyone who has been in the game for a long time'

Young players to look out for: Rupesh Amin, David Sales, Wayne Ritzema, Ed Smith, Mouhssin Ismail

Other sports followed: Football (Liverpool FC), American football, golf, skiing

Injuries: Stress fracture of the lower back, operation at the end of September but missed no cricket

Relaxations: 'Playing on my PlayStation, golf, a day at the races. Listening to sweet soul and swing music and riding the Groovy Train of the old skool'

Extras: Scored 52 not out on first-team debut against South Africa A in 1996. Took a wicket with his first ball in the Sunday League. Father used to play in the 70s band Hot Chocolate

Opinions on cricket: 'Lunch should be 45 minutes and tea should be 30. As far as the structure of the game is concerned, I favour four American football-style regional leagues, playing each side in the league twice plus inter-divisional games culminating in play-offs (top team and wildcards) and a final. One-day cricket should not be touched. Bonus points should be scrapped and, as in Australia, bonus points should be awarded for first innings wins and bonus points for winning the game overall. This would eradicate the boring draw.'

Best bowling: 1-31 Essex v Cambridge University, Fenner's 1997

1997 Season

	M	Inns	NO	Runs	HS	Avge	100s	50s	Ct	St	O	M	Runs	Wkts	Avge	Best	5wI	10wM
Test																		
All First	1	0	0	0	0	-	-	-	1	-	15.3	2	67	2	33.50	1-31	-	-
1-day Int																		
NatWest																		
B & H																		
Sunday																		

Career Performances

	M	Inns	NO	Runs	HS	Avge	100s	50s	Ct	St	Balls	Runs	Wkts	Avge	Best	5wI	10wM
Test																	
All First	1	0	0	0	0	-	-	-	1	-	93	67	2	33.50	1-31	-	-
1-day Int																	
NatWest																	
B & H																	
Sunday	2	1	0	7	7	7.00	-	-	1	-	48	40	3	13.33	3-40	-	

WILSON, E. J.   Worcestershire

Name: Elliot James Wilson
Role: Right-hand bat, right-arm
medium bowler
Born: 3 November 1976, London
Height: 6ft 2in **Weight:** 13st
County debut: No first-team appearance
Parents: Alec and Faye
Marital status: Single
Family links with cricket: None
Education: Felsted Prep School; Felsted
School; University of Durham
Qualifications: 10 GCSEs, 3 A-levels
Career outside cricket: Student
Off-season: Studying at Durham University
Overseas tours: Felsted to Australia 1995-96
Overseas teams played for: Pinetown CC,
Durban, South Africa 1995-96
Cricketers particularly admired: Nick
Knight
Young players to look out for: Tim Phillips
Other sports followed: Rugby, football and athletics, 'all sports really'
Injuries: Back operation, missed all of the 1997 season
Relaxations: Sport and seeing friends
Extras: Scored 950 runs in 10 2nd XI championship games in 1996, while scoring more than 3,000 runs in the season. Essex League Batsman of the Year in 1996. Broke Nick Knight's school record with 1,200 runs in 16 innings at an average of 120. Art scholar to Felsted School. Uncle Nev won yachting two-tonne World Cup Championship and was New Zealand touring car champion. Great Grandad went to the South Pole with Shackleton in 1907-09
Opinions on cricket: 'Why are the young lads who have the temperament which enables them to achieve in a match situation discarded to allow opportunities for other young lads who simply look the part, but always seem to underachieve? Surely technical abilities can be relatively easily developed through experience, while temperament is a natural gift that cannot be learned.'

---

97. Who finished the England A tour to Kenya
and Sri Lanka as leading run-scorer?

WILTON, N.   Sussex

Name: Nicholas Wilton
Role: Right-hand bat, wicket-keeper
Born: 23 September 1978, Pembury
Height: 6ft **Weight:** 12st
Nickname: Rodders, Froggie
Parents: Graham and Susan
Marital status: Single
Family links with cricket: Dad played local club cricket. Brother captains both school and club U12
Education: St Johns CE Primary School; Beacon Community College; City of Westminster College
Qualifications: 10 GCSEs, CFE in Sports Studies, completed 1st grade in Advanced GNVQ in Leisure and Tourism
Off-season: Touring South Africa with England U19 for Test series and Youth World Cup
Overseas tours: England U19 to South Africa 1997-98
Young players to look out for: Stephen Peters, Graeme Swann, Mark Currie
Other sports followed: Football (Arsenal FC), 'have just taken up golf'
Relaxations: 'Spending time with girlfriend, Amy.' Music, cinema, films
Extras: Played for Sussex Colts since the age of ten (U11 to U19). Played for Sussex 2nd XI in 1996. Retained and registered by Sussex in 1997 while spending a season with the MCC Young Cricketers. Has represented England at U14, U17 and U19 levels. Missed two-thirds of the 1997 season with a dislocated shoulder. Part of the England U19 squad which won the U19 World Cup in South Africa during the off-season
Opinions on cricket: 'A two-divisional County Championship should be introduced to raise the standards and make the game more competitive. More day/night cricket should be played to increase interest.'

WINDOWS, M. G. N.   Gloucestershire

Name: Matthew Guy Newman Windows
Role: Right-hand bat, left-arm bowler
Born: 5 April 1973, Clifton, Bristol
Height: 5ft 7in **Weight:** 11st
Nickname: Steamy

County debut: 1992
1st-Class 50s: 11
1st-Class 100s: 2
1st-Class catches: 35
Place in batting averages: 167th av. 24.60
(1996 162nd av. 29.53)
Strike rate: (career 46.50)
Parents: Tony and Carolyn
Marital status: Single
Family links with cricket: Father (A.R.)
played for Gloucestershire (1960-69) and
Cambridge University
Education: Clifton College; Durham
University
Qualifications: 8 GCSEs, 3 A-levels, BA
(Hons) in Sociology
Overseas tours: England U19 to Pakistan
1991-92; Durham University to South Africa
1992

Cricketers particularly admired: Graham Gooch, Mike Procter
Young players to look out for: Vikram Solanki
Other sports followed: Rugby (Bristol RFC), rackets
Relaxations: Listening to music, sleeping, watching television, 'a couple of pints with my mates'
Extras: Played for Lincolnshire and in England U19 home series v Sri Lanka 1992. Public schools rackets and fives champion. 1994 Gloucestershire Young Player of the Year. Holds the record for highest individual score for Durham University (218 not out)
Opinions on cricket: 'We have to bowl too many overs in a day resulting in a heavy fine rate. The county circuit offers us great camaraderie.'
Best batting: 184 Gloucestershire v Warwickshire, Cheltenham 1996
Best bowling: 1-6 Combined Universities v West Indies, The Parks 1995

1997 Season

	M	Inns	NO	Runs	HS	Avge	100s	50s	Ct	St	O	M	Runs	Wkts	Avge	Best	5wl	10wM
Test																		
All First	8	15	0	369	84	24.60	-	2	7	-	7	1	51	0	-	-	-	-
1-day Int																		
NatWest																			
B & H																			
Sunday	5	2	0	13	8	6.50	-	-	-	-								

Career Performances

	M	Inns	NO	Runs	HS	Avge	100s	50s	Ct	St	Balls	Runs	Wkts	Avge	Best	5wI	10wM
Test																	
All First	40	75	4	2064	184	29.07	2	11	35	-	93	90	2	45.00	1-6	-	-
1-day Int																	
NatWest	3	3	0	42	33	14.00	-	-	-	-							
B & H	1	1	1	16	16 *	-	-	-	-	-							
Sunday	38	34	2	610	72	19.06	-	2	7	-	48	49	0	-		-	-

WOMBLE, D. R. Derbyshire

Name: David Robert Womble
Role: Right-hand bat, right-arm fast bowler
Born: 23 February 1977, Stoke-on-Trent
Height: 5ft 11in **Weight:** 12st 2lbs
Nickname: Wombz
County debut: 1996 (one-day)
Parents: Michael and Marjory
Marital status: Single
Family links with cricket: Father plays club cricket
Education: Parkhall County Primary; St Thomas More RC High School; Stoke-on-Trent Sixth Form College; Leeds Metropolitan University
Qualifications: Preliminary cricket award
Cricketers particularly admired: Ian Botham, Dominic Cork
Young players to look out for: Andrew Harris, Mike Longmore
Other sports followed: Football (Stoke City), rugby, squash
Relaxations: Music and going out
Extras: Played for the National Association of Young Cricketers. Released by Derbyshire at the end of the 1997 season
Opinions on cricket: 'Brilliant, although maybe too much one-day cricket.'

---

98. Who won the Test series between Sri Lanka and Zimbabwe played in January 1998?

	M	Inns	NO	Runs	HS	Avge	100s	50s	Ct	St	O	M	Runs	Wkts	Avge	Best	5wl	10wM
Test																		
All First																		
1-day Int																		
NatWest	1	1	0	6	6	6.00	-	-	-	-	4	0	17	0	-		-	-
B & H																		
Sunday																		

Career Performances

	M	Inns	NO	Runs	HS	Avge	100s	50s	Ct	St	Balls	Runs	Wkts	Avge	Best	5wl	10wM
Test																	
All First																	
1-day Int																	
NatWest	1	1	0	6	6	6.00	-	-	-	-	24	17	0	-		-	-
B & H																	
Sunday	1	0	0	0	0	-	-	-	-	-	18	29	0	-		-	-

WOOD, J.   Durham

Name: John Wood
Role: Right-hand bat, right-arm
fast-medium bowler
Born: 22 July 1970, Wakefield
Height: 6ft 3in **Weight:** 15st 7lbs
Nickname: Woody
County debut: 1992
1st-Class 50s: 2
1st-Class 5 w. in innings: 4
1st-Class catches: 14
Place in batting averages:
(1996 308th av. 6.92)
Place in bowling averages: 134th av. 49.18
(1996 138th av. 48.69)
Strike rate: 61.09 (career 54.56)
Parents: Brian and Anne
Wife and date of marriage: Emma Louise,
30 October 1994
Children: Alexandra Mae, 7 April 1996
Family links with cricket: Father played league cricket for many years and brother
plays cricket in the Bradford League
Education: Crofton High School; Wakefield District College; Leeds Polytechnic

Qualifications: 6 O-levels, BTEC Diploma and HND in Electrical and Electronic Engineering, senior coaching certificate
Off-season: Working for Euro Copy in the north-east
Overseas tours: Durham CCC to South Africa 1994-95
Overseas teams played for: Griqualand West Cricket Union, South Africa 1990-91; TAWA, New Zealand 1993-95; Wellington, New Zealand, 1993-95
Cricketers particularly admired: Wasim Akram, Ian Botham, Wayne Larkins
Young players to look out for: Michael Gough
Other sports followed: Football (Newcastle United), rugby league (Wakefield Trinity), golf and snooker
Injuries: Twisted ankle, rib injury, hip and back, out for a total of seven weeks
Relaxations: 'Spending time with my family and swimming with my daughter'
Extras: Played in the Bradford League. Made his debut for Durham (Minor Counties) in 1991
Opinions on cricket: 'We need to improve the general standard of wickets. Still wish I could have been a football player.'
Best batting: 63* Durham v Nottinghamshire, Chester-le-Street 1993
Best bowling: 6-110 Durham v Essex, Stockton 1994

1997 Season

	M	Inns	NO	Runs	HS	Avge	100s	50s	Ct	St	O	M	Runs	Wkts	Avge	Best	5wl	10wM
Test																		
All First	6	8	4	72	21 *	18.00	-	-	4	-	112	14	541	11	49.18	4-73	-	-
1-day Int																		
NatWest																		
B & H																		
Sunday	8	6	1	27	11 *	5.40	-	-	2	-	58	5	278	11	25.27	4-17	-	

Career Performances

	M	Inns	NO	Runs	HS	Avge	100s	50s	Ct	St	Balls	Runs	Wkts	Avge	Best	5wl	10wM
Test																	
All First	51	76	15	779	63 *	12.77	-	2	14	-	7039	4880	129	37.82	6-110	4	-
1-day Int																	
NatWest	5	1	0	1	1	1.00	-	-	-	-	228	168	4	42.00	2-22	-	
B & H	6	4	0	36	27	9.00	-	-	-	-	348	224	5	44.80	3-50	-	
Sunday	32	23	7	165	28	10.31	-	-	4	-	1356	1191	32	37.21	4-17	-	

WOOD, M. J. Yorkshire

Name: Matthew James Wood
Role: Right-hand opening bat
Born: 6 April 1977, Huddersfield
Height: 5ft 10in **Weight:** 11st 10lbs
Nickname: Chud, Woody
County debut: 1997
1st-Class 50s: 1
1st-Class catches: 1
Parents: Roger and Cathryn
Marital status: Single
Family links with cricket: 'Father played at
local club Emley. Mother made the teas,
sister was the scorer'
Education: Emley Primary School;
Kirkburton Middle School; Shelley High
School
Qualifications: 9 GCSEs, 2 A-levels, NCA
coaching award
Career outside cricket: 'None yet'

Off-season: Playing and coaching in New Zealand
Overseas tours: England U19 to Zimbabwe 1995-96; Yorkshire CCC to West Indies
1996-97
Overseas teams played for: Somerset West CC, Cape Town 1995-96
Cricketers particularly admired: Martyn Moxon, Matthew Horne, Darren Gough
Young players to look out for: Anthony McGrath, Alex Morris, Mark Gilliver
Other sports followed: Football (Liverpool FC and Emley FC)
Injuries: Sprained ankle, out for ten days
Relaxations: Socialising with friends, eating out, sleeping, occasional golf
Extras: Played for England U17 against India. Spent two years on the Yorkshire
Academy before graduating to the full staff in 1996
Opinions on cricket: '2nd XI cricket should be played over four days and more often
on county grounds. Floodlit cricket should become more frequent including every
county to generate interest.'
Best batting: 81 Yorkshire v Lancashire, Headingley 1997

---

99. Who holds the record for the most runs scored by a
wicket-keeper in the County Championship?

O vodafone

645

1997 Season

	M	Inns	NO	Runs	HS	Avge	100s	50s	Ct	St	O	M	Runs	Wkts	Avge	Best	5wI	10wM
Test																		
All First	1	2	0	102	81	51.00	-	1	1	-								
1-day Int																		
NatWest																		
B & H																		
Sunday																		

Career Performances

	M	Inns	NO	Runs	HS	Avge	100s	50s	Ct	St	Balls	Runs	Wkts	Avge	Best	5wI	10wM
Test																	
All First	1	2	0	102	81	51.00	-	1	1	-							
1-day Int																	
NatWest																	
B & H																	
Sunday																	

WOOD, N. T. Lancashire

Name: Nathan Theodore Wood
Role: Left-hand opening bat, right-arm off-spin bowler
Born: 4 October 1974, Ossett, Yorkshire
Height: 5ft 7in **Weight:** 10st 5lbs
Nickname: Peckar, Rodders, Woderwick
County debut: 1996
1st-Class 50s: 2
1st-Class 100s: 1
1st-Class catches: 3
Place in batting averages: 86th av. 36.07
Parents: Barry and Janet
Marital status: Single
Family links with cricket: Father played first-class and Test cricket (Yorkshire, Derbyshire, Lancashire and England). Uncle (Ron) played first-class cricket (for Yorkshire)
Education: Altrincham Prep School; William Hulme's Grammar School
Qualifications: 8 GCSEs, coaching awards
Off-season: Employed by Lancashire

Overseas tours: England U18 to South Africa 1992-93, to Denmark 1993; England U19 to Sri Lanka 1993-94; Lancashire CCC to India and South Africa 1997
Cricketers particularly admired: David Gower, Michael Holding, Viv Richards
Young players to look out for: Chris Schofield, Richard Green
Other sports followed: Football (Manchester United) and rugby (Sale RFC)
Relaxations: Dining out, being with friends, listening to music
Extras: Played in junior one-day Internationals against Zimbabwe, India, South Africa and Sri Lanka. Played in U19 Tests against West Indies and Sri Lanka. Holds highest opening partnership record for Lancashire 2nd XI of 340 with P.C. McKeown and highest first-wicket partnership for Lancashire against Surrey (259 with M.A. Atherton)
Opinions on cricket: 'There is a lot of nonsense spoken about the structure of the first-class programme. The standard of our domestic game would improve if we reduced the number of games and increased the prize money substantially. Think the introduction of 12-month contracts at Lancashire is a step forward. Do cricket's marketing men undersell the game?'
Best batting: 155 Lancashire v Surrey, The Oval 1997

1997 Season

	M	Inns	NO	Runs	HS	Avge	100s	50s	Ct	St	O	M	Runs	Wkts	Avge	Best	5wI	10wM
Test																		
All First	10	15	2	469	155	36.07	1	2	3	-	4.1	0	38	0	-	-	-	-
1-day Int																		
NatWest																		
B & H																		
Sunday																		

Career Performances

	M	Inns	NO	Runs	HS	Avge	100s	50s	Ct	St	Balls	Runs	Wkts	Avge	Best	5wI	10wM
Test																	
All First	11	16	2	470	155	33.57	1	2	3	-	25	38	0	-	-	-	-
1-day Int																	
NatWest																	
B & H																	
Sunday																	

WREN, T. N. — Kent

Name: Timothy Neil Wren
Role: Right-hand bat, left-arm medium bowler
Born: 26 March 1970, Folkestone
Height: 6ft 3in **Weight:** 14st 7lbs
Nickname: Bear, Balou
County debut: 1989 (one-day), 1990 (first-class)
1st-Class 5 w. in innings: 3
1st-Class catches: 12
One-Day 5 w. in innings: 1
Strike rate: 26.00 (career 60.96)
Parents: James and Gillian
Marital status: Single
Education: Lyminge Primary; Harvey Grammar School, Folkestone
Qualifications: 6 O-levels, NCA coaching certificate
Career outside cricket: Plumbing and central heating engineer
Overseas teams played for: Universals, Zimbabwe 1989-90
Cricketers particularly admired: Aravinda De Silva, Carl Hooper, Curtly Ambrose
Other sports followed: Rugby, football (Lyminge)
Relaxations: 'Golf, reading, eating out, walking my dog'
Opinions on cricket: 'Too much talk of major changes. Not too much wrong with our cricket. Stop looking at other countries as a way to improve our cricket. Standard of pitches is not good enough, also sides are allowed to get away with sub-standard pitches.'
Best batting: 23 Kent v Sussex, Hove 1995
Best bowling: 6-48 Kent v Somerset, Canterbury 1994

1997 Season

	M	Inns	NO	Runs	HS	Avge	100s	50s	Ct	St	O	M	Runs	Wkts	Avge	Best	5wI	10wM
Test																		
All First	1	1	1	11	11 *	-	-	-	-	-	8.4	1	22	2	11.00	2-22	-	-
1-day Int																		
NatWest																		
B & H	1	0	0	0	0	-	-	-	-	-								
Sunday	3	0	0	0	0	-	-	-	1	-	17	0	96	0	-		-	-

Career Performances

	M	Inns	NO	Runs	HS	Avge	100s	50s	Ct	St	Balls	Runs	Wkts	Avge	Best	5wI	10wM
Test																	
All First	30	34	13	141	23	6.71	-	-	12	-	4024	2416	66	36.60	6-48	3	-
1-day Int																	
NatWest	2	2	1	1	1 *	1.00	-	-	-	-	120	92	1	92.00	1-51	-	
B & H	8	3	1	11	7	5.50	-	-	2	-	324	256	13	19.69	6-41	1	
Sunday	35	12	9	34	7 *	11.33	-	-	6	-	1329	1080	22	49.09	3-20	-	

WRIGHT, A. J.   Gloucestershire

Name: Anthony John Wright
Role: Right-hand bat, off-spin bowler
Born: 27 July 1962, Stevenage, Hertfordshire
Height: 6ft **Weight:** 14st
Nickname: Billy
County debut: 1982
County cap: 1987
Benefit: 1996
1000 runs in a season: 6
1st-Class 50s: 66
1st-Class 100s: 18
1st-Class catches: 213
One-Day 100s: 4
Place in batting averages: 197th av. 21.89
(1996 201st av. 24.41)
Strike rate: (career 74.00)
Parents: Michael and Patricia
Wife and date of marriage: Rachel, 21
December 1986
Children: Hannah, 3 April 1988; Beth, 19 August 1992; Joseph, 29 November 1993
Education: Alleyn's School, Stevenage
Qualifications: 6 O-levels
Overseas tours: Gloucestershire to Sri Lanka 1987 and 1993, to Barbados 1980,
1985, 1988, to Namibia 1990, to Kenya 1991
Cricketers particularly admired: Mike Gatting, Malcolm Marshall, Dermot Reeve,
David Gower
Other sports followed: Soccer ('life-long Chelsea supporter'), rugby (Bristol RFC)
Relaxations: 'Celebrating any Arsenal defeat and hacking my way around a golf
course'
Extras: Captain of Gloucestershire for 1990-93
Opinions on cricket: 'I feel that it is vital that the game is introduced to as many

youngsters as possible. Unless kids are at private schools they are unlikely to get a chance to participate – a shocking situation!'

Best batting: 193 Gloucestershire v Nottinghamshire, Bristol 1995
Best bowling: 1-16 Gloucestershire v Yorkshire, Harrogate 1989

1997 Season

	M	Inns	NO	Runs	HS	Avge	100s	50s	Ct	St	O	M	Runs	Wkts	Avge	Best	5wI	10wM
Test																		
All First	13	22	3	416	79	21.89	-	1	11	-								
1-day Int																		
NatWest	2	2	0	178	177	89.00	1	-	1	-								
B & H	3	3	0	76	41	25.33	-	-	-	-								
Sunday	12	12	0	236	69	19.66	-	1	5	-								

Career Performances

	M	Inns	NO	Runs	HS	Avge	100s	50s	Ct	St	Balls	Runs	Wkts	Avge	Best	5wI	10wM
Test																	
All First	276	484	38	13095	193	29.36	18	66	213	-	74	68	1	68.00	1-16	-	-
1-day Int																	
NatWest	30	29	2	1260	177	46.66	3	9	11	-							
B & H	47	44	0	1350	123	30.68	1	8	10	-							
Sunday	183	172	17	3853	96	24.85	-	25	67	-	26	22	0	-		-	-

WRIGHT, A. S. Leicestershire

Name: Ashley Spencer Wright
Role: Right-hand bat, right-arm medium bowler
Born: 21 October 1980, Grantham
Height: 5ft 11in **Weight:** 12st
Nickname: Ash
County debut: No first-team appearance
Parents: Keith and Anna
Marital status: Single
Family links with cricket: Father very keen cricketer and senior coach
Education: Redmile Primary School; Belvoir High School; King Edward VII, Melton Mowbray
Qualifications: 9 GCSEs
Career outside cricket: None
Off-season: 'Would like to play in Australia or South Africa'

Young players to look out for: Darren Maddy, Jimmy Ormond, Graham Napier
Other sports followed: Football (Leicester City, Notts County), rugby (Leicester Tigers) and squash
Relaxations: Swimming, listening to music and cinema
Extras: Hit a highest score of 158 against Staffordshire U15
Opinions on cricket: 'Pleased to see more younger players given a chance to play at higher levels.'

WYLIE, A. Worcestershire

Name: Alex Wylie
Role: Left-hand bat, right-arm fast bowler
Born: 20 February 1973, Tamworth
Height: 6ft 2in
County debut: 1993
Education: Bromsgrove School; Warwick College of Agriculture
Extras: Returns to county cricket in 1998 after announcing his retirement in 1995 due to persistent back problems
Best batting: 7 Worcestershire v Middlesex, Worcester 1995
Best bowling: 1-50 Worcestershire v Nottinghamshire, Trent Bridge 1993

1997 Season (did not make any first-class or one-day appearances)

Career Performances

	M	Inns	NO	Runs	HS	Avge	100s	50s	Ct	St	Balls	Runs	Wkts	Avge	Best	5wI	10wM
Test																	
All First	3	5	1	14	7	3.50	-	-	-	-	342	216	2	108.00	1-50	-	-
1-day Int																	
NatWest																	
B & H																	
Sunday																	

YATES, G.   Lancashire

Name: Gary Yates
Role: Right-hand bat, off-spin bowler
Born: 20 September 1967,
Ashton-under-Lyne
Height: 6ft 1in **Weight:** 12st 10lbs
Nickname: Yugo, Pearly, Backyard, Zippy
County debut: 1990
County cap: 1994
1st-Class 50s: 3
1st-Class 100s: 3
1st-Class 5 w. in innings: 3
1st-Class catches: 26
Place in batting averages: 219th av. 19.40
Place in bowling averages: 89th av. 33.20
Strike rate: 62.58 (career 80.74)
Parents: Alan and Patricia
Marital status: Single
Family links with cricket: Father played in
Lancashire Leagues
Education: Manchester Grammar School
Qualifications: 6 O-levels, Australian Coaching Council coach
Career outside cricket: 'Getting more involved in family business (Digical Ltd),
selling diaries, calendars and business gifts.'
Off-season: 'Working in family business'
Overseas tours: Lancashire to Tasmania and Western Australia 1990, to Western
Australia 1991, to Johannesburg 1992, to Barbados and St Lucia 1992
Overseas teams played for: South Barwon, Geelong, Australia 1987-88;
Johnsonville, Wellington, New Zealand 1989-90; Western Suburbs, Brisbane 1991-92;
Old Selbornian, East London, South Africa 1992-93; Hermanus CC, South Africa
1995-96
Cricketers particularly admired: Michael Atherton, Ian Botham, John Emburey
Young players to look out for: Andrew Flintoff
Other sports followed: All sports, especially football (Manchester City), golf, motor
rallying
Injuries: Finger infection, out for four weeks
Relaxations: Playing golf, watching football and good films, eating
Extras: Played for Worcestershire 2nd XI in 1987; made debut for Lancashire 2nd XI
in 1988 and taken on to county staff in 1990; scored century on Championship debut v
Nottinghamshire at Trent Bridge. Rapid Cricketline Player of the Month April/May 1992
Opinions on cricket: 'Would like to see more points awarded for rained-off games or
draws. This would hopefully help to abolish contrived matches. Hope four-day cricket

is here to stay.'

Best batting: 134* Lancashire v Northamptonshire, Old Trafford 1993
Best bowling: 5-34 Lancashire v Hampshire, Old Trafford 1994

1997 Season

	M	Inns	NO	Runs	HS	Avge	100s	50s	Ct	St	O	M	Runs	Wkts	Avge	Best	5wI	10wM
Test																		
All First	11	13	3	194	39	19.40	-	-	7	-	302.3	57	963	29	33.20	5-59	1	-
1-day Int																		
NatWest	2	1	1	34	34 *	-	-	-	-	-	22	3	88	2	44.00	2-15	-	
B & H	5	4	1	32	14	10.66	-	-	2	-	50	4	214	6	35.66	2-36	-	
Sunday	16	10	7	85	18	28.33	-	-	4	-	92	2	455	15	30.33	3-29	-	

Career Performances

	M	Inns	NO	Runs	HS	Avge	100s	50s	Ct	St	Balls	Runs	Wkts	Avge	Best	5wI	10wM
Test																	
All First	66	87	34	1496	134 *	28.22	3	3	26	-	11062	5821	137	42.48	5-34	3	-
1-day Int																	
NatWest	12	7	5	69	34 *	34.50	-	-	1	-	780	457	11	41.54	2-15	-	
B & H	26	10	2	97	26	12.12	-	-	6	-	1260	862	28	30.78	3-42	-	
Sunday	74	31	16	252	38	16.80	-	-	19	-	2640	2215	76	29.14	4-34	-	

YOUNG, S. Gloucestershire

Name: Shaun Young
Role: Left-hand bat, right-arm
fast-medium bowler
Born: 13 June 1970, Burnie, Tasmania
County debut: 1997
Test debut: 1997
Tests: 1
1st-Class 50s: 30
1st-Class 100s: 10
1st-Class 5 w. in innings: 8
1st-Class 10 w. in match: 1
1st-Class catches: 56
One-Day 100s: 1
Place in batting averages: 81st av. 36.48
Place in bowling averages: 98th av. 34.50
Strike rate: 74.34 (career 70.67)
Off-season: Playing Shield cricket for
Tasmania

Overseas teams played for:
Tasmania 1991-1997
Overseas tours: Young Australia to England 1995
Extras: Has been rated as Tasmania's most valuable non-international player of the decade. He continues to press his claims for international one-day representation. He is one of the few genuine all-rounders on the first-class scene in Australia. He toured England in 1995 with Young Australia and was signed by Gloucestershire to replace Courtney Walsh for the 1997 season. Was called up to the Australian squad for the sixth Test against England at The Oval in 1997 and subsequently made his Test debut in the same game
Best batting: 237 Gloucestershire v Derbyshire, Cheltenham 1997
Best bowling: 5-36 Tasmania v Pakistan, Devonport 1991-92

1997 Season

	M	Inns	NO	Runs	HS	Avge	100s	50s	Ct	St	O	M	Runs	Wkts	Avge	Best	5wI	10wM
Test	1	2	1	4	4 *	4.00	-	-	-	-	8	3	13	0	-	-	-	-
All First	19	31	4	985	237	36.48	2	5	10	-	396.3	111	1104	32	34.50	4-26	-	-
1-day Int																		
NatWest	2	2	1	14	14 *	14.00	-	-	-	-	14.3	1	63	1	63.00	1-20	-	
B & H	5	4	0	140	67	35.00	-	2	-	-	42.2	3	196	9	21.77	4-54	-	
Sunday	14	14	2	457	146 *	38.08	1	2	4	-	80	2	444	15	29.60	3-32	-	

Career Performances

	M	Inns	NO	Runs	HS	Avge	100s	50s	Ct	St	Balls	Runs	Wkts	Avge	Best	5wI	10wM
Test	1	2	1	4	4 *	4.00	-	-	-	-	48	13	0	-	-	-	-
All First	90	147	25	4951	237	40.58	10	30	56	-	15125	7300	214	34.11	7-64	8	1
1-day Int																	
NatWest	2	2	1	14	14 *	14.00	-	-	-	-	87	63	1	63.00	1-20	-	
B & H	5	4	0	140	67	35.00	-	2	-	-	254	196	9	21.77	4-54	-	
Sunday	14	14	2	457	146 *	38.08	1	2	4	-	480	444	15	29.60	3-32	-	

> 100. Who has scored two half-centuries in a
> Test match on the most occasions ?

THE UMPIRES

BALDERSTONE, J. C.

Name: John Christopher Balderstone
Role: Right-hand opening bat, slow left-arm bowler
Born: 16 November 1940, Huddersfield
Height: 6ft ½in **Weight:** 13st
Nickname: Baldy
Appointed to 1st-Class list: 1988
Appointed to Test panel: Stand-by umpire in 1991
One-Day Internationals: 1
Counties: Yorkshire, Leicestershire
County debut: 1961 (Yorkshire), 1971 (Leicestershire)
County cap: 1973 (Leicestershire)
Test debut: 1976
Tests: 2
1000 runs in a season: 11
1st-Class 50s: 102
1st-Class 100s: 32
1st-Class 5 w. in innings: 5
One-Day 100s: 5
1st-Class catches: 210
Parents: Frank and Jenny (deceased)
Wife and date of marriage: Angela, January 1991
Children: Sally, 15 September 1970; Michael, 3 January 1973
Education: Paddock County School, Huddersfield
Qualifications: Advanced cricket coach, soccer coach
Career outside cricket: Professional footballer 1958-78, cricket and soccer coach
Off-season: Coaching cricket
Overseas tours: Leicestershire to Zimbabwe 1981, to Oman 1984
Cricketers particularly admired: Willie Watson, Brian Close, Fred Trueman, David Gower, Ray Illingworth
Young players to look out for: Alec Swann
Other sports followed: All sports
Relaxations: Golf
Extras: 14 one-day Man of the Match Awards. Played a first-class cricket match and football league game on the same day in 1975 (Leicestershire v Derbyshire, Doncaster v Brentford).Was the first man to act as 'third umpire' in Test in England, in the second Test against Australia at Lord's in 1993. Umpired first one-day International, England v South Africa 1994
Opinions on cricket: 'Still too much knocking of English cricket by media etc. There

is still some good cricket and cricketers around, it just takes time to develop.'
Best batting: 181* Leicestershire v Gloucestershire, Leicester 1984
Best bowling: 6-25 Leicestershire v Hampshire, Southampton 1978

First-Class Career Performances

	M	Inns	NO	Runs	HS	Avge	100s	Ct	St	Runs	Wkts	Avge	Best	5wI	10wM
Test	2	4	0	39	35	9.75	-	-	1	80	1	80.00	1-80	-	-
All First	390	619	61	19034	181*	34.11	32	210	-	8160	310	26.32	6-25	5	-

BIRD, H. D.

Name: Harold Dennis Bird, MBE
Role: Right-hand opening bat
Born: 19 April 1933, Barnsley
Height: 5ft 10in **Weight:** 11st 7lbs
Nickname: Dickie
Appointed to 1st-class list: 1969
Appointed to Test panel: 1972
Appointed to International panel: 1994
Tests umpired: 68
One-Day Internationals umpired: 91
Counties: Yorkshire, Leicestershire
County debut: 1956 (Yorkshire),
1960 (Leicestershire)
County cap: 1960 (Leicestershire)
1000 runs in a season: 1
1st-Class 50s: 14
1st-Class 100s: 2
1st-Class catches: 28
Parents: James Harold and Ethel
Marital status: Single
Education: Burton Road Primary School; Raley School, Barnsley
Qualifications: MCC advanced cricket coach
Career outside cricket: 'Cricket is my life'
Off-season: After-dinner speaking and umpiring overseas
Cricketing superstitions or habits: Twitch of the shoulders, wears distinctive white cap
Other sports followed: Football
Cricketers particularly admired: Gary Sobers, Dennis Lillee, Viv Richards
Cricketers particularly learnt from: Gubby Allen, Johnny Wardle
Young players to look out for: Anthony McGrath (Yorkshire)
Relaxations: Listening to recordings of Barbra Streisand and Diana Ross
Extras: Has umpired 160 international matches to date, including three World Cup

finals at Lord's (1975, 1979, 1983); also umpired at the World Cup in India in 1987. Umpired the Queen's Silver Jubilee Test, England v Australia 1977, the Centenary Test, England v Australia 1980 and the MCC Bicentenary Test, England v Rest of the World 1987. In 1982 he umpired the Women's World Cup final in Christchurch, New Zealand. During the mid-1980s he umpired several times in the various competitions staged at Sharjah, UAE. To date he has umpired 34 Cup finals all over the world, as well as the finals of other cricket events such as The Best All-rounder in the World, The Best Batsman in the World and the World Double Wicket competition. In 1977 he was voted Yorkshire Personality of the Year. He is an MCC member and author of four bestselling books, *Not Out*, *That's Out*, *From the Pavilion End* and *Dickie Bird: My Autobiography*. Despite lucrative offers to join the 'Packer circus' and to visit South Africa with rebel tours, he remained loyal to the TCCB and to the established game on which he had been brought up in Yorkshire and which had given him so much in life. In June 1986 he received an MBE in the Queen's Birthday Honours List. With David Shepherd and Steve Bucknor became the first ICC officially-sponsored umpires in 1992, and was appointed to stand in Zimbabwe's first Test match (against India) in Harare. Subsequently, in Zimbabwe's second Test against New Zealand (also in Harare), he became the first umpire to officiate in 50 Test matches, having passed Frank Chester's world record of 48 Tests at Bulawayo six days earlier. Umpired all three Tests in West Indies home series against Pakistan in 1993. In 1994 he umpired Tests in New Zealand, England, Pakistan and India. Made Honorary Life Member of Yorkshire CCC in March 1994. Umpired in the Australia versus Pakistan Test series in 1996. Was voted the Yorkshireman of the Year in 1996. Awarded an honorary doctorate from Sheffield Hallam University for his outstanding services to cricket. Made an honorary Life Member of the MCC and of Leicestershire CCC. Retired from the Test scene after the second Test against India at Lord's in 1996. Was awarded an honorary doctorate degree in Law at Leeds University in July 1997 for his services to cricket. Stayed in the bestseller list with his book *Dickie Bird: My Autobiography* for several weeks in 1997

Opinions on cricket: 'The greatest game in the world. A game to be enjoyed by young and old. I have consistently advocated playing through all light unless the umpires are convinced that there is genuine physical danger to the batsman.'

Best batting: 181* Yorkshire v Glamorgan, Bradford 1959

First-Class Career Performances

	M	Inns	NO	Runs	HS	Avge	100s	Ct	St	Runs	Wkts	Avge	Best	5wI	10wM
Test															
All First	93	170	10	3314	181*	20.71	2	28	-	22	0	-	-	-	-

BOND, J. D.

Name: John David Bond
Role: Right-hand bat
Born: 6 May 1932, Kearsley, Lancashire
Nickname: Jackie
Appointed to 1st-class list: 1988
Counties: Lancashire, Nottinghamshire
County debut: 1955 (Lancashire),
1974 (Nottinghamshire)
County cap: 1961 (Lancashire)
1000 runs in a season: 2
1st-Class 50s: 54
1st-Class 100s: 14
1st-Class catches: 222
Education: Bolton School
Extras: Captain of Lancashire 1968-1972,
during which time Lancashire won the Gillette
Cup three years in succession (1970, 1971,
1972) and the John Player Sunday League in
1969 and 1970. He moved to Nottinghamshire
in 1974 and was a Test selector in the same year. He was appointed cricket manager at
Lancashire CCC in 1980 and held the position until 1986
Best batting: 157 Lancashire v Hampshire, Old Trafford 1962

First-Class Career Performances

	M	Inns	NO	Runs	HS	Avge	100s	Ct	St	Runs	Wkts	Avge	Best	5wI	10wM
Test															
All First	362	548	80	12125	157	25.90	14	222	-	69	0	-	-	-	-

BURGESS, G. I.

Name: Graham Iefvion Burgess
Role: Right-hand bat, right-arm
medium bowler
Born: 5 May 1943,
Glastonbury, Somerset
Appointed to 1st-class list: 1991
County: Somerset
County debut: 1966
County cap: 1968
Testimonial: 1977
1st-Class 100s: 2
1st-Class 5 w. in innings: 18
1st-Class 10 w. in match: 2
1st-Class catches: 120
Education: Millfield School
Extras: Played Minor Counties cricket for
Wiltshire 1981-82 and for Cambridgeshire
1983-84

Best batting: 129 Somerset v Gloucestershire, Taunton 1973
Best bowling: 7-43 Somerset v Oxford University, The Parks 1975

First-Class Career Performances

	M	Inns	NO	Runs	HS	Avge	100s	Ct	St	Runs	Wkts	Avge	Best	5wI	10wM
Test															
All First	252	414	37	7129	129	18.90	2	120	-	13543	474	28.57	7-43	18	2

CLARKSON, A.

Name: Anthony Clarkson
Role: Right-hand bat, right-arm off-spin
Born: 5 September 1939, Killinghall, North Yorkshire
Height: 6ft **Weight:** 14st
Appointed to 1st-class list: 1996
County: Somerset
County debut: 1963
County cap: 1969
1000 runs in a season: 2
1st-Class 100s: 2
1st-Class catches: 52
Parents: Joe (deceased) and Clarrie
Marital status: Engaged to Cheryl

Children: André, September 1964; Chantal, 27 May 1967; Pierre, 1 May 1969
Family links with cricket: Father was a league professional
Education: Killinghall C of E; Harrogate Grammar School; Leeds College of Building; Bradford Polytechnic; Brunel College, Bristol
Qualifications: 9 O-levels, past member of highway technicians
Career outside cricket: Architectural, Civil Engineering and Surveying Consultant
Off-season: Working and completing the renovation of house
Other sports followed: Golf and rugby ('especially league')
Relaxations: Golf, DIY, and gardening
Extras: First English player to score a century in the Sunday League

First-Class Career Performances

	M	Inns	NO	Runs	HS	Avge	100s	Ct	St	Runs	Wkts	Avge	Best	5wI	10wM
Test															
All First	110	189	12	4458	131	25.18	2	52	-	367	13	28.23	3-51	-	-

CONSTANT, D. J.

Name: David John Constant
Role: Left-hand bat, slow left-arm bowler
Born: 9 November 1941, Bradford-on-Avon, Wiltshire
Nickname: Connie
Appointed to 1st-class list: 1969
Appointed to Test panel: 1971
Tests umpired: 36
One-Day Internationals umpired: 30
Counties: Kent, Leicestershire
County debut: 1961 (Kent), 1965 (Leicestershire)
1st-Class 50s: 6
1st-Class catches: 33
Extras: County bowls player for Gloucestershire 1984-86
Best batting: 80 Leicestershire v Gloucestershire, Bristol 1966

	M	Inns	NO	Runs	HS	Avge	100s	Ct	St	Runs	Wkts	Avge	Best	5wI	10wM
Test															
All First	61	93	14	1517	80	19.20	-	33	-	36	1	36.00	1-28	-	-

DUDLESTON, B.

Name: Barry Dudleston
Role: Right-hand opening bat, slow
left-arm bowler, occasional wicket-keeper
Born: 16 July 1945, Bebington, Cheshire
Height: 5ft 9in **Weight:** 13st 7lbs
Nickname: Danny
Appointed to 1st-class list: 1984
Appointed to Test panel: 1991
Tests umpired: 2
One-Day Internationals umpired: 1
Counties: Leicestershire, Gloucestershire
County debut: 1966 (Leicestershire),
1981 (Gloucestershire)
County cap: 1969 (Leicestershire)
Benefit: 1980 (£25,000)
1000 runs in a season: 8
1st-Class 100s: 32
1st-Class 200s: 1
One-Day 100s: 4
1st-Class catches: 234
Parents: Percy and Dorothy Vera
Wife and date of marriage: Louise, 19 October 1994
Children: Sharon Louise, 29 October 1968; Matthew Barry, 12 September 1988
Family links with cricket: Father was a club cricketer
Education: Stockport School
Qualifications: O-levels, junior coaching certificate
Career outside cricket: Managing director of Sunsport Ltd (tour operators)
Other sports followed: Most
Cricketers particularly admired: Gary Sobers, Tom Graveney
Cricketers particularly learnt from: Vinoo Mankad
Relaxations: Television, bridge, wine, golf
Extras: Played for England U25. Suffered badly from broken fingers, breaking fingers
on the same hand three times in 1978. Played for Rhodesia in the Currie Cup 1976-80.
Acted as 'third umpire' in the third Test against Australia at Trent Bridge 1993
Opinions on cricket: 'It is still the greatest test of skill and character – beautiful to

watch when played well. Am worried about the declining standards of behaviour.'
Best batting: 202 Leicestershire v Derbyshire, Leicester 1979
Best bowling: 4-6 Leicestershire v Surrey, Leicester 1972

First-Class Career Performances

	M	Inns	NO	Runs	HS	Avge	100s	Ct	St	Runs	Wkts	Avge	Best	5wI	10wM
Test															
All First	295	501	47	14747	202	32.48	32	234	7	1365	47	29.04	4-6	-	-

HAMPSHIRE, J. H.

Name: John Harry Hampshire
Role: Right-hand bat
Born: 10 February 1941,
Thurnscoe, Yorkshire
Height: 6ft **Weight:** 13st
Nickname: Hamp
Appointed to 1st-class list: 1985
Appointed to Test panel: 1989
Tests umpired: 11
One-Day Internationals umpired: 6
Counties: Yorkshire, Derbyshire
County debut: 1961 (Yorkshire),
1982 (Derbyshire)
County cap: 1963 (Yorkshire),
1982 (Derbyshire)
Benefit: 1976
Test debut: 1969
Tests: 8
1000 runs in a season: 15
1st-Class 50s: 142
1st-Class 100s: 43
1st-Class catches: 445
1st-Class 5 w. in innings: 2
One-Day 100s: 7
Parents: Jack and Vera
Wife and date of marriage: Judith Ann, 5 September 1964
Children: Ian Christopher, 6 January 1969; Paul Wesley, 12 February 1972
Family links with cricket: Father (J.) and brother (A.W.) both played for Yorkshire
Education: Oakwood Technical High School, Rotherham
Qualifications: City and Guilds in Printing
Off-season: Coach to Zimbabwe 1992-97
Overseas tours: MCC to Australia and New Zealand, 1970-71

Overseas teams played for: Tasmania, 1966-69, 1977-79
Cricketers particularly admired: Peter May, Gary Sobers
Other sports followed: Most sports
Relaxations: Gardening and cooking
Extras: Captained Yorkshire 1979-80. Played for Tasmania 1967-69 and 1977-79. Scored a century (107) in his first Test match, against West Indies at Lord's 1969. Appointed manager/coach of the Zimbabwe Test squad for their first Test matches against India and New Zealand. Umpired four Tests in Pakistan 1989-90
Best batting: 183* Yorkshire v Surrey, Hove 1971
Best bowling: 7-52 Yorkshire v Glamorgan, Cardiff 1963

First-Class Career Performances

	M	Inns	NO	Runs	HS	Avge	100s	Ct	St	Runs	Wkts	Avge	Best	5wl	10wM
Test	8	16	1	405	107	26.86	1	9	-						
All First	577	924	112	28059	183	*34.55	43	445	-	1637	30	54.56	7-52	2	-

HARRIS, J. H.

Name: John Henry Harris
Role: Left-hand bat, right-arm
fast-medium bowler
Born: 13 February 1936, Taunton
Height: 5ft 11in **Weight:** 13st 5lbs
Nickname: Arry, Boater, JH
Appointed to 1st-class list: 1983
County: Somerset
County debut: 1952
1st-Class catches: 6
Parents: Jack and Freda Harris, Bill and
Doris Rowlan
Wife and date of marriage: Morag Elspeth
Jane, 20 October 1984
Children: Karen, Andrew, Mark and Tim
Family links with cricket: 'Grandfather
(Harry Jernie) was head groundsman at
Somerset CCC for 25 years'
Education: Priory School, Taunton; Coopers
Lane, Grove Park, London

Qualifications: Qualified coach and football and basketball referee
Career outside cricket: Devon League Cricket Inspector of grounds
Off-season: 'Holiday in the USA with our friends Phil and Karen Kyle in Kansas,' DIY and getting fit walking the dogs
Other sports followed: Golf ('poorly') and squash

Relaxations: DIY, Glen Miller music, Bournemouth Symphony Orchestra, television 'and a few drinks with my friends at the D&E squash club'
Extras: Made his debut for Somerset aged 16 years 99 days. Played Minor Counties cricket for Suffolk (1960-62) and Devon (1975). Two overseas tours with the MCC as umpire. Umpired the first Master World Cup in Bombay. Stepped down as Chairman of the First-Class Cricket Umpires' Association after five years
Best batting: 41 Somerset v Worcestershire, Taunton 1957
Best bowling: 3-29 Somerset v Worcestershire, Bristol 1959

First-Class Career Performances

	M	Inns	NO	Runs	HS	Avge	100s	Ct	St	Runs	Wkts	Avge	Best	5wI	10wM
Test															
All First	15	18	4	154	41	11.00	-	6	-	609	19	32.05	3.29	-	-

HOLDER, J. W.

Name: John Wakefield Holder
Role: Right-hand bat, right-arm fast bowler
Born: 19 March 1945, St George, Barbados
Height: 6ft **Weight:** 14st
Nickname: Benson, Hod
Appointed to 1st-class list: 1983
Appointed to Test panel: 1988
Tests umpired: 10
One-Day Internationals umpired: 14
County: Hampshire
County debut: 1968
50 wickets in a season: 1
1st-Class 5 w. in innings: 5
1st-Class 10 w. in match: 1
1st-Class catches: 12
Parents: Charles and Carnetta
Wife: Glenda
Children: Christopher 1968; Nigel 1970
Family links with cricket: None
Education: St Giles Boys School; Combermere High School, Barbados; Rochdale College
Qualifications: 3 O-levels, MCC advanced cricket coach
Off-season: 'Idling'
Young players to look out for: Alex Tudor
Other sports followed: Football (Manchester United)
Relaxations: Keeping fit and helping coach the Rochdale Indoor Cricket Team which

plays in the National League in the winter
Extras: Umpired four Tests in Pakistan 1989-90
Best batting: 33 Hampshire v Sussex, Hove 1971
Best bowling: 7-79 Hampshire v Gloucestershire, Gloucester 1972

First-Class Career Performances

	M	Inns	NO	Runs	HS	Avge	100s	Ct	St	Runs	Wkts	Avge	Best	5wI	10wM
Test															
All First	47	49	14	374	33	10.68	-	12	-	3415	139	24.56	7-79	5	1

HOLDER, V. A.

Name: Vanburn Alonza Holder
Role: Right-hand bat, right-arm
fast-medium bowler
Born: 8 October 1945,
St Michael, Barbados
Nickname: Van
Appointed to 1st-class list: 1992
County: Worcestershire
County debut: 1968
County cap: 1970
Test debut: 1969
Tests: 40
1st-Class 50s: 4
1st-Class 100s: 1
1st-Class 5 w. in innings: 38
1st-Class 10 w. in match: 3
1st-Class catches: 98
Overseas tours: West Indies to England
1969, 1973, to India, Sri Lanka and Pakistan
1974-75, to Australia 1975-76, to England 1976, to India and Sri Lanka 1978-79 (as
vice-captain)
Extras: Made his debut for Barbados in the Shell Shield competition in 1966-67
Best batting: 122 Barbados v Trinidad, Bridgetown 1973-74
Best bowling: 7-40 Worcestershire v Glamorgan, Cardiff 1974

First-Class Career Performances

	M	Inns	NO	Runs	HS	Avge	100s	Ct	St	Runs	Wkts	Avge	Best	5wI	10wM
Test	40	59	11	682	42	14.20	-	16	-	3627	109	33.27	6-28	3	-
All First	311	354	81	3559	122	13.03	1	98	-	23183	948	24.45	7-40	38	3

JESTY, T. E.

Name: Trevor Edward Jesty
Role: Right-hand bat, right-arm medium bowler
Born: 2 June 1948, Gosport, Hampshire
Height: 5ft 9in **Weight:** 11st 9lbs
Nickname: Jets
Appointed to 1st-class list: 1994
Counties: Hampshire, Surrey, Lancashire
County debut: 1966 (Hampshire), 1985 (Surrey), 1988 (Lancashire)
County cap: 1971 (Hampshire), 1985 (Surrey)
Benefit: 1982
One-Day Internationals: 10
1000 runs in a season: 10
50 wickets in a season: 2
1st-Class 50s: 110
1st-Class 100s: 35
1st-Class 200s: 2
1st-Class 5 w. in innings: 19
1st-Class catches: 265
1st-Class stumpings: 1
One-Day 100s: 7

Parents: Aubrey Edward and Sophia
Wife and date of marriage: Jacqueline, 12 September 1970
Children: Graeme Barry, 27 September 1972; Lorna Samantha, 7 November 1976
Education: Privet County Secondary Modern, Gosport
Overseas tours: International XI to West Indies 1982; England to Australia and New Zealand 1982-83
Overseas teams played for: Border, South Africa 1973-74; Griqualand West 1974-77, 1980-81; Canterbury, New Zealand 1979-80
Cricketers particularly admired: Sir Garfield Sobers, Barry Richards
Relaxations: Watching football, gardening, golf
Extras: One of *Wisden*'s Five Cricketers of the Year 1982. Left Hampshire at end of 1984 when not appointed captain and offered the captaincy of Surrey for 1985 season
Best batting: 248 Hampshire v Cambridge University, Fenner's 1984
Best bowling: 7-75 Hampshire v Worcestershire, Southampton 1976

First-Class Career Performances

	M	Inns	NO	Runs	HS	Avge	100s	Ct	St	Runs	Wkts	Avge	Best	5wI	10wM
Test															
All First	490	777	107	21916	248	32.71	35	265	1	16075	585	27.47	7-75	19	-

JONES, A. A.

Name: Alan Arthur Jones
Role: Right-hand bat, right-arm
fast-medium bowler
Born: 9 December 1947, Horley, Surrey
Height: 6ft 3in **Weight:** 14st
Nickname: Jonah, Buckets
Appointed to 1st-class list: 1985
One-Day Internationals umpired: 1
Counties: Sussex, Somerset,
Middlesex, Glamorgan
County debut: 1964 (Sussex),
1970 (Somerset), 1976 (Middlesex),
1980 (Glamorgan)
County cap: 1972 (Somerset),
1976 (Middlesex), 1980 (Glamorgan)
50 wickets in a season: 4
1st-Class 5 w. in innings: 23
1st-Class 10 w. in match: 3
1st-Class catches: 50
Parents: Leslie and Hazel
Wife: Marilyn
Children: Clare Michelle
Education: St John's College, Horsham
Qualifications: 5 O-levels, MCC advanced coach, NCA staff coach
Off-season: 'Recovering from the summer'
Overseas teams played for: Northern Transvaal 1971-72; Orange Free State 1976-77
Other sports followed: All sports
Cricketers particularly admired: Tom Cartwright, Brian Close
Young players to look out for: Darren Altree and Ashley Giles (Warwickshire), Jason
Laney (Hampshire)
Other sports followed: Golf
Relaxations: Reading, cooking and travel
Extras: Won two Championship medals with Middlesex (1976 and 1977). He was the
first person to play for four counties – only one other player has done so since
Best batting: 33 Middlesex v Kent, Canterbury 1978
Best bowling: 9-51 Somerset v Sussex, Hove 1976

First-Class Career Performances

	M	Inns	NO	Runs	HS	Avge	100s	Ct	St	Runs	Wkts	Avge	Best	5wl	10wM
Test															
All First	214	216	68	799	33	5-39	-	50	-	15414	549	28.07	9-51	23	3

JULIAN, R.

Name: Raymond Julian
Role: Right-hand bat, wicket-keeper
Born: 23 August 1936,
Cosby, Leicestershire
Height: 5ft 11in **Weight:** 13st 6lbs
Nickname: Julie
Appointed to 1st-class list: 1972
One-Day Internationals umpired: 3
County: Leicestershire
County debut: 1953
County cap: 1961
1st-Class 50s: 2
1st-Class catches: 381
1st-Class stumpings: 40
Parents: George Ernest and Doris
Wife and date of marriage:
Megan, 3 April 1993

Children: Peter Raymond, 1 February 1958;
John Kelvin, 13 October 1960;
David Andrew, 15 October 1963; Paul Anthony, 22 September 1967
Family links with cricket: Father and two brothers all played local cricket. Two sons play local cricket
Education: Cosby Primary School, Leicestershire; Wigston Secondary Modern
Qualifications: Cricket coach, decorator and gardener
Career outside cricket: As above
Off-season: Watching the England tour to Sharjah and West Indies
Overseas tours: MCC to West Africa, 1975
Cricketers particularly admired: Gary Sobers, Keith Andrew
Young players to look out for: Ben Hollioake, Michael Powell (Glamorgan), James Ormond, Jason Laney
Other sports followed: Football (Leicester City FC), boxing, rugby (Leicester Tigers)
Relaxations: Gardening, holidays, travel
Extras: Youngest player to make debut for Leicestershire (aged 15 years). Youngest wicket-keeper to play first-class cricket in 1953. Took six catches in an innings, Leicestershire v Northants, Kettering 1965. Played for the Army 1955-57. Gave eight LBW decisions in succession, Glamorgan v Sussex at Cardiff 1986. Has umpired three B&H semi-finals and one Gillette Cup semi-final. Has just completed 25 years on the first-class list. Was awarded one-day International between England and India at The Oval in 1996 and has been the stand-by umpire in three Tests. Umpired three one-day Internationals. Captained Leicestershire 2nd XI from 1968 to 1971
Opinions on cricket: 'The four-day game is good. There is too much one-day cricket.'
Best batting: 51 Leicestershire v Worcestershire, Worcester 1962

First-Class Career Performances

	M	Inns	NO	Runs	HS	Avge	100s	Ct	St	Runs	Wkts	Avge	Best	5wl	10wM
Test															
All First	192	288	23	2581	51	9.73	-	381	40						

KITCHEN, M. J.

Name: Mervyn John Kitchen
Role: Left-hand bat, right-arm
medium bowler
Born: 1 August 1940,
Nailsea, Somerset
Appointed to 1st-class list: 1982
Appointed to Test panel: 1990
Appointed to International panel: 1995
Tests umpired: 13
One-Day Internationals umpired: 14
County: Somerset
County debut: 1960
County cap: 1966
Testimonial: 1973
1000 runs in a season: 7
1st-Class 50s: 68
1st-Class 100s: 17
1st-Class catches: 157
One-Day 100s: 1

Education: Blackwell Secondary Modern, Nailsea
Extras: Was third (replay) umpire for two Tests in 1994
Best batting: 189 Somerset v Pakistanis, Taunton 1967

First-Class Career Performances

	M	Inns	NO	Runs	HS	Avge	100s	Ct	St	Runs	Wkts	Avge	Best	5wl	10wM
Test															
All First	354	612	32	15230	189	26.25	17	157	-	109	2	54.50	1-4	-	-

LEADBEATER, B.

Name: Barrie Leadbeater
Role: Right-hand opening bat, right-arm medium bowler, slip fielder
Born: 14 August 1943, Leeds
Height: 6ft **Weight:** 13st 1lb
Nickname: Leady
One-Day Internationals umpired: 4
Appointed to 1st-class list: 1981
County: Yorkshire
County debut: 1966
County cap: 1969
Benefit: 1980 (joint benefit with G.A. Cope)
1st-Class 50s: 27
1st-Class 100s: 1
1st-Class catches: 82
Parents: Ronnie (deceased) and Nellie
Marital status: Widowed
Wife and date of marriage: Jacqueline (deceased),
18 September 1971
Children: Richard Barrie, 23 November 1972; Michael Spencer, 21 March 1976; Daniel Mark Ronnie, 19 June 1981
Education: Brownhill County Primary; Harehills Secondary Modern, Leeds
Qualifications: 2 O-levels
Career outside cricket: HGV driver
Off-season: 'Looking after my sons. Especially Michael who was seriously injured in a road traffic accident that also killed my wife'
Overseas tours: Duke of Norfolk's XI to West Indies 1970
Overseas teams played for: Johannesburg Municipals 1978-79
Other sports followed: Table tennis, golf, snooker, football (Leeds United)
Cricketers particularly admired: Colin Cowdrey, Clive Rice, Richard Hadlee, Gary Sobers, Michael Holding
Cricketers particularly learnt from: Brian Close, Willie Watson, Arthur Mitchell, Maurice Leyland
Relaxations: 'Taking care of my family'
Extras: Acted as 'third umpire' in the fourth Test against Australia at Headingley 1993
Opinions on cricket: 'Disappointed in players who lack self-control and professional pride and set bad examples to young players and public alike. Public should be regularly and properly informed during stoppages in play. Stoppages for bad light cause more frustration for public, players and, not least, umpires and a change in regulations may be needed soon if the game is to retain its support and credibility. The recent theory of the

wicket-keeper standing between the leg stump and the return crease when the slow left-arm bowler is operating over the wicket should be made illegal. It is grossly negative and against the spirit of the game.'

Best batting: 140* Yorkshire v Hampshire, Portsmouth 1976

First-Class Career Performances

	M	Inns	NO	Runs	HS	Avge	100s	Ct	St	Runs	Wkts	Avge	Best	5wl	10wM
Test															
All First	147	241	29	5373	140	*25.34	1	82	-	5	1	5.00	1-1	-	-

LLOYDS, J. W.

Name: Jeremy William Lloyds
Role: Left-hand bat
Born: 17 November 1954, Penang, Malaya
Height: 5ft 11in **Weight:** 12st
Nickname: Jerry
Appointed to 1st-class list: 1998
Parents: Edwin William and Grace Cicely (Jackie)
Wife and date of marriage: Janine, 16 September 1997
Children: Kaeli, 16 November 1991
Family links with cricket: Father played cricket in Malaya. Brother Chris played for Somerset 2nd XI
Education: Curry Rivel Primary School; St Dunstan's Prep School; Blundell's School, Tiverton
Qualifications: MCC Advanced Coach since 1974

Career outside cricket: Coaching and setting up Western Province Youth Programme 1992-95 in South Africa
Off-season: Umpiring in South Africa
Overseas teams played for: St Strithian's Old Boys, Johannesburg 1978-80; Toombull DCC, Brisbane 1980-82; North Sydney District 1982-83; Orange Free State 1983-84; Preston (Victoria) 1986
Young players to look out for: Nick Boulton (Somerset)
Other sports followed: Golf, football (Tottenham Hotspur), American football (San Francisco 49ers)
Relaxations: Reading, music and spending time at home with my family
Opinions on cricket: 'Not enough time spent on specifics in the game. Too many nets for the sake of it. In South Africa the Test players are being destroyed by over-touring.

There is far too much one-day cricket – young players are being brought up on it. Maybe that is why they can't play Shane Warne!'

Best batting: 132* Somerset v Northamptonshire, Northampton 1982
Best bowling: 7-88 Somerset v Essex, Chelmsford 1982

First-Class Career Performances

	M	Inns	NO	Runs	HS	Avge	100s	Ct	St	Runs	Wkts	Avge	Best	5wI	10wM
Test															
All First	267	408	64	10679	132*	31.04	10	229	-	12943	333	38.86	7-88	13	1

MEYER, B. J.

Name: Barrie John Meyer
Role: Right-hand bat, wicket-keeper
Born: 21 August 1931, Bournemouth
Height: 5ft 10in **Weight:** 12st 5lbs
Nickname: BJ
Appointed to 1st-class list: 1973
Appointed to Test panel: 1978
Tests umpired: 26
One-Day Internationals umpired: 23
County: Gloucestershire
County debut: 1957
County cap: 1958
Benefit: 1971
1st-Class 50s: 11
1st-Class catches: 707
1st-Class stumpings: 118
Parents: Deceased
Wife and date of marriage: Gillian,
4 September 1965

Children: Stephen Barrie; Christopher John; Adrian Michael
Education: Boscombe Secondary School, Bournemouth
Career outside cricket: Salesman
Off-season: Coaching and umpiring in South Africa
Other sports followed: Golf (handicap 9), football (was a professional footballer for Bristol Rovers, Plymouth Argyle, Newport County and Bristol City)
Cricketers particularly learnt from: Andy Wilson and Sonny Avery (coaches for Glos)
Relaxations: Golf, music, reading
Extras: Umpired 1979 and 1983 World Cup finals
Best batting: 63 Gloucestershire v Indians, Cheltenham 1959
            63 Gloucestershire v Oxford University, Bristol 1962
            63 Gloucestershire v Sussex, Bristol 1964

First-Class Career Performances

	M	Inns	NO	Runs	HS	Avge	100s	Ct	St	Runs	Wkts	Avge	Best	5wI	10wM
Test															
All First	406	569	191	5367	63	14.19	-	707	118						

PALMER, K. E.

Name: Kenneth Ernest Palmer
Role: Right-hand bat, right-arm
fast-medium bowler
Born: 22 April 1937, Winchester
Height: 5ft 10in **Weight:** 14st
Nickname: Pedlar
Appointed to 1st-class list: 1972
Appointed to Test panel: 1978
Appointed to International panel: 1994
Tests umpired: 24
One-Day Internationals umpired: 20
County: Somerset
County debut: 1955
County cap: 1958
Testimonial: 1968
Test debut: 1965
Tests: 1
1000 runs in a season: 1
50 wickets in a season: 6
1st-Class 50s: 27
1st-Class 100s: 2
1st-Class 5 w. in innings: 46
1st-Class 10 w. in match: 5
1st-Class catches: 156
Parents: Harry and Cecilia
Wife and date of marriage: Jacqueline, 24 September 1994
Children: Gary Vincent, 6 September 1961
Family links with cricket: Father played club cricket and did the cricketer's double
13 times. Son played for Somerset, as did brother Roy, also a Test umpire
Education: Southbroom Secondary Modern, Devizes
Off-season: Working around new bungalow, playing snooker and squash and travel
abroad umpiring for the MCC
Overseas tours: Commonwealth XI to Pakistan 1962; International Cavaliers to West
Indies 1963-64
Cricketers particularly admired: Gary Sobers, Richard Hadlee, Viv Richards, David

Gower, Michael Holding, Malcolm Marshall
Cricketers particularly learnt from: Father and Maurice Tremlett
Other sports followed: Football (Manchester United) and rugby (Bath and England)
Relaxations: Car enthusiast
Extras: Called into Test side while coaching in South Africa 1964-65. Umpired two B&H finals and two NatWest finals and was twice on World Cup panel in England. Won Carling Single Wicket Competition 1961. Did the 'double' in 1961 (114 wickets, 1036 runs). With Bill Alley holds the Somerset record for 6th wicket partnership. Has umpired five Benson & Hedges finals and five NatWest finals
Best batting: 125* Somerset v Northamptonshire, Northampton 1961
Best bowling: 9-57 Somerset v Nottinghamshire, Trent Bridge 1963

First-Class Career Performances

	M	Inns	NO	Runs	HS	Avge	100s	Ct	St	Runs	Wkts	Avge	Best	5wI	10wM
Test	1	1	0	10	10	10.00	-	-	-	189	1	189.00	1-113	-	-
All First	314	481	105	7771	125	*20.66	2	156	-	18485	866	21.34	9-57	46	5

PALMER, R.

Name: Roy Palmer
Role: Right-hand bat, right-arm fast-medium bowler
Born: 12 July 1942, Hampshire
Height: 6ft 3in **Weight:** 12st 7lbs
Nickname: Arp
Appointed to 1st-class list: 1980
Appointed to Test panel: 1992
Tests umpired: 2
One-Day Internationals umpired: 8
County: Somerset
County debut: 1965
50 wickets in a season: 1
1st-Class 50s: 1
1st-Class 5 w. in innings: 4
1st-Class catches: 25
Parents: Harry and Cecilia
Wife and date of marriage: Alyne, 5 November 1983
Children: Nick, 7 October 1968
Family links with cricket: Brother of Ken Palmer, Test umpire and former Somerset player; nephew Gary also played for Somerset

Education: Southbroom Secondary
Modern, Devizes
Young players to look out for: Dean Cosker
Relaxations: DIY and reading
Extras: Won two Man of the Match Awards in the Gillette Cup
Best batting: 84 Somerset v Leicestershire, Taunton 1967
Best bowling: 6-45 Somerset v Middlesex, Lord's 1967

First-Class Career Performances

	M	Inns	NO	Runs	HS	Avge	100s	Ct	St	Runs	Wkts	Avge	Best	5wl	10wM
Test															
All First	74	110	32	1037	84	13.29	-	25	-	5439	172	31.62	6-45	4	-

PLEWS, N. T.

Name: Nigel Trevor Plews
Role: Right-hand opening bat
Born: 5 September 1934, Nottingham
Height: 6ft 6in **Weight:** 16st 8lbs
Nickname: Plod, Sarge
Appointed to 1st-class list: 1982
Appointed to Test panel: 1988
Appointed to International panel: 1994
Tests umpired: 11
One-Day Internationals umpired: 16
Parents: Deceased
Wife and date of marriage:
Margaret, 24 September 1956
Children: Elaine, 1961; Douglas, 1964
Education: Mundella Grammar School,
Nottingham
Qualifications: School Certificate in
Commercial Subjects, RSA Advanced
Book-keeping
Career outside cricket: Nottingham City
police for 25 years (Det. Sgt in Fraud Squad for 15 years)
Off-season: National Grid International Panel Appointments
Other sports followed: Football, table tennis, swimming
Relaxations: Hill-walking, reading, travel, cricket administration
Extras: Played local league and club cricket in Nottingham. Toured as umpire with
MCC to Namibia 1991. Has now umpired in 11 Tests and 16 one-day Internationals

Did not play first-class cricket

SHARP, G.

Name: George Sharp
Role: Right-hand bat, wicket-keeper
Born: 12 March 1950,
Hartlepool, County Durham
Height: 5ft 11in **Weight:** 15st 7lbs
Nickname: Blunt, Razor, Sharpie
Appointed to 1st-class list: 1992
Appointed to International panel: 1996
Tests umpired: 1
One-Day Internationals umpired: 1
County: Northamptonshire
County debut: 1967
County cap: 1972
1st-Class catches: 565
1st-Class stumpings: 90
Parents: George and Grace
Wife and date of marriage: Audrey,
14 September 1974
Children: Gareth James, 27 June 1984
Education: Elwick Road, Hartlepool
Qualifications: NCA coach

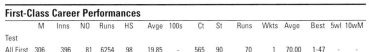

Career outside cricket: Director of GSB Loams Ltd, suppliers of soil and turf for
sports areas
Off-season: Working for GSB Loams Ltd
Overseas tours: England Counties XI to West Indies 1974
Cricketers particularly admired: Alan Knott, Bob Taylor, Keith Andrew
Other sports followed: Football (Newcastle and Middlesbrough)
Relaxations: Golf
Best batting: 98 Northamptonshire v Yorkshire, Northampton 1983

First-Class Career Performances

	M	Inns	NO	Runs	HS	Avge	100s	Ct	St	Runs	Wkts	Avge	Best	5wI	10wM
Test															
All First	306	396	81	6254	98	19.85	-	565	90	70	1	70.00	1-47	-	-

SHEPHERD, D. R.

Name: David Robert Shepherd
Role: Right-hand bat, right-arm
medium bowler
Born: 27 December 1940,
Bideford, Devon
Height: 5ft 10in **Weight:** 16st
Nickname: Shep
Appointed to 1st-class list: 1981
Appointed to Test panel: 1985
Appointed to International panel: 1994
Tests umpired: 30
One-Day Internationals umpired: 63
County: Gloucestershire
County debut: 1965
County cap: 1969
Benefit: 1978 (joint benefit with J. Davey)
1000 runs in a season: 2
1st-Class 50s: 55
1st-Class 100s: 12
1st-Class catches: 95
One-Day 100s: 2

Parents: Herbert and Doris (both deceased)
Marital status: Single
Education: Barnstaple Grammar School; St Luke's College, Exeter
Career outside cricket: Teacher
Off-season: Assisting brother in local post office/newsagent
Other sports followed: Rugby, football, most ball sports
Cricketers particularly admired: Gary Sobers, Mike Procter
Relaxations: All sports, philately, television
Extras: Played Minor Counties cricket for Devon 1959-64. Only Gloucestershire player to score a century on his first-class debut. Umpired the MCC Bicentenary Test, England v Rest of the World, at Lord's in 1987. With Dickie Bird and Steve Bucknor was one of the first umpires officially sponsored by the ICC. Known for his superstition regarding 'Nelson' score 111, and multiples – 222, 333 etc. Was England's umpire at the 1995-96 World Cup in India and Pakistan
Best batting: 153 Gloucestershire v Middlesex, Bristol 1968

First-Class Career Performances

	M	Inns	NO	Runs	HS	Avge	100s	Ct	St	Runs	Wkts	Avge	Best	5wl	10wM
Test															
All First	282	476	40	10672	153	24.47	12	95	-	106	2	53.00	1-1	-	-

STEELE, J. F.

Name: John Frederick Steele
Role: Right-hand bat, slow left-arm bowler
Born: 23 July 1946, Stafford
Height: 5ft 10in **Weight:** 11st 7lbs
Nickname: Steely
Appointed to 1st-class list: 1997
County: Leicestershire (1970-83),
Glamorgan (1984-94)
Parents: Alfred and Grace
Wife and date of marriage: Susan,
17 April 1977
Childen: Sarah Jane, 2 April 1982; Robert
Alfred, 10 April 1985
Family links with cricket: Uncle Stan
played for Staffordshire. Brother David
played for Northamptonshire and England.
Cousin Brian Crump played for
Northamptonshire and Staffordshire
Education: Endon School, Stoke-on-Trent;
Stafford College
Qualifications: Advanced cricket coach
Career outside cricket: Work study officer. Fireman with Staffordshire Fire Brigade
Off-season: Cricket coaching in South Africa and the UK
Overseas teams played for: Springs HSOB, Northern Transvaal 1971-73; Pine Town
CC, Natal, South Africa 1973-74, 1982-83; Natal, South Africa 1975-76, 1978-79
Young players to look out for: Anthony Cottey
Other sports followed: Soccer (Stoke City, Port Vale) and golf
Relaxations: Music and walking
Extras: Played for England U25. 1st wicket record partnership for Leicestershire of 390
with Barry Dudleston versus Derbyshire in 1979. Won two Man of the Match Awards in
the Gillette Cup and four in the Benson and Hedges Cup. Won the award for the most
catches in a season in 1984 and was voted Natal's Best Bowler in 1975-76
Opinions on cricket: 'Would like to see two divisions in the County Championship.'
Best batting: 195 Leicestershire v Derbyshire, Leicester 1971
Best bowling: 7-29 Natal B v Griqualand West, Umzinto 1973-74
7-29 Leicestershire v Gloucestershire, Leicester 1980

First-class career performances

	M	Inns	NO	Runs	HS	Avge	100s	Ct	St	Runs	Wkts	Avge	Best	5wI	10wM
Test															
All First	379	605	85	15053	195	28.94	21	414	-	15793	584	27.04	7-29	16	-

WHITE, R. A.

Name: Robert Arthur White
Role: Left-hand bat, off-break bowler
Born: 6 October 1936, Fulham
Height: 5ft 9in **Weight:** 'Fluctuates'
Nickname: Knocker
Appointed to 1st-class list: 1982
Counties: Middlesex, Nottinghamshire
County debut: 1958 (Middlesex),
1966 (Nottinghamshire)
County cap: 1963 (Middlesex),
1966 (Nottinghamshire)
Benefit: 1974
1000 runs in a season: 1
50 wickets in a season: 2
1st-Class 50s: 50
1st-Class 100s: 5
1st-Class 5 w. in innings: 28
1st-Class 10 w. in match: 4
1st-Class catches: 190
Wife: Janice – 'still married, must be a record in the modern game'
Children: Robin and Vanessa
Education: Chiswick Grammar School
Qualifications: Matriculation and cricket coaching certificate
Career outside cricket: Fireworks salesman
Off-season: Working
Other sports followed: All sports – golf, football, ice-hockey and horse racing in particular
Cricketers particularly admired: 'Gary Sobers more than anyone else'
Cricketers particularly learnt from: 'I tried to learn from everyone I encountered'
Young players to look out for: 'All of them'
Relaxations: Theatre-going
Extras: Made independent coaching trips to South Africa 1959, 1960, 1966, 1967, 1968. Together with M.J. Smedley broke the Nottinghamshire seventh wicket record with 204 v Surrey at The Oval 1967
Opinions on cricket: 'There is so much verbal noise on the field these days (mainly in my opinion to distract the batsman), that I, if still a player, would wear earphones and carry a Walkman so that I could listen to soothing music and obliterate the verbals. Those people who saw me play would no doubt say that I would have had time just to hear the "Minute Waltz".'
Best batting: 116* Nottinghamshire v Surrey, The Oval 1967
Best bowling: 7-41 Nottinghamshire v Derbyshire, Ilkeston 1971

First-Class Career Performances

	M	Inns	NO	Runs	HS	Avge	100s	Ct	St	Runs	Wkts	Avge	Best	5wl	10wM
Test															
All First	413	642	105	12452	116*	23.18	5	190	-	21138	693	30.50	7-41	28	4

WHITEHEAD, A. G. T.

Name: Alan Geoffrey Thomas Whitehead
Role: Left-hand bat,
slow left-arm bowler
Born: 28 October 1940,
Butleigh, Somerset
Appointed to 1st-class list: 1970
Appointed to Test panel: 1982
Tests umpired: 5
One-Day Internationals umpired: 13
County: Somerset
County debut: 1957
1st-Class 5 w. in innings: 3
1st-Class catches: 20
Extras: Acted as third (replay) umpire in the
fifth Test against Australia at Edgbaston 1993
and in two Tests in 1994
Best batting: 15 Somerset v Hampshire,
Southampton 1959
Best bowling: 6-74 Somerset v Sussex,
Eastbourne 1959

First-Class Career Performances

	M	Inns	NO	Runs	HS	Avge	100s	Ct	St	Runs	Wkts	Avge	Best	5wl	10wM
Test															
All First	38	49	25	137	15	5.70	-	20	-	2306	67	34.41	6-74	3	-

WILLEY, P.

Name: Peter Willey
Role: Right-hand bat, off-break bowler
Born: 6 December 1949, Sedgefield,
County Durham
Height: 6ft 1in **Weight:** 13st 4lbs
Nickname: Will, 'many unprintable'
Appointed to 1st-class list: 1993
Appointed to International panel: 1996
Tests umpired: 5
One-Day Internationals umpired: 2
Counties: Northamptonshire, Leicestershire
County debut: 1966 (Northamptonshire),
1984 (Leicestershire)
County cap: 1971 (Northamptonshire), 1984
(Leicestershire)
Benefit: 1981 (£31,400)
Test debut: 1976
Tests: 26

One-Day Internationals: 26
1000 runs in a season: 10
50 wickets in a season: 2
1st-Class 50s: 101
1st-Class 100s: 44
1st-Class 200s: 1
1st-Class 5 w. in innings: 26
1st-Class 10 w. in match: 3
1st-Class catches: 235
One-Day 100s: 9
Parents: Oswald and Maisie
Wife and date of marriage: Charmaine, 23 September 1971
Children: Heather Jane, 11 September 1985; David, 28 February 1990
Family links with cricket: Father played local club cricket in County Durham
Education: Seaham Secondary School, County Durham
Off-season: 'House husband'
Overseas tours: England to Australia and India 1979-80, to West Indies 1980-81 and
1985-86; with unofficial England XI to South Africa 1981-82
Overseas teams played for: Eastern Province, South Africa 1982-85
Cricketers particularly admired: Malcolm Marshall
Other sports followed: All sports
Relaxations: Gardening, dog walking
Extras: With Wayne Larkins, received 2016 pints of beer (seven barrels) from a brewery

in Northampton as a reward for their efforts in Australia with England in 1979-80. Youngest player ever to play for Northamptonshire at 16 years 180 days v Cambridge University in 1966. Banned from Test cricket for three years for joining England rebel tour of South Africa in 1982. Left Northamptonshire at end of 1983 and moved to Leicestershire as vice-captain. Appointed Leicestershire captain for 1987, but resigned after only one season. Released by Leicestershire at end of 1991 season to play for Northumberland in 1992. He was appointed to the first-class umpires list in 1993 and on to the international panel in 1996. Umpired the Australia against West Indies series in Australia during the off-season

Opinions on cricket: 'I think the fun has gone out of the game for many of the players. Not enough hard work and practice is done to improve playing standards throughout the first-class game. Players of average ability are being paid silly money in the modern game, by clubs, so they may not need to try and improve their standards. Why does the English game need overseas coaches? Why do we also need team managers?'

Best batting: 227 Northamptonshire v Somerset, Northampton 1976
Best bowling: 7-37 Northamptonshire v Oxford University, The Parks 1975

First-Class Career Performances

	M	Inns	NO	Runs	HS	Avge	100s	Ct	St	Runs	Wkts	Avge	Best	5wI	10wM
Test	26	50	6	1184	102	*26.90	2	3	-	456	7	65.14	2-73	-	-
All First	559	918	121	24361	227	30.56	44	235	-	23400	756	30.95	7-37	26	3

These mobile phone offers will knock you for six!

2 exclusive offers brought to you jointly by The Professional Cricketer's Association and The Carphone Warehouse

EXCLUSIVE NOKIA 3110 PACKAGE

Choose the FREE Nokia 3110 Mobile Phone package and **save yourself over £135** in the first year!

Free Nokia 3110 Digital Mobile Phone **worth £19.99**

Free Connection to **vodafone worth £35**

Free Calls up to £7 per month **worth up to £84 a year**

Free 3 year warranty & next day delivery

EXCLUSIVE NOKIA 6110 PACKAGE

Purchase the Nokia 6110 mobile phone for just £99.99 and receive a package **saving you over £115** in the first year!

Free Connection to **vodafone worth £35**

Free Calls up to £7 per month **worth up to £84 a year**

Free 3 year warranty & next day delivery

HOWZAT!

To order call FREE now on

0800 000 925

(quoting PCA)

Carphone Warehouse
COMMUNICATION CENTRES

PCA
PROFESSIONAL CRICKETERS ASSOCIATION

ROLL OF HONOUR
1997

ROLL OF HONOUR 1997

BRITANNIC ASSURANCE CHAMPIONSHIP

		P	W	L	D	T	Bt	Bl	Pts
1	Glamorgan (10)	17	8	2	7	0	50	57	256
2	Kent (4)	17	8	4	5	0	44	60	252
3	Worcestershire (7)	17	6	3	8	0	49	54	228
4	Middlesex (9)	17	7	4	6	0	33	56	219
5	Warwickshire (8)	17	7	2	8	0	32	51	219
6	Yorkshire (6)	17	6	3	8	0	41	54	215
7	Gloucestershire (13)	17	6	6	5	0	35	60	206
8	Surrey (3)	17	5	5	7	0	39	52	192
9	Essex (5)	17	5	6	6	0	39	55	192
10	Leicestershire (10)	17	4	1	12	0	37	54	191
11	Lancashire (15)	17	5	6	6	0	34	54	186
12	Somerset (11)	17	3	3	11	0	38	64	183
13	Nottinghamshire (17)	17	4	3	10	0	26	55	175
14	Hampshire (14)	17	3	5	9	0	42	41	158
15	Northamptonshire (16)	17	3	9	9	0	33	48	156
16	Derbyshire (2)	17	2	9	6	0	32	59	141
17	Durham (18)	17	2	8	7	0	22	56	131
18	Sussex (12)	17	1	10	6	0	24	57	115

(1996 positions in brackets)

NATWEST TROPHY

Winners: Essex
Runners-up: Warwickshire

BENSON & HEDGES CUP

Winners: Surrey
Runners-up: Kent

AXA EQUITY & LAW LEAGUE

		P	W	L	T	NR	Pts
1	Warwickshire (4)	17	13	4	0	0	52
2	Kent (10)	17	12	4	0	1	50
3	Lancashire (9)	17	10	4	1	2	46
4	Leicestershire (12)	17	9	5	1	2	42
5	Surrey (1)	17	9	5	0	2	42
6	Somerset (5)	17	9	6	0	2	40
7	Essex (17)	17	9	6	1	1	40
8	Worcestershire (8)	17	8	6	1	2	38
9	Northamptonshire (6)	17	8	6	0	3	38
10	Yorkshire (3)	17	8	7	1	1	36
11	Gloucestershire (16)	17	7	6	0	4	36
12	Nottinghamshire (2)	17	7	7	0	3	34
13	Glamorgan (13)	17	5	9	0	3	26
14	Derbyshire (11)	17	4	9	0	4	24
15	Hampshire (15)	17	5	11	0	1	22
16	Middlesex (7)	17	3	10	1	3	20
17	Durham (18)	17	3	13	0	1	14
18	Sussex (14)	17	2	13	0	2	12

(1996 positions in brackets)

FIRST-CLASS AVERAGES

1997

1997 AVERAGES (all first-class matches)

BATTING AVERAGES - including fielding
Qualifying requirements : 6 completed innings at an average of over 35

Name	Matches	Inns	NO	Runs	HS	Avge	100s	50s	Ct	St
Hick, G.A.	18	28	6	1524	303*	69.27	6	4	20	-
James, S.P.	18	30	4	1775	162	68.26	7	8	14	-
Maynard, M.P	18	25	7	1170	161*	65.00	3	7	21	-
Ponting, R.	8	12	3	571	127	63.44	2	2	7	-
Lehmann, D.S.	17	27	2	1575	182	63.00	4	10	9	-
Johnson, N.C.	12	18	5	819	150	63.00	2	5	13	-
Thorpe, G.P.	14	23	4	1160	222	61.05	3	6	17	-
Elliott, M.T.G.	12	19	0	1091	199	57.42	4	5	7	-
Law, S.G.	17	28	2	1482	175	57.00	5	8	19	-
Ramprakash, M.R.	19	30	4	1453	190	55.88	6	7	9	-
Nash, D.C.	6	8	2	332	100	55.33	1	1	4	-
Waugh, S.R.	13	17	0	924	154	54.35	4	4	9	-
Tweats, T.A.	7	13	2	590	189	53.63	1	1	7	-
Hayden, M.L	17	30	3	1446	235*	53.55	4	7	13	-
Ealham, M.A.	18	30	10	1055	139	52.75	3	6	12	-
Morris, H.	17	28	4	1262	233*	52.58	4	3	14	-
Leatherdale, D.A.	17	25	8	886	129	52.11	2	5	15	-
Turner, R.J.	17	28	7	1069	144	50.90	1	7	51	2
Barnett, K.J.	15	24	3	1055	210*	50.23	3	5	3	-
Rose, G.D.	18	26	9	852	191	50.11	2	3	7	-
Crawley, J.P.	16	25	2	1141	133	49.60	3	7	11	-
Weston, W.P.C.	17	29	5	1190	205	49.58	4	3	7	-
Knight, N.V.	11	17	3	689	119*	49.21	2	3	8	-
Lloyd, G.	16	24	2	1073	225	48.77	4	5	17	-
Moody, T.M.	14	21	1	973	180*	48.65	3	4	14	-
Saleem Elahi	8	13	0	625	229	48.07	1	3	6	-
Prichard, P.J.	17	27	2	1184	224	47.36	3	9	10	-
Kallis, J.H.	16	25	3	1034	172*	47.00	4	4	15	-
Curran, K.M.	15	26	4	1032	159	46.90	2	6	8	-
Russell, R.C.	19	29	6	1049	103*	45.60	1	8	52	5
Byas, D.	20	33	4	1319	128	45.48	3	9	24	-
White, G.	10	17	2	681	145	45.40	1	4	8	-
Ecclestone, S.	13	23	2	951	133	45.28	3	4	12	-
Fordham, A.	9	17	2	673	85*	44.86	-	6	10	-
Lewis, J.J.B.	18	32	4	1252	210*	44.71	3	5	10	-
Smith, B.F	13	19	5	624	131*	44.57	2	2	3	-
Langer, J.L	6	10	3	312	152*	44.57	1	1	5	-
Wells, V.J.	18	27	0	1200	224	44.44	3	6	10	-
Warren, R.J.	10	17	2	664	174*	44.26	1	4	12	1
Nixon, P.A.	19	25	9	708	96	44.25	-	4	57	4
Rollins, A.S.	17	29	3	1142	210	43.92	3	6	11	-
Harden, R.J.	7	11	2	395	136*	43.88	2	1	3	-
Waugh, M.E.	13	20	3	746	173	43.88	2	3	11	-

Name	Matches	Inns	NO	Runs	HS	Avge	100s	50s	Ct	St
Whitaker, J.J.	16	23	2	919	133*	43.76	3	4	5	-
Keech, M.	10	16	4	518	127	43.16	2	1	10	-
Bailey, R.J.	17	30	5	1078	117*	43.12	3	5	18	-
Smith, E.T.	18	30	3	1163	190	43.07	2	6	7	-
Ripley, D.	17	24	6	772	92	42.88	-	6	30	7
Johnson, P.	16	27	5	942	96*	42.81	-	8	12	-
Brown, A.D.	14	21	1	848	170*	42.40	3	2	11	-
Boon, D.C.	18	30	3	1144	117	42.37	3	8	19	-
Smith, R.A.	14	23	1	918	154	41.72	2	4	4	-
Jones, D.M.	7	12	1	458	99*	41.63	-	5	8	-
Stewart, A. J.	15	26	2	994	271*	41.41	2	3	39	-
Penney, T. L.	16	24	5	784	99	41.26	-	6	11	-
Hemp, D.L.	18	31	4	1107	138	41.00	3	5	9	-
Grayson, A.P.	19	28	3	1022	105	40.88	1	6	20	-
Alleyne, M.W.	19	30	4	1059	169	40.73	1	8	14	-
Sutcliffe, I.J.	13	20	2	727	130	40.38	2	3	6	-
Blewett, G.S.	12	18	1	686	125	40.35	2	4	17	-
Fairbrother, N.H.	16	24	2	887	132	40.31	2	4	19	-
Astle, N.J.	10	16	0	644	100	40.25	2	3	11	-
Pollard, P.R.	10	17	5	480	115*	40.00	1	1	8	-
Wagh, M.A.	18	31	2	1156	125*	39.86	4	5	14	-
Marsh, S.A.	18	27	6	837	142	39.85	1	3	61	2
Habib, A.	9	14	4	397	175*	39.70	1	1	4	-
Bicknell, D.J.	9	15	0	594	162	39.60	2	1	1	-
Austin, I.D.	17	25	4	825	95	39.28	-	8	6	-
May, M.R.	9	17	2	588	116	39.20	2	3	2	-
Shah, O.A.	11	16	2	548	104*	39.14	1	2	14	-
Gatting, M.W	19	29	2	1053	160*	39.00	2	4	23	-
Giles, A.F.	16	20	4	624	97	39.00	-	5	4	-
Hussain, N.	16	28	0	1081	207	38.60	4	3	17	-
Taylor, N.R.	16	28	1	1033	127	38.25	3	5	3	-
Blakey, R.J.	18	24	6	680	92	37.77	-	6	49	4
Dale, A.	19	27	4	860	142*	37.39	2	5	6	-
Wells, A.P.	18	31	1	1120	109	37.33	1	9	16	-
Hollioake, A.J.	16	25	1	891	182	37.12	1	6	15	-
Curtis, T.S.	13	21	1	742	160	37.10	4	1	9	-
Fulton, D.P.	16	29	3	953	110	36.65	1	4	23	-
Young, S.	19	31	4	985	237	36.48	2	5	10	-
Parsons, K.A.	10	15	3	437	74	36.41	-	3	12	-
Jones, R.O.	8	11	2	325	60	36.11	-	3	4	-
Maddy, D.L.	19	30	1	1047	103	36.10	3	5	18	-
Haynes, G.R.	17	25	3	794	70	36.09	-	6	5	-
Wood, N.T.	10	15	2	469	155	36.07	1	2	3	-
Athey, C.W.J.	12	21	2	682	138*	35.89	1	5	9	-
Taylor, M.A.	12	19	0	680	129	35.78	2	4	8	-
Bevan, M.G.	11	16	3	463	104*	35.61	1	3	6	-
Clarke, V.P.	19	30	6	847	99	35.29	-	5	9	-
Spiring, K.R.	17	28	3	876	150	35.04	1	4	7	-
Robinson, D.J.	14	22	1	735	148	35.00	2	3	13	-

BOWLING AVERAGES
Qualifying requirements : 10 wickets taken at an average of under 30

Name	Overs	Mdns	Runs	Wkts	Avge	Best	5wI	10wM
Anthony, H.	42	11	113	10	11.30	6-34	1	1
Donald, A.A.	387.5	123	938	60	15.63	6-55	3	1
Smith, A.M.	512.2	125	1464	83	17.63	6-45	5	3
Reiffel, P.R.	188.4	49	520	28	18.57	5-49	2	-
James, K.	161.1	37	504	27	18.66	8-49	2	1
Brown, D.	521.3	135	1560	81	19.25	8-89	4	1
Saqlain Mushtaq	254.5	75	617	32	19.28	5-17	4	2
Bloomfield, T.	85	17	258	13	19.84	5-77	1	-
Phillips, B.	282.1	73	877	44	19.93	5-47	2	-
Hutchison, P.	233.1	56	741	37	20.02	7-38	3	1
Warne, S.K.	433.4	112	1154	57	20.24	7-103	4	-
Kallis, J.H.	34.3	61	655	32	20.46	5-54	1	-
McGrath, G.	363.4	104	1012	49	20.65	8-38	2	-
Azhar Mahmood	290.5	66	829	40	20.72	5-66	1	-
Tufnell, P.C.R.	561.5	174	1205	55	21.90	7-66	3	1
Ilott, M.	332	91	946	43	22.00	7-59	1	-
Betts, M.	329	77	1085	49	22.14	9-64	3	1
Waqar Younis	441.4	83	1551	68	22.80	8-17	3	1
Watkin, S.L.	508.2	143	1393	61	22.83	7-41	2	-
Edwards, A.	103.2	19	389	17	22.88	5-34	1	-
Hartley, P.J.	170	39	532	23	23.13	5-34	1	-
Martin, P.	474.2	136	1342	58	23.13	8-32	3	1
Hewitt, J.	437	96	1389	60	23.15	6-14	2	-
Newport, P.	177.2	56	444	19	23.36	7-37	1	-
McCague, M.	312.4	55	1125	48	23.43	7-50	4	-
Malcolm, D.E.	526.1	81	1761	75	23.48	6-23	5	2
Gillespie, J.N.	198.4	43	692	29	23.86	7-37	2	-
Astle, N.	209	44	525	22	23.86	5-46	1	-
Illingworth, R.K.	206.1	79	442	18	24.55	7-79	1	1
Rose, G.D.	488.5	124	1563	63	24.80	5-53	1	-
Welch, G.	540.5	151	1625	65	25.00	6-115	3	1
Sheriyar, K.	445.5	94	1575	62	25.40	6-19	3	1
Cowan, A.	420	106	1334	52	25.65	5-45	3	-
Williams, N.	101	16	336	13	25.84	5-55	1	-
Kasprowicz, M.	267.2	50	1010	39	25.89	7-36	1	-
Lewis, J.	418.5	98	1401	54	25.94	6-50	3	-
Alleyne, M.	360.1	89	1148	44	26.09	6-64	3	-
Hindson, J.E.	96.4	24	287	11	26.09	4-28	-	-
Oram, A.	226.4	55	684	26	26.30	4-53	-	-
Such, P.M.	725.1	218	1739	66	26.34	6-55	6	1
Silverwood, C.E.W.	478.4	108	1531	58	26.39	7-93	4	1
Ormond, J.	345.3	72	1162	44	26.40	6-54	3	-
Caddick, A.R.	702.4	139	2156	81	26.61	6-65	6	-
Bicknell, M. P.	385.2	94	1174	44	26.68	5-34	1	-
Gough, D.	334.4	70	1149	43	26.72	5-56	3	-
DeFreitas, P.A.J.	574.1	132	1810	67	27.01	7-64	5	2

Name	Overs	Mdns	Runs	Wkts	Avge	Best	5wI	10wM
Austin, I.D.	448.4	131	1218	45	27.06	4-44	-	-
Thomas, S.D.	405.3	58	1444	53	27.24	5-24	3	-
Millns, D.J.	408.4	87	1341	49	27.36	6-61	2	1
Croft, R.B.D.	666.1	159	1698	62	27.38	5-33	1	-
Bates, J.J.	227.2	71	525	19	27.63	5-89	1	-
Brown, S.	590.3	126	1855	67	27.68	5-58	4	1
Shoaib Malik	123	24	333	12	27.75	3-49	-	-
Herzberg, S.	102	25	281	10	28.10	3-100	-	-
Mushtaq Ahmed	513	146	1407	50	28.14	6-70	3	-
Haynes, G	287.1	68	875	31	28.22	3-46	-	-
Taylor, J.P.	455.4	81	1532	54	28.37	7-87	3	1
Evans, K.P.	457.5	103	1277	45	28.37	6-40	2	-
Leatherdale, D.A.	219.3	46	742	26	28.53	5-56	1	-
Johnson, R.L.	429.2	80	1429	50	28.58	4-26	-	-
Thompson, J.B.deC.	223.2	30	890	31	28.70	5-89	1	-
Tolley, C.	363	87	1005	35	28.71	6-61	1	-
Dean, K.	234.4	47	811	28	28.96	4-39	-	-
Davies, M.K.	234.2	71	674	23	29.30	5-46	1	-
Lewis, C.C.	291.4	66	970	33	29.39	5-42	1	-
Robinson, M.A.	448.2	87	1426	48	29.70	6-78	2	-
Curran, K.M.	215.2	57	715	24	29.79	4-32	-	-
Shoaib Akhtar	194.2	35	747	25	29.88	5-62	2	-
Igglesden, A.P.	152	23	538	18	29.88	4-67	-	-

WHYTE AND MACKAY RANKINGS 1997

BATTING

Rank	Player	Total
1	M.R. Ramprakash (Middlesex)	496
2	G.P. Thorpe (Surrey)	487
3	S.P. James (Glamorgan)	482
4	N. Hussain (Essex)	404
5	M.P. Maynard (Glamorgan)	402
6	J.P. Crawley (Lancashire)	396
7	A.J. Stewart (Surrey)	384
8	D.L. Hemp (Warwickshire)	366
9	D. Byas (Yorkshire)	365
10	A.P. Wells (Kent)	362
11	H. Morris (Glamorgan)	359
12	M.W. Alleyne (Gloucestershire)	358
13	G.A. Hick (Worcestershire)	350
=	J.J.B. Lewis (Durham)	350
=	M.A. Butcher (Surrey)	350
16	R.C. Russell (Gloucestershire)	349
17	M.P. Dowman (Nottinghamshire)	346
18	M.A. Ealham (Kent)	343
19	J.E. Morris (Durham)	342
20	K.J. Barnett (Derbyshire)	341

BOWLING

Rank	Player	Total
1	A.R. Caddick (Somerset)	540
2	A.M. Smith (Gloucestershire)	537
3	D.R. Brown (Warwickshire)	529
4	R.B.D. Croft (Glamorgan)	484
5	S.L. Watkin (Glamorgan)	477
6	G.D. Rose (Somerset)	463
7	P.M. Such (Essex)	455
8	A.R.C. Fraser (Middlesex)	429
9	P.J. Martin (Lancashire)	423
10	J.P. Hewitt (Middlesex)	419
11	P.A.J. DeFreitas (Derbyshire)	410
12	D.E. Malcolm (Derbyshire)	409
13	G. Welch (Warwickshire)	399
14	J.P. Taylor (Northamptonshire)	398
=	D. Gough (Yorkshire)	398
16	M.A. Robinson (Sussex)	391
17	M.P. Bicknell (Surrey)	388
18	C.E.W. Silverwood (Yorkshire)	369
19	S.J.E. Brown (Durham)	365
20	A.P. Cowan (Essex)	363

1997 PCA Awards Dinner at the Cafe Royal, London

PROFESSIONAL CRICKETERS'
ASSOCIATION

1967

Formation of the Professional Cricketers'
Association

1971

The launch of the PCA Player Awards

1975

The creation of a pension scheme

1978

The introduction of the minimum wage

1982

The establishment of The Cricketers'
Association Charity

1985

The standardisation of contracts

1997

The formation of PCA Management Ltd.

The launch of the PCA Business Partnership

First edition PCA Annual Yearbook

The first televised PCA Awards Dinner

Rt. Hon. John Major MP, presenting the awards

1998

The launch for the PCA Hall of Fame

The launch of the PCA Affinity Credit Card

The PCA Cricket in the Community
programme

The formation of FICA

PCA MANAGEMENT LTD

PCA Management Ltd, Hawkstone Park, Weston-Under-Redcastle, Shrewsbury, Shropshire, SY4 5UY. Tel: 01939 200202 Fax: 01939 200699

PCA AWARD WINNERS

HAYTER CUP
THE PCA PLAYER OF THE YEAR

1970	Mike Procter and Jack Bond
1971	Lance Gibbs
1972	Andy Roberts
1973	Peter Lee
1974	Barry Stead
1975	Zaheer Abbas
1976	Peter Lee
1977	Mike Procter
1978	John Lever
1979	John Lever
1980	Robin Jackman
1981	Richard Hadlee
1982	Malcolm Marshall
1983	Ken McEwan
1984	Richard Hadlee
1985	Neal Radford
1986	Courtney Walsh
1987	Richard Hadlee
1988	Graeme Hick
1989	Jimmy Cook
1990	Graham Gooch
1991	Waqar Younis
1992	Courtney Walsh
1993	Steve Watkin
1994	Brian Lara
1995	Dominic Cork
1996	Phil Simmons
1997	Steve James

ARLOTT CUP
PCA YOUNG PLAYER OF THE YEAR

1990	Mike Atherton
1991	Dominic Cork
1992	Mark Lathwell
1993	Malachy Loye
1994	John Crawley
1995	Andy Symonds
1996	Chris Silverwood
1997	Ben Hollioake

GOLDBLATT UMPIRES CUP

1997	Peter Willey

WATERFORD CRYSTAL
PCA SPECIAL MERIT AWARD

1997	Alistair Brown

THE PRIMARY CLUB

PO Box 12121
London NW1 9WS
Tel: 0171 267 3316
Fax: 0171 485 6808

Derek Underwood, the patron of the Primary Club, qualified for membership in some style in 1965. Playing for Kent against the South Africans he was out first ball twice in the same match.

However, members do not have to be playing Test or county cricket when the ultimate disaster strikes in order to qualify for the club. As long as you are out first ball at ANY level of cricket you are eligible to join The Primary Club.

Why join? The Primary Club is a charity (Registered Charity No. 285285) and all profits from subscriptions, donations and the range of items for sale (ties, sweaters, shirts, mugs, umbrellas, etc.) go to pay for sporting and recreational facilities for the blind and partially sighted. All the club's workers are volunteers.

For many of us sport is an important part of our every day lives; for the blind and partially sighted, sport can mean so much more. The confidence and sense of achievement they get from mastering a physical skill helps them a great deal in tackling the problems of their lives.

MEMBERSHIP APPLICATION

Name

Address

Joining subscription:	
To include City tie – £15	
To include Club tie – £15	
To include City & Club tie – £25	
To include Bow tie – £15	
Lady, to include brooch – £10	
DONATION	
TOTAL REMITTANCE TO: THE PRIMARY CLUB' £	

Please photocopy this form rather than spoil the book

TIES AND OTHER ITEMS FOR MEMBERS

The City tie has several small reproductions of the club emblem embroidered on navy blue fabric – the Club tie has a single larger one on green. A colour leaflet of the full range of clothing and other items will be sent to members.

DEED OF COVENANT

If you wish to consider making a donation under a 4 year (or more) charitable deed of covenant, please tick the box, but do not include this donation in your present remittance. Further details and a form of deed will then be sent to you. Such a deed does not increase the cost to you of your donation but enables the Club to recover income tax. ☐

INDEX OF PLAYERS BY COUNTY

*denotes not registered for 1998 season. Where a player is known to have moved in the off-season he is listed under his new county.

DERBYSHIRE

ALDRED, P.
BARNETT, K.J.
BLACKWELL, I.D.
CASSAR, M.E.
CLARKE, V.P.
CORK, D.G.
DEAN, K.J.
DEFREITAS, P.A.J.
GRIFFITHS, S.P.
HARRIS, A.J.
HAYHURST, A.N.
JONES, D.M.*
KHAN, G.A.*
KRIKKEN, K.M.
LACEY, S.J.
MAY, M.R.
OWEN, J.E.*
ROBERTS, G.M.
ROLLINS, A.S.
SAEED ANWAR
SMITH, T.M.
SPENDLOVE, B.J.
STUBBINGS, S.D.
TWEATS, T.A.
VANDRAU, M.J.
WOMBLE, D.R.*

DURHAM

BETTS, M.M.
BOILING, J.
BOON, D.C.
BROWN, S.J.E.
CAMPBELL, C.
COLLINGWOOD, P.
COX, D.M.

DALEY, J.A.
FOSTER, M.J.
GRAHAM, J.
HUTTON, S.
KILLEEN, N.
LEWIS, J.J.B.
LUGSDEN, S.
MORRIS, J.E.
PRATT, A.
ROSEBERRY, M.A.
SAGGERS, M.J.
SEARLE, J.P.
SPEAK, N.J.
SPEIGHT, M.P.
WALKER, A.
WESTON, R.M.S.*
WOOD, J.

ESSEX

ANDREW, S.J.W.*
COUSINS, D.M.
COWAN, A.
FLANAGAN, I.N.
GOOCH, G.A.*
GRAYSON, A.P.
GROVE, J.
HIBBERT, A.J.E.
HODGSON, T.
HUSSAIN, N.
HYAM, B.J.
ILOTT, M.C.
IRANI, R.
LAW, D.
LAW, S.R.
NAPIER, G.R.
PETERS, S.

POWELL, J.C.
PRICHARD, P.J.
ROBINSON, D.D.J.
ROLLINS, R.J.
SUCH, P.M.
WILLIAMS, N.F.
WILSON, D.G.

GLAMORGAN

BUTCHER, G.P.
COSKER, D.
COTTEY, P.A.
CROFT, R.D.B.
DALE, A.
DAVIES, A.P.
DAWOOD, I.
EVANS, A.W.
JAMES, S.P.
JONES, S.P.
LAW, W.L.
MAYNARD, M.P.
METSON, C.P.*
MORRIS, H.*
PARKIN, O.T.
POWELL, M.J.
SHAW, A.D.
THOMAS, S.D.
WAQAR YOUNIS
WATKIN, S.L.

GLOUCESTERSHIRE

ALLEYNE, M.W.
AVERIS, J.M.M.
BALL, M.C.J.
CAWDRON, M.J.

INDEX OF PLAYERS BY COUNTY

CHURCH, M.J.
CUNLIFFE, R.J.
DAVIS, R.P.*
DAWSON, R.I.
GANNON, B.W.
HANCOCK, T.H.C.
HEWSON, D.R.
LAWRENCE, D.V.
LEWIS, J.
LYNCH, M.*
READ, C.M.W.*
RUSSELL, R.C.
SHEERAZ, K.P.
SMITH, A.M.
TRAINOR, N.J.
WALSH, C.A.
WILLIAMS, R.C.J.
WINDOWS, M.G.N.
WRIGHT, A.J.
YOUNG, S.*

HAMPSHIRE

AYMES, A.N.
BOVILL, J.N.B.*
CONNOR, C.A.
DIBDEN, R.R.
FRANCIS, S.R.G.
GARAWAY, M.
HANSEN, T.M.
HARTLEY, P.J.
HAYDEN, M.L.
JAMES, K.D.
KEECH, M.
KENDALL, W.S.
KENWAY, D.A.
LANEY, J.S.
LOUDON, H.J.H.
MARU, R.J.
MASCARENHAS, D.A.

MILBURN, S.*
MORRIS, A.C.
MORRIS, Z.C.
PATEL, C.*
RENSHAW, S.
SAVIDENT, L.
SMITH, R.A.
STEPHENSON, J.P.
UDAL, S.D.
WHITAKER, P.
WHITE, G.W.

KENT

COWDREY, G.R.
EALHAM, M.A.
FLEMING, M.V.
FORD, J.A.
FULTON, D.P.
HEADLEY, D.W.
HOCKLEY, J.B.
HOOPER, C.
HOUSE, W.J.
IGGLESDEN, A.P.
KEY, R.W.T.
LLONG, N.J.
MARSH, S.A.
MASTERS, D.D.
MCCAGUE, M.J.
PATEL, M.M.
PHILLIPS, B.
PRESTON, N.W.*
SMITH, E.T.
STANFORD, E.J.
THOMPSON, J.B.
WALKER, M.J.
WALSH, C.D.
WARD, T.R.
WELLS, A.P.
WILLIS, S.C.

WREN, T.N.*

LANCASHIRE

ATHERTON, M.A.
AUSTIN, I.D.
CHAPPLE, G.
CHILTON, M.
CRAWLEY, J.P.
FAIRBROTHER, N.H.
FLINTOFF, A.
GREEN, R.J.
HARVEY, M.E.
HAYNES, J.J.
HEGG, W.K.
KEEDY, G.
LLOYD, G.D.
MARTIN, P.J.
MCKEOWN, P.C.
RIDGEWAY, P.M.
SCHOFIELD, C.
SHADFORD, D.J.
TITCHARD, S.P.
WASIM AKRAM
WATKINSON, M.
WOOD, N.T.
YATES, G.

LEICESTERSHIRE

BRIMSON, M.T.
CROWE, C.D.
DAKIN, J.M.
HABIB, A.
JOHNSON, N.C.*
KIRKBY, S.
LEWIS, C.C.
MACMILLAN, G.I.*
MADDY, D.L.
MASON, T.J.

INDEX OF PLAYERS BY COUNTY

INDEX OF PLAYERS BY COUNTY

QUIZ ANSWERS

1. Jon Lewis/Paul Collingwood
2. Jon Lewis (Durham/Essex), Peter Bowler (Leics/Derbyshire), Neil Taylor (Kent/Sussex)
3. Bangladesh
4. Bangladesh/Kenya/Scotland
5. Saeed Anwar, 194 Pakistan v India, Independence Cup, May 1997
6. Desmond Haynes
7. Paul Smith, ex-Warwickshire
8. Graham Gooch, Mike Gatting, Graeme Hick, Tim Robinson, Bill Athey
9. Dean Headley; George and his son Ron both played for the West Indies
10. Syd Lawrence
11. Chetan Patel
12. Adam Hollioake
13. Michael Bevan
14. Sri Lanka beat Pakistan
15. Sanath Jayasuriya
16. Mark Butcher
17. Courtney Walsh
18. Geoffrey Boycott
19. Nick Knight and David Hemp
20. Mark Powell, Glamorgan
21. Rodney Marsh and Alan Knott
22. Sajeena De Silva
23. Paul Franks and Chris Tolley
24. England U17 – it was a tournament open to non senior major cricket-playing nations, but England agreed to take part if they fielded a younger side
25. Peter Such
26. Stephen Rhodes took David Bairstow's record
27. Tom Moody
28. 118 balls including 11 sixes and 19 fours
29. Ben Hollioake
30. Stephen James
31. Desmond Haynes, 8,648 runs @ 41.37
32. Millfield School beat Nottingham High School
33. Sri Lanka beat India
34. Sanath Jayasuriya and Roshan Mahanama
35. Sir Garfield Sobers
36. Chris Cairns, whose innings off 157 of 89 balls against Kenya in September 1997 included 14 sixes
37. Adam Hollioake
38. Stuart Law
39. Caldy
40. Graham Gooch, 3,582 runs @ 58.72
41. Graham Thorpe, 453 runs @ 50.33
42. Andrew Caddick, 24 wickets @ 26.41
43. The Grace brothers
44. Matthew Elliott, 556 runs @ 55.60
45. Glenn McGrath, 36 wickets @ 19.47
46. Karen Smithies
47. Bradfield Waifs beat Old Tonbridgians
48. Mark Nicholas
49. Pakistan beat England
50. Matthew Fleming
51. Steve James
52. Ben Hollioake
53. Peter Willey
54. Graham Lloyd, 73 balls v Leicestershire, June 1997
55. Lancashire
56. Paul Hutchison
57. 1969, Tony Lewis
58. Graeme Hick, 1,524 runs @ 69.27
59. Steve James, 7
60. Graeme Hick, 303 not out v Hampshire
61. Allan Donald, 60 wickets @ 15.63
62. Mike Smith, 83 wickets
63. Steve Marsh, 63
64. Trevor Ward, 30
65. Melvyn Betts, 9 for 64 Durham v Northamptonshire
66. Peter Martin, 13 for 79, Lancashire v Middlesex
67. Waqar Younis, 9
68. Steve Waugh
69. Stephen Fleming, New Zealand v Zimbabwe, Harare 1997
70. Herbert Sutcliffe, 119, The Rest v Cowdray's XI, 25 September 1923
71. Durham University
72. Owais Shah
73. Kevin Curran
74. Robin Smith
75. Wasim Akram
76. Hassan Raza, 15 years 215 days, 204 not out Karachi v Bahawalpur
77. Worcestershire, 415
78. Sussex, 239
79. Hampshire, 429
80. Glamorgan, 263
81. Mark Ramprakash, 6,828 runs @ 58.86
82. Steve Watkin, 319 wickets @ 25.70
83. Mark Alleyne, 4,661 runs @ 33.29, 173 wickets @ 29.01
84. South Africa beat Sri Lanka
85. Matthew Maynard
86. Alec Stewart
87. Carl Hooper
88. 1928 against England
89. Australia beat New Zealand
90. Aamir Sohail
91. His own. He took 8 for 75 in Barbados in 1994
92. Makhaya Ntini
93. Steve Waugh
94. Australia
95. Gary Kirsten
96. Shane Warne
97. Darren Maddy
98. Sri Lanka (2-0)
99. J.M. Parks, 16,380 runs @ 34.55
100. Allan Border, 13 times